China

World Social Change

Series Editor: Mark Selden

Perilous Passage: Mankind and the Global Ascendance of Capital, by Amiya Kumar Bagchi
Anarchy as Order: The History and Future of Civil Humanity, by Mohammed Bamyeh
Water Frontier: Commerce and the Chinese in the Lower Mekong Region, 1750–1880, edited by Nola Cooke and Li Tana
Empire to Nation: Historical Perspectives on the Making of the Modern World, edited by Joseph W. Esherick, Hasan Kayali, and Eric Van Young
First Globalization: The Eurasian Exchange, 1500–1800, by Geoffrey C. Gunn
Istanbul: Between the Global and the Local, edited by Caglar Keyder
The Origins of the Modern World: A Global and Ecological Narrative, by Robert B. Marks
The Politics of Greed: How Privatization Structured Politics in Central and Eastern Europe, by Andrew Schwartz
Leaving China: Media, Mobility, and Transnational Imagination, by Wanning Sun
Masters of Terror: Indonesia's Military and Violence in East Timor, edited by Richard Tanter, Gerry van Klinken, and Desmond Ball
Through the Prism of Slavery: Labor, Capital, and World Economy, by Dale W. Tomich
Politics and the Past: On Repairing Historical Injustices, edited by John Torpey

China

Its Environment and History

Robert B. Marks

ROWMAN & LITTLEFIELD PUBLISHERS, INC.
Lanham • Boulder • New York • Toronto • Plymouth, UK

Published by Rowman & Littlefield Publishers, Inc.
A wholly owned subsidiary of The Rowman & Littlefield Publishing Group, Inc.
4501 Forbes Boulevard, Suite 200, Lanham, Maryland 20706
http://www.rowmanlittlefield.com

Estover Road, Plymouth PL6 7PY, United Kingdom

British Library Cataloguing in Publication Information Available

Library of Congress Cataloging-in-Publication Data

Marks, Robert, 1949–
China : its environment and history / Robert B. Marks.
p. cm. — (World social change)
Includes bibliographical references and index.
ISBN 978-1-4422-1275-6 (cloth : alk. paper) — ISBN 978-1-4422-1277-0 (electronic)
1. Human ecology—China—History. 2. Human geography—China—History. 3. Nature—Effect of human beings on—China—History. 4. Environmental degradation—China—History. 5. China—Environmental conditions. I. Title.
GF656.M37 2012
304.20951—dc23 2011036804

∞™ The paper used in this publication meets the minimum requirements of American National Standard for Information Sciences—Permanence of Paper for Printed Library Materials, ANSI/NISO Z39.48–1992.

Printed in the United States of America

Brief Contents

Detailed Contents

List of Illustrations

MAPS

FIGURES

Acknowledgments

This book is among the largest and most complex that I have attempted, and although my name is on the title page as the author, I could not have completed the project without the help of lots of other people and institutions.

For their willingness to read, critique, and comment upon the entire book manuscript, I thank especially David Bello, Steve Davidson, Anne Kiley, John McNeill, and Mark Selden. Numerous others were willing to respond to email queries and phone calls or at other times and places to talk with me about sources or issues of interpretation, and I thank them all: David Bello, David Christian, Kent Deng, Lee Feigon, Edward Friedman, Daniel Headrick, Paul Kjellberg, Peter Levelle, Joseph McDermott, Nicholas Menzies, Andrew Mertha, Ruth Mostern, Micah Muscolina, Anne Osborne, Walter Parham, Peter Purdue, Cheryl Swift, Jonathan Unger, Donald Wagner, Robert Weller, Adam Witten, and Ling Zhang. Darrin Magee was not only willing to allow me to use a map from his dissertation, he volunteered to redraw it.

Colleagues at other colleges and universities were kind enough to invite me to visit and present aspects of my work. I want to thank both Jim Scott for inviting me to present parts of chapter 6 at Yale University's Program in Agrarian Studies, and seminar members for a lively discussion. Tom Lutze and Abby Jahiel invited me to present aspects of my work at Illinois Wesleyan University, and Scott O'Bryan invited me to lecture on my book at Indiana University. Edward Friedman and the East Asian Studies Program at the University of Wisconsin–Madison invited me to present parts of chapters 5 and 7. I presented portions of chapter 7 at a conference organized in honor of Maurice Meisner, and I want to thank those who were there for their comments, but especially Tom Lutze and Carl Riskin. Cecily McCaffrey hosted me at Willamette University. Johanna Waley-Cohen has invited me to a conference at NYU, and although that will be after I have sent this book's page proofs off, drafting the paper for that conference has prompted me to see aspects of my argument more clearly.

I was able to take the entire 2007–8 academic year to draft most of the book thanks to a sabbatical leave granted to me by Whittier College, coupled with a Faculty

Research Grant (HR-50349-07) from the National Endowment for the Humanities. Additional funding has been provided by the Richard and Billie Deihl Endowment, which funds the endowed chair that I currently hold. I thank them all for their financial support.

Several colleagues have graciously given me permission to use and quote from material that they are working on but that is not yet published, and I thank them too: Desmond Cheong, Hugh Clark, Jack Hayes, Jeffrey Kinzley, Peter Levelle, Tim Sedo, Elena Songster, and Ling Zhang.

Students in my Imperial China class the past several years have read and commented upon various drafts of the book manuscript: T. C. Collymore, Cameron Cuellar, Laura Jennings, Ben Mitchell, Leah Sigler, Dillon Trites, and Victor Velasquez (fall 2008); Melanie Abe, Andrew Choi, Matthew Evans, Bryan Herring, Korrine Hilgeman, Avinash Jackson, Brian Mao, Cody McDermott, Melissa Samarin, Chaz Smith, Katrina Thoreson, Andres Villapando, and Stephen Wishon (fall 2009); Courteney Faught, Cookie Fuzell, Timothy Lang, Ryan Raffel, Sue Rubin, Darren Taylor, and Matt Wiley (fall 2010). Additionally, I used selected parts of the book in a course on World Environmental History and in my East Asian and Modern Chinese history classes. I thank all those students for giving me feedback for how undergraduate students might read and understand this book.

At Whittier College, Joe Dmohowski, Mike Garabedian, and Cindy Bessler in Wardman Library helped locate and bring to Whittier College numerous books and articles from around the world. With his knowledge of Excel, Robert Olsabeck helped me format tables and graphs. Rich Cheatham lent me his vast experience with film and graphics when I needed to get old photos ready for digital publication. Darren Taylor translated the table of contents of a couple of Chinese-language texts, and worked on the translation of a couple of passages. The Whittier College history department, especially the current department chair, Elizabeth Sage, has been supportive of my work and understanding of my periodic absences from campus. Departmental assistant Angela Freeland has helped with more than copying and tea, although both of those are important. Hong Cheong at the UCLA Chinese Studies Library helped me locate some raw books in their collection that were not in the stacks.

At the press, Susan McEachern has long been a supporter of this project. As editor, not only did she read the manuscript and make suggestions for improving it, she helped realize my hope that the book contain quite a few maps and other graphics. Janice Braunstein oversaw copyediting and typesetting; Susan's assistant, Grace Baumgartner, kept the project on schedule. To make several of the maps, I used base maps from Map Resources and received help from Josh Brock in technical support for some routines using Adobe Illustrator and Photoshop to be able draw and print the map I wanted. Gregory Veeck, Clifton W. Pannel, Christopher J. Smith, and Youqin Huang gave permission to use several maps from their book, *China's Geography: Globalization and the Dynamics of Political, Economic, and Social Change*, also published by Rowman & Littlefield.

Portions of chapter 7 have been published previously in *Radicalism, Revolution, and Reform in Modern China Essays in Honor of Maurice Meisner*, and I want to thank Lexington Press for permission to use that material. I also want to thank

Cambridge University Press for permission to use several images from various volumes of Joseph Needham's *Science and Civilization in China*. Several sections of this book are based on my previously published *Tigers, Rice, Silk, and Silt: Environment and Economy in Late Imperial China*, for which I hold the copyright.

Alas, this book was in the final stage of production when an important new work came my way that I was not able to incorporate. David Bello has a new book manuscript tentatively entitled *Fencing in Forest, Steppe, and Mountain: Environment, Identity and Empire in Qing China's Borderlands* which he asked me to read just as this manuscript was in page proofs. Had I had David's material and insights sooner, I would have incorporated both into this book. That I didn't means that readers will soon have a marvelous new book to add to their reading lists.

Without the work of generations of scholars and the help of those mentioned above, this book would not have been possible. I thank them all from the bottom of my heart for all they have meant to me. But in the end, this book is mine, and I take sole responsibility for whatever is good and right about it, but also for whatever mistakes, omissions, oversights, or questionable interpretations or inferences remain.

Finally, my wife, Joyce P. Kaufman (who is a very productive scholar in her own right), and I have shared the often very lonely work of composing our various books, and giving each other love, comfort, and acceptance when our unruly manuscripts were not being kind to us. Our black Labrador Stanton has laid quietly by our desks for hours waiting for that brief moment of excitement when one of us would get up and say "Let's go for walk!"

Chapter 1

Introduction

Problems and Perspectives

Four thousand years ago, the place we now call China was among the most biologically rich and diverse places on earth. Today, the Asian elephant—which once thrived throughout the region—has been displaced to the furthest reaches of China's southwest, the South China tiger is on the verge of extinction, the Yangzi River dolphin is probably extinct, and a couple of Yangzi giant soft-shell turtles in two zoos are all that remain of that species. And those are just the "star species" we know about; hundreds of other species have gone extinct nearly unnoticed. Biologists estimate that nearly 40 percent of all remaining mammal species in China are endangered, and that 70–80 percent of plant species are threatened. This book tells the story of how and why that massive environmental transformation happened.

Mostly, the story involves humans in China, and what they have done to their environment over the past four thousand years. Paradoxically, the very biodiversity of the region was the reason that it has supported from one-quarter to one-third of the world's human population at any given time, with peoples in different parts of China exploiting the vast and diverse natural treasure trove not merely to sustain their immediate lives but also to increase their populations. At first, the footprint of humans was light; humans mostly hunted for sustenance, or gathered food from the forests, grasslands, or wetlands. But with the development and subsequent spread of agriculture, and the attendant clearance of forests for farmland, that began nearly ten thousand years ago, the effects of human population changed dramatically. More recently, in the twentieth century, rapid industrialization and the rise of a consumer culture accelerated the transformation and degradation of nature in China. The "success" of the peoples of China over the past four thousand years in establishing and maintaining their particular form of civilization is, then, the chief reason for ecological change in China.

That last phrase—"in China"—is startlingly illustrated by a recent map of the range of the tiger (*Panthera tigris*) published by the International Union for the Conservation of Nature for their "red list of endangered species."[1] Whereas tigers once roamed throughout much of the space labeled "China," by 2009 the tiger had been extirpated

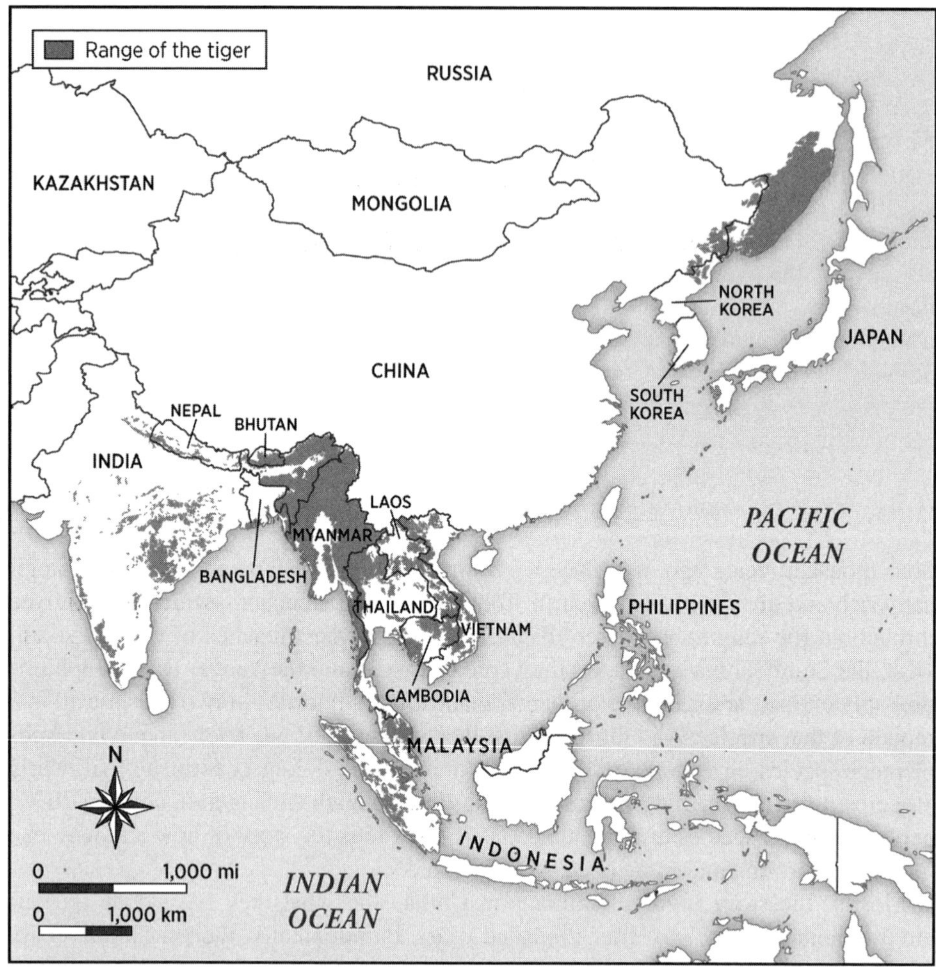

Map 1.1. The Range of the Tiger, ca. 2009 *Source:* Adapted from The IUCN Red List of Threatened Species, "Panthera tigris," www.iucnredlist.org/apps/redlist/details/15955/0.

from within Chinese borders (see map 1.1). That correspondence between the range of the tiger and China's borders is not accidental.

To be sure, natural forces—in particular climate and climate change—also drove environmental change. But by the early 1800s, it was apparent to the Chinese that the major cause of environmental change in their world was human action. Indeed, by then, most of China, including the very soil itself, had been touched or worked (and reworked) by human hands, leaving very little of "nature" left natural. That which remained pristine progressively shrank in size, and remained chiefly in places too remote for humans to access easily—high mountains, deep river valleys, underground rivers. In the last decades of twentieth century, these places and others like them that contain habitat for endangered species have been placed into protected nature preserves, places that have now become space contested between those who want to preserve biological and natural diversity and those who want economic "development." This book will conclude with the unresolved battles being waged to preserve perhaps the last bit of natural beauty and biodiversity left in China in a remote region known as the Three Parallel Rivers, in Yunnan Province.

We will confront several paradoxes in this environmental history of China. On one hand, a primary storyline concerns the ways in which the Chinese transformed their environment (deforesting it, channeling water, moving mountains or cutting through them, etc.) through the establishment of a particularly successful combination of family farming with the strategic interests of the state. And, as we will see, the transformations of the Chinese environment not only were extensive but also caused episodic and long-term ecological damage that resulted in mounting environmental crises. Yet another storyline is how the Chinese agricultural system turned out to be exceptionally sustainable over long periods of time: how else can we explain how land that was farmed three thousand years ago is still being farmed, and how rice paddies and the waterworks to maintain them, built one thousand years ago, still produce vast amounts of rice? To be sure, part of the answer involves the application of chemical fertilizers, but only recently; over long centuries, Chinese farmers became exceptionally good at recycling nutrients back into their soil.

China's environmental history is not just the story of the ways in which the natural environment conditioned human settlement of the land, and the ways that people then altered their environment. Certainly, the story involves the natural environment, but it also explores the relationship of how the people who became Chinese interacted with other peoples, different from them, who also inhabited the region. These non-Chinese—who, as we will see in the coming chapters, numbered at least in the hundreds of different peoples, tribes, and ethnicities—also derived their sustenance from the environment, often in ways quite different from those by which the Chinese did. Sometimes these non-Chinese were hunter-gatherers, sometimes farmers, sometimes pastoral nomads—and sometimes combinations of some or all of these. These peoples, too, as we will see, often dramatically altered their environments; ecological change in the part of the world we call "China" was not all brought about only by the people we call "Chinese." The extraordinary diversity of China's natural environment meant that within it were numerous ecological niches where people could, and did, exploit the environment to sustain and reproduce themselves and their cultures.

The most successful people, at least on their own terms, turned out to be the Chinese. As with any name for a contemporary people or a place that is projected back in time (in this case, for several thousand years), numerous problems arise when using the name "Chinese." Simply put, there weren't any "Chinese" when this narrative begins; like the space we call "China," they came into being only as a result of a very long historical process. Sometimes they referred to themselves as Yin, Xia, Hua, Han, Tang, or so forth, depending in part on the ruling elite who structured their political space. For our purposes, I will refer to the stock of people who became today's Chinese as "Han Chinese." The term "Han" comes from an early dynasty when the people of that time referred to themselves as "Han," as well as from current ethnographic usage that identifies the "Han" ethnicity as Chinese.

With these ambiguities and caveats in mind, we will see that from their early states in what is now north and northwest China, Chinese expanded to the east, south, and west, encountering the non-Chinese inhabitants of those regions with military force backed by sophisticated social, economic, and political institutions. Humans exploited nearly every ecosystem in some way: deserts, mountains, jungles, and even oceans that might appear to have been uninhabited in fact turn out to have been contested borderlands where much of China's environmental history was fought out over millennia.[2] Indeed, at various times, nomadic peoples of the steppe or the northeastern forests so efficiently tapped their natural resources that they could mount significant military challenges to the Chinese, sometimes even conquering and ruling them.

In this complex, interactive process engaging different peoples and their environments, many non-Chinese peoples nonetheless were eliminated, assimilated, or forced to flee, thus allowing the Chinese to take their land and transform the environment into Chinese-style farms. Contrary to what is often assumed, the Chinese did not expand from a core region in the Yellow River plain of north China into a pristine wilderness. Other people were already in that wilderness, people who had established ways of supporting their populations from that natural environment. The story of China's environmental history in many ways thus entails the Chinese seizing of land from peoples who were already there (peoples who, as we will see, had themselves perhaps supplanted earlier peoples) and who had altered the "natural" environment to suit their way of life, and then the remaking of the environment in a particularly Chinese way, marked by settled agriculture based on farming families tilling the land and paying taxes to a central state.

Unfortunately, we know little about these other peoples and their relationship to the environment, largely because they either had no writing system to leave records of their own, or because their written languages have been lost. One major exception in all this is the Mongols, whose views toward their landscape and environment have been captured by anthropologist Dee Mack Williams, and subsequently compared with Chinese views. To Chinese, who were comfortable enclosing their space and marking it off with boundaries and walls, nomadic Mongols of the inner Asian grasslands, known as the steppe, had a much more "expansive spatial orientation," in Williams's words, with a significant tolerance for dry (and sometimes even sandy) landscapes that were not "opened" by the plow for tilling.[3] At various points, we will explore Chinese-Mongol interactions and perceptions of the other, for that relationship—which in many ways became a symbiotic one—constitutes a significant dynamic in Chinese history that warrants address in nearly every chapter of this book.

With a few notable exceptions, then, what we know about China's environmental history mostly comes from Chinese sources: the Chinese had a writing system and left records that we can interrogate for evidence about their relationship to the environment. Archeological finds of the remains of material culture, such as pottery and building foundations, also tell us things, and we will use evidence from those sources, too.

Mostly, however, historians have had to rely chiefly on Chinese sources. The Chinese, of course, have told their history from their perspective, and for quite some time other historians too have seen Chinese history from the point of view of Chinese sources. This has lent a heroic tinge to the traditional storyline of Chinese history: *Chinese spread the benefits of their high civilization to less advanced peoples, bringing them within the fold of Chinese civilization.* The Chinese saw themselves as the font of culture and civilized values; all other peoples they encountered were at best "barbarians" who could be introduced to, then transformed by, Chinese culture. Those of the barbarians who resisted were to be dealt with militarily—unless, as we will see, they were protected by invisible microbes to which Chinese were not immune, such as the complex of deadly diseases in the tropical and subtropical south.

Chinese and their chroniclers enmeshed in a discourse about their "civilization" for the most part framed their views of new environments by their encounters with other peoples not like them: both the "barbarians" and their wild environments were meant to be tamed and civilized. From the Chinese point of view and the historians who have consciously or unconsciously written Chinese history from that perspective, the Chinese have been an active, "progressive" force, while the non-Chinese peoples and the environment have merely been acted on. In the nature-culture dualism, Chinese-centered narratives thus see the Chinese as being above, or outside of, "nature"—that is what it means, after all, to be "civilized." Both the other peoples and the environment were there to be transformed—and they were.[4] What this Chinese-centered view of the world overlooks, of course, are the ways in which Chinese were transformed by other peoples and environments. That becomes an interesting dynamic as Chinese migrated out of their northern homeland into unfamiliar environments further south and west.

The nature of our sources thus leads to the question of what can be actually known about China's environmental history. Those sources require that we see events, landscapes, and environments from Chinese perspectives. But we will also "read" those sources in light of contemporary understandings of ecological processes. Much early ecological thinking, especially that published in the United States and Europe since World War II, posited a steady-state model of climax ecosystems. The idea was that natural processes would lead to ecosystems such as particular kinds of forests dominated by one or more combinations of plants: fire sparked by lightning might burn down much of that forest, but it would recover to the same climax stage by going through identifiable succession stages.

Over the past several decades, however, that steady-state view of ecosystems has been replaced by one that sees natural processes as much more chaotic, as not necessarily progressing through succession stages to a "climax ecosystem."[5] In part, that changed perspective has been influenced by studies of global climate change and animal population dynamics, and by chaos theory itself. Natural change to ecosystems is much more chaotic (and hence less predictable or knowable) than previously assumed. Another significant reason for the new perspective on ecosystem change is the growing recognition that humans are part of ecosystems, and that their actions have long been a significant cause of environmental change. As a species, humans are not separate from nature but depend existentially on it.

Because humans have always been part of the natural environment, several scholars argue that "culture" needs to be included as an explanation in environmental change. The idea is that "attitudes, values, preferences, perceptions, and identities" shape the ways in which people use (or abuse) the land. While it is true that people make history and shape their environment through their actions, those actions are based (at least in part) on what those people think and believe.[6] Thus, at various points in this book, we will pay attention to those beliefs: not just the beliefs of "Chinese" or other peoples but also, in later chapters, the more global and "modernist" belief that nature can be known and controlled through science.

Nonetheless, in trying to assess and understand the causes of environmental change, I intend to focus on more material considerations, structures, and dynamics. Ecologists and environmental historians speak of "driving forces" of environmental change.[7] Some of these forces, such as global climate change, are natural. Others are anthropogenic, and include human population dynamics, the formation and interactions of states, and the various modes of the extraction, production, consumption, and exchange of products originating in natural environments. Understanding peoples' economies is critically important, because—for better or worse—nearly everything that counts as "economic" involves a transformation of some part of nature. And that gets to the nub of the problem for environmental historians and is the core of contemporary concerns about the environment: economic growth, development, and progress almost invariably involve using natural resources and dramatically altering or degrading the natural ecosystems on which all life on earth—ours included—depends.

Given those caveats and perspectives, what can we learn about earth environmental systems by looking at Chinese history? Even from a Chinese point of view, the progress of civilization was not without reverses and setbacks, as climate change, fierce resistance by other peoples protecting their own space, and periodic successful invasions by mounted nomadic and pastoral peoples pushed and pulled the Chinese in various directions. Nonetheless, by 300 BCE, Chinese had so thoroughly transformed their North China homeland that some were already bemoaning the loss of their historical forests.[8] During the height of the Han era (ca. 200 BCE–200 CE) two thousand years ago, Chinese military might extended far west along what we now know as the Silk Road and into the tropical far south. By one thousand years ago (during the Song dynasty, 960–1279 CE), the Chinese already had more than a millennium of experience with a powerful state. Markets had come to allocate most resources, an economic "efflorescence" was bringing China to the verge of a self-sustaining industrial revolution,[9] and China's population of 120 million accounted for about one-third of the entire world.

But China's success at establishing, spreading, and then maintaining its particular way of extracting energy from the environment had long-term costs. By 1800, China had become so deforested that it was facing a pre-modern energy crisis; the landscape had been so worked and reworked by human hands that animals such as tigers and elephants had been pushed to the furthest peripheries; and some Chinese had become aware of the extinction of species.[10] In the first half of the twentieth century, political collapse, foreign invasion, and civil war added to China's environmental degradation, and while the victory of the Chinese Communists in 1949 ended the civil war, Mao Zedong and his followers soon launched a concerted effort to dominate and control what they believed to be a malleable nature in the pursuit of building an industrialized socialist state.[11] Since 1980, the pursuit of rapid industrial growth in the context of a global market economy has driven even more environmental degradation, including such serious air and water pollution that organizers and athletes participating in the 2008 summer Olympic games accounted for it in their planning.

Even for all its environmental degradation, China paradoxically remains one of the most biologically diverse places on earth. Indeed, it is one of twelve mega diversity countries. The reason for China's diversity is its tremendous variety of ecosystems. With the highest and lowest points on earth, glaciers and coral reefs, and deserts and tropical rainforests, among other places, China has a vast number of ecological niches for its native species to exploit.[12] China is home to 30,000 types of seed plants (13,000 of which are in the far southwestern province of Yunnan—where, as we will see, many are endangered), second only to the Amazonian rain forest of Brazil and

Columbia, and 6,300 species of vertebrates, accounting for 14 percent of the world total. And yet four thousand years of Chinese occupation and transformation of its land has put nearly 400 of those species (that we know of) at risk of extinction, largely because habitats in China have become so fragmented that the areas remaining are no longer sufficient to sustain healthy natural populations, putting entire species at risk of extinction.[13]

To put China's 400 endangered species into global perspective, since 1600 there have been just more than 500 recorded species extinctions worldwide.[14] There have probably been many more species extinctions in China over the past millennia, largely because of habitat destruction and fragmentation. Whereas most of China was once forested, today healthy forests remain on the margins of China, mainly in the far southwest and northeast. Plants and animals cannot hang on for long under those circumstances, though in the past twenty years the Chinese government has established hundreds of protected areas for endangered species. Whether these preserves will stem the tide of species extinction remains to be seen, but all of humanity has a stake in the success (or failure) of China to maintain its biodiversity.

In a nutshell, China's environmental history is a story of the simplification of environments, peoples, and institutions. Where four thousand years ago there were extraordinary natural and human diversity, agriculture and farming subsequently created simpler, less complex ones. Where there were hundreds (if not thousands) of different peoples, Chinese have proliferated, and other peoples have disappeared. Where there were numerous ways to organize states and societies, the Chinese way subsequently marched across the landscape.

This book thus is an environmental history of China, and a story that needs to be told, and understood, because of its profound implication not only for China but also for the world. Broadly understood, environmental history explores the mutual interaction over time between people and their environment, in particular the ways in which the environment conditioned human settlement, and the ways in which human activity in turn altered the environment. Environmental change thus alters the course of human and natural history. And because the story of China's natural environment also includes the various peoples who lived there, the story is more than a millennia-long "war against wild animals," as one historian put it[15]—although it is in part that. The Chinese also waged war against non-Chinese peoples, many of whom the Chinese often saw as being not much more than animals themselves, as the Chinese state expanded into frontier areas to gain control of new resources. In the process of these attempts to establish Chinese hegemony over the natural and human world, both natural species and other peoples have vanished.

Before sketching this book's chapter contents, I would like to comment on this book's intended audience, and on the sources used in this book. Because I think the topics are important, and because I hope to reach the broadest readership possible, I have composed the narrative assuming that most readers will not know much about China or its history, and so have provided that context when needed. Moreover, as careful readers will note by perusing the notes, this book relies on scholars whose work is published in English, not in Chinese. While the narrative at times draws on Chinese-language sources in the areas of my specializations in late imperial and modern Chinese history, it aspires as well to provide a synopsis of English-language scholarly literature that is relevant for constructing an environmental history. Many of these sources are widely scattered and not easily accessible, so part of this book's contribution is to synthesize them into a broader historical narrative.

Certainly, we need to be modest about what is, and what can be, known about China and its environment. In writing this book, I have become ever more impressed, awed, and humbled by the scholarship I have consulted. This book would have been impossible without the impressive achievements of those who have preceded me. In addition, gaps still exist in the available scholarship that are only very slowly being filled by new and exciting work—some of which work I use and cite here. But much more work is in need of being done—and if other scholars find holes in my argument, omissions in my materials consulted, or variations in my interpretations of the evidence, I hope they (or their graduate students) get to work. There is much scholarship to be done on many questions in this field that yet need addressing. I hope this book will stimulate some of that new scholarship.

PLAN OF THE BOOK

A certain tension exists between my aim of providing an environmental history of China and my desire to provide sufficient context for nonspecialists to be able to place environmental changes into a Chinese historical context. Mostly, histories follow periodizations based on major political or socioeconomic developments or changes within specific political units, usually the modern nation-state. Those political demarcations do not show up from space—they are artifacts of the human imagination. Rather, the world's ecosystems cross political lines. Environmental history therefore tends toward the global, and toward periodizations that decenter the nation-state from historical narratives. Processes of deforestation, or changes in energy sources and usage—for instance—are not bounded by nation-states or their historical periodizations.

How then, should one organize an environmental history? In a recent book on global environmental changes in the twentieth century, J. R. McNeill arranged his narrative in terms of the various natural spheres that make up the earth and its environment, from the lithosphere to the stratosphere, and examined the ways in which human activity has altered those spheres.[16] Following that example, one could approach China's environmental history topically, with chapters on land, water, forests, mountains, human population, animals, and air.

I considered such an approach but decided against it for two major reasons. I want to make this book accessible to nonexperts, and thus for my purposes need to provide some of the standard chronology and periodization. Locating China's environmental history within that framework will also allow us to examine the interconnections between environmental change and a standard historical narrative, to assess the impact of humans on the Chinese environment.[17] Moreover, the space bounded by "China" is big—including nearly 600 ecosystems—and part of the story includes considering how environmental conditions have set limits to how expansive China could get.

China's history typically is periodized into ancient, imperial, and modern periods, with the 2,100-year imperial period divided by ruling dynasties into the early, middle, and late imperial periods (see figure 1.1). This book is not organized by dynasty, but because it will refer to those periods and dynasties, figure 1.1 highlights the overlap of this book's chapters with China's dynasties and names for other historical periods and also summarizes the major landmarks in China's environmental history.

Existing environmental histories of China tend to focus either on the history of the People's Republic of China (1949–present) or on aspects of the ancient or imperial period. The twentieth-century divide, in particular that set by the Chinese Communist victory in 1949, has not yet been crossed by an environmental history. In part, this is because the rapid social, political, and economic changes of the last half century appear to have set China on such a radically different path as to render the preceding millennia irrelevant. But by engaging all of China's history from the Neolithic to the present, this book integrates Chinese environmental history into a single narrative, providing the context for evaluating the extent to which its more contemporary history does indeed constitute a separate and perhaps more significant episode.

The book is written in chapters that correspond to what I think are major environmental themes within China's more traditional historical periodization. Because the pace of environmental change (especially human-induced change) often is much slower than political or even social change, the chapters can cover rather long periods of time; chapters 2–4 each treat a thousand years or more of Chinese environmental history. Chapters 5–7 cover shorter periods, both because we know more about more recent eras, and because the pace of environmental change quickened during these times. For the aid of readers, each chapter is divided into several major subsections (please refer to the detailed table of contents).

Chapter 2 sets the environmental and human stage by looking at the origins of agriculture and the growth of states to about 1000 BCE. Chapter 3 covers ancient and early imperial China from 1000 BCE to 300 CE, and shows how the establishment of a powerful central state created a vast empire that sent Chinese far from their north China heartland and that "developed" settled agriculture throughout much of the region, deforesting much of the North China plain as early as two thousand years ago. The impact on the environment resulting from the collapse of the early empire is considered in chapter 4, as is the transformation of the very different environment of central and southern China under the creation of the powerful new agricultural technology of wet-rice agriculture that supported a much larger human population during the middle imperial period, from 300 to 1300 CE. In China's late imperial period, from about 1300 to 1800 (chapter 5), the ecological limits of the empire were being reached, its peripheries exploited and transformed, and its inner highlands and mountains settled by people who were supplying their food needs using New World food crops. The reaching of the ecological limits of the empire, and the using up of resources in an agrarian economy, bounded the empire's ability to capture and process solar energy, leading to ecological degradation and an increasingly severe environmental crisis as China entered its modern period (chapter 6). As chapter 7 describes, the Communist-led regime that came to power in 1949 proved to have the organizational capacity to rapidly industrialize China's economy, precipitating a host of new environmental issues, challenges, and responses not just for its citizens but for the world more broadly. In the conclusion (chapter 8), I assess the meaning and significance of China's environmental history in terms of both Chinese and world history.

Book Chapter	*Era*	Approx. Dates	Chinese period or dynasty	Technological innovation	Traction & power	Population size	Social formation	Climate	Environmental Impacts	Energy regime
Chapter 2	*Neolithic*	9000 BCE		Fire	Human muscle	?	small bands	Warming	Few to none	Somatic; Gathered biomass
		8000 BCE		Stone and wood tools		?	Small settlements	Warm and wet		
		7000 BCE		Domestication of rice and millet		?	Villages with cultivated rice	warming and drying		Locally farmed and gathered biomass
		6000 BCE				?	Villages cultivating millets	Cooling and drying	Loess land farming	
		5000 BCE	Yangshao Dapenkeng	Glazed Pottery		?	Settled agriculture more broad		Some forest clearing	
		4000 BCE				?	Proto-bellic states			
		3000 BCE	Longshan	Soybeans		?	Chinese interactive zone			
	Ancient	2000 BCE	Xia	Bronze	Oxen	?	States; cities		Forest clearance for farms	Extensive agriculture
		1500 BCE	Shang	Local irrigation; water control; silk	Horse	4–5 million	Writing	Rapid cooling ca. 1000 BCE	Forest clearance for farms more extensive	
Chapter 3		1000 BCE	Zhou	Chariots		4–5 million		Cold shock	Colonization Yellow River valley	
		500 BCE	Warring States	Iron and steel	Water		Multi-state Private property	Cooling	Deforestation in the north plain	
	Early imperial	250 BCE	Qin 221–207 BCE				Empire		Resources mobilized by the state	
		1 CE	Han 202 BCE–220 CE	Iron plows pulled by horses; collar harness	Cavalry	58 million	Markets		N. China plain deforested; ag. Intensifying	
Chapter 4		300 CE	Ten Dynasties			60 million	Estates		War and depopulation	
	Middle imperial (Medieval)	500	Sui 589–607 CE			45 million	Equitable fields	Warming	Population shift to south	
		750	Tang 607–907 CE	Wet rice paddies		50 million	Buddhist monasteries		Grand Canal Colonization of south and west	Intensification of agriculture
		1000	Song 960–1279	Coal for iron and steel		66 million	Market exchanges	Cool	Poldering Yangzi R. valley; highly intensified ag.	Biomass with increased use of coal
Chapter 5		1300	Yuan 1279–1368			115 million			Mining and deforestation in Southwest	Advanced organic regime
	Late imperial (Early Modern)	1500	Ming 1368–1644	Variolation against small pox		110 million		Cooling; cold shocks	Upland exploitation and deforestation	;
Chapter 6		1800	Qing 1644–1911			350 million		Warming	Conquest of NW	
	Modern	1900	Republic 1911–1949			500 million	Nation State	Cooling	Environmental degradation and crisis	
Chapter 7		1950	PRC 1949 Socialist industrialization	Chemical fertilizer coal, steam; nuclear weapons		583 million		Warming	Rapid industrialization w/in B.O.R.	Fossil fuels
		2000	PRC Market Capitalism, 1980–	Petroleum		1300 million (1.3 billion)			Rapid industrialization	Nuclear energy

Fig. 1.1. Timelines for China's Environmental History

Chapter 2

China's Natural Environment and Early Human Settlement to 1000 BCE

This book looks at a very long period in human history—nearly ten thousand years from the Neolithic to the present, and thus more than most. Before beginning, I want to warn readers not to look back in Chinese history and assume that the way things turned is the only way Chinese history and the relationship of Chinese to their environment could have unfolded. Sometimes we may think that the present is somehow the inevitable result of previous history, and we its ordained beneficiaries.[1] In most cases (and China's environmental history is one), the present is not the only outcome possible—things could have turned out quite differently, making the history we are telling rather different, too.

The way Chinese history turned out was not predetermined but rather was contingent on several exceptionally important turning points when China and its history could have been very, very different, and hence the relationship of Chinese to their environment very different as well. As we pursue this story, we will have to be highly attuned to those moments, for they were important not just for the people of China but for China's flora and fauna as well.

Calling a place "China" and its people "Chinese," though, commits the historical fallacy of projecting current circumstances back into the past. There was, of course, no "China" ten thousand years ago, or even four thousand years ago; indeed, numerous peoples of varying languages and cultures were living in the geographical region we now call "China." The process by which the place that we call "China" came into being and subsequently became a modern country was a historical process with many contingencies. Nonetheless, we need a shorthand term to discuss the area that ultimately became China, so I will use "China" to refer to the eastern part of the Eurasian landmass, from the Tibetan plateau to the Pacific Ocean, between about 20 and 50 degrees north latitude.[2] Those who are not Chinese and who do not want to be under current Chinese jurisdiction might object to this kind of cartographic imperialism; I am mindful of their concerns. As we will see, the process by which the area called

"China" became inhabited by the people we call "Chinese" was the result of a very long and contested process, extending in some important ways to the very present.

This chapter will start with an overview of China's natural environment, which was exceptionally diverse, providing large numbers of niches for a wide variety of plants and animals to exploit. In that environment, climatic and other changes that ended the last Ice Age also created conditions in which people could domesticate plants and begin farming. That happened as early as 9,500 to 8,800 years ago in the Yangzi River valley, where some people began to cultivate rice, and by eight thousand years ago in north China, where dry farming based on millet emerged. Over several thousand years, as agriculture provided food for growing populations, villages came under control of rulers, and the first states emerged. Farming, coupled with these states' interactions, wars, and strategic concerns, drove early large-scale transformations of China's environment.

NATURAL ENVIRONMENT

Landforms

Both the earth's climate and its landmasses are constantly changing. Geologists know that the current continents are drifting on the earth's mantle, and that they all came from one giant continent called Pangaea that began breaking up about 200 million years ago. As the plate that became Eurasia rotated clockwise, the part that became India slammed into it. That collision raised up the Himalayan Mountains and created the Tibetan plateau, changing not only the geography of Asia but also its climate.

Prior to the uplift of the Himalayas, the Asian plate was without mountains, allowing warm, moist air from tropical oceans to flow over it, resulting in a subtropical climate far to the north that included all of modern China. From a rather level topography, the uplift of the Himalayas and Tibet created landforms arrayed from west to east in three great topographic steps.[3] By about 1 million years ago, both the Himalayas and the Tibetan plateau had reached their current height. The highest peak in the Himalayas is Qomolungma (Mt. Everest), at nearly 29,000 feet—indeed, the entire Tibetan plateau is more than 10,000 feet above sea level.

This change in the Asian landmass created new weather patterns as a monsoonal pattern developed in the rain shadow of the new mountain range (this will be discussed in more detail in the section on climate).[4] When the uplift of the Himalaya Mountains and Tibetan plateau dried out much of the land to the north and east in their "rain shadow," thereby creating the Gobi desert, annual dry winds from the northwest picked up huge quantities of dust from that desert and deposited it across northwest China. In the spring and summer, however, the winds reversed and blew from the Pacific into East Asia, bringing much-needed rain—as much 80–90 inches in the south, and 20 inches in the north. This annual swing of winds from the dry northwest in the winter to the warm and moist Pacific air in the spring and summer is called the monsoon, and has had a significant effect on the patterns of China's natural environment.

Another consequence of the western uplift was the increasing aridity of Inner Asia, which saw the creation of deserts in the Xinjiang region and dry steppe across Inner Mongolia, and the formation of what is known as loess across much of north and north-

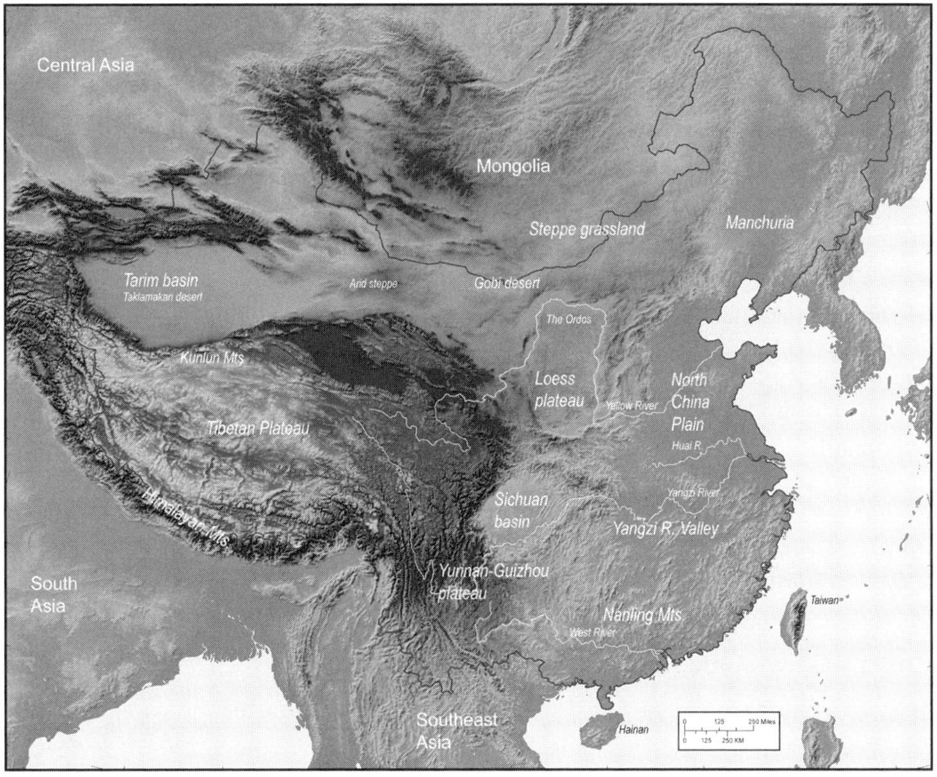

Map 2.1. China's Major Physical Features

west China. Loess was created when the dry winter winds picked up dust from the desert regions and then deposited it further east. So much dust was deposited this way that loess is up to 500 feet deep in some places, completely covering the landforms that preceded it. North China is still known for its dust storms, which make it difficult for the residents of Beijing, for instance, to keep the yellow dust out of their homes. In the winter of 1997, the winds were so powerful that the dust blew across the Pacific and could be seen as a yellow haze above California. However, loess is important for the development of agriculture in China as well as for being a conditioning feature of some of the first civilizations that developed in north China, and will be discussed again later in that context.[5]

The monsoonal rains, falling over a landmass that generally sloped from west to east and toward the Pacific Ocean, created China's rivers and drainage systems, yielding four major systems—the Yellow River in north China, the Yangzi River in central China, the Huai River between the Yellow and Yangzi Rivers, and the West River in south China (see map 2.1).[6] All these rivers play important parts in China's environmental history, and will be discussed as they arise. The Yellow River and its tributaries, for instance, will be part of the story of early Chinese states, partly taken up later in this chapter as well as in the next.

The global warming of some thirteen thousand to eight thousand years ago that ended the last Ice Age was also important to China's natural environment. Until then, most of

China had not been covered with an ice sheet, unlike western Eurasia or North America. In China, the species that were there before the Ice Age and glaciation elsewhere were still there afterward, giving us such splendid trees as the 200-million-year-old ginkgo biloba with its strangely shaped but beautiful foliage. After the last Ice Age, those species that did emerge in new niches added to the biological richness of the region, giving it a huge numbers of species. As a result, Asia in general, and China in particular, was particularly lush and biotically rich. Korea alone, for example, currently has 4,500 plant species, more than twice the diversity of England.[7] And of the 225,000 plant species in the entire world, China has thirty thousand, making it the biologically richest region in the whole Northern Hemisphere.[8]

During the last Ice Age, Northern Hemisphere glaciers had locked up so much of the earth's water that oceans were much lower than they are now, creating the well-known "land bridge" where the Bering Strait now separates Asia from North America. Importantly, Japan and Korea were also connected to the Asian mainland: the "coast" of China was much farther east than it now is. The melting of the glaciers raised the Pacific Ocean, covering the Bering Strait land bridge, separating the Japanese islands from the mainland, and moving China's coast progressively westward. The physical space we now call "China" had come into being.

China's Geographic Regions

The reason for China's extraordinary biodiversity, of course, is that it has such a variety of geography, climate, and soils. It spans 50 degrees of latitude and 62 degrees of longitude, and ranges in altitude from nearly 1,000 feet below sea level (the Turpan depression in modern Xinjiang province in northwest China) to more than 29,000 feet on the peak of Qomolungma (Mt. Everest). From the tropics of Hainan Island and south China, with annual mean temperatures in the 70s (in degrees Fahrenheit) and annual rainfall of 80 inches, to glacial conditions on the Tibetan plateau, with annual mean temperatures around 40 degrees and little rain, to the coniferous forests of the northeast (Manchuria), China has a vast range of climates. It also has most of the soil types found in the world.[9]

In light of this variety, there are nearly as many systems for dividing China regionally as there have been geographers, with most classifications ranging between eight and fifteen topographical/climatic regions.[10] For the purposes of this book, however, we will be a bit more general and refer to the regions of China as noted on map 2.2. Our story of the relationship of humans to the environment begins to unfold in Wei River valley of northwest China, and then moves to the Yellow River region of the North China plain (chapters 2 and 3), including the vast grasslands of the Eurasian steppe stretching from the northeast through the far west and crossing what is now Mongolia. The Yangzi River basin of central and eastern China enter the narrative in chapter 4, as do the Sichuan basin in west China, the Nanling Mountains and the Pearl River drainage basin in south China, and the southeast Chinese coast. The plateau and rain forests of the southwest, as well as the grasslands and deserts of the far west, become central to the story in chapter 5, and the high mountain plateau of Tibet enters the discussion in chapter 7. As the Chinese state became organized

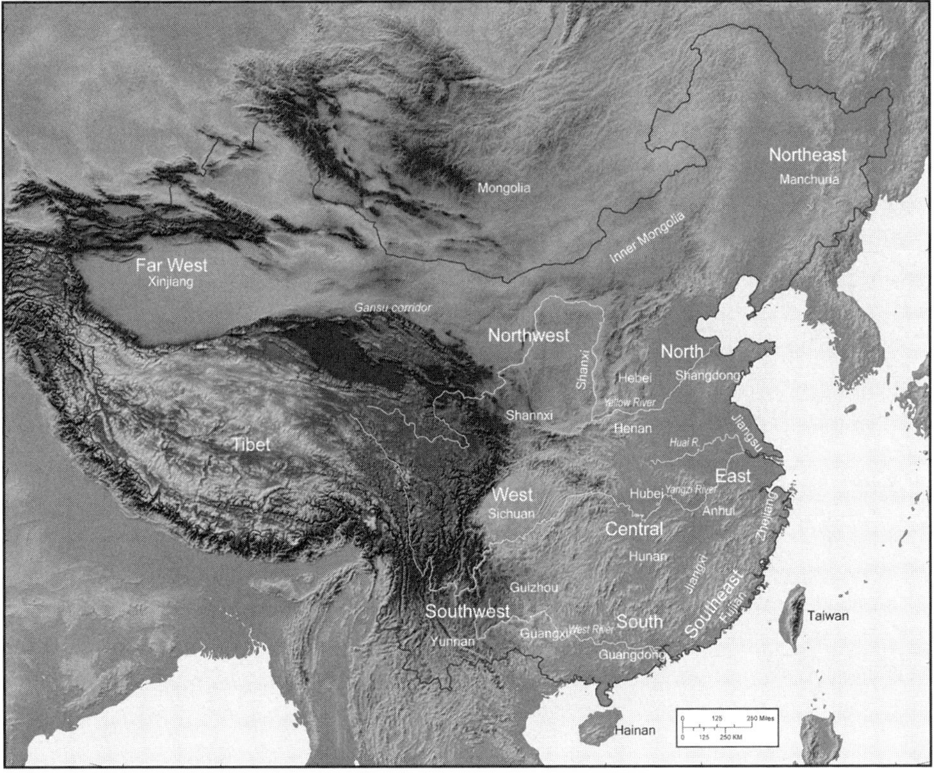

Map 2.2. **Geographic Regions of China**

and began to expand, these regions also acquired political designations, which for the sake of convenience I will associate with the names of modern provinces (see maps 2.2 and 2.4).

Forests and Ecosystems

We will introduce and discuss specific kinds of forests in the second part of this chapter, when the humans in our story encounter them. For now, suffice it to say that for most of China's history, the presence or absence of forests and their animal inhabitants served as indicators of the impact of Chinese on their environment. The reason is twofold. First, natural forest once covered nearly all of China, forming, in the words of forest expert S. D. Richardson, "an unbroken sequence of communities from tropical monsoon forest in the south to montane coniferous forest in the north."[11]

However, because of the rapid falloff in the amount of monsoonal rain reaching into the interior, according to Nicholas Menzies, "the forests of China are largely confined to the eastern half of the country. Grasslands and scrub predominate in the arid west, except in mountainous areas where sufficient water is derived from winter snowfall to support coniferous forests. . . . The historical geographer Wen Huan-Jan has identi-

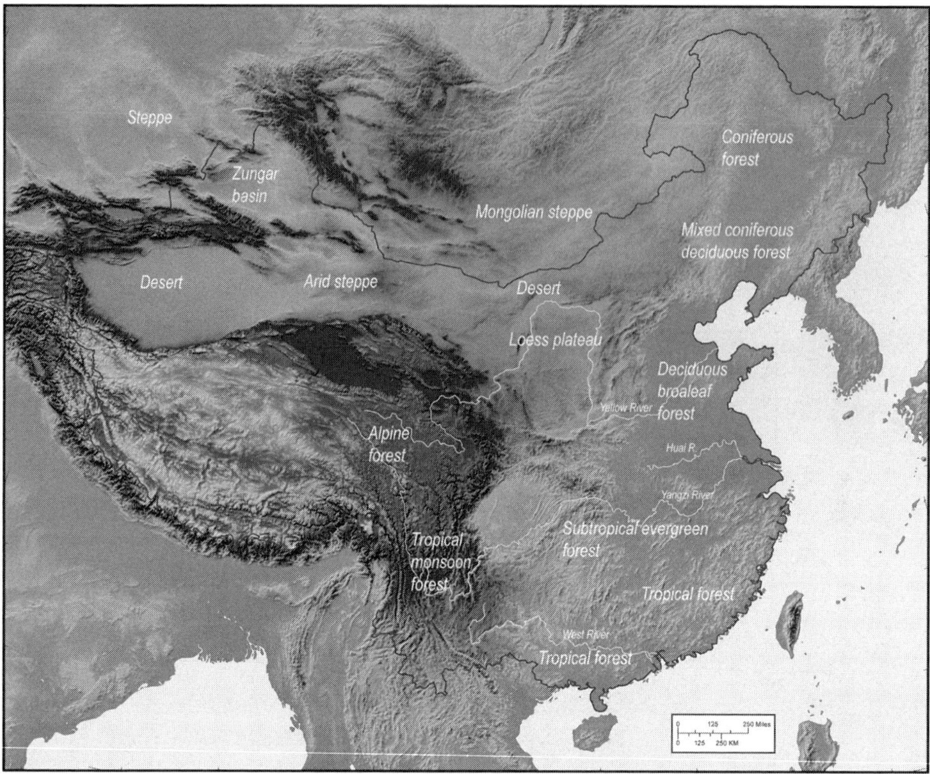

Map 2.3. Paleovegetation of China

fied five forest zones (not including the western grasslands and desert) which combine the biological factor of the dominant plant communities with the human factor of the history of exploitation of the forest. These are the boreal forest [of the northeast], the temperate forest of north China, the subtropical forest of central and southwestern China, and the tropical forest of southern China."[12]

Because the Chinese ultimately developed as a highly efficient agricultural society, they had to remove forests to make way for farms and farmland. In effect, the Chinese experienced an exceptionally long period of progressive deforestation of their land, starting with the development and spread of agriculture some ten thousand years ago. Map 2.3 shows what the land cover of China was about six thousand years ago. By the twentieth century, so little forest remained that scientists had to develop methods of reconstructing what forests had been there previously.[13] The story of how and why China became deforested is one of the main themes of this book, and is important because forests are important.

Forests are not merely stands of trees but, as noted above, "communities" that scientists now recognize as ecosystems, with varieties of organisms ranging from bacteria in the soil to the large mammals—often carnivores—at the top of the food chain, all interdependent and interacting with each other as well as with soil, water, and solar energy. The more species of plants and animals interacting in any given ecosystem, the more biologically diverse and hence healthy the ecosystem is.

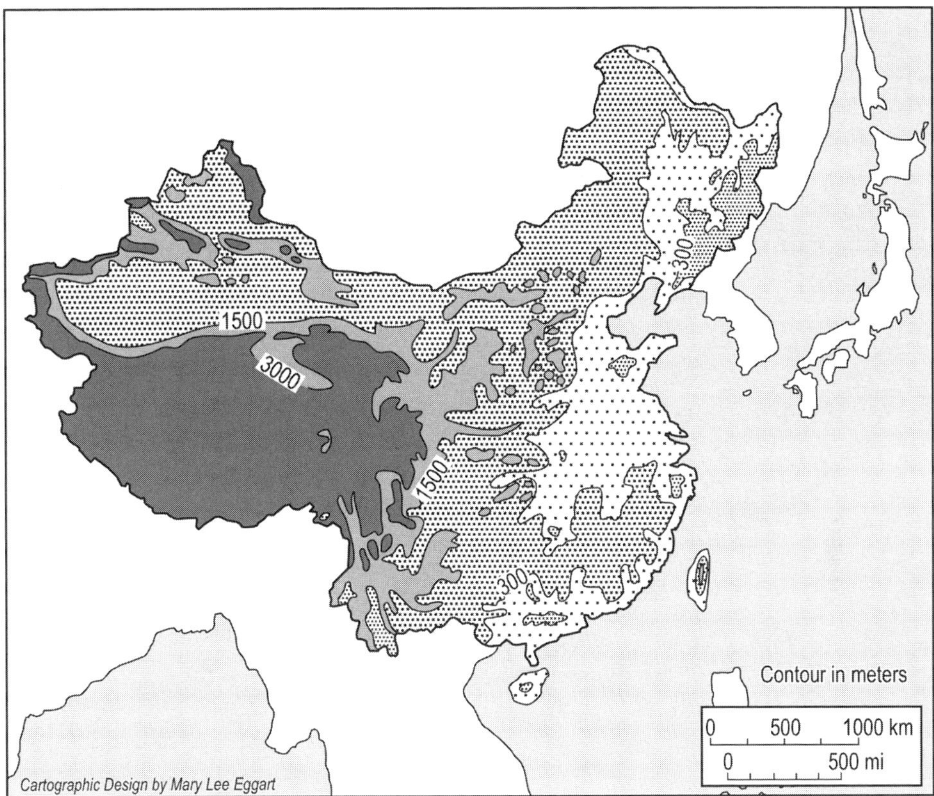

Map 2.4. China's Topography *Source:* Gregory Veeck, Clifton W. Pannell, Christopher J. Smith, and Youqin Huang, *China's Geography: Globalization and the Dynamics of Political, Economic, and Social Change,* second edition (Lanham: Rowman & Littlefield, 2011), 17.

Ecologist E. O. Wilson called the animals at the top of the food chain "star species," and others term them "umbrella species." An important reason for identifying star and umbrella species is that their existence can act as a barometer of human intrusion into and destruction of the natural environment. For instance, both the Asian elephant and the tiger require vast expanses of habitat to sustain themselves. Elephants consume huge amounts of foliage each day; herds of elephants graze though miles of territory daily. To accommodate elephants, a forest needs lots of trees with plenty of leaves, which means that where there are elephants, there are forests. The same was true of tigers; they inhabited forests.[14] While female tigers are territorial, male tigers roam widely in search of prey. The amount of territory required to support each tiger varies with the density of large prey—the more deer, for instance, the more tigers—and recent studies estimate that it requires between 20 to 100 square kilometers under good conditions to support a single tiger.[15] As the habitat required to support the tiger and the elephant declined, in the past just as today, so too did the populations of these two animals. Wilson cites biological studies showing a "rigorous connection" between the decline of rain forest habitat and that of species, so that when the rain forest is reduced by 90 percent, the number of species will have been reduced by 50 percent.[16]

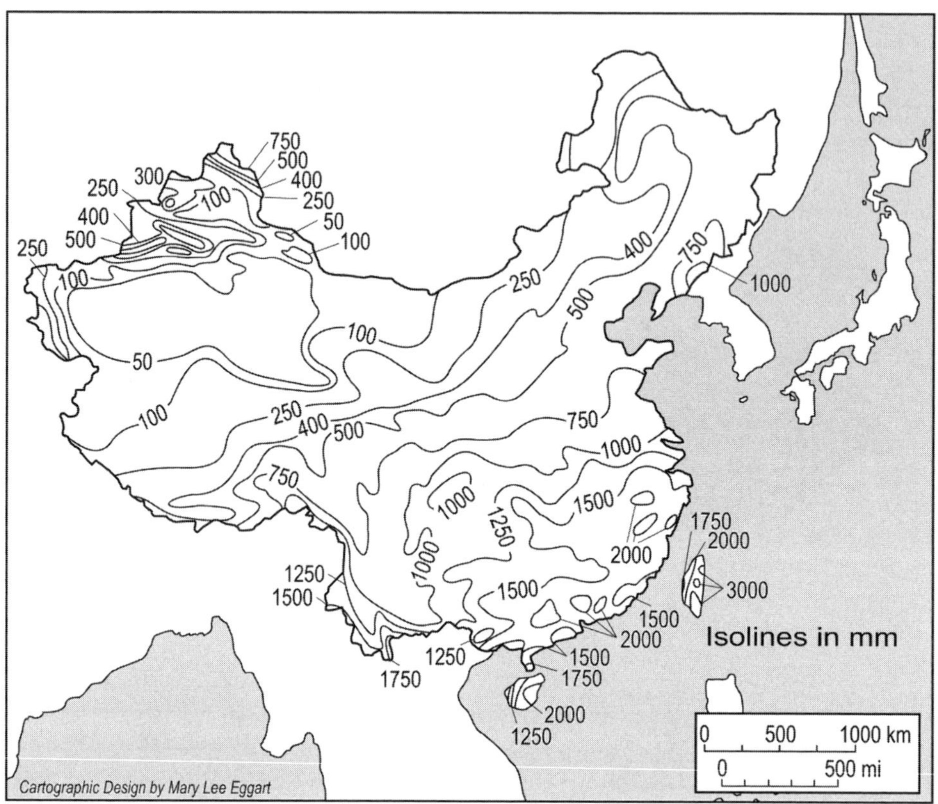

Map 2.5. China's Annual Precipitation *Source:* Gregory Veeck, Clifton W. Pannell, Christopher J. Smith, and Youqin Huang, *China's Geography: Globalization and the Dynamics of Political, Economic, and Social Change,* second edition (Lanham: Rowman & Littlefield, 2011), 19.

Traditional sources familiar to most historians of China have been used to chart the location of tigers and elephants, at least so far as the Chinese observers who left the records were aware, and thereby provide additional evidence concerning the timing and extent of changes in China's environment.[17]

China's Climate

Today, northwest and north China could be described as a temperate zone with freezing winter temperatures (but little snow) and warm to hot summers; central China occupies a subtropical zone with few freezing temperatures and hot, humid summers; south China is a tropical region with warm winters (seldom seeing frost or freezing) and hot, rainy summers (see map 2.5). But, as we now know, past climates have been both warmer and colder than present conditions, and climatologists have concluded that climate conditions coincided around the Northern Hemisphere, so that changes detected in Europe or North America also affected East Asia, and vice versa.

Climatologists have reconstructed past climates mostly on the basis of "proxy" data—that is, indirect evidence such as tree ring growth, ice layers in glaciers, and

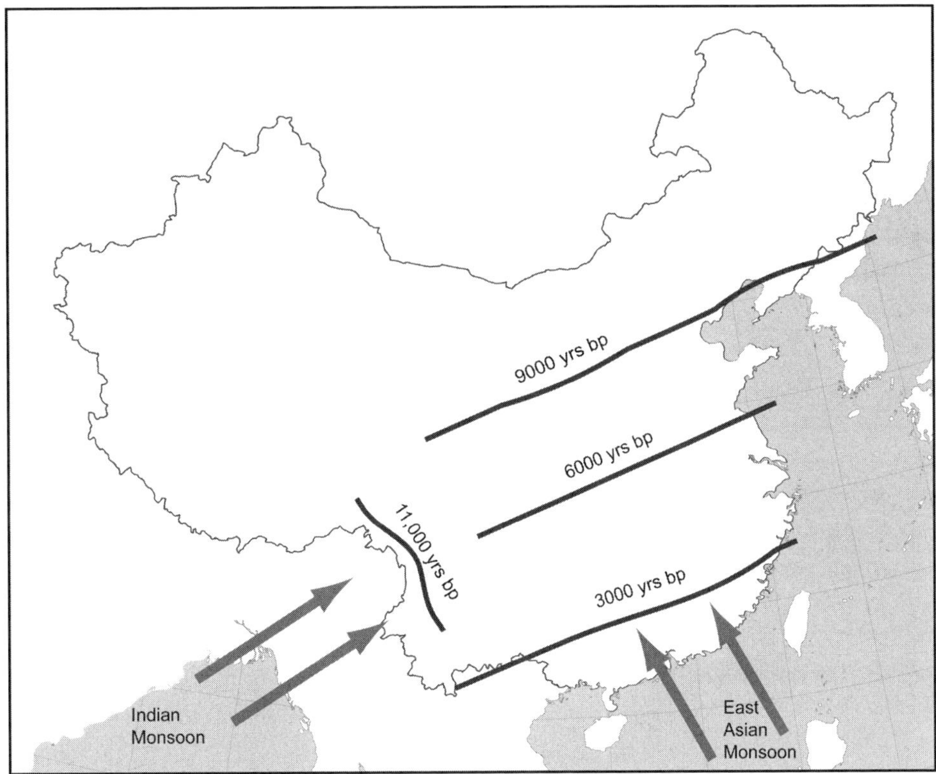

Map 2.6. Maximum Positions of the East Asian Monsoon Front *Source:* Adapted from Li Liu, *The Chinese Neolithic: Trajectories to Early States* (Cambridge: Cambridge University Press, 2004), 24.

sediment layers in lakes, marshes, and bogs, as well as archeological evidence.[18] What that evidence tells us is that after the last glacial age, the period from 6000 to 1000 BCE was warmer and wetter than at any time in the last eighteen thousand years. From then until the twentieth century, despite fluctuations, China mostly experienced a gradual cooling and drying as the East Asian monsoon weakened (see map 2.6). Of course, these climatic changes affected forest composition and the animals inhabiting it. In the North China plain around 6000 BCE, the warmer climate supported the alligator, rhinoceros, jackal, and Asian elephant, as well as substantial stands of bamboo—all species later found only much further south.[19]

But historians of China do not need to rely solely on proxy records to reconstruct past climates. For China, somewhat more direct evidence has been found in written records. As it is, China has the longest unbroken written record of all the world's civilizations. As early as 1500 BCE, rulers who wanted to know whether to take particular actions asked diviners who claimed to be able to ascertain answers from the ways tortoise shells and animal scapula cracked under heat; sometimes these questions and answers were carved onto the shells or bones, which came to be known as "oracle bones" (see figure 2.1) when archeologists unearthed them in the twentieth century.

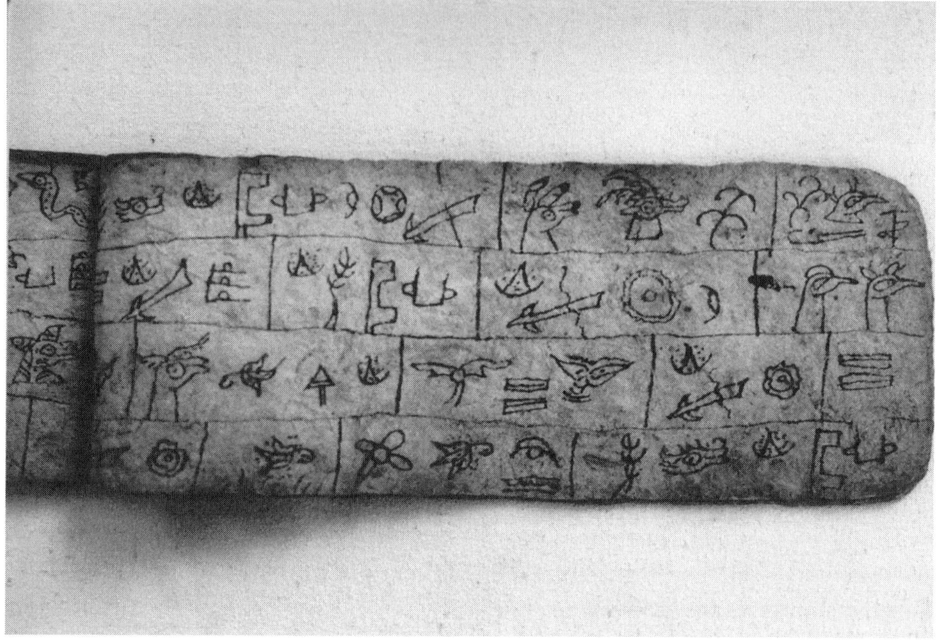

Fig. 2.1. An "Oracle Bone" *Source:* Author.

Two thousand years ago, those ideographs were standardized into a script that can easily be read today. Subsequent Chinese states produced piles of written records that historians periodically compiled into dynastic histories, and since the advent of printing and books by about a thousand years ago, significant amounts of primary sources have survived intact, or partially so. The last dynasty, the Qing (1644–1911), produced so many records that more than 9 million separate surviving documents are now housed in the world's largest history archive in the Imperial Palace Museum, of no small use to climatologists, who have used those records to reconstruct China's past climates.[20]

The first scholar to use those written records to reconstruct an important aspect of China's environmental past was the meteorologist Zhu Kezhen. The idea of climate change is of course relatively recent, dating to the early twentieth century and calling into question the assumption that climate has remained more or less constant during human history. The problem for early climatologists was that instrumental records dated only from the late nineteenth century. Zhu Kezhen, who received a Ph.D. in meteorology from Harvard University in 1922, thought that China's vast store of historical records might be helpful, and began combing through Chinese sources on his return home. Over the next fifty years, Zhu studied and wrote on various aspects of China's historic climates, publishing his results in 1972 in the modestly entitled "A Preliminary Study of the Climatic Fluctuations in China over the Past 5000 Years."[21] His research is summarized in figure 2.2,[22] which charts his reconstruction of past temperatures in terms of deviations in degrees Celsius from the mid-20th-century mean.

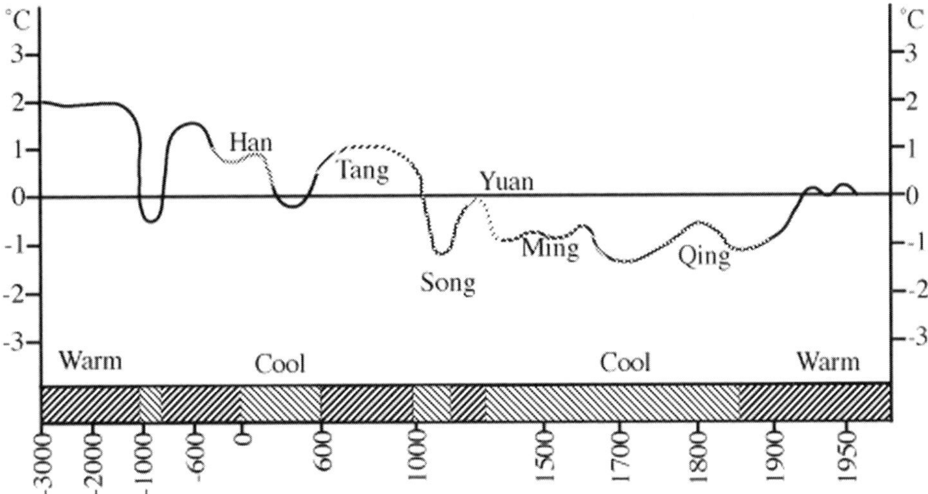

Fig. 2.2. Zhu Kezhen's Reconstruction of China's Climate Changes *Source:* Robert B. Marks, *Tigers, Rice, Silk, and Silt: Environment and Economy in Late Imperial South China* (New York: Cambridge University Press, 1998), 49.

This chart is significant (and justly famous) not just for its findings but also for Zhu's innovative methods and use of Chinese written sources.[23] Zhu classified his sources into four periods:

i. From 3000 to 1100 BCE, providing information based on oracle bones.
ii. From 1100 BCE to 1400 CE, providing information based on dynastic histories with little regional specificity, except for poems and other literary sources.
iii. From 1400 to 1900 CE, providing information based on local gazetteers.
iv. From 1900 onward, providing information based on instruments.

From the oracle bones, Zhu compiled records of prognostications about rain or snow, harvests, spring plantings, and animal sightings (e.g., elephants and rhinoceros in north China), concluding that the ancient period was generally warmer than the twentieth century. The dynastic histories and other sources yielded vast amounts of phenological observations (e.g., dates of tree and flower blossoming, bird migrations), as well as specific dates for snowfall, frost, and freezing or rivers and lakes. From the fourteenth century on, local officials began producing gazetteers (accounts of specific towns and counties), more than five thousand of which are extant, yielding an even larger amount of phenological data with which Zhu produced even more finely grained reconstructions of climate—concluding, for instance, that the period from the 1620s into the early eighteenth century was relatively cold, a finding preceding later European work on "the Little Ice Age."[24]

The impact of climate on China's history is complex. On the one hand, we do know that China's climate has changed over the millennia, and that people, plants, and animals reacted to changes in both temperature and the amounts and timing of rainfall.[25] But climate change did not wholly determine what people did, and hence what their culture and history was like; people responded to climatic and environmental changes in ways that ameliorated those environmental challenges. Those human responses may well have induced other problems, but the point is that humans did not merely react to their environment—they also changed it.

In summary, the physical space we now call China spanned an exceptional number of ecosystems, from tropical rain forests and coral seas in the south to the highest mountains on earth in the west, to grassland and desert in the northwest and an unbroken forest stretching from the south to the northern grasslands. In light of the vast numbers of ecosystems and ecological niches involved, as well as China never having had glaciers, it should not be too surprising that China was home to an immense number of different animal and plant species—China was species-rich. Such an environment was also hospitable to another kind of animal searching for sustenance from its surroundings—humans.

HUMAN SETTLEMENT AND PRE-HISTORY

To separate this chapter into sections on the natural environment and human settlement is to make a false dichotomy, because humans and their ancestors have been part of China's environment for hundreds of thousands of years. Until about ten thousand years ago, the story of humans in Asia is part of the general story of human evolution, with all that is uncertain and debatable about that record.[26] Suffice it to say here that fossil remains of upright walking *homo erectus* have been dated to 1 million years ago in Java, implying their existence on mainland Asia as well, and that the famous fossils of Peking Man (*homo erectus*) have been dated to about 500,000 years ago. Peking Man probably hunted, used crude stone tools, and used fire, although all of those conclusions have been contested.

By the time anatomically modern humans (*homo sapiens*) migrated out of Africa and through Southeast Asia into East Asia,[27] fire- and tool-using hominids were already there. These early humans disappeared from Asia about fifty thousand years ago (in Europe between thirty-three thousand and twenty-four thousand years ago), possibly driven out of existence by competition for food from the more technologically advanced modern humans. The total population of the earlier hominids probably never exceeded ten thousand individuals, so their environmental impact was small. So, too, was the impact of early human hunter-gatherers, although some paleobiologists suspect that their hunting prowess may have been responsible for the disappearance of several large animals such as the wooly mammoth and saber-toothed tiger. Whatever the case, it is certain that the major change in terms of the human relationship to their environment came with the emergence of agriculture, beginning about 9,500 years ago, not just in China but in at least four other parts of the world as well (the Fertile Crescent of ancient Mesopotamia, in what is now Mexico and the Andes in Mesoamerica, and on what is now the eastern coast of the United States, about 4,500 years ago, and probably also in west Africa and New Guinea).

China thus was one of the few places on earth where agriculture not only developed early but also became a mainstay of human society, and agriculture is thus central to the story of China's environmental history. Readers might think of it this way: hunters and gathers depended on maintaining their environment more or less unchanged to ensure the supply of the game and fruits and nuts that sustained their populations. They probably did use fire in the forest to clear out the underbrush and to allow fresh grasses to grow so as to attract deer and kill them more easily.[28] But the forest remained. Settled farming, on the other hand, requires that clearings in the forest be made and, when accompanied by the farmers' settlement in permanent villages, that those clearings be maintained. Farming increased the food supply by making its production more certain, and thus the human population increased in number as well, creating a need for more farmland. The technologies of farming and settled agriculture are thus significant ways in which humans have interacted with and transformed their environment.

The Origins of Agriculture in China

The transition to agriculture that some of the world's people made is sometimes called the "Agricultural Revolution" and sometimes the "Neolithic [New Stone Age] Revolution." Both terms refer to the process by which peoples who had previously gained their sustenance from hunting and gathering, moving either periodically or annually with the ripening of fruits and grains or the migration patterns of deer or ducks, began to plant crops and to domesticate animals. Agriculture was a gradual process in each of the areas it originated, beginning probably with a phase we might think of as gardening, when most food still came from hunting and gathering. Over time and for reasons scholars debate, but which probably include increasing population density, more and more food—ultimately most—came from sown crops, or a fully agricultural way of life. This process took several thousands of years, leading some scholars to question whether the term "revolution" is appropriate. I think it is, because regardless of how long a people took to change from hunter-gathers to farmers, the change represented a new and powerful relationship of humans to their environment, and created possibilities for new and more powerful or coercive forms of social organization.[29]

Scholars' understanding of the origins and spread of agriculture in China has changed over the past several decades. Because agriculture first emerged in Mesopotamia's Fertile Crescent, early accounts explained agriculture elsewhere in the world by "diffusion" from Mesopotamia. More recently, scholars have shown that agriculture developed independently in at least five regions of the world, China included.

But even there, the scholar who made the strongest initial case for the indigenous origins of agriculture in China argued that it developed first in north China, and then diffused along with the power and wealth of that first core throughout China and to the rest of Asia as well.[30] What we now know, though, is that agricultural practices emerged about the same time in several places in north and south China, with annual varieties of wild rice in the south and two types of millet in the north being planted and harvested.[31] How and why that happened in China in particular, or elsewhere in the world, is not known. Likely it had to do with the end of the last period of glaciation when the general warming of the earth led to the geographic spread of grains and grasses that held the possibility of being gathered, planted, and then harvested. Perhaps the warming climate had enlarged the food supply of the hunting and gathering peoples, and their populations increased to the point at which they then encountered difficulty sustaining their new size by hunting and gathering alone. In any event, agriculture in China from the beginning was based on two types of farming: wet-rice farming in central and south China, and dry-land farming based on millet and later wheat and barley in the north.[32] Each of these will be discussed in more depth in the pages to come.

Being as human as you or me, the hunting and gathering peoples inhabiting Asia were neither stupid nor ignorant. In the couple thousand years from the end of the glacial period to about ten thousand years ago, they had come to have substantial and very deep knowledge about the plants and animals in their very biologically rich environment—after all, they had to survive. Hunter-gatherers had this knowledge of their environments, making successful agriculture possible. But farming required another change in the nature of cereal plants themselves. Hunter-gatherers around the Northern Hemisphere had stripped grains from the perennial forms of rice, rye, oats, barley, wheat, and probably millet, along with legumes, all of which had been perennials. For farming to be possible, those cereals had to become annuals, with seeds that were then not just consumed by humans, but planted by them. How and why those grains developed annual forms is not known with any certainty, but plant biologists think that the stress of climate change—both increased aridity and high and fluctuating annual temperatures after the last Ice Age—induced the emergence of annual forms of cereals.[33] In Robert Whyte's words, about ten thousand years ago "an explosion of annuality . . . in a remarkably short period of time" made food crops available to humans for annual planting and harvesting.[34] Only then could cereal crops become "domesticated."

Rice Environments in Central and South China

A tropical evergreen broadleaved forest covered the southern hills of the Yangzi River basin, while a tropical rain forest, including brackish mangrove swamps, stood in south and southeast China. Among the forests of the world, these are the most species-rich. According to Wang Chi-wu, an expert who was among the first to reconstruct China's forest types, "the composition of the rain forest is characterized not only by the exceedingly rich flora but by the great diversity of plant species in a unit area, features which are not surpassed in any other type of plant community. The forest contains a wide range of life-forms to fit every possible niche . . . It is, in fact, a community of communities."[35]

Later Chinese found much use for products of the southern Chinese forest. Two Ming-era Guangdong province gazetteers (published in 1558 and 1602) list more than sixty different kinds of trees. For several, the 1558 edition also glossed their uses and their relative abundance. Pine (*song*) was most plentiful; camphor (*zhang*) grew so tall (50–60 feet) that half the lumber for a house could be cut from one tree; cedar (*bo*) could be used to carve Buddhas; cypress (*shan*) was used for lumber to build houses, boats, and furniture; *gao* was very suitable for furniture; and the cutting tong tree (*la*

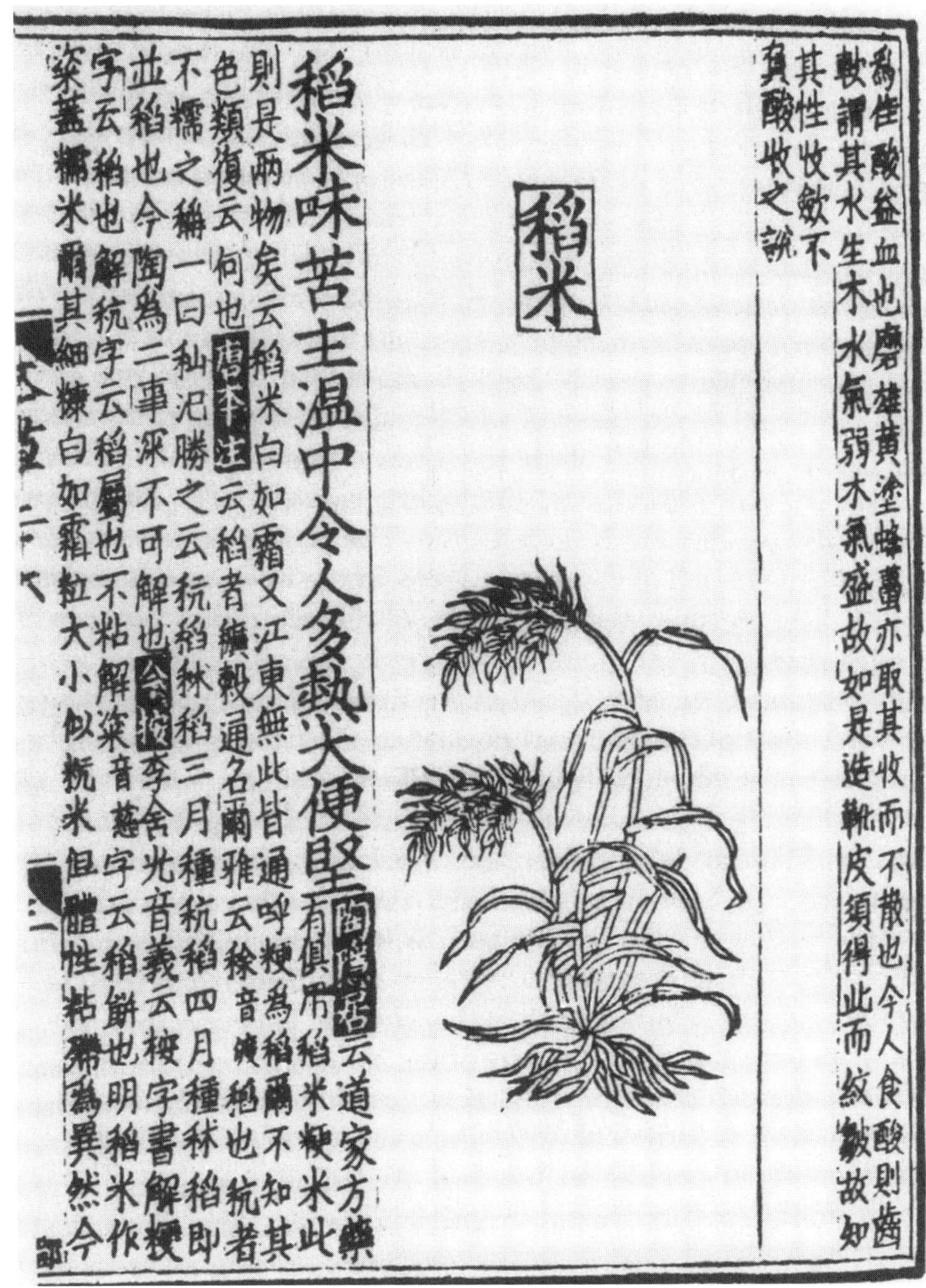

爲佳酸益血也磨雄黄塗蜂蠆亦取其收而不散也今人食酸則齒軟謂其水生木水氣弱木氣盛故如是造靴皮須得此而紋皺故知其性收斂不負酸收之說

稻米

稻米味苦主温中令人多熱大便堅陶隱居云道家方藥有俱用稻米粳米此則是兩物矣云稻米白如霜又江東無此皆通呼粳爲稻爾不知其色類復云何也唐本注云稻者穬穀通名爾雅云稌稻也秔者不糯之稱一曰秈氾勝之云秔稻秫稻三月種秔稻四月種秫稻即並稻也今陶爲二事深不可解也今按李含光音義云稉字書解粳字云稻也解秔字云稻屬也不粘解粢音慈字云稻餅也明稻米作粢蓋糯米爾其細糠白如霜粒大小似秔米但體性粘滯爲異然今

Fig. 2.3. The Rice Plant *Source:* Francesca Bray, *Agriculture,* vol. 6 part 2 of Joseph Needham, *Science and Civilization in China* (New York: Cambridge University Press, 1984), 483. Reprinted with permission.

tong) yielded good lumber. Writing in 1178, Zhou Qufei identified the remarkable *wu lan* wood found in Qinzhou, "used for the making the rudders of great ships . . . Rudders that are produced elsewhere do not exceed 30 feet in length and are adequate to control a [large] ship of 10 thousand piculs capacity . . . Only rudders produced in Qinzhou are close-grained, sturdy, and almost 50 feet in length . . . Ten to twenty percent of purchasers come to the spot because the length of the materials makes it difficult to transport by sea."[36]

To be useful did not require being cut, for many trees provided oils and varnishes (the lacquer tree and the tong-oil tree, for instance), or had leaves or bark that could be distilled for spirits (the *zhi fo* tree), or yielded seeds or leaves used in medicine (from the *dang* tree) or pesticides (from the *yuan* tree). Still others provided raw material for weaving into cloth (the *mu mian*, or kapok tree and the *guang lang* palm). Ironically, the banyan (*yong*) was included as a "local product" precisely because its economic uselessness did lend it a usefulness of sorts: "The wood is twisted and turned, and cannot be used to make utensils, nor as lumber. It does not burn, and so cannot be used as fuel. It has absolutely no use, so it is not harmed. It can shade more than 10 *mu*, though, so people rest under it."[37]

Among the vast number of plants and animals the people of southern and central China of ten thousand years ago had come to know quite well was rice, a grain that had grown wild in freshwater swamps and along the edges of lakes, ponds, and rivers. A particularly rich area of wild rice was in central Yangzi region around Dongting Lake. No doubt the Neolithic peoples had long gathered wild rice, and had come to know its characteristics and value quite well. Following paleobotanists, Bray argues that wild rice originated along rivers and swampy places in a band that spread from northern Southeast Asia into northeastern India, including south and central China.[38]

Wild rice is a perennial, so cultivation required its mutation into an annual form that may have thrived at the edges of marshes that went through annual drying cycles, thereby selecting for an annual form. Even with that mutation, though, cultivation required human intervention. Archeological evidence shows that Neolithic peoples gathered and consumed both the perennial and newly annualized forms of wild rice as long as ten thousand years ago in places of south and central China.[39] The earliest hard evidence of cultivated rice in China comes thousands of years later from sites in the Yangzi River valley. However, whenever, and wherever precisely it happened, people in south and central China began cultivating rice, possibly picking it out as weed that grew among their taro plants. By 5000 BCE, wet rice cultivation was widespread in the Yangzi River valley, on the island of Taiwan, and at places in the current provinces of Hunan, Jiangzi, Guangdong, and Guangxi. Along with clear evidence of cultivated rice (both *Oryza sativa japonica* and *O. sativa indica*), these archeological sites reveal a large number of wild animal bones and shells; these people also had domesticated chickens, pigs, and dogs, used finely chipped stone axes, adzes, and arrowheads, and fired their own pottery. In other words, by 5000 BCE, the cultivation of rice as the basis of settled farming communities from south China north into the Yangzi River valley of central China was already widespread and well established.[40]

We might imagine small village settlements near water sources, with people of the village periodically tending their standing rice crop and probably selecting as seed for the next harvest grains from among the largest, most prolific, best-tasting, or healthiest plants in a process agronomists now call "selective breeding." We know that this happened, because in the historic period, hundreds of varieties of rice, with varying characteristics for different environments and uses, were developed and used. Indeed, rice is among the most adaptable of all major food grains.[41]

In Steven Mithen's recent interpretation of the archeological evidence, cultivation of annualized forms of wild rice likely first emerged in the middle reaches of the Yangzi River valley just after the dramatic global temperature increase known as the Holocene began, around 10,000 BCE. At a site near the current village of Pengtoushan in Hubei province, hunter-gatherers around 9500 BCE began to select the annualized forms of wild rice, probably for their larger size, and then to broadcast the seeds into mud flats after the monsoonal floods receded. Unlike wild rice (*Oryza rufipogen*), which germinates over a month or so, planted rice plants all germinate simultaneously, and hence when ripe can be harvested at the same time. Even more evidence from the same time period of annualized rice was found in a limestone cave further down the Yangzi in present-day Jiangxi province. Evidence over the next three thousand years shows a mixed use of wild and domesticated varieties of rice, but by 6500 BCE nearly all the evidence of rice found with human settlements was of domesticated *Oryza sativa*. By 6800 BCE, people in the middle Yangzi region were not only farming rice but also making clay pots to both store and cook it. By 5000 BCE, this whole technology had been transplanted further down the Yangzi River to its delta region, which, as we will see in chapter 3, became the most agriculturally rich region in China by about 1000 CE—because of rice.[42]

As paleobotanist Hui-lin Li points out, however, rice alone could not support a viable agricultural system; the Neolithic rice farmers in south China and the lower Yangzi River valley planted and harvested a number of aquatic flowering plants to supplement their food supply: "Little known to people elsewhere, these are crop plants of a distinct system of farming, a wetland agriculture developed only in the special environment peculiar to the Yangzi basin. . . . Aquaculture . . . has been practiced in China since Neolithic times."[43] In addition, the Neolithic farmers supplemented their diet with plentiful ducks and fishes.

Malaria

And where there was water and a particular kind of mosquito, there likely was malaria, a debilitating and often deadly endemic disease. Unlike plague, smallpox, or cholera, malaria is not spread directly from host to host, but rather requires a specific kind of mosquito (*Anopheles*) that is infected with a particular genus of protozoa. Malaria thus requires a specific environment to exist, and cannot spread beyond that environment. South and southwest China had that kind of environment.

Tropical forests with plenty of standing or slow moving water, such as those originally covering south China and the Yangzi River valley, were especially good breeding grounds for parasites of all kinds. Malaria probably is as old as modern humans, evolving with them in their African homeland and migrating with them as they spread into hospitable environments throughout Eurasia, south China included.[44] However and whenever malaria became established among the human population of south and southwest China, it was there among the Neolithic population that domesticated and planted rice. The degree to which those peoples had developed some natural immunities, used drugs derived from natural sources, or adopted routines designed to avoid infection just is not known, but some of each of those adaptations were needed to enable people to continue to live there. By the second century BCE, a Chinese medical treatise identified a plant now known as the *qinghao* plant ("sweet wormwood;" *Artemisia annua L*) as being effective against malaria;[45] did the rice-growing people of the Yangzi River valley and the south coastal regions know it, too? Possibly. We'll delve more into the subject in future chapters.

The Yangzi River Valley

The cultivators of rice in the Yangzi River valley lived in an environment slightly different from that of the peoples to their south. Here the Yangzi River flowed through a mixed deciduous and evergreen broadleaved forest. Average temperatures today remain above freezing, but around 5000 BCE temperatures were warmer than they are today, and supported more of the semi-tropical forest found in south China. At the higher, cooler elevations, the forest included oaks, poplars, and maples among the more recognizable species; a notable "relic" from hundreds of millions years earlier which survived in China is the "ginkgo," or "maidenhair tree," with its brilliant gold fall foliage. Conifers included junipers, pines, and cypress.

The peoples in the Yangzi River valley had domesticated rice by 5000 BCE but also continued to gather large numbers of other plants from their environment, many of which came from ponds, lakes, and rivers, such as water chestnut, water spinach, and cattail. They lived in dwellings built along riverbanks on pilings above the water, and had domesticated the dog, pig, and water buffalo; they made and used pottery for storage and cooking. The peoples further upriver clearly lived in villages and also made pottery, in their case emblazoned with dragon designs. From these beginnings, the Yangzi River valley, in particular its lower reaches, became one of the most agriculturally rich and developed regions of China.[46]

The Environment for Millet in North China

When we come to the Neolithic settlement and environment of north China, we encounter important differences from those to the south. The forest, from just north of the Yangzi River through the North China plain to eastern Manchuria, was a deciduous forest dominated by oaks with stands of maple. On drier sites, pines were common, and higher yet stood coniferous forests. In the northeast, dense coniferous forests covered both valleys and mountains.

But a bit further west, about the last bend in the Yellow River before it flows east into the ocean, began a different kind of landscape called the loess highlands.[47] As mentioned earlier, loess soil began as dust carried from the deserts further north and west, and deposited over this part of northwest China. The loess was deposited in two major areas, and by different processes. In the western portion, covering the modern provinces of Gansu, Shaanxi, and western Shanxi (map 2.7), loess was laid down by dust storms in depths up to 250 meters. These loess highlands were probably not forested but were covered by a scrub brush known as *Artemisia*.[48] Over several millions of years, this loess then slowly eroded into the Yellow River and was carried further downriver to the east, where it was deposited as alluvium in the Yellow River flood plain in Hebei, Henan, and Shandong provinces. There, an oak and maple forest covered the flood plain.

There are many characteristics of loess that imparted important particularities to agriculture when it developed there. Loess is incredibly fertile soil, is easily worked, and, where it was the deepest, probably was not forested but was likely rather a scrubby grassland, possibly savanna with scattered trees along rivers and streams. As Hui-lin Li points out, grasslands are not good habitat for pre-farming hunter-gatherers, who need the greater protection and food supplies that a forest provides. "The forest does not offer the kind of . . . plants which are man's staple crops. Important staple crops are all sun-loving, high-energy-producing plants. . . . It was at the boundary between woodland and grassland, in an intermediate savanna environment, that cultivation began."[49] That area corresponds with the encircled region on map 2.7 identified as the "approximate border of the nuclear area" where north China agriculture first emerged.

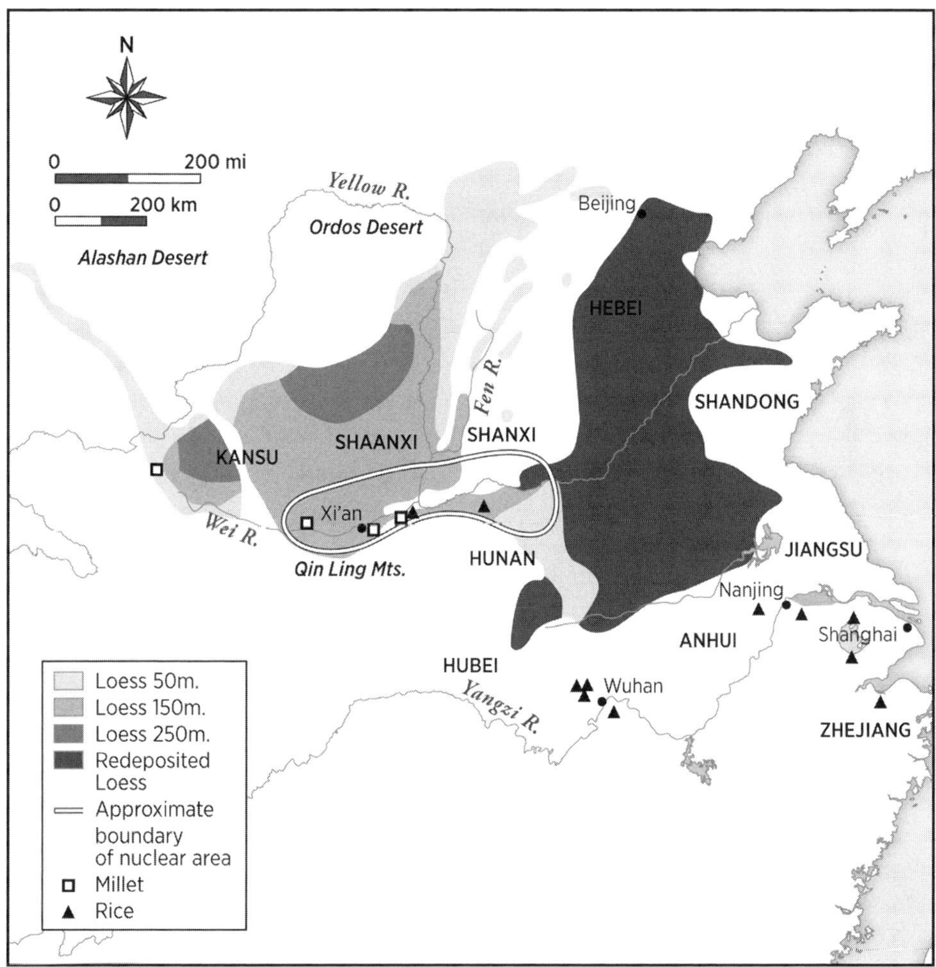

Map 2.7. The Distribution of Loess in China *Source:* Adapted from Ho Ping-ti, *The Cradle of the East: An Inquiry into the Indigenous Origins of Techniques and Ideas of Neolithic and Early Historic China* (Chicago: University of Chicago Press, 1975), 24.

As summarized by Menzies, "The picture of the original landscape of north China which emerges . . . is neither of dense forest nor of a barren steppe, but rather of a mosaic of vegetation. There was a fairly thick forest around rivers and other permanent sources of water. The plains were probably covered in rather sparse deciduous woodland, opening out to savannah grasslands with scattered trees or brush in the northwest, in what is now northern [Shanxi] province, and most of the Ordos plateau of Inner Mongolia. Denser deciduous woodland was found in the foothills of the mountains, with scrub and brush or drought-tolerant species on south-facing slopes. Coniferous forests dominated the higher elevations above about 1,500 meters with larch and spruce forming the highest forests just below timberline."[50]

In this environment, the first grains domesticated were forms of millet (foxtail millet, *Setaria italica*, and broomtail millet, *Panicum miliaceaum*) that had developed as annuals, meaning that they reproduced each year from seeds produced the previous year, making them good candidates for planting. Millet also had other qualities that recommended it, including the ability to self-fertilize and to hybridize with other strands, making it highly adaptable to various environments. Recent archeological studies show that millet farming did indeed develop around eight thousand to seven thousand years ago at the ecotone between grassland and forest on the loess highland, as warming temperatures brought more rainfall to the area. As the climate continued to warm and bring

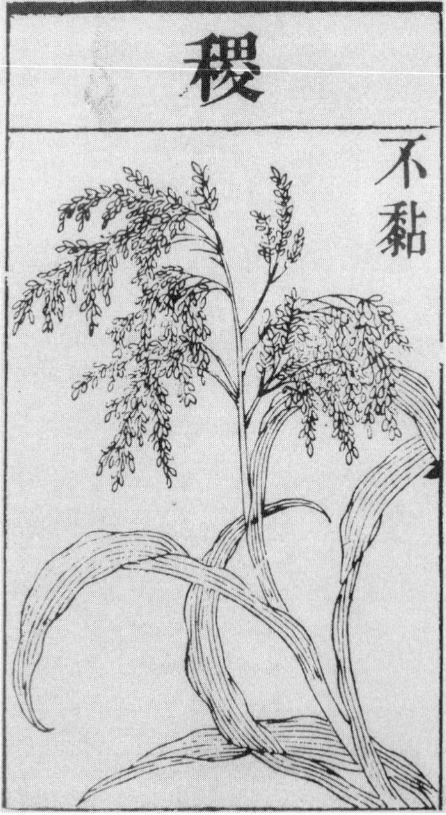

Fig. 2.4. Millet Plants (*Setaria* and *Panicum*) *Source:* Francesca Bray, *Agriculture*, vol. 6 part 2 of Joseph Needham, *Science and Civilization in China* (New York: Cambridge University Press, 1984), 438, 439. Reprinted with permission.

more moisture, this rain-fed farming spread as far north as Mongolia before climatic cooling and drying beginning about 3,500 years ago pushed farmers south once more.[51] The most studied of the Neolithic agricultural villages is Banpo, a five-thousand-year-old site near the present-day city of Xian.[52]

As historian Ho Ping-ti points out, loess soils are quite fertile, with nutrients continually brought to the surface by capillary action after rains. The water table, though, is so low that few if any trees could ever establish roots systems and flourish. Grasses thus covered the loess. "In all likelihood . . . [the] farmers first cleared the grass by burning. Using stone hoes and spades, they broke up the virgin sods, and very probably they also had wooden digging sticks. Without experience in field agriculture, they would almost certainly plant millet soon after the sods were turned over. It should not have taken them long to learn that the yield of the first year was meager but the yields of the second and third years were much better. During the first year the nitrogen in the soil is mostly consumed by the various microorganisms, which are the main agent in decomposing plant residues. By the second year, when the plant residues have already been decomposed, the various microorganisms, instead of continually tying up the nitrogen in the soil, release it to nourish the seed plants."[53]

Over the centuries, numerous varieties of millet developed, either by cross-breeding or chance, so that, as with rice, there were varieties for almost any growing situation, as early as five thousand years ago.[54] Although rice yields more than millet (per grain volume sown), millet is more productive than wheat, the grain favored farther west in Eurasia. At several of these early north China sites, the people had created numerous seed-processing tools, including pestles and mortars, and had domesticated the dog and pig; evidence of continued reliance on natural sources of food come from numerous wild animal bones found mingled in the kitchen middens. As archeologist K. C. Chang cautions, though, we should not underestimate the cultural sophistication of these peoples, as both flutes and bones with inscriptions resembling later ideographs have been found.

By 5000 BCE, the Neolithic peoples inhabiting China had developed cultural regions distinguished largely on the basis of the kinds, shapes, and decorations of the pottery they produced. Most of those on the North China plain belong to what archeologists have called the Yangshao culture area (which lasted for three thousand years, until 2000 BCE), which remains the most studied and best-known of all Neolithic cultures, with more than one thousand identified sites. These people were a millet-farming people who lived in villages, some of which clearly had shamans. The Dawenkou people lived further east, on the low hills and lakeshores of the Shandong peninsula highland. They, too, were millet farmers, but with slightly differently shaped and differently colored pottery. In the south, the Hemudu and Qing-lian-kang cultures around the Yangzi River valley cultivated rice, as did the Dabenkeng and Yue on China's southeast coast.[55]

Although questions about the origins and development of agriculture in China abound, and probably never will be solved definitively, agricultural historian Bray thinks that "it is quite clear . . . that as early as the –5th millennium [5000 BCE] the two distinct agricultural traditions that we associate today with north and south China had already emerged, namely the cultivation of dry land cereals, especially millet, in the northern plateaux and plains, and the cultivation of wet rice in the river valleys and deltas to the south of the Huai [River, about half way between the Yellow and Yangzi Rivers]."[56]

Nitrogen and Fertilizer

For agriculture to be sustained year after year, especially on the same plots of land, farmers had to learn about a plant's needs for nutrients beyond just sunlight and water. Among the most important is nitrogen, an element in chlorophyll, the green substance that, in the presence of sunlight, transforms carbon dioxide into food for the plant. Although nitrogen is plentiful in the earth's atmosphere, it is not present in a form usable by plants—it must first be "fixed" in the soil. This fixing occurs naturally by the death and decay of other plants, and by lightning strikes. But to capture the energy needed to concentrate food production in agriculture, farmers needed to find ways to get nitrogen into the soil used by their crops (even if they didn't know then what nitrogen was as such).

Both green manure (that is, chopped up leaves and other organic material) and animal manure contain high amounts of nitrogen, but another source is a category of plant called the legume—for China in particular, a member of that category called the soybean. Legumes fix nitrogen into the soil by the action of microbes associated with their roots, and do so without depleting the nutrient. Because of this, planting legumes in rotation with other crops adds nitrogen to the soil instead of taking it out. Wild species of the soybean have been found in wet lowlands in southern and eastern China, as well as in Taiwan and Korea. Domestication probably occurred much later than for the main grain crops, perhaps in the second millennium BCE, but the soybean had certainly become an integral part of the cropping repertoire by about 1000 BCE, though only in those areas having sufficient rainfall or water supply: the soybean requires lots of water.[57]

Summary

After the last Ice Age had ended, humans came to inhabit many ecological niches in north, northwest, central, east, and south China, gaining their sustenance from the opportunities offered by their environment. People may have spread throughout most of China, although the archeological evidence of their presence has not yet been found. Meacham, for instance, thinks that Neolithic peoples had settled on the continental shelf off what is now the southeast China coast, only to be pushed inland as the great ice sheets melted and the sea level rose by 100 feet, covering (possibly forever) evidence of their existence.[58] A region of the earth as species-rich as China is, even as it is today, would have provided countless opportunities for humans to find ways of gaining their sustenance from their environment.

In most places, that environment would have been forested, providing both game for hunting and plenty of dangers to survival as well, ranging from poisonous snakes throughout the tropical and subtropical forests to tigers, leopards, and wolves in other forests. Nonetheless, plenty of peoples the world over, even to this day, hunt and gather in forests (e.g., in Borneo and the Amazon), surviving because of what they have learned about their environment. Some of those Neolithic peoples in China, as Hui-lin Li points out, would have inhabited wooded areas bordering open marshes, grasslands, sea coasts, or savannas. And it was the people living in these kinds of places who took advantage of an extraordinary natural change in the genetics of cereal grains, from perennial to annual types, that made farming—the conscious planting of seeds for food—possible for the first time. Clear evidence shows that this happened in at least two places in China—first in the Yangzi River valley (and possibly all along China's southeast coast), where rice cultivation developed, and then in the loess highlands, where farming centered on millet emerged.

As it turns out, both loess-based millet farming and wet-rice agriculture have particularities that would be extraordinarily important for the subsequent course of Chinese history. Both systems were highly "self-sustaining." In the north, because of the fertility and workability of the loess soil, the soil could be planted almost continuously, year after year, without being exhausted or needing long fallow periods. Similarly, in wet-rice cultivation, the rice plant receives much of its nutrients directly from the water. The type of soil is irrelevant—it *becomes* rice paddy after years of being worked. To be sure, over time farmers in both regions found that adding fertilizers (both green and manures) raised productivity. But both systems supported higher population densities and, because the land was not left fallow, provided fewer options for pastures for use in raising livestock.

As a result, Chinese agriculture was to become centered on intensively cropped cereal production, and would support relatively high populations living in settled villages near their permanent fields.[59] Pasture for grazing cattle or horses was minimal (and hence so too was meat from those animals in the Chinese diet). In short, the particular environments in which the various peoples inhabiting Neolithic China found themselves presented particular bundles of opportunities, at least two of which led to the emergence of distinct forms of agriculture in which the same plots of land could be tilled year after year without being left fallow. The significance of these particular environmental conditions tended to push Chinese agriculture in both the north and the south into the form of small farms tended by families, and to leave little room for livestock. Both of these features would be extraordinarily important in the development of a particularly Chinese kind of agriculture that would predominate, and transform, the Chinese landscape into the twentieth century: peasant families farming small plots under the aegis of a central state.

PREHISTORIC ENVIRONMENTAL CHANGE

From the end of the last ice age about twelve thousand years ago through the Neolithic period to about 2000 BCE, China's environment changed substantially, both because of natural causes and human-induced change. Natural and anthropogenic sources of environmental change also interacted in the prehistoric period, as they would for the next four thousand years to the present day. Perhaps because they occur over periods thousands of years long, the largest environmental changes appear to have been natural. In particular, the East Asian monsoon, which brought rain to mainland China, weakened over those millennia, as we saw in an earlier section (see map 2.6). And as the monsoon weakened, the climate cooled and became drier, with subtropical forests and their animal complexes retreating from the North China plain toward the Yangzi River valley.

Changes in the monsoon pattern were largely responsible for at least two changes in the course of the Yellow River during the Neolithic period. For most of that period, the Yellow River flowed to the north, where it discharged into Bohai Bay (map 2.8). But somewhere between 3650–3000 BCE, its course shifted to the south of the Shandong highlands and emptied into the Yellow Sea. Another shift occurred between 2900–2200 BCE, when the river switched back to its northern course.[60]

To the humans who lived and farmed on the North China plain, these shifts in the course of the Yellow River were massive floods. Compounding the flooding, according to archeologist Li Liu, may have been rising sea levels that resulted in a substantial "marine transgression," with the ocean moving east as much as 100 kilometers; coastal inhabitants, too, would have experienced that environment change as a massive flood. Li thinks that these environmental changes contributed to the large-scale population movements noted at the time.[61] She also thinks that "climatic fluctuations may not have been the only source of the flooding. Soil erosion caused by increased Neolithic agriculture in the loess regions along the tributaries and middle reaches of the Yellow River may have contributed to a higher sediment content in the waters, raising the bed and the banks of the river, and leading to more extensive flooding on the eastern plains."[62]

Those floods, no doubt, were the context for the formation of the flood myths of early China that were handed down generation after generation until finally being written down in various accounts of the origins of the Chinese people. In these myths, the great sage-king Yu is credited with bringing order (and land) out of an originally flooded world by directing the flood waters into four channels that became major rivers: the Yellow, Wei, Huai, and Yangzi Rivers.[63] How Chinese and other peoples thought of themselves and their relationship to their environment is important to understanding the processes of environmental change, and will be a topic taken up further in coming chapters.

Whether or not Neolithic farmers in the loess lands contributed to those great floods, agriculture did begin to alter the Chinese environment. By about 5000 BCE, people in several parts of China were farming. These regional prehistoric farming communities, generally identified with the Yangshao Neolithic culture, are the ones out of which a "Chinese interaction sphere" and the earliest identifiably Chinese states later formed. With the vast numbers of ecological niches that the Chinese environment provided, no doubt there were other peoples, too, who had begun the transition to agriculture; we simply do not have an archeological record to show who or where they were. The ones discussed above, though, did share agriculture, and in the three millennia after its emergence, especially from 5000 to 2000 BCE, farming began to change the Chinese landscape.

While millet farming originated in the semi-arid savanna of the loess highlands in the Wei River valley, migrating peoples spread it north (as we saw earlier) and then east into the forested plains of the Yellow River valley and the North China plain (see map 2.9). There, much of the underlying soil too was loess, but was deposited as alluvium as the Yellow River flooded and changed course over the millennia. As farming villages

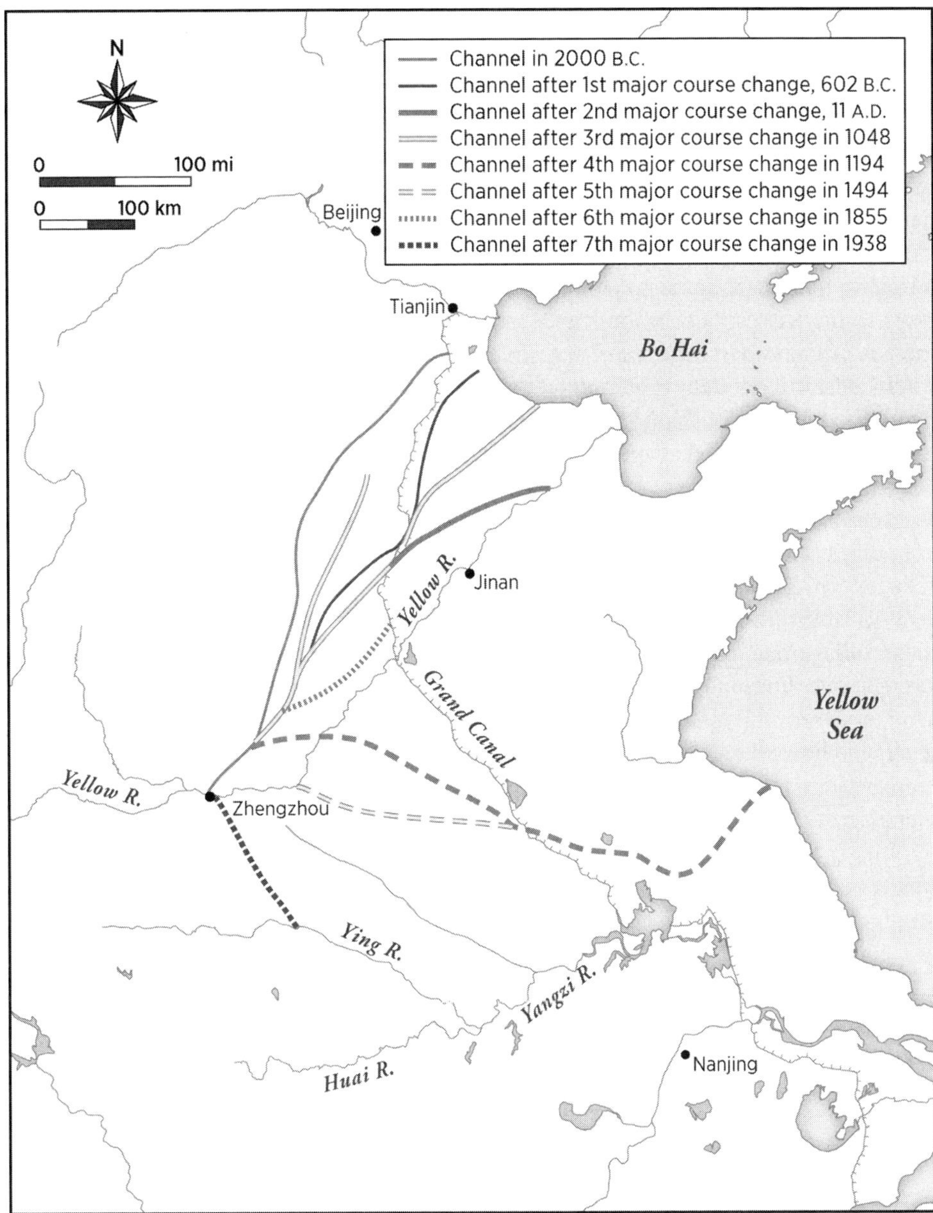

Map 2.8. Changes in the Course of the Yellow River *Source:* Adapted from Jiongxin Xu, "A Study of Long-Term Environmental Effects of River Regulation on the Yellow River of China in Historical Perspective," *Geografiska Annaler: Series A, Physical Geography* 75, no. 3 (1993): 61.

developed in this area, contact was made with the rice-farming peoples to the south in the lower Yangzi River region, and, with a climate that was warmer and wetter than it is now, rice was added to the mix of grains grown in the lower reaches of the Yangzi River. The establishment and growth of farming villages on the North China plain in the period around 3000 BCE is identified as the Longshan culture of north China.

There, cultivated land needed to be cleared land, and the Yangshao peoples developed the techniques necessary to remove forest to make way for farms (see map 2.10). At first, a clearing in the forest near the village might have sufficed. But over time, and with growing technological sophistication and possibly need for food because of a growing population, additional forest had to be cleared. Cutting trees down, even with highly honed stone axes, was laborious, and simply setting fire to a forest was unpredictable and dangerous; precision was needed. A later Chinese source describes a process by which individual trees were killed by ring-barking, the practice of cutting a ring around a tree trunk to prevent water and nutrients from being carried from the roots to the leaves: "Once the leaves are dead and no longer cast any shade ploughing and sowing may begin, and after three years the roots will have withered and the trunks decayed enough to be burned out. The fire burns below the surface of the soil and kills the roots."[64] With this method, specific amounts of forest were cleared in a predetermined size and shape, leaving a sharp edge between farm and forest, between "culture" and "nature."

There is little evidence, though, that the Neolithic farming peoples anywhere in the area that became China altered their environment on a large scale. Farmers lived in villages with populations of hundreds of people; the largest may have been one thousand to fifteen hundred people on an area about the size of four football fields. How many villages such as this dotted North China around 3000 BCE? That is very hard to say, but one thousand years later, around 2000 BCE, there might have been one thousand or so farming villages.[65] However large or small these Neolithic farming villages were, and however many of them were, they did mark a beginning of the separation of humans from their surrounding environment. These people no longer lived at encampments in the forest, gathering and hunting their sustenance from it—they either lived in villages on the savanna or cleared the forest and made space for themselves, their fields, and their domesticated animals. And in doing so, they made themselves easier targets for those wanting to expropriate their crops.

THE FORMATION OF A CHINESE INTERACTION SPHERE, 4000–2000 BCE

No matter how and why settled agriculture emerged in China when and where it did (and elsewhere in the world for that matter), climate changes no doubt would have to be included in the explanation. But would a cooling or a warming climate have most stimulated agriculture? The evidence here is ambiguous, for in the thousands of years considered so far, China's climate had both cooled and warmed as agriculture was developing. Nonetheless, it seems safe to say that a warmer and wetter climate would encourage greater yields from agriculture, both because of a longer growing season and the possibility of harvesting two crops over a growing season, and because growing food plants flourish with more water and solar energy. And larger harvests meant the possibility of substantial surpluses of food that Neolithic villagers needed to store and protect against outside threats, whether human, animal, or climatic. Those agricultural surpluses also meant that villagers would be able to support a segment of population that did not need to labor in the fields to procure their own food but could rely on others to supply it them, either willingly or by force: a ruling elite. This combination of a generally warm and wet climate, rising surpluses of food, and the emergence of rulers prevailed over the two millennia from about 4000 to 2000 BCE when a definable system of interacting states and proto-states developed in north China, constituting what historian K. C. Chang has called a "Chinese interactive sphere."

Over the couple of thousand years from the emergence of the first agriculture-based regional culture zones discussed above until about 4000 BCE, both the sophistication of agriculture and of the societies based on it continued to grow, and the interaction among them increased, too. As K. C. Chang has concluded, "When the chronologies of the various cultural types and systems are carefully traced, it becomes apparent that by approximately 4000 [BCE] some of the adjacent regional cultures had come into contact as an inevitable result of expansion. . . ."[66] For Chang and other scholars, the formation of those "interaction spheres" is exceptionally significant, and "for the first time . . . the interaction sphere may be referred to as 'Chinese.' . . . By 3000 [BCE], the Chinese interaction sphere can properly and appropriately be called China, as it became the stage where Chinese history began to play out, with its clearly defined actors, events, motivations, and story lines."[67]

No doubt because of the wealth and power made possible by agriculture, this "interaction zone" intensified most quickly in north China. There, archeologists have uncovered and studied numerous village sites, and it is there as well that the first identifiable Chinese states emerged. Why this occurred on the North China plain, and not in south, east, or central China, is not known. No doubt the particular environmental conditions of north China favored the widespread adoption of millet-based agriculture, whereas the watery conditions necessary for rice were not as easily replicated, or as abundant. Archeological sites in south, central, and east China have been found, and they do reveal agricultural and cultural sophistication, but they are not as numerous as in north China. Thus it was it was in the north that the accumulating wealth made possible by agriculture led to new social structures bifurcated between a ruling elite and a farming population. As Ping-ti Ho has shown, Neolithic agriculture was sufficiently advanced that one farm could produce a surplus capable of supporting more than just the one farming family who tended it, "thus releasing segments of the population to pursue nonagricultural activities, and hence to give rise to a certain degree of social division of labor. There was also great potential for sustained population growth."[68]

Out of this mixture of village-based agriculture and social stratification arose what might be termed confederations of villages, brought together for defense and raids against others, out of which the first Chinese states emerged. When and where that happened first is not easy to pinpoint. But in the period from about 2400 to 1000 BCE, historians and archeologists have identified three states—the Xia, Shang, and Zhou—that overlapped in time and perhaps space, that were competing and opposed political groups, and that shared a common culture. Archeologist K. C. Chang thinks that the Xia state came first and was centrally located where agriculture first developed in the region covering both the loess highlands and the edges of the North China plain; the Shang came somewhat later and were based to the east of the Xia on the forested North China plain; and the Zhou, the last, were situated to the west in the Wei River valley. Chang dates Xia archeological sites from 2400 to 1200 BCE, Shang from 1800 to 1100 BCE, and Zhou from 1400 to 700 BCE.[69]

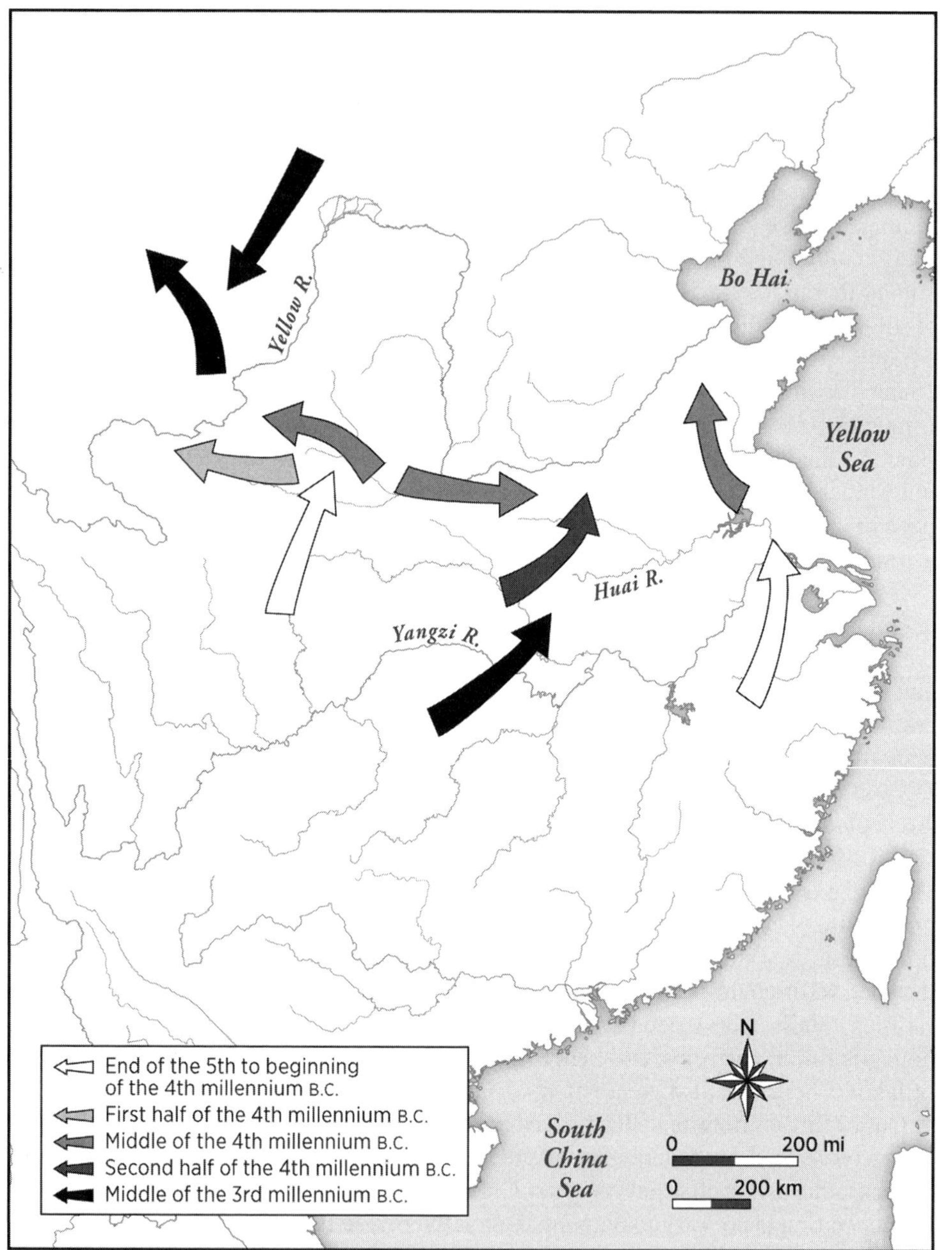

Map 2.9. Neolithic Migrations in China *Source:* Adapted from David N. Keightley, *Origins of Chinese Civilization*, 219.

That these north China cultures had become states with a ruling, warring elite and a population of farmers bound to work for the elite is clear. The ruling elites, composed of warriors and shamans, did not work the fields but rather lived off the surplus of food grown by the village agriculturalists. The evidence for the emergence of stratified societies comes mostly from archeological excavations of gravesites throughout

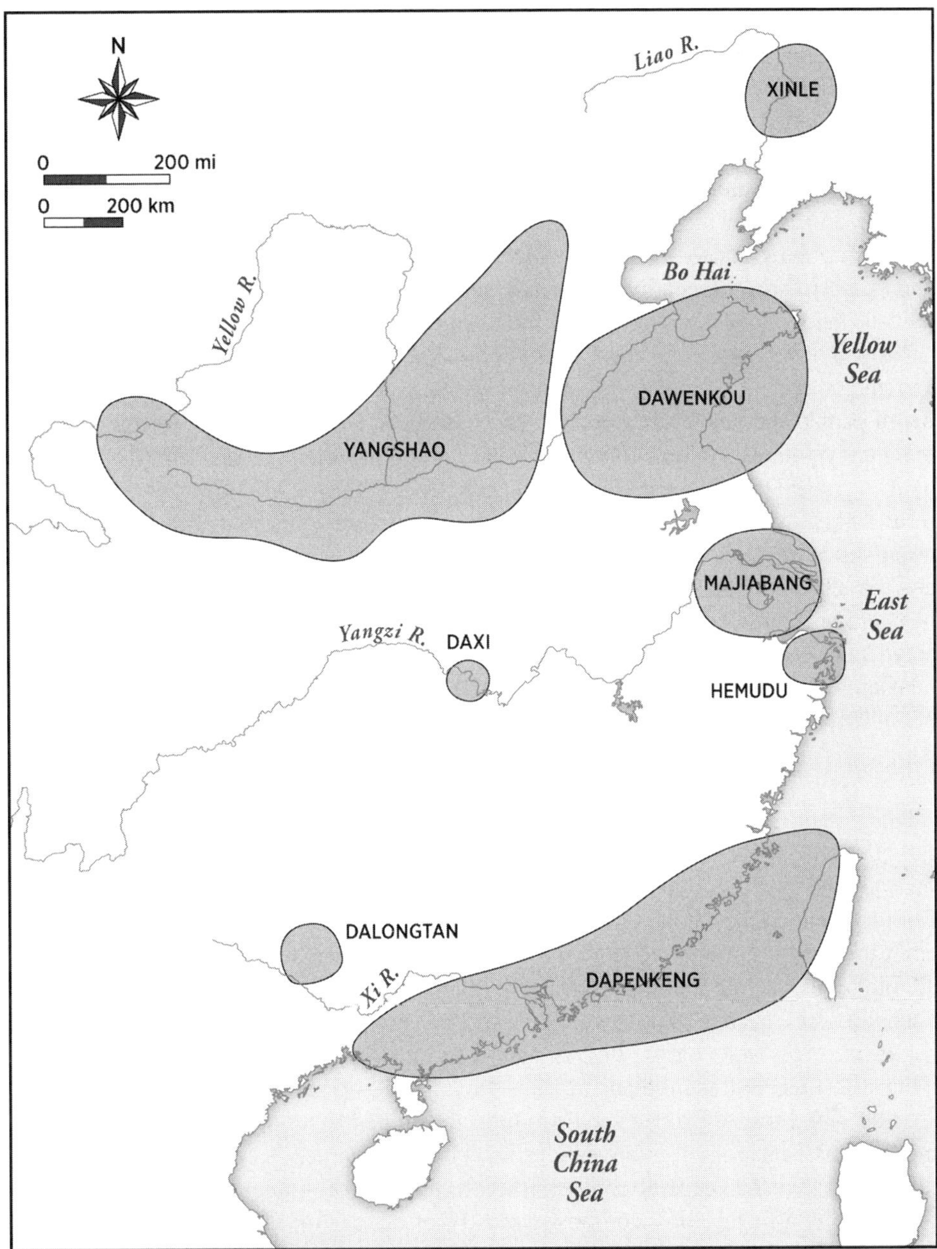

Map 2.10. Major Regional Cultures in China *Source:* Adapted from Lowe and Shaughnessey eds., *The Cambridge History of Ancient China,* 49.

the Chinese interaction sphere, showing clearly that some people had come to accumulate larger amounts of wealth and power than others, and to make expressions of that political power manifest in the materials they took with them to their graves. We have no idea what these peoples believed about the afterlife, but their actions are clear evidence of the creation of what early Chinese historians called "the ten thousand states" ruled by elites who extracted and divided wealth, and who conducted war against others.

Scholars do not know the extent to which the Xia and early Shang societies had developed cities, which might be understood here as concentrations of large numbers (in the thousands) of people who did not do agricultural work, including the ruling elite, warriors, priests, and artisans. Certainly the elite buried their dead in places that were important to them, which may well have been near their residences. How they extracted grain from the villagers is also not known, although some combination of shamanism and military force, especially over newly subdued people, was no doubt the key. As we will see below, by about 1500 BCE, the Shang were in fact building walled cities.

Most probably, some of these rulers became better at extracting resources from their agriculturalists, at fighting, at making more effective weapons, and at increasing the number of people and the territory under their control. As a later Chinese source put it about these early political entities, "Ritual and war . . . are the affairs of state."[70] Also, this was likely a gradual process over the two millennia from 4000 to 2000 BCE. But in the period from 2000 to 1500 BCE, other social developments were coincident with the creation of the first unambiguous urban centers and warmaking states in China—bronze technology and writing.[71] With the combination of ruling elites, warmaking ability, advanced technology, and a means of keeping written records of earthly and cosmic affairs, the first identifiably Chinese states emerged in the North China plain, the most notable being the Shang. But before discussing the Shang in more detail, we need to take a look at the development of a powerful new technology available to the Shang rulers—bronze.

BRONZE-AGE CHINA: TECHNOLOGY AND ENVIRONMENTAL CHANGE, 2000–1000 BCE

Broadly understood, technology is the way humans interact with and transform the environment as they seek to extract energy to sustain themselves and to reproduce. In simple terms, the more energy extracted, the more likely the population will increase. Technological change thus usually represents greater efficiency at extracting and using resources and energy. Fire is such a technology, as is agriculture. And among the greatest technological leaps humans have made is the development of metallurgy, starting with bronze. Bronze seems to have developed first not for use as farm implements but for fashioning into weapons used by ruling elites to control human populations and the resources they could extract from the environment.

Bronze is a metal alloy composed mostly of copper to which tin and sometimes other metals have been added to increase the amalgam's strength beyond that of copper alone. The earliest known bronze industry in China is dated to about 2000 BCE in an area at the far western edge of northwest China, and although that is later than bronze in Iran and Iraq, the conclusion of experts in Chinese metallurgy is that bronze technology had indigenous origins in China.[72]

Copper and tin are minerals that need to be extracted from ores deposited in the earth. And those ores, like other minerals such as gold and silver and organic substances such as coal and oil, are not distributed evenly across the face of the earth but come to be where they are as a result of vast geological processes that formed the crust of the earth and the continents. Just as some places on earth have coal and oil deposits, so, too, some places on earth had copper and tin deposits.[73] The place that became the Chinese interaction sphere happened to sit on top of large quantities of both. Without those deposits or access to them, no amount of human ingenuity would have invented bronze, and most likely what later became known as Chinese "civilization" would not have developed.

The bronze industry in China developed differently than in other parts of the world, in part because of good luck (vast deposits of the requisite metal ores) and in part because of the development of Chinese states having large supplies of laborers coerced into such work. It also developed in the context of an exceptionally advanced and sophisticated ceramic pottery industry with large numbers of experts aware of the general principles of heating and forming clay vessels who would have been very sensitive to the idea that heated or molten metal could be easily formed into shapes with which they were already familiar. Once that step was taken, Chinese bronze was cast, not hammered, in vast quantities because of the abundant supplies of copper and tin, and used for ritual vessels as well as weapons and tools. As archeologist Robert Bagley observed, casting had significant social consequences: "Casting more than hammering encourages division of labor and invites the organization of efficient workshops limited in size only by the resources and requirements of the patron."[74]

As Franklin concludes, "In the context of early China, the sheer scale of bronze production is as impressive as the quality of the craft. Such a level of bronze production demands, as a prerequisite, a well-organized large-scale mining and smelting industry. It seems to me that this could not have been in effect without a large pool of forced labor, a pool much larger in number than the workers required to produce the objects."[75] As we will see, one of the defining characteristics of the Shang social order was its large number of unfree subjects who could be coerced into agriculture, and thus presumably into dangerous and unpleasant tasks such as mining and smelting as well.

At first bronze production was small-scale, but by 1500 BCE, large-scale foundries covering an area about the size of three football fields (10,000 sq. m.) were busily at work at sites near the current city of Luoyang, much further south on a tributary to the Yangzi River at Xin'gan in Jiangxi province, and probably elsewhere as well, although archeological evidence is as yet lacking.[76] In other parts of the world where bronze technology emerged, it did so in places where either or both copper or tin was found, but not both, implying the necessity of long-distance trade. As far as I can tell, both ores were available to the metalworkers in Chinese states, although it is entirely possible that one cause of wars among the Chinese states was the strategic need of some states to control the sources of both metals so as not to be dependent on trade for supplies. For the later Shang era ca. 1200 BCE, copper and tin may have come to the capital city of Anyang from thousands of miles away.[77]

The amount of bronze cast in China from 1500 to 500 BCE is quite astounding, leading Bagley to conclude that the term "Bronze Age China" is apt. Larger numbers of bronze vessels used for the storage, preparation, or serving of food and drink—probably for ceremonial purposes—have been unearthed over the past century. One such vessel cast around 1200 BCE weighs 875 kg (nearly a ton), and a tomb from the fifth century BCE was filled with ten tons of bronze objects.[78]

The method of bronze casting that developed in China requires vast quantities of metals, and wastes a huge amount in the process. The abundance of copper and tin ores is what sets Bronze Age China apart from bronze-age states in other parts of the world, the Near East in particular, where the more precious metals were shaped and conserved by hammering. The huge amounts of bronze cast in China imply vast mining and transportation enterprises that brought refined ores to foundries in cities.

The Shang bronze industry thus burned considerable amounts of wood fuel for mining, smelting, and casting. In light of the vast distances that copper and tin were transported from the mines to the bronze workshops in the capital city, both would have been refined at the mine head to varying degrees before shipping. These mines no doubt had substantial impacts on their immediate environment. As with the iron industry in later centuries, the limits on production of those metals, too, may have been set by local supplies of wood: when forests were depleted, the mine was abandoned. When the copper and tin arrived at the capital workshop, additional piles of wood were needed for final refining and combining to make the bronze before casting. How much wood all of this required is not known, but air quality no doubt deteriorated when the foundries fired up their furnaces. Did nearby forests provided adequate supplies; or was local deforestation one of the reasons the Shang moved their royal residence more than once? Or did the careless disposal of their industrial and human wastes befoul water supplies? As yet, we do not know the answers to these questions.

Bagley suggests that the record reconstructed from findings of vast quantities of bronze objects shows that "urban societies arose in the middle Yellow River region during the first half of the second millennium [BCE]. About 1500 [BCE] a major state [the Shang] formed there and expanded outward to rule, perhaps only briefly, large territories. By about 1300 [BCE] that state had retreated, perhaps under pressure from newer powers that had formed on its borders. For the next few centuries thereafter, civilized China was a network of interacting powers. . . ."[79] These interactions, whether peaceful trade, migration, alliances, or violent warfare, began creating elements of shared culture, including bronze technology and a hierarchical social structure—a state with central cities, armies, and coerced labor for both manufactured goods and agriculture. The formation and interaction of states in China intensified the need for resources and energy, and hence enlarged the human footprint on the Chinese environment.

The Bronze Age Shang State, 1500–1050 BCE

The early state that became central to much of the interactions on the North China plain, the Shang, shows clear evidence of having been quite large and populous, with a large city from which its rulers governed the countryside and warred against other similar rulers. The foundations for buildings that have been excavated at an early site dated around 1500 BCE (Erlitou, near the current city of Luoyang) show large structures, probably palaces, of more than 100 meters on a side.[80] "If the compound was a setting for ceremonies performed on the porch of the hall," Bagley suggests, "an audience of several thousand could have watched from within the enclosure."[81] An even larger, later site dated from 1500 to 1300 BCE (at Erligang, near the current city of Zhengzhou) covers 25 sq. km and had a city wall nearly 7 km around, 60 feet wide at the base, 30 feet tall, and in sections 2,385 feet long, which Paul Wheatley figures would have taken ten thousand laborers eighteen years to complete.[82]

The Shang thus were city- and wall-builders. Their capital cities near the present cities of Luoyang and Zhengzhou were large indeed, with tens of thousands—maybe up to one hundred thousand residents, including the royal family, priests, and warriors, as well as workers in bronze, ceramic, and munitions factories. These cities did not emerge out of the increased trade among the north China villagers but were placed in specific locations by the ruling elite, and then enclosed with massive walls. The walls were tamped earth, constructed by compressing earth and stone into wooden forms of manageable size, which were then lifted higher and higher until the desired height was reached. The walls were defensive, and not for protection from the elephants and tigers in the surrounding forests but from other warring states. How many of those there were in the neighborhood is not known, but later written sources refer to "the ten thousand states." That figure no doubt was figurative, but it does suggest a large number of states similarly structured to the Shang. Chang counts thirty-three Shang names for states it had contact with.[83]

Anyang

The grandest of all Shang archeological finds is the city of Anyang, dated to 1200 BCE. With Anyang, we have clear evidence of the existence of a highly stratified, urban society with a cohesive ruling elite, a large number of artisans, a productive agriculture, bronze used not just for ritual or cooking vessels but for war as well, composite bows aimed by skilled archers, chariots pulled by a team of horses for both transportation and battle, and importantly, a written script to communicate with each other and with ancestors and gods. By the time the Shang built Anyang, it had become a very sophisticated state that contained many of the elements that became the distinctively Chinese way of organizing their society and economy, and interacting with their natural environment.

Anyang is also significant because with the discovery of large numbers of surviving written documents, identifiable people, motivations, and events can be known. The documents take the form of "oracle bones" (see figure 2.1) which a ruler's specialists used to divine what the future might bring—for example, whether the king should take any particular action, such as go on a hunt, conceive a child, or go into battle; many concerned agriculture (the harvest, land clearance, etc.) or war. Heat applied to the bones or shells produced cracks that produced the divination.

Since these written characters are well formed and number about a thousand in the Anyang finds, archeologists presume that writing had been developed earlier but that because the medium likely was grass, bamboo, or some other degradable material, evidence simply has not survived. Being quite durable, two hundred thousand of the oracle bones and turtle shells have survived, along with their writing; forty-eight thousand of these have been used by scholars. Since being discovered in the 1920s, most of the oracle bone writing has been deciphered, in part because philologists realized that they are an early form of the Chinese writing system that has been in use for more than three thousand years.[84]

Shang Social Organization

The archeological and written records show that Anyang was then the capital city of the Shang state, and served as the royal seat for nine kings, starting with Wu Ding around 1200 BCE and ending 150 years later when the Shang state was conquered by one of the other competitors in north China, the Zhou. Anyang itself was large, some 15–24 sq. km, but probably not walled. At the center of the city lay the royal palaces, temples, and altars, surrounded by an industrial area for bronze foundries, pottery, jade, and weaponry. Farther out were small houses built partly below ground, probably for workers and soldiers. Beyond these were the burial tombs, mostly for royalty. Outside of the city lay villages surrounded by agricultural fields, and royal estates, and somewhere beyond the edge of direct Shang political and military control (anywhere between 10 and 50 miles) were the other hostile states.

Shang society was complex and hierarchical. The king represented the royal lineage, which in King Wu Ding's time around 1200 BCE stretched back sixteen generations to about 1500 BCE, ritually commemorating them and periodically asking their advice and favors via divination. Royalty included the king's sons and the minor lineages they headed, as well as more distant relatives who had their own lineages. Other powerful people unrelated to the king also had lineages, led their own men into battle, and were allowed to cast bronzes with their family insignia. Those who did the divining numbered about 120 men and were linked to the royal family but were not allowed to conduct the rituals of ancestor worship themselves. Outside the city, the king commanded a bevy of officers and minor chiefs, many of whom were expected to raise and lead troops on their own account in service to the king. More distant chiefs who sent tribute to the Shang king, mostly the turtle shells and cattle scapula used in divination, likely acted more independently the farther in time and space the Shang king was from their initial appointment.

The Shang king was centrally concerned with all aspects of agriculture, not merely with divining whether or not the harvest would be good but with opening new land, planting, and inspecting the farms and the work of the laborers. The cultivated plants included the two kinds of millet as well as rice and mulberry—"the all-important food tree for the silk worm. Oracle records contained the characters for mulberry, silkworm, and silk." Archeological remains of silk survive, indicating that by Shang times, sericulture was an important part of the Chinese agricultural system.[85] The king's estates apparently provided for the needs of the royal family, the ruling elite, the foundry workers, and other artisans, as well as of the military officers and whatever full-time troops they commanded. The king led hunts on his lands, which not only provided a significant amount of meat for the elite but also provided military training. Fires not only drove game toward the hunters but also prepared additional land for tilling.

Food

The point of agriculture, of course, was to improve the food supply available to the human population so it could not just survive but in fact increase. For that, more food than was necessary simply to reproduce the existing population was required. Millet or rice by themselves are not "food," but are turned into food through the cultural practices that make those raw materials into palatable, if not enjoyable, food and drink—what people actually ate.

Millet and rice were cooked into a form of stewlike congee; for the elite, meats or fish cut into "morsels" were added. Seasonings such as salt and vinegar were used, too, as were various legumes (soybeans became important around 1000 BCE). Of the common people's food we know less than of the elite's, for the elite have left written records of their ritual uses of food, and their feasts.

One source, which is a song "summoning the soul" of a departed loved one to return, tempts the soul with delectable dishes concocted from both domesticated and gathered or hunted wild sources—rice, broom corn, millet, salt, ox ribs "tender and succulent," stewed turtle, casseroled duck, braised chicken, wine, and liquor among them.[86]

Aside from the cultivated grains and vegetables, much of the meat in the Shang diet was game. Deer bones have been found in such quantities that E. N. Anderson thinks deer might have been domesticated. He also concludes, though, that "hunting was practiced on a vast scale, netting every sort of game from elephants and rhinoceri to rabbits and deer. Fish and turtles of every sort were eaten. Presumably the sacrificial animals that gave up their shoulder blades and shells [for the oracle bones] wound up in the stew pot. Trade brought some exotic artifacts to the area; central China was scoured for turtles, and some species originated from south China. Marine shells and whale bones indicate trade with people on the coast."[87]

The Shang food supply thus was not dependent solely on millet or animals raised on farms but included a vast array of wild animals as well as fruits, nuts, and berries. The Shang may have begun transforming the North China plain into farms, but there was still plenty of forest to provide a rich and varied diet that was not dependent on the vagaries of weather and the size of the harvest but on nature. Additionally, the forest was tempting to farmers who might want to flee the exactions of the Shang state.

Shang "Civilization" and "Barbarian" Others

Most of the Shang population were unfree people living in settlements in the countryside whose labor could be tapped to open new lands, plow, plant and harvest the fields, muster for military campaigns, cut and transport wood to the city for fuel and production, build city walls, work the foundries, and make tombs for the royalty. The tomb of Lady Fu Hao, who was a consort of King Wu Ding, with its extraordinary collection of bronzes, jades, and other materials, shows how powerful the Shang royalty was, not just for mobilizing the vast labor and material supplies to cast bronzes weighing more than 200 kg each but also for constructing the tomb itself. Historian Patricia Ebrey estimates that it took thousands of laborers to dig the forty-foot-deep hole for the tomb, construct the burial chambers, and fill the hole with layer upon layer of rammed earth. Not just Lady Hao's tomb but hundreds of others also offered up clear evidence of human sacrifices, most beheaded and buried in the tomb, as well as chariots and horses. The written sources also show that Lady Hao was an active member of the Shang elite, performing rituals herself, running an estate outside of the capital city, and even leading military campaigns, once with thirteen thousand troops, against other peoples to the west, northwest, and east.[88]

Of these other peoples, a few merit mention. The Qiang were west of Shang, probably in the steppe, for the Qiang were sheepherders. The Qiang also were a favored source of Shang war captives, brought back to Shang to be enslaved to work and clear fields, or as human sacrifices. Sometime during the third millennium BCE wheat (and probably barley) was introduced into the Qiang area, probably from areas further west. The Shang themselves did not plant or harvest wheat but did use it in their rituals. They thus spied on the wheat harvest of neighboring tribes, and the Shang king "engaged in raids on the basis of such intelligence."[89] The Zhou were in the Wei River valley just west of Shang, and became the Shang state's greatest nemesis, ultimately subduing the Shang in 1045 BCE. Indeed, drawing on the work of other scholars, David Keightley has produced maps based on Shang interactions with other states to show the extent of the "interaction sphere" on the North China plain, showing it to be rather dense, and with large numbers of non-Shang entities.[90]

North China thus was more than just the Shang, including as it did numerous other peoples and states. Shang wars with those states continued until about 1050 BCE, leading ultimately to the defeat of the Shang state by one of their competitors to the west, the Zhou, which then claimed to have established not just a successor state to the Shang but universal kingship over "all under heaven," or their known world. Because all the extant sources come from the victorious Zhou, historians understand that the Shang acquiesced to Zhou claims, but it is not known why (or even whether) the other peoples in the Chinese interaction zone would have submitted as well. Not surprisingly, much of the history of the early Zhou period, as we will see in the next chapter, was consumed by wars against these other peoples, and a distinction between the "civilized" Chinese "barbarian" others emerged.[91]

ENVIRONMENTAL CHANGE, 1500–1000 BCE

The Zhou conquest and state will be taken up in the next chapter. Here, however, I want to conclude by examining what we can know about the processes of environmental change from about 1500 to 1000 BCE. Mostly, I will have to draw inferences from what we do know, since almost no direct evidence survives.

First, the northern and western limits of Shang settlements, villages and cities included, coincides with a line demarcating at least 20 inches of rainfall under today's climatic conditions. As discussed earlier, the climate in the second millennium BCE was warmer and wetter than at present, so the area probably received more rain than now. Whatever the amount, to the north and west of the 20-inch line are grasslands and deserts not capable of sustaining agriculture; grasslands, however, could support grazing of sheep, goats, and horses—though there is no evidence that Shang or Zhou people ventured there to do so. But, as we will see in the next chapter, other peoples did exploit those ecosystems. The southern limit of Shang settlement was just south of the Yangzi River. As best as we can now ascertain, at that time, Shang civilization was carved out of a deciduous broadleafed forest dominated by oaks, extending south to the mixed deciduous, semitropical forest of the Yangzi River valley. The Shang had become expert at exploiting the resources from those forest ecosystems.

If the earlier Neolithic villagers had begun to make a break with their environment by clearing fields from the forest, the Shang put an exclamation point to the separation from the countryside and the forest by building walls. Their capital cities had populations in the tens of thousands, with Anyang by 1200 BCE having as many as 230,000 people, most of whom were artisans or other workers. But Anyang was not the only Shang city. There were as many as 700 other named places, probably walled outposts, settled by those entitled to have family names and lineage ancestral rites, all members of the ruling elite. How many of those there were is unclear, but later sources mention hundreds. Since those "states" did not survive the competition with the Shang, and later with the Zhou, little is known about them, including about their social organization or population size. All told, though, there might have been as many as 4–5 million people living in these various places on the North China plain.[92]

How much farmland would food for that population require? The answer to that is a function of agricultural yields (i.e., how much could be harvested from a given amount of seed planted), the amount of food need supplied by hunting, and the technology available for farming. Over the millennia surveyed in this chapter, all of those factors changed, with agriculture becoming more productive—but probably not much more so than somewhat later. A later source from the first century BCE, presumably reflecting improvements through that time, nonetheless suggests rather high millet yields in the north, especially in the loess-soil areas. [93]

Shang farmers also had domesticated oxen (a source for the manure mentioned above), and also had used a stone or wooden plow to break open the ground. No evidence of a bronze plow has yet been found, but agricultural historian Bray would not be surprised if one is found. Even without a metal plow, Bray thinks Shang agriculture was as advanced as any in the Neolithic world, and was certainly productive enough to support an elite, troops, and workers who relied on food produced by farmers. There is clear evidence that bronze was used to make an array of agricultural tools, sickles included. Bray also thinks that this technological basket allowed agriculture to spread and the population to grow.[94] The use of plows and fertilizer also implies settled agriculture, and the use of the same plot of land for several years in a row, rather than a fire-driven shifting cultivation. Settledness also enabled the ruling elite to keep tabs on their farmers and not let them run away.

Given that the actual tools used for clearing land and for farming were wooden or stone, such as a wooden spade called *lei*, or stone axes, historian K. C. Chang thinks that the most important input into agriculture and hence for transforming the north China environment was unfree human labor under the command of the king. As one oracle bone inscription put it: "The king ordered the *zhong-ren* ('the multitude') and said: open new fields so that there will be a good harvest."[95] According to another Chinese historian, the *zhong-ren* "were farmers, and were the fighting men in wars. They usually occupied a very lowly position opposite the . . . nobility. They had no title to land . . . and were securely tied up with agricultural collectives, controlled by the . . . rulers, were conscribed to become soldiers, paid tribute, and performed labor services. When they were soldiers they would become slaves when captured, and if they refused to become soldiers they and their families would instantly become slaves also. Their lives and their possessions were controlled by the king and the nobles, being in essence their tools and possessions."[96] As we will see in subsequent chapters, the Chinese state has played a significant role driving economic development and environmental change ever since.

Assuming a population of some 4–5 million people by the late Shang (ca. 1100 BCE) and agricultural yields of about one *shi* measure per *mu* land measure, that would mean that about four thousand to five thousand square miles of farmland had been cleared from the north China oak forest (if it were continuous, that is an area some 60–70 miles on a side). As we have seen, though, the fields were in the midst of forests that also provided important sources of game. Certainly in the more densely populated regions such as those around the capital cities of Anyang, Zhengzhou, and Luoyang, much of the surrounding countryside would have been cleared, with patches cleared around other settlements. Mostly, north China as seen from the air would have been forested with patches cut out for farms. This interpretation is buttressed by the Shang oracle bone graph for "farming" which, according to Mark Elvin, shows "activity being carried on in the midst of trees."[97]

The Shang state went to war to acquire farmland from neighboring states. As a Chinese historian explained: "That the Shang state would enter into the territory of another state to open up new fields is a bit curious but not incomprehensible. The ancient states had different economies and uneven societal developments. When agricultural states had population increases and new field requirements, they could go out to look for uncultivated land and would turn neighboring hunting areas and grazing pastures into farming fields. This the ancients had a term for: *ji tian*. . . . *Ji tian* meant to cultivate new land in another state."[98]

As early as three thousand years ago, then, the Chinese were having a significant impact on their environment. Farming had created a new horizon between "culture" and "nature" in ancient China, and in fact created a new front for human interaction with nature. Fields with ripening millet (or rice, in the south) attracted pests, some of which could be deterred in various ways, but larger ones, such as deer and wild boar, could do extensive damage to the standing crop, perhaps even making a village lose much of its grain. Most likely the standing harvest increased the numbers of deer and pigs hanging out in the forests on the edge of the farmland. But it also turns out that pigs and deer are also the preferred prey of tigers, and so tigers, too, would have migrated toward their newly increased food sources. We know so little about Shang folk beliefs that we do not know if the villagers considered the tigers helpful in keeping the deer and pig population down, or as threats to human existence, or both. But tigers and elephants did count among the images cast onto bronzes, perhaps the most famous of which are those on the bronzes of Lady Hao.[99]

Elephants, too, inhabited the forests of north China, as did rhinoceros, which preferred habitat that included ponds for their daily immersions. These three animals were so large, powerful, and dangerous that it is unlikely that the villagers ever hunted them. But the royal family did arrange hunts, not just for deer meat for their table but also for tigers, elephants, and rhinoceros. To be sure, those three did provide meat and other delicacies, but we can imagine that the hunting and killing of these animals also served to demonstrate the military power of the rulers, establishing their right to rule over humans by their ability to keep the wild beasts away (or at least at bay). The royal hunts resulted in large kills, implying dense wildlife populations in nearby forests, as oracle bone inscriptions attest. The greatest catch recorded on one was 348 elaphures (a kind of large deer). [100]

K. C. Chang thinks that domesticated animals were a more important source of meat for the royal table, with bones of dog, cattle, water buffalo, sheep, horses, and pigs having been found or mentioned in the oracle bones. "The number of cattle used in rituals is truly amazing: 1,000 cattle in one ritual once, 500 once, 400 once, 300 thrice, 100 nine times, and so on. . . . One gets an inkling from these numbers about the size of the herd." Chang thinks that elaphure, while not domesticated, may have been kept in large enclosures to ensure an easily accessible supply of venison.[101]

Chariots and the Yellow River give us two additional perspectives on the question of land clearance in ancient China. First, the Shang oracle bones refer to the Yellow River simply as "the River." We know that the silt that gives the river its yellow appearance comes from erosion of loess deposits, covered over by oak forest in most of the area I have been discussing so far. Although archeologist Li Liu suggests that Neolithic farming might have increased the silt load of the Yellow River in the third millennium BCE and hence the floods that led to that river's change, the Yellow River may, of course, have flooded during the Shang, but its course did not radically shift. It was first dubbed the "Yellow" River a thousand years later during the Han Dynasty, by which time both land clearance and subsequent erosion had sent vast quantities of yellow silt into the river.

On the other hand, chariots needed open space to be effective. To be sure, most archeologists and historians of Shang China think that the chariots were not used for combat, but probably rather to carry generals or royalty as they oversaw battle preparations and progress. Nonetheless, the chariots were large, with axles up to nine feet long, and a team of horses pulled them. As Bagley notes, chariots made an abrupt appearance in north China around 1200 BCE, implying the assistance of skilled charioteers from Central Asia, as well horses from there, too, implying regular, if not friendly, contact with nomadic peoples from the grasslands to the north and west of Shang territory to supply horses and charioteers.

Energy Regime

All living things need energy to grow and reproduce. Except for some life forms that extract energy from heat generated from inside the earth or by chemical reactions, most life forms on earth have derived their energy needs directly or indirectly from the sun. Plants use solar energy to produce chlorophyll and more plant matter, animals eat the plants, animals eat other animals, and dead organic material is consumed and decomposed by bacteria that return minerals to the earth to be taken up as nutrients by plants.

For most of human history, and for most of the time covered by this book, people have provided for their energy needs by tapping into annual flows of solar energy. Plants grown for food are digested, and the energy to move muscles releases heat, sometimes in adequate amounts to keep the body warm. Clothing and shelter also provide protection against the elements. But even those would have been insufficient to keep people on the North China plain warm through the winter. People needed fires, and fires came from wood.

Fortunately for the Shang and earlier inhabitants of north China, the region was largely a deciduous hardwood forest dominated by oaks and elms. As we have also seen in this chapter, most of the Shang farmland was carved out of the forest, with trees felled one by one, rather than by burning down the forest. Using fire to clear forests for farmland is not only dangerous but also wastes much fuel wood. The Shang practice of cutting individual trees probably was not only for self-preservation but also for firewood.

How much firewood the 4–5 million inhabitants of Shang China burned each year, and hence how many trees they felled, is only open to guess. A small proportion of those inhabitants were royalty, and they certainly would have burned wood to stay warm. Not only did the bronze industry use vast amounts of wood, but the size of the bronze vessels that were produced also suggests that huge fires were built under them to cook food. What about their subject peoples? That we do not know. We are not even quite sure if they lived in separate abodes or in larger collective housing. Fires were needed to cook food, and some of those hearths may well have been indoors, where the heat could be captured, especially in winter. Over the past millennia, as forests have disappeared and wood for heating has become in very short supply on the North China plain, villagers have constructed their homes so that indoor fires for cooking heated a brick surface above them called a *kang* that then became the warm bed for the family for the night. Were such structures used 3,500 years ago?

Environmental historians increasingly see the way societies store and use energy as important demarcators in various stages of social and economic development. Energy is used to do work, and the more energy that is tapped and the more efficiently it is used, the more work (and hence wealth and power) can be realized.[102] For agricultural societies such as the Shang, storing energy for future use was always a problem. Grains could be kept at most for a couple of years before rotting, and trees of course could live for a century or more, but the expenditure of human energy would be required to cut those trees down. Significantly, among the more efficient stores of energy in a solar-driven agricultural regime were humans and animals. John R. McNeill has called such pre-industrial energy regimes "somatic" for their dependence on human and animal muscle to do work. For states, the more people under a ruler's command, the more energy that could be deployed against others or for other tasks. For commoners, farm animals and other livestock were also stores of energy to be tapped for conversion into human energy as food, or to do work.[103] And for a solar-driven agricultural somatic energy regime, changes in the amount of solar energy reaching the earth to be captured by plants could be critical to survival.

Not surprisingly, much of the Shang divination was about agriculture and the fate of the annual harvest. From the spring through late fall, according to Keightley, "the king and his diviners would have been continually and urgently involved in rituals, forecasts, and prayers designed to nourish and protect the growing grain and ensure its safe harvest and storage." Worried about early or late killing frosts, droughts, locusts, wind, and rain—not to mention enemy attacks—"a successful harvest meant that the dynasty would endure, that the Powers had demonstrated their approval. Peasants, diviners, and the king had labored together and would labor once again as the stores of grain dwindled and grew stale, and inexorable cycle of the seasons, with its rituals, anxieties, and triumphs, repeated itself year after year." [104]

Despite the threats to the harvest, Keightley thinks that the Shang experienced a "benevolence of the climate and the fecundity of the environment . . . [that] contributed to the general optimism about the human condition and human nature that characterizes much early Chinese religion, legend, and philosophy."[105] But much like the modern world, the Shang may have built their assumptions about the natural world in a time of climatic stability, and were unprepared for the shocks to their system that climate change might induce.

Climate Change and the Fall of the Shang

The climate coinciding with the Bronze Age Shang state at its height was considerably warmer and wetter than at present—maybe as much as 5–8 degrees Fahrenheit warmer. Rain may have fallen more regularly on the North China plain than it does now, making conditions for agriculture much more favorable. Some oracle inscriptions even record two crops annually of millet and rice in the Anyang area. An entire way of life built on assumptions about the climate being stable can be called into question when the climate changes, as it did for the Shang around 1100 BCE. For reasons climatologists cannot identify, the climate suddenly became colder and drier shortly after the Shang capital Anyang was built, contributing to the difficulties the Shang kings faced, and probably to their destruction by the conquering Zhou around 1050 BCE. Colder weather decreases the harvest by shortening the growing season and making killing frosts in the planting season and during the harvest more likely. Complete harvest failure in some places would have been likely, leading to food shortages not just for the villagers but, more important, also for the royal elite, soldiers, and foundry workers. Declining food supplies also led to fewer births, and hence to a declining population. Villagers fled to the woods or other states in substantial numbers, decreasing the labor and military force available to the Shang royalty. Little wonder that the Shang kings divined constantly about their crops.

Certainly, the colder weather would have affected agriculture in all of the states alike, not just the Shang. Indeed, the cold may have affected the neighboring Zhou state even more adversely, it being further west and at a higher elevation than the more fortunate Shang. Did declining agricultural yields make the Zhou more bellicose and covetous of Shang resources, leading to war? Or did the Zhou have some social or agricultural innovations that enabled them to maintain their economic, political, and military power in the face of declining temperatures? Again, we do not know, and later Zhou sources do not tell us.

What Zhou sources do tell us is a moral story about why the Shang lost and the Zhou forces won: the last Shang kings were evil, and the Zhou kings were good and humane. This moral-based claim to legitimacy was articulated as the Zhou idea of the "Mandate of Heaven": Heaven mandates the king to maintain order in the universe, understood as cosmic, natural, and human affairs, and as long as the king fulfills his duties, he retains the mandate to rule. But disorder in the universe, such as evidenced by the poor rule of the last Shang kings, under which the people were so poorly treated that they fled, would lead Heaven to withdraw the Mandate and confer it on another—in this case, the Zhou. The Zhou would keep it as long as they maintained order in the universe, and probably attributed the cooling climate to the Shang moral failings.

The Zhou story of their legitimation as rulers holding the Mandate of Heaven made the contest a bilateral one between them and the Shang. But why that was we do not know. Zhou sources airbrush out of the story the other states we know were at war with the Shang. For despite what selective memory or construction of reality the Zhou were attempting to pull off, the reality of the Chinese world is that it was one defined by war: preparation for war, engagement in war, and preparation for war again. What we might call interstate war was the conditioning factor of life for states and people in the period from 1500 to 1000 BCE, and that fact is significant for understanding processes of environmental change in ancient China.

CONCLUSION

Over the period covered in this chapter, from the origins of settled agriculture in both north and south China, people mostly exploited opportunities that the environment they were in offered them, including the still poorly understood mutation of perennial forms of millet and rice into annual forms that could be harvested and planted. To be sure, the people who were observing and experimenting had to have the insight to take advantage of that change, and they did so. Moreover, the environments that sustained rice farming and millet growing had peculiarities that conferred a distinctive cast to Chinese agriculture from its very origins. The north China soil that the millet grew in—the loess—was distinctive in that it held many nutrients that rose to the surface year after year by capillary action, pulled up by surface evaporation. Farms on this soil did not need to leave soil fallow. For different reasons but with a similar result, rice could draw most of its nutrients from water, and so that soil too did not have to be left fallow. One result was that Chinese farming could sustain increasingly large and densely settled human populations.

That was one instance of the ways in which humans interacted with the environment that they encountered, and in the process created something new—farming—that in turn would have a rather dramatic impact on the environment through progressive cutting down of forest to make way for farms. And although China's Neolithic and early state peoples certainly altered their environments to be more suitable for them and the plants and animals that they were selecting for survival and propagation, nonetheless they were more at the mercy of natural forces, especially weather and climate, than not. A society that becomes agricultural and settled depends on weather patterns remaining pretty much the same year after year so they can plan (hope) for a life-sustaining harvest. It is little wonder that the Shang kings spent so much time consulting their gods about whether or not the harvest would be good, or whether to raid neighboring peoples' fields. The Shang combination of a particular kind of agriculture carved from forests that provided additional resources for a central state that could concentrate resources to cast bronze weapons and mobilize warriors allowed the human population to increase to 4–5 million, quite a successful adaptation. At least until a rapidly cooling climate precipitated the fall of the Shang and the rise of the Zhou.

By about 1000 BCE, there is substantial evidence that the people who came to be Chinese certainly had an impact on their environment, from mining and smelting copper for bronze to building cities and clearing forests for farms. In competition with others, they created states that were profligate users of natural resources and mobilizers of unfree human labor power. Ruling elites were quite cognizant of the role of agriculture and secure food sources in increasing their populations, and hence their power. As hierarchical societies formed with elites determined to extract the maximum from their environment to enhance and perpetuate their power, the impact on the Chinese environment proceeded apace, and increased dramatically over the next thousand years, as we will see in the next chapter.

Chapter 3

States, Wars, and Farms

Environmental Change in Ancient and Early Imperial China, 1000 BCE–300 CE

As we saw in the previous chapter, by 1500 BCE the driving forces of environmental change included the establishment of a Shang central state that engaged in wars with non-Shang peoples, pushed the development of agriculture to increase the population under their command, and refined bronze technology both for domestic uses and in war. As a result, by about 1000 BCE, the activities of those 4–5 million people cut back the deciduous broadleaf forest to provide space for farms and fuel for domestic uses and the bronze industry.

The area that became China had given rise to two distinctive kinds of settled agriculture, with dry-land farming in the north based on millet, and wet-rice cultivation in south. The line demarcating the two regions lay between the Yangzi and Yellow Rivers, about along the Huai River. China was one of four or five places in the Neolithic world about seven thousand years ago where settled agriculture produced more food than the direct producers required for their own subsistence. As we will see, in this chapter we will need to expand our horizon to the grasslands to the north and west of the North China plain to bring into our narrative both the pastoral nomadic peoples there who learned how to exploit the peculiarities of that ecosystem, and the ways in which those peoples and the Chinese interacted.

STATES, WAR, AND ENVIRONMENTAL CHANGE IN ANCIENT CHINA, CA. 1000–250 BCE

An agricultural surplus enabled the emergence of a new elite that built and lived in cities and made war on other similarly organized groups. By 1200 BCE the Shang state was one of several competing polities in north China. Thus not only was China one of the few places in the world where agriculture originated, but it was also one of the few places in the world to give rise to war.[1] Along with agriculture, states and war thus became significant driving forces in environmental change in China.

The combination of settled agriculture, a ruling elite, and war created a situation where rulers had a strong interest in exploiting their environment to bolster their power against rivals. Let's discuss a little more precisely the connection between state power and the natural environment. Humans need energy to survive, and the more energy they can tap collectively beyond what they need for their own survival and reproduction, the more power the collective group—via the state—can wield. Until fossil fuels were used, most sources of energy came from collecting and using plants that converted solar energy into food sources accessible and digestible by humans or animals. Agriculture is the primary means by which humans capture concentrated accumulations of solar energy in plants such as millet and rice. And as stores of energy, humans were prizes to be captured.

In this world, expanding agriculture thus expanded energy supplies; humans and animals were essentially stores of energy—little batteries, if you will.[2] Power meant the ability to control and mobilize these human and animal sources of energy, although a solar-energy regime placed definite limits on the power any pre-industrial state could wield. For the Shang state, this energy was organized and tapped under their direct control to farm, to conduct war, and to clear forest for farming—under the Shang ruling elite, the people were not free. The Shang state was very good at mobilizing humans for this transformation of their environment. The resulting pressure meant that increasing both agricultural production and population was a high priority for the Shang state, leading to very early pressure on the forests of China. We do not know when the clearance of forest for farms began to lead to something we might call deforestation, but archeologist Gina Barnes thinks that by about 1000 BCE this was certainly happening: "[T]here is no doubt that the agricultural practices of the Neolithic and later historic peoples contributed to massive deforestation across the eastern loess lands and the Central Plain."[3]

Forests are not simply trees but ecosystems with species embedded in a trophic web feeding on each other—microbes feed on decaying organic matter, freeing minerals and nutrients available for new plant growth, which is then (sometimes) consumed by other animals, and so on. Cutting down forests to make way for farms thus reduces the habitat available for "wild" nonhuman species, in the sense of those animals not controlled by humans. The forests of north China, as we saw in the previous chapter, provided habitat for numerous species, including elephants, tigers, rhinoceros, numerous kinds of deer, wild boar, and birds and plants of all kinds, all of which required a forest environment to live. As that forest was removed and fragmented, the space available for the larger species especially shrank, and their disappearance is a rough indicator of the scope of environmental change. We know, for instance, that by about 1000 BCE, the range of the elephant had been pushed from its previous range all over China, including the North China plain, south to about the Huai River valley (see map 3.1).[4]

It would be an overstatement to think that the north China deciduous forests had been lost by 1000 BCE, for that certainly was not the case. But it does seem fair to say that by that time, agriculture, population growth, technological development, rulers and their ideas, war, and environmental change had become so intertwined in ancient China that figuring out which came first is a chicken-and-egg problem. Suffice it to say that in China a complex of economic, social, political, and military forces had

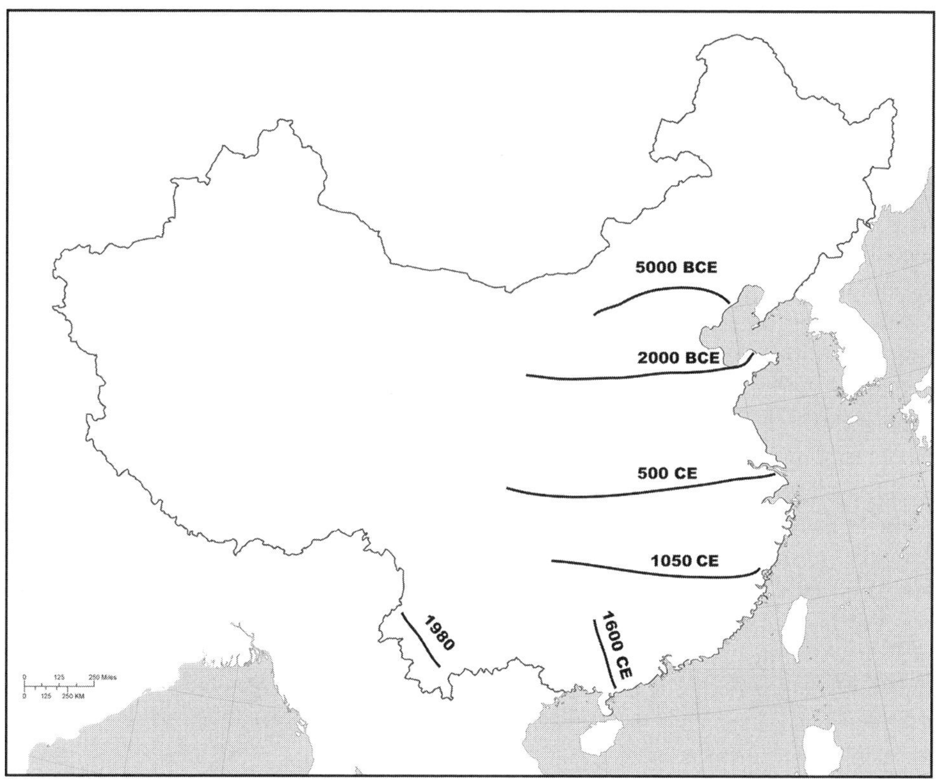

Map 3.1. Northern Limits of the Asian Elephant (*Elephas maximus* L.) *Sources:* Adapted from Richard Louis Edmonds, *Patterns of China's Lost Harmony: A Survey of the Country's Environmental Degradation and Protection* (London and New York: Routledge, 1994), 29; Elvin, *The Retreat of the Elephants,* 10.

become so fully developed by 1000 BCE that it remained a driving force of environmental change for the next three thousand years.

The period considered in this chapter, from about 1000 BCE to 300 CE, is thus one in which Chinese states and their actions are important for understanding the processes of environmental change in ancient China. As is true with almost any period covering 1,300 years, there is much change over that time. The period begins with the conquest of the Shang by the Zhou, who established their rule over north China, extending their sway east and south. Within a few generations, the Zhou system broke down, with Zhou vassals asserting their independence, giving rise to hundreds of small states and periodic wars. These wars led to a process of consolidation, resulting in larger, more powerful territorial states locked in war. By 250 BCE one of those states, the Qin, set about unifying China by conquering all the other Chinese states, completing the task in 221 BCE and establishing the first empire. Although the Qin dynasty was short-lived, the one that followed it, the Han, continued many of the Qin's innovations, so we can speak of the Qin and Han collectively as China's "early empire," with successor states holding on until 317, when nomadic invasions ended any hope of a reunited empire ruling over China. So important in Chinese history were the Qin and Han eras that our name for "China" derives from the Qin (pronounced "chin"), and the Chinese people call themselves "Han."

This period is also significant because the agrarian empire that was created during the Qin and Han dynasties came to be the form that most Chinese states embodied for the next two thousand years, until the early twentieth century. As we will see, the Chinese agrarian empire was one characterized by family farms supporting a centralized bureaucratic state, with their taxes and labor linked by a monetized market economy.[5] As simple as it sounds, this combination of a central state with farming families linked by markets proved to be a distinctively Chinese way of organizing their society, and of transforming nature.

One of the most important dynamics established during this period was the one between two different environments and the peoples who learned how to exploit the energy resources available in those ecosystems. So far we have focused almost exclusively on the ways in which the environment of north and south China made possible the invention of agriculture, using plants that had mutated and other natural resources to sustain a settled way of life. But the grasslands to the north and west were not so hospitable to human habitation. The further west and north one traveled from north China, the less the summer monsoons could bring rain, and the drier the climate became, resulting in grasslands of greater or lesser lushness, semi-arid desert, and desert. Over the same period of time that Chinese were learning how to farm and build an agrarian society, other peoples learned how to use the resources of the grasslands to sustain their lives and societies.

Nomadic Pastoralists of the Steppe

This chapter begins not with a continuation of the story of farming and how that changed the Chinese environment but with the peoples and environment to the north and northwest in the vast grassland known as the steppe that ranges across the Eurasian continent from Manchuria in China's northeast to the Hungarian plains (see maps 2.1, 2.2, and 2.3). At first glance, that may seem strange, since it appears to be outside the scope of an environmental history of China. But it seems warranted nonetheless, not just because China came to incorporate the eastern portion of these grasslands but also because the grasslands and their pastoral inhabitants had such a profound effect on the course of China's history.

Just as the particular environmental conditions in north and central China had provided the opportunities for farming based on millet and rice to emerge there, so too did the vast grassland known as the steppe provide a different environment from which another kind of human adaptation could arise: the horse-riding pastoral nomads of Central Asia. The horse was domesticated and herded by 4000 BCE, and there is evidence of horse-riding (to tend herds) shortly thereafter. Raiding followed riding, but mounted archery and militaristic styles of nomadic pastoralism probably had to await the Iron Age and the invention of the short compound bow around 1000 BCE. Horse-riding pastoralists tending their herds of goats, sheep, and horses migrated east across the steppe from the Ukraine north of the Black Sea to the Altai Mountains in the fourth millennium BCE, and then into the northern oases of the Tarim Basin by 2000 BCE.[6]

As Thomas Barfield assessed the nomads' significance in world history, "Though relatively few in number and seeming to lack even basis for state organization, for more than 2,500 years they nevertheless managed to create great empires that continually terrorized and periodically conquered powerful sedentary states in northern China, Iran and Afghanistan, and Eastern Europe."[7] Attila the Hun and Chinghis Khan are but two of the best-known nomadic invaders known to Europeans and Chinese, but there were numerous other successful nomadic empires as well. Because of their importance in establishing an exceptionally important symbiotic relationship with China, setting in motion one of the key dynamics in Chinese and nomad history—indeed, becoming part of China's environmental history—we need to examine the environment in which nomadic pastoralists emerged, as well as their history.

Bounded on the north by the thick forests, swamps, and tundra of Russia and Siberia, and on the south by the agrarian civilizations of Iran, Anatolia, Turkestan, and China, the grassland running from the Black Sea in the west to Manchuria in the east was broken into two zones by the Altai, Pamir, and Tianshan mountains: a western section of the Russian and Kazak steppe at about sea level that was more closely connected with the Near East and eastern Europe, and the eastern section on the Mongolian plateau at about four thousand feet above sea level that was oriented more toward China.[8] "Horse-riding pastoralists historically occupied [these] grasslands and mountain pastures . . . [with] rolling plains of grass, scrub land, and semi-desert punctuated by high mountain ranges. . . ."[9]

Because humans cannot digest grass, and because the low annual rainfall meant that the grasslands could not be successfully farmed, for several millennia the steppe constituted a great barrier to the expansion of human settlement, leaving that vast ecosystem to animals that could eat and digest grass. Indeed, the grassland supported a large and varied population of animals. Chief among those was the horse, the domestication of which played an important role in the rise of a pastoral nomadic way of life.

Other notable animals included the kulan, the wild ass of Mongolia. It has been described as "nearly as fast as a race horse . . . almost from birth [it] can escape its chief predator, the wolf. . . . Like other ungulates of the arid regions, the kulan can live on scant fare: brackish water and dried grass are all it gets some seasons." The kulan was never domesticated; neither was a horse that came to be known as Przewalski's horse. Also native to the steppe grasslands was the Bactrian camel, probably the ancestor of the domesticated two-humped camel. The saiga, an antelope at home on the steppe, is able to withstand blowing winds and subzero weather: "Its bulging nose is as useful as it is bizarre: the nostrils open downward as protection against windblown snow and sand." A huge bird known as a great bustard weighed thirty pounds and preferred walking to flying. Buboc marmots dug networks of burrows, pushing the subsoil up into mounds four feet high that then alter the chemistry of the soil and make possible the growth of plants, such as feather grass and fescue, that otherwise would not grow there. [10] Predators included the grassland wolf.

In short, the steppe was not inhospitable to animal life. Indeed, around 5000 BCE the herds of horses, wild asses, camels, and antelope probably would have been quite large, if not in fact huge. The high-plateau grasslands of Tibet supported large ungulate populations even into the late twentieth century.[11] In the grasslands of central North America, for example, Andrew Isenberg has estimated that there might have been as many as 30 million bison around 1800.[12] That similarly large herds of grazing animals roamed the Eurasian steppe seems likely.

The animal herds on the Central Asian steppe thus would have been very attractive to humans. Anthropologists think that the first attempt to capture and domesticate the horse was around 4000 BCE in Central Asia east of the Ural Mountains, where "these environments created conditions favorable to the breeding of animals, and [where] agriculture could also be practiced."[13] Horses were first domesticated as a food source (especially in winter), and herded along with sheep and goats. Riding probably emerged about the same time, and horses probably began pulling wagons by 3000 BCE. "Wagons and horseback riding made possible a new, more mobile form of pastoralism. With a wagon full for tents and supplies, herders could take their herds out of river valleys and live for weeks or months out in the open steppes between the major rivers."[14]

By about 2000 BCE, bronze technology enabled the production of lighter and more mobile chariots that could be used both for transport and for war. "Leaving the protection of river valleys they began to migrate across the grasslands with large herds of animals"; by 1200 BCE, nomads on chariots invaded Iran and India;[15] as we saw in the last chapter, the chariot made a sudden appearance in Shang China about the same time.[16] Although seen as barbaric or at best primitive by ancient Chinese and the Greeks and Romans, nomadic pastoralism "is in fact a sophisticated economic specialization"[17] and creative human use of an extensive ecosystem, using horses, cattle, sheep, goats, and camels to make the energy stored in the grasses available for human use. Steppe peoples tended their herds, and hence to that extent were pastoral, but because their herds followed the fresh grasses that sprouted in the spring, they moved with them, and to that extent were nomadic. The horse and cart made that human adaptation to the steppe ecosystem more efficient, and spread these peoples and their way of life across the steppe.

Horse riding was probably practiced as early as the horse was domesticated, by about 4000 BCE, but it was not until about 1000 BCE that saddles and improved bits and bridles gave nomads greater control over their horses,[18] and the compound bow transformed mounted archers from skilled hunters into feared mounted warriors. "The steppe nomads now combined a mobile economy with a powerful mobile military. This new culture soon displaced the semi-nomadic, riverine agricultural settlements and even began to threaten neighboring sedentary civilizations. . . . Marginal farmers from China, forest hunters from Siberia, and the more sedentary inhabitants of the steppe itself all adopted a fully nomadic style of life to more efficiently exploit the Central Eurasian grasslands."[19] In other words, nomadic pastoralism was such a successful way of using an otherwise untapped ecosystem that people of vastly differing cultures, languages, and places all adopted the same practices, and in the process developed a new common steppe culture spanning much of the Eurasian continent.

Nomadic pastoralism was based on an annual cycle of moving herds of sheep, goats, cattle, camels, and, of course, horses from pasture to pasture. Sometimes the movement was horizontal, as the herds followed the new grasses from the southern plains further north, or vertical, taking herds from the valleys in the spring into mountain pastures in the summer. Either way, the pastoralists moved with the seasons, and developed portable shelters called yurts (also called a gir) that they carried from one encampment to the next, going and returning to the same pastures in the spring and summer, and to the same camps in the winter. If all went well, the herds would be fattened by the fall and available for slaughter, or sufficiently strong to survive the cold winters.[20]

How much environmental change the nomadic pastoralists brought to the steppe is not known, but some can be assumed. Their herds had to have consumed grass that wild animals would have relied on, and hence wild populations would have been reduced by a certain amount to make way for the domesticated sheep and horses. Did the trampling of the steppe disrupt the marmots and their transformations of the grasslands? Were different species of grass transplanted from region to region in the dung the domesticated herds dropped along the way? Did the dung improve the grasslands and the meadows for the herds, or make the grasslands better for them and worse for indigenous species? Those are all questions whose answers we do not have, but it does seem quite certain that the nomadic pastoralists did not simply pass over steppe ecosystems without changing them in some unknown but substantial ways.

Although the horse was the pride of the nomads' herds, sheep and goats provided most of the nomads' sustenance and usually constituted the largest herds. These animals reproduce faster than horses or cattle, devour almost anything on the grasslands and provide milk and wool while alive—and meat and leather afterward. Milk from all the animals was fermented into kumis, and the wool was processed into felt used both for weatherproof clothing and as cover for their yurts. In short, the animals in the nomads' herds transformed the energy available on the vast grasslands into forms consumable by humans. Without this important relationship, humans would have found life on the steppe difficult, if not impossible.

But live they did, and by about two thousand years ago there might have been about 1 million pastoralists spread across the steppe. The smallest social group probably was the household that followed its herds to grazing lands that it traditionally used. In winter, the larger camps would have been composed mostly of patrilineal relatives, although there was a great scope for women and their activities. Mostly, the extended family was the group within which nomadic life was lived out—except, as we will see, when relations with outsiders such as other nomads or sedentary societies such as the Chinese prompted larger pan-nomadic organizations such as chieftains or confederacies.[21]

One of the reasons for these broader political organizations is that the nomadic pastoral way of life did not produce much above subsistence needs for its members, leaving very little room for the rise of a ruling elite. And yet we do know that nomads developed a warrior aristocratic elite from which leaders (called *shan yü* by Chinese observers) were chosen. Other men were followers, and all male nomads (and sometimes women too) would be expected to become warriors at a moment's notice, for raiding other tribes or agrarian societies provided the booty that was then distributed by the leader to his followers.[22] "Rulers of steppe empires . . . did not expect to support themselves by extracting revenue from their nomadic subjects, rather the reverse.

They used the military might of their nomad followers to extract revenue from outsiders which could not only pay for the administration of the empire but also could be redistributed among the potentially rebellious component tribes to keep them happy."[23]

This is where nomads begin to enter "history": those who were attacked, such as the Iranians or Chinese, were literate and wrote about these encounters. For the Chinese of the Central Plain of north China, these contacts did not come until about 500 BCE during an era known as the Warring States period, which we will discuss in more detail later in this chapter. But because nearly all of the written records about nomads come from people who were threatened by them, such as the Chinese, the accounts reflect the views of those "civilized people" about others in and around their world. But the nomads were not the only "barbarians" to the Chinese.

Other Non-Chinese Peoples

The Chinese of the period ca. 1000 BCE called themselves either Xia or Hua, and considered that they inhabited the Central Plains (*Zhongguo*) around which lived peoples they either knew or guessed about, but none of whom they considered to be as advanced ("civilized") as they were; these peoples thus were various kinds of "barbarians." To the north, all non-Chinese were known as the Northern Di; to the south, all were Man; to the east, the Yi; to the west, the Rong. Within those broad categories, the Chinese of the central plains gave specific names to peoples as they encountered them. Based on archeological and linguistic evidence, we now know that the space that became China in ancient times was inhabited by a rich array of peoples of different cultures and languages, including the pastoral and nomadic peoples to the north.

One problem we face is that the names for these peoples almost always were embedded in Chinese civilizational discourse that defined others as "barbarians." In many cases, these labels may have been embedded in Chinese fantasies, and in others the same label was applied to very different peoples—or, alternatively, the peoples of a region changed, but the Chinese label remained the same. Martin Fiskesjö notes that Chinese "civilization" needed "barbarians" to define itself by the difference, and discusses the fascinating case of the Chinese rediscovery of "the ancient Miao" during the Song dynasty (960–1279 CE).[24] Heather Peters examined similar problems of connecting an ancient archeologically definable culture—the Yue south of the Yangzi River valley who cultivated wet rice, used water buffalo, built their houses on stilts above the water, and tattooed their faces—to later peoples and modern ethnicities, in particular the Tai.[25] Recognizing the slipperiness of those Chinese labels, and the modern politics surrounding ethnicity in China,[26] we nonetheless have few alternatives to using them to refer to the various peoples the Chinese encountered.

According to E. G. Pulleyblank, peoples known to the Chinese as the Miao and Yao inhabited south China, from the Yangzi River valley down to where the Tai and Vietnamese (Mon-Khmer speakers) lived. The Tai, whose tongue is now the national language of Thailand and Laos, migrated out of south China in the last thousand years or so (probably having been pushed by Chinese). Other Tai speakers in south China include the Kam, Zhuang, and Xi in Hunan, and possibly the Kelao or Lao in the southwest. Austronesian languages are far-flung from Hawaii to Madagascar, and are related to the diverse languages on Taiwan Island. Along the southeast coast were the Yue, with languages related to Mon-Khmer—as were the Yi, of the Huai River marshes as far north as Shandong province. Further to the northeast in Hebei were the Mo and in southern Manchuria down through the Korean peninsula were the Mo-wei and Eastern Hu.[27] Although we cannot now be certain, all of these peoples with different languages and cultures probably had developed their own ways of extracting sustenance from their particular ecosystems, sometimes by farming (both settled and shifting) but probably mostly by hunting, gathering, and fishing. The archeological record confirms the existence of numerous different kinds of non-Zhou tribal peoples within and bordering Zhou territory.[28] We will encounter these peoples and more as the Chinese of the central plain consolidate their power and extend it into regions inhabited by these peoples, setting in motion complex processes of interaction, as well as sending many of these peoples into flight from the more powerful Chinese.

The Zhou Conquest: Colonies and Forests, 1050–750 BCE

By 1050 BCE, various peoples on the central plain of north China whom the Shang had preyed on began to actively oppose the Shang. Certainly the Shang had angered those from whom they stole wheat, especially the Qiang whose villages were periodically raided to provide humans for their sacrifices. However the anti-Shang coalition came together, it was led by the Zhou, a people to the west of the Shang, in the loess lands of Wei River valley just west of where it entered the Yellow River (see map 3.2). Also included in the anti-Shang alliance were the Qiang and peoples known as the Yong, Shu, Mao, Wei, Lu, Peng, and Pu.[29] In 1045 BCE the Zhou-led alliance defeated the Shang and set up their own state, the Zhou dynasty, which reigned for 700 more years. And because the Zhou were the literate ones who left whatever records we have, mostly we learn about the virtue of the Zhou and the evil of the Shang. The other peoples who participated in the Shang overthrow mostly disappeared from the written record, either assimilated via marriage into the Zhou system or conquered and vanquished.[30]

The center of Zhou power was in the Wei River valley, an area that came to be called Guanzhong, meaning "within the passes" (see map 3.2). This was the area where dry-land farming first developed in north China (see the previous chapter), and by 1000 BCE it had become very productive indeed. The easily worked loess soil could be farmed annually without fallow periods, fresh water came from the Wei River, and the timber for building and firewood could be cut and hauled from the Qinling Mountains to the south. The Qinling Mountains also provided a natural defense, and access to the Wei River valley to the east was choked off by the pass cut by the Wei River before it joined the Yellow River. The Zhou built their capital city Hao on the southern bank of the Wei River.

To control their newly won territories, Zhou rulers created a decentralized political system sometimes described as feudal, sending family members, allies from the war, and even some Shang royalty they could trust to rule various parts of their new territory in the name of the king. The Zhou royal family kept significant lands around their

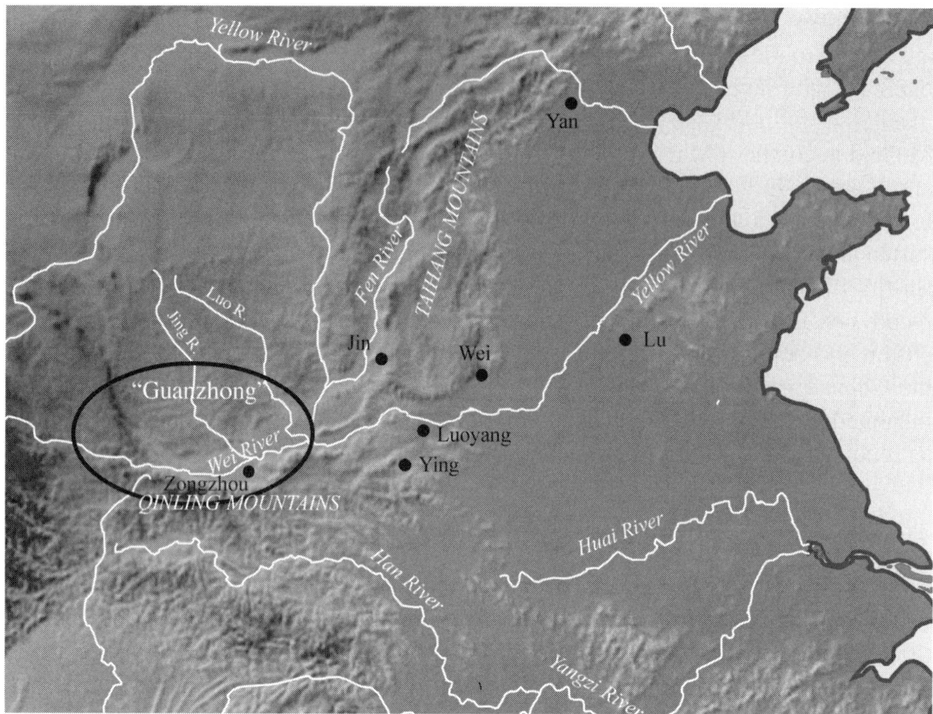

Map 3.2. Zhou China. The central region of the Zhou in the Wei River valley, called "Guanzhong," is encircled; later colonies in the lower course of the Yellow River are noted.

capital city, now called Zongzhou, along the Wei River, for themselves. In return for their lands, the rulers of the vassal states were expected to be loyal to the Zhou family, and to send troops to defend the Zhou king when required.

The Zhou colonies were agents of environmental transformation. Sent out into the wilderness, or to newly conquered lands, the Zhou vassals built walled towns, or garrisons, from which to assert their claims to the land. Several vassals in turn granted land to their own subvassals, who then began clearing the forest and creating farms, poetically describing their efforts in heroic, military language in which trees and forests were enemies, and the resulting clearings for farms and fortifications were good.[31]

The most effort to bring the environment under control was made to the east of Guanzhong on Yellow River plain (see map 3.2) in lands inhabited by the "Eastern Barbarians," the Yi. There, the land was fairly flat and densely forested, and because the Yellow River periodically flooded and flopped around, it was not a safe place to build garrison cities or to farm. Garrison towns thus had to be located on higher ground to the north or south of the channel of the lower Yellow River. Nonetheless, that alluvial plain was quite fertile, and could be settled when the Yellow River was diked to prevent flooding. As we will see, the diking of the Yellow River began somewhat later, and was to have a profound effect on the environment and history of the North China plain.

The evidence thus indicates that during the early Zhou there was still plenty of virgin land, not just on the North China plain but even in the core area of the Zhou state in the Wei River valley. Around 800 BCE, for instance, the ruler of a Zhou vassal state called Zheng decided, for unknown reasons, to move his domain from where it was founded to a place further east, to a new site near the Zhou capital, Zongzhou. Even there, around the Zhou capital, the new land was described as "full of thorns and bushes," and according to historian Cho-yun Hsu, "the settlers had to make considerable effort in its reclamation."[32]

The early Zhou period (to about 750 BCE) thus saw a significant clearance of forests and concomitant ecological change beyond the former Shang heartland in the North China plain, to the east, northeast, and northwest. We know little about the histories of the states of Chu in the Yangzi River valley at that time, or of Shu in the Sichuan basin, or of the emerging Wu polity in south China. What we know about the non-Zhou peoples is based on archeological finds, and those indicate that these states were at least as technologically as advanced as the Zhou, and in some ways—in particular when it came to iron, perhaps even more advanced. Their societies, too, were hierarchical, with ruling elites and farming commoners, but because of the existence of written sources, we know more about how early Zhou society was organized.

Early Zhou society was quite similar to Shang society, some differences in basic beliefs notwithstanding. At the top was the king and the royal family, ruling from their capital city, at first at Zongzhou but after 770 BCE at Luoyang. The family members, allies, and some former Shang royalty whom they dispatched to rule on their behalf constituted an aristocracy that was expected to be loyal to the king by sending troops when the king called. All lived in, and ruled from, walled cities, connected with the capital by roads sufficient to carry chariots and carts. Since vast numbers of bronzes were cast, we assume that, as when the Shang ruled, large numbers of artisans and foundry workers lived in or near the walled cities. Working the land of both the royalty and the aristocracy were peasants held in varying degrees of bondage. Almost everything—food, clothing, and so forth.—was produced on a lord's domain.[33]

Until about 500 BCE, when iron became widely available, Zhou farmers used stone or wooden plows to open their fields; some proportion of these stone plows were pulled by men, and others were pulled by teams of oxen. Hoes were also used to break up the soil. In the easily eroded loess lands, the plowing technique included ridging to minimize soil erosion. Main crops continued to be the two strains of millet, although rice was planted in the lower Yangzi River and in south China—areas not tributary states of the Zhou—and wheat and barley became increasingly important. Where Shang rulers had determined the best time for sowing the seed by divination, by Zhou times the use of calendars and observations of tree and shrub flowerings became commonplace, and, one would assume, more accurate.

As Bray concludes, both Shang and Zhou agriculture had had to be sufficiently productive for the farming population to support a large population of non-farming rulers and their artisans. She notes that ox-drawn plows had been used in the Shang. "Without high-yielding crops or even irrigation . . . to boost agricultural production, the Shang farmers must surely have used ox-ploughs to till their fields. There was an economic necessity to do so, they were familiar with the principles of animal traction, and the plough was probably known to their . . . predecessors and certainly to their Bronze Age contemporaries in Tonkin."[34]

Like the Shang, the early Zhou period was one in which there was an abundance of land but a relative shortage of labor to work it. Under those conditions, the farming population was held in various kinds of bondage to their lords, who did not want them running off into the forest. As we will see below, circumstances changed later during the "Warring States" period (481–221 BCE), when peasants unhappy with their prospects under a particular lord could hope to improve their lots by fleeing to another state that had more attractive terms of employment. In the early Zhou, though, the only alternative to working the fields and supporting the nobility was to head into the forest.

Agricultural workers had to be kept in their villages producing grain, because the consequences to a vassal state of a declining population and food supply would prove to be disastrous. In a world of war against others in the early Zhou state system, or against the depredations of outsiders from the grasslands, grain and people were power, and control over those sources of power were essential to rulers. So subjects had to be kept on the farms.

The reasons for keeping one's farmers from fleeing back into the forest changed as the balance between the amount of land and labor available began tipping as both virgin forests for clearance declined, and the population increased. Signs of this change appear very early in the Zhou period, in 913 BCE in an inscription on a bronze vessel cast for the occasion. Virgin land in this area was becoming short, so one lord had to acquire additional land from another by paying for it. The seller then reneged after receiving payment, setting in motion a legal suit of sorts. A royal panel listened to the evidence, and decided the fields had been sold, marked them off, and awarded them to the complainant.[35] Apparently this was one of many such incidents, most of them adjudicated by the Zhou royal court. However, as the power and influence of Zhou royalty declined, regional lords began settling their disputes over land using their own military forces. Additional pressures on land resources came as estates were broken up and parceled out to new families who then competed with neighbors over land resources. Conflict over land and its resources fueled the increasing conflict among the hundred or so new states that were emerging from the declining Zhou system, and demand for resources to fight the wars put additional strain on the environment.

Chinese of the early Zhou period were beginning to develop the idea that humans should dominate and control nature, an idea that was to become fully articulated and implemented centuries later during the Han dynasty. Zhou conquerors explained their victory over the Shang in terms of a new concept, the Mandate of Heaven. The idea was that Heaven had given a mandate to the Shang rulers, not merely to rule but to rule well—to maintain order in the universe. The last Shang kings abused that trust, and Zhou texts depict them as monsters, starving and killing their own people. In the Zhou interpretation of their victorious war, Heaven then revoked the mandate from the Shang and bestowed it on the Zhou,[36] who then conquered the Shang and restored order by subduing nature. A Zhou ruler then "drove the tigers, leopards, rhinoceroses, and elephants far away, and the world was greatly delighted."[37]

There is much apocryphal in early Zhou accounts, but they do begin to lay out early Chinese beliefs and actions about their environment—that it was there to be transformed and exploited—not necessarily in the orgy of violence celebrated earlier by the Zhou, but through the calming and civilizing influence of their sovereign. The proper natural order was one in which humans dominated the landscape, and thus the wild animals had to be driven away. Of course, the tigers, leopards, and elephants were indeed dangerous to humans, especially as humans increasingly destroyed their habitat and made their lives more difficult. But it is clear that the ancient Chinese were less interested in "living in harmony with nature" than they were in humanizing it.

Wars, Warring States, and the Creation of the First Empire, 750–200 BCE

In the half-millennium or so after 771 BCE when "the dog barbarian" invaders forced the Zhou royal house to flee to the east, China underwent significant changes, all of which affected the ways in which Chinese interacted with, and understood, their environment. Politically, the decline of Zhou royal control over their vassals led to the establishment of a couple hundred states, most of which were at war with others at one time or another, or were consolidating power over non-Chinese peoples within their realms. These wars led to territorial consolidation, with about twenty major states emerging by 400 BCE as the most powerful players in a multistate system. The destruction of states led to the fall of their ruling elites and downward social mobility, while skill at state administration and war led to the rise of men because of their martial abilities, not their birth. Ideas about how the state should best use its human and natural resources were explicitly articulated, as were ideas about what constituted the ideal state. State revenues came to be collected as taxes on harvests, leading to private ownership of land and to peasant families taking responsibility for their own production decisions. Markets for land and commodities developed. States to the south and east that had not been part of the Zhou system increasingly entered into the wars to their north, bringing an even greater part of what we now call "China" into military and political interaction with their neighbors. Iron was first used around 500 BCE, and its use spread widely to agriculture (especially plows) and then later to war (e.g., mass production of iron swords, arrowheads, and crossbow mechanisms). Rising agricultural productivity led to significant population increases, and larger and more destructive wars, some with armies exceeding one hundred thousand troops. Widespread deforestation and environmental destruction became palpable, and warnings sounded.

And all that was before one of the Warring States, the state of Qin, around 250 BCE, began wars of conquest designed to eliminate all of its rivals, leading in 221 BCE to the establishment of the first empire (the Qin and Han dynasties). With the rise and fall of that empire, political, economic, social, and environmental patterns were established that affected China for the next two thousand years. In retrospect, then, the period from 750 to 200 BCE was thus a transition from a warring multistate system (see map 3.3) to a unified, agrarian empire. During these 500+ years, there were more than a thousand recorded wars, most of which occurred during the last 250-year period, aptly named the Warring States (481–221 BCE) period.

A competitive multistate system had significant consequences for how Chinese states organized themselves and interacted with their natural environment. The heads of all of these states, plus the new non-Zhou states of Wu, Chu, and Yue that

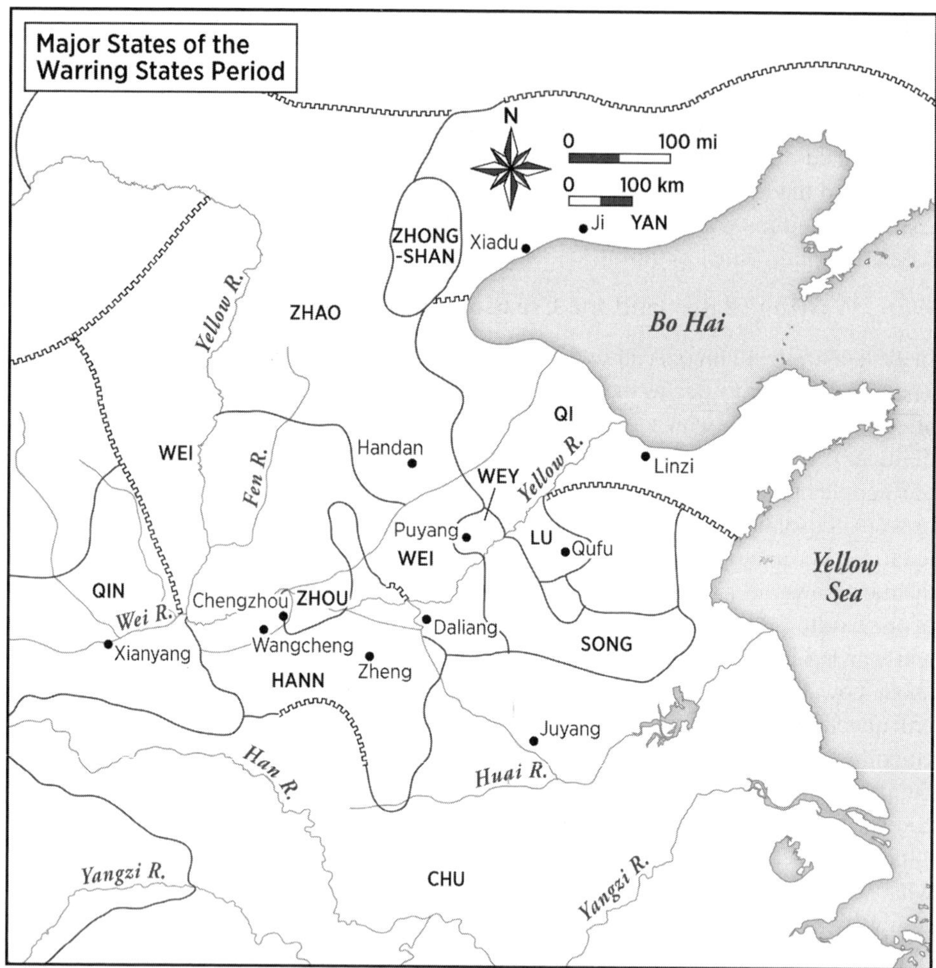

Map 3.3. Major States of the Warring States Period *Source:* Adapted from Michael Lowe and Edward L. Shaugnessey, *Cambridge History of Ancient China* (New York: Cambridge University Press, 1998), 594.

developed in and to the south of the Yangzi River valley, were well aware that war, preparing for war, and paying for war were the most important acts of any state, and that those priorities created the political, social, and religious machinery necessary for skillfully warring. Dominating others required dominating the social as well the natural environment. And the primary purpose of agricultural development was the provision of tougher "sinews of war."[38] The needs of state security drove political concepts, agricultural innovation, and, of course, population increase, all of which were then harnessed to the chariots of war.

War drove political innovation, social change, and attacks on nature. To gain access to the agricultural wealth produced by the farming population, ruthless leaders of several states eliminated their aristocracies and began to create something approaching a bureaucracy of civil and military officials beholden to the king for their positions. State revenues increasingly came from taxes, which transformed aristocratic manors into private property. The establishment of borders created a need for a state to reclaim forested land, now understood as wasteland, for agriculture, and to entice farming families to migrate; the states that gave the better "deals," including land ownership and the possibility to rise economically and socially without feudal barriers of birthrights—such as Qin, Wei, Han, and Zhao—attracted migrants and hence larger farming populations. As Cho-yun Hsu put it, "thus a certain number of plebeians became independent farmers working land that had never been part of a manor."[39] More forest gave way to farms.

As populations grew, so too did the number and size of cities. Paradoxically, Warring State China became urbanized and commercialized. The city of Linzi in the state of Qi was densely populated with 350,000–400,000 workers, merchants, and service personnel. States built roads within their borders, created money, and conducted a thriving trade with other states. If one state became too powerful, others formed alliances to thwart it. All in all, it was a period of considerable fluidity, with some social classes and people rising, others falling, some getting rich and powerful, and others losing their fortunes or political fortunes. And into this mix came a powerful new technology, iron-making.

Iron and Steel in Ancient China

Just as bronze technology developed elsewhere earlier than in China among the peoples of the Central Asian steppe, so too did iron.[40] By 1000 BCE, when bronze technology was being highly refined in the early Zhou, iron had already become an integral part of nomadic economic and political development, and it was used in all aspects of life and war.

Within the territory of present-day China, clear evidence for iron smelting dates from around 500 BCE, not in one of the core Chinese warring states but in the state of Wu south of the Yangzi River. That region had been settled by a people who by the time of the Zhou conquest of Shang already had a developed bronze industry. Wu used bronze not just for ceremonial castings, as the Zhou did, but for agricultural tools as well, tipping wooden spades with bronze for use in wet-rice farming. They also cast bronze harvesting knives and harvesting hoes, so their agriculture was at least as advanced as the Zhou. By the sixth century BCE, during the time of the Warring States, Wu had become a powerful state and recognized force by Chinese states to their north. But Wu was then conquered by the even-more powerful Yue state, which became the core of the Yangzi River valley state of Chu.

Iron was long known as a byproduct of bronze smelting, and historian Donald Wagner speculates that the people of Wu, being less hierarchically organized than Zhou states and very interested in improving agriculture, had an incentive to look for a less expensive material than bronze to use for their tools. However that happened, by 500 BCE iron implements were being placed in Wu graves, and by the fourth century BCE iron technology had spread much more widely along the Yangzi River valley.[41] Presumably both the smelting technique and the quality of the iron improved enough to be noticed by the Chinese states to the north, which also began producing large amounts of iron. Since both the nomads to the north of Chinese states, and the state of Wu to the south, had iron technology, perhaps it spread among the western non-Chinese peoples and thence into the south, or perhaps the technology developed independently in both regions. But when China's warring states learned of it and its uses in war, it spread rapidly among those warring states, too.

Iron ore was rather widely distributed throughout China, so once the technology became known, iron smelters rapidly spread. Mines tended to be opened where ore deposits were in forests with access to a stream or river. Ironworks were in effect large plantations located in forests (burned to produce the charcoal necessary for the furnaces smelting the iron ore) and waterpower from a stream or river (to pump the bellows). Wagner estimates that producing 800 tons of pig iron a year—which these ironworks were capable of doing—required about four square miles of forest. "The limiting resource in pre-modern iron production," Wagner says, " is wood, not ore."[42] So iron manufacturing also created a demand for wood, adding to the environmental pressure caused by population growth, agriculture, and wars. As we will see in the next chapter, by about 1000 CE the North China plain and nearby hills had been deforested, drying up the sources of charcoal for the iron industry, but resulting in the innovative use of coal for the same purpose.

Iron was used to manufacture swords, knives, drill bits, saws, crossbow parts, belt hooks, and helmets, as well as leg, hand, and neck cuff irons to hold slaves. In agriculture, iron was used for hoes, spades, shovels, and especially plowshares, and many ironmasters became very rich men. In both war and agriculture, iron increased efficiency and output, contributing to rising populations within Chinese states, and to the size and destructiveness of armies.

Whether burning charcoal for the iron smelters contributed to deforestation is an open question. According to Anthony Barbierri-Low, "Deforestation caused by indiscriminant harvesting of trees for charcoal production can lead to extensive erosion and even permanent changes in climate. In one tragic incident from the Han, it led to the death of more than one hundred workers. The story is told from the perspective of a boy named Dou Guangguo, who was kidnapped from a poor family around 190 BCE, when he was four or five years old, and sold into slavery. After his slave contract was sold from one master to another, he eventually found himself making charcoal for a private iron industrialist in Yiyang, near Luoyang in present-day Henan. He and his fellow slaves had apparently denuded most of this hillside on which they were working, for one night while they slept, the entire mountain gave way and buried more than one hundred men and boys alive."[43]

Wagner, on the other hand, argues that the iron industry did not lead to deforestation. The number of trees felled for the charcoal certainly was impressive, he says, but a forest that was managed for that purpose might well have been able to provide adequate supplies of trees for the charcoal and not cause ecological devastation.[44] But as the next section of this chapter on resource constraints makes clear that that level of forestry management was unlikely to have been achieved in the early empire.

War and the Use of Natural Resources

The wars and emergence of a multistate system; rapid social change, with new classes rising and old ones falling; urbanization, with concentrations of populations using money and markets to consume food and products they themselves did not make; and new iron technology all began to place pressure on natural resources, and to raise in some minds the idea that natural resources were not unlimited—a new idea that began dawning in the midst of the wars and the demand on natural resources.

As a book called the *Guanzi* composed around 250 BCE observed, "When the state is wasteful, it exhausts resources. When its resources are wasted, its people are impoverished. Therefore it is said: 'It is vital for the state to be judicious in setting limits, to be frugal in dress, to be economical in the use of resources, and to prohibit extravagance.' Those who do not understand such calculations cannot make proper use of their states."[45]

The *Guanzi* goes on to detail those limits. "Even though the mountains and forests be extensive and the grass and trees lush, proper times must be set for the closing and opening [of the mountains and forests]. . . . Even though the rivers and lakes be extensive, pools and marshes widespread, and fish and turtles, plentiful, there must be regulations set on the use of nets and lines. Boats and nets cannot be the only resource for there to be success. It is wrong to be partial toward grass and trees or favor fish and turtles, and it is inadmissible to subvert people from the production of grain. Therefore it is said: 'When the former kings prohibited work in the mountains and marshlands, it was to expand [the efforts of] the people in the production of grain.'"[46]

Certainly, the *Guanzi* expresses awareness that natural resources were limited, and that the successful state should have a ruler who puts limits on their exploitation so that the resources are not exhausted. The overriding concern of a ruler, though, was with maintaining the strength of the state, not in preserving the environment. Paradoxically, the Warring States period demonstrated that few states indeed were successful, so the *Guanzi* no doubt was raising warnings to rulers based on the failures of substantial numbers of states. The pressures of war clearly were more compelling than the advice to conserve the natural resources within a state.

Nonetheless, it is also clear that highest priority for these rulers was the production of grain to sustain and increase the number of people available to be mobilized by the ruler. The *Guanzi* therefore contains a substantial amount of information about agriculture and the ecological bases for successful farming, starting with an agricultural calendar. But the text also relates the level of the water table to the likelihood of drought or flood, and includes an entire section on "categories of land." As translator Allan Rickett observes, the *Guanzi* "remains unique in its detailed treatment of soils and plant ecology and is certainly one of the earliest works of its kind in any language."[47]

The *Guanzi* grouped soils into five categories with their characteristic plants and trees, depth of water tables, and grains that do best in those conditions. Another section relates associations of plants with particular settings. For example, "At the top of some high mountains, there are areas known as 'hanging springs.' The land there is not dry. Characteristic plants are madder and *wan*. The characteristic tree is the larch. Digging down two *chi* [a linear measure], one reaches the water table. . . . On the lower slopes of mountains, characteristic plants are varieties of bindweed and wormwood or mugwort. The characteristic tree is the thorn-elm. Digging down three times seven or twenty-one *chi*, one reaches the water table."[48]

That such detailed ecological knowledge in ancient China coincided with serious pressures on the environment, and perhaps even substantial environmental damage, should not be surprising. The modern environmental movement arose under similar circumstances.

The Warring States and Non-Chinese Peoples

Chinese states warred not only among themselves but also against non-Chinese peoples. The Zhou classified these peoples as "barbarians," in part because of what they ate and how they prepared it: "The people of those five regions—the Middle States, and the Rong, Yi (and other wild tribes among them)—all had their several natures, which they could not be made to alter. The tribes to the east were called Yi. They had their hair unbound, and tattooed their bodies. *Some of them ate their food without its being cooked with fire.* Those on the south were called Man. They tattooed their foreheads, and had their feet turned in toward each other. *Some of them ate their food without its being cooked with fire.* Those on the west were called the Rong. They had their hair unbound, and wore skins. *Some of them did not eat grain-food.* Those on the north were called the Di. They wore skins of animals and birds, and dwelt in caves. *Some of them did not eat grain-food.*"[49]

The Rong and the Di, arrayed from northeast of the Zhou warring states to the northwest, probably were pastoralists, not nomads, and acted as a buffer between the Zhou states and the nomadic societies developing in the steppe to their north; the Di may have "descended from mountain-dwellers who had been settled for several millennia."[50] Among the various non-Zhou peoples with which Zhou states had long-standing contacts, based mostly on war, it appears that the Di played an important role both as tormentor of Zhou states, and unwittingly as a buffer between Zhou civilization and the steppe nomadic pastoralists, whom Zhou states may not even have known about. Di peoples conducted a struggle against Zhou states for a couple of centuries, building cities, armies, and economies to defend their lands. On the other hand, by the middle of the fourth century BCE the Di were also building defensive fortifications against the steppe nomads to their north. The Di and the Rong were not nomads, but the Zhou considered them "barbarians" nonetheless: "Those whose ears cannot hear the harmony of the five sounds are deaf; those who eyes cannot distinguish among the five colors are blind; those whose minds do not conform to the standards of virtue and righteousness are perverse; those whose mouths do not speak words of loyalty and faith are foolish chatters."[51] We do not have any Di or Rong sources, but we might well wonder what they thought of the Zhou warring states to their south.

Meanwhile, from the ninth through the third century BCE, according to historian Nicola Di Cosmo, all across the nomadic steppe, "the herds of horses, cattle, and sheep grew. . . . As in other parts of Inner Asia, the growth of [nomad] economies was accompanied by the rise of a military warlike aristocracy."[52] In other words, as Chinese states warred, the steppe peoples to the north of the Rong and the Di were getting stronger, economically, politically, and militarily. But the Chinese seemed quite unaware of these "momentous events that were occurring in the steppe region," as Di Cosmo put it.[53]

The Chinese states did pay attention to the Rong and the Di, though, and expanded at their expense. In 771 BCE, Rong attacks drove the Zhou royal court from their capital in Guanzhong further east to a new capital at Luoyang. In the centuries afterward, Zhou states, Qi in particular, mounted numerous campaigns against the Rong, finally conquering them in the seventh century BCE. Another state, called Jin, eyed the lands of the Di: "The marshes and deserts of the Di will be to the Jin like a metropolitan area. Wouldn't it be right to expand the territory of Jin?"[54] Numerous Jin attacks against the Di in the seventh to sixth century BCE, for both booty and their lands, led to Di's elimination by the fifth century BCE and incorporation into Chinese states. By about 400 BCE, both the Rong and the Di were gone (however that might have come about), and Chinese states along the northern frontier, in particular Qin, Zhao, and Yan, came into direct contact with the mounted nomadic pastoralists of the steppe.

Pastoral Nomads and Nomadic "Invaders"

That peoples of the steppe came into military conflict with the expanding Chinese states between about 450 and 330 BCE is a given. The question of whether the Chinese were attacked and invaded by "barbarians," as Chinese sources tend to describe the relations, or whether instead the Chinese states advanced to the north and took lands the nomadic pastoralists considered theirs, is a different story. According to Nicola Di Cosmo, after the Rong and Di had been eliminated, Chinese states began advancing northward with their infantries against the people of the steppe. Not having horses or cavalry of their own, the Chinese states began to use a technique they had pioneered in wars against Chu to the south, and among themselves: building walls. The first "long wall," as it was

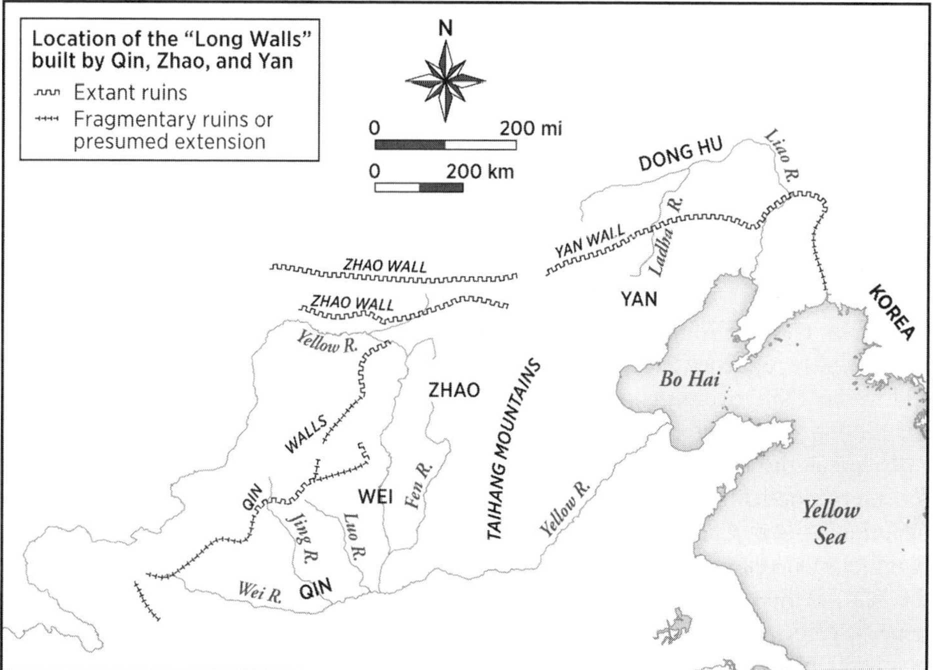

Map 3.4. "Long Walls" of the Warring States Era *Source:* Adapted from Nicola DiCosmo, *Ancient China and Its Enemies: The Rise of Nomadic Power in East Asian History* (New York: Cambridge University Press), 141.

called (see map 3.4), was built by the state of Qi for protection against Chu. Later, other states built walls between themselves as well.

Chinese warring states thus knew how to build long, sinuous walls of tamped earth and stones, and after pushing the nomadic pastoralists from their pastures and homelands, they built walls for protection against the nomads' horses and cavalry: Wei did so in 353 BCE, Qin and Zhao around 300 BCE, and Yan in 290 BCE (see map 3.4). In Joseph Needham's words, the walls were designed "to break the shock tactics of the nomadic horse archers, or of cavalry belonging to [one of the Chinese states] which had adopted such tactics."[55] By about 300 BCE, then, long walls built "in the middle of large stretches of grassland" separated the pastoral and agrarian peoples within (i.e., to the south) the walls, from the nomadic pastoralists to the north. Over the course of the next century, Chinese encroachment on nomads' lands—the Chinese called all of these people "Hu"—pushed the disparate tribes into a mighty steppe federation known as the Xiongnu that would become a "formidable opponent" of the Chinese.[56]

The new Xiongnu federation pushed the Chinese forces and their colonists back, and the Qin state began building a "great" long wall to consolidate their gains in the steppe. From this point of view, what was to become the Great Wall of the Qin and Han dynasties was in fact an offensive move by the Chinese designed to secure lands taken from the Xiongnu, Xiongnu wars against the Chinese were in reaction to Chinese aggression, and the Xiongnu were not the "barbarian" aggressors against the "civilized" Chinese.

Nonetheless, that first Great Wall (there was another built during the fifteenth century; see chapter 5) did become a great dividing line between two very different ways of life and of interacting with the natural environment, and frontier relations between Chinese and the nomadic pastoralists became a key piece of Chinese history for the next two thousand years. The Qin Great Wall was of such a vast scale that some began to express fears that it would interfere with "the given pattern of Nature," as Needham put it. When Meng Tian, the engineer sent by the First Emperor of Qin to design and build the Great Wall, was ordered to commit suicide after the emperor had died, Meng Tian lamented: "Indeed I have a crime for which I merit death. Beginning at Lintao, and extending to Liaodong, I made ramparts and ditches [for the Great Wall] over more than 10,000 *li* [3,500 miles], and in that distance it is impossible that I did not cut through the veins of the earth. This is my crime."[57] This may or may not have been an early reference to later Chinese beliefs about *feng shui*, or the powers of "wind and water" that govern geomantic forces, but it does show both the will to dominate nature, and the regret at having done so.

The Wall did not completely separate agrarian China from the nomadic grassland, for interactions of all kinds—"peace, war, and trade" in the words of one Mongolian historian[58]—kept Chinese and mounted steppe pastoralists tied together for the next two thousand years. But there are two points worth considering about the nomads and the Wall at this point in our story. First, the Wall did come to define something of a boundary between sedentary Chinese agriculture to its south, and nomadic pastoralism to its north. As long as Chinese could not conquer the nomads, Chinese would continue to see them as a threat. Two distinct ways of life based on two distinct human adaptations to different environments had come into existence in East Asia, and through their continuous interactions came to define each as "the other." Second, Chinese sources depict themselves as the "civilized" victims of unprovoked attacks by "barbarians" who desired the food grains and silks of China. To be sure, the peace pacts that Chinese concluded with nomadic pastoralists often included regular payments of rice, silk, and gold. But the mounted steppe pastoralists did not need access to Chinese agriculture because (as some have assumed) that was the only way they could get adequate carbohydrates (from grains) in their diet. According to Di Cosmo, nomads grew food when and where they could, and the Chinese were not the only ones with whom they could trade horses for grain. The nomads thus did not have a structural need to raid China. On the contrary, Di Cosmo argues, it is more likely that Chinese states needed the resources of the steppe, in particular horses for their cavalry and grasslands for pasture, than vice versa.[59]

Whatever the cause for their constant interaction, by at least 200 BCE, Chinese and mounted steppe pastoralists had established a symbiotic relationship across two vastly different ecosystems. Sometimes Chinese states would push into the steppe to try to control or eliminate nomad forces, seldom with any lasting success; sometimes, nomadic forces would attack Chinese outposts, and in one case (the thirteenth-century Mongol invasion), conquer China. Only in the mid-eighteenth century did rulers of China attempt a "final solution" to the "problem" of nomads, a story that will be taken up in chapter 5. Until then, steppe nomads and their particular environment were very much a part of Chinese history.

Summary

The Chinese world in 250 BCE was quite different from the one 500 years earlier, with the Zhou system having given way to a vibrant, if violent, multistate system. These wars drove increasingly intensive use of natural resources, and an emerging conscious that the bounty of nature could be exhausted, causing serious problems for states that did exhaust their natural resources, up to and including extinction. To that extent, the period was formative in Chinese conceptions of nature, a topic that will be taken up in greater detail later in this chapter.

Still, in 250 BCE the people in the Chinese world had had more than 200 years' experience with a multistate system, and there seems to be little reason to expect it to have led to anything else. After all, the multistate system that emerged in Europe around 1500 CE has existed for the past 500 years, with little evidence that that system will change into anything else. But in China, the multistate system of 250 BCE was gone a mere thirty years later, having fallen to the unifying power of one of those states, Qin, and its ruler, King Cheng, who took the new title of "First Emperor" when his armies vanquished the last competitor in 221 BCE. But the end of wars among Chinese states did not lead to a kinder, less exploitative relationship to nature. Instead, internal peace under the long-lived Han dynasty (202 BCE-220 CE) allowed the human population to boom to nearly 60 million people, and for the expansion of farmland to deforest much of the North China plain.

ENVIRONMENTAL CHANGE IN THE EARLY EMPIRE, 221 BCE–220 CE

Although composed of two dynasties with important differences, the "Early Empire" is considered as one period because of significant continuities from the Qin (221–207 BCE) to the Han dynasty (202 BCE-220 CE). Most importantly, the institutions of a centralized bureaucratic state, first created by the Qin, were used by the Han as well, softened a bit by the adoption of Confucianism as the official state ideology. After defeating all the other Warring States and unifying China under Qin control,[60] many advisors to the king thought that reestablishing some kind of feudal system such as that of the Zhou would make the most sense. One of the king's strongest advisors, Li Si, instead argued that the king should take the opportunity to sweep the feudal institutions and states into the dust bin of history, replacing rule over China with a new system and a new title for its ruler—Emperor (*huangdi*), not simply "king." As the First Emperor, the ruler of Qin appointed officials to rule commandaries on his behalf; if they did not perform adequately and follow specific rules and regulations to the letter, the Emperor had them removed.

But more than just a bureaucratic empire, the Qin attempted to impose uniformity throughout the empire. Weights, measures, and currency were standardized, as was the written language. Private weapons were confiscated, and the state sought to control knowledge and learning, and to suppress ideas that were not useful to the state. When Li Si heard that certain scholars were "praising the past to criticize the present," he had the offending books rounded up and burned. And, according to later legend, he had 460 scholars buried alive.

The Qin dynasty was short-lived for many reasons, but mostly because the First Emperor died in 210 BCE, his sons were incapable of ruling, the state imposed high taxes and labor demands, mostly to build the First Emperor's palace and tomb and to reinforce what came to be known as the Great Wall. Both of those projects were so huge and used so much timber that forests on Inner Mongolia's plateau and on a nearby mountain were destroyed to build the palace, and a 250-mile section of the Great Wall used up nearby forests as well.[61] When a revolt broke among peasants ordered to labor on the Great Wall, there was little if any support for the Qin, and quite a bit of support for change.

In the civil wars that followed, forces loyal to a commoner general named Liu Bang emerged victorious over the forces of an aristocrat. Liu Bang then founded the Han dynasty, and, following the Qin innovation, called himself "emperor." Because Qin rule had been considered harsh, Liu Bang reverted to the loose control of the Zhou system and parceled out large territories to his comrades and family members to rule as vassal states, retaining the right to appoint local officials and to hold them accountable to the emperor.

The weaknesses of the Han neofeudal system were apparent soon enough, and the third Han emperor, Wu (r. 141–87 BCE; also known as Han Wu-di, "Emperor Wu of Han") sought to rein in the power of the new aristocracy and to gain access to the revenues that they had kept for themselves. Wu needed revenue and troops, but wealthy landowners—both the Han aristocracy and merchants who had put together landed estates—stood in his way. Using whatever pretexts necessary, he confiscated many of their estates and enforced a principle of equal inheritance among all their sons to break up their lands, wealth, and power. As a result, the state became one of the largest landowners. To get capable men to govern, he reached an understanding with Confucian scholars, establishing an imperial academy in the capital city of Chang'an to teach the Confucian classics and to serve as a recruiting ground for officials. And to gather more revenue for the state and his military, he monopolized the production and sale of iron, salt, and liquor, and controlled wholesale grain markets.

Han Colonialism, the End of the Xiongnu Steppe Nomads, and the Beginnings of Desertification

A major driving force in Emperor Wu's quest to increase state revenues by reasserting central authority was the need to strengthen the military to defend China against attacks from the Xiongnu, who had organized themselves into a large federation. As we saw earlier, in 215 BCE, Qin forces had taken nomad lands within the great bend of the Yellow River, and built a wall to consolidate those gains. Spurred by these losses, a steppe leader forged various nomadic peoples into a vast confederation called the Xiongnu. After the Qin collapse, the Xiongnu continued to grow in power at the expense of other Inner Asian nomadic peoples.[62] Within a short time, the Xiongnu grew to control much of the Inner Asia steppe, an area perhaps as large as 2 million square miles (larger than that controlled by the Qin and early Han) with a population of more than 3.5 million people. "Furthermore," notes historian Chun-shu Chang, "as conditioned by their nomadic lifestyle, every able-bodied Xiongnu man was a fighting cavalryman—a natural soldier riding and shooting on horseback—and there were at least 500,000 of them."[63]

Emperor Wu's predecessors had tried to deal with the Xiongnu threat. Just two years after declaring himself emperor of the new Han dynasty (202 BCE-220 CE), Liu Bang sent an army of charioteers supported by footsoldiers against the mounted Xiongnu. The Xiongnu cavalry easily outmaneuvered and defeated the slower Han army, and the emperor sued for peace. The deal included not only giving the Xiongnu grain, cloth, and gold but also sending a Han princess to become the Xiongnu leader's primary consort as well as recognizing the Xiongnu federation as an equal to the Han Chinese. Using the Great Wall as the dividing line, the Xiongnu would rule over "all the people who draw the bow" north of the wall, while the Han would rule over all those south of the Wall who wear hats and sashes.[64] This "peace-through-marriage" policy continued for the next seventy years while both the Xiongnu and the Han strengthened themselves. During those years, the Xiongnu conducted thirteen raids against the Han, twice threatening the Han capital of Chang'an. From the Chinese point of view, the "peace" policy was not working, but they were still recovering from their civil wars and in any event still did not have a cavalry to go on the offense against the Xiongnu. Mobile military force forged in the steppe ecosystem clearly had bested the ponderous Han army growing out of farms on the North China plain.

Then, Emperor Wu transformed China's military into one with a large cavalry, using the superior military techniques of the Xiongnu against them. In a series of

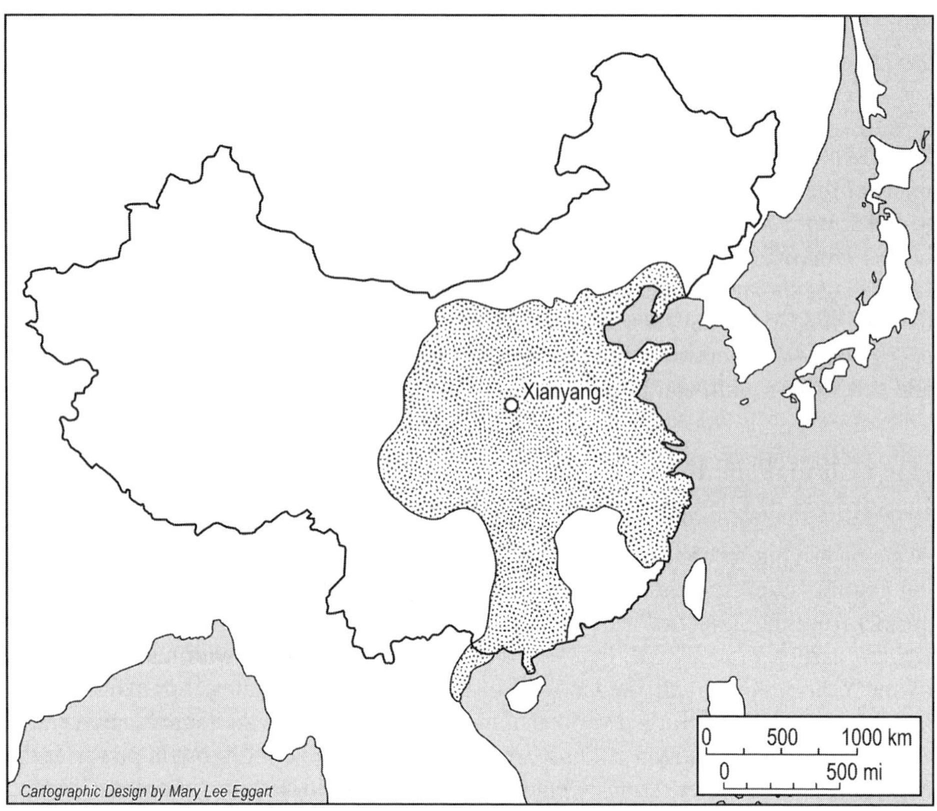

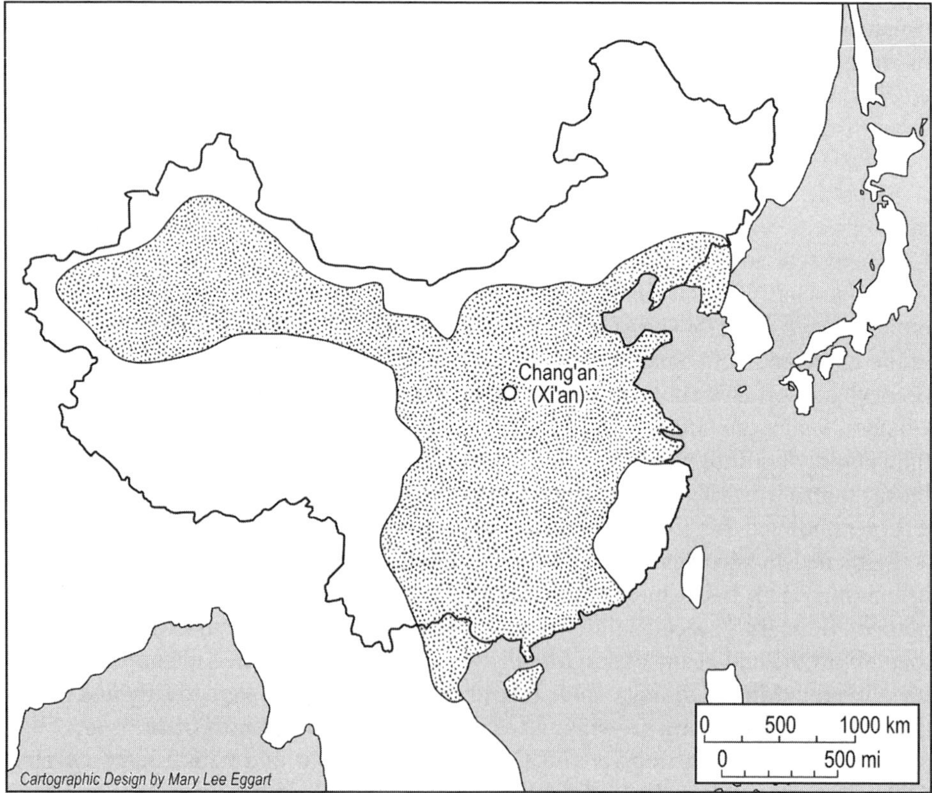

Map 3.5. Qin and the Han Dynastic Territories *Source:* Gregory Veeck, Clifton W. Pannell, Christopher J. Smith, and Youqin Huang, *China's Geography: Globalization and the Dynamics of Political, Economic, and Social Change,* second edition (Lanham: Rowman & Littlefield, 2011), 62, 65.

campaigns beginning in 129 BCE that lasted four decades, Chinese forces destroyed the Xiongnu and five other Central Asian states. In all, "more than 12.5 million people were mobilized . . . as Han soldiers marched to the edges of the Gobi desert and inner Central Asia."[65] Veterans from these campaigns were then sent as far south as Vietnam and southwest to Yunnan to begin to colonize those areas as well; the extent of the Han empire at its height is depicted in map 3.5.

Emperor Wu's military campaigns and the conquest of new territories had important environmental and ecological underpinnings and consequences. Foremost, the Chinese agricultural system as it had developed (for at least the preceding two thousand years!) had not included much pasture for grazing animals. Chinese agriculture intensively used land that did not need to be left fallow, and hence common Chinese farmyard animals included pigs and chickens but not horses, goats, or sheep—those were the animals herded by mounted pastoralists on the grasslands.[66]

After their first humiliating defeat by the Xiongnu, Han officials knew that they needed a cavalry, and that needed horses. Thus a few years before Wu became emperor, the Han set up thirty-six pastures in northern and western border regions for breeding warhorses. Some thirty thousand slaves were sent to raise the horses, and by Emperor Wu's time the number of horses totaled more than 450,000. From those, the best were selected for military training, and cavalry men, too, were trained, another impressive logistic feat. Of Emperor Wu's 500,000 men in arms, half were professional cavalrymen. This was the army that Emperor Wu threw at the Xiongnu. Not only did the newly mobile Han army kill or capture tens of thousands of Xiongnu, but in two of the campaigns it seized about 1 million horses, sheep, cattle, and other domestic animals.[67]

But Emperor Wu wanted not just to defeat the Xiongnu but to annihilate them. For this purpose, killing and capturing them was insufficient. He understood the ecological basis for the nomadic lifestyle, and determined that the solution to the problem of the Xiongnu was to transform their grasslands into farms operated by Han Chinese who would be settled in the regions seized from the Xiongnu. In two great colonization projects, starting with the area in the Gansu corridor called "West of the [Yellow] River" (He Xi) and then continuing further northwest into the Tarim Basin, a million or so Chinese were relocated from the more densely populated North China plain. The remaining Xiongnu were not killed but were instead settled on these lands "West of the River" with the expectation (or hope) that settled village life and proper education would transform them into civilized Chinese. The effort succeeded as long as the Han state was there to protect the Chinese farmers and school the Xiongnu, but those conditions would not outlast the dynasty.

As Chun-shu Chang shows,[68] the colonization and subsequent environmental transformation of the steppe was planned down to the last details. First, military watchtowers were built, followed by garrison towns sited near water and arable land first opened and farmed by soldier-farmers. Then houses were built and stocked with furniture and agricultural tools into which the Han Chinese were moved and set to farming. As the colonization project progressed and succeeded, civilian government replaced military rule, and the entire region was integrated into the Han empire.[69]

The colonization of former Xiongnu grasslands had lasting environmental consequences: the steppe grassland was opened by the plow to farming followed by wind erosion and desertification when the power of the Han state withered. "From an economic standpoint," Chang concludes, "it represented the region's transformation from an uncultivated area of nomadic cultures into an agricultural domain. . . . [T]he colonization of He Xi [West of the River] represented the victory of agricultural over nomadic society, a continuing process in North and East Asia in which the domain of the nomads gradually shrunk due to the expansion of agricultural civilizations. . . . [T]he transformation was carried out by the Han government through an ingenious design—the *tun-tian* [military-agricultural colony]. Emigrants from the 'old world' of the Han empire populated the region. These colonists, from almost every section of the empire, settled in their new world according to a systematic plan and were rigidly organized in every way."[70] Further to the west, in the Tarim basin, where desert predominated, oases rather than grassland were "developed,"[71] a practice, it turns out, that in the long term was more sustainable than plowing under grasslands.

As we will see in coming chapters, the Han military-agricultural colony scheme of *tun-tian* was then adopted by later Chinese dynasties—in particular the Tang (618–907), Song (970–1279), Ming (1368–1644), and Qing (1644–1911) and, in some important ways, by Chinese governments to this day—for the same purposes and with similar outcomes. In what is perhaps an overly confident assessment, and one certainly revealing his Han Chinese prejudices, historian Chang concludes that "the Han frontier system was a great heritage in the historical and political context of Imperial China."[72] But that "heritage" included outcomes that were arguably genocidal and environmentally destructive. Not only were non-Chinese eliminated, but also the transformation of grasslands into farms depended on the protection of the Chinese state. Even Chang recognized that these newly colonized territories "did not belong to the empire when China was weak."[73] But the farmland did not simply revert to grassland. The grasslands had taken millennia to evolve, and when iron plows broke up the sod to get at the soil, and water was brought to the crops not by rainfall but by irrigation ditches channeling water from rivers fed by annual snowmelt, a new "built environment" dependent on Han Chinese farmers emerged. Without them and their water, the former grasslands turned into desert,[74] much the same way that portions of the American Midwest became the Dust Bowl in the 1930s.[75]

Thus most of the area that we call "China" first came under the control of a single political entity during the Qin and Han dynasties (see map 3.5). Qin armies conquered the southern state of Yue as far south as Vietnam, incorporating it into the empire as well. Although the Qin was short-lived (221–207 BCE), its successor, the Han (202 BCE–220 CE) continued the military conquest of rivals, pushing into the far northwest during the second century BCE, cutting the Xiongnu off from their Tibetan allies the Qiang, and establishing a protectorate as far west as the Pamir mountains in Central Asia. The Han armies were large—100,000 to 300,000, and the campaigns lasted years. With the establishment in 221 BCE of the first empire, for four centuries Chinese states controlled a vast territory filled with resources that could be mobilized for state purposes. The ability to assemble and project such power lay in the growing Chinese ability to tap and organize sources of human and natural energy, and to create a communications network to hold it together.

Han Roads and the Opening of New Lands

Roads are tools of political and economic integration, and serve also to open up new areas to further economic development and migration to frontier areas. And

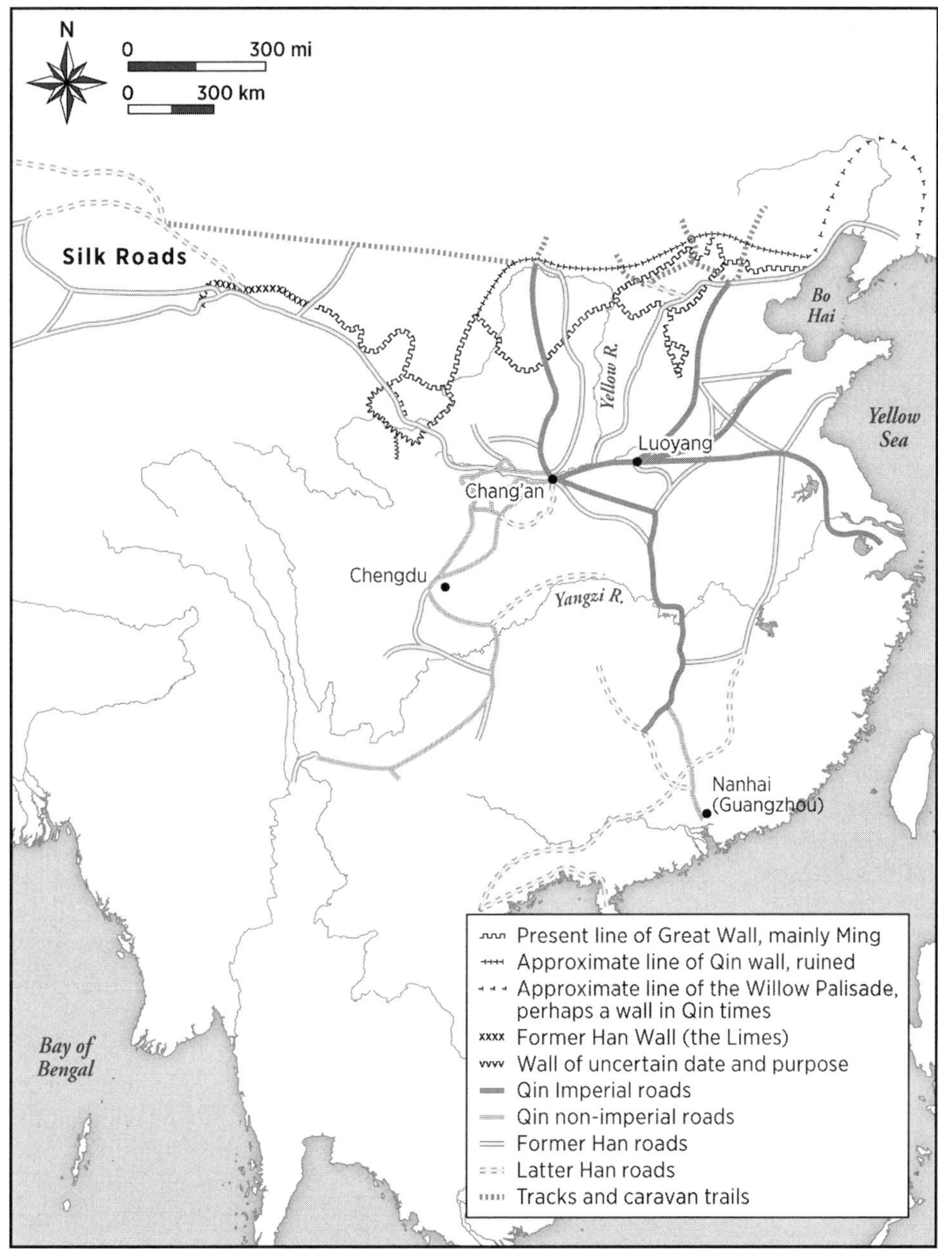

Map 3.6. The Han Road System *Source:* Adapted from Joseph Needham, with the collaboration of Wang Ling and Lu Gwei-djen, *Civil Engineering and Nautics,* vol. 4 part 3 of Joseph Needham, *Science and Civilization in China* (New York: Cambridge University Press, 1971), insert on page 1.

because nearly all economic activity has environmental consequences, roads also foster environmental change, as the contemporary fate of the Amazon rainforest reminds us. Two thousand years ago in China, in addition to being empire builders, the Qin and Han were road-builders. Before unifying China, the Qin had already had an extensive road system. After proclaiming the creation of the empire, the First

Emperor ordered the construction of a vast network of roads radiating out from the capital at Chang'an (near the present-day city of Xian) in all directions: "[E]ast to the uttermost bounds of Qi and Yan [in Shandong], south to the extremities of Wu and Chu, around the lakes and rivers, and also the coasts of the sea; *so that all was made accessible* [emphasis added]. These highways were 50 paces wide, and a tree was planted every 30 feet along them. The road was made very thick and firm at the edge, and tamped with metal rammers. The planting of the green pine-trees was what gave beauty to the roads. Yet all this was done (only) so that (Qin Shihuang Di's) successors (on the throne) should not have to take circuitous routes."[76]

The Han emperors continued the Qin road-building projects, expanding from five to seven the major arteries flowing from the capital to every corner of the empire. The most impressive of these roads, according to Joseph Needham, was the one built from the capital southwest over the Qinling Mountains to the agriculturally rich Sichuan basin. This road was called the "Five-Foot Way" because of the numerous places along mountain precipices and cliffs where it was no more than five feet wide. Needham calls the engineering of this road "heroic," and given the difficulties in building it, that was probably an apt description. The point of building this road was not just to ensure military control over this region but also to tap its agricultural and environmental riches.[77]

Not only did the roads bind the empire together, but they also spurred agricultural development in the areas they opened up, especially to the south, southwest, and northwest. Han engineers "opened up for the first time (the territory of) the southwestern Yi peoples. Cutting through the mountains, they constructed a great highway more than a thousand *li* [about 350 miles] in length, in order to extend the territory of Ba and Shu (Sichuan)."[78] Another road penetrated the Korean peninsula. While these roads into the frontier initially had strategic purposes, they had the effect of "opening up" those areas to Chinese settlement and to connection with the rest of the empire. Forest products flowed out of Yunnan and down the West River to Nanhai (Guangzhou), while in what is now southern Manchuria, the plain along the Yalu River between Korea and Beijing became available for Chinese settlement and farming. More environmental transformation followed the roads.

All told, the Qin and Han road builders constructed between 20,000 and 25,000 miles of main roads. And main they were. The thoroughfares were nine lanes wide: the inner lanes were reserved for imperial use, while merchants and others used the outer lanes. The roads served as the backbone of a post-station system, with post offices nearly every two miles with stables and couriers ready for relay service, way stations every ten miles for overnight lodging, and every fifteen miles or so a market for supplies. These roads and the postal system were in use for two millennia, from the Han through the last dynasty in the early twentieth century.

The walls that the Chinese built to enclose steppe lands thus did not mean that the Chinese world was closed off from the rest of the Eurasian continent—far from it. To outflank the Xiongnu, Han Emperor Wu had sent an emissary across the Taklamakan Desert into what became Xinjiang province, over the Pamir Mountains and along the Talus River into Central Asia to find allies. While he did not find any groups militarily strong enough to help check the Xiongnu, he did find thriving trading cities and what even the Chinese called "civilization." On returning, the emissary informed Emperor Wu, and eventually a road from the capital at Luoyang west toward the oases was built, connecting China to the Central Asian trade, protected along much of the first two thousand miles by an extension of the Great Wall. This network of roads and trade routes later became known as "the Silk Road," ultimately going all the way to the eastern Mediterranean and the Roman Empire. Eventually two roads were built around the Taklamakan Desert, the first circling to the north, the other to the south connecting a string desert oases fed by mountain snow meltoff.[79] Owen Lattimore noted, additionally, the environmental reasons why the Silk Road hopped desert oases: the Taklamakan protected merchants from raids by nomads of the steppe.[80]

Trade along the route was segmented, so few if any single individuals made the entire trip.[81] But food plants such as peaches, apricots, and pears traveled west out of China, and grapes and alfalfa (the latter to feed Emperor Wu's horses) went to China. Of course silk went out from China, but so, too, did vast amounts of cinnamon from south China. Small amounts of Chinese wrought iron (which those further west could not yet manufacture), along with jade, moved west as well. Also during the early Han, "donkeys, mules, and camels came in through the Great Wall in long chains."[82] And as we will see shortly, unseen biological agents may well have accompanied all of these goods, contributing to outbreaks of epidemic disease, much like the later Columbian Exchange between Old and New Worlds, but on a smaller scale.[83]

More important in terms of the sheer bulk of goods moving between China and elsewhere was the southern sea route from the south China city of Nanhai (later called Guangzhou), through the Straits of Malacca, and into the India Ocean where it intersected with pre-existing trade routes from the Red Sea and the Persian Gulf. For bulky goods, water transport is much, much cheaper and more convenient than land transport, and the evidence is that there was a brisk ocean-borne trade linking China to the Indian Ocean, with hundreds of ships carrying 600–700 people and 260 tons of cargo each. Additionally, scholars are now identifying what some call a third "Southwestern Silk Road," centered on what becomes Yunnan province and linking that part of Asia overland with Tibet, southeast Asia, and Burma and Bengal in the Indian Ocean. The point is that ancient "China" was not isolated from the rest of the world—ancient Asia was in fact already quite interconnected, allowing for the exchange or people, goods, agricultural products, animals, and diseases.[84]

Empire, Agriculture, and Deforestation

Qin and Han rulers not only created a centralized, bureaucratic empire, marking a sharp break with its feudal past. They also self-consciously based that empire on agriculture, preferring to tax independent farming families than to allow commerce or industrial wealth to create power centers out of the control of the state. That decision, as we will see, meant that while Chinese states continually had to deal with the problems attendant on the concentration of land ownership in the hands of wealthy owners, China would be an agrarian empire.

But that outcome, as important as it would be for the ways in which Han Chinese interacted with and transformed their environment, was not inevitable. The place that became the Chinese empire might instead have been a multistate system driven by cities and urban commercial and industrial development. As Cho-yun Hsü has argued, "In the years of turmoil from the fifth to the third century B.C.[E.], there was the strong possibility of developing a predominantly urban-centered economic life rather than a rural-based agrarian economy."[85] Markets, cities, profit, and contractual reciprocity all had emerged by then. That China instead developed as an agrarian empire had a huge impact on the way in which the Chinese interacted with, and transformed, their environment. That course was largely set during the Early Empire.

Many of the elements needed for a productive agricultural base had been set in the previous centuries during the Warring States period. Iron plows, the knowledge and use of fertilizer (mostly animal and human waste), grains appropriate for particular soil conditions, land preparation, and the like were known, and were written down in texts as guides to farming. Nothing was more important, though, than the creation of a class of free and independent small farmers whose taxes supported the state. That was a conscious choice on the part of the state. The First Emperor of Qin vastly preferred an agrarian economy to the much more freewheeling, commercial life of Warring States cities, and not only encouraged farming but also actively discouraged commerce. So, too, did Emperor Wu of Han, who monopolized major industries (iron and salt in particular), suppressed trade, and taxed merchant wealth out of existence—all to encourage farmers who received grants of land and tax remissions to bring frontier lands under the plow.[86]

New crops from Central Asia, intensive farming methods for millet and rice, the increased cultivation of autumn-sown and spring-harvested crops like wheat and barley, and cash crops such as mulberries for silkworms, hemp for cloth, sesame for cooking oils, and indigo for dyes all increased agricultural output, supporting a significant population increase, in particular on the North China plain. Although we do not know how much the population had increased from the beginning of the Han era, according to a census taken in 2 CE, there were about 60 million Han Chinese, most of them densely packed north of the Yangzi River, and a core in the Sichuan basin in the west. Some had migrated to south China, to Yunnan in the southwest, or as farmer-soldiers along the northwest frontier, but these numbered in the several hundreds of thousands each (see map 3.7).

Agriculture continued to become more and more efficient, enabling farmers to produce significant surpluses that could be used to sustain even larger numbers of people who did not need to grow their own food—government officials and functionaries, and soldiers mostly, but artisans and merchants as well. Iron plowshares fitted with a mouldboard and pulled by a team of oxen enabled one farmer to till, and then sow, larger amounts of land than ever before. Iron sickles and scythes sped harvesting, and iron implements of all kinds boosted agricultural productivity. Plows became specialized, including those designed to open up recently cleared land: "There were ploughs with sharply pointed shares for opening new land, heavy plows with giant shares for trenching, and, most commonly, broad-shared ploughs with mould-boards for tilling arable fields. The large clods thrown up by the turnploughs required breaking up, and thus we see the drag-harrow developing in China towards then end of the Han; the ridge-and-furrow system is better suited to sowing in rows than to simple broadcasting,

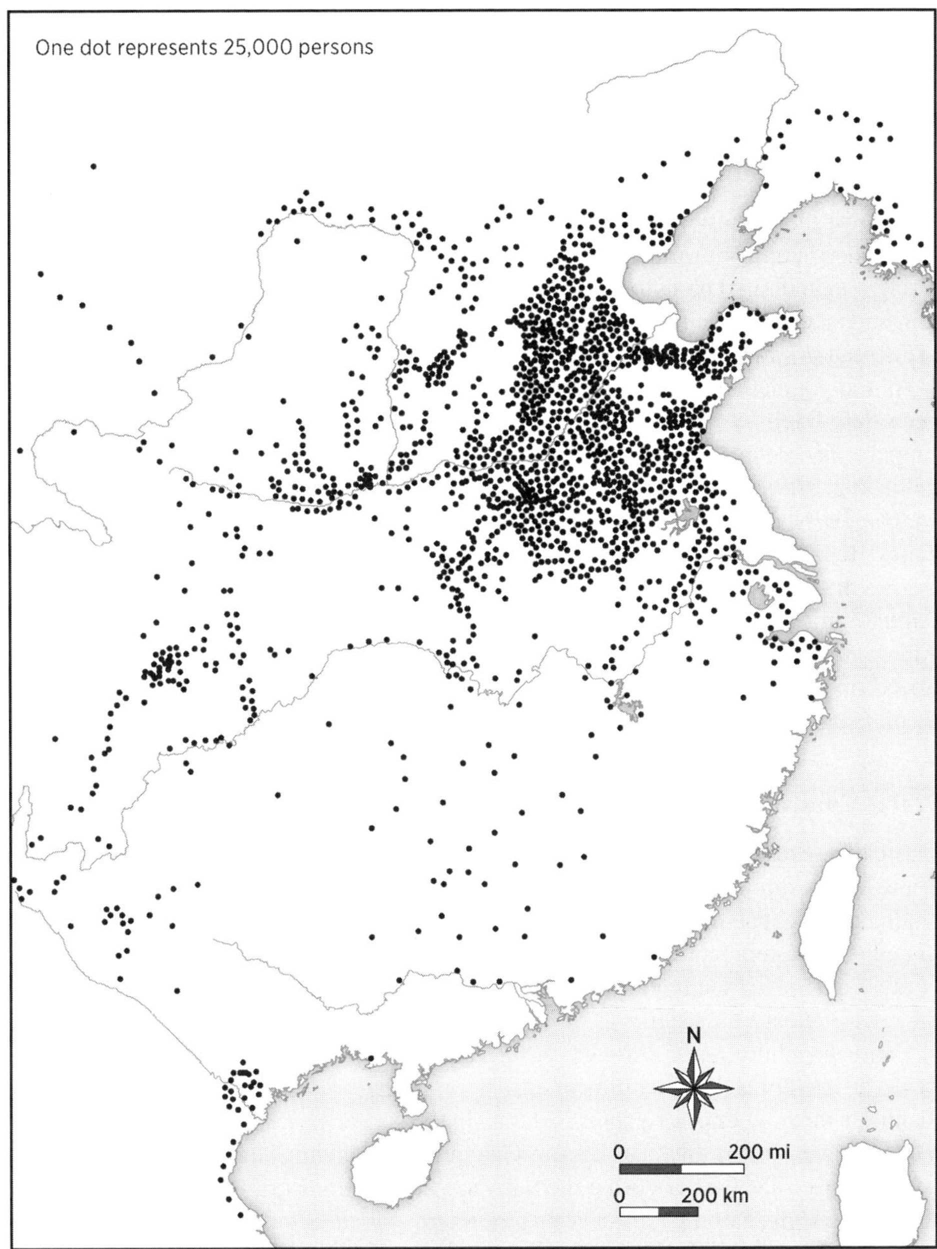

Map 3.7. The Population Density of Han China, ca. 2 CE *Source:* Adapted from Denis Twitchett and John K. Fairbank, eds., *The Cambridge History of China,* vol. 1 (New York: Cambridge University Press, 1987), 241.

and the seed-drill also appears in China during the Han."[87] Plows were used not just on dry-land millet and wheat fields but in wet-rice fields as well.

The different types of plows largely corresponded to two types of soil and ecologies in north China: the light loess soils of the Guanzhong area, and the heavier alluvial soils of the Yellow River valley. As we saw in the previous chapter, the loess soils might have been fertile but they were light, and the major problem farmers faced was in conserving soil moisture.[88] In the loess lands, the plows were light and penetrated only three or four inches of soil. There, agriculture was quite productive. As Shih Sheng-han concluded, "agriculture in [Guanzhong, the loess lands of the Wei River valley] is principally well-advanced dry-farming adaptive to an arid climate."[89] "Further down the Yellow River," Bray explains, "a different system of cultivation was desirable to cope with much heavier soils . . . [needing] the mouldboard plow. . . . Using a mouldboard plow to turn up ridges has additional advantages: . . . it is easy to thin and space the plants correctly, it makes hoeing much more convenient . . . [and] if the seed is sown in rows rather than broadcast, less seed is required."[90]

As the population density in map 3.7 implies, most of the North China plain had been deforested by the middle of Han dynasty, and perhaps much earlier: the First Emperor had decreed that trees be planted along his roads, and that memorial forests be planted as well. By the Han, previously forested hills on the Shandong peninsula were being planted with fruit and other trees of economic value.[91] Most the Wei River valley was sparsely forested loess land to begin with, but the Yellow River valley and the North China plain had been covered with a thick oak and maple deciduous forest; farmers' iron axes cut down those forests, and their plows opened up the heavier soils. Although the Taihang and Qinling mountains retained their forest cover, forests on the North China plain were no more, and neither were the animals that had inhabited them. Natural ecosystems became agro-ecosystems.

Water Control

The Chinese transformation of environments during the early imperial period was impressive. Wars with steppe nomads led to Han colonization and farming of grasslands; states encouraged the development and spread of agriculture, which an integrated road system facilitated; and the growing population intensified land use on the North China plain, leading to increasing deforestation. Another tool for transforming the environment was water.

From the Zhou period through the Early Empire, important improvements were made in the storage and control of water for irrigation, and for flood control. Bray identifies three types of irrigation systems. In the southern rice-growing regions of the Yangzi River, inland Sichuan, and in Guangdong, individual farmers dug out ponds and tanks to collect water during the rainy season, and to distribute it as needed to the rice paddies. In central China, river water was dammed to form reservoirs, and water was released to fields through sluice gates into canals and to the fields by the force of gravity. In the Yellow River system in the north, states organized and funded large-scale irrigation works characterized by contour canals, so called because they brought water from rivers to fields in canals that followed the contour of the land. The most famous of those was the Zheng Guo canal.

The Zheng Guo canal (figure 3.1) was started in 246 BCE on the loess plateau north of the Wei River by the state of Qin (the one which was to unify China under its rule). The idea for this project was to build contour canals about 120 miles long to

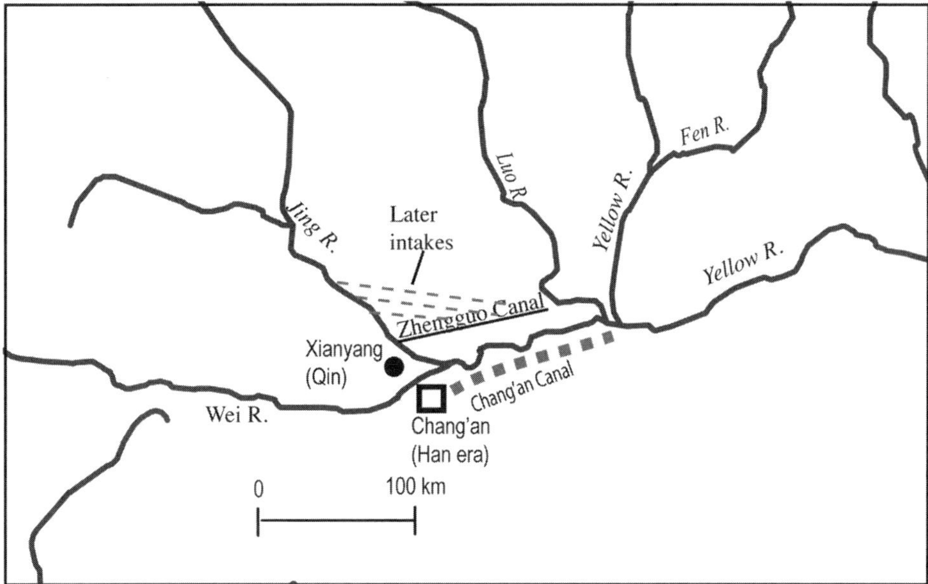

Fig. 3.1. The Zheng Guo Canal

direct water from the Jing River to the Lou River, along the way releasing water for irrigation. In its first decades of operation, the Zheng Guo canal irrigated more than 4 million mu (possibly as much as 650,000 acres, or a thousand square miles) of land, greatly increasing the economic might of the state of Qin.

The Zheng Guo canal almost immediately began experiencing ecological difficulties, and over the centuries much work and capital had to be invested to keep it operating (which it didn't for long periods of time). First, the water from the Jing River had become heavily silt-laden, initially a blessing for farmers, since "it served as both irrigation and fertilizer."[92] The silt raised the level of the Luo River, which had to be dredged, and the Jing River eroded its bed, lowering it below the intake level on the Jing River, with its silt getting increasingly sterile as it scoured into lower soil levels. An adjunct canal system had to be built to keep the water flowing to the fields.[93]

Another of the Qin state's water projects, the Dujiangyan, or Capital River Dam, was so brilliantly conceived that it continues to function to this day, more than 2,200 years later. By 300 BCE, the state of Qin had conquered Shu to its south and west, in the current province of Sichuan. Sichuan is a bowllike basin, with rivers tumbling steeply out of the mountains into a broad plain. Shu engineers had already built an irrigation system on the Min River where it entered the plain. The problem was that the Min flowed southward, not eastward through the Shu capital or the fertile Chengdu plain where irrigation water for wet-rice agriculture was sorely needed. The solution that Qin engineers came up with was to divert half of the Min eastward into a new channel. For the diversion, an ingenious artificial island called the "fish mouth" was constructed, and for the new channel, a cut through high bluffs had to be made, removing a huge amount of earth, and then a new channel was dug through the plain

Fig 3.2. The Ling Canal. Photo shows the spillway constructed to raise the level of the north-flowing Xiang River and divide it into two channels, the new, higher level then being connected by the 16-km Ling Canal to the south-flowing Li River. *Source:* Author.

to connect with the Yangzi River further east. Not only does this water system still function (although, as we will see in chapter 7, it has been threatened by plans to build hydroelectric dams), but, according to Stephen Sage, it so increased the rice yields of the Sichuan basin that the state of Qin had the additional resources necessary to complete its plan to unite the empire under its control.[94]

A final example of Qin hydraulic engineering comes from the far south with a canal called the Ling Canal, variously translated as the "Marvelous" or "Magical" Canal. To conquer the south (now the provinces of Guangdong and Guangxi), Qin armies had to traverse a low mountain range separating the Yangzi River basin from the south. Water transport being much faster and economical, especially for large numbers of troops with their equipment, Qin engineers sought a way to connect a north-flowing tributary of the Yangzi with a south-flowing tributary of the West River that emptied into the South China Sea. Built in 230 BCE under the direction of the Qin engineer Shi Lu, the Ling Canal connected these two river systems with water flowing in opposite directions off the watershed. The means by which the problem was solved remain a masterpiece of ingenuity, and much too complex to describe; suffice it to say that the translation of "Ling" as "marvelous," "magical," or "ingenious" is apt[95] (see figure 3.2).

The success of these major water projects, along with countless other smaller ones, gave ancient Chinese the belief and confidence that they could master and control nature—or, at least, that the emperor, the "Son of Heaven," could. But even that belief would be tested over the next two millennia by the Yellow River.

The (Yellow) River[96]

When what had been called simply "The River" became known commonly as "the Yellow" River is a matter of some scholarly discussion,[97] but as early as 1 BCE Chinese engineers estimated that Yellow River water was about 60 percent silt, a figure that seems implausibly high but that was confirmed by twentieth-century studies. The yellow silt began flowing into The River because the surrounding lands had been cleared for agriculture, and for bronze and iron smelting. The loess is very dustlike, and without a cover of vegetation was hence easily eroded, leaving deep gullies in more recent times. Farmers in the Warring States and Early Empire knew that moisture in the soil needed to be conserved to minimize erosion, and so had adopted various methods to preserve rainfall and moisture, rather than allow it to run off. Nonetheless, those measures were insufficient to prevent runoff and erosion.

Farmers also knew that the silt that was then periodically deposited on the flood plain was quite fertile, and so farmed there—but they did not establish villages there because of the danger caused by the annual flooding. Rulers of states, too, understood the annual flooding but began instead to channel the floodwaters with dikes rather than allow the floods and the attendant problems. The earliest diking of the Yellow River came in the seventh century BCE on its lower reaches where it flowed through the state of Qi, with the intended effect of knitting the nine strands of the river into a single channel, thereby increasing the land available for farming.

The dikes prevented flooding but created another problem that bedeviled the people on the North China plain for the next 2,500 years, and created challenges for governments and engineers alike. Because most of the rain on the North China plain came in the summer monsoon, the flow of the river slowed considerably in the dry periods afterward. A slowing river allowed the silt to settle out in the riverbed, and the riverbed therefore rose a bit each year, at an average rate of about three feet per century. As the riverbed rose, the likelihood of flooding increased, and so too did the problem of how to deal with the flooding.

Two schools of thought developed for how to deal with the problems of flooding and silting of the Yellow River, broadly reflecting Confucian and Daoist views (discussed more in the next section of this chapter). Those with more Daoist leanings argued that the river (mostly) should be allowed to follow its own "natural" course, with relatively low dikes built a very long way from the riverbed—basically simply defining a flood plain. Confucians tended to want to build higher dikes to confine the river to a narrower course (much as they wanted to define proper human behavior). Neither approach proved totally effective over the next two thousand years, but Yellow River dikes did get higher as the silt deposits raised the river bed—until unusually heavy rainfall broke the dikes and flooded the surrounding plain. The Yellow River dikes were breached first in the early Han dynasty in 168 BCE and again in 131 BCE (and not closed until 109 BCE), with the Han aristocrat whose lands north of the river were flooded clamoring for more and higher dikes, which apparently were built along the course of the river, leading to more breaches in 39 and 29 BCE. Joseph Needham concludes that these dikes "in no way solved the problem and the stage was set for the historic breakout of 11 [CE]"[98] which changed the course of the river. Despite later and even more heroic attempts to contain the Yellow River, it periodically broke through the levees, and, even more destructively, completely changed course several times over the next two thousand years; two of the more noteworthy cases in the twelfth and nineteenth centuries will be discussed in coming chapters.

Cities and Eating

That the Early Empire was self-consciously agrarian should not obscure the fact that China was home to some of the largest and best-run cities in the world at the time, even compared with the Roman Empire. The cities that had arisen during the Warring States period did not wither and disappear, but became nodes in the great transport system. The capital city of Chang'an probably had close to a half-million residents (maybe more), with lively commercial, manufacturing, and educational districts. The imperial academy had thirty thousand students studying the Confucian classics in preparation for a career in the state bureaucracy.

So China during the Early Empire was not farm after farm without any city. But it was a society in which the taxes from the small, dependable farming families supported the lives and lifestyles of the urbanites.

Whatever common people might have eaten—and that differed depending on whether they lived in the cities or farmed—we do have more information about what the wealthy offered guests at important ritual occasions, and that was an extensive and varied list of food and drink. In addition to cooked rice and millet, K. C. Chang lists seven meat dishes, including bear's paw and panther's breast, both wild animals; seven bird dishes, all but one (chicken) wild, including snow goose and crane; fish and turtles; and among the vegetables edible rush shoots, which would have been gathered from a marsh. Used as a spice, cinnamon came from the bark of a tree that grew only in the far south, while hazelnuts and honey were gathered from forests. Additionally, several kinds of alcoholic beverages were served, most fermented from grains to produce various kinds of wines. The poor probably subsisted on soybeans and wheat, which though "coarse, . . . can nevertheless satisfy our hunger," according to a Han source.[99] Thus although thoroughly agrarian, Han-era Chinese still consumed substantial amounts of game, implying the continued presence of forests not too far removed from cities.

Imperial Hunting Parks

If, as Cho-yun Hsü argues, farmers during Han times came to think that the quality of their harvest had more to do with the efforts they expended than the vagaries of the weather, and hence that common people came to believe that they had some control over natural processes, that belief was accentuated among the ruling elite. Since Shang times, rulers and royal families had their hunting grounds, not just to supply the royal household with a variety of game to supplement their diet but also to train leaders and troops for war, and increasingly to serve as the site of hunting rituals to demonstrate the dominion of humans (or at least the ruler) over nature: "While the Zhou had emphasized hunts as actual training and a practical means of securing sacrificial victims, the official hunts of Han China in the great parks were primarily pageants or demonstrations of the all-encompassing range of imperial power, a range which included even beasts and plants."[100]

The First Emperor of Qin had a huge hunting park built on the edge of his capital city, Xianyang on the northern bank of the Wei River, and Emperor Wu of Han constructed an even larger one connected with his capital of Chang'an on the opposite side of the Wei River. Lewis calls the Han imperial hunting parks "nature preserves" where the Han emperors "hosted religious rituals, grand imperial banquets, the reception of foreign guests, the great ritual hunts, and even served such mundane purposes as agriculture and pasturage. They contained wild animals, mountains, rivers, exotic flora, and many palaces."[101] A poem celebrating the Han hunting park mentions boars, wild asses, camels, onagers, mares, stallions, donkeys, and mules.[102]

During the annual winter hunt, the emperor demonstrated his dominion over nature by the massive slaughters of beasts, killed in the service of the all-encompassing power of the imperial state and, according to Lewis, in turn sanctioning the equally brutal use of force and violence against others in the human world: "The systematic equation of the violence of men with that of wild animals had become a basic element in the displays of the killing power of the Han rulers."[103] Warfare thus was rendered "natural." Of course, equating the violence of human society with nature had its risks, as such an equivalence might call into question the "civilizing mission" that the Han rulers also believed they had, bringing both nature and non-Chinese under the purview of their universalizing civilization. Such were the power and glory of the Han dynasty, though, that Chinese since have called themselves "Han."

Summary

The Early Empire was critically important in setting patterns that governed Chinese interactions with their environment for the next two millennia. Chinese built walls to keep the nomadic invaders out, thereby defining the northern reach of Chinese-style settled farming. Within the walls, Qin and Han engineers and workers built a vast highway system that linked the east, south, west, and southwest together, as well as to the capital. Officials, orders, soldiers, and mail could get from one end of the empire to the other quite expeditiously, while millions of tons of grain could be transported to the capital and to other cities. For the most part, peasant farmers made decisions about what to crop in the context of markets and prices for their commodities. Very light taxes on millions of farming families supported a centralized bureaucracy that by all accounts ruled efficiently enough. Wealth tended to be accumulated and invested in land, and although that led to farming families' losing ownership of their land to the Great Families, they remained tenants on their own farms, paying rent to landlords. As we will see, the dynamics created by a centralized bureaucratic state administering the empire and raising an army to protect against nomadic invaders, and by the relations between an independent small family-based farms and large landowners, structured much of Chinese history for the next two thousand years.

The course of Chinese history might have been different. The politics, society, and economy of the Warring States period were quite different, with commerce and urban wealth being much more important. How and why the state of Qin decided to end that multistate system is an interesting story that we are not able to tell here. Suffice it to say that when the King of Qin had vanquished all of the competing states, most of his advisors urged him to reinstate a feudal system much like that of the early Zhou. One of his advisors strongly argued for creating something new and stronger—a centralized bureaucratic empire—that would last "for ten thousand generations."[104]

Those were two exceptionally important turning points in the course of Chinese history, but so, too, were decisions made by both Qin and Han rulers during the Early Empire. The first was to base the empire on agriculture, suppressing private commerce and manufacturing and hence the private fortunes and power that might have been created from that base. The second was to base agriculture on independent peasant family farms, not on large estates owned and controlled by lords who directed the labor of unfree serfs on their lands. The latter might have developed, and at later points in Chinese history in fact did. But the ecologies and technologies of Chinese agriculture continued to favor small plots intensively farmed by families making their own decisions. To be sure, those families might lose ownership of their land and become tenants, but they still farmed on their own account. As it was to turn out, this system was almost endlessly replicable across the land, as long as there was an imperial state to support it. The combination proved to be a powerful force transforming the environment and making it "Chinese."

ANCIENT CHINESE IDEAS ABOUT NATURE AND THE ENVIRONMENT

To discuss "Chinese ideas about nature" presupposes both that we know what the concept of "nature" means in English, and that there is something comparable if not similar in Chinese. Both sides of that equation are problematic and have been contested. In European traditions, "nature" for a long time was understood to be separate from humans (or "man"), and assumed a dichotomy or separation between "nature and culture" or between "man and nature." Greek dramas were driven by storylines pitting man against other men, man against himself, or man against nature. European religious or philosophical traditions that placed humans outside of nature then also could place humans and their needs above nature. More recently, in the midst of growing global ecological crises, ecologists and philosophers have begun to see humans as part of nature, and hence that the fate of humans and the natural world are intertwined. But that debate is hardly settled.

Compounding the ambiguity in our interpretation of early Chinese discussions about humans and their relationship to the natural environment is that until the twentieth century, there was not a word in Chinese that has the same meaning and connotations of the English-language word "nature" that separated "the world out there" from humanity. When early Chinese philosophers discussed "human nature" or the "nature of things," they used a term (*benxing*) that means "the inherent quality of a thing." When the Zhou conquered the Shang and explained it by reference to "Heaven" (*tian*) having given its mandate (*ming*) to rule to the Zhou, the word for "heaven" is sometimes taken to be something like nature, at least to the extent that it points to a constancy that is beyond humankind, "a kind of inherent force," in Robert Weller's words, "directing the world."[105] Sometimes combinations of Chinese characters also get at something that approaches the concept of "nature," as in the triad "heaven, earth, and mankind" (*tian di ren*) or the unit "heaven and earth" (*tiandi*), pointing to all in the universe except for humanity.[106] The term that perhaps comes closest to the modern concept nature is *ziran* ("that which is self-so").[107] However, none of these terms were static, and over the past 2,500 years they have been dynamic, reflected on, and contested.[108] In short, there is a long and very interesting history of the "concept of nature" in China that we can only begin to touch on here.[109]

Because the meaning and interpretation of these various terms have been debated by Chinese over time, there is not an unchanging, essential "Chinese view of nature." Often it has been assumed that there is, especially by those in Europe or the United States trying to point out the destructive relationship between "man and nature in the West," contrasting that with a supposedly more "harmonious relationship of man with nature" in "the East" in general, or China in particular. That view has been popularized by various European or American writers,[110] as well as by a common interpretation of Chinese landscape painting, a form that flourished for more than a thousand years from the Tang dynasty (618–907) on, that often depicts humans as small figures within a larger mountainous or watery landscape.[111] As we will see throughout this book, the idea that the Chinese have had a harmonious relationship with nature is far from the truth.

As we have seen so far, Shang-era rulers tended to see the quality of their harvests, and their fates, as more dependent on "heaven" (*tian*) than on their own actions, although the Shang were quite active in transforming their environments into farms. As discussed earlier, the early Zhou (ca. 1000 BCE) expressed the idea that they succeeded the Shang because the Zhou had received "the mandate of Heaven" (*tian ming*) to rule. The idea of the "mandate of heaven" exemplifies what some have identified as China's "correlative cosmology," where actions on earth and in "heaven" were interrelated.[112] Introduced in the early Zhou, this way of thinking about the relationship of humans to the cosmos flourished during the Han dynasty in the hands of a state philosopher who argued, for instance, that the Chinese character for "king" of three parallel horizontal lines representing heaven, earth, and man was tied together by a single vertical line linking all three (王), the "king."

Chinese reflection on what we might call "nature" and the relationship of the human world to it emerged around 500 BCE with the development of a special social stratum called the *shi*, sometimes translated as the "literati," or those with the time and position to think about things. Given the nature-transforming thrust of the early Zhou colonizing efforts, coupled with the emergence of warring states which contested with each other and sought to most efficiently exploit natural resources so as not to face defeat on the battlefield and political extinction, it is not too surprising that the early Chinese philosophical disputes that took place during the so-called Hundred Schools of Thought had as their background "a destructive practice that views nature primarily as the realization of human purposes and one that is not even slightly characterized by empathy" toward nature.[113] The most noteworthy of these schools were Confucianism (named after the thinker named Confucius), Daoism (named after the "Dao," or "The Way"), and Legalism, or more aptly "statism," the idea that the state and its power take precedence over all else. It is also important to keep in mind that these ideas took form in north China, in particular with the Yellow River plain and the loess plateau in mind as the natural environment. When Chinese began moving into the very different environments of the warmer, wetter south, new ideas about nature emerged then too, as we will see in the next chapter.

Confucius

Confucius (551–479 BCE) lived at a time of great political, social, and economic change, when the Zhou feudal system was breaking down into warring states, with old nobility losing their ranks and positions and new social classes rising. Confucius neither liked nor approved of these changes, and sought answers to the problem of how to establish and maintain social order in what he understood to be the ways of the Zhou dynasty founders. He thought that the patriarchal family and detailed attention to the rules of proper behavior and ritual among all classes would be the way to assure social and political order. He was concerned with human behavior and order, and not much concerned with what we might call religious ideas (e.g., the existence of a god or gods and humans' relationship to them). Confucian state functionaries charged with water management thus tended to want to force water into strictly controlled channels, and those encountering other peoples to see the clothes they wore, the food they ate, and the musical instruments they played all as markers of whether they were (or even could become) "civilized."

Those who were inspired by Confucius's ideas ("Confucians") sought to develop and extend them. Mostly, "Confucians are principal advocates of the development of a world of culture from a nature experienced as hostile . . . [They] define the human being precisely in terms of his difference from animals, which lack that what is specifically human, namely morality, manners, and social differentiation."[114] Humans form societies, Confucians thought, precisely because alone a human would succumb to wild beasts. Man thus "disposes over the world of [wild] things, tames wild animals and brings cowed vermin under his control." The resulting society thus is an expression of "man's nature" (*ren zhi xing*).

Daoism

Reacting to what they conceived as Confucian stiffness and conformity to social norms, Daoists thought that people should follow "the Way," the *Dao*, to be natural. Following one's own nature (*benxing*), like water flowing downhill, would be the way to simplicity and to harmony. The ideal Daoist world would be sparsely populated with enough space between people that they would not intrude on each other. Clearly, that vision of human society was being negated by the growing population and consequences of the Warring States period.

Of all the philosophical schools, Daoists were especially skeptical of the benefits of "civilization," if by that was meant something such as what Confucians saw as a necessary and potentially good human society separate from, if dominating, the natural world. Daoists pined for a time when people had not become alienated from the cosmos around them, but were instead part of a harmonious whole: "an age of perfect virtue," in the words of one Daoist philosopher, where "people sauntered along their way and gazed about with blank eyes. In that time there were no paths and ramps on the mountains and no boats upon the bridges. . . . There were vast numbers of animals and grasses, and trees reached their natural growth. Wild animals could be taken for walks on leashes, and one could climb up to the nests of magpies and other birds."[115]

But then the state, war, and large-scale economies—actions by people building "civilization"—ruptured that oneness. Daoists contrasted "the developed world of civilization" with the "idea of the unity of nature," and blamed civilization (and Confucians) for destroying this primal harmony.[116] But rather than seeking the destruction of culture and civilization, many Daoists sought individual solutions by fleeing to mountain redoubts and living as recluses where they could "follow the way," shed the trappings of civilization, and become one with nature.

Later Confucians

The Daoist admonition to "act naturally" had raised the question of just what "nature" and "human nature" meant, since those ideas had not yet arisen, and fourth-century BCE followers of Confucius took up that challenge, in particular the one regarding human nature. Next to Confucius, the most important philosopher in the classic Confucian tradition was Mencius (372–289 BCE). He had taken up the question of what constituted human nature, concluding that it tended to be "good," and used a particularly interesting parable about the environment to explore that issue:

> The trees on Ox Mountain were once beautiful. But being situated on the outskirts of a large state, the trees are hewn down by axes. Could they remain beautiful? Given the air of the day and the night, and the moisture of the rain and dew, they do not fail to put forth new buds and shoots, but then cattle and sheep also come to graze. This accounts for the barren appearance of the mountain. Seeing this barrenness, people suppose that the mountain was never wooded. But how could this be the nature of the mountain? So it is also with what is preserved in a human being; could it be that anyone should lack the mind of humanness and rightness? If one lets go of the innate good mind, this is like taking an axe to a tree; being hewn down day after day, can it remain beautiful?[117]

We do not know which state Mencius was referring to, nor do we know if Ox Mountain was a real place. He was using the story of the deforestation of Ox Mountain to make an argument about the innate goodness of humans, and the necessity to properly cultivate that goodness. That being said, the parable makes sense both to us, and presumably to the people of 300 BCE China, because they had seen with their own eyes the deforestation of mountains, and knew both the causes and consequences of that deforestation. That Mencius could build a parable around that reality demonstrates how pervasive state-driven environmental change was during the Warring States period.

Mencius was not simply a "philosopher," but also considered himself to have ideas that would be useful to the rulers of the various Warring States. He considered land management to be important and counseled the development of conservation practices, as did other thinkers writing about the same time. Mencius thought that humans were above animals, and were their masters, but he did acknowledge that because we humans could feel badly seeing an ox cringe in fear before being sacrificed, humans (kings included) could and should have empathy for other humans. He thought that extensive royal reserves took land from farmers and animals, and that royalty and the rich ought to be moderate in their consumption and housing so as not to deplete resources. But as we will see below, like the advice of others who provided similar counsel, "Mencius' advice was not taken seriously enough by the rulers of China."[118]

Accepting the basic Confucian premise that culture and society were good, Xunzi (312–230 BCE) parted company with Mencius in arguing that humans by nature tend to be evil. Man's instinctual nature needed to be suppressed and controlled, and a cultivated and controlled one developed. So "Xunzi celebrates the regulating, active role of man with regard to nature. . . . Xunzi's 'domesticating' of nature confers upon it a new order tailored to many and reaching human perfection in terms of human needs."[119] Both humans and the human-dominated nature need the strong hand of the state to keep them in line. This line of thinking was taken up by advisors to the king of the state of Qin, Shang Yang (d. 338 BCE) and Han Fei Zi (280–233 BCE), who created a political philosophy that celebrated the state and its power over people and nature.

Legalism

Legalists were most interested in promoting the power and primacy of the state above all else, and believed in controlling people and nature. As the *Guanzi* put it: "One controls the people as one controls a flood. One feeds them as one feeds domestic animals. One uses them as one uses plants and trees." Farming and cereals were essential to state power. Compared with a well-ordered state such as Qin, in lesser ones "the farmland lies uncultivated and the state capital is empty. . . . [T]he elite among the commoners will esteem profit and think little of military bravery. The masses will be addicted to quaffing and feasting, and detest farming. In a situation like this, the state's coffers will be exhausted, and food, drink, firewood, and vegetables lacking."[120]

The Qin state feared a shortage of labor, not just for farming but also for military service, and introduced numerous reforms to make Qin attractive to farmers who might flee from other states, in particular reforms designed to spread land ownership from the nobility to the common people. Where other states still had aristocracies, in Qin farmers could be free to own their land, and to make their own cropping decisions. Qin did not invent the idea of taxes on farmer's produce, a 10 percent tax having been introduced in the state of Lu in 594 BCE, but Qin revenues came from a hefty 50 percent tax on the harvest.

To pay the tax, Qin farmers had to be productive, and they were, helped and encouraged by the minister of agriculture. The minister's responsibility was "to open up the grassy lands for farming, appropriate the crop for the cities, and extend the territory, stockpile grain, and increase the population." Working under the minister of agriculture, forest wardens were "to see that the rules about fires are enforced, so respect is shown to the hills, wetlands, forests, and thick vegetation. This is because these are the sources of materials." The director of works was "to breach dikes to release flood waters, and to ensure the through flow in the irrigation and drainage channels, to repair the levees and embankments, and to have the storage reservoirs in readiness so that even if the seasonal floods exceed due measure, no harm is done to the cereal crops, and that, even if there is a year of severe drought, there is grain to be sickled for harvest." The director of farming helped farmers with the timing of planting, and with the proper techniques of cultivating the various crops.[121]

Legalist ideas were important for the course of Chinese history and the relationship of Chinese to their environment, because Qin forces united China and established a new political form, the imperial state, that came to be the form of all Chinese states for the next two thousand years, even if they expressed revulsion at the harshness of Qin rule. Moreover, Qin Legalists were not the only ones expressing ideas about the environment.

Resource Constraints and the Control of "Nature"

Warring State-era texts reveal an increasing awareness that the bounty of nature was not endless, and that care had to be taken not to exhaust all natural resources, in particular food sources: "The ruler of a state, in the spring hunting, will not surround a marshy thicket, nor will Great officers try to surprise a whole herd, nor will (other) officers take young animals or eggs. In bad years, when the grain of the season is not coming to maturity, the ruler at his meals will not make the (usual) offering of the lungs, nor will his horses be fed on grain." Additional admonitions included not destroying bird nests or even insects; "unformed insects should not be killed, nor creatures in the womb, nor very young creatures, nor birds just taking to the wing, nor fawns, nor eggs should be destroyed."[122]

Qin and Han laws from statutes known as "Monthly Ordinances for Four Seasons" understood that the unchecked tendencies of humans would be not just to interfere with important natural ecological processes but also to damage human livelihoods, deplete natural resources, and needlessly kill animals. Two in particular are prescient in pointing to directions China would nonetheless follow, the "Ordinances" notwithstanding. "Do not encroach on waters and marshes, [or] drain ponds . . . Only then will people everywhere be able to catch fish." "Do not burn mountain forests. This refers to setting forests on fire for hunting, as that harms fowl, beasts . . . snakes, insects, plants and trees."[123]

These comments indicate a growing awareness of the impact of humans on the natural environment, and sounded warnings about the consequences of unrestrained harvesting of wild food sources. Not only would "plants and trees decay prematurely," for instance, but "states would be kept in continual fear . . . there would be pestilence among the people . . . and the first sown seeds would not enter the ground."[124]

By 200 BCE, Chinese and their states had learned how to use human and natural resources to extend control over other humans and over their environment—as long as a strong central state was maintained—and continued to do so during the Early Empire. Intellectuals in the Confucian and Daoist traditions may have raised warnings about the constant state-driven push for agricultural development, but the idea of the benefits of agricultural development always seemed to be stronger and more dominant.

Historian Cho-yun Hsü, whose work on the Warring States period and Han agriculture I have consulted for this chapter, made some very interesting observations about how farmers at the time understood the relationship between the forces of nature and the size of their harvest. During the Warring States period, Hsü argued, farmers were very much aware that weather conditions had a greater effect on the harvest than anything that they might do as farmers. "Nature apparently had far more influence on the crops than man did," Hsü concluded about the Warring States period.[125] Indeed, we saw that attitude toward natural forces as early as the Shang. But by the Han period, with the massive remaking of the landscape by the state and its farmers, with their knowledge of soils and plants, and with their ability to get water to go where it was needed, a significant change had come over farmers, their abilities, and their attitude toward nature: "Without the confidence that man could control at least some natural conditions, the Han farmer would not have asserted himself so persistently to find ways of enhancing his productivity."[126]

Here we have the expression of an attitude that would become integrated into the Chinese way of farming, despite warnings from intellectuals or philosophers, or artistic depictions of Chinese people "in harmony" with their surroundings: the confidence that Chinese farmers could—and should—transform the natural environment into farms. And that is what happened to the forests on the North China plain during the Han era.

Certainly, that impulse to control nature was exceptionally strong among Han Chinese, but that, and its effects in transforming the Chinese landscape even in ancient times, was not the only way Chinese related to their environment or to the processes of nature. Chinese in cities or on the farm could not see everything.

Epidemic Disease

The Early Empire created almost perfect conditions in which to incubate epidemic disease and pandemic outbreaks. Scientists now know that most human infectious diseases such as measles, mumps, chicken pox, and influenza originated among domesticated animals. When those pathogens first made the jump from animal to human, the disease no doubt was deadly. But after generations of contact with those diseases, the human body built up various immune responses, and by even three thousand years ago, those diseases had become what we now call "childhood" diseases; nasty and unpleasant for children, but not especially deadly, except to those adults who had not contracted the disease as children. Moreover, because most people with animals lived in villages, the spread of those pathogens probably remained localized.

During the Qin and especially Han dynasties, not only were many more farmers living in close contact with farm animals, thereby incubating more human disease pathogens, but the roads and markets also led them periodically into towns and cities where pathogens could pass quickly among huge, densely packed human populations, after which the efficient highway system could spread those diseases around the empire or, via the overland and sea lanes, elsewhere throughout Asia.

Somewhat surprisingly, the incidence of pandemics in ancient China—or at least the written evidence of them—is slight.[127] We know of at least one pandemic in 243 BCE. Donald Hopkins thinks that epidemic was smallpox, spread to China a few years earlier from Central Asian steppe via the Xiongnu.[128] A few more epidemics (again, probably smallpox) spread during the early and later Han periods but only became more regular from 151 CE on, contributing to the causes of the collapse of the Han dynasty and its end in 220 CE.

We do not know what those epidemics were—though Hopkins is quite certain they were deadly smallpox—but whatever they were, they were virulent. One in 16 CE reportedly killed six to seven out of every ten of a general's troops, and another in 46 CE reportedly killed two-thirds of the population; similar numbers died in a 208 outbreak. A Chinese doctor who lived late in the third century described the victims as having symptoms we associate with smallpox: "Recently there have been persons suffering from epidemic sores which attack the head, face, and trunk. In a short time, these sores spread all over the body. They have the appearance of hot boils containing some white matter. While some of these pustules are drying up, a fresh crop appears. If not treated early, the patients usually die. Those who recover are disfigured by purplish sores which do not fade until after a year."[129]

THE END OF THE EARLY EMPIRE

Not only did the general patterns of social, economic, and demographic growth contribute to the spread of infectious disease, so too did increasingly difficult conditions for vast numbers of rural and urban poor during the last part of the Han dynasty. Rural farmers had been losing ownership of their land for some time, tilling plots of land but paying rent to increasingly wealthy and powerful "Great Families." We do not know the full extent of the rural impoverishment, but anecdotally it was palpable to rich city folk, one of whom described a farmer "with skin as rough as mulberry back" and whose "feet resembled bear paws" as less than human—maybe more like a plant, or perhaps "a bird or a beast."[130]

By the Han, Chinese farming may have been exceptionally successful and productive. But farmers existed not necessarily because that was how they chose to gain their sustenance but because their bodies and the resources they produced could be controlled and mobilized. If the human body was host to micro parasites such as viruses, bacteria, or other small creatures, additional macro parasites such as the state and landowners fed off farmers.[131]

Whatever the causes, and those surely included lost land, epidemic disease, famine, and control of governmental power slipping into the hands of venal advisors and eunuchs, there was misery enough in rural areas, especially in the eastern part of the empire where farmers were losing marketing opportunities as well, to fuel a massive peasant revolt. And when it came in 184 CE, coalescing around millenarian religious ideas spread by Daoists proclaiming the imminent arrival of a new and better world, the Han dynasty soon came apart as the three generals charged with suppressing the revolt decided instead to divide the empire among themselves; the last Han emperor abdicated in 220 CE.[132]

The empire remained divided among three competing states until 280 CE, when one of them succeeded in reuniting China under the name of the Jin dynasty. That effort proved short-lived when in 311 the capital city of Luoyang—population around 600,000—was attacked and sacked by resurgent Xiongnu armies, leaving it a rubble with piles of corpses and roving packs of dogs, followed in 317 by the sacking of Chang'an. The destruction of those two capital cities ended any hopes of continuing the Early Empire, and marks both the end of that phase of Chinese history and the beginning of another, to be taken up in the next chapter.

CONCLUSION

During the 1,300 years covered in this chapter, China underwent remarkable changes, not just in its social and political organization but also in its environment. Where late Shang-era tombs were filled with bronzes adorned with images of tigers and elephants, and early Zhou texts celebrate their rulers taming the world by driving away those wild animals, Han-era tombs a millennium later contain models of farm houses and animals, and detailed paintings of kitchen scenes. Nothing so aptly captures the domestication of China north of the Yangzi River from a Shang-era forest with scattered farm clearings into an intensely farmed landscape inhabited by nearly 60 million people. Farms replaced forests, and pigs and oxen replaced forest-loving tigers and elephants, at least in north China. During the Early Empire, much of north China had been deforested to become one large farm.

But it wasn't just any farm: it was a particularly Chinese kind of farm and farming. For reasons that are contingent both on the state of Qin's deciding to end the Warring States era, thereby uniting China under a single central empire, and on Han emperors, too, favoring an agrarian base for state revenues, Chinese agriculture became based on peasant families intensively tilling their own farms. Landownership may have become periodically concentrated in the hands of "the Great Families," but they did not farm themselves, or supervise peasant farming; mostly, they collected rents. Although these relationships among the Chinese state, peasant farmers, and large landowners would change over the course of the next two millennia, as we will see in forthcoming chapters, they formed the triad on which much of the Han Chinese encounter with their environment was based.

If farming was one form of human adaptation to the environment, the development of pastoral nomadism was another. Nomads following their herds across the vast grasslands of Central Asia became fierce warriors and competitors with Chinese states for natural resources, especially pastures and horses, that both Han and steppe warriors needed for their militaries. Based on different ecologies and hence different societies and militaries, nomadic and Chinese states clashed first during the Qin and Han dynasties, with the Chinese state under Emperor Wu of the Han proving the stronger. But keeping the nomads under control, or at least at bay, required Chinese occupation of arid grasslands, and the only way the Chinese knew how to do that was to turn the steppe into farms, and to move Chinese into the colonized territories. As long as the Chinese state was strong enough to provide protection for the farming colonists in these agriculturally marginal places, the strategy could work, at least in the short run. Over longer periods of time, especially when the Chinese state weakened or collapsed, those farms would be abandoned and the turned-over sod blown away, leaving an advancing desert. Just as relations among the state, peasants, and landlords formed one of the dynamics of Chinese history for the next two millennia, so too did relations between Han Chinese and nomadic pastoralists of the steppe, each with their own ecological base.

Over the 1,300 years covered in this chapter, the Chinese population on the North China plain had increased from about 5 million to 60 million, the oak and maple forest had been removed and the landscape scraped of its original vegetation to make way for farms, Chinese troops had pushed the nomads out of the steppe to the north and Chinese settlers had converted the grassland into farms, waterways had been redirected to irrigate a vast acreage of farmland, roads linked the far-flung empire and penetrated into new territories where Han Chinese could displace indigenous peoples, and the "River" became yellow because of erosion and siltation, and was diked to prevent flooding. Chinese political structures and ideas, social and family organization, and particular forms of farming replaced the multitude of natural and human forms that had preceded them. What had been a diverse human and natural environment in north China had been radically simplified.

But why had the Han Chinese focused their expansive energies to the north, rather than to the south? In part, of course, the mounted nomads presented a greater threat. But both the Qin and Han states had sent their militaries to conquer the south as far as northern Vietnam. The south, though, presented environmental obstacles not encountered in the steppe. Besides hostile peoples, not only was the warm and moist climate inhospitable for the grains northern Chinese had learned to farm—in particular the two kinds of millet and the wheat and barley that had been imported from the Middle East—but also the south hosted numerous deadly diseases that the northerners feared. There was, in short, a steep disease gradient in the south that northern Chinese could not easily climb, at least not until they were forced south by a greater fear of nomadic invaders, and subsequently learned how to transform the watery environment of the south into highly productive rice paddies. And that is the story of the next chapter.

Chapter 4

Deforesting the North and Colonizing the South in the Middle Imperial Period, 300–1300 CE

A significant shift in the history of China and its environment unfolded over the thousand years from 300 to 1300 CE. On the North China plain, already largely deforested during the Han dynasty, the Yellow River completed a centuries-long process of overflowing its banks and dikes, abandoning its former course to the Yellow Sea and taking a new one further south to the East China Sea, leaving vast tracts of the North China plain under mounds of sterile sand. This historic shift occurred in the context both of continuing pressure on China from nomadic pastoral steppe peoples known as Mongols who conquered China during the thirteenth century, and of a booming iron and steel industry that finished off forests in north China and sparked a coal-fueled industrial revolution that was then cut short as a consequence of the Mongol wars of conquest. And under the pressures of nomadic armies and conquerors, as Han Chinese started colonizing the south, the population center of China shifted from north to south, too (see figure 4.1).

The millennium covered in this chapter is bracketed on one end by fourth-century nomadic invasions that spelled the end of Chinese rule in their north China home, and on the other end by another series of twelfth- and thirteenth-century invasions that ended with the conquest of China by the most formidable nomadic force ever, the Mongols led by Chinghis Khan. Thus the two great powers that arose in very different environments in eastern Asia—the steppe nomadic pastoralists and the Han Chinese—continued to confront each other over these centuries in an uneasy symbiotic relationship. The early empire of the Qin and Han was followed by several centuries when there was no significant central state, but that changed in 589 CE when a brief new state, the Sui (589–618), reestablished the empire, to be followed by the longer-lived Tang (618–907) and Song (960–1279) dynasties. The Mongol conquest and rule of China as the Yuan dynasty (1279–1368) marks a transition from the middle empire to late imperial China, the topic of the next chapter.

Facing ecological and military pressures, Han Chinese began a massive migration into the south, pushing other peoples who were there first out of the way, and then transforming their new environments with the new technologies bundled up in

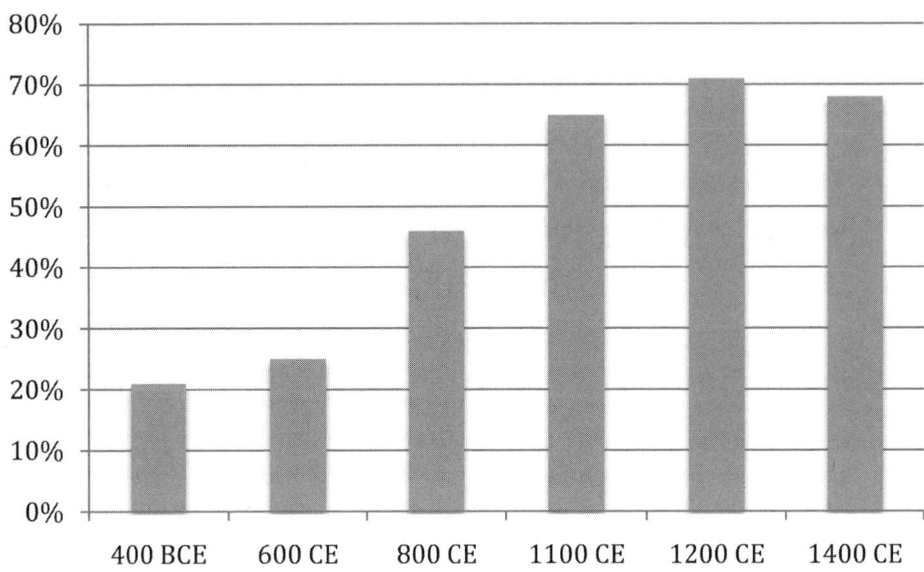

Fig. 4.1. Percentage of China's Population in the South *Source:* Based on Robert M. Hartwell, "Demographic, Political, and Social Transformations of China, 750–1550," *Harvard Journal of Asiatic Studies* 42, no. 2 (1982): 368.

wet-rice agriculture.[1] Largely because of the nomads and their attacks on China, the political, economic, and demographic center of gravity of China shifted progressively from the northwest further east and finally south. From the original home of the Zhou, Qin, and Han dynasties in the northwest, in particular the Wei River valley, where their capitals were established, China's dynastic capitals shifted east from Chang'an to Luoyang during the Tang dynasty (618–907), further east to Kaifeng during the first part of the Song dynasty (960–1127), and then south to Hangzhou in the lower Yangzi valley during the Southern Song (1127–1279). Nearly 80 percent of China's population had lived in north and northwest China during the Han dynasty, a proportion that fell to 75 percent by the early seventh century. The south had only 25 percent of the population during the Han, but nearly 50 percent by 750 CE; then "the proportion [in the south] climbed to 65 percent in 1080 and 71 percent by 1200."[2] That historic shift in the geographic distribution of the Han Chinese population entailed a significant encounter with the peoples and environments of south and west China as the Tang and Song states pursued colonial projects there.

As Han Chinese moved—or rather were pushed—out of their north China environment increasingly toward the south, they had to adapt to a new warmer and wetter environment that posed numerous challenges and fears—in particular from hostile non-Chinese who fled further south after losing wars and land to the Han Chinese, but also from diseases such as malaria and dengue fever. But the Han Chinese migrants to the south also came to master a powerful new agricultural technology—wet-rice cultivation—that gave them immense new sources of wealth and power to confront their nomadic foes to the north, as well as to conquer others and transform environments in south, southeast, and west China.

The fourth-century Han Chinese who fled their homes in the historic core of north China looked back, not just in fear that the nomadic cavalry might overtake them on their flight south, but with hope that they would be able to return from their exile to the place they knew and loved. But that would never happen. It took more than a century for the exiles to get used to the idea that the Yangzi River valley was their home. As they settled in, north China became a battleground among competing steppe tribes that had moved into the power vacuum and the remaining Han Chinese, who barricaded themselves in forts and garrisons. This was the beginning of the development of south China,

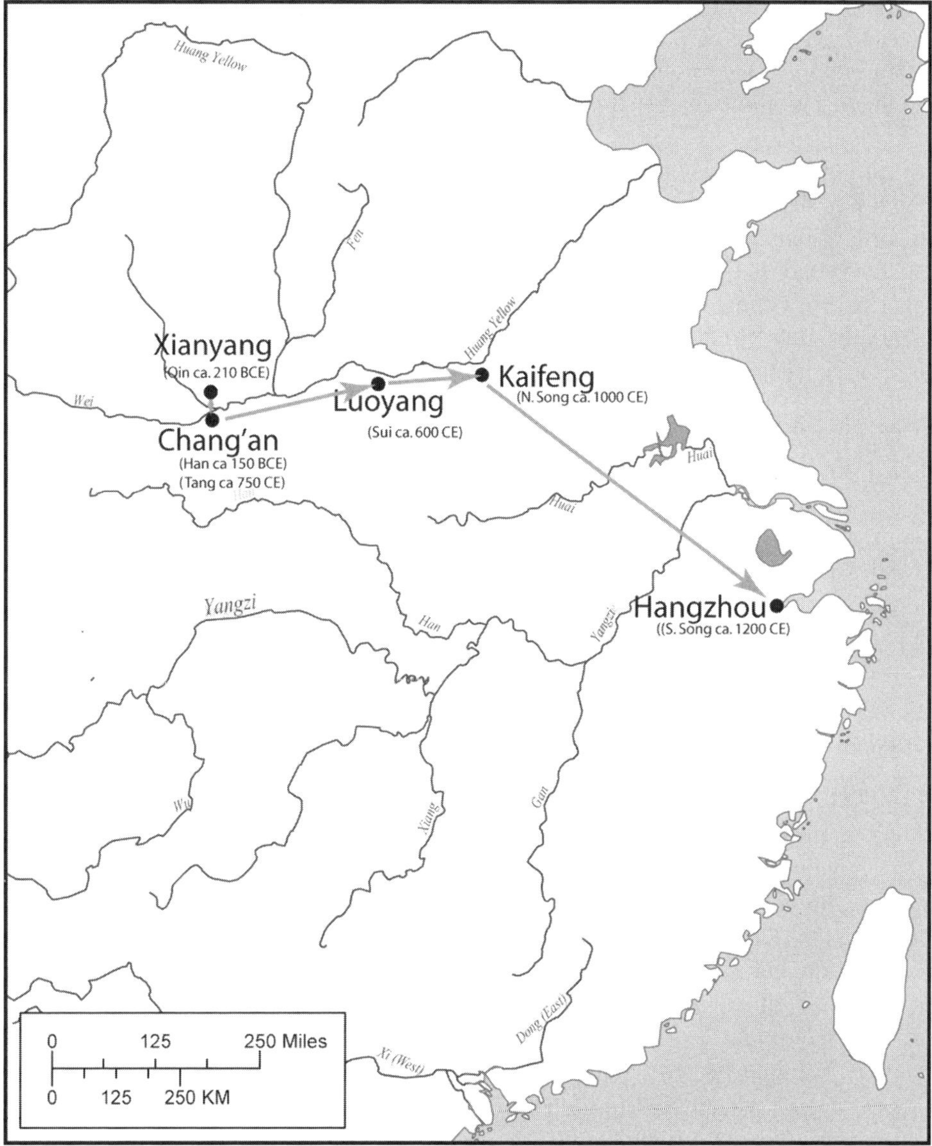

Map 4.1. The Southward Shift of China's Capital Cities

and a marked contrast with north China, leading to the regionalization of China into north and south, with the south soon having the bulk of the Han Chinese population.

NORTH CHINA: WAR, DEPOPULATION, AND THE ENVIRONMENT, 300–600 CE

The sacking in 311 of the Jin capital of Luoyang, and then in 317 of the former Han capital of Chang'an by nomadic invaders, put an exclamation point on processes that had been transforming north China since the late second century. Then, peasant rebellions accompanied by plague, famine, and poor harvests—probably brought on by a cooling climate (see figure 2.1)—caused a sharp population decline, both from the heightened mortality, but also because those who could fled south to the safety of the lower Yangzi Valley. The population of Han-era China had reached its height of about 60 million around the time of the 2 CE census, for 150 years later, the recorded population was slightly smaller, at some 56 million people. Nearly all of those people lived in north China, on the North China plain, in the Wei River valley where the Zhou state had formed, or in the fertile Sichuan basin. The population of what was to become the other half of China, from the Yangzi Valley south to Guangzhou, was more sparsely populated, home to few Chinese and to many more non-Chinese peoples. By the time the Han dynasty finally succumbed in 220 CE, some people at the time believed, in historian L.S. Yang's words, that only "one-tenth of the Han population was left."[3]

That population figure, no doubt, was understated, for farms may have been abandoned not because the people had died, but because they had fled. To be sure, the death and destruction had been great, and with evidence of cannibalism, we can be sure that food supplies had become so low that many places in north China experienced a demographic crisis. Still, several millions had begun the migration out of north China to the Yangzi Valley. Whatever the causes, and whatever the actual population left in north China, the generals who became the rulers of "the three kingdoms" that succeeded the Han dynasty endeavored to get agricultural production going again by relocating people into military colonies, giving them the seed and tools to begin farming again, and paying taxes to support the military. However effective those policies may have been is not known, for the recorded population in 280 when the Jin reunited the three kingdoms under its single rule was merely 16 million. Again, that figure is surely too low, for the newly organizing states did not have the wherewithal to accurately count all the people in their areas, and the owners of large estates had sheltered their tillers from being counted as well—but the evidence of a real crisis ravaging the Han Chinese population is clear enough.

Rebellion and internecine struggle among the Jin founder's sons left north China in a state of war and destruction in the early fourth century. According to the *History of the Jin Dynasty*, "many suffered from hunger and poverty. People were sold as [slaves]. Vagrants became countless . . . [and] there was a plague of locusts. . . . Virulent disease accompanied the famine. Also the people were murdered by bandits. The rivers were filled with floating corpses; bleached bones covered the fields. . . . There was much cannibalism. Famine and pestilence came hand in hand."[4]

And so, with the sacking of the Jin capital city of Luoyang in 311 and of Chang'an in 317 by nomadic invaders who left little standing or living, images of a greatly depopulated north China become more frequent and compelling. "A contemporary witness," according to Arthur F. Wright, "who had made a tour of inspection reported that previously rich farmlands were covered with weeds and that only 20 percent of the Chinese population remained—mostly the old and weak."[5] After Luoyang was sacked, a visiting Sogdian merchant wrote home that "the palace and walled city were set on fire. . . . [They] are no more!"[6] Xiongnu troops plundered the royal tombs, took what they wanted, and returned to their steppe homeland with their booty. When Chang'an was sacked a few years later, the ruling Chinese elite fled in great numbers—hundreds of thousands—to the Yangzi Valley, where they established a government in exile. We will have more to say about that shortly; it was there that the Han Chinese settlement and development of south China, from the Yangzi River valley to the South China Sea, began.

Even before the sacking of Luoyang and Chang'an, Chinese society had become increasingly militarized to the point that land-wealthy Great Families had become more and more like a hereditary military class, gaining their status from a weakened state that needed their support, their armed men from the peasant families who fled to them seeking protection from the elements and other military men, and, increasingly, their armed cavalry from among the Xiongnu who had begun settling within the Great Wall even before the fall of the Han. After the fall of the Jin dynasty and the hasty departure of the ruling elite to the safety of the south, north China was open to wave after wave of nomadic invaders who fought with each other for the spoils of war. The Chinese who remained retreated behind defensible walls or easily defended redoubts in the hills. From the fourth to the fifth century, north China was dotted with hundreds of these forts, and their "chiefs squabbled with one another for power at the grassroots level and were alternately coerced and courted by barbarian rulers. . . . The fortified community of refuge would remain the basic building block of local power in north China for several generations after the Jin collapse [in 311]."[7]

Over this "stability" came ruler after ruler, most of nomadic "barbarian" stock, nonc lasting for very long—but they did muster tens of thousands of cavalry and even more footsoldiers to protect what they had, and to poach on others. North China was a vast war zone for more than a century. The accounts of death, destruction, and cruelty are depressing to recount,[8] but at some point the mounted invaders realized that among the booty they had to capture were the energy stores of humans—Han Chinese farmers, to be precise—for use working land and growing food. But rather than finding a farming community and "capturing" it in place for this purpose—most Chinese had retreated behind defensible walls—their tactic was to capture Han Chinese by the thousands, round them up, and take them to the invader's captured and secure land.

Unlike the densely populated North China plain during the Han dynasty, where land had become in relatively short supply and people were numerous, in the depopulated destruction of fourth-century north China, land had become plentiful, but the people to work it were very few, and hence were very valuable. "Human populations, therefore, were prominent among the spoils of victory, and successful campaigns were frequently followed by the forcible transfer of thousands or even tens of thousands of people from the newly occupied areas to the core territories of the victor. In some cases military campaigns were little more than gigantic slave-raids, with the occupied territories being abandoned after the population had been removed. Captives taken in this way tended to be concentrated in the vicinity of the victor's capital."[9]

These conditions—a general depopulation, vast tracts of untilled land, tens of thousands of people being forcibly moved from one place to another, others living inside forts or garrisons for protection—all seem to have been nearly perfect for some kind of serfdom to have emerged across north China. Both the new Chinese military men who protected their local populations, as well as the marauding nomadic cavalrymen, would seem to have had a strong interest in keeping the tillers of the land, not just on the land, but on their land. Maybe fear kept large numbers of north China peasant farmers from running away, or maybe their "protectors" understood that productive peasant farmers were essential to their survival as well. The peasant farmers may not have been free, but they did not lose control over farming decisions to their overlords. Thus, whatever the dynamics or the reasons, it does look as if the various initiatives taken to encourage agriculture and get the rural economy producing again did assume that the basic productive unit would be the Chinese farming family. Even at the end of the Han, when the empire was being divided under the control of various generals, one of the most famous, Cao Cao, established military colonies on abandoned land where peasant families were given plots of land to farm in return for providing taxes to support Cao Cao's armies.

The invading nomadic conquerors of the fourth and fifth centuries also developed similar schemes, and put them into writing on the assumption that their decrees would have the force of law. An indicator of the loss of farmland following the carnage of the collapse of the Han and the nomadic invasions was the variety of attempts by the various Chinese and non-Chinese rulers of north China to get farmers to bring the land back under the plow by guaranteeing land to farming families, and restricting the land that the wealthy could own or control. But there were many complicating factors. "In the first place, there was the usual antagonism between nomad pastoralists and agriculturalists, the conquering Xianbei and the conquered Chinese, on the one hand, and on the other, an increasingly marked distinction between the tribal aristocracy, who made common cause with the Chinese gentry, and the ordinary warriors, herdsmen, and serfs composing the backward and impoverished tribal masses. In the second place, once the wars had ceased, the demographic structure of the North—which had been violently disturbed by the invasions—began to pose the same problem as before and with even greater force. This was the problem of the continuous pressure exerted by a rapid increase of population in the most fertile part of the [North China] plain." Even there, though, there were areas with plenty of available land.[10]

But land alone would not provide an adequate base for the nomadic invaders to transform themselves into states or proto-states; for that they needed farmers tilling fixed parcels of taxable land. Nomadic invaders realized that they could not just kill off all the Chinese in north China, or leave them with no resources to live. But the practice of forcibly removing large populations from one place to another, along with the general depopulation of north China, did mean that there were vast tracts of farmland that were deserted for several generations. And there's an important ecological question, too: what happened to that land?

On the one hand, war and catastrophic collapse of human populations often give the environment time to recover from human exploitation. Forests that have been cut to fuel iron smelting or farms can regrow over the centuries, and rivers and lakes that have been silted by farm run-off can run clear again (including the Yellow River), and with those ecosystems healing, animal populations can recover. In most cases, abandoned farmland that had been carved out of a forest often reverts to forest cover, as has happened in parts of New England since about 1950, or in the cases cited by anthropologist Sing Chew.[11] Other places, too (parts of Italy and France after the fall of the Roman empire, for instance), saw the regrowth of forests in such circumstances.

An early sixth-century text on agriculture thus suggests that farmland must be "reclaimed" from "waste": "When clearing land in mountains or marshes for new fields, always cut down the weeds in the seventh month; the weeds should be set on fire once they have dried out. Cultivation should only begin in the spring. Larger trees and shrubs should be killed by ring-barking. Once the leaves are dead and no longer cast any shade ploughing and sowing may begin, and after three years the roots will have withered and the trunks decayed enough to be burned out. Once the ploughing of the waste is completed, draw an iron-toothed harrow across twice. Broadcast millet and then the bush-harrow over the field twice. By the next year it will be fit for grain land."[12]

There are several reasons to doubt that much of north China's farmland saw the return of forest, and hence also of the animal community, during the centuries following the fall of the Han dynasty. First, to regrow, a forest would have had to have a source of seed. It may well have been that such large swaths of forest had been removed during the Han that little if any remained as a source of seeds. Also, north China was crossed and recrossed by armies, and that too would have kept brush, let alone a healthy forest, from regrowing.

But I suspect that the major reason that forests did not return to north China is because the nomadic peoples brought grazing animals with them. One nomadic tribe boasted in 366 that they had several hundred thousand armed archers, and that their pastures supported a million horses. And that's just one tribe, to which numerous others must also be added. It is not unlikely that former Han Chinese farms on the North China plain became pasturage for millions of horses. Not only horses, but also—and perhaps even more effective in keeping trees and bushes away—sheep, and goats. A herd of fifty to a hundred goats can clean off a small mountain and keep it free of trees for a very long time. So the relative depopulation of north China and the extensive abandonment of farms there did not inevitably lead to the return of forests, but rather, most likely, to the extension of pasture for the nomads' grazing herds.

Moreover, "relatively depopulated" does not mean "depopulated." Even the extremely low population figure for 280 CE of 16 million is still 16 million people, and probably more, most of whom farmed. During the Han dynasty, parts of the North China plain, especially those in the flood plain of the Yellow River, had become densely populated, and apparently remained so through much of the death and destruction of the fourth century CE. When one nomadic tribe's army captured the capital of another's in 370 in the heart of the North China plain, it was claimed that it gained 157 districts with 2.5 million households, or perhaps nearly 10 million people.[13] They apparently were left where they were, to farm and provide taxes.

The invading nomadic armies underwent another modification that helped them gain and retain their hold on north China. Understanding the truism that conquerors cannot rule from horseback, several quickly started bringing Han Chinese into their service. Literacy and learning had not died with the Han dynasty, and there were plenty of Chinese who had continued to study the Confucian classics and understood the principles of good governance enshrined in Han dynasty practice. These Chinese had to confront the question of working for the conquerors, but enough did so to help the conquerors form states with rulers, laws, and taxes. The most successful conquerors adopted Chinese names for their states, and even fashioned themselves as "dynasties," although the question of whether a ruler was succeeded by his son or vanquished by a rival remained an open question. The steppe peoples, too, had to confront the question of how far they could use the Chinese, or become "like" the Chinese, without losing their own identity. That may have been a moot concern, for "identities" are very slippery when a people moves to a new social and natural environment and begins interacting with it in ways that both change. Intermarrying greatly facilitated those genetic and social changes. In other words, just as Chinese armies under Emperor Wu of the Han had to adapt their military tactics to conditions on the steppe by creating a cavalry, so too did mounted steppe warriors have to adapt to the environmental and cultural conditions of the North China plain.

In historical retrospect, the most successful of the northern nomadic pastoral groups was the Xianbei, who ultimately defeated all rival states, including the Chinese one in the south, reuniting all of China in 589 CE under the Sui dynasty. As early as 493, one of their rulers had begun a process of adopting Chinese customs, language, and ways of ruling, banning the wearing of tribal clothing and the speaking of non-Chinese languages at court, and adopting Chinese surnames. Most importantly, he resettled a vast number of his officials and warriors south to Luoyang, which at the time was not much more than a garrison outpost after having been razed nearly two centuries earlier. The city had to be rebuilt, and when it was, it was largest walled city on earth.[14] With the 150,000 Xianbei as the core, Luoyang quickly grew to a bustling city of 600,000, and the Xianbei living there became increasingly like Chinese, not simply by adopting Chinese culture, but also by intermarrying with elite Chinese women. The Xianbei were not unanimous in this policy, and that disagreement resulted in various civil wars and the destruction, yet again, of Luoyang in 534, but the power of the Xianbei state (then called the Zhou, after the historic Chinese Zhou dynasty), grew until it was one of three contending for control of north China. By 580, the Xianbei had defeated their north China rivals, a senior official by the name of Yang Jian seized control and declared himself emperor of the new Sui dynasty in 581, and then conquered the south in 589.

Climate changes may have precipitated the scramble for power in the north, and weakened the Chinese regimes in the south. The general cooling that followed the end of the Han dynasty seems to have eased by the sixth century, just as the Xianbei were rebuilding Luoyang and consolidating their power on the North China plain. But in 536, just two years after civil war had destroyed Luoyang, geologists think that a massive volcanic eruption at Rabaul, just off the coast of what is now New Guinea, sent a huge plume of ash and dust into the atmosphere, producing what later became known as a "nuclear winter,"[15] with solar radiation being partially blocked from reaching the earth for several years. The global cooling shortened growing seasons, and hence clipped harvests and the taxes that states relied on. Whether this cooling was coincidental or causal of the success of the Xianbei in seizing control of all of China has not yet been sorted out.[16]

ENVIRONMENTAL CHANGE IN THE YANGZI RIVER VALLEY

Even prior to the sack of Luoyang in 311 and of Chang'an in 317 CE, hundreds of thousands of Han Chinese—maybe up to a million or so—had fled south to the relative safety of the Yangzi River valley or even further south to Nanhai (later Guangzhou), while even earlier Han Chinese had migrated south as part of the Qin army conquest and Han dynasty development projects; the south therefore was not fully frontier nor terra incognita when the new wave of refugees arrived.

One of those fleeing the chaos in the north was a young man in his early 20s by the name of Ge Hong. Ge's ancestors had already moved south and settled on the northern bank of the Yangzi River during the Han dynasty, and had served as administrators and generals in both the Han and the Jin administrations. In 303, Ge was called on to form a militia to defend against rebels, and he did so successfully. Rather than collect his rewards from the emperor and remain in the north, Ge accepted a position as military councilor to a friend who had been appointed governor of the far-south port city of Nanhai (now known as Guangzhou).

Ge's patron was killed en route, but Ge continued south to Nanhai anyway, ultimately becoming a recluse in the mountains to the east of Nanhai. What we know of Ge Hong comes from the reputation he then established as a Daoist philosopher and alchemist, and from several of his writings that have been preserved.[17] Mostly he is known for his Daoist inquiries into what it meant to explore the inner regions of the mind and body, his experiments with many elixirs purporting to cure various illnesses and confer immortality, and his Confucian informed musings on the affairs of state. But recently another volume of his writings has gained newfound relevance, and puts Ge Hong into China's environmental history. Much of south China was malarial, and among the various elixirs, potions, and herbal remedies Ge Hong collected into a book he titled *Emergency Preparations Held Up One's Sleeve* was one for the preparation of a cure for the fevers that we now know as malaria. Soak the leaves of the *qinghao* plant, he counseled, wring the water out, and drink it. As we will see in chapter 7, in the late twentieth century Chinese researchers rediscovered this text, as well as the fact that *qinghao*, now known scientifically as *Artemisinin annua*, actually contains a substance that does indeed cure malaria.[18]

For our purposes in this chapter—1,700 years before that scientific confirmation of the power of this herbal remedy—we can infer that Ge Hong had to have gathered that remedy from among the locals he encountered, possibly the lowland Tai-farming population or the various non-Han Chinese peoples such as the Yao or Zhuang who had fled to the hills of the south to escape the clutches of the Han or Sui states,[19] and who had discovered and used *qinghao* to cure malarial fevers. How widespread that knowledge was among the south China population simply is not known. Even more curiously, although Ge Hong included the remedy in his book, for the next 1,700 years it was overlooked by the Han Chinese, and a highly effective cure—not merely a palliative—for malaria did not spread widely enough to halt the ravages of malaria throughout southern, central, and southwestern China. Malaria thus remained endemic, awaiting new blood from the north.[20]

And it came. With the loss of the Jin capital in the early fourth century came south to the Yangzi River valley not just the imperial family, but also the aristocrats who had lived in the capital region, along with their families, military retainers, tenants, and even neighbors seeking their protection—altogether hundreds of thousands more. On the southern bank of the Yangzi River they established a new city, Jiankang (later known as Nanjing) as the capital of the exiled Jin dynasty. They brought with them the ideas, institutions, and cultural norms from the North China plain, and expected to reproduce them in the south.

To a certain extent the expectation of being able to do that would seem unreasonable, given the wildly different natural environment of the south: "The landscape was dramatic: the wildness of the Yangzi gorges, wide stretches of shimmering lakes and, along the seacoast, craggy mountains rising from the narrow coastal plain. The human landscape was stranger still, for the Chinese of the Yangzi Valley spoke dialects the northerners often could not understand at all, and these people had traditions and all manner of customs that the northerners had never encountered. Moreover, beyond—and often surrounding—the centers of southern Chinese settlement were aboriginal people, 'barbarians' who led a primitive life as yet unaffected by Chinese influence."[21]

Beside the new capital and its immediate region, the closest area of Han Chinese settlement was around Lake Tai and Hangzhou Bay, a few score of miles southeast of Jiankang. Other centers of Chinese settlement had developed further up the Yangzi River where the Han River enters the Yangzi from the north, and even further upstream in the Sichuan basin. Added to these were a couple of outposts on the China Sea, Nanhai and Jiaozhou in what is now northern Vietnam. Over the next thousand years, the natural environment of this entire region would be transformed by Han Chinese farmers under the protection of a Chinese state into the most productive and wealthiest agricultural region on earth.

Whereas roads and chariots had provided the means of transportation on the North China plain, in the water world of the south, boats and rivers became the primary mode of transportation. "All of these [new] Chinese settlement areas were situated in low-lying plains and river valleys where the terrain was well suited to the cultivation of rice in flooded paddy fields. Between them lay vast expanses of forested hills and mountains inhabited by aboriginal peoples such as the Man, Liao, Li, and Xi, most of whom had yet to be assimilated to the Chinese way of life. In this warm, watery, mountainous, and heavily forested environment, so different from the dusty plains of the north, the Yangzi River and its major tributaries such as the Han, Xiang, and Gan Rivers were the threads that connected the various Chinese centers of the south to one another."[22]

The military strength of the Han Chinese in their new southern home, though weak at first, improved, and was used to "civilize" the frontier. One general, for instance, surrounded a large marsh just north of the mouth of the Yangzi, set it ablaze, and captured ten thousand families that fled the inferno—only to be enlisted as military households. As we will see shortly, what those families were doing in a marsh was farming rice. Other generals also sought to add to their troop strength by raiding and capturing the peoples in the hills and mountains. The Liao people in the hills around the Sichuan basin were captured, as were the Li in the Nanling mountains separating the Yangzi Valley from the southernmost Guangdong province, and the far-flung Man people, who could be found just about everywhere else, and who resisted Chinese encroachment fiercely, especially in the fifth century. In one campaign, a Chinese general captured 28,000 Man prisoners, and in another more than 200,000 were captured and enrolled as military households supplying troops to the Chinese. Despite the scale of these military campaigns against these peoples, they were not easily nor completely conquered, with conflicts continuing, as we will see, for another thousand years. The Han Chinese wars against the native peoples was also a war against their environment, for the point of removing the non-Chinese peoples and settling Han on their lands was to transform the region into farms—not the dry-land farms of the north, but watery rice paddies.

Wet-rice Cultivation

The south was a land of water and forested hills and mountains, not at all offering itself up easily for agriculture. That it did become home to agriculture required vast effort and much investment of labor and capital, most of which was provided by the aristocratic families who were attached to the royal family. They claimed vast tracts of frontier land, especially around Lake Tai, which became the center of development and ultimately one of the richest agricultural places in the world. These families not only had the support of the court for their efforts but also had their own military force to protect them, and when necessary, the Jin court at Jiankang as well. Working at first from stockades and then walled towns, work parties began to transform the landscape of the south, starting in the lower Yangzi region, into well-tended and watered rice paddies. To a certain extent, these outposts were much like the Zhou-era colonies, and they had the same purpose: hewing farmland out of forest and swamp.

We saw in chapter 2 that rice had been cultivated in the south for several millennia, in the lower Yangzi region, in its middle reaches, and in the far south around what became the outpost and port of Nanhai. The non-Chinese peoples there had developed the sophisticated cultivation techniques necessary for wet-rice cultivation, and by the Warring States period the state of Chu had drawn on the wealth and resources based on the rice harvest to construct a state and military power that had contended with the other Warring States on the North China plain. Thus the south was neither devoid of people nor a complete backwater when the fourth-century nomadic invasions of the north forced Han Chinese south into the Yangzi valley.

Han Chinese quickly adopted the techniques of wet-rice cultivation, and used the wealth that was thus created to support their state and society. The best example of that comes from the lower Yangzi region south of the mouth of the Yangzi near what became the cities of Hangzhou and Suzhou, an area that became the center of agricultural wealth in the Yangzi delta region (see map 4.2). The rich rice fields there were not just for the taking, but required an immense effort over several centuries to create. And in the

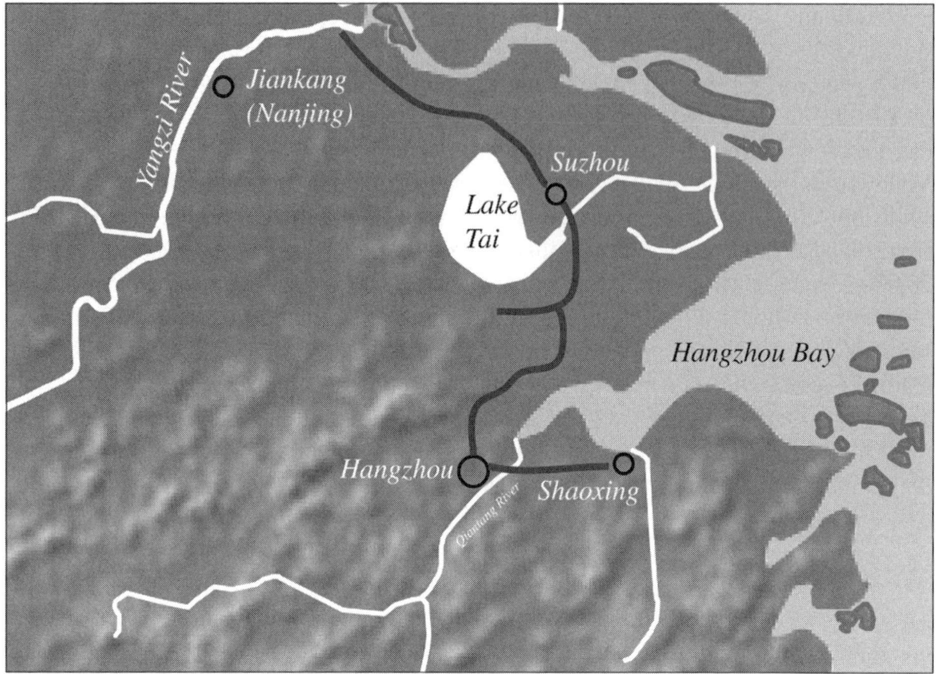

Map 4.2. The Lower Yangzi Region. Rivers are depicted as white lines, and canals as dark lines.

process, the Han Chinese created technologies and models for transforming the watery southern landscape into productive rice paddies.

The Yangzi delta and the Hangzhou littoral was not really ready for human settlement when Chinese first began migrating there, and those who were already there as early as the Yue kingdom in the third-century BCE inhabited the upland areas or the alluvial fans and slopes that came down from the upland areas, not the swampy river valley. Indeed, the lowlands "resisted the access of settlers over a long period. Though they were very extensive in the dimensions, these areas in earlier times were covered with brackish water. The amount and level of such water fluctuated considerably either in response to the seasonal variations in the amount of stream water from the uplands or in accordance with the ebb-and-flow movement of the tide. . . . People in the elevated plains could sustain their lives by their production of dry and wet crops, while those in the low-lying plains near Hangzhou Bay and the sandy elevations along the eastern coast enjoyed good access to salt production and fishing."[23]

For Han Chinese to be able to settle and farm the swampy, marshy river valleys of the south, they would need not just rice as a crop, but a means by which to transform the swamps into productive rice paddies. That would entail the construction of miles upon miles of earthworks called "polders," and the construction of those required vast amounts of capital and labor. Those conditions would not become available until later in the Song era, and will be taken up later in this chapter. In the meantime, smaller steps were taken on this new frontier.

During the Qin and Han dynasties of the Early Empire, the Lower Yangzi was sparsely populated, but after a decision in 140 CE to create arable land by damming and diking the numerous small streams that flowed out of the upland hills, some Han Chinese farmers struck out for the southern frontier. The dams created a large artificial reservoir, called Mirror Lake, with a circumference of 148 kilometers and an area of 20,600 hectares. Regulating the water levels in the lake, and letting it out at required times, were forty-three floodgates and sluices, creating a significant amount of new farmland. A few years later, in 173 CE, another man-made reservoir, called South Lake, was created that provided water to the growing city of Hangzhou and that regulated water so as to create additional farmland, and around 300 CE a canal for commercial traffic was constructed from the port town of Xixing to the Cao'e River. All these water control projects had been conceived, directed, and built by Han Chinese government leaders.

But why is all this important? First, wet-rice cultivation has several peculiarities that require precise control of water, both in terms of timing and amounts. To ensure that the rice plant thrives, the water depth throughout the field needs to be uniform. That means that not only did the land have to be properly prepared and leveled, but also embankments had to be built around each field, along with sluice gates to let water in and out. Because of these requirements, rice paddies tended to be small so as to ensure the proper leveling of the soil in preparation for the rice.

Second, the rice plant is unique among food grains in that it gets most of its nutrients from the water, so that the kind of soil is less important than the water supply. In fact, the soil that becomes best for wet rice is actually created over time in the process of continued flooding and drying; rice paddy fields actually improve in fertility and workability over time, rather than lose fertility as is the case with dry-land farming. "The distinctive feature of wet-rice fields is that, whatever their original fertility, several years' continuous cultivation brings it up to a higher level which is then maintained almost indefinitely. . . . This transformation requires years of hard work, *in return for decades if not centuries* of stable yields."[24]

Third, rice is both nutritious and is exceptionally high-yielding, especially in comparison with dry-field crops such as millet and wheat. From their harvest, dry-land farmers needed to keep one-third to one-fourth of the crop simply for seed for the next year's planting. Rice yields so much more grain that farmers needed just five percent of the harvest for seed. Add to that the fact that the rice fields are in a warmer climate, so farmers could get two or sometimes even three crops annually, sometimes of rice, sometimes other crops, from the same plot of land, supporting an increasingly large and dense population.

And finally, because of the amount of labor required to grow rice and the small plot size involved, Francesca Bray has argued persuasively that rice-growing encourages family farming rather than labor directly supervised by an estate owner or his agents. Supervising laborers to make sure that the field was leveled and that the growing plants were properly spaced, weeded, and picked free of insects, was almost as much labor as doing the actual work. Bray thinks that this fact tipped the balance in favor of the actual tillers of the rice fields, and so short-circuited the development of a manorial economy—that is, one where large amounts of land were not only owned as estates but also worked and managed by their owners. Instead, although the wealthy could own huge amounts of land, as apparently the aristocrats who had fled south in the early 300s did, ultimately it made more sense for them to rent their land to farming families who made their own decisions about what, when, and how to farm.[25]

The point is that this family-farm wet-rice technology developed first in the lower Yangzi region, and then spread via government initiative throughout south China. As Shiba Yoshinobu put it, "from the earliest times the Chinese were distinguished for the pervasive tendency to settle in lowland areas, while they proved themselves to have a genius for developing both the advanced technology and the organization needed for draining and taming wild lowlands."[26] The techniques of wet-rice cultivation would not just drain and tame lowland river valleys, which is of course what the entire Yangzi River valley system was, but also under expert farm family supervision work its way up slopes and eventually to the tops of hills and mountains by terracing the fields like steps (see figure 4.4d, page 134). Although the end result was by no means inevitable, as we shall see, by the early twentieth century much of lowland south China had been transformed into irrigated rice paddies.

Just as the creation of farmland from oak forests on the North China plain changed those ecosystems into simpler agro-ecosystems managed by people to maximize their collection of energy produced by plants, so too did the creation of rice paddies create a new agro-ecosystem. To be sure, the purpose was the same as a dry-land farm. But the standing water proved attractive to various species of birds, especially after rice farmers introduced carp and other fish into the paddies both to harvest and to eat weeds and mosquito larvae. Frogs also found the watery and muddy environment to be congenial, as did predators including tigers that preyed on the frogs.

The continuing story of the spread wet-rice agriculture throughout south China during the Song dynasty (960–1279 CE) will be taken up in a later section of this chapter. The main point here is that because the environment of the south was so different from the north, Chinese had to develop new agricultural techniques to transform it into farms. Rice paddies were the foundation of that technology, and coupled with the development of levees to control floodwaters, would massively transform the watery southern environment.

NORTH AND SOUTH REUNITED IN THE MIDDLE EMPIRE: THE SUI, TANG, AND SONG DYNASTIES, 589–1279 CE

After nearly four centuries of disunity, the Chinese empire was reconstituted in 589 CE as the Sui dynasty (589–618 CE) under the leadership of Yang Jian, a man of mixed Turko-Chinese blood and background, who took the imperial title "Emperor Wen ('The Cultured') of Sui." Although the tasks of reunification undertaken by him and his son proved to be long-lasting, the Sui itself was short-lived. The succeeding Tang dynasty (618–907) was militarily powerful and expansive, pushing Chinese rule far to the northwest and reconstituting the basic outlines of the empire established by the Han dynasty under Emperor Wu. Tang expansion was checked in 751 in a battle with Central Asian Muslim armies at the Talas River, and shortly afterward in 755 one of the Tang generals rebelled, ushering in a period of long but steady decline.

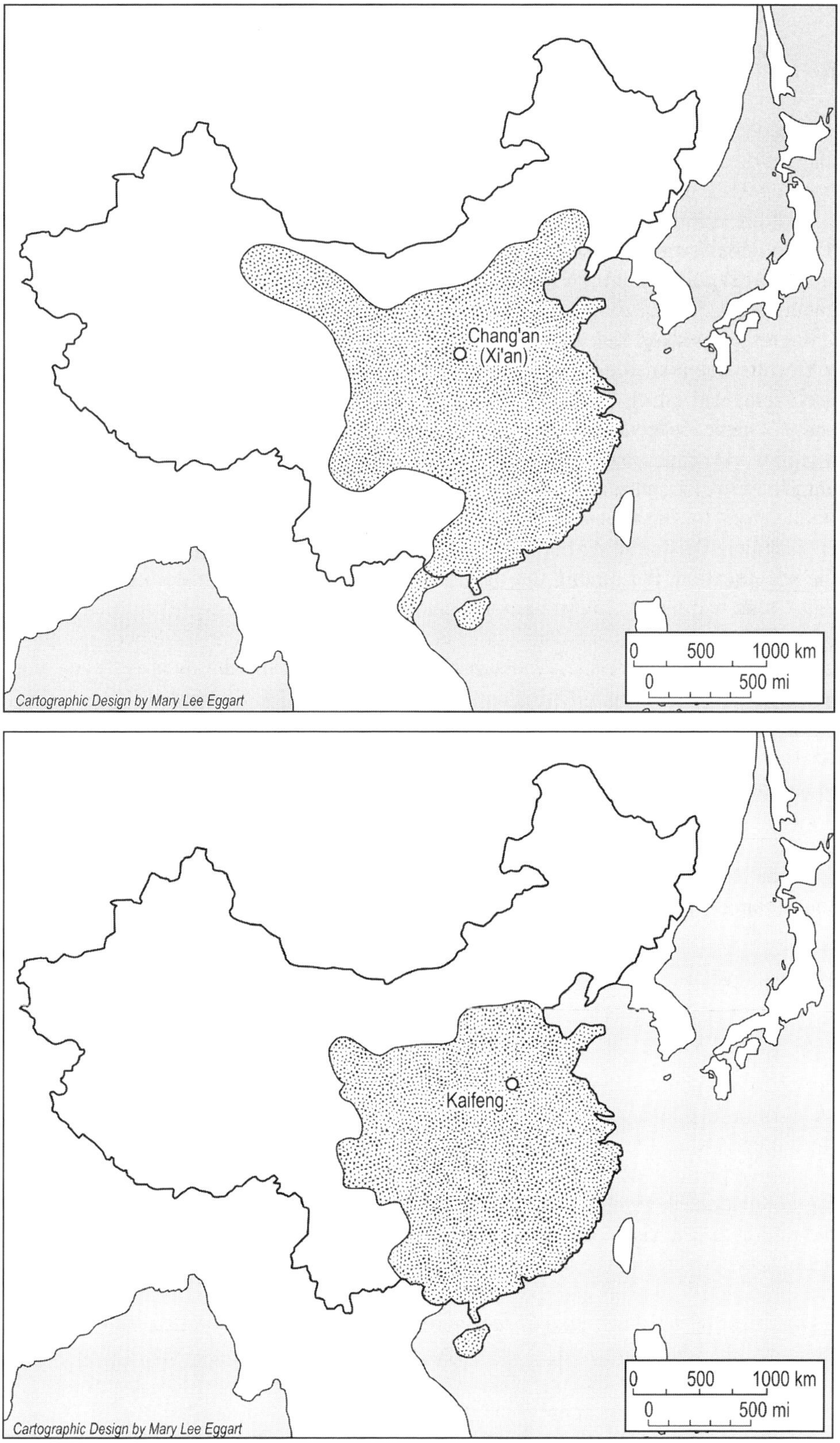

Chang'an
(Xi'an)
0 500 1000 km
0 500 mi
Cartographic Design by Mary Lee Eggart

Map 4.3. The Territorial Extent of the Tang (top) and Song (bottom) Dynasties *Source:* Gregory Veeck, Clifton W. Pannell, Christopher J. Smith, and Youqin Huang, *China's Geography: Globalization and the Dynamics of Political, Economic, and Social Change*, second edition (Lanham: Rowman & Littlefield, 2011), 67, 69.

When the Song (960–1279) picked up the threads of the empire, it was much smaller than before, with large amounts of the north and northwest again under nomadic control.[27] Despite newfound wealth and power coming from an exceptionally productive agriculture, a military supplied and supported by new industries, and a population that doubled, the Song still were not able to fend off nomadic advances on their territory, and in 1127 abandoned the north for the south. The rise of a new nomadic empire under the leadership of Chinghis Khan ultimately spelled the end of the Song when Chinghis's grandson Kubilai completed the conquest of the Song in 1279.

Despite the nomadic attacks and the conquest of the Song empire, the empire itself remained intact. That the empire was reunified and then remained unified was not inevitable. Indeed, what we now call China might have become a four-state (or more) world, each part more or less culturally and economically distinct. That an empire emerged and not an alternative system of competing states had tremendous implications for the course of China's history and for the relations of Chinese to their environment. Historian Arthur F. Wright identified numerous factors that account for the reunification, but among the most important was first the historical knowledge that China had been a unified empire, and the fact that those who kept that knowledge alive—Confucian scholars—considered the Han dynasty to have been not just a golden age, but recoverable. And second, the founder of the Sui dynasty, Yang Jian, was a man who had the ambition and ruthlessness to make the attempt.[28]

The task would be immense, and not just because of the military challenges but also because of the very different physical environments that underlay a unified empire. We have already seen how during the Han dynasty Chinese from north China tried and failed to conquer and hold the steppe from nomadic warriors. Those warriors adapted more successfully to the conditions on the North China plain, but the watery south was very different from the arid and flat north: horses had a much tougher time as weapons of war in the south. Harder, too, would be creating the links that held north and south together.

War and Water in Reuniting China under the Sui Dynasty (589–618)

The story of how Yang Jian, the founder of the Sui dynasty, reunified China makes the stuff of legend, plays, song, and novels, and for those who want to follow that, there are plenty of sources.[29] Suffice it to say here that reuniting the various non-Chinese states of north China was relatively easy and bloodless. The conquest of the Chinese in the Yangzi River valley, in a state that by then called itself the Chen dynasty, looked as if it would be more difficult, even though the north had many more resources, including population: there may have been more than 32 million people in north China by the middle of the sixth century, as opposed to perhaps 5 million in the Yangzi River valley, concentrated in the lower Yangzi around the capital of Jiankang. But the south was protected against invasion by the Yangzi River, and so Yang Jian began preparing a large fleet of warships, both far upriver in the Sichuan basis, and on the coast. Surprisingly, the Chen state in the Yangzi River valley folded quickly, and the Sui moved to buy the southerners' acquiescence with assurances and positions, but especially with a 10-year tax remission.

As the Emperor Wen-di of Sui, Yang Jian concentrated his energies on the institutional and cultural elements necessary for reunification, including building a new capital city near Luoyang in the north near all the previous dynasties' capitals along the Wei River, and when he died (some say under questionable circumstances) in 604, his second son, who became Emperor Yang, had been prepared to rule and follow his father's example of "filling out of the Han model of a Chinese empire"[30] after crushing his brother's attempt to usurp the throne. Emperor Yang-di was energetic, extravagantly building a new capital further downstream on the Yellow River at Luoyang, the city that had been the capital of the Jin dynasty, then sacked, then rebuilt, then sacked again. He also continued a massive canal building project begun by his father that subsequently became known in English as the Grand Canal. Because of the importance of these canals in Chinese environmental history, it behooves us to take a closer look before returning to examine the Tang dynasty record.

The Grand Canal

The founder of the Sui probably did not have a grand vision for connecting north and south China via an inland canal, since he simply started by redigging a hundred mile stretch of an old Han canal that linked his capital on the Wei River with the Yellow River in order to get food supplies from the better-endowed North China plain. His son, though, began an ambitious project in 605 CE of building new sections of canal and connecting others from the Yellow River all the way down south to Hangzhou south of the Yangzi River delta. He also constructed a branch that went northeast from near the confluence of the Luo and Yellow Rivers up to the present-day city of Beijing (see map 4.4). The number of people required for all this work is not precisely known, with reports of anywhere from 1 million to 5 million men and women being mobilized for the work at any one time.[31] However many workers were required, the canal, though a massive public works project, was speedily completed.

The route of the Grand Canal was changed after the Mongols conquered China in the thirteenth century and established their capital at the present site of Beijing. The Mongols straightened the canal by eliminating the section that had connected the cities of Chang'an and Luoyang, going in a more northerly direction over the Shandong peninsula and solving numerous engineering problems that arose from having a canal traverse more than a thousand miles with two significant elevation increases of more than a hundred feet. As Needham observed, "Here was a great work of engineering indeed, all the more remarkable when one remembers that in its course it had to connect with two of the greatest rivers in the world (the Yangzi and the Yellow) and one of the most changeable [the Yellow]."[32]

The significance of the Grand Canal for the subsequent course of the history of China and of the relationship of Chinese to their environment cannot be overestimated. Together with natural water ways, the Grand Canal linked China into what would become a single political and economic unit, making it possible for rulers in the north to tap the natural and agricultural resources of the entire empire. Additionally, the Sichuan basin was already tied to Chang'an with the road the had been built during the Han, and the "Magic Canal" linked the Yangzi River valley via the Xiang River to the far south over the Nanling mountains via the Li River. An additional overland route connecting the Yangzi Valley to the south came in the mid-700s when a grand minister who was from the far south "chiseled" a pass through the Nanling mountains

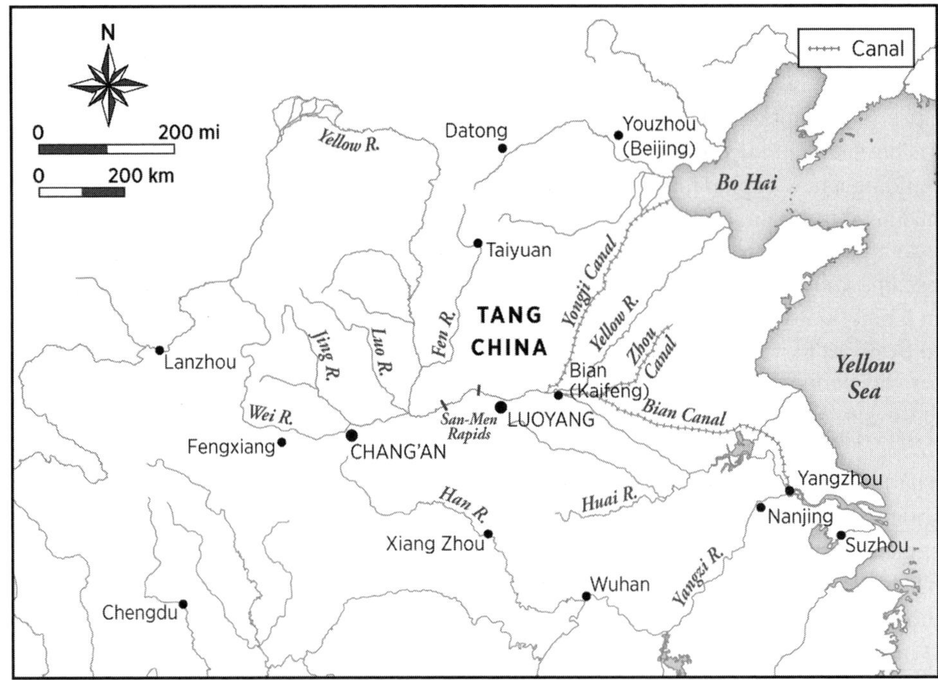

Map 4.4. North China's Canal System, Late Tang *Source:* Adapted from Frederick Mote, *Imperial China, 900–1800* (Cambridge: Harvard University Press, 1999), 18.

at the headwaters of the Gan River connecting with the North River flowing down to the port of Guangzhou.

"The canals also had a political use," according to Arthur Wright. "China had only recently been forcibly reunified after a long period of disunion. The ability to display the wealth and majesty of the new monarch throughout the empire was an important advantage; obviously the ability to get armed men and supplies by boat to areas of potential dissidence was even more important. Southeastern China below the Yangzi was already in the process of being settled, and the extension of the canal system to [Hangzhou], for example, greatly stimulated its growth from a frontier outpost to a thriving commercial city."[33]

Despite the importance of the new canal system, the Sui and later dynasties did not abandon the road system that had been built during the Early Empire; indeed, there are indications that the Sui canal builders put additional roads along the canal levies. The two systems just had different purposes, with the road system serving mostly for the postal system and other imperial communications, and the water ways for commerce and the movement of bulk goods, especially rice, from where it was grown in the lower Yangzi delta region north to the capitals of the Sui, Tang, and Song dynasties. Transportation of bulk goods such as grains becomes prohibitively expensive if it is moved over land in carts, however they were pulled. Water transportation is less than "dirt cheap," and before the advent of railroads in the nineteenth century, only water transport enabled bulk food grains grown in one region to be transported over long distances.

Most of the river valleys in China thereby became accessible to ports and cities further down stream, making it possible for farmers upriver to grow food and export it downriver to growing urban areas, and then to buy manufactured goods or other necessities such as salt in markets. As we will see, both the development of the river valleys in the south would take several centuries more, and the establishment of an integrated market system as well required some important changes (unplanned as they were) that would come in the middle of the Tang dynasty (which will be examined more below). But neither would have been possible without the integrated water transport system that the Grand Canal created, for the first time in Chinese history, in the early 600s.

Building and maintaining the Grand Canal dramatically altered the environment of the North China plain in ways that would create recurring dramas and nightmares for the people living there. To maintain water in the canals that otherwise would drain into either the Yellow River in the north, or the Huai and Yangzi Rivers in the south, required not just locks and weirs to hold the water in the canal (and then all the machinery to pull grain boats up and over or through these impediments). Streams and rivers flowing westward down the Shandong peninsula were redirected and dammed to capture their water for the canal. Silt from the Yellow River and its tributaries also settled out in the canal, requiring periodic dredging. The intersections of the canal with major rivers required intense maintenance and the development of deep knowledge about river hydrology. And because the Grand Canal was crucial for supplying food to the troops and rulers in the north, it became the single most important strategic resource of all Chinese dynasties until the late nineteenth century, requiring vast inputs of energy and resources to maintain. And when those inputs lagged, the highly engineered hydraulic system could break down, sending catastrophic floodwaters across the North China plain.

HAN COLONIZATION OF THE SOUTH AND SOUTHEAST

For Chinese in their north China world, "the south" had varying meanings. At first it meant the Yangzi River valley and the lower Yangzi, the unfamiliar warmer world of water and rice that they fled to after the capitals of Luoyang and Chang'an had been sacked in the early fourth century. After the empire was reunited under the Sui-Tang dynasties, and Chinese had more than two centuries' experience living and farming in the lower and middle reaches of the Yangzi River, "the south" came to mean even further south, over the line of low mountains called the Nanling, or "Southern Mountains," separating the Yangzi drainage basin from what was called Lingnan, or "south of the [mountain] ranges," the area generally covered by the current provinces of Guangdong and Guangxi. That now became "south China." Up the southeast coast was Min, a region settled later.

Chinese followed two major routes into south China over the low mountains that formed the southern limits of the Yangzi River drainage basin. In addition to the route into the northern karst region around Guilin (see figure 4.2) made possible by the Magical Canal discussed in chapter 3, a route further east followed the Gan River in Hunan south (upstream) until it was necessary to go by foot over the Meiling Pass to a tributary

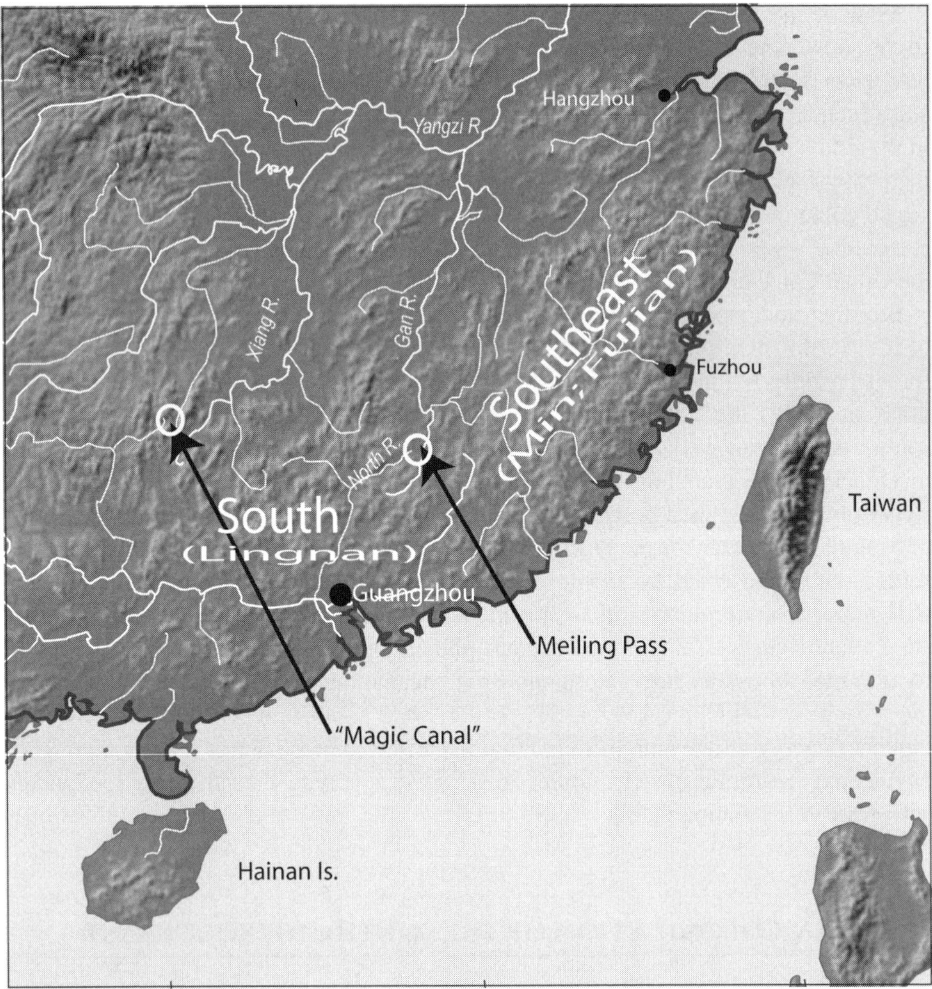

Map 4.5. South and Southeast China

on the North River that would take the travelers all the way south to the port of Guangzhou. To improve the passage, in 716 a southern native who had risen to become chief minister of the Tang dynasty was commissioned to build an easier road over the pass, which he did by having the Meiling Pass "chiseled" (see figure 4.3).

During the Tang (618–907) and Song (960–1279) dynasties, both of these regions became more tightly incorporated into the Chinese world as Han Chinese migrants, some forced and some voluntary, began settling in the numerous valleys that carried streams and rivers through the folded crust of the earth, leaving a landscape of hills and valleys very much unlike the flat North China plain. Moreover, non-Chinese peoples already inhabited nearly every part of that new space. The south and the southeast may have been frontiers to the Chinese, but these regions were home to many others who were there first.

Fig. 4.2. The Karst Region along the Li River near Guilin *Source:* Author.

"South of the Mountains": Lingnan

Nearly the entire frontier south of the Yangzi was a kaleidoscope of peoples and environments. To the Dian, Lao, and Yi peoples of Sichuan we can add the Western Quan of the Yunnan-Guizhou plateau, the Xie, Western Zhao, and Man of Guizhou, the Xie and Zhou of Hunan, the Eastern and Western Ou, the Min, and the Yue on the southeast coast. Over the Nanling mountains in the far south were the Tai-speaking Zhuang farming in river valleys, the Li in the Hainan Island highlands, the Miao in the hills further south, the Dan living on the rivers, and, later, the Yao in the hills, among many others. And because Lingnan included not just the present provinces of Guangdong and Guangxi but Annam in what is now northern Vietnam, there were the Moi in the Annam mountains and the Muong natives of the Red River basin, as well as the Huang, the Ning, and the Nong, and the Wu-hu in the mountains separating Annam from Lingnan. To the Han Chinese, all of these people and more were collectively known as "Man" ("barbarian") or, generically, "Lao."[34]

Like the peoples elsewhere in China, those living in the south had devised various strategies for obtaining their livelihood from a variety of environments. Mostly, the distinction between the wet-rice farming populations in the river valleys, and hunting and gathering peoples who also practiced shifting, or swidden, agriculture in the hills, held true for most of Lingnan as well. The Tai-speaking peoples of the river valleys had been farming wet-rice for centuries, and may well have been among the original inhabitants of the region. The highlands peoples used fire to burn off the forest and then to plant crops for a years or two before moving on to another part of the forest to burn. As early as the Han dynasty,

Fig. 4.3. The Meiling Pass *Source:* Author.

it was said of the Mo Yao, "a shoeless people," that "by sowing in fire they open up the spines of the mountains." After the fall harvest, they hunted in the deciduous forest of the uplands: "The woods are red, the leaves wholly changed; the plain is black, the grass newly burned."[35] The grass probably was burned to encourage new shoots that would bring deer to the clearings where they could be captured or killed.

These upland forest dwellers also cleared forest by girdling, topping, and felling trees, creating spaces among the tall forest canopy for sunlight to reach the forest floor where taro and other root crops could be planted with digging sticks. But the fires to burn the felled trees, to open space for deer, or to clear for planting, sometimes were quite spectacular, as a Chinese observer in the eighth century put to poem:

> Wherever it may be, they like to burn off the fields . . .
> Up the mountain they go and set fire to the prostrate trees . . .
> The red blaze forms sunset clouds far off,
> Light coals fly into the city walls.
> The wind draws it up to the high peaks,
> It licks and laps across the blue forest.
> The blue forest, seen afar, dissolves in a flurry,
> The red light sinks—then rises again . . .
> They drop their seeds among the warm ashes;
> These, born by the "essential heat" [yang],
> Burst into buds and shoots.
> Verdant and vivid, after a single rain,
> Spikes of trumpet vine come out like a cloud.[36]

Northern Han Chinese first conquered Lingnan in the third century BCE when armies of the First Emperor of Qin descended through the Nanling mountains over the "Magical Canal," leaving behind a garrison force of several hundred thousand troops, most of whom intermarried with natives, as had the man who was Chinese commander when the Qin was crumbling and the Han consolidating its power, General Zhao To, who took the title of "King of Nan Yue." Although Zhao To eventually came to an accommodation with the Han state (he stopped calling himself "Emperor" and reverted to "King"), he was mostly independent. It was his troops that marched south and captured Annam in what is now northern Vietnam, incorporating it under his rule. Sui and Tang rulers too reunited the empire and sent their troops south into Lingnan again in the seventh century to colonize it.

In Lingnan, Tang dynasty (618–906) wars against the natives began as skirmishes in the early seventh century, and became especially fierce toward the end of the eighth century. To be sure, the later Song-era wars against the natives in Sichuan, as we will see later in this chapter, had been driven by state policy, while those against the natives of Lingnan appear to have been in response to native attempts to drive the Chinese out. As Schafer observes, "The reconquest of the native peoples of [Lingnan] by the Tang soldiery and the establishment of a Chinese administration there . . . give a false impression of finality. The triumph of the [Chinese] over the [natives] was never complete."[37]

During the Tang dynasty, Schafer lists eighty-four "insurrections" of the native peoples of Lingnan that required Chinese military response. Mostly, those insurrections came from the subject peoples of Annam, who eventually secured their independence from direct Chinese rule, and the native peoples of western Lingnan in what became Guangxi province. For reasons that are not clear, the native peoples of central and eastern Lingnan appear to have accepted Chinese rule and customs; they were quite “cooked” by the Tang dynasty. The natives of Guangxi, though, remained rather “raw,” even those in the so-called bridled and haltered districts.

Since the records are all from Chinese documents, we do not really know the reasons for all the revolts, but the consequences for what the Han Chinese called “the native rebels” were often severe. One uprising in 728 that captured forty Chinese walled towns must have been quite large and spectacular, as was the following Chinese suppression that yielded 60,000 native heads. Another uprising in 756 apparently mobilized 200,000 natives to burn Chinese settlements in western districts, carrying off captured Chinese as slaves. Schafer curtly concludes: “After 866 there was relative peace,”[38] because of the massive Tang military presence and repression.

To consolidate Chinese rule over the defeated peoples, the Tang state established military farm colonies, the agricultural military colonies called *tun-tian* pioneered by the Han dynasty for the colonization of the northwest, using the soldiers who had been involved in the campaigns. As we saw in the previous chapter, the Qin and the Han had used similar strategies, so Tang rulers had precedents to follow. Altogether, twenty-four colonies in five prefectures in Lingnan were established in the early ninth century,[39] an indication of how difficult it was for Chinese from the north to migrate to the far south. The other mechanism the Tang used to control these territories was to cast a Chinese administrative net over the region, appoint Chinese officials in areas reliably Chinese, and appoint native chieftains to oversee the “bridled and haltered” districts of native peoples in malarial areas that tended to kill off Chinese from the north. In Lingnan, most of those districts were in the western half, in what became Guangxi province.

As we will see later in this chapter, the pattern of human settlement of Lingnan was somewhat different from that of Sichuan in the west. In Sichuan, Han Chinese farmers had quickly settled and cleared the river valleys after the native peoples had either been assimilated or pushed into the hills, and much of the region was deforested by the eleventh century. In Lingnan, malaria kept Chinese out of many of the low-lying river valleys, and their preferred area of settlement was in the northern hills. Malaria-resistant Tai tilled the lowlands, while Li, Miao, Yao, and others burned the hills for their shifting agriculture.

Both the native peoples and Chinese migrants thus altered their environment to meet their needs, but the available evidence indicates that during the Tang, most of Lingnan remained forested.[40] To be sure, the original deciduous forest in upland areas may have been burned off to be followed by a secondary forest of conifers and firs. And forests composed of trees with economic value, in particular the dense stands of cassia that produced fragrant cinnamon in the northern hills of Guilin (“Cassia Forest”), also disappeared. According to Edward Schafer, by about 1000 CE, “it appears that Chinese cinnamon hunters and aboriginal fire-cultivators together . . . removed a good part of the primeval forest in [Guilin].”[41]

Palms of various kinds also provided resources—food, fuel, fiber, and shelter. Among the most noteworthy were the banana and the coconut, but also the coir palm from which water-resistant rope could be braided. The areca palm yielded nuts which when processed and chewed (so-called betel nut) gave a buzz similar to caffeine, and an alcoholic “toddy” was brewed from the sap of the sugar pine.[42]

Another prized natural resource of Lingnan was pearls harvested from oyster beds just off the Leizhou peninsula. Pearls had made their way north since early Han times and by Tang times were periodically overharvested to the point of collapse. One such collapse in 742 CE led to the establishment of a supervisory office to maintain oyster beds by limiting the amount of pearls that could be gathered, and production resumed twenty years later.[43]

Nonetheless, more thoroughgoing environmental change in south China would have to await larger and denser populations of Han Chinese. Chinese military power and administrative skill were no match for malaria, so much of western Lingnan (in what became Guangxi province) as well as Yunnan further west remained in native hands, preserving conditions that led to another set of wars between Chinese troops and the native peoples (and their hidden ally, the malaria-bearing mosquito) in later centuries, topics to be taken up in the next chapter.

The Southeast Coast

This theme of Han Chinese migration into areas inhabited by other peoples was recapitulated up the coast in the southern part of what became Fujian province.[44] There, the inhabitants called Yue, settlers from the South Seas who spoke an Austronesian language, gained their livelihood mostly from fishing and hunting, and probably practiced some kind of swidden rice farming. Much of southern Fujian (then called Minnan) where these people lived was saltwater swamp, the home of the large and very dangerous saltwater crocodile (*Crocodylus porosus*). Inland mountains cut this region off from the inland migration routes Han Chinese followed into Lingnan, and so Han Chinese filtered into the region later and slower than they had into Lingnan.

By the eighth century, though, there were increasing numbers of Han Chinese migrants, many of whom tried to accumulate wealth by farming in that difficult environment. Historian Hugh Clark has reconstructed the story of a Han Chinese by the name of Wu Xing who constructed a weir across the Mulan River both to back up fresh water to irrigate nearby fields, and to prevent the tidal bore from inundating rice fields with salt water. "The Yanshou weir was the first of a series of projects that controlled the flooding and opened the land to the dense settlement and intensive exploitation that had developed even by the 11th and 12th centuries. Through a network of dikes and retention ponds, the weir both controlled the waters of the streams flowing from the northern fringe of the . . . flood plain and the main course of the Mulan River and checked the tidal incursions that had rendered much of plain a saline wasteland."

Han Chinese not only did battle with the environment and the crocodile, but with the natives as well. Chinese forced the Yue peoples out of the river valleys, Han Chinese armies dealt with "unruly" elements in the hills, and the Tang state established a military colony to rule over the region. Many indigenes fled, possibly to highlands elsewhere,[45] but others "opted to coexist with the [Han Chinese] immigrants, and so to adopt" their culture. The Yue people disappeared along with the saltwater crocodile, replaced by Han Chinese and their farms and culture.

Thus Lingnan and the southeast coast in Tang times were inhabited by both Chinese and by several other non-Chinese peoples. Unlike the Sichuan experience, which we will examine shortly, the Han Chinese in Lingnan were not able to easily displace the Tai farmers in the lowlands. In part, that was because the early Chinese conquerors had intermarried with the Tai natives; Zhao To, "the King of Nan Yue" built his power base in large part by intermarrying and allying with powerful Tai leaders. But an even greater barrier to Chinese penetration of the lowlands was a feared disease, malaria. "Prior to the Tang period, said Xu Songshi, [Lingnan was still a region] of forests and swamps, roamed by elephants, rhinoceros, pythons, lions, and tigers."[46] Many of the accounts of Chinese military action against natives in the south count losses of 25 percent from malaria alone, and the great Tang rebel Huang Chao in the late ninth century fled north out of Lingnan after 30–40 percent of his troops died of malaria.[47]

DISEASE REGIMES NORTH AND SOUTH

Malaria in the South[48]

To Han Chinese from the north, all of the south looked diseased. In the words of Liu Xun: "The mountains and rivers of Lingbiao [i.e., Lingnan] are twisted and jungly; the vapors concentrate and are not easily dispersed or diffused. Therefore there is much mist and fog to cause pestilence." As is now known, of course, malaria is caused by a parasite transmitted to humans from a particular kind of mosquito, the *Anopheles*. Because of the linkages among parasite, mosquito, and human host, malaria requires a specific set of environmental conditions to exist, and cannot spread beyond those limits. Malaria thus is not a disease such as plague, smallpox, or cholera that can spread broadly and fast through human populations regardless of where they reside, but is limited to certain environments.

Tropical forests such as those originally covering Lingnan are especially good breeding grounds for parasites of all kinds. But the particular parasites that cause malaria in humans—several species of the single-celled protozoa belonging to the genus *Plasmodium*—were not there just waiting for human hosts to invade, but rather arrived with their human hosts when they migrated into south China. To be sure, malaria is found in monkeys, apes, rats, birds, and reptiles, many of which inhabited south China's tropical forests, but these forms are not infectious to humans. Human malaria is a very old disease, not merely evolving with humans, but even influencing the process of natural selection. The disease probably originated in tropical Africa, and only later spread elsewhere with the Neolithic revolution.[49] Whether it was brought into southern China by the original settlers in the area, or was spread among an indigenous population by later arrivals, is not known. But however and whenever malaria became established among the human population of south China, it was there among the indigenous Tai population long before the first Chinese migrants arrived.

Anopheles mosquitoes carry three species of plasmodium harmful to humans, and each causes a different kind of malaria. Two cause intermittent fevers and are not particularly virulent, even in non-immune populations, but the one caused by *p. falciparum* "is the most dangerous form of malaria."[50] Depending on the parasite, the clinical manifestations of malaria (including fever with or without paroxysm, sweating, and chills, vomiting and diarrhea, anemia, and hardening of the spleen) occur as the brood of the parasite undergo schizogony together. That all three forms of malaria were found in south China is clear from the classification of fevers given by Zhou Qufei in the late twelfth century. In the "lighter kind (*qingzhe*), the fevers come and go." In the "serious kind (*zhongzhe*), there is only fever and no chill." And in the "really serious kind (*geng zhongzhe*), fever continues without letting up."[51] Zhou may have been in error about ranking the severity based solely on the periodicity of fever, but clearly he identifies three kinds of fever, all consistent with scientific understandings of malaria. Which of the three was predominant in south China can only be guesswork, but given what is known about the general epidemiology of the parasites and the fact that the malaria in south China was often fatal to newcomers in the region, *p. falciparum* probably was the most prevalent.

With rainfall coming in the spring and summer when temperatures were in the range considered optimal for mosquitoes to breed, with pools of water forming in depressions in the earth's surface but especially in the swamps left by the annual flooding of the river systems, and with relatively high humidity, both the parasite and the *Anopheles* mosquito could flourish in many places in south China. Since the parasite lived in both the mosquito and in humans, the environmental conditions that brought both into contact provided the environment for malaria. Humans, as a host to the parasite, thus are a prerequisite to the existence of malaria: no humans, no malaria.

The Han Chinese in-migrants to the south understood neither the causes of malaria, nor the environmental link to the mosquito, but they did have enough knowledge of where the disease was and where it wasn't to guide decisions about where to settle—and where to remain. Possibly, they had access to local anti-malarial treatments preserved in Ge Hong's writings. Most came south via either the Meiling Pass or the "Magical" Ling Qu canal (see map 4.5), and then settled in northern Guangdong and Guangxi provinces. This was in part because those were the first regions "south of the mountains" they encountered, and in part because those regions were free of malaria. Once settled, they tended to remain there, and the primary reason given was fear of malaria in other areas. According to the genealogies of several lineages that trace their roots to Nanxiong in the Nanling Mountains, during Song times fear of malaria kept them from migrating elsewhere in Lingnan, even in the face of mounting population pressure in northern Guangdong.

Settlement patterns provide indirect evidence that malaria existed in the flood plains in the lower reaches of major rivers in the south, but not in upland areas. Malaria cannot exist without human hosts to provide a "reservoir of malaria infection,"[52] so areas uninhabited by humans thus could not have been malarial. As noted above, an indigenous population of Tai peoples lived in the river valleys and along the coast, providing the infectious reservoir of humans that allowed malaria to become endemic: uninfected *Anopheles* mosquitoes picked up the parasite from an infected human and passed it along to a person uninfected or not recently infected. Interestingly, though, communities in which malaria is endemic also develop a certain immunity to the disease.

The Tai population in southern China, especially those who lived in the lower reaches of the river valleys, may have had knowledge of the curative value of the *qinghao* plant, and possibly could also have acquired a certain level of immunity to malaria before Han Chinese even appeared on the scene. But for those without acquired immunity—such as Han Chinese migrants from north China—the disease would have been deadly. Besides malaria, other tropical diseases too no doubt ravaged newcomers from the north, posting warning signs for later arrivals. Indeed, the Yao, too, settled in the hills and avoided the flood plains, perhaps as much because of their fear of tropical diseases as because of their preference for the hills. If malaria was one reason Chinese (and Yao) initially avoided settling in river valleys in the south, then to settle there Chinese either had to acquire immunity to malaria as the indigenous Tai peoples had, or change the ecological conditions so they were no longer so conducive to breeding *Anopheles* mosquitoes. The best piece of direct evidence for the gradual acquisition of immunity comes from a Ming-era author, Wang Linting, who claimed that "in the Tang and Song, malaria in Lingnan was wherever [Chinese] in-migrants (*qian ren*) lived. But by the end of the Song, when the worthies and ministers fled [in the face of the Mongol invasion], [the earlier migrants] had become more like the locals [in not contracting malaria]."[53]

Contagious and Epidemic Disease in the North

Malaria is a disease grounded in a particular environment and with a specific vector (the mosquito) that may make it deadly, but it is not directly contagious—it does not spread from person to person, but only via bites from an infected mosquito. A similarly spread disease is cholera, in that the bacteria that spreads it is contained in contaminated water, human waste, and food; humans get infected through these vectors. In Chinese history, a disease called *huoluan* that had characteristics like those of modern cholera periodically afflicted large numbers of people.[54] Tuberculosis, too, probably infected Chinese from at least the Han dynasty, reaching epidemic proportions in the nineteenth and twentieth centuries.[55] Tuberculosis, cholera, and especially smallpox could reach epidemic scale in ancient China. In such diseases, the microscopic infectious agents can spread directly from human to human—they are highly contagious. Moreover, the spread of these diseases followed the sinews of the built environment now holding the Chinese empire together—the canals and waterways—without which these diseases would have remained local disasters and not spread as epidemics.

For these diseases to spread thus requires other humans, usually in sufficient densities as found in cities, and connected to each other via trade routes. Epidemics thus require a particular kind of environment, but one that is built rather than natural. These conditions were satisfied during the Tang era, when there were at least two series of highly contagious and deadly epidemic outbreaks, one in the 630s and the other two centuries later in the 830s. However, because the Chinese sources refer to these outbreaks by the generic name of *yi*, "epidemic," or *da yi*, "great epidemic," historians cannot be sure just what the actual disease was. As Denis Twitchett explained, "By the Tang period the Chinese had known smallpox for at least three centuries. When it first appeared in south China about 317 AD it was attributed to the barbarian peoples from the steppe who had over-run much of Northern China. Typhoid, dysentery and cholera were also well known. Lastly bubonic plague appears to have been described for the first time in . . . an imperially sponsored compilation completed in 610. Which of these diseases caused the [Tang] epidemics . . . is impossible to determine from the Chinese sources."[56]

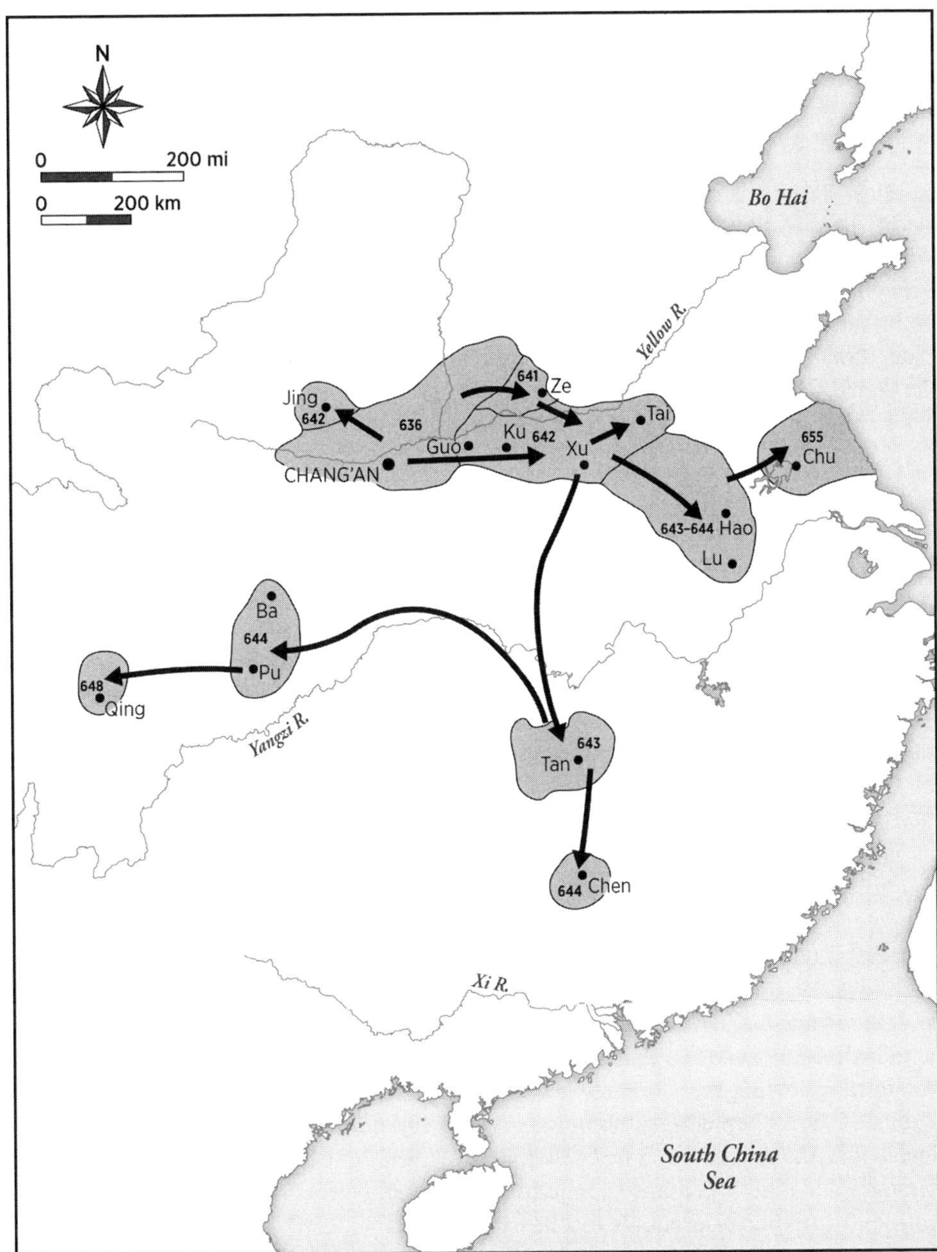

Map 4.6. Epidemics of 636–55 *Source:* Adapted from Denis Twitchett, "Population and Pestilence in T'ang China," in *Studia Sino Mongolia: Festschrift für Herbet Franke,* ed. Wolfgang Bauer (Weisbaden: Steiner, 1979), 44.

The first outbreak began in 636 in north China in the region around the Tang capital city of Chang'an. Twitchett thinks that because bubonic plague had been ravaging the Middle East and Constantinople, "it is tempting to see in the Chinese epidemic of 636 an outbreak of plague that had spread along the land route from Soghdiana and Iran," the old Han Silk Road route that Tang armies were advancing along. "Whatever its origins, we can follow the spread of the infection along trade routes within China" (see map 4.6). As Twitchett concludes, "this epidemic is the only case of pestilence in Tang China where we can actually plot the progress of infection, which followed almost exclusively water routes used for the shipment of grain, or major post roads."[57]

Unlike this first great epidemic, later outbreaks in the eighth century seem to have started in China's sea ports along the southeast coast from the Yangzi River south to Guangzhou, and to have spread from there. In 762, for instance, there was a terrible epidemic in the region around Lake Tai where wet-rice agriculture was beginning to support a large and dense population. With the Grand Canal completed, this entire region "was a major centre of water-borne traffic" on the Yangzi, the southern extension of the Grand Canal, and by sea to Japan and Korea. Moreover, because there had not been any famine or other food supply problems and yet "more than half the population died," Twitchett thinks that "it seems likely that the epidemic was a new infection to which the local Chinese population had little resistance that came from abroad by sea."[58]

The epidemic that began in 832 and continued for the rest of the decade "was a catastrophe on a national scale." Probably an outbreak of bubonic plague "on an unprecedented scale," the epidemic followed a series of major floods that destroyed crops and caused famines not just in north China, but also, for the first time, in south China. Although he could not map this outbreak as cleanly as the 630s epidemic, Twitchett is quite certain that it spread rapidly by water transport and jumped from city to city joined by water routes. The losses and destruction caused by the combination of floods, famine, and epidemic disease "may also have been a factor in the steady growth of endemic lawlessness, and loss of government control in the Yangzi provinces in the 830s and 840s when banditry, piracy, and clandestine traffic in smuggled salt became major problems," and contributed to the outbreaks of rebellions that ultimately brought down the Tang dynasty in 906.[59]

Besides these social and political consequences, "it is clear that these epidemics must have had some considerable effect on population trends. Both series of pestilences were accompanied by very high mortality, at least locally." Although Twitchett recognized that "it is of course quite impossible to quantify these losses," it "is equally certain that [the statistics that do exist] show a real decline of population" of up to one-third following the 636 outbreak. No statistics exist to measure the demographic results of the 832 epidemic, but because the anecdotal evidence suggests it was more severe than the earlier one, Twitchett concludes that these epidemics had an impact on demographic trends, perhaps enough to keep the population of Tang China within the limit of 10 million households reached in Han and Sui times. As we will see below, that limit was smashed during the next dynasty, the Song (960–1279), in large part because new agricultural technologies so vastly increased the food supply.

NEW AGRICULTURAL TECHNOLOGIES AND ENVIRONMENTAL CHANGE

Even in the lower Yangzi River delta, an area that was to emerge as the most agriculturally productive region of China, Han Chinese settlement and wet-rice farming started first in more elevated areas, as I discussed earlier in this chapter. The lowlands were not effectively farmed until new water control technologies developed between the ninth and twelfth centuries. The challenges to farming the river lowlands were not just the broadleaf evergreen forests; as we have seen, Chinese had been quite capable of removing forest for farms for at least two thousand years. The main environmental impediments were malaria and flooding, a natural consequence of the monsoonal rains which sent annual deluges down the Yangzi River, overflowing the banks of the river into flood plains, lakes, and swamps from the middle course of the river 1,000 miles downstream to its mouth.

The main problem that rice farmers faced that had to be solved thus was flooding. If a farmer were to clear the forest, annual floods in the summer and fall would submerge the land (and the crop) just when the rice crop was growing or being harvested. The solution that the Han Chinese devised was the "enclosure," or polder, an earthen levee completely surrounding an area and protecting it from flooding. In those circumstances, farmland would be below the level of the surrounding river or floodwaters, making possible both flood protection and a regular source of water for irrigation[60] (see figures 4.4a–d).

Such undertakings were beyond the capacity of individual farming families, and required vast amounts of capital and labor. Some extremely wealthy landowners were able to mount these projects, at first by encroaching on lakes that had been created as reservoirs, but such actions drew the protests of other land owners, who depended on the reservoirs for irrigating their farmland, and hence the attention of government officials. After the end of the Tang dynasty in 906 CE and a period of division known as the Five Dynasties (907–960 CE), a powerful new dynasty known as the Song (960–1279) came to rule China.

Faced with threats from nomadic peoples to the north, the Song state was constantly improving and increasing its military, raising the largest standing army in the world, more than a million strong. Such a large army meant the Song had a need for revenue, mostly generated by taxes on agricultural production. The Song state thus had a strong interest in increasing agricultural production, and its officials in the lower Yangzi delta region organized the creation of numerous huge polders in lowlands that vastly increased both the amount of land that could be farmed, and hence annual harvests and taxes. By one account, from the late eleventh century into the early twelfth century, several *millions* of acres of new farmland were developed inside the enclosures in the Yangzi delta region.[61] The result was a vast region of rice paddies linked by a dense network of canals to irrigate rice paddies and to serve as a transportation network.

The threat to the Song from their nomadic rival to the north, the Khitan Liao, also prompted the Song state in the early eleventh century to defend itself by digging a series of ponds on their northern border that Khitan horses could not cross. To keep water in these ponds, Song engineers diverted seawater, rerouted rivers, and built dikes and dams. Once those ponds were built, they could be maintained only at great cost. And so Song statesmen, familiar now with the wet-rice technology of the lower Yangzi River region, had the brilliant idea that military colonies (the *tun tian*) established to man the border and maintain the ponds could feed themselves by planting rice. Because the weather was too cold, the experiment failed; but the ponds did deter the Khitan, and also provided a breeding ground for huge mosquitoes and swarms of

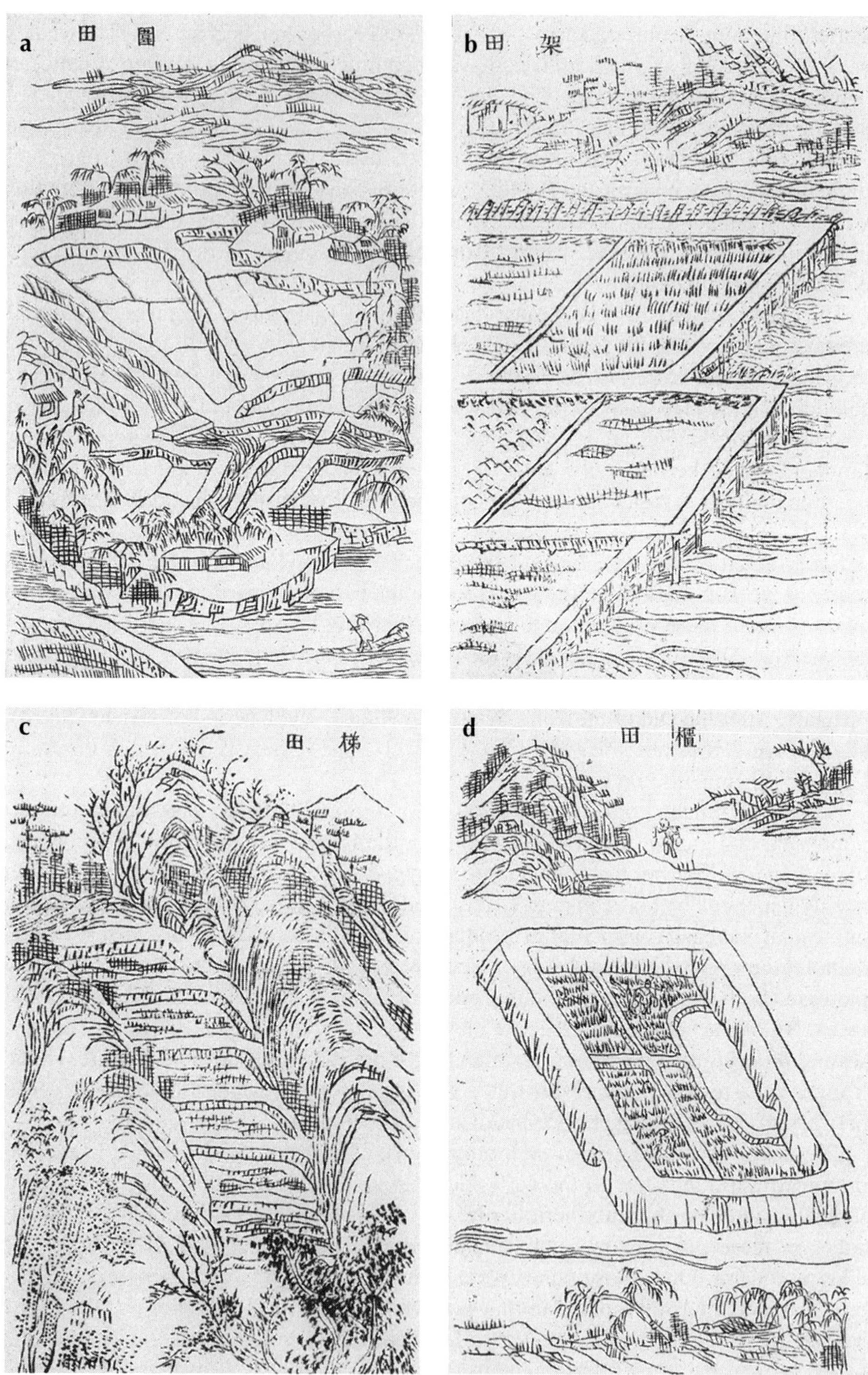

Figs. 4.4 a–d. Types of Diked and Enclosed Fields *Source:* Wang Zhen nong shu (Wang Zhen's agricultural treatise) (n.p., 1911), 6a, 11a, 10a, 12a.

biting black flies.[62] That experiment failed, but the effort to create a vast expanse of rice paddies in the Yangzi River delta succeeded.

The creation of polders was accompanied by other improvements that vastly increased both the total output of grain, and the productivity of the land, especially for rice. Through the process of selective breeding, farmers began developing new strains of rice suitable for many local environmental conditions, including soil, nutrients, and even taste.[63] Like all plants, the rice plant is subject to mutations induced by solar radiation damage to its DNA. Not all mutations benefit farmers, but some do and are noticed and selected; one of the most important adaptations was the development of early-ripening strains. The greatest leap in that direction came with the importation, early in the eleventh century, of a new rice seed from Champa (in what is now northern Vietnam) that ripened in sixty days rather than the usual 150–180 days. The new early-ripening drought-resistant varieties meant that land could be sowed with two or even three harvests of rice, or one each of rice and wheat in the same year.

Through decades or centuries of experience with wet rice, farmers in upland areas discovered that annual drying of paddy improved its workability, fertility, and productivity. In those areas, farmers planted one crop of rice followed by one of wheat or vegetables. In the lower-lying fields newly enclosed within the huge polders, farmers found it difficult if not impossible to drain the water from the paddies and so could not dry the fields out for planting wheat or vegetables. Over time, new ways of subdividing the polders into smaller, more easily managed parcels developed, along with the cross-village cooperation needed to manage water supplies, so that even those fields that had more swamplike qualities could be dried out annually. When that became possible, so too did the extension of double- and triple-cropping to ever more extensive areas, converting forest and swamp to rice paddies.[64]

But the early-ripening variety also extended the rice-growing area beyond the well-watered polders. According to Ping-ti Ho, "since the extent of lowlands suitable for the cultivation of indigenous late- and medium-ripening rice is rather limited, the drought-resistant early-ripening varieties in the course of time brought about a major revolution in land utilization and more than doubled the area of rice culture in China. Directly by way of doubling China's rice area and indirectly by promoting a better cropping system, the long-range effect of early-ripening rice on China's food supply and population growth was prodigious."[65] Where the population of Han and Tang China had topped out at about 10 million families, under the Song it doubled to 20 million families, or between 100–120 million people.

The innovations wrought by early-ripening rice slowly spread throughout southern China. "Within two centuries of the introduction of Champa rice the landscape of the eastern half of China's rice area had already been substantially changed. By the thirteenth century much of the hilly land of the lower Yangzi and Fujian where water sources and climatic and soil conditions were not sufficiently favorable to the cultivation of [longer-ripening rice varieties] had been turned into terraced paddies." In subsequent centuries, early-ripening rice and the practice of double- or triple-cropping spread throughout south China.[66]

Other improvements to agriculture in the lower Yangzi included the perfection of sluice gates to regulate water through the enclosures into fields, a treadle water pump and a water wheel to bring water into (or out of) irrigation ditches. As a result of all of these improvements, in what historian Mark Elvin calls "the revolution in farming," wet-rice agriculture in the lower Yangzi region became the most productive in China. During the Song dynasty and the one that followed, as much as 40 percent of the state's tax revenue came from the lower Yangzi region alone, an indication of how much rice was produced there.

Weeds and Fish

Where ever the earth gets disturbed, whether naturally by fire, landslides, or even asteroid collision, or intentionally by people scraping away the natural vegetation for gardens or farms, plants specialized to take advantage of the opening move in to colonize. For humans, these unwanted plants are "weeds." "More often than not they are plants that evolved to fill the minor role of colonizing bare ground...and that found themselves wonderfully preadapted to spread across the expanses stripped clean by the Neolithic farmer's plow or sickle."[67] Because the point of farming was to give favored plants the maximum solar energy, water, and nutrients to grow so as to provide the resulting energy for humans to consume, unwanted plants—the weeds—had to be removed.

Weeds were a bane the farmer's existence in China as elsewhere, and like farmers everywhere, weeds emerged as a result of the interaction of humans with their environment, with plants that were already there being selected by the act of farming to proliferate in farmers' fields. What precisely those weedy plants might have been in north China we do not really know, but we do know that farmers in north China became excellent weeders, and developed tools (hoes of varying kinds) and techniques for keeping unwanted plants out of their fields. Hoeing may have started along with the development of agriculture in north China, and by the time of the Han dynasty farmers had all kinds of hoes, spades, and scrapers to use for particular crops. Moreover, because "the climate is dry so that centuries of manuring have produced a thin, impermeable crust of salts on the surface of the soil, it is only by hoeing immediately after every rainfall that plants can really benefit from the moisture."[68]

In the rice-growing south, flooding to irrigate paddies might have been one way to suppress weeds. A Han-era historian noted that in the south farmers "plough with fire and weed with water."[69] Still, in the irrigated rice paddies of south China, various kinds of rush and marsh plants competed with the rice plant, although Bray thinks the most invasive weed through Asian rice paddies is "barnyard millet." Farmers pushed these weeds and others into the paddy mud as a kind of green fertilizer, and learned how do so with their toes, or if by hand, with "weeding claws" fitted to protect finger tips. Additionally, rice paddies were drained two or three times to dry out, not just to kill weeds but also to aerate the soil and encourage root development. [70] Weeding of rice paddies was shown to increase yields by 45 percent, so the obverse is also true: weeds are exceptionally good at making the most of the sunlight, water, and nutrients available to them, robbing the intended crop of all of those.[71]

Weeding was such noxious labor that it was a communal village activity in the north, and in the south rice farmers learned how to enlist fish to help. Although there are no records of when the practice started, except for a few tantalizing references from as early as the Warring States period, with the massive development of rice paddies during the Tang and Song eras, raising fish in rice paddies was well understood and apparently widely practiced. One Tang-era writer said that in the south, "land on the hillside is watered but the flat areas near the houses are hoed into fields. When spring rains come, water collects in the fields around the houses. Grass carp fingerlings are then released into the flooded fields. One or two years later, when the fish are grown, the grass roots in the plots are all eaten. This method not only fertilizes the fields, but produces fish as well. Then, rice can be planted without weeds. This is the best way to farm."[72]

The fish mostly used were common carp, crucian carp, grass carp, or silver carp. Not only did the carp eat weeds, their feces contain nitrogen and potassium that plants need. Moreover, the carp ate insects and their larvae, including those of *Anopheles* mosquitoes, the main vector of malaria.[73] How widespread the use of carp in rice paddies was is not really known, nor is it known whether the farmers understood that the carp may well have reduced the incidence of malaria. Most likely they did know that carp kept down the weeds and added to the family diet when eaten and to income when sold.

A famous historian once observed that for most of human history the energies of the direct producers of food (villagers, peasants, farmers) have been sapped both by micro-parasites (the bacteria, viruses, and protozoa attacking human bodies) that cause diseases and increased mortality, and by macro-parasites (rent-taking landlords and tax-taking states) that also shortened lives.[74] To those we now can add "agro-parasites": the weeds and vermin that consumed the nutrients intended for crops, and the growing, standing, or harvested grains. For just as human bodies fought off disease-causing bugs, and peasant farmers resisted (as best they could) the exactions of social and political elites, so too did they expend tremendous amounts of time, energy, and creativity dealing with agro-parasites.

Technological Diffusion

The new rice-growing agricultural technologies spread from the lower Yangzi to other areas of south China. Since China was a unified empire, officials brought with them their knowledge of the new techniques to other areas that they recognized were not as advanced. Wood-block printing, invented in China in the ninth century, contributed to the distribution of the knowledge of the best agricultural practices. The two most impressive books were entitled *The Essentials of Farming and Sericulture*, a compilation sponsored by the state, and the second the privately authored *Wang Zhen's Treatise on Agriculture*.[75] An earlier treatise, the *Qi Min Yao Shu*, describing best practices in the loess highlands, was also printed and distributed.[76]

The invention of the new agricultural technologies and dissemination by the new technology of printing did not necessarily mean that the practices would spread rapidly throughout south China. The reason is that their effective use required both large amounts of capital and a large supply of labor, neither of which existed in much of south China even as late as the Song dynasty. Much of the south remained a subtropical frontier, so much so that Song emperors exiled their critics there, hopefully to die of a tropical disease—or, at least, not to be heard from again. But to the slow natural increase in population in south China were added invasions and conquest, first of northern China in 1127 by nomadic peoples, and then by 1279 of all of China by the Mongols. Both of these conquests sent additional Chinese fleeing south; in 1127 the Song dynasty fled its capital at Kaifeng and reestablished its government first at Nanjing, the "Southern Capital," and then further south in Hangzhou. But before turning to that episode in Chinese history and its impact on processes of environmental change, we must consider some other extraordinary changes in China's society and economy that also affected its environment.

Landed Estates

A primary agent of the agricultural innovations that transformed both the economy and the landscape of south China from the late Tang through the Song was a new form of land tenure: the large private estate. The equitable land system (*jun tian*) of the Sui and first half of the Tang broke down after the An Lushan Rebellion of 755. Officials and other wealthy families began grabbing the land and assembling it into their private estates, using the wealth and revenue to consolidate their political positions. The extent to which these estates were contiguous parcels worked by various kinds of unfree labor varied. In the least developed parts of the Song empire, the estates probably were compact and the labor mostly unfree, while in the most economically advanced and densely populated parts of China, especially in the lower Yangzi and along the southeast coast, the estates most likely had been assembled from large numbers of small plots worked by peasant farming families who paid rent to the landowner. Moreover, the best estimates of historians are that a substantial amount of land remained owned and tilled by peasant families.[77]

Despite the continued existence of both a smallholder sector and large amounts of land in south China held by non-Han Chinese, the large private estate had the resources necessary to invest in the vast poldering and irrigation projects needed for wet-rice agriculture. According to Peter Golas, "Unlike most smallholders, landlords possessed the capital that might be invested in new tools, draft animals, irrigation works, and other aids to higher yields."[78] To be sure, the Song state also had an interest in disseminating those innovations throughout the empire, but it was largely the wealthy who could implement them. The rising productivity on the nearly 100 million acres of land under cultivation during the Song[79] supported a doubling of the population from some 50–60 million in the Tang to 100–120 million by the mid-Song.

Buddhist Monasteries

An unexpected engine of environmental transformation in middle imperial China was the Buddhist monastery. During the Han dynasty, Buddhist ideas had filtered into China from merchants along the Silk Road, but mostly Buddhism was considered interesting evidence of another advanced civilization by Chinese scholars in the comfort of the imperial academy in Chang'an. By the late Han, there was misery enough among the increasingly impoverished peasant class, but it took the collapse of the Han dynasty and then the invasion and sacking of Luoyang and Chang'an by nomadic invaders in the early fourth century CE to create the death and destruction that gave widespread credence to the first of Buddhism's Four Noble Truths: all life is suffering.

Buddhist ideas spread rapidly among the impoverished and conquered Chinese on the North China plain, and among the Han Chinese aristocrats who had fled south to the lower Yangzi, where they set up their government in exile and tried to recreate the glories of the Han dynasty. The "barbarian" conquerors, too, came to accept Buddhism, creating both a common belief system among all these peoples, as well as a link between north and south China.

Buddhism spread not just because its main message spoke to the conditions of life many people found themselves in, or because the ideas were rich and complex enough to engage an otherwise intellectually idle aristocracy, but especially because the rulers of the various states favored and supported Buddhist establishments, in particular monasteries. Buddhism grew rapidly during the sixth century CE as rulers provided funds for the building of massive statues of the Buddha, gave monasteries the right to taxes from nearby lands, and allowed them to build in the hills and highlands that were not part of the various "equitable land" redistribution plans but were considered "state" land. To ensure that their names would be remembered for all times, wealthy landowners also donated their country estates and city mansions to Buddhist monasteries. These processes continued from the fourth-century era of division, through the Sui dynasty and into the Tang.

By the Sui dynasty in the seventh century, there were about 4,000 great monasteries throughout north and south China,[80] each with twenty to forty monks overseeing scores of agricultural workers and other servile people who worked lands totaling hundreds of acres. Gernet estimates that as many as three million serfs, slaves, and other unfree persons worked the estates of the great Buddhist monasteries, so these were large enterprises indeed.[81]

It is not that there were not others who had equally as large estates, for from the sixth century on, Tang aristocrats too owned vast estates. But the Buddhist monasteries had an interesting distinction: monasteries were built on untilled hilly, mountainous, or otherwise unused land. According to Gernet: "It is significant that the law which at the beginning of the Tang dynasty endeavored to protect farmland and to maintain the principle of lifetime allotments [of the "equitable fields" system] was, on the contrary, much more lenient with regard to fallow lands: these alone were susceptible to appropriation" and transfer to Buddhist monasteries. It wasn't that these untilled fields were not used, for they were, but not for grain: "they were planted with trees, consisted of gardens and pastures, and were situated on hills, hillocks, or in valleys. . . . It was within such untilled islets, which had emerged in the middle of irrigated fields, or uneven terrain, on mountains, in valleys, or on hillsides, that most of the monasteries were established."[82]

The Buddhist community did not simply sit in their hilltop monasteries meditating. The monasteries were economic units—big and powerful ones—that undertook the "reclamation" of the hill lands for agriculture, pasture, orchard, and timber. In difficult conditions, all of this work required large amounts of labor, which they commanded, and significant amounts of capital, which their devotees donated to them. In 707, a Tang official complained: "Extensive constructions of monasteries are undertaken, and large mansions are built. Even though for such works trees are felled to the point of stripping the mountain, it does not suffice to supply all the beams and all the columns required, [so more are imported]. Though earth is moved to the point of obstructing the roads, it does not suffice for the [production of bricks required for] walls and partitions, [and so more are brought in]."[83]

Gernet thinks that that construction of monasteries led to the deforestation of certain regions, but that the loss of forest "became perceptible only with time and did not give rise to undue concern."[84] The reason for lack of concern seems to have been two-fold. First, the monasteries apparently transformed the original forest cover into various kinds of productive trees or shrubs, such as tea plantations, fruit orchards (especially oranges, apparently), and pasture for horses and sheep. Historian Denis Twitchett also thinks that the "most important activity of the upland industries was probably lumbering. We have ample proof that timber and bamboo, the dominant building materials, constituted an important trade. . . . Timber . . . was often transported considerable distances. . . . In this industry, the manpower at the disposal of monasteries must have given them an important advantage."[85] Besides being an agent of deforestation, monasteries in the hills and mountains indirectly contributed to further deforestation when their fortunes declined. One very large monastery in the hills of Shanxi, formerly very wealthy with vast land holdings, fell on hard times by 836 CE. Then, "we . . . are told that its forests had been destroyed by firewood gatherers—evidence that timber had been a considerable part of its resources."[86]

Being adept at extracting resources from highlands, Buddhist monasteries benefitted immensely from various dynasties' explicit policies to bring new lands under the plow, especially in the west (Sichuan), the south (Lingnan), and the northwest. As we saw earlier in this chapter, the Tang state used considerable military power to subdue native peoples to the south and west, and then to cast an administrative net over them to impose Chinese rule. To establish an economic foothold in these areas, states in the north had created "agricultural colonies" and "military colonies," in the former case forcibly uprooting farmers from north China and resettling them in the reconquered arid northwest. But that was not all: these farmers were placed "at the disposal of the Buddhist monasteries, to serve as their agricultural workforce."[87]

But why, asks Gernet, did the state entrust to the Buddhist monasteries a task—land settlement and agricultural development in frontier regions—that should normally have come under state auspices? "There may have been several motives," he suggests. Among others, "[t]he establishment of colonies and the clearing of new lands for cultivation required significant funds, and the [Buddhist] Church, grown rich in this period of intense faith, disposed of the sums necessary for the purchase of plow animals, plowing implements, and other equipment."[88]

Much of what we know about the extent of Buddhist economic activity comes from the vigorous actions of the Tang state in the 840s to break up monastic economic power, selling off their lands to others who would be more likely to pay taxes on the property. Because much of the land was gobbled up by officials and others striving to put together estates of their own (and to keep as much of their lands off the tax rolls as well), the goal of increasing the tax base of the Tang state was unrealized, and its decline and fall was a matter of just a few more decades.

Paradoxically, whereas Buddhist monasteries in the fifth through ninth centuries played an important role in China's environmental history by being agents of ecological change, Buddhist monasteries that managed to hang on into the late twentieth century have become important resources for reconstructing what original forests might have looked like. For as China has industrialized and its increasing population terraced hills to the top with rice paddies, Buddhist monasteries, especially in the south, have kept both their calm and their forests, giving ecologists important clues about what the environment might have been like in past centuries.

Tang-era Attitudes (and Actions) toward Nature

Although Buddhist monasteries caused unseen damage to China's animal life because of the ecological changes they brought about, Buddhist religious ideas, especially the injunctions against killing, did contribute to new sensibilities about nature among cultured Tang-era urbanites, as did readings of certain passages in Confucian and Daoist texts. The desire of the royal family to protect the capital city of Chang'an from the ravages of soil erosion from nearby hills, as well as keep the streets and canals the city neat and clean, also heightened awareness of the natural environment; the Tang legal code imposed stiff penalties on those who let their filth drain into the streets or sewers. Joy in experiencing beautiful mountains and clear streams was expressed in poems and paintings.

For many early-Tang artists, "sketching from nature was the normal practice," yielding "visually convincing" studies of horses, birds, insects, and flowers. But representational painting did not continue much past the mid-Tang with the rise of landscape painting,[89] less representational and more metaphorical. Monumental Chinese landscape painting was dominated by panoramic views of mountains and streams, with humans depicted as but a small part of the whole composition. In the words of one master, "Mountains are larger than trees, and trees are larger than human figures. If the mountains are not stacked up by the score, and if they are no larger than the trees, they will not look imposing. And if the trees are not stacked up by thc scorc, and if they are no larger than human figures, they will not look large." Chinese landscape paintings were not meant to be realistic representations of nature but "a vision of the cosmos as a complex, hierarchically ordered paradigm of human society" in which the great mountain is "like a ruler among his subjects, a master among servants."[90]

Nonetheless, this emerging love of nature coupled with the knowledge of the baleful effects of deforestation, notably expressed during the reign of the Xuanzong emperor (713–755 CE), "did not suffice to save the forests of China," in the words of Edward H. Schafer.[91] Schafer notes that need for fuel led to the cutting down of the magnificent trees that had been planted along the thoroughfares of Chang'an, and that burning pines for the soot that became ink for the brushes of China's clerks and scholars had deforested the slopes of the Taihang mountains. "Attempts to prohibit the slaughter of animals" also ran up against economic demand for protected species such as "kingfishers, whose feathers were used in jewelry, . . . muskdeer, which provided a popular scent for ladies of fashion, . . . martens, whose fur gave style to martial hats, and . . . alligators, whose tough hides were used to cover drums. And a thousand other species were wanted too for the several parts of their bodies where found to be useful. . . . Inevitably some species were hounded into extinction, and others became very rare."[92] Schafer sadly concludes that while "all of the psychologically necessary elements to produce sound policy for the protection of nature . . . were present in Tang times . . . , they were ultimately ineffective."[93] Satisfying the material needs of a growing human population trumped the conservation of nature, even when that idea was held so strongly by a powerful ruler.

Buddhist religious convictions sparked at least one other flash of concern about the fate of animals, eight centuries later during the late Ming dynasty (a period taken up in the next chapter). At a time of social unrest and growing poverty but amid a burst of commercial expansion, a Buddhist monk in the late sixteenth century not only revived the idea of not killing animals, but added one of "liberating" them. The twin practices of non-killing and liberating animals meant not just, for example, freeing flies from spider webs, but purchasing and freeing caged birds and other animals on the way to be slaughtered. This compassion for animals then sharpened the concern of at least some of China's elite for the plight of the poor and the weaker members of human society as well.[94]

CHINA'S MEDIEVAL INDUSTRIAL REVOLUTION[95]

Developments from the ninth to the thirteenth century, roughly from the late Tang dynasty (618–907) through the Song (960–1279), mark a watershed in Chinese history, and must be considered if we are to understand and interpret the causes and consequences of environmental change during the next thousand years. The Sui and early Tang rulers had reunited the empire, using both military force buttressed by calculated use of Buddhism to cement ties between regions and between rulers and ruled, and the construction of the Grand Canal (and other waterworks), coupled with the road and post system inherited and revived from the Qin and Han era, to link the Yangzi River basin with the bases of political power further north, further strengthening the ties that bound the empire together.

Though militarily strong and in many other ways a brilliant flowering of Chinese civilization, the Tang dynasty did have a structural weakness that led both to its demise and to the rise of new institutions that would further strengthen the bonds holding the Chinese empire together. Until the devastating An Lushan Rebellion of 755, the Tang state had rigorously implemented periodic land redistribution under the "equitable fields system," and maintained a state-regulated market system.[96] In the century or more after the An Lushan Rebellion, the Tang state no longer had the capability to periodically redistribute land, or to regulate markets. As a consequence, land became privately owned—much of it grabbed by wealthy and powerful people, leaving the vast majority of Chinese farmers without claim to land ownership—and markets for commodities, land, and capital began to operate freely. For the next thousand years, private property in land, and markets for land, labor, and capital, would become integral aspects of the Chinese system, and, as we will see in coming chapters, those institutions would have significant consequences for the nature of environmental change as well.

Those changes alone would seem to have been sufficient to have caused a significant departure in the pattern of Chinese history from about 1000 CE on, but there were more changes that also had lasting consequences. The founder of the Song dynasty (960-1279), Song Taizu, looking back at the causes of the fall of the Tang, identified the relative independence of the Tang military, and the source of military leaders from an aristocracy, as serious weaknesses. To strengthen the Song central state, Song Taizu made the civil service examination system the primary means by which men from any social class could enter government service, eliminating the aristocratic monopoly on government service and fostering upward social mobility, and he established clear civilian leadership of the military.[97] Like private property and free markets, the civil service examination system would mark the Chinese empire until the twentieth century. And to ensure that accumulated wealth could not be passed down from generation to generation, challenging the power of the central state, he imposed the rule that family wealth had to be equally divided among all sons.

And still there were additional social and economic changes from the late Tang through the Song dynasty. By 750, the population had recovered from the disasters following the collapse of the Han dynasty, reaching perhaps 75 million. By 1200, the population had increased to at least 120 million, or an additional 45 million people (see figure 4.5). The food supply had to increase dramatically to sustain that many more people, or even more if those people were to enjoy a higher standard of living. Those facts alone had significant implications for China's natural environment.

Year	Population (millions)	Cultivated Land (millions shi mou)	Per Capita Acreage
2	59	571	9.68
105	53	535	10.09
146	47	507	10.79
961	32	255	7.97
1109	121	666	5.50
1391	60	522	8.70
1581	200	793	3.97
1657	72	570	7.92
1776	268	886	3.31
1800	295	943	3.20
1848	426	1154	2.71

Fig. 4.5. China's Population and Cultivated Land Area, 2–1848 *Source:* Kang Chao, *Man and Land in Chinese History: An Economic Analysis* (Stanford: Stanford University Press, 1986).

Most important, during the course of the Tang dynasty, north China had become substantially deforested. That process, of course, had been a very long one. To summarize briefly: The loess lands of north China, where the earliest Chinese states—the Shang and the Zhou—emerged, probably had no forest cover to begin with. But as the Shang and Zhou spread east along the Yellow River and into the North China plain, existing forest was removed for farms. That process of conversion increased during the Han dynasty as iron axes and plows made opening new land easier, and as a consequence the population of Han China swelled to nearly 60 million. The disasters and steep population decline following the end of the Han and the invasions by nomads probably gave the environment a breather from human pressure, but forests may well not have regrown in north China—despite having a century or more to do so—because of the widespread use of former farmland for horse, sheep, and goat pasture, all of which prevented forest from regrowing. Hence, when the empire was reunited by the Sui, and as peaceful conditions for more than a century after the founding of the Tang allowed the human population to increase, farms replaced pasture. And, as we have seen, the creation of thousands of Buddhist monasteries, many in the remaining hills or wooded areas of north China, contributed to the treeless landscape.

Given the general deforestation of north China by about 900 CE, one wonders about a growing energy crisis. Certainly, people needed fuel for heat and cooking, and, as we will see shortly, industry required fuel too, nearly all of which had come from wood. Indeed, the evidence for a shortage of wood in the iron and steel industry is direct and comes from the Song dynasty, but the evidence of an energy shortage among the populace is more indirect. Certainly, there was enough wood around for cooking, as it was famously said during the Song that "the things people cannot do without every day are firewood, rice, oil, salt, soybean sauce, vinegar, and tea. Those who are slightly better off cannot go without [additional garnishes] and soup. Though they be the poorest people, this must always be so."[98]

On the other hand, the method of cooking now identified as "Chinese"—stir-frying of small pieces of vegetables and meat—became the main way food was cooked. Unlike Han times, when grains were cooked whole and meats roasted or braised—both of which required hours and lots of wood for the stove—stir-frying is quick and uses much less fuel. Moreover, there is evidence that much food was not even cooked, but eaten raw. A visiting Buddhist monk not only found Chinese food bland, compared with his native India, but more shockingly that "in China, people of the present time eat fish and vegetables mostly uncooked."[99] By the Song, eating thinly sliced raw fish and meat became a fashion, especially among urbanites and the well to do; it was "sushi."[100] Despite being elements of a distinctive Chinese cuisine, stir-frying and sushi also reflect the fact that firewood was becoming scarce and hence more valuable and expensive—though not totally unavailable, at times rationed.[101]

Such scarcity of wood proved to be problematic for the iron and steel industry. Until the Song, iron and steel had relied on charcoal for both fuel and carbon for steel; charcoal is made from wood heated in the absence of oxygen, which when then reburned can reach the "white hot" temperatures needed to make iron (see chapter 3). But when demand for iron and steel spiked during the Song, firewood and charcoal shortages spurred a search for coal as a substitute. Not only was the Song economy expanding, and hence generating demand for iron to be used as currency and for iron farm implements, a major reason the need for increased iron and steel output came about was because of the strategic concerns of the Song state for defense against northern nomadic enemies. The Song army swelled to 1.25 million men, and so did the need for steel for arrowheads and swords, and for iron for everything from carts to watchtowers and even warships. To meet these needs, historian Robert Hartwell estimates, production of iron increased twelvefold between 850 and 1050 CE to 150,000 tons, ten times the amount produced during the Han dynasty, and comparable to the amount produced in England in the early eighteenth century.[102]

That increase was fueled (literally) by coal. If only charcoal had been used, a forest of 22,000 medium-sized trees would have been required each year—and forests that size near the iron ore mines in north China no longer existed. Instead, most of the needed 276,000 tons of fuel came from coal mines. Moreover, coal began to substitute for firewood in heating homes and cooking in north China, especially the capital city of Kaifeng, and for firing furnaces in the brick and tile industries too. By 1100, only coal was being sold in the markets of the capital, and "an observer noted that Kaifeng relied on coal to such an extent that not a single dwelling burned firewood."[103]

The burning of such large amounts of coal in a city the size of Kaifeng—maybe a million residents in the eleventh century—must have affected air quality, especially in winter, but we really do not yet know. Coupled with the iron and steel smelters within a couple hundred miles of the capital, the air had to have been at least periodically befouled, if not regularly shrouded in gray haze. More research needs to be done on the environmental consequences of China's brief spurt of fossil fuel–fired industrialization. What we do know is that "the last seventy-five years of the Northern Song dynasty was a period when north China became the center of significant, perhaps revolutionary, changes in the sources of fuel; a time when coal became the most important source of heat for both industrial and domestic use."[104] If China's nascent industrial revolution rivaled that of England in the early nineteenth century, it is not unreasonable to expect that both experienced similar kinds and extent of industrial pollution.

The use of the term "revolution" to apply to Song China no doubt is apt, and is strengthened by the idea that China's "medieval economic revolution," a term coined by Mark Elvin, was accompanied by revolutions in farming (as we have seen), in water transport, in money and credit, in markets and urbanization, and in science and technology.[105] But the incipient industrial revolution did not continue.[106] Historians have debated the question "why not" for decades, and have provided numerous and often very complicated arguments, but the simplest may simply be that Song China was invaded, conquered, and destroyed by a series of northern nomadic peoples, starting with the Khitan, Tangut, and Jurchen, all of whom established states of one kind or another in the tenth and eleventh centuries, with the Jurchen attacking and conquering Kaifeng in 1126–27, forcing the Song government to flee south to the lower Yangzi and to re-establish its capital in the city of Hangzhou. The border between the Jurchen state in north China, which called itself the Jin dynasty, and the Song, was established about halfway between the Yangzi River and the Huai River to its north. The Song consequently lost access to both its iron and coal mines on the Shandong peninsula, which fell into enemy hands. A century later the Jurchen were subsequently taken over by the Mongols, who then warred on the Song until a final push in the 1260s led to the demise of the last Song emperor in 1279 and the rule of all of China by the Mongols. A significant indicator of the destructiveness of these wars, invasions, and foreign rule is that the population declined from a peak of 110–120 million in 1200 to perhaps 75 million a century and a half later—a staggering loss of 35 million to 45 million people, enough to bring any industrial development to a halt. Kaifeng alone shrunk to less than 90,000 residents by 1330.[107]

COLONIZING SICHUAN AND CATEGORIZING OTHERS

In the meantime, like the Han and Tang dynasties before it, the Song was quite interested in colonizing frontier areas to tap additional resources necessary for maintaining a strong military. Where the Han had expended considerable energy colonizing the northwest, and the Tang colonizing Lingnan in the south, the Song trained most of its colonizing energies to the west on the province of Sichuan (see maps 2.1, 2.2, and 2.3).

Not as remote or exotic as Lingnan, Sichuan in China's west had been known to Chinese during the Warring States period as the southern kingdoms of Shu and Ba that had been conquered and appended to the state of Qin in the fourth-century BCE. This area later became the province of Sichuan, a basin ringed by mountains and connected with the rest of the Chinese world by the road over the Qinling mountains built during Qin-Han times, and later via the "Three Gorges" that the Yangzi River flowed through on its way east to the ocean. Those are the same Three Gorges that have recently been dammed and flooded in the largest hydroelectric power scheme in the world, a topic discussed in chapter 7.

Most of Sichuan, but especially its eastern and southern parts, was hilly and mountainous, and covered with a subtropical broadleaf evergreen forest. Early inhabitants of the region thus tended to settle on river terraces and around Lake Dian, where rice was cultivated as early as 1200 BCE (around the same time that the Shang city of Anyang flourished). By the Warring States period a people the Han Chinese called the Dian had created a culture based around wet-rice cultivation and domesticated animals (especially cattle) and had a relatively sophisticated bronze industry. Conquered by the Qin state in the fourth-century BCE, Chinese with iron plows and axes began moving into the lowlands settled by the Dian. Over the following centuries, the Dian were assimilated by the Han Chinese, and by 1000 CE were virtually extinct.

A second group, a "warlike confederation of tribes" called the Lao, appeared abruptly in the fourth century CE, apparently migrating in from further east and hence probably pushed there by advancing Han Chinese. The Lao settled in the lowlands along the rivers, and practiced shifting agriculture, burning part of the forest, planting taro or millet in the ashes, harvesting the crops for a couple of years before the nutrients released from the burned trees were exhausted, and then moving on to a new patch of forest. Whether they did so in a regular pattern, returning after twenty or thirty years to forest previously burned and regrown, or constantly moving to new ground, is not known.

What is known is that the Lao, gathering their sustenance from the lowlands, bore the brunt of the Han Chinese expansion. The Chinese were agriculturalists, and with their iron plows and axes, could more easily remove forest and break open the heavy soil. As the Han Chinese pushed the Lao out of the lowlands, some retreated to the hills and mountains, a niche for humans already taken by others (as we will see below), but mostly they accommodated themselves to the Han Chinese and accepted their economic and political dominance, largely because the Han Chinese had the military power of their well-organized state to back them up, a part of the story that we'll take up shortly.

A third people, the Tibertan-Burman speaking Nuoso, also known as the Yi, were also present when the Han Chinese arrived, but they were an upland people who preferred the resources and protection afforded by living in the hills. They created fortified villages on hilltops, accessible only by narrow trails, within which were their villages with fresh water supplies, gardens, and paddocks for their livestock, including sheep, oxen, and horses. The Yi were not easily conquered or assimilated by the Han Chinese; they apparently also had their own writing system.[108] Nor were they gentle stewards of their environment. In fact, according to historian Richard von Glahn, the Yi transformed the region's natural environment.[109]

In the mountains, the Yi set fire to the forests, not to make way for agriculture, but to create grasslands for their livestock. This way of life was quite successful, for as the Yi population increased, they moved lower down the hillsides until they got into lowland forests, which they also burned, and where they then practiced shifting cultivation. As Han Chinese battled the Yi for these lowlands, the Yi moved back up into their hilltop fortresses. "Even as Han settlers pushed into the more remote river valleys, the 'nests and lairs' of the natives dotted hills and forests all around them."[110]

These interactions among the various peoples who inhabited the same general area, and between the human population and their natural environment, took centuries to unfold. Even after the reunification by the Sui of the empire and then the rule of the Tang, the situation was complex and undetermined as to who or which strategy for extracting sustenance from the environment would prevail. What is clear is that the Dian, the Lao, and the Yi had all altered the environment to suit their needs, before, during, and after the Han Chinese began moving in. In Sichuan, the Chinese confronted not a virgin wilderness, but an environment already in the process of transformation by human action.

But during the Song era (960–1279 CE), the Han Chinese established their cultural hegemony, and then reshaped the Sichuan environment to meet their needs. Already during the Tang, wealthy and powerful Han Chinese—"local magnates," in von Glahn's words—had established garrisons from which they constantly encroached on native lands. Han Chinese farming families worked the fields during the day, and for safety retreated behind their walls at night. This working population also provided the bulk of the fighting force for the local magnates, for the Yi and Lao did not give up their lands without a fight. The Han Chinese might have slowly picked away at native lands and ultimately have dominated in any event, but during the eleventh century, the Song Chinese state saw the environment of Sichuan as a resource to be tapped to support their military—but the natives had to be subdued or destroyed. Bloody conflicts in the mid-eleventh century gave way to a generally expansionist frontier policy, with wars of conquest being waged against natives not just in Sichuan but also elsewhere in the southern frontier regions.

The Song state was interested in the iron and salt of Sichuan—and especially in the revenues it could capture from their extraction and sale in state monopolies—but the effect of the wars against the natives of Sichuan was to make the place safe for Chinese farming families. State lands were offered to immigrants, as were seed, tools, and tax exemptions for several years. Han Chinese population growth pushed non-Chinese out of the lowlands, and as the Chinese filled up the lowlands, they began to eye the hills and mountains to expand their farms. The major technological difficulty the farmers faced was that wet-rice cultivation required irrigation. In the lowlands and river valleys, those requirements could be met, but not in the hills. The solution there was to terrace the hillsides and dig ponds to capture the plentiful rainfall, then to plant the early-ripening varieties of rice. Much of Sichuan was transformed this way.

Not only did non-Chinese and Chinese agricultural practices lead to deforestation, but so too did logging. "In 1136 a memorialist protested that all along the frontier of southern Sichuan the Han inhabitants engaged in timber cutting, shipbuilding, and weapons manufacture, with the result that the 'forbidden hills' separating the Han from the native territories had been almost completely denuded."[111]

Organizational Context

To complete this section, we need to consider the organizational context within which the Sichuan environment was transformed. Removing forest and opening up land, let alone mining and timbering, are projects that require considerable amounts of labor and the ability to coordinate that labor for a collective end. We really do not know how the Dian, the Lao, or the Yi organized themselves, but the latter two have been described as "tribes," an imprecise term to be sure but one generally referring to groupings of several families headed by an elder (or a group of elders) who have respect and insight (if not magical powers), and hence the ability to command the labor of others.

The Han Chinese were organized differently. Mention has already been made of the "local magnates" who directed farming families to encroach on native lands. But the elemental unit of that organization was the peasant farming family: husband, wife, children, perhaps a grandparent or two. This was the unit that did the work, and that eventually made cropping and marketing decisions on what and how much to plant. In Sichuan, the actions of the Song state in building military support for its aggressive frontier policy undermined the power and position of the local magnates, and encouraged the formation of villages given corporate existence by the state, with village headmen (usually the more wealthy in the village) to organize payment of taxes and labor to the state. In some other provinces, such as neighboring Hunan, an additional organization emerged—the lineage—that tied families together and provided resources for collective effort, but that too was coincident with, or subsumed under, the corporate village.

Thus regardless of who actually "owned" the land that the peasant family farmed (the state, large landowners, the peasant family, "magnates"—as we will see, this could become very complicated), the decision-making economic unit was the Han

Chinese peasant farming family, most often living in villages of anywhere from a few families to several hundred. Of course peasant villagers on their own would not have been able to compete militarily with the better-organized and usually more "fierce" native peoples. So with the reestablishment of the Chinese empire under the Sui and Tang, and continuing in the Song, the Chinese state provided the military muscle to "pacify" the natives, whether by coercion, force, cooperation, or cooptation.

Chinese Views of "Barbarians" and Others

Over the incredibly complex natural and human environment of the frontier regions, first the Tang and then later dynasties cast an administrative net to capture, claim, and rule the frontier. The areas that had become reliably Chinese—that is, those areas mostly in the lowlands that had become marked by Han Chinese farming families living in villages—became "counties," administered by Chinese bureaucrats appointed by and responsible to the emperor. In areas that remained dominated by "natives," the Chinese attempted to find hereditary native chiefs who would be amenable to Chinese overlordship and who demonstrated that fealty by periodically offering up "tribute" to the agents of the Chinese state. These districts were known as "bridled and haltered" districts, or "loosely governed" (*jimi*) districts.

The "Cooked" and the "Raw"

This arrangement was, of course, one made from the point of view of the Chinese and especially the leaders of their states, and accepted (or not) by non-Chinese peoples of the frontier or inner periphery. Possibly from Shang times, and certainly from the Zhou, the Chinese central state had defined those outside of its domain generally as "barbarians." The Zhou tended to classify these barbarians into four types (the Eastern Yi, Eastern Rong, Northern Di, and Southern Man), and as the Chinese encountered more peoples, they gave them other names (e.g., Lao, Miao, Lolo or any of the other score already mentioned in this book). China's colonizing projects from the Han through the Song (and, as we will see in the following chapters, through the Ming and Qing to the present) have seen their rule as "civilizing" the "barbarians": transforming them (*hua*) through their acceptance of the Chinese sovereign, their education, and the recasting of their local ecologies into Chinese-style farms.

The Chinese referred to peoples who accepted this arrangement as "cooked" (*sheng*) barbarians, while those peoples who resisted Chinese rule were known as the "raw" (*shu*) barbarians. Over time, the cooked might even become Chinese (fully assimilated, we might say). The "raw," though, represented in many ways not just those peoples who the Chinese state could not control—the vast region of "Zomia," in James C. Scott's analysis[112]—but also environments and ecologies beyond the control and ability of the Chinese to transform. To that extent, Chinese depicted the "raw" barbarians in animalistic terms, putting elements of their writing system standing for "insect" or "dog" or "beast" with the homophone of the names for those peoples. The environments that the "raw" inhabited as well repelled the Chinese transformative capacities.[113] We will see these themes continued, especially in the next chapter.

Animals

And what about animals? We cannot know what happened to all species, so as I mentioned in the Introduction, one way to gauge ecological change is to follow two "star species," the elephant and the tiger, whose existence points to healthy ecosystems all the way down to the insects and bacteria decomposing the leaves on the forest floor.

We know that tigers were still present in north China during the era of division following the end of Han. To exist, tigers need forest cover, so the fact that tigers were to be found in some places in north China in the fifth century implies the existence of a nearby forest. But maybe not too much forest, for one of the reasons that tigers became "man-eating" and preyed on humans was because of the destruction of their habitat and food sources. So even by the fifth century, tiger habitat in north China was being constricted. We can be quite certain that just as forest was removed for farms during the Sui and Tang dynasties, tiger habitat, too, was removed. By the Song, probably the only place tigers continued to exist in north China was in whatever forest remnants remained, and in the vast swamps between the Huai and Yangzi Rivers.

So too with elephants. Where elephants were found throughout north China before 600 CE, with unity under the Sui and Tang and progressive deforestation of the North China plain,[114] elephants, too, disappeared from that part of China, and accounts of tigers and elephants during the Song dynasty come mostly from south China. According to Edward Schafer, "Elephants were still abundant in the mountainous parts of [Lingnan] in the ninth century, and we are not surprised to read of herds in coastal Lingnan in the tenth."[115] By the middle of the eleventh century, Mark Elvin thinks that elephants had been pushed not just from north China but from most of the Yangzi River valley as well. If so, then the forest cover of most of that region had been removed as well, although it seems likely that hills and uplands south of the Yangzi remained forested. Those areas would have continued to provide habitat for tigers, but not for the lowland dwelling elephants,[116] which were gone from most of Chinese-controlled territory by 1400.[117]

LANDSCAPES AND WATER CONTROL

North China

That north China had become deforested during the Tang, pushing the range of elephants and tigers mostly south of the Yangzi River, does not mean that north China was a featureless plain. In various places walled cities, some county seats and the others larger cities, rose off the plain. In rural areas, the land had become divided into strips several hundred yards long, largely because of the periodic redistributions of land under the "equitable fields" system and because of the use of ox-pulled plows. Whether or not those strips predate the Sui and Tang, and perhaps even follow the ancient "well field" system of the Zhou dynasty, as Frank Leeming has suggested, it is pretty clear both that farmers' fields were laid out by those strips, and that nearly all of the North China plain was laid out that way, with straight north-south and east-west lines[118] (see figure 4.6). Paths and roads followed those rectangular lines, and if rural north China in the twentieth century (even today, for that matter; see figure 4.7) is a guide, villagers planted trees

Fig. 4.6. Rectilinear Farmland Layout on the North China Plain *Source:* George B. Cressey, *Asia's Lands and Peoples* (New York: McGraw-Hill, 1963), 130.

Fig. 4.7. North China Farmland, ca. 2000 *Source:* Author.

along those lines as well. Hills, mountains, and seacoasts were not rectilinear, and so had the appearance of green bumps rising from the farmland.

Leeming is quite certain that the rectilinear landscape of the North China plain was totally absent in southern China. That assessment corresponds with my sense that the requirements of wet-rice agriculture prohibited the use of the equitable fields system from the Yangzi River valley on south. Besides, southern China much more resembled a crinkled-up piece of paper, with numerous streams and rivers running through hills and mountains, than a landscape easily turned into rectangles on the ground. The difference between north and south China thus was not merely geographical, cultural, or historical but visual as well. Mostly, the North China plain was exceptionally flat, giving rise to significant hydrological problems brought about by attempts to "control" the Yellow River.

Yellow River Water "Control"

The "Yellow" River may have had a respite following the collapse of the Han dynasty, for a fifth-century nomadic ruler who encamped within the great bend of the river exclaimed about the beauty of the place and its extensive grasslands, woods, and clear streams,[119] but by the Tang it was commonly referred to as "the Yellow River"[120] because of the huge amounts of yellow soil eroded from the loess lands and carried along by the river. Chinese and nomadic conquest states had had to contend with the River, and to devise strategies for dealing with the silt content. To periodically scour the riverbed by confining it closely between high dikes? To allow the flood waters to spread broadly between widely spaced dikes?

Either way, the Yellow River came to be defined by dikes, no matter how close or loosely they kept the river flowing, and the riverbed kept rising. The dikes needed annual maintenance and repair, so the state organized the work and required local villagers to work a certain number of days on it, itself providing the necessary tools and capital for the job. To raise the dikes, soil was dug from nearby the river, lowering the land nearest the river and heightening the difference between the river and the surrounding land. Seepage turned many of these depressions into swamps, and because the suspended salts in the Yellow River could not be flushed away, a swath of salinated land up to two miles wide followed the course of the River, rendering that land unproductive.[121]

When the Sui dynasty rulers built the Grand Canal and connected the drainage systems of the Yellow and Yangzi Rivers, a whole new set of issues arose: the Canal took in water from the Yellow River, and hence its silt content as well.[122] So the Canal had to be dredged, too; sometimes the intake of Yellow River water was stopped up and the canal dried so that it could be dredged, but this meant closing the canal for several months each year, defeating its main purpose of ensuring the flow of grain from the lower Yangzi River to the north to supply the Tang capital at Chang'an, and even more importantly, the Tang troops defending the empire from northern enemies. Water was acquiring a strategic significance.

When the new Song state established its capital at Kaifeng, on a section of the Canal near the confluence with the Yellow River, the strategic importance of both escalated in the minds of state officials. Northern enemies were not at all far away—the border with the Khitan Liao state was the Yellow River where it discharged into the Gulf of

Bohai. The Yellow River thus kept the enemy's mounted cavalry at bay, even after the Khitan had in turn been conquered by another nomadic group, the Jurchen.

Where the Yellow River turned north and branched its way to the Gulf of Bohai, Song officials had the choices conferred on them by past conservators of the River when variable amounts of monsoonal rain and winter snow melt sent unknown amounts of water gushing down the Yellow River: to cut diversion channels to lessen the force of the current, or to maintain the system of dikes, sometimes with jetties built into the stream to lessen its strength and sometimes with huge rolls of vegetation strategically placed to protect the dikes. Still, the Yellow River dikes were periodically breached, as in 1019, when the River flooded thirty cities, or again in 1048, when it opened several new courses, none of which was easily controlled. Still, the 1048 flood began eighty years of Yellow River flooding to its north into agriculturally rich Hebei province, causing vast economic, demographic, and environmental damage, a part of the story that will be taken up shortly.

With the Yellow River now more frequently breaching its dikes and flooding surrounding towns and farmland, Song officials debated what should be done to maintain the River as a strategic defense against the Jurchen, and built their plans and projects into state budgets, precipitating numerous political struggles over control over resources and complaints about the lack of resources to accomplish particular goals.

The debate was resolved in 1126 when Jurchen forces besieged Kaifeng, and in 1127 when they returned to take the city. In the winter of 1128, the Chinese governor of Kaifeng, trying to save the capital region from Jurchen forces, intentionally breached the Yellow River dikes some 50 miles north of Kaifeng, hoping the flood would stem the invasion and save the capital. He was mistaken in that judgment, and by 1194 the flooding and silting ultimately caused the Yellow River to seek a wholly new, southerly route to the ocean, taking over the course of the Qing River before invading the Huai River, and forming a huge new lake, aptly called "Vast Flood Lake" (*Hong ze hu*), before entering the sea south of the Shandong peninsula, and turning that part of the ocean into the "Yellow Sea." That mouth of the Yellow River was to remain there until the middle of the nineteenth century, when once again it was used to slow the advance of military enemy of the state, a story to be taken up in chapter 6.

Changing the course of the Yellow River also kept the River and its mouth to the sea in Chinese hands—a major success, if one can call it that. As Christian Lamouroux argues, "Hydraulic action was the ultimate recourse against enemy superiority, and more than a military option: it was necessary to keep the Yellow River within the empire, since it was a strategic resource that the Song had been developing for more than a century to defend itself against external attack. As it happened, nature was to put this program of defense into effect, in that it was precisely the waters of the Yellow River that, having captured the lower course of the Huai, were to serve as the new official frontier between the state of Jin and that of the Song once this latter had fallen back southward to their new capital at Hangzhou."[123] Hence the Song period is divided into the Northern Song (960–1127) and the Southern Song (1127–1279).

The southward shift of the mouth of the Yellow River had other ecological consequences as well, starting with the silt that settled out to make a rather large delta and several new outlets to the sea. But, curiously, the ocean currents also carried substantial amounts of that sediment another 200 miles south to Hangzhou Bay, the region

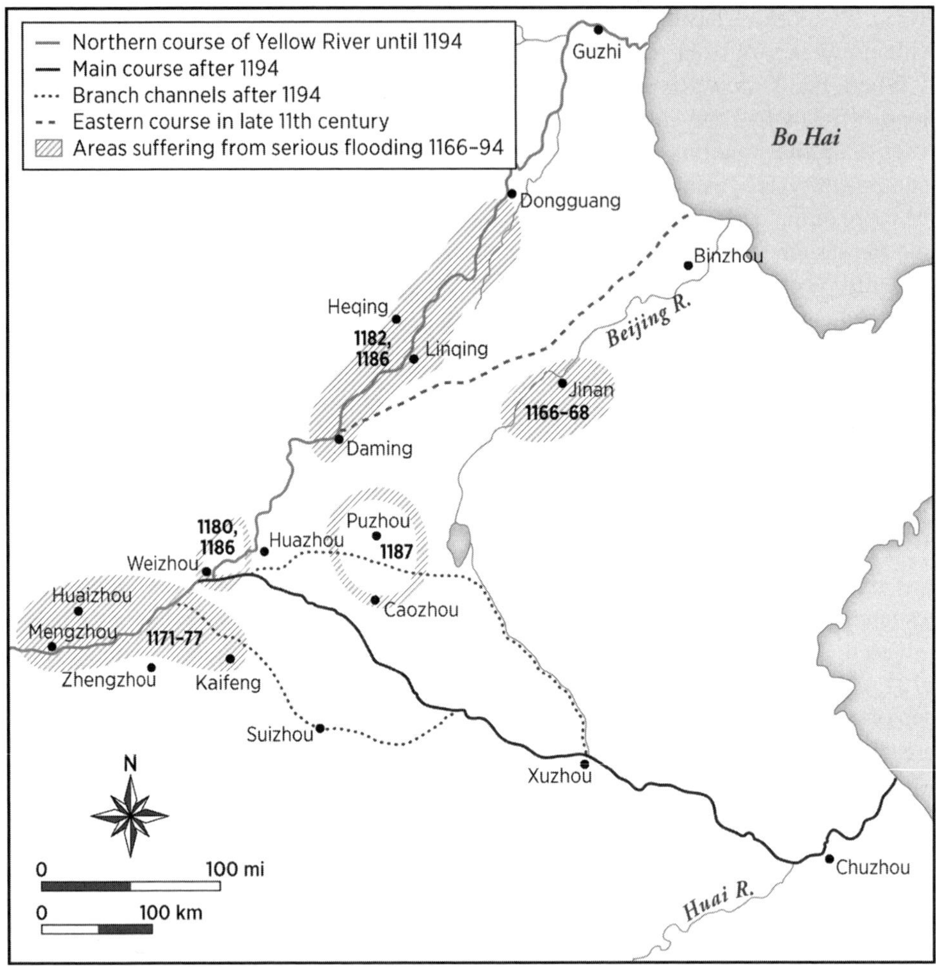

Map 4.7. The Change of the Yellow River's Course, 1194 *Source:* Adapted from Denis C. Twitchett and Herbert Franke, eds., *Alien Regimes and Border States, 710–1368,* vol. 6 of *The Cambridge History of China* (New York: Cambridge University Press, 1995), 246.

discussed earlier where the new water control technologies were enhancing wet-rice cultivation. To make a long but fascinating story rather short, the new silt from the Yellow River added to the land available to farmers along the coast in Jiangsu province, thereby increasing the amount of rice produced from this already agriculturally rich area. And because the Song government established their capital at Hangzhou after fleeing south, it had ready access to the agricultural and human wealth already being produced in the lower Yangzi region.[124]

Environmental Decline on the North China Plain, 1048–1128[125]

For nearly a millennium, the Yellow River had flowed in a course that led to its emptying into the Yellow Sea north of the Shandong peninsula. The 1194 shift of its course south by taking over the Huai River would have immense environmental consequences, especially in the nineteenth century, as we will see in chapter 6. But what is not well known is that before the largely human-engineered shift of the Yellow River into a southern course, flooding that began in 1048 sent the river on a more northerly course through portions of Hebei province that had not been flooded before.

Although the immediate causes of the 1048 flood are not known, the Yellow River broke through its northern banks about 50 miles north of the capital, Kaifeng. The floodwaters surged north through the nearly flat plain, emptying into the Yellow Sea near the present-day city of Tianjin. Historian Ling Zhang estimates that a million people died or fled. Officials were so caught off guard that they did not know how to respond, and in fact it took them eight years to figure out a course of action. Certainly, the long-term cause was the amount of silt that kept raising the riverbed in its lower reaches, pushing water levels higher and higher up stream. After the 1048 breach, about 70 percent of the Yellow River waters flowed in those new northerly flood channels, flopping about every year or two and causing immense damage, with about 30 percent continuing in its old channel. Officials thought about more evenly dividing the Yellow River waters between those two routes to lessen the likelihood of flooding, but the lesser amount of slower flowing water simply allowed more silt to build up. The silt buildup then led to another sizeable flood in 1068, and another rivercourse even further to the west. More floods hit in 1086, 1087, 1093–94, 1099, and 1108.

The flooding and shifting course of the Yellow River had severe environmental consequences. The silt that it deposited across the North China plain blocked up many smaller local rivers, causing them to change course or dry up altogether. To repair the dike ruptures, local residents chopped down trees and bushes from nearby hills and mountains in an attempt to shore up the embankments. In the words of historian Ling Zhang, "they ended up deforesting their province."[126] By the mid-1070s, the Taihang Mountains "lost their pine forests and became bald."[127]

Because the plain is so flat and the floodwaters could not drain away, the land was waterlogged and salinized. In the words of one official, "In places where river water stagnates, not an inch of grass grows; instead, white saline is generated."[128] Coupled with sterile silt, vast expanses of land lost their cover of vegetation, and wind blew the sand across the plain and into sand dunes: "Erosion followed, making sandization the severe environmental problem that would characterize Hebei from the eleventh century up to modern times."[129] Lakes and ponds silted up; even a city "was buried beneath the Yellow River's silt."[130] And the silt quickly became infertile: "After the [Yellow River's] water recedes," a Song-era history recorded, "the sediment is a fertile glutinous soil in the summer. It then becomes a yellowish dead soil in the early autumn. . . . Next it becomes a whitish dead soil in the deep autumn. After the first frost, it becomes sand completely."[131] Much formerly fertile land on the North China plain became sand. After Song officials intentionally tried to block the Jurchen invaders from attacking Kaifeng by breaching the southern embankments of the Yellow River, which eventually did turn south in 1194, the Yellow River's abandoned riverbed in the north became a source of sand that was picked up by winds into sandstorms that coursed over the region. A Korean visitor a few centuries later observed that "the white sand extends without end. In the wilderness, grass appears scarce, various crops do not grow, and human settlements are few."[132] Sandstorms then plagued the region for nine centuries.

The flooding in 1048 that changed the Yellow River to a northerly course, in the words of Ling Zhang, "initiated eight decades of progressive environmental degradation there."[133] And as the environment deteriorated, so too did agriculture, economic activity, and population density. As we will see in chapter 6, a similar story unfolded in the mid-nineteenth century when a combination of silt build up and declining state capabilities led to another change of course for the Yellow River.

South China: The Making of the Pearl River Delta[134]

These surprisingly interrelated processes of war and nature also came to bear on the creation of an important agricultural region in China, the Pearl River delta in the south. For the first millennium after Chinese settlers moved into Lingnan, what we now call the Pearl River delta and know as one of the most agriculturally rich and productive regions of China, second only to the Yangzi River delta, was not yet a delta, but in fact still was open sea, albeit a fairly shallow bay. Residents of Guangzhou, then called Nanhai, or "the south sea," looked out onto a bay dotted with islands.

In the 1975 Landsat photo in figure 4.8, Guangzhou is just about in the middle, just west of where two rivers merge; two thousand years ago, the area to the south and west that is now a delta was an open estuary. The Landsat photo also shows a fairly heavy amount of silt being carried in the water of the Pearl River estuary. It looks as if the creation of the Pearl River delta might have been a natural process by which silt naturally in the river water just naturally settled out to form the delta. But that's not what happened.

To be sure, silt carried downstream in the West, North, and East Rivers had been settling out in the bay, slowly creating the upper reaches of the delta. But because the silt content of these rivers was exceptionally low, the natural processes by which the delta was being created worked extremely slowly. Then, beginning in the eleventh century (during the Song dynasty), the delta began to grow more rapidly, and in the fourteenth century (during the Yuan dynasty) accelerated even faster. The series of four maps of

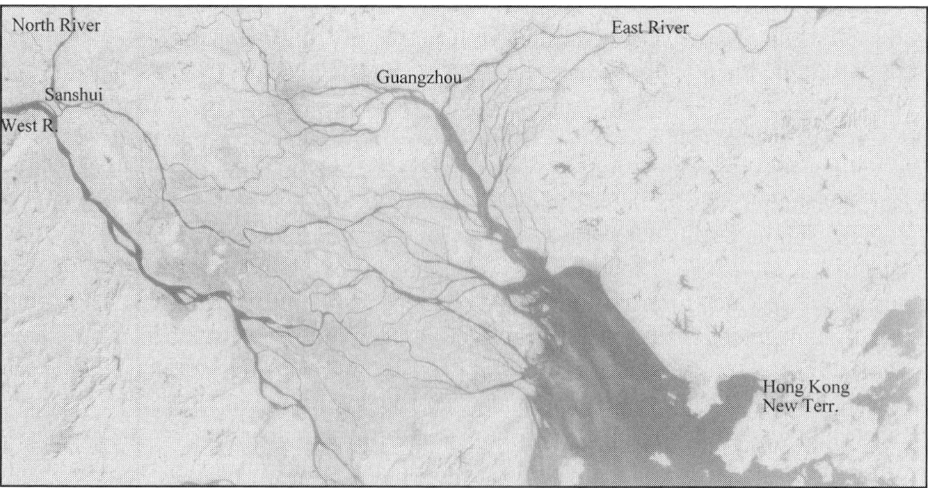

Fig. 4.8. Landsat Photo of the Pearl River Delta, December 14, 1975

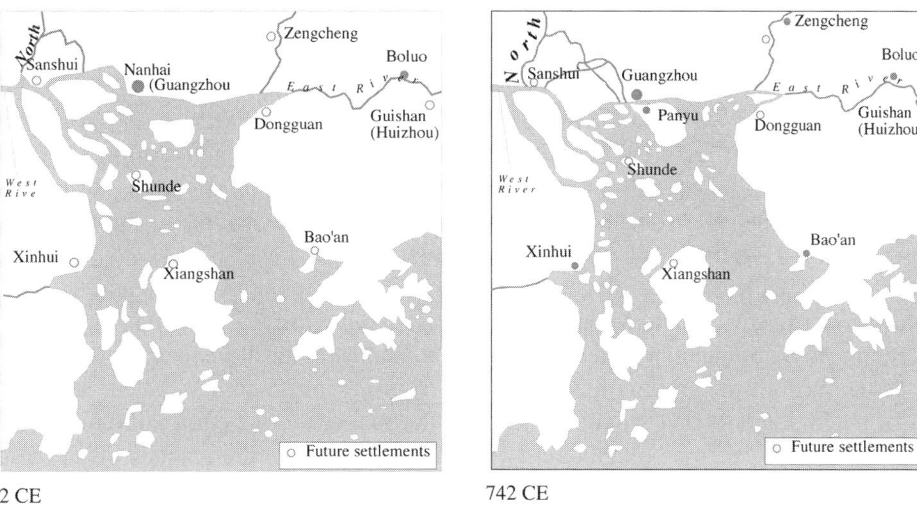

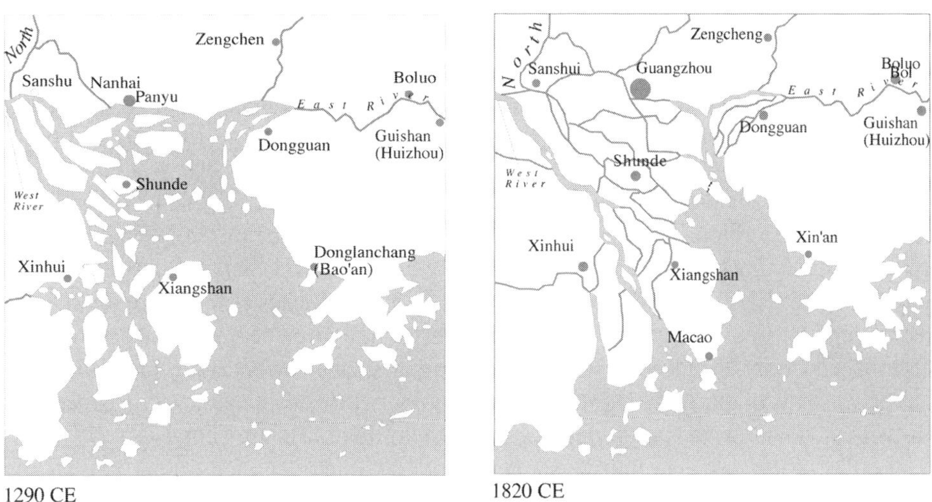

Fig. 4.9. The Pearl River Delta, 2–1820 CE *Source:* Robert B. Marks, *Tigers, Rice, Silk and Silt: Environment and Economy in Late Imperial South China* (New York: Cambridge University Press, 1998), 68.

the Pearl River delta (figure 4.9), chosen to correspond with the dates for which we have population data, shows the buildup of the delta. During the seven centuries from the Han to the Tang, the delta barely changed, with the bay remaining filled with water. By the Song dynasty, however, enough of the delta had emerged south of Guangzhou to block the view of the ocean, and by the Yuan dynasty alluvial sand bars appeared off the coast where the East River emptied into the bay. Certainly, though, the largest increases in the size of the Pearl River delta occurred from the Yuan dynasty on. Where virtually no change had occurred in the nine centuries after the founding of the Han, in the 300 years from 1290 to 1582, what had been the island of Xiangshan became connected to the mainland. Both the change in the shape of the delta over time, and the rate of the change itself, are interesting and significant: what accounts for both?

In the title to this section, I referred to the "making" of the Pearl River delta. I chose the word "making" specifically to refer to the action of humans, for—more than anything else—people made the Pearl River delta. Involved in this story are, in chronological order, the early settlement patterns and agricultural technology of the Chinese in-migrants; the building of water control projects in the lower reaches of the West, North, and East Rivers; the Mongol invasion of south China in the 1270s and the consequent displacement of the Chinese population from northern Guangdong to islands in the Pearl River estuary; and the creation of new lands off the islands in the estuary.

How much of the original forest the settlers burned off is not at all clear, nor is it clear whether the forest was given sufficient time to recover its composition of broadleaf evergreens before being burned off again, nor whether the scrubby *pinus massoniana* took the place of the broadleafs. What does seem to be quite certain, though, is that the slash-and-burn agriculture practiced in the upper reaches of the drainage system opened the hills to greater erosion and hence to a higher silt content flowing downstream in the West, North, and East Rivers.

Until the eleventh century, much of this silt did not reach the Pearl River delta, but rather was deposited in the flood plains in the lower reaches of the West, North, and East rivers. Much like the end of a garden hose under high pressure, the lower courses of these rivers flopped around from one outlet to another when monsoonal rains sent water gushing through the system, filling the flood plains with silt-laden water. When the floodwaters receded, silt and nutrients were left behind. Clearly, the flood plains of the lower reaches of these rivers, especially the area near the confluence of the West and North Rivers, thereby contained fertile soils with great agricultural potential. But they had two related problems: flooding and malaria. Before the upper reaches of the future Pearl River delta could become the densely populated, agriculturally rich center of the south China regional economy, the Chinese would have to either change the swampy environment of the flood plains of the West, North, and East Rivers, or else adapt to that environment, for the south China lowlands were not hospitable to northern Chinese people.

Flood Control[135]

South China experienced two kinds of water control problems: too much water, resulting in flooding, and too little or irregular supplies of water during the growing season; the summer monsoon rainfall pattern and the Pearl River drainage system accentuated both. When the monsoons brought the rain to Lingnan, most fell in the four summer months, swelling the often nearly dry riverbeds. From the west, all the rain gathered into the catchment basin that emptied into the West River, and then spilled from Wuzhou down into Guangdong province. From the north, all of the rain gathered into the North River. The West and North Rivers joined at Sanshui ("Three Rivers") some 10 miles west of the city of Guangzhou, forming the headwaters of the Pearl River delta. From the east, rain drained into the East River basin, pouring into the Pearl River to the east of Guangzhou.

The normal rainfall patterns thus poured huge amounts of water into the system in a very short period of time. Naturally, the lower reaches of the rivers flooded every year, depositing ever-greater amounts of silt eroded from the burned-off hills further upriver. As early as 809 (during the Tang dynasty), the construction of levees prevented the West River from following the southern of two branches to the confluence with the North River, restricting the flow to the northern branch. The levees not only opened a flood plain to agriculture, but also sent all the silt-laden floodwaters further downstream. Controlling the flooding at the confluence of the West and North Rivers thus was among the first large-scale water control projects in south China to be tackled.

Around 1100, work commenced on the Sang Yuan Wei (or Mulberry Garden polder). When it was completed, it was about 28 miles long and protected about 100,000 acres of land from flooding, inaugurating a new era of agricultural development in that part of south China. About the same time that the Sang Yuan Wei was being built, sea walls along the coast also were under construction. Nearly 48 miles of sea wall was constructed during the Shaoxing era (1131–62 CE), creating about 160,000 acres of arable land by protecting it from periodic inundation by tides and typhoons, and, no doubt, eliminating the mangrove forests there as well.

According to statistics compiled by Ye Xian'en and Tan Dihua, in Song times twenty-eight earthen work dikes or embankments were built in the upper reaches of Pearl River delta, totaling about 125 miles in length and protecting nearly 400,000 acres; during the Yuan dynasty an additional thirty-four embankments were built, adding about 100 miles to the length of the levee system. In other words, the embankments extended for about 200 miles (or about 100 miles of river, if dikes were on both banks), and protected about 20 percent of the cultivated land.

These flood control levees had the effect of pinning each river diked into a single course, so that rather than meandering and spilling into numerous courses during the monsoon season, rivers ran straight for the bay. The flood plains, of course, then were opened for agricultural production. But these waterworks begun in the Song had other environmental consequences as well. Draining the swampy backwaters that had remained after the flood waters receded altered the ecological conditions that had favored the malaria-carrying *Anopheles* mosquito, rendering the areas so opened less deadly to Chinese originally from the north.

Equally important, however, the flood control works channeled the silt away from the former flood plains and directed it further downstream to the headwaters of the Pearl River estuary. As a consequence both of the slash-and-burn agriculture in the hills and of the water control works, the amount of silt pouring into the Pearl River thus increased significantly from the eleventh century onward. The changes to the Pearl River delta that the increased amount of silt precipitated are evident in the maps of the delta. What is not evident, however, is that although more silt entered the upper reaches of the delta, it just might have continued to flow further into the bay had it not been "captured" by pioneers who fled to the safety of rocky islands in the estuary in the face of the Mongol invasion of the 1270s.

Fearing the Mongols more than malaria or adversity, and perhaps hoping to find additional maritime escape routes, the refugees fled the malaria-free hills in the way of the Mongol invasion route and settled on small islands that dotted the Pearl River estuary. Even today, the relics of that settlement pattern can be seen in the towns situated on what once were islands, but now are hills in an ocean of alluvial soil. Most expressive of this is the town of Shawan in the midst of the delta, which hugs the southern slope of the island/hill; Shawan means "bay of sand," which in 1276 no doubt it was.

How much cultivable land was available to the settlers of places such as Shawan in the fourteenth century is not known. No doubt some alluvium had been deposited by natural processes, perhaps speeded up a bit by the slash-and-burn agriculture practiced in the hill regions. As the water from the West and North Rivers flowed into the bay and around the islands, the current slowed on the "leeward" side, allowing the silt to settle out. But the new residents in the bay were not content to let slow natural processes create their agricultural land.

Fields Captured from the Sea[136]

In what became the Pearl River delta, settlers created new fields from the sand bars that formed wherever the current slowed sufficiently for the transported sediment to settle, but mostly on the downstream side of islands, or on the outward side of river bends. Called "*shatan*" ("sand flats") or "*shatian*" ("sand fields") (see figure 4.10), these fields truly were new, having literally arisen from the water. Unlike polders or enclosed fields that had been reclaimed from swamps or coastal flats, the *shatian* "grew" in the Pearl River, adding land where none had previously existed.

The particular topographical and hydrological conditions of the Pearl River estuary and the modifications to both caused by diking contributed to the creation of *shatian*. Before the Sang Yuan Wei and other dikes had been built at the headwaters of the delta, the floodwaters of the West and North Rivers spilled over the riverbanks, depositing the sediment in the swamps bordering the river channels. Some of the silt was carried further down into what was then a bay, creating the delta. But when the dikes were built to prevent flooding, the river course was fixed and the sediment did not settle until further downstream.

Certainly, some of the *shatian* emerged by natural processes, but the majority were constructed. The method of creating *shatian* was relatively simple, but did require years until the land was usable. When a sandbar arose by natural means close to the water level, rocks were thrown around its perimeter not merely to fix the existing sand in place, but also to capture more sediment. After a more substantial enclosure was built, the sediment was "transformed" by planting legumes (which fix nitrogen in the soil). After three to five years, the *shatian* would be ready for rice. According to the seventeenth-century writer Qu Dajun, a three-year fallow period followed three years of growing rice.

Once one *shatian* was created, more silt would build up on its downstream side. This silt would be captured by the process described above to create more *shatian*, and so on, until a whole series of *shatian* extended the cultivated land area to several thousand acres. These connected *shatian* were called "mother and child" (*mu zi*) *shatian*, rendering metaphorical the relationship between the original *shatian* and the one to which it had given birth. Continuing the Chinese metaphor, one could say that over time whole families or even lineages of *shatian* constituted the Pearl River Delta. But more to the point, the delta had been built by people working with natural processes, but in the unusual conditions created by the Mongol invasion of south China.

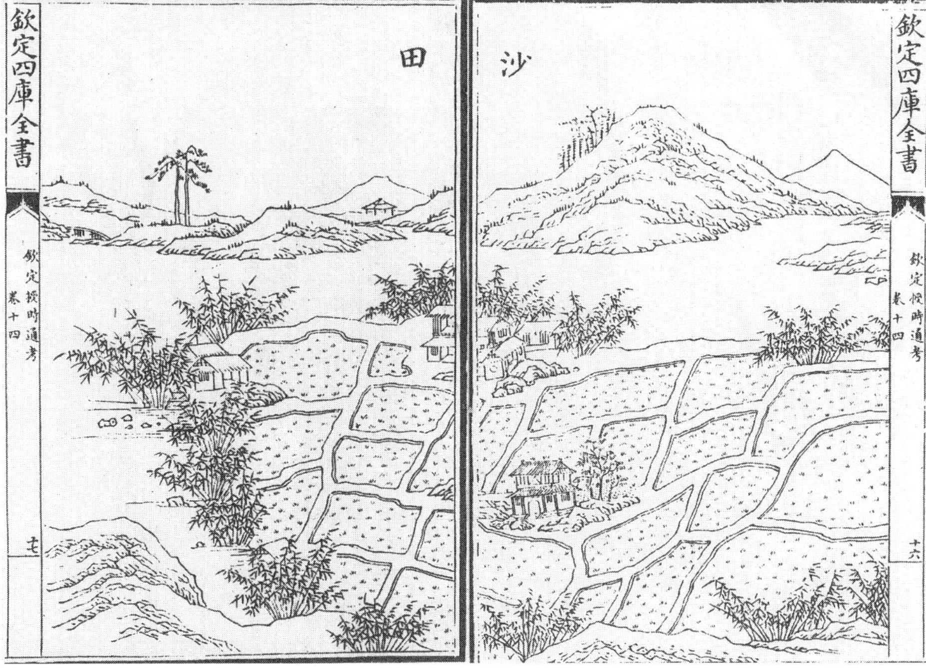

Fig. 4.10. Shatian *Source: E'ertai, Qin ding Shoushi tongkao,* 1742 edition original (Taibei: *Taiwan shangwu yinshu guan,* 1983 reprint) v. 732, 201.

The Pearl River Delta thus was not created by purely natural processes, and had not been simply waiting for Chinese to migrate from the north and reclaim it for agriculture. Rather, the creation of the delta was the result of a complex causal chain. Chinese immigrants into south China preferred to settle in the hills of northern Guangdong, fearful of the diseases in the river valleys further to the south. Their land clearing eventually increased the silt content of the rivers flowing south, but most of that alluvium never reached the bay, being deposited instead in the lower reaches of the North, East, and West river valleys. Only the construction of dikes and levees there in the Song directed the silt-laden waters into the upper reaches of the Pearl River estuary. Even then, that silt might have continued to flow farther out into the bay had it not been captured by refugees from the north who had fled from the Mongols to the islands in the bay. The creation of the Pearl River delta and its later emergence as the densely populated, agriculturally rich core of south China was thus a historically contingent, rather than naturally determined, outcome. One can only speculate as to whether or not the same pattern would have been followed had it not been for the "historical accident" of the Mongol invasion. Whatever the outcome may have been, by the time the Mongols were driven from China and the Chinese peasant army leader Zhu Yuanzhang succeeded in establishing the Ming dynasty in 1368, the development of the Pearl River delta had begun.

THE BUILT ENVIRONMENT: CITIES AND WASTE

From as early as the Shang dynasty, Chinese have been planning and building capital cities. Those cities have been central both in the governance of their territories and in their views of the cosmos, laid out to represent and tap cosmic energies to rule the earth. Nearly all have been walled, built by tamped-earth techniques pioneered in the Shang requiring vast armies of conscripted labor. Construction of buildings was almost always wood post and beam, so cities consumed a large amount of timber to build and maintain. And despite the massive ramparts, nearly all of China's political capitals have been conquered and sacked to demonstrate the fall of one power and the rise of another, requiring massive rebuilding projects drawing timbers from ever greater distances.

From the establishment of the centralized state under the Qin on, other walled towns and cities were built throughout the empire for the officials of the state, or as garrisons for their troops. Over the millennia from ancient times to the seventeenth century, one historian figures that the Chinese built 4,478 walled cities.[137] But not all towns and cities owed their origins to political considerations. During the Warring States period, the economy grew at a rapid rate, and China began undergoing a more "natural" process of urbanization. As centers of production and distribution, these cities connected a vast commercialized economy that further knit the Chinese empire together; I will have more to say about these cities and the market economy in the next chapter.

Over the millennium considered in this chapter, there were numerous capital cities, both for the Chinese who fled south in the fourth century and for the numerous nomadic peoples who attacked and settled in north China. After being reunited by the Sui at the end of the sixth century, four cities served as the capital for the empire: Chang'an for the Sui and Tang, Kaifeng and Hangzhou for the Song, and Dadu (Beijing) for the Mongols (see map 4.1). Significant numbers of studies exist treating each of those,[138] so here I will focus on the Tang capital of Chang'an, and place it (and by extension other Chinese cities) in the larger context of China's environmental history.

An Urban Exemplar: Tang Chang'an

Chang'an was first built by the early emperors of the Han dynasty beginning around 200 BCE, across the Wei River from the site of the capital built by the First Emperor of Qin.[139] The Wei River valley was the center of these early Chinese states, being strategically located in a defensible bowl surrounded by mountains to the south and hills to the north—it was Guanzhong, "within the passes." Two passes to the east connected it to the Yellow River plain, several hundreds of feet lower in elevation. The Wei River valley itself was fertile, and the loess hills to the north, too, were easily worked, and both provided an agricultural base to the Qin and Han states. To the west were desert and the oases along the Silk Road, and Chang'an anchored that trade route for the Chinese.

Destroyed in 311 CE by Xiongnu invaders, Chang'an declined along with the rest of north China during the succeeding wars, destruction, and population decline, until the site was chosen by the founder of the Sui dynasty for his capital. Rather than rebuild old Chang'an, Emperor Wen of Sui decided to create an entirely new city adjacent to the old. The new Chang'an was huge—nearly six miles east to west, and more than five miles north to south, defined by massive earthen walls. Inside the walls, emperor Wen's architects designed a city laid out on a grid, with eleven grand avenues running north to south and fourteen running east to west. The main north-south thoroughfares were 482 feet wide, and the east-west ones were more than 200 feet wide (by comparison, Fifth Avenue in New York City is 100 feet wide), flanked by ditches and lined with trees.

Into this grid were placed the imperial palace and government offices backing up against the north wall and facing south; grand markets were established in the eastern and western sections, and an additional 106 wards were planned for residential neighborhoods. Chang'an was still a work in progress when Emperor Wen took up residence, and he did what he could to populate the city by requiring his sons and other grandees to build city mansions there, and by endowing and building numerous Buddhist temples. Nonetheless, much of the massive Sui-era city was empty, with many of the southern wards given over to farming and a park around a large lake. The real grandeur of Chang'an was to await the Tang and its flourishing in the eighth century.

By then, Chang'an had not merely filled in its 31 square miles, but it had become home to the largest concentration of humans on earth—about one million residents. The Western Market was a raucous, multicultural place that offered goods of all kinds from all over the empire and from the Silk Road trade as well, and entertainment of all sorts. While the Western Market catered to the needs and interests of commoners and merchants, the Eastern Market was a more sedate affair, attracting the wealthy. There were nearly a hundred Buddhist temples, and the southern wards housed a "gorgeous" water park. The imperial residence, called Daming Palace, was removed from inside the walls of the city and relocated to a vast hunting park that had been built to the north of the city, extending all the way to the Wei River.

During the second half of the ninth century, Chang'an and its residents suffered mightily. The city was attacked, and many of its buildings were destroyed, in 881 CE by the rebel Huang Chao, and as the dynasty's fortunes crumbled by the turn of the tenth century, so too did Chang'an. As the dynasty fell, successors moved their capital further east to Kaifeng; Chang'an "was earth-heaps and waste-land." The lake that was at the center of the water park dried up and was converted to farmland. Although soldiers and others used the site intermittently, commoners cut down the city's weeping willows, pagoda trees, and elms for fuel, and by 1100 a curious visitor "found some ruined foundations . . . and little else but cultivated fields where the gilded halls of Tang had once stood."[140] What can the city of Chang'an tells us about the relationship of Chinese to their environment?

That is a huge question, but cities in general—and Chang'an is no exception—represent a physical separation from the natural environment and the creation of a new kind of environment, a built environment. Chang'an was walled off from the surrounding countryside, and its gates closed at night. To be sure, the north China countryside was rural and agricultural, and so was also a humanized environment. But the million residents of Chang'an never had to go outside the walls to get everything they needed; indeed, it is entirely possible that large numbers of those residents never left Chang'an, living their entire lives within its walls.

That all the necessities of life were available within the city meant that Chang'an was the center not just of political power, but of consumption as well. Each day, food and fuel for a million people had to be carted or shipped on one of the canals connecting the city to the Wei and Yellow Rivers (and hence to the Grand Canal) into the two main markets, and then stored, displayed, and sold. Foods and spices came from vast distances—the exotic Far South or the foreign far west (what we now call Central Asia)—and so people came to eat not just "food," but to prepare dishes with style, to develop a cuisine.

Among the importations and re-creations was "nature." The wealthy created gardens in their mansions, with ponds stocked with carp and flocks of ducks and geese, and parrots and singing birds in the trees. The most sought-for look was a "wild, natural" one with "fantastic stones and ancient pines, as austere as those in a painted picture." Flowering trees and shrubs of all kinds were planted, but especially prized were pink or purple peonies. The peony season peaked in the spring, when the flower market was well stocked with cuttings. For some time in the eighth century, peony connoisseurs competed to have the most beautiful blooms, and one man was said to have paid a fortune of several tens of thousands of copper cash for a single flower. Public gardens, too, were as meticulously appointed.[141]

Today we cannot be sure what all of this meant to Chinese at the time, but it seems to me to represent a separation from nature enforced by city life, a longing to be in nature (even if such a nature was un-natural), and an underlying assumption that natural processes could be man-made (literally), and thereby controlled. By the Tang, nature was no longer feared, at least for city folk, but merely exotic.

The control—or at least enclosure—of nature was most forcefully expressed by the imperial hunting park.[142] Like the city itself, the Tang emperors had not invented the idea of an exclusive hunting park. Clear evidence of royal hunting preserves went back to Zhou times, and the one created in Tang China north of Chang'an was explicitly modeled on the great Han-era preserve, which in turn followed a huge enclosure that the First Emperor of Qin had created. Although the Tang version was smaller (a mere 40 miles in circumference), it was stocked with every sort of animal for observing and hunting—bears, tigers, foxes, ducks, geese, even elephants and rhinoceros. Hunting had two functions: to provide meats for royal feasts, and to exhibit the emperor's ability to subdue nature, and hence to rule "All Under Heaven," as the realm of the Chinese emperor—the "Son of Heaven"—was known.

Where the Han emperors apparently engaged in mass campaigns to round up and slaughter vast numbers of animals in their hunting preserve, Edward Schafer argues that a change in attitude came about during the Tang dynasty. Confucian ideas about what it meant to be a "gentleman" in interpersonal relations was being extended to animals as well. Daoist ideas about allowing "nature" to find its own course led to a concern for the well-being of captive or caged animals. Perhaps most influential though were Buddhist ideas and strictures that animals must not be killed. The melding of these three traditions, according to Schafer, led to official edicts limiting the killing of animals and establishing hunting seasons. "The [Confucian] principle of humanity (*jen*) should be applied to plants and animals as well as to men, even within the park where the unconditioned majesty and ruthless domination of the Son of Heaven had always been displayed."[143]

But here we have to stop and consider for a moment the connection between articulated ideas about nature, and the actions of people who profess to holding those ideas. For as Schafer concludes, "in the long run this noble synthesis of ideas probably had little effect on imperial policy. The forests continued to be ravaged; their wildlife continued to be slaughtered. The Tang ideal sickened and died."[144]

The Tang example raises questions about the ideas about nature and its conservation or protection that people and societies hold, and what actually they do. In China, Mark Elvin observed that while Chinese may like a particular tree, they dislike forests,[145] preferring instead a humanized farming landscape within which cities comfort the ruling elite. And not just in China more than a thousand years ago. Surveying the twentieth century, John R. McNeill, too, found that even broadly held commitments to preserve nature does not prevent individuals from driving their own cars or consuming as much stuff as they can, adding to an already heavily polluted environment.[146] A plausible explanation, according to environmental historian J. Donald Hughes, is that "[m]any humans, particularly those who wield power, decide that other values, such as short-term survival or profit, are more important to them than long-term survival and sustainability. . . . In most societies, a minority that exploits resources has usurped power from a majority whose genuine, if not always conscious, interest is to maintain the sustainability of resources."[147] On the other hand, most agrarian societies, China's included, have found ways to avoid wallowing in their own filth.

Waste, Sustainability, and Nutrient Cycles

At the most basic level, cities are concentrations of people who do not produce their own food. Cities have to import food, via either direct expropriation or market exchanges, from rural producers. Farms are specialized kinds of energy converters and concentrators, having removed forms of vegetation that do collect and store solar energy but from which humans have difficulty tapping that energy in favor of forms (e.g., grains, vegetables, and fruits) that humans can directly transform into energy (or store in bodily fat). Using the chlorophyll in their leaves, plants use solar power to "photosynthesize" water and nutrients drawn from the soil into stored energy.

All agriculture thus removes nutrients from the soil, and at some point the nutrients decline to a point where agriculture is no longer viable and the farmers move to a new location (as was the case with shifting agriculture), or the soil itself becomes so depleted that northing will grow there again, permanently degrading the soil (as in desertification). To remain productive, settled agriculture thus requires methods of recycling nutrients back into the soil. Even Neolithic villagers, who both produced and consumed in pretty much the same area, needed to find ways to fertilize the soil. Legumes helped replace nitrogen, and green waste and animal manure also returned nutrients to the soil.

But imagine how much larger the scale of the problem became for Chinese society when vast quantities of food—enough to feed millions of people—were produced and then exported from the countryside to the cities. Because of some ecological peculiarities, Chinese farmers had advantages over farmers elsewhere in the world. The loess soil that underlay much of north China had the unique property of continually bringing nutrients buried in its depths over the millennia to the surface via capillary action. And the rice plant has the peculiar ability to absorb nutrients dissolved in water. Still, for most of human history, the major problem faced by farmers, including those in China, was the shortage of fertilizer.[148]

Both dry land and wet-rice farming thus needed additional nutrients, and the cities were a major source—human excrement—for recycled nutrients lost when food was exported to them. An American agronomist traveling in China at the turn of the twentieth century estimated that 1 million humans excreted 500,000 tons of waste annually, containing nearly 6 million pounds of nitrogen and tons of other nutrients.[149] The farms certainly could use that waste, and the Chinese rulers apparently were not willing simply to befoul their water supplies by dumping all that waste into the rivers. And so it was collected every night (hence its name, "night soil"), carted to barges, shipped back to the countryside, and prepared for use in the fields.

The full history of this vast recycling effort has yet to be investigated and told, but scholarship on night soil in the late imperial period sheds further light on the ecological linkages between urban and rural areas in China, in this case, in the wealthy lower Yangzi region centering on the city of Hangzhou. Not only did farmers make long journeys to urban areas to collect night soil, they organized its daily collection, thereby ensuring that cities and towns were cleaner and healthier than they otherwise would be,[150] but they also graded the quality of the night soil. Night soil quality was a function of the diet of urban residents: the wealthier, with their diets rich in proteins from regular and high-quality meals that included geese, fish, and meat, left the highest-quality—and hence the most prized, and thus highest-priced—night soil.[151]

Villagers, too, collected their waste, usually in pits or large crocks, for weeks or months so that the heat from decomposition would kill the larvae and eggs of parasites. That method, however, was not foolproof—at least by the twentieth century, a major health hazard to wet rice farmers was *schistosomiasis*, a parasite transmitted to humans via freshwater snails that distended the belly and caused intestinal inflammation as well as hardening of the liver. When this scourge began to afflict Chinese rice farmers is not yet understood.

Villagers also maintained compost heaps, and threw in weeds, grass, sandals, pulverized bricks and adobe—anything that was not fed to animals but had some likelihood of adding nutrients to the soil.[152] Another important source of nutrients was muck scooped up from canals, and placed on fields next to the canals.[153] Of course, farmers whose fields were closest to the cities and the canals had the greatest advantage of using these sources of recycled nutrients, since the cost of transporting the bulky material rose rapidly with distance; the further from cities, the less fertile the land and the poorer the people.

When Chinese farmers began such intensive fertilizing is not known for certain. An early eighteenth-century European traveler, Pierre Poivre, was impressed with the annual tilling of land without any fallow period: "That which must render this plan of agriculture the more inconceivable to Europeans, is the idea of their never allowing their lands to lie one season fallow . . . [the land thus] yield[s] annually two crops, and in those towards the south often five in two years, without one single season fallow." The reason for the continuous cropping was massive fertilizing: "They are familiar with marl; they employ also common salt, lime, and all sorts of animal dung, but above all that which we throw in our rivers: they make great use of urine, which is carefully stored in every house, and sold to advantage: in a word, everything produced by the earth is re-conveyed to it with the greatest care."[154] Such a highly developed system had to have developed centuries earlier.

On the one hand, Chinese farming practices in both north and south China, especially the use of human excrement collected from the cities, linked town and countryside in a great nutrient cycle and made their system of agriculture much more sustainable than European practices. That view of the exceptionality of Chinese farming is held to the present.[155] And the fact of the matter is that the soils prepared and farmed during the Song dynasty are still being farmed today (albeit since the 1970s with modern chemical fertilizer applications). To a certain extent, then, Chinese farming was environmentally sustainable.

On the other hand, there is always some leakage of nutrients and energy from any environment that cannot be replaced; we will see another example of that in a coming chapter when examining the "mulberry tree, fish pond" combination of south China. The scientific term for that inevitable loss of energy is called "entropy," and to stop it requires additional inputs of energy to restore "order." An environment modified by humans thus requires considerable effort to maintain. Thus, the Chinese state was continuously looking for ways to enhance the resources and energy available to it, and hence was territorially expansive. The Chinese empire expanded to the north against nomads (when it could), to the east and south against other non-Chinese, and as we will see in the next chapter, to the southwest and west as well. In each of these cases, treasure troves of natural wealth fell under Chinese control, flowing back into core Chinese areas. Those cores thus were "sustainable" in part because of Chinese conquest and exploitation of regions previously inhabited by other indigenous peoples. The creation, maintenance, and expansion (or contraction) of the Chinese empire thus had its underpinnings in basic environmental processes.

CONCLUSION

Over the course of the thousand years covered in this chapter (from 300 to 1300 CE), China and its environment underwent several remarkable changes. Nomadic invasions and the collapse of the Early Empire sent large numbers of Chinese fleeing their homeland on the North China plain for a more uncertain future in the wet and wild south, marking the beginning of a long-term shift in the bulk of China's population from north to south. Chinese took up wet-rice farming that had been pioneered by the non-Chinese indigenous people of the Yangzi River valley, and made numerous improvements, including the construction of dikes and levees to protect new rice paddies, and the introduction of early-ripening rice varieties that dramatically increased the production of food. Just as horses had pulled iron plows across the North China plain, so too did water buffalo give traction to the heavier iron plows needed to turn over wet paddy land. With these new technologies and military support from a reunified state, Chinese migrants pushed further south into Lingnan, west into Sichuan, and into Fujian along the southeast coast, not only transforming the landscape but also forcing indigenous peoples to assimilate, flee, or fight.

By about 1100 CE, at the height of the Song dynasty, the North China plain had been deforested, and an emerging iron and steel industry had to turn to coal for fuel. Coal was also used to heat homes in the great capital city of Kaifeng, and many historians think that China was on the verge of an industrial revolution—a transformation cut short by war with steppe nomads and the relocation of the capital south to Hangzhou. Throughout the south, wet-rice agriculture technologies allowed Chinese to alter the swampy environments by turning river valleys into rice paddies, pushing indigenous peoples into the hills and mountains where they continued their slash-and-burn, shifting agriculture among the deciduous and evergreen semitropical forests.

On both the North China plain and in the southern river valleys, Chinese farmers developed intensive techniques for recycling nutrients taken from the land as crops grew and fed both urban and rural populations. Agro-ecosystems replaced natural ones, concentrating solar energy into forms more readily usable by humans, not just sustaining existing populations but positioning China for a dramatic population increase when New World food crops became available in the sixteenth century, an important part of the story we'll take up in the following chapter.

Chapter 5

Empire and Environment

China's Borderlands, Islands, and Inner Peripheries in the Late Imperial Period, 1300–1800 CE

China's environmental history in the late imperial period unfolded in a context changed from earlier periods. Most importantly, the human population dramatically increased, especially in the south, and market exchanges came to regulate most economic interactions. Population size and density and the commercialization of the economy both had a significant impact on the environment so that by 1800 there were few areas of China untouched and unworked by human hands. The empire reached its maximum size, with the environments of borderlands, islands, and inner peripheries being exploited and transformed, with limits to the extent of the empire set. Much of China was deforested, and, as we will see in the next chapter, an environmental crisis was developing.

A NEW HISTORICAL AND INSTITUTIONAL CONTEXT

Population Size and Distribution

Humans, as we have seen, have been in China's natural environment for a very long time, gleaning the necessities of life—food, clothing, fuel, and shelter—from the natural environment. Hunting-gathering peoples had perhaps the lightest impact on the environment, both because of their relatively small numbers and because their way of life required them to maintain the environment in ways that continued to provide sustenance. Even when practicing shifting agriculture, these peoples generally allowed forests to regrow before returning to the same area after twenty or thirty years. As we will see, in the hilly and mountainous areas of south, southeast, and southwest China, those practices continued into the nineteenth and twentieth centuries. To be sure, the original forest was replaced with a secondary growth of trees more amenable to harvesting, but forest it was.

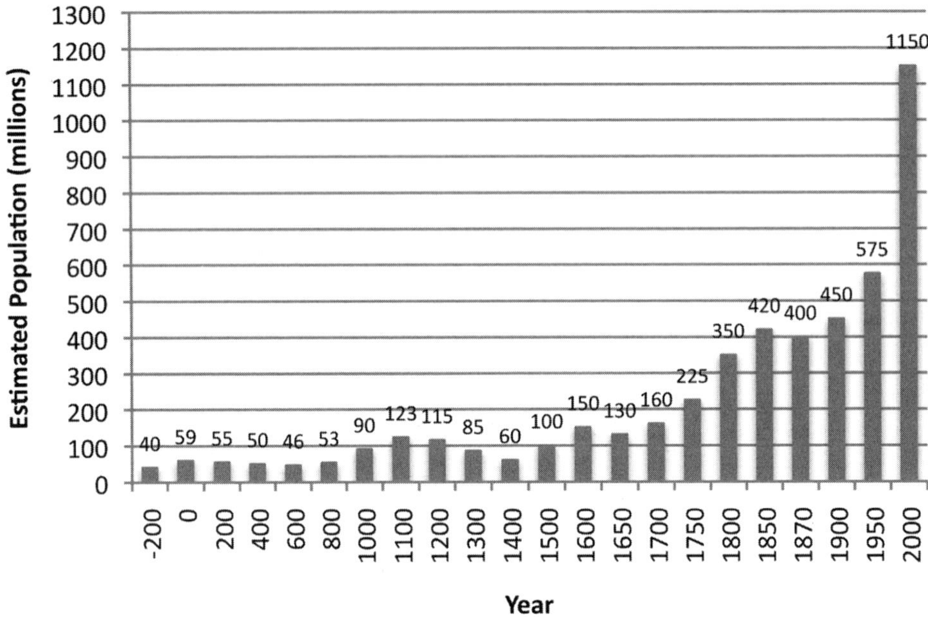

Fig. 5.1. China's Population, 200 BCE–2000 CE

Settled agriculture changed humans' relationship both to nature and to the natural environment. By 1000 CE, nearly all the North China plain had been turned into farmland. To be sure, those farms were an environment, but that environment was no longer "natural"; it was "built," like cities or walls. Human hands had changed the environment in order to concentrate the collection of solar energy transformers—that is, food crops—and to increase the amount of energy available to power humans and their society. As a result, the human population of China had grown to about 60 million people as long as two thousand years ago, and did not surpass that level until about 1000 CE (see figure 5.1).

The north China environment placed some limits on the amount of food that could be grown, in particular because the colder climate limited crops to one main harvest annually. As Han Chinese pushed into the warmer climes of the Yangzi River valley, particularly its lower reaches, the availability of a regular water supply for irrigation of wet-rice paddies, and the conscious use of early-ripening varieties, meant that two and sometimes three crops could be harvested from the same plot of land. Moreover, because rice paddies actually became more fertile over time, and the rice plant could obtain nutrients directly from the water, land did not need to be fallow for any period. The vast increase in agricultural output during the Tang and Song dynasties allowed the population of Han Chinese to increase to an estimated 110 million to 120 million by 1200.

But the Mongol conquest of China, which took much of the thirteenth century to accomplish, was devastating. By 1290, China's population had declined to 65–85 million and stayed at that level until 1400.[1] The Mongol tactics of "isolating major cities by devastating their hinterlands," historian Thomas Allsen writes, "meant that both urban and rural populations suffered grievous casualties and privation."[2] Mongol armies wreaked havoc by destroying north China's cities, "massacring their population, and even contemplating turning north China into pasture lands for their herds,"[3] just as their predecessors had done centuries earlier (see chapter 3).

Chingis Khan's armies leveled city walls and structures associated with farming. "Towns were destroyed from pinnacle to cellar, as by an earthquake. Dams were similarly destroyed, irrigation channels cut and turned into swamp, seed burned, fruit trees [turned into] sawn-off stumps. The screens of trees that had stood between the crops and invasion by the desert sands were down. The handiwork of thousands of years was leveled to steppe again; orchards were laid defenseless to the driving, all-penetrating sandstorms from steppe or desert. These oases . . . were nothing now but arid steppe, this by the nomads' aid making all once again its own."[4]

These Mongol tactics were less to inspire fear (although that was partly the point), and more that Mongols had different values about what constitutes the proper landscape and environment. Just as Han Chinese placed a high value on settled agriculture and their colonists turned other peoples' lands into farms, so the Mongols preferred to "let land lie untilled and be restored to its dignity as steppe."[5] And so Mongol herds grazed on the North China plain for a hundred years after it was conquered.[6]

Whether an outbreak of bubonic plague contributed to—or primarily caused—China's Mongol-era demographic catastrophe, when the population declined 30–40 percent from its high of 120 million around 1200 CE, is uncertain. The European Black Death that started in 1347 and took one-quarter to one-third of the population in parts of Western Europe is often considered to have spread via Mongol troops attacking the Black Sea port of Caffa, who were presumed to have brought it from China. William McNeill thinks the plague originated in a 1331 outbreak in Hebei province, and another historian says that "chroniclers claim that two-thirds of China's population had died since 1331."[7] Although environmental historian Radkau seems more certain that plague caused the population disaster, historians of China just cannot be sure whether an epidemic caused the deaths, and if so, whether the disease was bubonic plague.[8]

Whatever the case, the Mongol conquest solidified a major shift in Chinese population from north to south. Where two-thirds of the Chinese had lived in north China prior to the Mongols, and one-third in the south, those proportions were reversed afterwards (see figure 4.1 in chapter 4). In part, that was because much of south China was spared the Mongol death and destruction visited upon the north. When Kubilai Khan came to the Mongol throne in 1260 and shortly thereafter decided to finish off the conquest of all of China from his north China base in the new capital of Dadu (which later became Beijing), he also knew that the economic power of the Han Chinese lay in the south, and he wanted it captured, not destroyed. Although he let it be known that the southern Chinese ruling elite and landowners would be allowed to remain in place—unlike in north China—when his armies advanced against the Southern Song, large numbers of Chinese fled even further south, as we saw in the previous chapter. By 1279, the last remnants of the Song armies were destroyed, and all China became part of the larger Mongol empire (map 5.1).

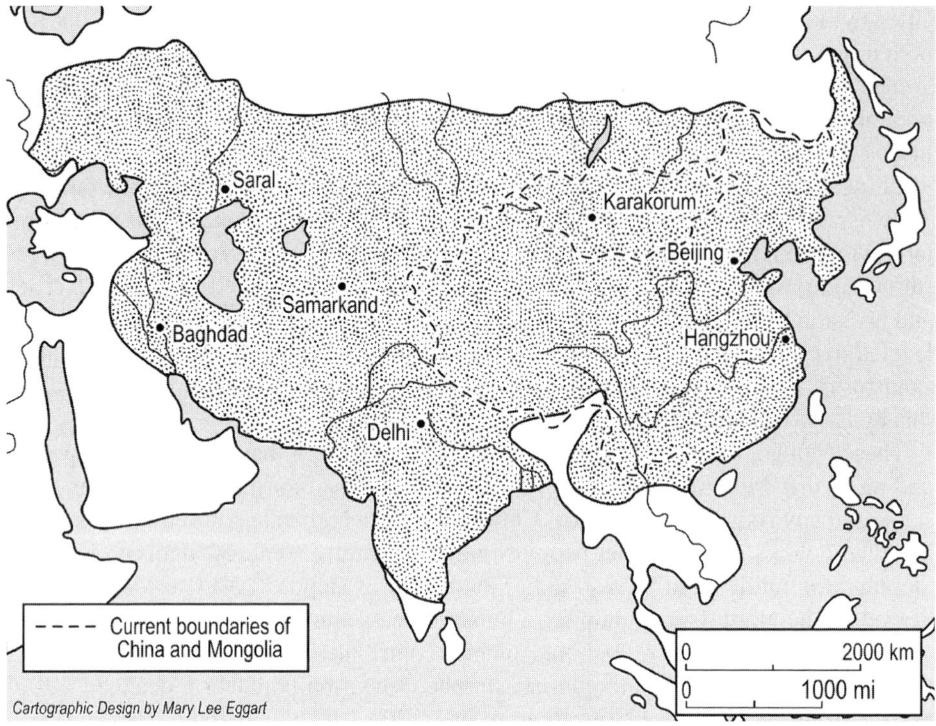

Map 5.1. The Mongol Empire *Source:* Gregory Veeck, Clifton W. Pannell, Christopher J. Smith, and Youqin Huang, *China's Geography: Globalization and the Dynamics of Political, Economic, and Social Change,* second edition (Lanham: Rowman & Littlefield, 2011), 72.

If the Mongol conquest of north had been brutal, their actual rule nevertheless did reunify a China that had been divided into north and south.[9] After Kubilai's relatively benign rule (d. 1294), succession squabbles among Mongol princes led to disinterest in China and the Mongol departure to their steppe homelands in the mid-1300s. After the Mongols left China and the Chinese empire was once again ruled by Han Chinese under the Ming dynasty (1368–1644), peace was reestablished and the population began a seemingly inexorable increase that continues to this day (with a few blips caused by war). From 85 million or so around 1400, the population increased to around 200 million by 1600 (and stayed there until 1700 because of wars and other disruptions), to 225 million by 1750, and to 425 million by 1850. That population increase was both cause and consequence of a better food supply, more land under the plow, enhanced agricultural technologies, and improved markets, all of which had an impact on China's environment.

Markets

Local markets where villagers exchanged products they grew or made, sometimes using money, sometimes just bartering, have existed in China for a very long time, going back at least to the late Zhou and Warring States periods. Markets in cities, too, have been around a very long time, giving urban residents an opportunity to buy food, cloth, and other products from the countryside. Thus it is not as if there have not always been many and varied markets throughout much of China and its frontier areas.[10] Nonetheless, an important change in markets and their place in the Chinese economy and society began in the late Tang, becoming much more institutionalized in the Song dynasty, and in many ways coming to define China's late imperial economy in the Ming and Qing periods as a "market economy" with many features historians of other parts of the world have called "early modern."

Before describing more the development of this Chinese marketing system over the past thousand years, I would like to indicate briefly why markets are important to understanding the processes of environmental change. While there are natural causes of environmental change (climate, volcanoes, wild fires, etc.), most of the driving forces we are considering here are human-induced. Indeed, the focus of this book is on human-environment interactions. While the number and density of people is an important indicator of the pressure on an environment, in particular because of the need for food and hence for farmland, markets can intensify and extend that human impact. Markets allow some regions to specialize in one or more products if the people there know they can depend of the markets for their regular supply of foods and other necessities that they no longer have to produce. This specialization not only increases the amount of goods and services available for everyone within the marketing system but also tends to simplify, sometimes radically, the natural environment as complex ecosystems give way to extensive tracts of monoculture, either for rice or wheat for instance, and nature is thereby simplified as humans replaced the ecosystems which had sustained a diversity of species with those suitable for growing a single crop.

Markets also link people in one area, which might have a limited demand for certain products, to a much larger population and demand, making it economically feasible to harvest products from remote regions. As we will see, this particularly happened with forests and timber products, which began to be cut and floated down rivers to meet the building and heating demands of cities. The demand of cities for these forest products in some cases reached out a thousand or more miles away, enticing some people who became specialized in extracting these mountain resources to cut and transport the timbers.

We will explore ways in which markets facilitated environmental change in late imperial China in this chapter. For now, I would like to take a few moments to describe what that marketing system was like, and how much of the space within China came to be organized into marketing systems.[11]

Through the end of the Tang dynasty, the markets that did exist were established and regulated by the state. From Zhou times on, trade had been "restricted to officially established commercial areas within cities, and to marketplaces set up by the government as needed along the main communication routes." Even into the mid-Tang, it was "not lawful to establish markets anywhere except in prefectural and county capitals unless permission to do so had been granted."[12]

The Tang government did not merely control the establishment of markets but also set the days and hours of operation, and, most important, the prices that could be charged for goods and products. For this purpose, detailed lists were drawn up and distributed to market operators and investigators, not just in the Tang capital city of Chang'an, where both the Eastern and Western markets were regulated but even out into outposts far from the center of Tang economic and political power.[13]

The ability of the Tang state to manage the economy was destroyed as an unintended consequence of the An Lushan Rebellion in the mid-750s.[14] Not only did the Tang state establish and regulate markets, but it also controlled the land and periodically redistributed it. After 756, the Tang government could no longer redistribute land, and so land fell into the hands of wealthy or powerful private people, and markets, too, became unregulated. Neither would be controlled by the state again until the Chinese Communists came to power in 1949. For a thousand years, private property and unregulated markets came to mark China's economy and its relationship to the natural environment.

During the Song, rural periodic markets began to be established with increasing frequency both in areas where population was increasing and hence becoming more dense, in particular in the lower Yangzi region, the area of China with the most people, and in areas, mostly throughout the south, where goods and products from mountainous regions were brought down to lowland markets for exchange for food, cloth, and salt. During the Song, but especially during the Ming and Qing, these markets began to coalesce into a hierarchically structured marketing system that then commercially linked most of the empire.

Climatic Changes

During the 500 hundred years covered in this chapter, the climate of China (as well as the northern hemisphere generally) continued to be generally cooler than the prior millennium (see figure 2.2 in chapter 2). Indeed, some historians refer to the climate during much of this time as "the Little Ice Age."[15] As we will see later in this chapter, exceptionally cold weather did settle over China in the seventeenth century, lowering temperatures and harvest yields, contributing to a major political, social, and economic crisis that gripped China and many other parts of the world as well.[16]

But the climate was not always getting relatively worse and making people's lives more miserable. Indeed, cooling in the middle of the fifteenth century, probably brought on by volcanic eruptions that spewed solar-reflecting sulfur into the atmosphere, was followed not just by climatic warming in the fourth quarter of the fifteenth century, but by China's recovering economic engine, which significantly expanded global activity into the sixteenth century.[17] Silver flowed from Japan to China, harvest yields improved, Europeans set out in small caravels to find water routes to the riches of Asia, in the process discovering "the New World" and its vast treasures of gold, silver, and foodstuffs from the New World, in particular maize, sweet potatoes, peanuts, and tomatoes, all of which found their way into Chinese and other peoples' planting rotations. So important were these combined global climatic, economic, and ecological changes that one scholar sees this more intensive linking of continents, peoples, and economies as marking the beginnings of modern world history.[18] This chapter of China's environmental history takes place in that broader context.

FRONTIERS AND BORDERLANDS

During the late imperial period considered in this chapter, roughly from the Yuan dynasty (the name chosen by the Mongols, 1279–1368), through the Ming (1368–1644) and much of the Qing (1644–1911) to about 1800, the boundaries of what became modern China were filled out. The first area to come under Chinese rule during this period was the southwest, which became the two provinces of Yunnan and Guizhou. Initially conquered by the Mongols in their quest to subdue the southern Song, the southwest remained under Chinese control during the Ming dynasty. During the Qing dynasty, the ruling Manchus conquered the far west, bringing Tibet, Xinjiang, and Inner Mongolia into the empire. Their homeland of Manchuria in the northeast became part of the Chinese empire as well, and the island of Taiwan also came under Chinese rule during the Qing dynasty. These frontier areas became the environmental "hot spots" of the late imperial period.[19]

The other hot spots were the upland hill and mountainous regions of China south of the Yangzi River. As population increased in the lowland river valleys, pressure mounted for some to migrate out.[20] Some of that pressure came from peoples from farther north who had been pushed out by the expanding Han Chinese state. Some of these people left the lowland valleys they had inhabited for similarly positioned farmland in the south and west. Some went to the frontiers, while others developed strategies for extracting a livelihood in the hills and mountains: "upland specialists," we might call them, whose occupation and transformation of the hills and mountains were facilitated both by the marketing system and the availability, from the early sixteenth century, on of New World food crops. The theme for this part of China's environmental story thus could be summarized as "outward and upward." We will start with what to China became the southwestern frontier.

The Southwest

Like the rest of what became Chinese territory south of the Yangzi River, the far southwest—the areas that would become the provinces of Yunnan and Guizhou, and the western half of Guangxi province—had been settled for millennia by people who had cultures and languages related to Tai and Tibeto-Burman rather than Chinese. In a word, they were not Sinitic (i.e., Han Chinese) people. Neither were they "simple" tribal people "at one with nature" gaining their sustenance from the woods and rivers. Rather, these were socially stratified societies with elites and commoners (sometimes in servile positions), politically sophisticated, and sufficiently powerful to engage and defeat Chinese and other armies—and even possessed of their own languages with which to record these accomplishments.

Indeed, although viewed as peripheral to China's central state, the region centered on Yunnan and encompassing parts of Tibet, Burma, Vietanam, and Bengal comprised its own rather well-integrated system that some have dubbed the "Southwest Silk Road." Among the goods flowing from Yunnan included tea and horses to Tibet (thus the name the Road of Tea and Horses), silver and copper bullion to Bengal, and a host of other goods such as silk, metals, jade, elephant tusks, lumber, herbs, spices, tin, and cotton, among other things. Two kinds of horses were raised in Yunnan, one adapted to cooler

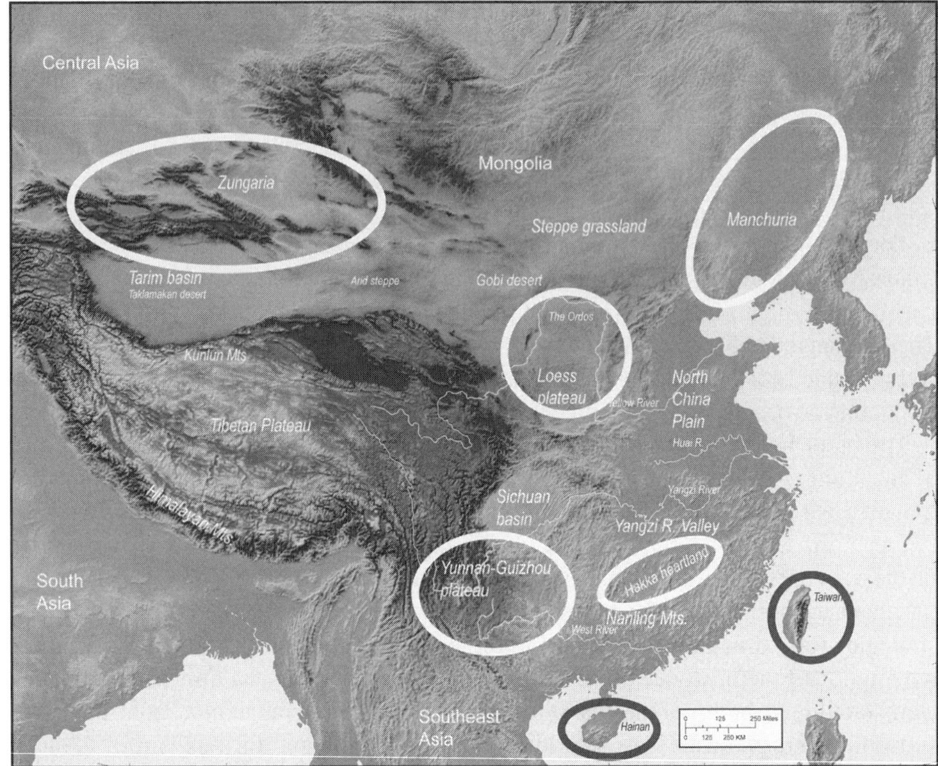

Map 5.2. Late Imperial Frontiers, Borders, and Hot Spots. Regions discussed in this chapter are circled.

climates and the other to subtropical conditions. Tibetans were quite interested in the former, and a brisk trade for horses engaged various Chinese states, in particular the Song after it lost access to steppe grazing lands, opening instead a dozen markets in Sichuan and Guangxi to acquire horses for its cavalry.[21]

Yunnan thus was of strategic importance to the Mongols when they settled on conquering China. In 1253 they captured the Dali kingdom in Yunnan, cutting off the supply of horses to the Song and opening a far western front from which to attach Song forces. The Mongols prized Yunnan's silver mines, set quotas for their production, and taxed the output. After Mongol rule collapsed and the Chinese empire was reconstituted under Ming rule, Yunnan silver (and hence Yunnan) became even more strategically important. As the Ming followed a policy of monetizing its economy with silver, Yunnan became central to the operation of the economy of the empire, and produced half of Ming China's national output of silver.[22]

So, over those centuries, Yunnan went from being in a central position in the regional Southwest Silk Road trading world to being a Chinese frontier. "Between 1400 and 1800," according to Jon Herman, "China's Southwest Frontier . . . was transformed from a poorly understood and seldom visited semiperiphery into an integral part of the Chinese empire. During these four hundred years China's Southwest Frontier changed in dramatic and fundamental ways, from an economically undeveloped and sparsely settled rural frontier inhabited almost exclusively by indigenous non-Han peoples to an increasingly commercialized region populated predominantly by Han in-migrants."[23]

In what became Yunnan province, the state of Nanzhao had emerged in the eighth century, an alliance of six native kingdoms. The Tang Chinese apparently thought Nanzhao could be enlisted in the struggle against the Tibetans, and so showered the Nanzhao ruler with titles and gifts. Nanzhao rulers understood their intermediate position between Tibet and Tang China and used that to their benefit, swinging their allegiance to one or the other as conditions permitted. For reasons that are unclear, both the Nanzhao and Tibetan kingdoms collapsed about the same time as the Tang, with a new kingdom called Dali emerging in Yunnan, and ruling the region until it was conquered by the Mongols in 1253. The Dali people remaining became known as the Dai, a literate lowland farming people who once had their own independent state.

Vast numbers of other peoples inhabited the huge number of environmental niches of the ecologically rich southwest.[24] From the Chinese point of view, the fierce Wa people inhabited their farthest frontier. A Mon-Khmer speaking people who were situated in the highlands between the Burmese and Shan states, the Wa too had a state that fended off both. The Wa region was structured with a densely populated core living in heavily fortified settlements, with other Wa further away but more likely to be in contact with Burmese or Chinese. According to Fiskesjö, the Wa united when confronting the Burmese or the Chinese, but warred against each other. "Internal warfare here . . . took the form of head-hunting, which intensified with the successive exhaustion of virgin land that could be opened up for shifting agriculture . . . Although most war victims were Wa, outsiders venturing into the central Wa lands might also prey to head-hunting."[25]

In the far southern part of Yunnan known as Xishuangbanna there were numerous mountain and river valley peoples, all having established particular kinds of relations with their natural environment. The Kammu lived "in jungles at the foot of mountains" among thick bamboo forests. Other peoples arriving at different times fought the Kammu for their lands, and the Kammu or others moved up or down the mountainside. Practicing slash-and-burn cultivation until well into the twentieth century, those annual movements gave people their ages (having been born when a particular plot was opened up). Elephants were an important part of Kammu livelihood, having domesticated and raised them.[26] To this day, this densely forested region is among the last refuges of elephants in China.

Another Xishuangbanna people call themselves the Akha, and are a Tibeto-Burmese speaking people. "For much of the past two thousand years, Akha farmers have lived in the mountains that now link China and mainland Southeast Asia and relied on shifting cultivation in hilly, wooded sites to grow upland rice and a rich array of vegetables. . . . Akha cultivation practices revolved around complex upland environments that varied greatly in elevation and microclimate. Akha farmers exploited these diverse sites by nurturing an astonishing array of trees and plants, whether wild or cultivated." Having developed a deep understanding of ecological processes in their mountains, the Akha nonetheless "refashioned their landscapes to meet daily needs, respond to emergencies, maneuver around state extractions, and to produce for markets."[27] The Akha experience makes an interesting point: humans can refashion their environments in ways that are sustainable.

In Guizhou, a mountainous region cut by fast-flowing rivers, peoples known to the Chinese as the Yi originally had been mountain dwellers but over time moved into the river lowlands to farm. Over the centuries, much of Guizhou become peopled by Yi as population pressure on the limited agricultural land led clans to break apart, apparently in exceptionally bloody encounters, with the loser migrating out to another river valley. The Yi clans "battled one another as well as non-Yi for control of fertile land, scarce water, and pristine pastureland."[28]

By the time the Nanzhao state was confronting Tang China, the Yi had fashioned the Mu'ege kingdom that dominated nearly all of modern Guizhou. Given titles by the Tang in the expectation (hope?) that they would be helpful in the Tang-Nanzhao tussle, the Yi and their kingdom entered into Chinese consciousness as one of the many "barbarian" tribes that might be amenable to Chinese culture. Clearly, the Yi were an aristocratic warrior society capable of fighting long and hard. For their part, Mu'ege leaders got something out of the relationship with China too—titles and other trappings of rule. This tributary relation continued through the Song, with Yi leaders periodically bringing as many as a thousand horses to the Southern Song capital of Hangzhou.[29]

The Mongol decision to conquer China spelled the end of both the Dali kingdom in Yunnan and the Mu'ege in Guizhou. Determined to outflank the Southern Song by going through the southwest and attacking Song forces from the south and the west, the Mongol commander Kubilai (who would become Khan) led the campaign against the Dali and Mu'ege from 1253 to 1255. A truce was affected, with the Mongols preferring to rule through existing political structures in a system called the *tusi*, or "native official" system. When a century later Chinese troops pushed the Mongols out and the Ming dynasty (1368–1644) was established, the Ming founder Hongwu continued to use the *tusi* system to keep control of the southwest. As we will see shortly in connection with Yunnan during the Qing dynasty, the use of "native officials" there was related to malaria and Chinese fear of contracting it and other tropical diseases.

As John Herman argues, the Mongol conquest of the southwest marked a turning point in the history of that region, in particular regarding how Chinese came to see it: as an integral part of the Chinese empire. And they began to treat it as such, with schemes promoting the rapid development of the southwest by Han settlers moved in from China proper. But the southwest was not an environment for "easy progress" of the Han Chinese.[30]

The entire region of Yunnan, Guizhou, and western Guangxi forms a mountainous plateau that slopes from the northwest to the southeast where the plains along the West River make extensive agriculture more possible. James C. Scott sees the region as part of what he and other scholars have called "Zomia," a highland region stretching across Southeast Asia but including China's southwest.[31] Most of the mountains in the Chinese part of Zomia are formed of limestone karst, which when heated and weathered by vast geologic forces formed fantastic shapes (see figure 4.2). Limestone underlies most of the region, too, and rivers can disappear into underground courses before appearing elsewhere. Cisterns, caverns, sinkholes, and hanging cliffs mark the region. In the western part of Yunnan, three major rivers—the Yangzi, the Mekong, and the Salween—race through deeply folded mountains with as much as 6,000 feet of difference between the mountain tops and the river (we will return to the environmental fate of this region, which becomes known as the Three Parallel Rivers Region of Yunnan, in chapter 7). The rivers are not navigable, and anyone wanting to traverse the area had to climb up and down numerous mountain spines. Only 6 percent of the land surface is flat enough, and contains adequately arable soil, to be farmed. The forest is mostly evergreen broadleaf, except in lower elevations where monsoon tropical forests grow.

Guizhou occupies the eastern part of the Yunnan-Guizhou plateau, and like Yunnan has a significant amount of karst; 70 percent of the province is covered with limestone, making agriculture difficult except in its few river valleys, which account for little more than 1 percent of the land area. Like Yunnan, the mountains and fast-coursing rivers made for difficult transportation, and are not usable for irrigation. It was said of Guizhou that "there is no level land within three miles, no fine weather for three days, and no person with three cents." Where much of Yunnan has a temperate climate because much of the province is at or above 5,000 feet above sea level, Guizhou has more rainfall as well as about 160 days of orographic rain. Southern Guizhou is monsoon forest on slopes and valleys, with the evergreen broadleaf forest typical of tropical regions elsewhere.

Western Guangxi shares many physical characteristics with Guizhou, including karst limestone formations, poor soil, and evergreen broadleaf forests. The eastern half of Guangxi is more suitable for farming along the West River and its tributaries, and thus population densities are highest there.

With such an extraordinary natural environment with an exceptional number of ecological niches, including "a subtropical labyrinth of mountains and plunging river valleys," the region supported a wide diversity of plant an animal species. "Snakes, monkeys, tigers, deer and many other animals and birds flourished in its forests. Malaria lay in wait in some places, though not in others."[32] Even by the end of the twentieth century, this region was believed to contain about 25 percent of China's flora and fauna, and a considerable amount of the entire world's. The significance of that biological diversity—and the growing fight to preserve it—will be considered in chapter 7.

The human diversity too was—and remains—quite extraordinary.[33] Most of those throughout the region who inhabited and farmed the malarial river lowlands tended to be Tai, probably the original Neolithic human settlers. But there were others, too, and there was considerable migration among these peoples within the southwest.[34] In Yunnan, the Achang were spread throughout the western mountains, but some farmed or raised livestock on river plains. On the intermediate slopes of the southern mountains were the Buddhist Bulang, who practiced swidden agriculture and had lost their independence to Tai suzerains. The Hani and Jinuo harvested tea from wild bushes on mountain slopes. Deep in the mountains were the Lahu and the Lisu, who hunted and fished. The Wa had originally been hunter-gatherers, too, but had migrated into the lowlands between the thirteenth and eighteenth centuries, only to retreat back into the mountains as Tai and Han Chinese occupied the best agricultural lands.[35]

In Guizhou, there were seven main ethnic groups—the Miao, Zhongjia, Gelao, Luoluo (Yi), Yao, Zhuang, Nong and Dong. Chinese first categorized the indigenous peoples into thirteen groups, but during the Qing dynasty as the Han Chinese tried to understand them in order to better conquer and rule them, they ultimately classified the Guizhou natives into eighty-two groups.[36]

However many indigenous people there were in the southwest—and the number was not great—their impact on the environment was light. By the time Han Chinese showed up in large numbers around 1400, there are numerous reports of tigers and elephants and descriptions of vast forests, all indicators of healthy ecosystems. To be sure, Tai farmers did transform small intermountain river valleys into farms, and small numbers of others practiced shifting slash-and-burn agriculture, but the mountains and valleys were too vast and inaccessible to be much affected by the peoples who called the place home.

But upon expelling the Mongols and proclaiming the establishment of the new Chinese Ming dynasty in 1368, the founding emperor Hongwu also laid claim to the southwest by sending letters to all of the local chieftains who had earlier submitted to the Mongols. This was the *tusi*, or "native chieftain," system; in return for maintaining a semblance of order and submitting tribute of local products, the indigenous rulers became hereditary chiefs with all the claims to rulership over their own people. Even so, it took Ming forces until 1382 to defeat Mongol forces in Yunnan, and local opposition to the Ming took another decade to suppress.[37]

But why did the new Ming state even want the southwest? As an agrarian empire, there appeared to be little opportunity to reap the benefits of taxing agriculture in a part of the empire apparently so ill suited to crops. That Ming Emperor Hongwu had a strong drive to colonize the southwest with Han Chinese migrants and officials is apparent, and the motivating forces included security against Mongols and Tibetans, access to strategic raw materials, in particular silver and copper but other minerals and natural resources as well, and taxes from settling Han Chinese soldier-farmers on "uninhabited lands"[38] using the tried-and true method of *tun-tian*, the agricultural-military colonies pioneered by the Han state in its conquest of the northwest, and the Tang and Song later in Sichuan and Lingnan.

With the local chieftains appointed and military opposition mostly eliminated, the Ming established military agricultural colonies throughout the southwest; two hundred fifty thousand Han Chinese soldier-farmers and their families took up residence in increasingly fortified garrison towns in the river valleys, took the land, and started farming. By 1400, perhaps a million or more Chinese had been moved into the southwest—and, in the words of historian John Herman, that was "only the beginning."[39]

Two additional waves of Han Chinese were either forcibly relocated to the southwest, or tempted there by Ming state promises of free seed and tools, and three-year tax exemptions. Prior to the arrival of the Han Chinese, agriculture in the southwest was limited by available land and by the lack of iron plows; indigenous peoples used wooden implements that could not break up heavier soils under forests but only the light alluvial soil in river valleys. Neither did they have oxen to pull the plows. So not only did the Ming state make iron plows available to the Han settlers, but it also drove tens of thousands of head of oxen there—thirty thousand in the five years between 1385–90 alone—to pull the heavy iron ploughs that broke up the forest soils.[40]

Initially, "nearly all the land distributed to these soldier-farmers was seized from the local non-Han population."[41] However much that was, by 1400 an additional 1.3 million mu (more than 200,000 acres) had been "cleared" in Yunnan, and by 1441 another million more in Guizhou. By 1597, an additional 1.7 million mu was "cleared." All this land then was administered under Chinese concepts of landownership, in particular the idea that it was owned (and hence could be sold to others). Not surprisingly, the various peoples in Yunnan, Guizhou, and western Guangxi periodically resisted, only bringing more Chinese force to bear against the "rebels." In the fifteenth and sixteenth centuries, Han Chinese armies of a hundred thousand or more were sent against the non-Han in wars lasting a decade or more. And, ironically, most of the troops in those "Chinese" armies were indigenous people from other areas pressed into China's military service.[42]

One of the largest and best-described uprisings occurred in 1465 among the Yao peoples of western Guangxi, an area of mountains making the Great Vine Gorge, through which the Xun River flowed. The gorge was named for a massive rattan vine that the Yao used as a footbridge. The area was also malarial. Whatever the immediate "causes" of the uprising, one can be sure that Han Chinese pressure on Yao lands was at the core, and under the leadership of one "Big Dog Hou," Yao bands conducted guerrilla warfare against Chinese troops, "appearing and disappearing among the mountains and valleys," according to the official Chinese history of the war. The Chinese Minister of War assigned General Han Yong to supplement his force of thirty thousand men with another composed of one hundred sixty thousand local fighters (who were likely to have had some resistance to malaria) and to attack the Yao camp above Great Vine Gorge. More than a thousand Yao were captured, and more than 3,200 were beheaded.[43] But that did not stop the uprising. General Han Yong ordered another campaign, this one blockading all the passes and setting the hills on fire. When some Yao escaped, the general "cut down the trees on the mountains and drove roads through them" to find them. Enticing the Yao into an attack, the general mowed them down with cannons and "burned the palisades by shooting fire arrows [rockets] at them." Another three thousand Yao had their heads taken. Historian Mark Elvin calls these campaigns to subdue the southwest an "eco-war" because of the planned destruction of habitat.[44]

Even so, the wars continued throughout the sixteenth century and into the seventeenth. As the Han, Tang, and Song states had discovered, the solution to the unrest ultimately lay in transforming the non-Chinese environment into farms to destroy the ecological basis of the indigenes' way of life, and hence their opposition to Chinese rule. In an early seventeenth-century Chinese plan, "More land will be opened up for farming. Day by day the settlements will become more densely populated. Once the division of land into fields has been correctly carried out, the local chieftains will not be able to make encroachments onto land not currently farmed by the commoner-civilians. . . . thus farming will be the means by which the settled population will grow."[45]

But it wasn't just the Han Chinese who transformed the forests into farms. In Guizhou in the 1570s, some of the native *tusi* appointees led the conversion of their land and people to Han-style farming, replacing the shifting, slash-and-burn practices used until then. In the words of a Han Chinese advisor, "The leaders of the Luoluo [Nasu] realize they can generate more revenue by farming like the Han than they can if they continue with traditional methods." Doing so required more labor power than was readily available from their own people, so these Nasu leaders "raid[ed] vulnerable Han settlements to obtain captives to work their reclaimed lands. By the turn of the [seventeenth] century, then, an extensive trade network . . . had developed to supply the expanding [Nasu] political economy with slaves."[46]

The transformation of the environment of the southwest thus was a complex interaction of Chinese political pressure and economic enticements with the existing political and class structure of the non-Chinese peoples. The co-optation of native leaders with Han Chinese values and rewards was a necessary part of Ming colonialism in the southwest.

The colonial project continued into the Qing dynasty. The Kangxi emperor continued the indirect rule of the *tusi* system, but his successors were much more interested in more efficiently gaining access to the minerals and timber of the southwest and thus attempted to impose direct rule. Either way, the Chinese state committed significant resources to the effort. According to a French Jesuit sent by the Kangxi emperor to map Guizhou, "In order to make them submit, or at least to contain them, large garrisoned areas have been constructed at unbelievable expense. . . . As a result the most powerful of these Miao are as if blocked off by forts and towns that cost the state a great deal, but which ensure peace. . . ."[47] Han Chinese militia sent into the province in a revival of the *tun-tian* system took land from the indigenous peoples, and used military force to protect themselves from the resulting rage and attacks. Han settlers also acquired land when locals defaulted on loans, and when Han men married non-Han and inherited their land.[48]

The Han Chinese population in the southwest thus surged; by the middle of the nineteenth century, Han Chinese in Guizhou outnumbered the original inhabitants. According to historian James Lee, "The rise in population can be divided into two periods. . . . Between 1250 and 1600 the population of the Southwest about doubled from 3 to 5 million; between 1700 and 1850 the population quadrupled from 5 to 20 million."[49] The increase in the first period was caused by the agricultural colonization of the southwest, but the even larger increase in the second period, as James Lee has shown, was almost all due to Han migrants coming to work the copper and other mines in Yunnan—a strategic consideration that had motivated the Ming state to colonize the southwest in the first place.

The first mineral to attract Han Chinese attention was silver in Yunnan, Guizhou, and northwestern Guangxi. For reasons that need not detain us here, the paper money that had been used and accepted during the Song and Yuan periods fell into disfavor by 1400, with merchants and others preferring silver instead; when the central government started accepting silver for tax payments in the 1430s and paper money fell to 2 percent of its face value, the Chinese economy switched to silver as the basis of its currency, creating a huge demand for silver.[50] Although some silver was extracted from the southwest and helped to monetize the Chinese economy and tax system, the Chinese economy was so huge, and demand for silver so great, that Ming China was soon importing vast quantities of silver from Japan, and, after the discovery of the

New World and its sources of silver, historians estimate that as much as one-half to two-thirds of all the silver extracted from the New World from 1500 to 1800 wound up in China. China cast a long economic and environmental shadow around the entire world.[51]

Like agricultural land, the lands of the indigenous peoples were taken for the mines, with the indigenes sometimes (often?) forced to work the mines. Hundreds of thousands of ounces of silver were mined and refined in the fifteenth century, until production of silver peaked around 1500 and China began importing vast sums from Japanese and New World mines. In addition to the silver ore being taken out, the silver was extracted from the rock using mercury, a highly poisonous liquid metal itself extracted from cinnabar. And there was lots of cinnabar to be mined in the southwest as well.

According to a Han Chinese critic of the environmental destruction caused by the mining of silver and cinnabar: "Along the banks of Guizhou's many treacherous rivers live men, both old and young, who refuse to leave the banks of the river to reside in town. With pans and pipes, they strain to gather a few fragments from the river. For many, standing in the river has caused their toes to rot and fall off, though the water they stand in is clear; their eyes are red and filled with tears, though their pupils have suffered irreparable damage. Because of the mining, the water appears red, and the clothing worn by the miners is stained red. When a miner obtains even the smallest amount of cinnabar, he proclaims success and becomes quite excited, for he knows he will eat well today. . . . Cinnabar satisfies neither eyes nor ears with enjoyment. [It has] perverted the spirit of concern for daily necessities."[52]

What these miners were suffering from was the effects of mercury poisoning. Especially as used in silver mining, in which miners had to get into pits with mercury, mercury poisoning caused hair and teeth to fall out and rotted soft tissue and inner organs whose failure led to a painful death.

After the silver mines gave out, copper mining flourished in Yunnan in the eighteenth and nineteenth centuries, with the peak of production in the mid-eighteenth century.[53] Like silver, copper was in demand as a currency. Officially valued at one-thousandth the value of silver (i.e., one thousand copper coins exchanged for an ounce of silver), copper was minted into coins that circulated for everyday use. Also like silver, copper was both mined and refined at the mine head, thus requiring vast quantities of charcoal: "It was the constant demand for pine charcoal for smelting that brought about the 'exhaustion of the mountains.' The production of 100 *jin* (about 133 pounds) of copper required 1000 *jin* of charcoal, so in the peak period, when production was 10 million *jin* [of copper], over 100 million *jin* of charcoal was burned. The refining kilns . . . consumed newly cut wood. As the ore from the old mines declined in quality more and more charcoal was needed for smelting. . . . Depletion of the fuel resources proceeded faster than exhaustion of the mineral deposits, and the indiscriminate felling of trees increased the danger of flooding. Thus the increasing decrepitude of the mines and the devastation of the mountains dealt an almost mortal blow to the [copper] industry."[54]

Even then, the difficult topography and lack of transportation made the transport of the refined copper from Yunnan to the mints in central and northern China difficult.

"Yunnan is on the frontier and the mines were all in the mountains: it was said that transporting 10 million *jin* of copper required a hundred thousand horses and oxen: the only alternative was manpower. The dredging of the Jinsha River (the upper reaches of the Yangzi River in Yunnan Province) brought about a considerable improvement, but it silted up later [because of the deforestation] and was only navigable as far as Huangcaoping, then the copper had to be carried down the Yangzi via Luzhou. [Later] the big mines were located in western Yunnan, where river transport is unavailable and the journey even more difficult; the copper had to be carried on packhorses . . . down to the Yangzi . . ."[55]

Just as the Song state had a strategic interest in colonizing Sichuan for the resources it could extract for its war efforts, so too did the Ming and Qing states have an interest in the southwestern provinces of Yunnan and Guizhou. The driving force then, though, was more economic than strategic, though when we return to consider Yunnan under the Qing in more detail later in this chapter, we will see that Qing visions of military conquest of Burma, bordering Yunnan to the south, were to be foiled by the *Anopheles* mosquito. In the meantime, the pressure exerted by the Han state continued to push more and more people into settled farming or into the hills to escape the grasp of the state and its native agents.

The Ordos Desert and the Great Wall

Even as the Ming state pursued a vigorous military strategy to incorporate the southwestern borderlands under its imperial control, military setbacks in the northern steppe borderlands forced the Ming to adopt a radically different strategy—building walls to keep the Mongols out. But building what then were called "long walls"—which when connected and reinforced in the fifteenth and sixteenth centuries became known to Europeans as the "Great Wall of China"—emerged from a major military disaster in the mid-fifteenth century.

Among the greatest fears of the new Ming rulers were the Mongols and the possibility that they would mount another invasion of China from their steppe homeland. The presence of Mongol forces in Yunnan is what prompted Ming concern for that region in the first place. But the homeland of the Mongols was in the grasslands to China's north, and that was the borderland that had the Ming founder's attention when he launched attacks on the Mongol capital at Karakorum. His successor continued campaigning in the steppe, and in the 1420s moved his capital from the relative security of Nanjing on the Yangzi River to Beijing (which the Mongols had called Dadu), closer to the frontier and just south of the defensive ponds the Song had built to protect themselves from the Khitan Liao. Some historians see the move of the capital as a defensive strategy of being "close to the Mongols," whereas a more recent assessment by Arthur Waldron suggests that these early Ming emperors simply had expected to incorporate the steppe into their empire.

That idea is new to some historians of China because they have tended to equate "China" with settled agriculture and the steppe with nomadism and pastoralism, seemingly two distinct "civilizations" based upon different ecosystems—the so-called distinction between the "steppe" and the "sown." But why shouldn't the "Chinese"

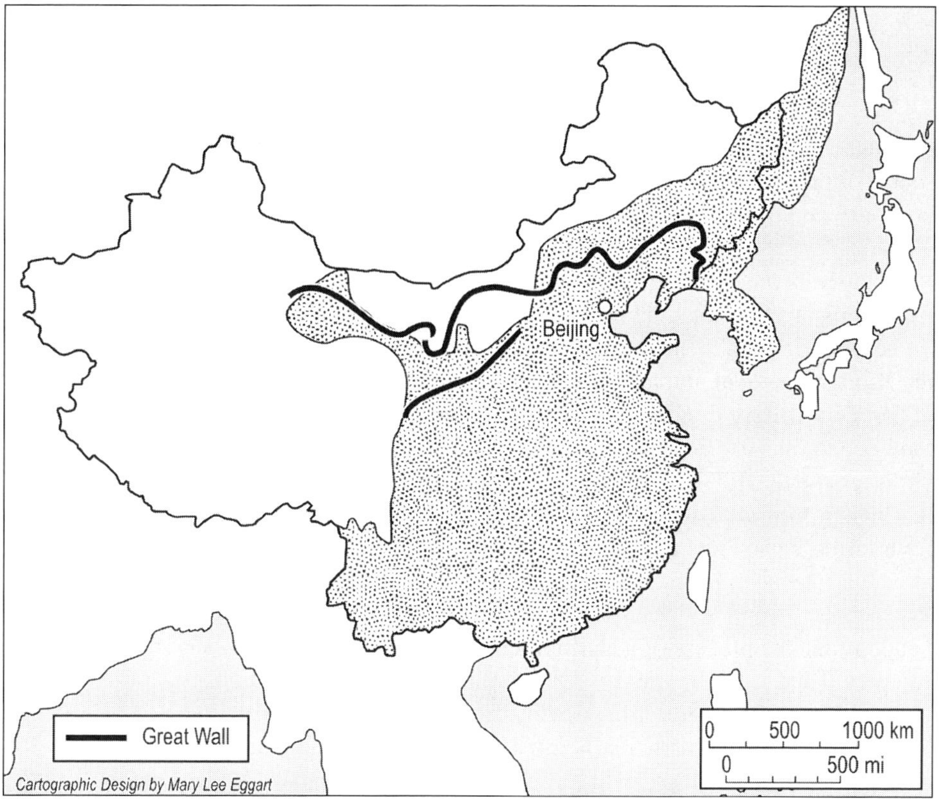

Beijing
Great Wall
0 500 1000 km
0 500 mi
Cartographic Design by Mary Lee Eggart

Beijing
0 500 1000 km
0 500 mi
Cartographic Design by Mary Lee Eggart

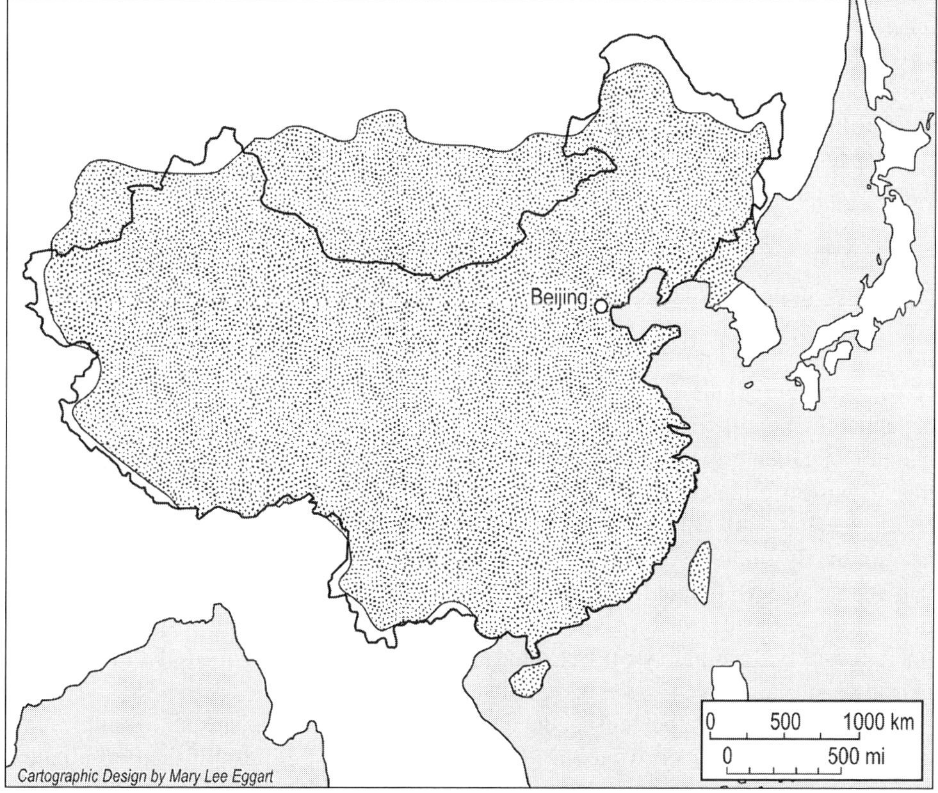

Map 5.3. The Territories of the Ming (top) and Qing (bottom) Dynasties. The Ming map depicts the location of the Great Wall. *Source:* Gregory Veeck, Clifton W. Pannell, Christopher J. Smith, and Youqin Huang, *China's Geography: Globalization and the Dynamics of Political, Economic, and Social Change*, second edition (Lanham: Rowman & Littlefield, 2011), 74, 77.

empire have expanded north to incorporate the steppe, just as it was expanding to the south? What we will see is that it in fact did, and that the building of the Great Wall was only an apparent demarcator of agrarian China from the steppe and its pastoral nomads.

As early as the Warring States period (403–221 BCE), Chinese had adapted to the conditions of the steppe. The state of Zhao, in particular, had been quite successful. To be sure, one of the rulers of Zhao had built a tamped-earth wall for defense against the Xiongnu and Hu nomadic warriors, but that wall was built north of the great loop of the Yellow River, and incorporated a significant segment of the steppe and its pastoral economy. As described by Owen Lattimore, the rulers of the state of Zhao were "frontiersmen" who adopted the mobile warfare techniques of the "barbarians" and fed their troops with meat from the cattle herds of the steppe rather than with grain from farms. Zhao "was a frontier state, modified by contact with nomads in a territory in which intensive, irrigated agriculture [such as that just to south in the Fen and Wei River valleys] was not the standard of taxation and administration." That Zhao did not continue the process of adapting to the steppe, Lattimore says, was because it was conquered and ruled by the new Qin empire in 221 BCE[56] (see chapter 3).

During the Ming, the Ordos desert, the area within the great northern loop of the Yellow River, was of particularly important strategic importance, for the Ming had to decide what to defend and what to attack. According to Waldron, "Enclosed within this Yellow River loop is the Ordos desert . . . an expanse of some fifty thousand miles, nearly the size of New England. . . . [I]t is a compact and easily defended territory hospitable only to nomads. . . . Ecologically, the territory is mixed. Parts are pure desert. . . . But other parts of the Ordos are ideal for nomads, with good grazing land. . . . Furthermore, sedentary Chinese could settle in those places where [Yellow River] water made irrigation possible." By the end of the Ming, 369 miles of canals irrigated thousands of acres of farms in the Ordos.[57] Moreover, "in Ming times, climate in the northwest [of China] was also probably more favorable than it is today. The areas just south of the Ordos, where walls were eventually built, were moister and they could support agriculture. . . . This fact makes sense of names, such as Yü-lin, which means 'elm wood,' for a place that . . . appears to have been forested, although today it is menaced by encroaching sand dunes."[58]

The strategic significance of the Ordos is that whereas the Yellow River might appear to make a defensible line for the Ming, especially where it flows north from Ningxia and then east toward Dongshen, the fact of its inner ecological systems meant that it was hospitable to nomads who might use it as a base from which to launch attacks against Chinese cities in the Fen, Wei, and Yellow River valleys to the east and south. By the time the Ming dynasty was founded, Chinese had understood this fact for centuries, although no dynasty had a simple or even workable solution for maintaining control over the Ordos. The Ming founder established forward garrisons for defense, but ultimately all but one of those were withdrawn by the 1430s—for reasons historians have not yet been able to disentangle.

Whatever the cause, the consequence of that withdrawal was fateful. Mongol tribes began uniting, and by the 1440s a leader had emerged who established an alliance stretching from Korea to Xinjiang. Wanting better terms of trade with China but rebuffed in his peaceful approaches, the Mongol leader began raising his army and "threatened to conquer China as their ancestors had done."[59] The new Ming emperor, the 21-year old Zhentong, ignored the advice of his Minister of War and decided not merely to launch a pre-emptive attack against the Mongols in an area where the Ming Chinese had forgotten how to fight with cavalry but also to lead the troops himself. Near a postal station named Tu-mu some 60 miles northwest of Beijing, the Chinese troops were ambushed and defeated, and the emperor taken prisoner. "The defeat at Tumu was a disaster for the Chinese."[60]

Put on the defensive, the Ming decided to abandon the forward military pressure on the Mongols and to adopt instead the defensive strategy of building walls, starting in the Ordos along the line separating the steppe from Chinese agricultural communities. The success of this wall in keeping Mongol cavalry out spurred a wall-building spree over the next century that resulted in what came to be called "the Great Wall," putting extreme financial strain on the Ming empire because of the cost involved—and ultimately contributing to the empire's weakness and collapse in the mid-seventeenth century. In the meantime, Ming garrisons set fire to a 15–30 miles swathe of "wasteland" north of the Wall "to deprive barbarian cavalries of feed for their horses." As a late Ming statesman put it, "although it [the burning] takes a considerable effort, one may have a peaceful winter."[61]

But in one of the great ironies of history, the Great Wall ultimately proved irrelevant in keeping northern invaders out and hence became a very large monument to massive Ming spending. The mid-seventeenth conquerors of China came from north of the Great Wall, and while they were Manchus from the forests and plains of Manchuria, not the Mongols of the steppe, their empire did come to include the nomads of the steppe, making the Great Wall a historic relic of no strategic importance when the Manchus came to incorporate the Mongols and other peoples of the steppe into their state, the Great Qing empire (1644–1911).

The Seventeenth-Century Crisis[62]

During the seventeenth century, China was beset by numerous overlapping and interweaving crises: peasant unrest and uprisings, banditry and piracy, foreign and domestic trade dislocations, epidemic disease, invasion by Manchus followed by 40 years of war, and harvest failures caused by decades of exceptionally cold weather. People died from wars, starvation, and disease, all of which resulted in a severe decline in population throughout the empire, from perhaps 150 million in 1600 to 120 million by 1650, with recovery not beginning until the 1680s, at the earliest.

Historians looking at the world in the seventeenth century have commented on how widespread social and political disorder was, not just in China but in Russia, England, and France also. With such a global reach, these historians have wondered about a "general" global crisis in the seventeenth century, and have searched for common causes in all of them. The most significant factor common to all was a global climate event known as the "Little Ice Age."[63] Defined as the period from the late-fourteenth to the mid-nineteenth century, the term "Little Ice Age" should not be read to mean uniformly colder temperatures, nor should it be interpreted to mean that each year during this period was colder than the one preceding or following. Indeed, even during the "Little Ice Age," some years and even decades were rather warm. But on balance, though, global temperatures cooled enough for glaciers to keep growing rather than receding.

In China, the coldest decades appear to have been the 1610s, 1630s, 1650s, and 1680s. The impact of the Little Ice Age can be seen even in the subtropical south, in Lingnan. After the cold snap of 1614, two years of drought began with the late harvest of 1616 and continued until the winter wheat harvest in the spring of 1618. The drought affected the most densely populated parts of Guangzhou and Huizhou prefectures, leading to reports of "dearth" (*ji*), "famine" (*da ji*), and "disturbances" in most of the county cities of eastern Guangdong. Additionally, regular outside supplies of grain to Guishan city (Huizhou) dried up, prompting the prefect to organize a small relief effort.[64]

The significance of the climatic turn toward a colder, drier regime around 1614 lies in the impact these conditions had on agricultural yields.[65] Obviously, droughts, especially those that lasted for more than a single year, so seriously slashed harvest yields that the gazetteers glossed those years as experiencing "hunger" (*ji*) or "famine" (*da ji*). But more subtly, lower temperatures and less rain also placed downward pressure on harvest yields. Although good data to demonstrate this phenomenon for the seventeenth century are lacking, we do know from better data in the eighteenth century and from modern studies that cool temperatures lower the grain harvest yields by shortening the growing season: for each day the growing season is shortened, the skimpier the harvest.[66]

In upland areas of south China where peasant farmers planted just one crop, such as in the northern Guangdong hill region, colder temperatures may have had less of an impact than in the double- or triple-cropping areas to the south. Even in rich alluvial fields of the Pearl River delta, where farmers could get two or three crops, a shortened growing season could force farmers to choose between harvesting a first crop before it was fully ripe to ensure that the second crop could be planted in time for harvesting, or taking the risk that the second crop would not have sufficient time to ripen, and in the next year lowering the risk of frost damage by planting one less crop altogether. The incidence of harvest failures, food shortages, and dearth thus increased with the onset of colder temperatures in the decade of the1610s, peaking in the middle of the century. [67]

In north China, epidemics swept both town and countryside in two great waves in the 1580s and 1640s. And in both cases, the epidemics followed on the heels of natural disaster–induced famines. As summarized by Helen Dunstan, the precipitating sequence of events in the 1640s in the Lower Yangzi region included "floods resulting from the prolonged torrential rains of 1640, the drought and locust-plague of 1641, the prolongation of the drought and famine into 1642 and 1643, aggravated by further ruinous floods in the last summer of 1642, the rise in the price of rice. . . . By the winter of 1641 'there was no rice for sale on the market, or even if there was, people walked past without inquiring.'" What common people did eat was "chaff, leaves, bark, roots of grass . . . human flesh, wild goose droppings and clods of earth."[68]

Famine conditions and starvation diets lower human resistance to diseases of all kinds, which are more often than not the actual cause of deaths during famines—not actual starvation. In conditions of drought and poor sanitation, typhoid can spread quickly. Typhus and dysentery are common "famine fevers." What the actual diseases were that spread from the lower Yangzi River into the North China plain in the mid-seventeenth century is not known with certainty, since most Chinese accounts simply refer to the epidemics as "pestilential airs." On the basis of first-hand accounts, Dunstan thinks there were several, including dysentery, some kind of killing-fever, possibly meningitis, and bubonic plague. In places directly hit, mortality rates might have reached 90 percent, although that would not have been the case throughout the affected regions. But historians are quite certain that the death and destruction of the 1640s was significant.[69]

Not all of that was caused by the natural disasters, famines, and epidemics, for those were accompanied by two massive peasant rebellions that were both cause and consequence of the disasters. The details of those uprisings can be found elsewhere,[70] but for our purposes they effectively spelled the end of the Ming dynasty in 1644 when the last emperor hung himself on a hill to the north of the Imperial Palace in Beijing. But instead of the peasant rebels from within China founding a new dynasty, Manchus from north of the Great Wall invaded, helped by Ming generals who preferred Manchu rule to that of peasant rebels. After conquering China, the Manchus not only ruled over China "within the Great Wall," but by the mid-eighteenth century conquered the remaining nomadic empires to their north and west.

The Great Hunt in the Northeast

The Manchu conquest of China lasted nearly forty years, from the time they took the capital of Beijing in 1644 until the last internal rebellion was put down in 1683. During that time they were most interested in consolidating their power by tracking down the last remnants of Ming loyalists, winning over the Chinese elite so that they would not resist their Manchu overlords, and suppressing the peasant rebel armies that had brought down the Ming in the first place.[71]

Prior to their conquest of China, the Manchu state had formed only recently from a number of tribes inhabiting the forests and steppe northeast of the Great Wall (see map 2.2). Their great leader Nurhaci began melding numerous tribes into a single state under his rule, and even had a language created to solidify their identity as "Manchu." His state had close ties to various Mongol tribes to his west, solidified by intermarriage of princes and princesses. Chinese who "had gone native" and adopted Manchurian customs and language too came to serve the Manchu state. Indicating the Manchu intent to take at least part of north China, in 1616 Nurhaci declared the establishment of the "Latter Jin dynasty," harkening back to the Jurchen state that had taken part of north China from the Song six centuries earlier. His successor later changed that dynastic name to "Qing" to indicate a larger objective—the conquest of all of China. That the Manchus did, and they ruled China as the Qing dynasty for over 250 years, until 1911.

As the Manchu rulers were consolidating their rule over China, they also decided to isolate their homeland so as to provide a basis to maintain their strengths and their identity. For several millennia, Han Chinese had migrated into the plains of southern Manchuria, and so had a toehold there and in Mongolia too. But both through imperial fiat, and the planting of the "Willow Palisade," the Manchus determined to keep Manchuria for the Manchus by keeping the Han Chinese out.[72] The Manchu rulers thought that their way of life and that of the Han Chinese were fundamentally incompatible, and that Han Chinese ways (drinking, gambling, and extravagant feasting) would be corrupting.[73] The Manchus also forbade nomadic peoples from grazing within 15 miles of the Great Wall, a policy that allowed vegetation to return and that halted (if only temporarily) processes of desertification.[74]

Although the Manchus did farm in the river valleys, much of Manchuria was old growth pine forest that harbored a vast quantity of wildlife, from the Amur tiger and brown bear at the top of the food chain to fur-bearing animals such as sable mink, a variety of fish (including the huge sturgeon), and birds of all kinds, including storks. Additionally, a very valuable root called *ginseng*, believed by Chinese to have a variety of medicinal properties, grew on the forest floor. With such a variety of wildlife, hunting and gathering had been an important part of Manchu life, and played a significant role in the raising and training of Manchu warriors.

After capturing Beijing and settling into the Ming imperial palace, Manchu rulers relied on Manchuria to supply them and the imperial household with all kinds of foods and furs. Indeed, David Bello argues that although the Manchu state was initially dependent "on the region's biodiversity for its very existence,"[75] over the first half century or more of its rule, it developed hunting and gathering policies for Manchuria that were linked with Manchu identity, policies that Bello calls "imperial foraging." The Manchus established an entire bureaucracy to oversee the procurement of game and supplies from specially designated enclaves throughout Manchuria, as well as licensing foragers and imposing tribute quotas on them. Tigers, bears, leopards, fish, feathers, storks, and pine nuts, among other forest products, were foraged from Manchurian forests and sent to Beijing.

By the early 1700s, "elite demand approached mass consumption," and shortages began appearing, raising concern among China's Manchu rulers. "[T]here are indications that intensification of hunting and gathering [to meet that demand] . . . as well as illicit poaching and environmental degradation related to [illegal] Han migration, seem to have contributed to the depletion of resources." But rather than seeing these "shortages" as possibly indicating that the wildlife populations were being ravaged to the point of collapse, China's Manchu rulers "interpreted shortfalls in anthropogenic terms that were centered on human idleness, incompetence, or greed" and so intensified the foraging. Where pine nuts earlier had been easily gathered, as low-hanging fruit, as it were, by the late eighteenth century "the only way to obtain pine nuts and pinecones was to cut down trees." Bello concludes that although the Manchu imperial foraging, intensified by Han in-migration, did not permanently exhaust the most valuable resources of the northeast, the "extractions proved unsupportable by the early nineteenth century."[76] The Manchus may not have deforested the northeast—indeed, as we will see in chapters 6 and 7, the forests were left there for Japanese and Russian to extract in the first half of the nineteenth century, and for the Communist rulers of the People's Republic of China to exploit—but they did deplete its wildlife.[77]

China Marches West[78]

As the Manchu state had been forming in the early seventeenth century, to the west a new Mongol state was also forming in the Zunghar basin (see map 2.2): the Zunghar empire. Formed out of four western Mongol tribes that had spent most of their time fighting with each other and with the Mongol tribes to their east who had formed close ties with the Manchus, the Zunghars emerged as a major threat to the new Manchu-led Qing empire. Located in the grassland steppe, the first really successful Zunghar leader attempted to increase the resources available to his state by encouraging settled farming in the steppe where possible, in particular in the Ili River valley and around the oasis towns ringing the Taklamakan desert (through which the Silk Road had gone in centuries past), and by mining and casting cannons.

Simultaneously, the Russian empire was pushing east into Siberia, and there were numerous clashes between Russia and the new Qing state along the Amur River. Two treaties between the Russians and the Manchu Qing state—the 1689 Treaty of Nerchinsk and the 1727 trade Treaty of Kiakhta—established a border between the Russian and Qing empires. There are many aspects of those treaties that are still noteworthy, but for our purposes the most important is that the negotiated boundaries of China now included the grasslands in what was to become Inner and Outer Mongolia, and everything to the south of that line, including the areas of Zungharia and Tibet. One could argue that the treaties with Russia were a form of cartographic imperialism that freed Manchu forces to conquer regions Russia did not care to contest, and vice versa: Russia had all of Siberia from which to extract its tribute.

As soon as was possible, in the late seventeenth century, the Manchus sent expeditions against the Zunghars. The Qing emperor Kangxi (r. 1661–1727), himself a Manchu warrior, considered it a matter of personal triumph to be able to defeat the Zunghar leader Galdan, and spent much time and effort in the attempt. But these first Qing attempts ultimately failed because the Zunghars could rely upon the tried-and-true defensive measures of steppe warriors in conflict with Chinese forces by retreating into the grasslands. Ultimately, the Chinese troops, who depended on supply lines from north China, would stretch their logistical support to the limit and either be defeated or be forced to retreat.

Galdan's death in 1698 apparently led to a Qing victory over the Zunghars, but the Kangxi emperor had been more interested in the personal, man-to-man conflict and victory than in directly ruling over Zungharia, so he settled for the promise of the new Zunghar leader, Tsewang Rabdan, to become a tributary state to the Qing. What the Manchu rulers had come to consider China's northwest was only apparently "pacified."

The Zunghar state not only survived but grew in strength during the first half of the eighteenth century. But the death of their last leader Galdan Tseren in 1745 led to internecine warfare, leading to another opening for the Qing to attempt to defeat the Zunghars. This time the wars were led by the Qianlong emperor (r. 1736–95), who was interested not merely in defeating the Zunghar leader but in eliminating Zungharia and the Zunghar people from the face of the earth, much like Emperor Wu of the Han had tried with the Xiongnu. With the extraordinary resources made available by a booming Chinese economy and rapid extension of commercial activity and establishment of markets for the movement of goods, capital, and labor, the Qianlong emperor succeeded not just in defeating Zungharia but in achieving his "final solution" to the problem of steppe-based attacks on China.

The Qianlong emperor issued several edicts that led to the extermination of the Zunghar people. "Show no mercy at all to these rebels. Only the old and weak should be saved." In historian Peter Perdue's words, "The emperor deliberately targeted young and able men in order to destroy the Zunghars as a people. . . . Old men, children, and women were to be spared and sent as bondservants to other Mongol tribes and Manchu bannermen, but they would lose their tribal identity."[79] The result, in the words of a later Chinese statesman, was that out of the million or so Zunghars, "40 percent died of smallpox, 20 percent fled to the Russians and Kazakhs, and 30 percent were killed by the great [Chinese] army. . . . [Across the steppe] there was not one single Zungharian tent." As Perdue concludes, "Zungharia was left as a blank social space, to be refilled by a state-sponsored settlement of millions of Han Chinese peasants, Manchu bannermen, Turkestani oasis settlers, [Muslim] Hui, and others."[80]

The newly conquered and cleansed Zungharia was renamed Xinjiang, meaning "New Frontier." To the Zunghars, of course, it had been a core region, not a periphery. It was a "new frontier" only to the Chinese and their Manchu overlords. But in their hands, Zungharia was transformed into a frontier. Using the *tun-tian* Chinese technique of military-agricultural colonies, Chinese troops were settled in the region and set about on a continuous campaign of bringing the fertile lands of the steppe under the plow. Not all the grasslands could be turned into farms, but those that were near sources of water for irrigation could be. So too could the desert lands around the oases of the Tarim basin, where snowfed rivers could be used to irrigate farms. In the 60 years from 1760 when the first colonies were formed until 1820, more than 1 million mu (about 17,000 acres) were registered as farmland, and Han Chinese farmers were plowing up grasslands, just as their ancestors had done nearly two millennia earlier during the Han dynasty (see chapter 3).

Establishing farms on marginal grasslands works as long as the climate cooperates by supplying sufficient water for irrigation, and as long as farming techniques preserve the fertile topsoil. These conditions held for most of the eighteenth and nineteenth centuries. But, as we will see in chapter 7, once the grasslands were disturbed by plows, as likely an outcome as productive farms was the loss of farmland to erosion, and the advance of deserts in grasslands never able to reestablish themselves.

The Qing conquest of Zungharia, and its transformation into a frontier zone to be farmed and exploited, is one part of the environmental story of China's new west. Another part includes the story of disease—in particular, smallpox. For most of the period covered in this book, the nomads of the steppe and the settled agriculturalists of China had had periodic contact, ranging from wars to trade. Despite that interaction, the ecologies of the steppe and of the sown were very different. Their peoples had developed different ways of gaining their necessities of life from their environments, causing the disease pools of these two ecozones to remain mostly separate.[81]

That separation proved especially dangerous to the various peoples of the steppe, for unlike the more densely populated Chinese to their south and Russians to their west, they had little experience with the ravages of smallpox, and thus had had little opportunity to develop some level of societal immunity. Even in a community with some levels of immunity to smallpox, an outbreak could kill a quarter of those infected. And the loss of life was much higher in communities in which few had already survived the disease once. The Chinese, in fact, had much experience with smallpox. They understood its etiology, and knew when and how to quarantine houses and neighborhoods. In the sixteenth century, Chinese doctors even began to understand an early form of inoculation accomplished by placing the scabs of infected patients into the noses of children to induce an immune system reaction to the weakened smallpox virus. This process, known as "variolation" for its use of variola, or scabs, was later used by the Manchu rulers of China to inoculate their children. One of the reasons the Kangxi emperor had been selected over his brothers to rule the empire is that he had survived smallpox as a child and thus was immune; in 1687 he initiated regular inoculation of the royal family.

Mongols, too, knew of the virulence of smallpox, and limited their contact with Chinese to avoid the disease. They carefully chose which members would attend the markets that were established to trade their horses with Chinese for grain, tea, and cloth. Should one of their tribe be afflicted, they knew enough to isolate the tent and only to approach it from downwind to deliver food and water. Still, contact with Chinese increased the likelihood that not just Mongols of the steppe would contract smallpox but that so, too, would the forest tribes of Siberia north of the Amur river. There, smallpox wiped out 50–80 percent of the natives who contracted it.[82] It is thus not too surprising that up to 40 percent of the Zunghar population was wiped out by smallpox. To that extent, their unfortunate experience is similar to that of the natives of North America and the Pacific Islands.

"The elimination of the [Zunghar] state," in Perdue's words, "gave the Chinese imperial rulers [the Manchus] the largest area they had ever controlled, including the present boundaries of the People's Republic [including Tibet] plus the present-day Mongolian Republic, the Ili valley in Kazakhstan, part of Kirghizia, and parts of Siberia north of the Amur River."[83] Nearly simultaneously, the limits of the empire in the southwest were reached as well. Still, an additional part of the story of the eighteenth-century colonial expansion of the Chinese empire into new territories and ecosystems is the incorporation of two large islands, Taiwan and Hainan. There, however, the outcome of the story was surprisingly different than that of the one leading to the extermination of the Zunghars.[84]

ISLANDS AND THEIR ECOLOGICAL TRANSFORMATIONS

During China's late imperial period, two large tropical and semitropical islands—Hainan and Taiwan—became thoroughly enmeshed in China's political economy and thus experienced processes of environmental change similar to that in China's southwestern frontier, in particular Han Chinese–driven agricultural development and the consequent deforestation. Although they are similar in size (around 35,000 square kilometers, or the size of Massachusetts), they have different ecosystems and histories of relations with the Chinese mainland. Hainan Island, just 15 miles south of the Leizhou peninsula on the mainland, is a tropical island well south of the Tropic of Cancer, whereas Tawain, a bit further north, sits astride the Tropic of Cancer about 100 miles off China's southeast coast. Because of the distance and difficulties of navigation in the Strait of Formosa, Taiwan was relatively isolated from direct involvement with the Chinese state until the sixteenth century, while Hainan was in and out of Chinese control from the Han dynasty on.

Hainan Island

Bounded on the north by coral reefs and pearl-yielding oyster beds, Hainan Island was covered by tropical forests that varied from monsoon forests in the coastal lowlands and the tropical evergreen and deciduous forest common to the mainland on the lower slopes of the island's central mountains to a tropical rain forest on its windward southeastern side. Hainan Island is not as species-rich as the tropical forests of South America or Southeast Asia, but it is rich enough, with more than 3,500 species of plants. Long known by Han Chinese as a place "without horses or tigers," Hainan's forests did support leopards, muncjacs and sambar deer, gibbons, macaques, and hundreds of species of snakes, many of them poisonous. It was also malarial, probably courtesy of some of the early in-migrants.

Whoever the original inhabitants may have been, archeological evidence shows continuous human habitation from about three thousand years ago by a people the Chinese later called the Li, but who called themselves Shem, Chem, Tam, or Dan.[85] Like other aboriginal peoples of China's south and southwest, the Li were Tai-speaking and obtained their sustenance from the land by a combination of shifting, slash-and-burn cultivation of yams and dry rice, and hunting and gathering from the forests. The Li thus transformed their environment, but their numbers were too small for those actions to have made much impact on the island's ecosystems. When troops of the First Emperor of Qin first landed on the island around 200 BCE, followed by Han dynasty troops and civil administrators, the Li were found throughout the lowlands, and clearly had a well-developed agricultural economy that included the skilled weaving of textiles.

According to an official Han Chinese history written about 100 BCE: "The people all wear a costume of linen, like an unlined blanket, which is pierced through the center so that the head may pass through. The menfolk are tillers and farmers, planting millet, rice, ramie, and hemp. The womenfolk are mulberry- and silkworm-cultivators, and they weave and spin. There are neither horses nor tigers. The people possess five kinds of livestock. The mountains abound in sambar and muntjacs. As for weapons, there are pikes, shields, knives, wooden bows and crossbows, and bamboo arrows—though sometimes they have points of bone."[86]

Han Chinese contact with the island and with the Li waxed and waned with the early dynasties, with the Chinese presence limited mostly to the northern plain across the strait from the mainland. By the Tang dynasty (618–907), Chinese claimed to govern the entire coastal strip, and while Li remained in the lowlands, Chinese now made note of Li who inhabited the highlands further inland, and a trade between lowland

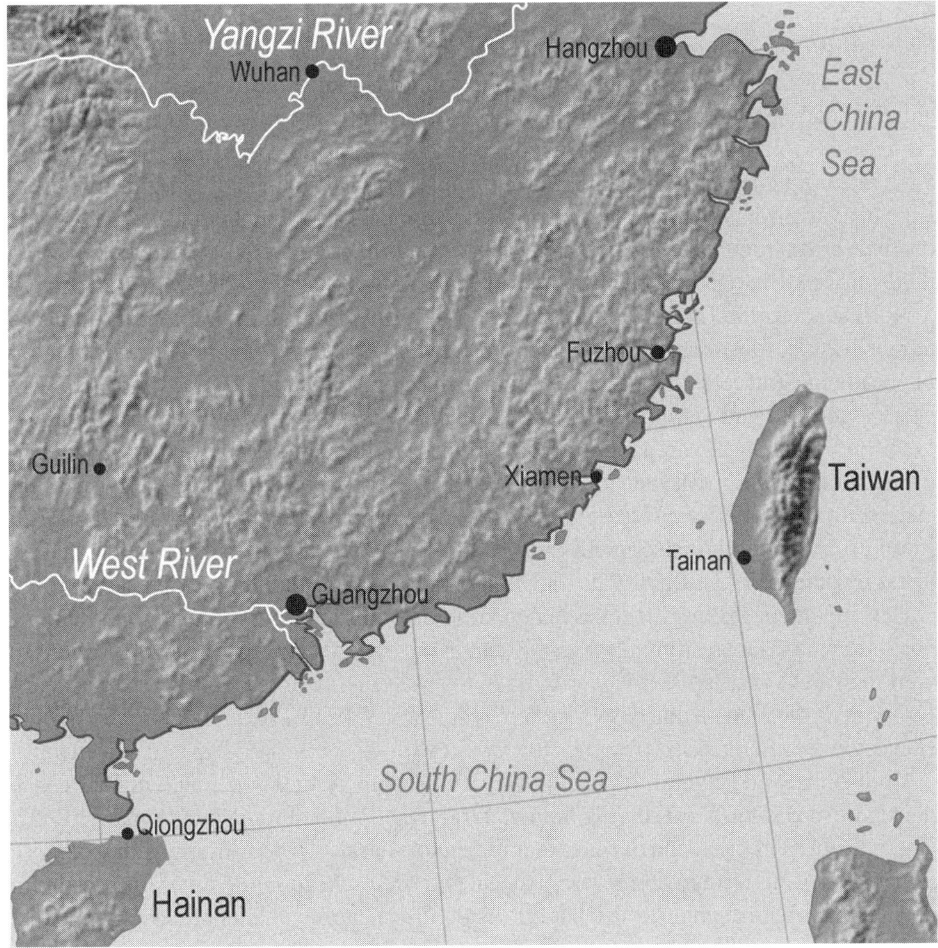

Map 5.4. The Islands of Taiwan and Hainan in Relation to Mainland China

and upland areas began. Especially prized by Han Chinese was a particular kind of aromatic wood called "sinking aromatic," a dense, diseased resinous heartwood of the tropical tree known as garro, or aloeswood, that was heavier than water, and hence "sinking." The highland Li traded these aromatics and their finely woven textiles with lowlanders in exchange for salt, cereals, and iron hatchets and axes.[87]

During the Song, a more permanent Chinese administration was established, and Han Chinese settlers spread in the lowlands all around the island. The Chinese then distinguished between the "*shu*," or "cooked" and therefore "familiar" and "safe" Li, who accepted Chinese administration, and the "*sheng*," or "raw" and hence dangerous Li, who maintained their distance as well as their independence.[88] But not all Chinese migrants insisted on imposing their agricultural ways on the Li. Some instead learned from the Li how to live on the island. These Han migrants took up Li customs and finally became Li themselves.[89] But just as the Song-era "forward policy" in Sichuan and elsewhere resulted in conflict with the natives, so too did violence flare on Hainan Island, with eighteen major Song-era conflicts between Han and Li. Whether these were caused by Chinese land grabs or attempts to impose Chinese administrative and military rule is not known, but most likely the former, given the evidence from other frontier regions already cited in this book. As Anne Csete cautiously observes, "Although precise data on settlement patterns of Han farmers is lacking, such attacks [by Li on Chinese] may have been organized to defend Li territory from encroachment."[90] Han Chinese farmers cleared the forests and planted wet rice, whereas the Li way of life depended on the continued existence of forests, even if portions were periodically burned for shifting fields.

Wars against the Li continued under Mongol rule of China. Although substantial numbers of Li acquiesced to Mongol rule, large numbers of others did not, resulting in "massive" military campaigns against them in the 1290s. "The [Mongol] Yuan forces sacked every Li settlement on the island, and forced the surrender of 626 Li townships. . . . The Yuan army was the first to penetrate to the very heart of Hainan, where Yuan soldiers carved the words 'cavalry troops of the great Yuan came here' on a stone marker at the foot of Five-Fingers Mountain."[91] Besides subduing the Li for a while, the Mongol achievement included a census of the island, indicating a nearly equal number of Li and Han Chinese, about one hundred fifty thousand each.

Despite the Mongol military campaigns, Li continued to resist Chinese encroachment on their lands. And as Mongol rule crumbled in the early fourteenth century, Li headmen with their battle-hardened troops moved in to take control from fleeing Yuan officials. By the time the Ming dynasty was proclaimed in 1368, Li had been in control of Hainan Island for several decades.

During the Ming dynasty (1368–1644), the amount of cultivated land on the island doubled, from some 2 million mu around 1400 to 3.8 million mu by 1615. Most of this land was tilled by Han Chinese farmers, and a good deal was seized from Li territory in the mid-sixteenth century. Until then, Hainan had been ruled by the Chinese state as were other frontier regions, by the "loosely haltered" (*jimi*) "native chieftain" *tusi* system. The Ming state granted Li headmen hereditary *tusi* rule in return for periodic ritual acceptance of Ming rule and a willingness to continue to allow trade and export of island products. Thus the lowland-highland trade established as early as the Tang dynasty, of grain, silk, and iron products for aromatics and other mountain forest products, continued. But so too did a constant trickle of Han Chinese settlers up river valleys, further and further inland, and hence into increasing contact with the "raw" *sheng* Li.

Periodic conflict flared into a major islandwide war in the early 1500s, apparently brought on by wealthy Han Chinese's buying up farmland from the state military colonies, and further encroaching on Li lands as well. By 1550, local Chinese officials teamed with a high court minister who had been born on Hainan to advocate the rapid settlement of key areas of the island by Han Chinese, so to eliminate the Li and their threats to Chinese control. The idea was to move troops from military colonies where the Li had been "good citizens" to areas further inland. A local official "identified fertile land in specific Li townships . . . [and] advised that roads be built . . . through the heart of the mountains." State Minister Hai Jui wrote: "Although the land inhabited by the Li has tall mountains and steep ridges, within there are many level areas and fertile fields. These could be enlarged. . . . Nowadays it is very common for everyone to take over land after a suppression campaign. . . . [We should] move Han cultivators into [these districts]."[92]

But not all Ming officials saw the Li as the enemy. After all, many had accepted Chinese customs and rulers, and had adopted Chinese-style agriculture, become settled, and paid taxes. To the Chinese, they had been *hua*, or "transformed." To some Chinese administrators, the real enemy was the *unhealthy environment* that the Li, by cultivating and becoming more like Chinese farmers, were improving: "[At the beginning of our dynasty] the Li people were few and the land was uncultivated and wild. The mountain mists still had not cleared. But now [1503], there are many crowds of people, the land is open and cultivated, and eighty to ninety percent of the mountain fogs have already been dispersed."[93] The Han Chinese and their ways of settled farming were clearly understood as positive transformers of the environment from raw, wild, and threatening, to subdued, conquered, and life sustaining (at least for the Han). The Han Chinese thus had come to see themselves, as the high official Hai Rui intimated, as having the power not just to "cook" the "raw" barbarians and hence to "civilize" them, but to "improve" the very environment as well.

By the mid-sixteenth century, Han Chinese had aggressively pushed inland, following the Nandu River from its mouth on the north shore of Hainan, south into the heart of the island. Officials then began identifying other areas suitable for Han Chinese settlement, and were eyeing the Changhua River valley, flowing through the southwestern quadrant of Hainan Island. However much land Han Chinese seized from the Li, and how much was transformed into farmland, is not known with any precision. We do know that settlers were encouraged to use fire to burn the forests not just out of the river valleys but up into the hills as well. Periodic firings kept any forest from regrowing, encouraging instead the growth of a tough tropical grass known as cogon that also grows in the Philippines and Vietnam under similar circumstances. By 1950, when just 7 percent of the forest cover of Hainan remained, most of the island had become savanna, grassland, or shrub.[94] Most of this transformation happened from the mid-eighteenth century on, but the process got its start around 1550.

Fortunately for the forests and various species inhabiting the island, political instability and, ultimately, the collapse of the Ming dynasty, followed by the Manchu conquest of China, left Hainan relatively untouched by aggressive outside forces until the early eighteenth century. The Ming wars of conquest, the flight of people from areas near administrative towns or military garrisons, left the island with little organized agriculture and much "wasteland" when Manchu-led troops began to secure the island, and apparently to seize the best houses and land for themselves.[95]

When Manchu-led troops arrived around 1700, the island looked relatively depopulated. An official reported that "there were uncultivated hills as far as the eye could see, broken-down towns and dilapidated villages. There were neither flames nor smoke from cooking fires." Nonetheless, demand for "sinking" aromatics remained sufficiently strong that another official worried that private collection and sale to Han merchants would soon exhaust the supply of the rare aromatic.[96] The large number of Li revolts lasting until 1700 also belied the depopulated picture. By using Li against Li, and rewarding with ranks and titles those who cooperated with the new Qing, Li resistance was overcome, and Hainan Island experienced 60 years of relative peace from about 1700 to 1760.

The island population increased mostly due to a slow but steady migration of Han Chinese, and the economy became ever more integrated with that of the mainland by the markets that popped up everywhere, especially in the northern half of the island. Whereas exotic mountain forest products had been the main exports from Hainan Island in early centuries, by the eighteenth century sugar cane and rice—two staple commodities—dominated exports. Officials debated what to do about the interior mountainous areas still inhabited by the "raw" *sheng* Li: some advocated building roads through the island to settle Han Chinese, but the most agreed-upon tact was to leave them alone; the raw *sheng* Li, it was believed, would tend to adopt Chinese agricultural methods and to trade peacefully with Chinese merchants. "The [Li] people were faithful, ignorant and primitive, maintaining remnants of extreme antiquity. Later on the Li gradually split into the [raw] *sheng* and [the cooked] *shu*. . . . The raw *sheng* Li 'eat their own strength' (are self-supporting) while the cooked *shu* Li have gradually become crafty and dishonest. The raw *sheng* Li were 'unopened' and innocent until outsider scoundrels used many methods to tempt them to make profits, so that they gradually lost their old ways."[97]

However much the first half of the eighteenth century was "peaceful," population growth, migration of Han Chinese to Hainan, and commercialization of the broader Chinese economy continued to put pressure on mountain resources and relations between the indigenous Li and the Han Chinese, finally erupting in a major Li rebellion in 1767. Apparently angered by high interest charged by Han Chinese merchants and poor treatment at the hand of Han landowners, two Li leaders decided, in Anne Csete's words, "to drive the Guest people [i.e., Han Chinese] from their region by killing them."[98] The end result was predictable: the Li leaders were captured and beheaded, their followers imprisoned, and the Han Chinese protected by their military. But Chinese state officials were not certain about the wisdom of then settling Han Chinese on Li land.

By the time of the 1767 revolt, Li and Han had become quite economically interdependent. Chinese merchants advanced silver to cooked *shu* Li who contracted with the raw *sheng* Li to clear land, plant betel nut and sugar cane, and gather aromatics. Some officials thought it would be best for Li and Han to be separated, to protect the Li from unscrupulous Han. But higher officials understood the importance of the lowland-upland trade to both Chinese and Li: "Most of the cane, aromatics and other products come from the hills and valleys of Li townships. Now that the Guest people [i.e., Han Chinese] are forbidden to make private loans to Li people or to demand high interest, unless we think of a way for them to trade, the goods will rot where they stand and the Li people will certainly be in dire straights."[99] The solution was to allow markets, but for officials to regulate prices and market days. Furthermore, the really wild *sheng* Li should be left alone: "They live in their lairs and eat from the land. They are ignorant and fierce, no different from dogs or sheep. They should be left alone to do as they want as before."[100]

The area that was to be left to them was the last remaining wilds of the inaccessible Five-Fingers Mountain region. But unlike refugees from the Han Chinese state on the mainland who might always have highlands even further away to escape to, the *sheng* Li of Hainan Island were increasingly encircled and pushed higher up the slopes of

Five-Fingers Mountain, encircled by their cooked brethren and by increasing numbers of Han Chinese. By the late eighteenth century, then, Han Chinese and domesticated *shu* Li who had accepted Chinese rulership and customs, especially the Han Chinese way of farming, had come to inhabit nearly all of Hainan Island, turning it under their plows and trading mountain resources for silver. The desire to get their hands on increasingly rare mountain goods led Han Chinese and *shu* Li as well to extort goods from other Li: "Some people 'borrow' official rank and put on the angry looks of an office runner to demand 'tribute' of aromatics, pearls, flowering pear, large [tree] branches, ocean-boat wood, wildcat skins, cotton, Li bronze, can and bamboo, deer antler velvet, deer whips, bear gallbladder, flowering bamboo, Sapan wood and other products."[101]

That is quite a list, and indicates that the ecosystems of Hainan Island were being pillaged for their natural resources. Li resisted as best they could; the nineteenth century was one of almost constant Li uprisings and Han Chinese reprisals. By the end of the century, Chinese officials once again were proposing "development," including a road across the island, as a way to resolve the endemic Li violence. Only the advent of the Chinese Communist regime in 1950 would bring political order. By then, only 25 percent of the island remained forested, and over the next twenty years a variety of developmental schemes hatched in Beijing would bring that down to just 7 percent.[102] Hainan Island became an independent province in the 1990s, and since then has been fast transforming itself into "China's Hawaii," golf courses and all.

The Island of Taiwan

Were it not for the Dutch in the early seventeenth century, the Chinese state might never have taken an interest in the island of Taiwan, and the course of its environmental history no doubt would have been quite different. But different enough it was in any case. Situated 100 miles off the coast of Fujian province, for most of the period covered so far in this book, Taiwan attracted little Chinese interest. To be sure, the occasional Han Chinese mariners or farmers had made it to the island, but they were few and far between. But in the sixteenth century, first the Portuguese, then the Spanish, the Dutch, and the English all tried to get a piece of the action in the thriving Asian maritime trade, with the Dutch constructing a fort on Taiwan in 1624. The Dutch remained there until dislodged in 1661 by a Ming loyalist, whose forces in turn held on until 1683. By then it was clear to the Manchus that Taiwan was of considerable strategic importance.[103]

The island had its peculiarities (map 5.5). Slightly larger than Hainan, Taiwan is shaped like a tea leaf. A mountain range fell sharply off its eastern coast, which thus was rugged, and with few inlets or even space for human settlement. The mountains sent the monsoon winds up its windward side, which got dumped with huge amounts of rainfall, while the western leeward side, comprising about two-thirds of the island, was more gently sloping, with less rainfall and apparently some grasslands; not all of the island was forested. "In the seventeenth century," according to John Shepherd, "forests and tall grasses covered Taiwan's largely uncultivated plains as well as its mountains. These areas were teeming with herds of deer, 'sometimes two or three thousand in a flock together.'"[104]

The aboriginal peoples on Taiwan first arrived some three thousand to four thousand years ago, followed by several others. By the time Taiwan was noticed in the sixteenth century, as many as twenty different and mutually unintelligible languages may have been spoken on it. The aborigines were broadly classified as the mountain and plains aborigines, with most ecological niches taken by the time Dutch arrived. Finding people there but no farming, the Dutch had to import Chinese farmers and settle them around their fortress (called "Zeelandia") in order to supply it with food.[105]

The aborigines on Taiwan, who numbered about fifty thousand, hunted and gathered, and specialized in deer hunting and head hunting. With such a low density, they lived in more or less permanent villages, practiced shifting cultivation when needed, and had grasslands they considered their own, where they hunted both the plentiful deer herds and wild boar in the forests. The villages were well protected "by impenetrable rings of dense, prickly bamboo," apparently needed because of the almost constant warring and head hunting.[106]

To say that the Dutch and the Chinese found the native peoples of Taiwan fierce would be something of an understatement. But the island teemed with deer, the natives knew how to kill them, and there was a huge market in both Japan and China for deer skins, dried venison, and other deer parts that the Dutch were eager to supply. "The most numerous species were the sambar, Formosan sika, and muntjac. The large-antlered sambar and muntjac would graze in open country on grasses, herbaceous vegetation, and cultivated fields, as well as browse in woodland on trees and bushes. The smaller muntjacs, with simple, spike-like antlers, preferred to browse selectively in the deeper mountain forests."[107] In exchange for deer skins, the Dutch provided iron, salt, and cloth.

The story of what happened to Taiwan in the seventeenth and eighteenth centuries is familiar enough by now—but has some important differences. During the eighteenth century, population increases on the Chinese mainland, in particular in the coastal provinces across the strait in Fujian and Guangdong, sent increasing numbers of Han Chinese settlers to Taiwan. These Han Chinese farmers began transforming the deer fields into farms, but interestingly they did not displace the aborigines or push them into the mountains. Rather, because of the existing village structure and some sense, however ill defined, that the aborigines had about "their" land, village heads leased out their land. That does not mean that there weren't conflicts between Han and plains aborigines, for there certainly were. Moreover, as the Han population increased and farmland stretched even closer to the mountains, conflicts with the mountain aborigines increased Qing state concern over what policies to follow.[108]

According to Shepherd, a major consideration of the Qing state was the cost of occupying the island and defending the local Han Chinese population. Although the farmers paid the land tax, the taxes collected were insufficient to cover the costs of administration and the military. Given the strategic importance of the island, the Qing were in no mood to abandon the island, but neither were they interested in a continuous war with the mountain aborigines. Perhaps they were learning lessons from Hainan, where, as we have just seen, wars between the Chinese state and the Li continued into the twentieth century.[109] The Qing state thus tried to segregate Han Chinese farmers and the plains aborigines from the mountains by building walls,

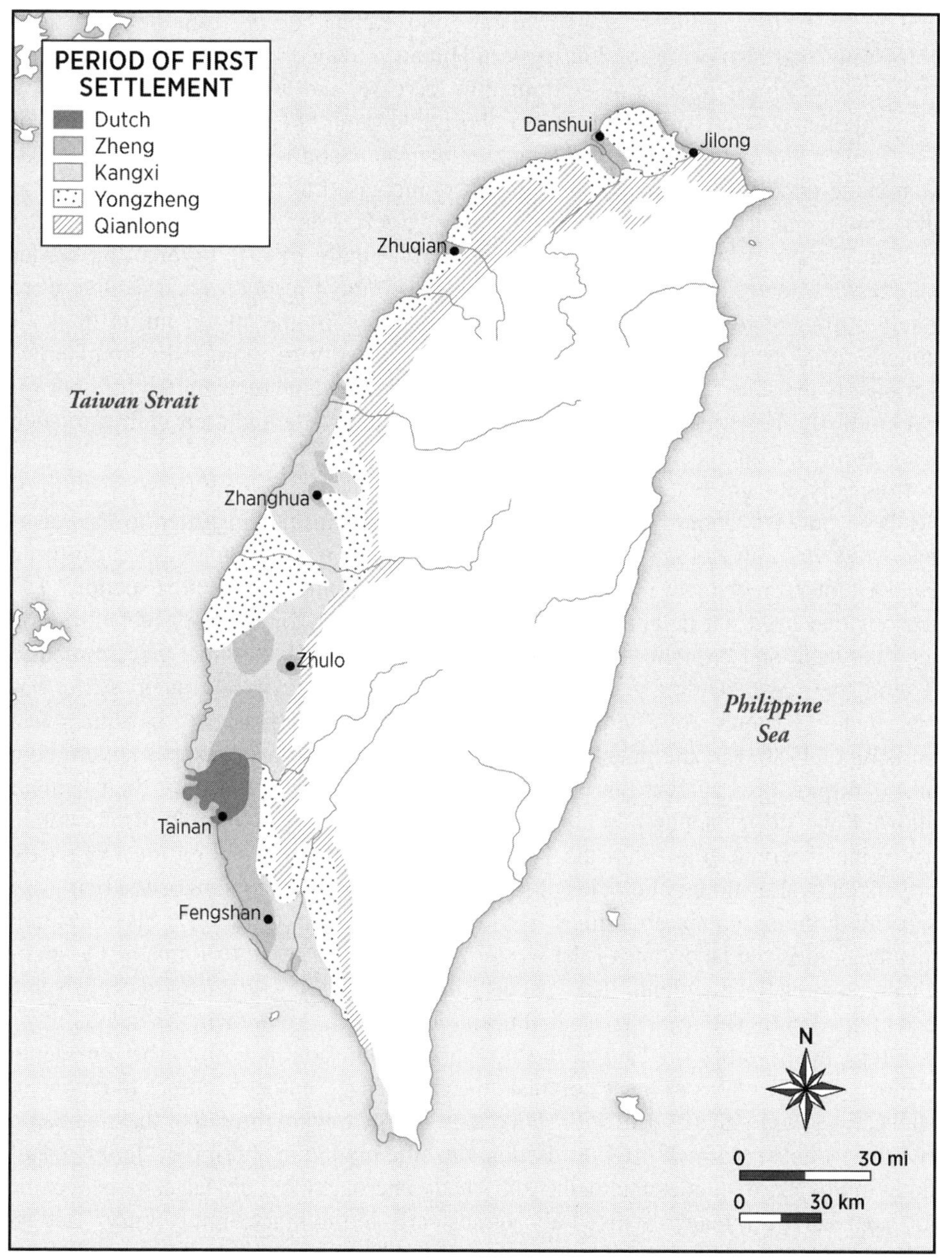

Map 5.5. The Island of Taiwan *Source:* Adapted from John Shepherd, *Statecraft and Political Economy on the Taiwan Frontier, 1600–1800* (Stanford: Stanford University Press, 1993), 175.

digging trenches, and, in 1722, erecting stone stele prohibiting any further migration into mountain aborigine territory. In the areas already settled by Han Chinese, the state created the requisite administrative machinery—counties and prefectures—to keep order among the Chinese population.[110] As we will see shortly, the idea of building walls to separate the transformable "cooked" barbarians from the more hard-core "raw" was also being tried in western Hunan province with the Miao.

The Han Chinese population continued to increase, and with the larger population came greater pressure on the protected aboriginal lands. From a total population of about one hundred thirty thousand Chinese and plains aborigines in 1684, when Taiwan came under Qing control, the population increased to more than eight hundred thousand a century later (the increase coming largely from in-migration), and to 2.5 million (or more) by 1900.[111] The Qing state repeatedly tried to enforce the border between Han and mountain aborigines. "But government resources and resolve were rarely sufficient to enforce such a radical policy against the steady influx of land-hungry immigrants, and the government had repeatedly to redraw the boundaries. Ultimately the state retreated from a total prohibition on Han reclamation [of aboriginal land] . . . The tribes were in most cases too weak to defend their claims to such lands from Han encroachment."[112]

Ironically, the greatest threat to Qing control of Taiwan came not from the aborigines but from Han Chinese immigrants. Three main groups had migrated to Taiwan—two from the prefectures of Chuanzhou and Zhangzhou in Fujian, and the third the Hakka (upland reclamation specialists we will discuss more in the next section). For reasons that need not detain us, the Fujian groups had a long history of feuding on the mainland, and brought their grudges to Taiwan. The Hakka, too, were forced to defend their own particular cultural mores. As a result, intercommunal strife was high, leading to numerous outbreaks of violence before the massive Lin Shuangwen uprising of 1786. Lin attempted to link up with mountain aborigines, but government agents turned them against Lin with stories about how Lin would seize their lands if allowed in—stories apparently confirmed by rebel behavior. Not only did mountain aborigines become allies with the Qing state, but after the rebellion the Qing state organized twelve military colonies of plains aborigines to stand guard on the boundary separating the mountain aborigines from the fractious Han Chinese.[113] "By the nineteenth century, the landscape of the western Taiwan plain resembled that of Fujian or Guangdong on the mainland. The vast deer herds of the early seventeenth century had been wiped out. The forest cover had been cleared. Han settlement prevailed."[114]

Inter-Chinese strife on Taiwan did not subside, but continued into the nineteenth century, and the plains military colonists were mobilized numerous times to put down Han Chinese uprisings or deal with Han bandits. Only toward the end of the nineteenth century were the plains aborigines used against the mountain aborigines. In the meantime, in Shepherd's understatement, "the steady encroachment of Han settlers became too oppressive for many civilized aborigines early in the nineteenth century," and so substantial numbers migrated to the narrow coastal plain on the east coast, and the only river valley there. On a northeastern plain inhabited by the Kuvulan tribe, Han Chinese migration began suddenly in the early nineteenth century, and the Kuvulan "were totally unprepared for the onslaught of Chinese settlers."[115]

In the late-nineteenth century, as foreign steamships plied China's coastal waters and their sailors periodically washed up on Taiwan's shores only to fall victim to head-hunting aborigines, pressure built for the Qing state to do something. The imperial court thus endorsed policies of "opening the mountains and pacifying the aborigines," and sent the plains aborigine military colonists against the mountain aborigines. These campaigns "in the late 1880s against the mountain aborigines were intended to end head-hunting and open the mountains to allow tea planters and camphor workers to take advantage of booming international markets for Taiwan's tea and camphor."[116] China's defeat by Japan in the first Sino-Japanese War of 1894–95 transferred Taiwan to the control of Japan, which ruled it as a colony from 1895 to 1945, transforming it into a rice and sugar bowl for Japan's domestic market.[117]

LAND COVER, LAND USE, AND LAND OWNERSHIP

Most of the non-Han peoples whose land was seized and farmed by Han Chinese employed various forms of collective decision making about the uses of the lands they occupied. We would hard pressed to call those arrangements "ownership." For peoples who were mobile, either because they followed their herds over the grasslands, or because they practiced shifting cultivation in the hills, the concept of "private" property rights did not make much sense. Various collective groups—whether organized by kinship group, monastery, or community—did make decisions about who got to use which lands at which times of the year. Mostly, those decisions allocating access to land reflected various kinds of social hierarchies, with those who were higher up getting more and better resources. The non-Han peoples were not egalitarian, nor did they leave their environments unchanged. We have seen numerous cases already of the extensive alteration of environments by these various peoples, and in chapter 6 we will see how extensively Tibetans and others in far western China dramatically deforested their mountains and valleys to make pastures for their yaks, sheep, and goats.

The Han Chinese had a very different property regime based on private ownership of land. Land ownership did not arise out of Chinese farmers' desire to protect their rights, but because the state needed a dependable and expandable tax base to undergird its power. Private ownership of farmland by farmers first emerged during the Warring States period as states were struggling for advantage over others, and by the Han dynasty became the fiscal basis of the Chinese state. Although the Sui and Tang state exerted claims to the right to redistribute land (the "equitable fields system"), and large landlords periodically encroached on peasant farmers' lands, the ideal for the Chinese state was an efficient system that taxed farmers. The attempts of landowners (whether large or small) to protect their wealth led to all kinds of ingenious means of avoiding taxes and hiding the actual ownership of land, but those practices did not obscure the point that the Chinese wanted to make its subjects and its land "fiscally legible."[118]

To a significant degree, the expansion of Han Chinese rule to the south, southeast, southwest, and southeast was driven both by a felt need to expand its tax base and because of the density of population in its core regions of north and east China (see figure 5.2). The population density in those regions was a function of the amount of flat, tillable land (the North China plain and the rice paddies of the lower Yangzi), and the early settlement and farming there. Also, Scott thinks that there was a logic to the linkages among settled farming, state power (not just in China but in Southeast Asia too), and pressures to colonize new lands: "[S]edentary agriculture leads to property

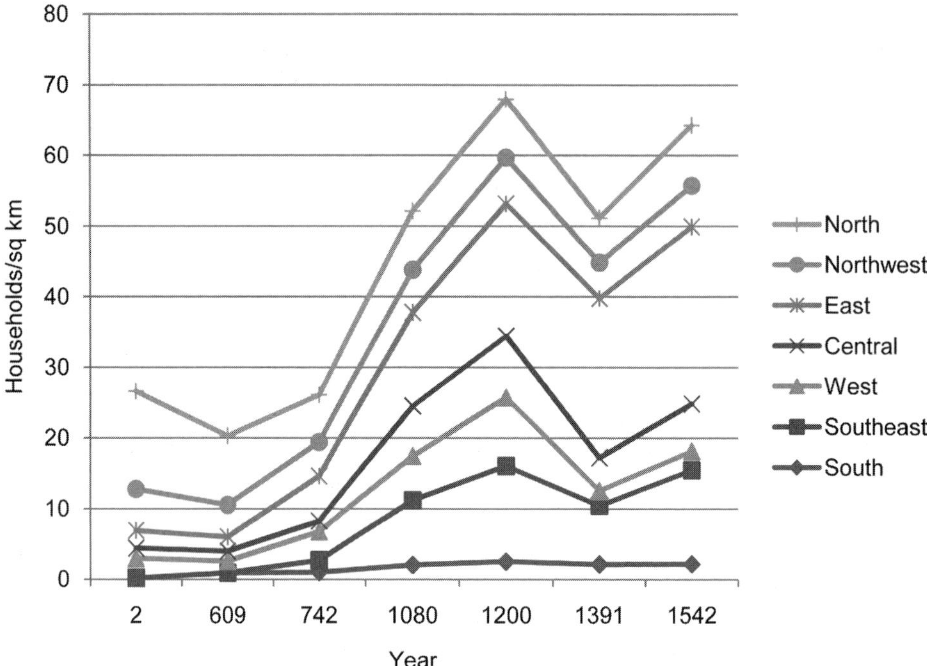

Fig. 5.2. China's Population Density by Region, 2–1561 CE *Source:* Based on Robert Hartwell, "Demographic, Political and Social Transformations of China, 750–1550," *Harvard Journal of Asiatic Studies* 42, no. 2 (December 1982): 369.

rights in land, the patriarchal family enterprise, and an emphasis, also encouraged by the state, on large families. Grain farming is, this respect, inherently expansionary, generating, when not checked by disease of famine, a surplus population, which is obliged to move and colonize new lands."[119]

The Chinese colonial enterprise, as we have seen during the Han, Tang, Song, Ming, and Qing dynasties, led to the capturing of lands that had very different land use principles, and the imposition of Han Chinese rules for land use upon them, either immediately and directly, or over a long period of time and sometimes indirectly, as in the use of the *tusi* system throughout the newly colonized lands of the south, west, and southwest. And with changes in the rules for land use came changes in land cover, mostly deforestation, not just in China's colonial frontiers but in its inner peripheries as well, as we will see in the next section.

There, the ownership rights to forests and other land in hilly and mountainous regions was more ambiguous, because the Qing state asserted implicit rights to all that land. "Though state ownership had not been expressly stated, once people started to exploit land resources and disputes arose between various users, the government would allocate usage rights, begin levying taxes, and by implication, establish its ownership."[120] Besides conflicts among competing private parties over ownership of these "wastelands," government officials during the Qing sometimes acted as entrepreneurial developers, claiming rights over vast tracts of land and scheming with wealthy patrons or friends to acquire the rights to the land. A rather egregious and well-documented case concerned Guangxi province in during the early eighteenth century.[121] But because the Qing state was most interested in maximizing tax revenues, so, too, did it have an interest in making as many people and as much land "fiscally legible" as possible, and thus it encouraged the "reclamation" of "wasteland."[122]

EXPLOITATION OF INNER PERIPHERIES

Where the strategic concerns of the Ming and Qing states drove consolidation and ecological transformation of the southwest borderlands and the islands of Taiwan and Hainan, and the attempt to demarcate the Chinese "civilized" agrarian empire from the nomadic warriors to its north and west led to the building of the Great Wall, demographic and economic processes and forces drove settlement of the interior hills and mountains in the lower and middle Yangzi regions, the southeast, the southwest, and the far south.

Highland Specialists: The Hakka and the "Shack People"

As population recovered from the Mongol conquest in the numerous river valleys from the Yangzi River valley south into Lingnan, the supply of good river bottom farmland became relatively low. Migrants looking for farmland thus had to look to forested upland areas, and to learn techniques from peoples already there. Various non-Han peoples had figured out how to use these upland ecosystems (perhaps like the Akha of Yunnan, discussed earlier in this chapter), and apparently were willing to share their understandings with newcomers who then became specialists in exploiting upland ecosystems. Markets had existed in China for a very long time, but during the Ming the population increase spurred the consolidation of a broader marketing system, making it possible for some people to specialize in nonfood crops and to rely on the market for their food supply. But especially important for the movement of larger numbers of Han people from the lowlands into the highlands was the availability of new kinds of foods from the Americas that were especially adapted for those environments. Markets and these new crops combined to render the exploitation of China's inland upland resources unsustainable and environmentally destructive.

The idea of the "Columbian exchange," first articulated by Alfred Crosby, usually refers to the biological exchange between the New World and the Old World, in particular Europe and the Mediterranean, following Columbus's "discovery" of the Americas.[123] But the maize (corn), potatoes, sweet potatoes, peanuts, and tobacco that Aztec and Incan farmers grew also spread very quickly to China and had dramatic ecological consequences there. Clear documentary evidence of all of these crops in China shows up by the 1550s, and the foremost authority on the question, historian Ho Ping-ti, argues that the crops had to have been planted for twenty to thirty years prior to that for them to have been noticed.[124] Just as the introduction of early-ripening rice strains around 1000 CE led to massive economic shifts and developments ultimately leading to the transformation of the environment of south China, so too was the introduction of New World crops to Chinese farming of epochal importance, making possible the exploitation of new niches in China's interior highlands and the transformation of upland environments.

The two groups primarily responsible for exploiting upland environments from the sixteenth through the twentieth centuries are called the Hakka (literally, "guest families") and the *pengmin*, or "shed people." Through a very interesting process, the Hakka became an ethnic group that exists to this day, though the shed people were more ephemeral. But both shared important similarities, even though the areas they settled were different.

The origins of the Hakka are unclear and are debated among historians and ethnographers, but the latest work suggests that they were Han Chinese who had migrated into the mountainous periphery along the borders of the current provinces of Jiangxi, Fujian, and Guangdong in several waves from Han times through the Song and into the Qing. However and whenever the Hakka arrived, they encountered an indigenous people called the She. The She had already developed a subsistence basket of slash-and-burn agriculture relying on rough grains and primitive tools. It appears that the She assimilated to the Hakka, for by about 1500, the region was largely home to the Hakka, a people with a dialect and customs that distinguished them from Han Chinese farmers in the lowlands.

With the availability of the New World food crops, the Hakka developed a new subsistence strategy that led to their migration throughout the mountainous areas of the south: Hakka felled upland forests to open fields to plant maize. "In penetrating new territory, either sweet potato or maize, usually the former, was the first crop to be planted in the fields that had been newly carved out of the [mountainside] forest."[125] But unlike the She or the Yao, who were highland subsistence farmers with little or no interaction with lowland Han society, the Hakka took advantage of marketing opportunities for mountain products. "[S]ubsistence agriculture was a means rather than the end: the ultimate objective was production for the market. This was true not only of the miners, charcoal burners, lumberjacks, and papermakers . . . but also of many [Hakka] farmers. Hemp, ramie, and indigo were the cash crops most widely cultivated by the Hakka. . . . Tea, sugarcane, and tobacco were also important commercial crops in many Hakka settlements."[126]

Starting in the mid-1500s, from the area that historian Sow-Theng Leong calls the "Hakka heartland" (see map 5.2), Hakka migrated throughout the mountainous regions of south and southeast China. But the interesting and significant thing about their migrations, according to Leong, is that they were not random but rather were specifically targeted at those regions close to tributaries of major river systems. The topography of the south—with hills and mountains folded throughout the area and Han Chinese villages and towns along the rivers—made it possible for the Hakka to take their upland skills and market their products to close-by towns and cities. "With accumulated capital they were leasing tracts of mountain land from [Han] landlords, called *shanzhu* (mountain landlords). . . . The Hakkas invited the poor among the She people in Shandong to clear the forests by the slash-and-burn technique."[127] In short, markets and New World food crops made the Hakka assault on the subtropical forests of the southern mountains possible.

Although those who came to be called the *pengmin*, or "shack people," shared characteristics of upland exploitation with the Hakka, they tended to work the mountains further north than the Hakka, in Jiangxi, Anhui, and Zhejiang provinces. Nor did the term designate an ethnic group. First used by the state in the mid-seventeenth century to identify a new group of migrants, the term *pengmin* "was highly elastic, indicating a range of persons, modes of existence, and economic activities,"[128] but generally referred to people—mostly men—who set up temporary shacks to exploit the highlands, and who then moved on after the fertility of the land had been depleted. New World food crops and markets for upland products enabled the *pengmin* to exploit the mountains, as they had for the Hakka.

Han Chinese settlers had begun settling in the Gan River valley of Jiangxi province as early as the Han dynasty, and then progressively moved upriver, possibly displacing the indigenous Yao and She. More arrived during the Tang and Song periods, with Han Chinese occupying the river lowlands by the end of the Southern Song. According to Stephen Averill, "the bulk of the region's thickly wooded mountains remained largely unsettled by Han Chinese" until a new wave of immigrants arrived in the sixteenth and seventeenth centuries—these were the *pengmin*, or "shack people." They probably arrived not from the north but from areas to the south and east in the mountainous areas of Guangdong and Fujian. They may have been Hakka, or possibly She, but coming from already "heavily settled mountainous areas with extensive repertoires of mountain products (including crops of New World origin . . .) and long experience in opening and cultivating steep, wooded hillsides."[129]

Like the Hakka, the shack people of the Jiangxi highlands were miners, lumberjacks, and papermakers, all of whom grew their own food on land slashed and burned from the mountain sides. According to a Chinese official, "poor people from Fujian and Guangdong" migrated to the Jiangxi hill country, rented tracts of mountain land, and "drew upon the mountains [for materials] to build shacks. They used the first five years to open waste land [i.e., the mountain forests], planting crops such as dry rice, beans, potatoes and yams. After five years the soil was rich, and they began to plant *shan* seedlings; while the seedlings were not yet tall, food crops could still be cultivated. In this way the migrants invested and saved for ten years, taking wives, building houses, and secretly laying a good foundation [of wealth]."[130]

Along the lower elevations, and anywhere else that ponds could be dug for irrigation water, rice paddies, in Averill's words, "rose in terraced stacks on formerly wooded and brush-choked land. Narrow paths crisscrossed the surrounding mountain slopes, providing access to small hillside plots of sweet potatoes, peanuts, tea, and other dry crops, and to the large stands of timber and bamboo where wood products and medicinal roots were harvested."[131] Although this kind of transformation of the mountain ecosystem sounds more or less "sustainable," it did have long-term consequences. Again, historian Averill: "Over the years, deforestation and erosion also became progressively more significant. . . . By the twentieth century . . . as the ground cover decreased, flooding and other erosion-related problems also progressively developed. One of the most consequential of these was a gradual silting up of the region's larger streams and rivers that . . . had severely curtailed their usability by boats or large timber rafts."[132] Whereas the environmental damage in the Jiangxi highlands appears to have been gradual, in other areas in the Yangzi River drainage basin the process was much faster, and the consequences more disastrous.

The Central Yangzi Region—Hunan and Hubei Provinces

Translated into English, the names of the two provinces straddling the Yangzi River in central China—Hunan and Hubei—mean "South of the Lake" and "North of the Lake." The lake in question is Dongting Lake. Today the lake is the second largest in China, and through the millennia it has acted as a great regulator of water levels in the Yangzi River. The Yangzi has its origins in the melting glaciers of Tibet, winds its way through Yunnan and Sichuan, irrigating much of the Chengdu basin, before cascading through the "Three Gorges" into the broader plains of central China.

Two major tributaries flow into the Yangzi through central China. To its south, the major river draining Hunan province is the Xiang River, which has its source in the Nanling Mountains and flows northward, emptying into Dongting Lake before its waters join the Yangzi. North of the Yangzi, the Han River flows southeast through Hubei province, joining the Yangzi at the present-day city of Wuhan (see map 5.6). The lower reaches of the Han River form an "inland delta," with numerous branches both serving the irrigation needs of farmers and making numerous connections to the Yangzi, especially at times of high water flow.[133] Joining the Yangzi further downriver, the Han River does not flow directly into Dongting Lake, but floodwaters from the Han can make a wall of water that pushes Yangzi floodwaters back up into Dongting Lake. The lake thus was an essential part of the natural hydrological cycle of the Yangzi River in central China.

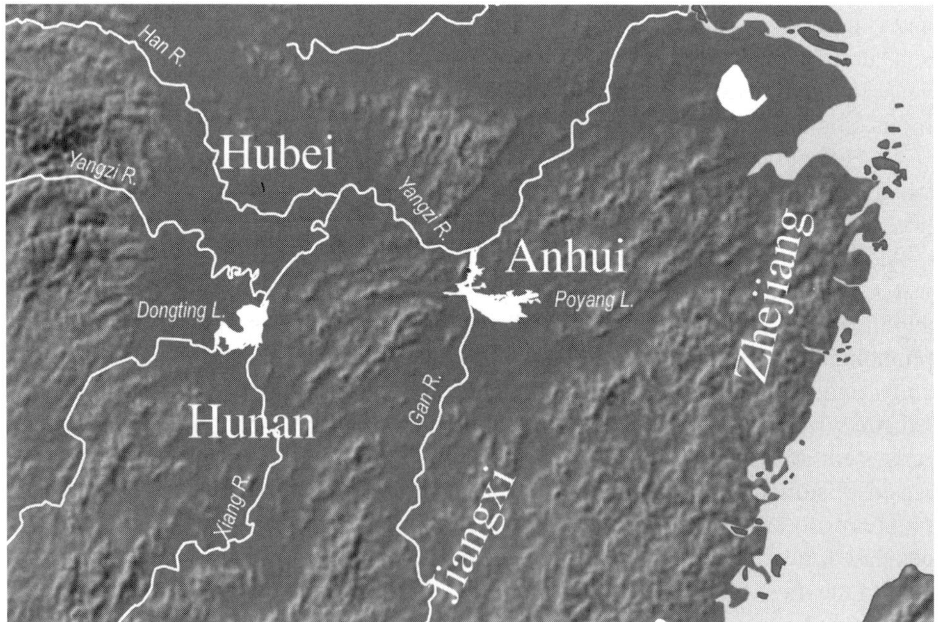

Map 5.6. Central and Eastern China

Bordering the North China plain, Han Chinese settled Hubei first, probably during the Han dynasty. Being a watery world, the first dikes were built in the third century, protecting the outpost of Jiangling from the floodwaters of the Yangzi. The southern bank of the Han River was diked in the tenth century to protect farms in the middle of the province. After the Song court fled the invading Jurchen to Hangzhou (see chapter 4), additional dikes were built between the Han River and the Yangzi, creating an inland sea to prevent nomadic horsemen from reaching the Yangzi and invading the Southern Song further downriver. Additional dikes built during the Southern Song along the northern bank of the Yangzi protected additional land from flooding and encouraged significant numbers of immigrants to open new land for farms. Using the wet-rice technologies developing at the time in the Lower Yangzi, enclosures also created polders throughout the "inland delta," and farmers began selling surplus rice downriver to the cities in the lower Yangzi.

Increased efforts to control the waters of the Han and Yangzi Rivers came during the Ming dynasty. The Ming founder Hongwu established military colonies in Hubei as he was doing elsewhere, relocating soldiers and their families to repair existing dikes and build new ones and to open land for reclamation, farms, and more people. Another major effort came in 1394 when the emperor sent students from the Imperial College throughout the empire to organize the reestablishment of water control works. According to Pierre-Etienne Will, "we are told that during the following winter a total of 40,987 reservoirs and dams, 4,162 canals, and 5,418 dikes and embankments were created in this way."[134]

The active role of the Ming state in building these dikes continued into the sixteenth century. State policy encouraged land reclamation, immigration, and the creation of irrigation systems. As a result, numerous large land owners created their own embankments and polders, and sought tenants to reclaim and till the land within the enclosures. With the increased number of people and farms in Hubei that could be threatened by flooding of the Han and Yangzi Rivers, additional resources were thrown into the task of building dikes to keep the rivers pinned to their courses. At the same time, eunuchs of the Jiaqing emperor (1522–66) had additional dikes built further up the Han River for the stated purpose of protecting the tomb of the emperor's father, who was buried there. As soon as the dikes made the surrounding alluvial plain safe for agriculture, the eunuchs snatched up huge tracts of land for themselves and their families.

The consequences of all this dike building are not hard to fathom, and are comparable to those that contributed to forming the Pearl River delta (see chapter 3). Normally, the summer rains would raise the water level of Han river, and the excess water would spill out into the numerous lakes and swamps to its south; as the water level receded, the waters would gradually drain into the Yangzi. With the southern bank of the Han River now diked, there was no place for the water to go, so the river bed rose higher and the river became more violent, significantly increasing the risk of disastrous flooding, especially downriver. The diking of the Han River thus led to a divergence of interests between those living upsteam and those downstream, and although some level of cooperation over water control measures might have been "rational," intervillage squabbling and inaction by the state were the more normal outcomes. As a result, those living downstream began building their own dikes and enclosures to protect their settlements and to make more swamps and lakes candidates for "reclamation," which they were. By the late Ming, the hydrology of the entire Han River drainage basin had been altered by human action, with the accompanying belief that the waters could be controlled.

Of course, they could not be. With the wars at the end of the Ming, the death or flight of the population, and then the conquest by the Manchus, such a large complex as the hydraulic system in Hubei was impossible to maintain, breaks in the dikes were not repaired, and numerous areas remained "flooded" (or more precisely, returned to a more natural state) for decades. The new Qing dynasty, though, had an interest in settling the population, getting farms and agriculture going again, and bringing peace and prosperity to the empire, and so invested considerable resources in shoring up the dikes of the Han River in Hubei province. This effort began in the 1650s but did not really take off until the 1680s, after internal rebellions had been suppressed.

Letting the floodwaters escape through the gaps opened in dikes certainly was one option facing Qing officials. Improving the outflow of water to lessen the likelihood of disastrous flooding had been discussed by Chinese statesmen for a very long time, going back to the issues faced by diking the Yellow River. So that policy option had supporters. But so too did those who argued, in effect, for "diking at any cost." That voice came to be heard most insistently by the mid-eighteenth century as growing population pressures and an apparent empirewide spike in rice prices caused the emperor to decide that increasing food supplies was the best course of action. And so when wealthy local interests built their own enclosures to further constrain the natural flow of water, officials looked the other way—until the reclamation of lakes, swamps, and bottom land increased the threat of flooding not just downstream in the Han River basin but even further down the Yangzi River in the agricultural heartland of the empire, the lower Yangzi River delta. To continue with that part of the story, we need to look "south of the lake" to Hunan province.[135]

Dongting Lake plays a central role in the normal hydrology of the Yangzi River. As the mountain snows melt at its source, the water level in the Yangzi begins to rise in June, peaking in August or September. What would otherwise be floodwaters drain into Dongting Lake, whose level rises as much as 40 feet above its low point. Additionally, Dongting Lake serves as the outlet for four rivers, the largest being the Xiang River, draining Hunan province. Ringed by mountains on the east, south, and west, rainfall from the summer monsoons collects in the basin and flows northwards into Dongting Lake. Under "normal" conditions Dongting Lake "breathed in" the excess waters of the Yangzi and of the Hunan rivers, and then let them out again in the fall and winter as the level of the Yangzi fell. For those regions downriver, this action of Dongting Lake kept the Yangzi River flowing quite steadily throughout most of the year.

However, if there were heavy rains in Sichuan or in the areas north of the Yangzi, which also had rivers draining into the Yangzi, especially the Han River, then the cresting rivers from Hunan met a wall of water in Dongting Lake, and had nowhere to go but to back up into the surrounding region. All of this action was quite "natural," and did not cause "floods" until people started settling in and around Dongting Lake, changing its hydrology and that of the Yangzi River as well.

The history of human settlement of Hunan is similar to that of other regions south of the Yangzi. Han Chinese began migrating into areas already inhabited by various indigenous peoples as early as the Han dynasty, pushing them into the hills and farming the river valleys. Han numbers really were small, and the region remained sparsely settled through the Song and Yuan dynasties. As he had done elsewhere, the first Ming emperor, Hongwu, established military colonies in Hunan to make it safe for Han civilians to follow. Even so, in 1400 there were only about 2 million people in the province, mostly in the area around Dongting Lake and the eastern banks of the Xiang River. Two hundred years later there were 5–6 million people. The biggest surge in population came during the eighteenth century, when the population rose to 17 million by 1800 and then to 20 million by 1850.

As in other areas, the influx of Han Chinese pushed others who had been farming in the valleys out, into the surrounding uplands. In the case of Hunan, those people appear to have been those whom the Chinese called the Miao, and whom others know as the Hmong of the western border region of Hunan and Guizhou. By the early Qing, there were already several tens of thousands of Miao there "practice[ing] intensive agriculture in narrow valleys and high plateaus, supplemented by fishing and hunting."[136] The Miao were hunter gatherers who also farmed, and where known as a bellicose people armed with "formidable muskets, crossbows, spears, and knives." They also worked silver for ornaments and iron for farm implements and weapons.[137] During the early eighteenth century, Qing administrators debated whether to handle the Miao as "raw" or "cooked" barbarians. Deciding the former, the Qing unleashed "devastating" military campaigns against the Miao in the 1720s, and implemented policies intended to transform Miao society and culture, including the seizure of their land. That led to a huge Miao revolt in 1737: "By decisive, brutal action, the Qing state opened Guizhou's lands to unrestrained economic exploitation andits people to harsher forced cultural assimilation."[138] That did not happen, leading to tensions, skirmishes, and ultimately a major Miao uprising in 1795. The result was not that the region became open to Han farmers, with the Miao defeated or pushed out, but rather a rapproachment that left the Miao in the hills of western Hunan, being recognized as an autonomous region in the PRC after 1950.[139] Their farming, fishing, and lumbering activities do not appear to have caused much problems for the watersheds flowing downriver into Dongting Lake. Han in-migrants, though, did.

In the fifteenth and sixteenth centuries, migrants came because of the reputation Hunan had for its fertile, relatively unpopulated land around Dongting Lake and along the Xiang River. Using the wet-rice technologies perfected in the lower Yangzi region, dikes were built around swamp and marshland as protection against flooding and to provide water for irrigation, and then the lands were transformed into rice paddies. Some of these early polders were huge, encompassing thousands upon thousands of acres. After a lull in polder construction in the seventeenth century because of the civil wars and Manchu conquest, dike construction surged again in the eighteenth century as the new Qing state financed numerous projects designed to get agricultural production going again. These state-financed projects then were followed by civilian projects authorized by the state, and then by a host of illegal, private diking projects.

As a result, Dongting Lake became hemmed in by dikes, its surface area shrank as water was taken for land, and as early as the sixteenth century the various waterways that allowed Yangzi River water out were blocked up. As Peter Perdue put it, "As the channels grew fewer and the dikes higher, the Yangzi was directed into Hunan with even greater force, raising the water level of the lake and producing greater floods."[140] Attempts in the eighteenth century to limit dike building failed because local interests wanted their polder lands protected, and as dike repairs became more expensive and less frequent in the nineteenth century, flooding became disastrous: eighteen major floods from 1831 to 1879 destroyed crops, cities, and many of the dikes. A similar story has been told about Xiang Lake further down the Yangzi River in Zhejiang province.[141]

The lowland flooding was exacerbated by deforestation of the surrounding mountains by the highland specialists, the "shack people" who began migrating in from Jiangxi province in the sixteenth century, and in greater numbers in the eighteenth century. As in Guangdong, Fujian, and Jiangxi provinces, these new arrivals "developed a trade in forest products, cutting trees and planting new food crops like sweet potatoes, tobacco, and sorghum. Jiangxi immigrants also dominated the trade in 'wood ears,' an edible tree fungus. . . . [T]hey cut down the withered trees on which the fungus grew and in the winter opened shops to sell the wood ears they had harvested."[142]

As a result, by the mid-eighteenth century, Perdue reports evidence "that the limits of land clearance were nearly reached. . . . Mountains were stripped bare and swamps were drained to produce the maximum amount of cultivated land. Forests that abounded in wood, bamboo, ramie, fiber, and charcoal exhausted their production as cultivated fields spread. . . . Even wild areas . . . whose mountains were filled tigers and leopards when the area was first opened to Han settlement . . . in the 1720s, reported, by the 1760s, that the wild animals had disappeared and that 'all the mountains have been turned into cultivated fields.'"[143] Not surprisingly, denuded mountain slopes sent silt into the rivers and down into Dongting Lake, raising the lake bed and increasing the likelihood of flooding.

By the mid-eighteenth century, officials had begun debating the wisdom of allowing more and more dikes to be built around Dongting Lake, with one side arguing that with a rising population and food prices, more land was needed to be "reclaimed" from the "waste" represented by the marshes and swamps around Dongting Lake. The other position recognized that the increasing settlement and farming of the area had increased the possibility of local flooding, and worried about the government's ability to respond to the emergencies, and to fund the relief and repairs that would inevitably follow in the wake of a flood. A 1747 prohibition on building additional dikes or filling in upland reservoirs for more farmland was mostly ignored, as private parties continued to "reclaim wasteland."

By the early nineteenth century, Chinese officials were more acutely aware of the ecological dangers they were facing, and that the dangers were more than just local (i.e., the region around Dongting Lake) but in fact extended all the way down to the Yangzi delta region. An official by the name of Wei Yuan understood that although the extensive diking of Dongting Lake may have kept the polder lands there safe from flooding, the floodwaters were just directed downriver to the four provinces where was some of the most densely settled and productive farmland in the entire empire—the lower Yangzi. As Wei Yuan put it, "Which is more important: protecting the fields of few polders [in Hunan], or protecting the fields of four provinces along the Yangzi River?"[144] To protect those downriver fields, Wei Yuan advocated destroying all the dikes around Dongting Lake except for those that protected cities. Locals whose economic interests would have been hurt actively opposed the destruction of the dikes, and the state water patrol that would have been ordered to carry out the task said it was too busy protecting boats on Dongting Lake from pirates to do the job, even if it were given to them. As a result, nothing was done. The dikes not only remained but fell into disrepair, and disastrous floods swamped the area.[145]

One might think that that paralysis of action in Hunan, with the disasters there, might have saved the provinces downriver from flooding. But the lower Yangzi area was experiencing its own ecological problems.

The Lower Yangzi Highlands[146]

As we saw in the previous chapter, the lower Yangzi region was the center of the agricultural revolution in wet-rice farming from the eighth through the thirteenth centuries. Diked polders controlled water for irrigating rice paddies in the area from Hangzhou north to Lake Tai, and then north of the Yangzi River in Jiangsu province poldering turned vast tracts of the region into the most agriculturally productive place not just in China but probably the world. Highly productive rice paddies spread as far as the eye could see, requiring regular and regulated water supplies to remain productive.

Jutting up from the low-lying plains south of the Yangzi River and around Hangzhou are mountains rising higher than 3,000 feet, with some peaks around 6,000 feet. Because the slopes are steep and abrupt, they look higher than those numbers suggest. Whereas the lowlands had been turned into farmland by the sixteenth century, into the eighteenth century the mountains in the lower Yangzi region contained basins and river valleys that had not yet been exploited. Officials described one such area as "in the midst of myriad mountains. There is no water for irrigation, or else there is no arable to plough. The stony barren soil barely can be depended on for three months' food."[147] That assessment, of course, assumed the usual kind of farming carried out in the lowlands, not the kind of exploitation made possible by the highland specialists known as the *pengmin*, or "shack people."

Some "shack people" had filtered into the region in the mid-sixteenth century migrations discussed above but the evidence suggests that there were very few; numerous counties in the mountains were described like the area in the previous paragraph: "In the west of Huzhou, the various mountains extend far into inaccessible gullies and lonely precipices. There are many stones and the soil is thin. It is not that suitable for millet or rice. In the past there were none who farmed it."[148] But in the eighteenth century, officials began to take note that "shack people" had begun entering the region and "reclaiming" land in the mountains.

Importantly, though, these were not the same "shack people" that had been migrating up into the mountains since the sixteenth century, but rather Han Chinese locals from river valley farming villages who were being pressed off the land because of rising population pressure on available resources. They saw that the original "shack people" could make a living in the highlands, and began adopting their methods of highland exploitation. But as G. William Skinner observes, "some ecological tricks may have been lost in transmission"[149] because of the vast environmental damage to the lower Yangzi highlands that followed in their wake.

Unlike the Hakka people in the highlands of Guangdong, Guangxi, and Jiangxi province, those entering the lower Yangzi highlands did not adopt a regime relying on sweet potatoes and planting and harvesting of *shan*, the Chinese fir, in the process keeping the soil on the mountains, minimizing erosion and the silting of rivers and streams. Instead, these new shack people relied on New World maize, and that was to have a major ecological impact.

According to Anne Osborne, maize not only required less labor than sweet potatoes but had other advantages as well. It could be planted at most times in the growing season, and once in the ground could be left unattended until ripe. Even then, the cobs could be left on the stalk without fear that rain or pests would destroy them. Corn could be dried and hung over the beams of the shacks for storage, not requiring investment in separate facilities. Maize could be ground into flour and baked or mixed into a gruel. The cobs could be fed to pigs, and corn could be distilled into alcohol.[150] All of these apparently appealed to the new shack people who were not particularly interested in improving the thin mountain soil to cultivate and harvest *shan* fir trees. And so the shack people "flocked to maize like ducks to water."[151]

Once the original forest was removed and the trees sold downstream as timber or fuel, the shack people planted maize in acidic soils with a modest humus content. Being a heavy feeder, maize depleted the fertility of the upland soils within a couple of years, a hard layer of subsoil formed that made continued farming impossible, prompting the shack people to move on to another part of the forest and start all over again. By the mid-eighteenth century, there were so many shack people in the mountains that an official complained that "their shacks and workshops overlook each other throughout the whole highland area."[152]

Both the numbers of shack people and their methods led to increasingly grave environmental degradation of the mountain ecosystems. In the words of Anne Osborne: "Deprived of forest cover, exposed to erosion, and depleted by production of hungry crops, the soil rapidly returned to its natural state of infertility, lack of humus, acidity, and podzolization or latosolization. In such soil, maize does not grow well, and neither will the traditional dryland crops. . . . The land was often abandoned and the shack people moved on. But the locals had roots in the narrow valleys and plains beyond. . . . When the exposed mountain clearings eroded, . . . sand, gravel and sterile subsoil washing down from the scarred mountains blanketed their own fertile fields."[153]

By the early nineteenth century, local observers and officials were quite aware of the environmental damage. According to one official, "various local people . . . all said that before the mountains were reclaimed, the soil was firm and the rocks were solid. The grass and trees grew closely, rotten leaves accumulated, and in several years it could reach a depth of two or three inches. Whenever it rained, it fell from the trees to the fallen leaves, from the leaves to the earth and rocks, it passed through the cracks in the rocks and trickled and formed a spring. The flow of the water was slow: it flowed down but the earth did not wash down with it. Its downflow always was slow. Therefore the fields below received it, but it was not a disaster, and if for half a month there was no rain, the high fields still were watered by the water [retained in this way]. Now they lay bare the mountains with axes and clear the earth with hoes and plows. Even before each shower is finished, the sand and rocks wash down and quickly flow into the mountain streams, which are filled in and silt up. They are unable to store water. The water flows straight down to the bottom fields, and only then it stops. The bottom fields are ruined, and there is no way to water the mountain fields. This amounts to harming fields that produce grain in order to benefit laborers [i.e., the shack people] who pay no taxes! . . . Rich land becomes stones and bones, there were mudslides and erosion, and fields that produced rice were covered with sand and gravel. Innumerable ones have been eaten up and are gone."[154]

Paradoxically, at the same time that those fields were being rendered sterile, additional fields were being carved from lakes, reservoirs, and river bottomland by wealthy and powerful landowners. Much as with the situation in the Dongting Lake area, landowners encroached on Lake Tai, South Lake, and Mirror Lake, all in the area between Hangzhou and the Yangzi River. And as with the "land reclamation" in the Dongting Lake area, all of these newly diked fields reduced the surface area available to store water, simultaneously increasing the likelihood of drought in times of no rain, and worsening the floods when it did rain. As we will see in chapter 7, the loss of natural places to store water for irrigation led the rulers of the People's Republic of China after 1949 to embark on a crash program of building dams, a decision that would have continuing implications for the people and environment of China.

By the mid-nineteenth century, officials in the lower Yangzi region tried to address the mounting ecological crises facing them by the "prohibition of further reclamation around water margins in most of the lower Yangzi region; prohibition of any new highland reclamation by outsiders . . . ; prohibition of maize production by locals or immigrants and its replacement by crops that would hold the soil; [and] blanket expulsion of short-term migrant labor" used in mountain enterprises. As Osborne ruefully concludes, the economic interests of the wealthy in lowland and highland areas conflicted, the state was unable to enforce the prohibitions listed above, and with the shack people's security threatened, they became even more rapacious in their exploitation of mountain resources. "Economic growth based on highland reclamation was clearly unsustainable."[155] But it did not stop.

THE ECOLOGICAL LIMITS OF EMPIRE

The techniques of "highland reclamation" allowed Han Chinese migrants in the southwestern borderlands, in particular Yunnan province, to attack the high country there, too. In addition to the copper mining discussed earlier in this chapter, Han Chinese agriculture brought vast changes to the southwestern landscape. Until the eighteenth century, most Chinese had settled around a few garrison towns located in the river valleys. That changed in the early 1700s with a new aggressive strategy to colonize Yunnan and Guizhou[156] using the tried-and-true *tun-tian* method of garrisoning soldiers there then moving in Han Chinese migrants. And they did indeed come in, in two major waves in the 1720s and 1770s, following the troops.

Whereas early Chinese arrivals practiced intensive agriculture in the few river valleys, in the eighteenth century New World crops and techniques learned from the Hakka and "shack people" allowed Chinese to penetrate the "vast, mountainous expanses of forest" in the southwest. Although the indigenous highlanders had practiced slash-and-burn agriculture, they had also allowed the forest to regrow on a twenty- to thirty-year cycle, as the Hakka had done. But, mirroring the experience of the lower Yangzi highlands, the addition of maize to the upland crops depleted the soils. "By the early nineteenth century, Chinese settlers were opening such lands in even the most remote mountains [of Yunnan], felling trees at rapid rates, and introducing new crops to highland soils." According to Giersch, "even indigenes turned away from highland pursuits of hunting [and] gathering." By the early nineteenth century, a European traveler "found that the deep forests of [southern Yunnan] 'had almost entirely disappeared,' replaced by a denuded landscape of intensive agriculture" and hills covered with tea bushes.[157]

But what about that tea? Wasn't tea an environmentally sustainable use of hills and mountains? Perhaps.

The tea plant is an evergreen perennial originating in the tropical and subtropical zones of the mountains of Yunnan. During Han times the tea plant was grown successfully in the Sichuan basin, and processed tea was available to tea drinkers in the centers of the Han empire. By Tang times, tea had become such an integral part of the Chinese diet that it was considered one of life's daily necessities, and an important book was written for connoisseurs on the steeping and imbibing of tea. In the Song, Yunnan *pu'er* tea became justly famous, and constituted the major item the Song state tried to trade with Tibetan tribesmen for horses for the Song cavalry.[158]

Along the way of its transplantation from Yunnan to Sichuan and then the hills of south and southeast China, the tea plant changed from the single-stemmed variety growing from 20 to 60 feet high found in Yunnan to a multi-stemmed bush growing to 9 feet but pruned to a few feet high for ease of picking. Under good conditions, the tea bush could thrive for a century. During the Song and into the Ming, tea cultivation spread as demand increased. With the advent of foreign demand in the eighteenth century, in particular by the English, tea planting and production increased yet again.[159]

As an eighteenth-century official in one of those tea districts in northwestern Fujian province wrote: "Formerly (we) tilled fields, now (we) till mountains. Formerly we planted only rice, panicled millet, beans, and wheat; now what is planted on the mountains is melon, or tea, tung nuts, pin, cedar, or bamboo: all of these can supply daily needs."[160] In northwestern Fujian, tea was planted on hills just above the rice paddy fields, with bamboo and timber harvested higher up.

The increase in tea production during the eighteenth century apparently was part of the highland repertoire of the "shack people," with some of the same consequences noted earlier. As noted in the mid-1820s, "Recently because of the opening up of mountains to [tea] cultivation, there is no way to stop the runoff of water down into the valleys. . . . When there are downpours, muddy soil is washed down and fertile [lowland] soil becomes stony earth in which grains will not grow. . . . Thus as a consequence mountain and lowland cultivators fight one another and foment lawsuits."[161]

Thus, even though forest cover was replaced with tea shrubs, and even though some tea plantations apparently were in operation for centuries, the current state of things was not sufficient to halt the erosion when the shack people responded to the growing demand for mountain resources, tea included. The tropical and subtropical forest was multistoried, with heavy rainfall broken by numerous tiers of leaves until it dropped onto the leaf litter of the forest floor. In the hills of south and southeastern China, the stubby tea plants were all that stood between the heavy rainfall and eroding hills, and they proved insufficient for the task, whether in the land of its origin, the southern hills of Yunnan, or the regions of its transplantation.

Another reason tea could be planted and harvested in the hills is that at those elevations the possibility of encountering malaria lessened. As David Bello notes, "Eighty-four percent of Yunnan is mountainous, and three distinct ranges, collectively called the Hengduan Mountains, alternate with three major river systems running through [the province]. One effect of this combination has been the emergence of malarial zones in the river basins, forests, and foothills while zones at higher elevations remain malaria-free."[162] Ever since Han Chinese and then Mongols attempted to conquer and rule Yunnan, their efforts had been compromised by malaria that kept northern Han Chinese from settling, and hence ruling, most of the province directly, giving rise to the indirect *tusi*, or native chieftanship system. As one Manchu official explicitly stated, "the Ming's former division of the area into native- and central government–controlled zones originally arose from the new frontier's malarial (*yanzhang*) climate, to which Chinese officials were not accustomed."[163]

One of the non-Chinese peoples who inhabited Yunnan were the Miao (the Hmong), and as with indigenous peoples the Han Chinese encountered elsewhere as they expanded their empire, those who accepted Chinese overlordship in return for titles and central state support were called the "civilized" *shu*, while those who did not were the "wild" *sheng*. In Yunnan, both kinds of indigenous peoples inhabited malarial areas, which was the main reason Han Chinese administrators and soldiers stayed out of those areas. But, as noted above, a number of Han Chinese poured into the southwest to take up mining, and called for the Qing state to abolish the native chieftainships so they could live under Han Chinese rule. Direct rule conferred Chinese institutions such as the legal structures for land ownership, leading the Qing government to consider bringing the region under direct control. A major problem was that the areas inhabited by the "wild" tribals tended to be in a frontier no-man's-land with Burma. To establish direct control thus required confronting, defeating, and perhaps incorporating, Burmese territory into the Chinese empire.

But the Qing military campaigns in the late 1760s to do so ended in disaster. As one official recounted, "I have seen Myanmar [Burma], and it is nothing more than a southwestern tribe. Its people are neither brave nor vigorous, their weapons dull. They fall short of Chinese troops and preserved themselves only because of rugged terrain and virulent malaria."[164] Even the Qianlong emperor, who presided over the Burma campaigns, admitted that "Myanmar has awful conditions. Human beings cannot compete with Nature. It is pitiful to see that our crack soldiers and elite generals die of deadly diseases for nothing. So [I am] determined never to have a war again [with Myanmar].[165]

David Bello's investigation of the ways in which malaria conditioned Han Chinese expansion into Yunnan goes beyond the limits malaria placed on direct Han Chinese administration, or even the limits malaria placed on the expansion of the empire—which it did in both cases. Bello's sophisticated analysis shows that "malaria was instrumental in delineating and differentiating administrative space in Yunnan in bioethnic terms."[166] The indigenous peoples, both "civilized" and "wild," had some levels of resistance to malaria which the Han Chinese did not, a significant marker of ethnic difference between Han and Miao. "Malaria was a major constituent of the fundamental structure through which Qing imperial agency operated in frontier Yunnan. The environmental conditions created by the disease functioned to keep Han and tribal physically separated in every sense, and this separation in turn made the native chieftanship system an integral component of dynastic control of the province—even though the presence of large numbers of unsupervised tribals certainly limited and often undermined dynastic control as well. . . . Yet this contestable division of provincial space was not entirely the product of conflicting human ambition, for behind the clamor of its tribal and imperial creators rises the relentless whine of mosquitoes."[167]

Malaria was not the only deadly disease awaiting Han Chinese migrants into Yunnan. Chinese at the time considered malaria to have been a part of the environment and thought of it as *zhang* or *zhang-yi*, encountered and contracted in warm, swampy, low-lying places where mists formed and tannins in decaying vegetation turned standing waters a dark brown. They did not know about the mosquito vector responsible for bringing malaria to people, but they did know that if they avoided those kinds of environments—or moved from them—they would not contract malaria.

The same was not true with bubonic plague, which could spread rapidly and then jump from area to area or region to region, from one environment to one completely different—to the Chinese, these diseases were *yi*, pestilence or epidemic disease, or *da-yi*, major epidemics. Whereas Chinese recorded *zhang* in the "geography" section of local gazetteers, *yi* or *da-yi* were recorded in "great events" sections of the gazetteers; *zhang* was endemic to a region, whereas *yi* and *da-yi* were episodic. Nevertheless, southwestern Yunnan province contained two areas that later epidemiologists have called "plague reservoirs," or places where plague was endemic among certain rodent populations; in Yunnan those were the Oriental vole, a field mouse, and the yellow-chested rat. Both rodents and humans contracted the disease from the bites of insects, most commonly rat fleas.

Casual contact with an infected rodent by a hunter, logger, or trapper who wandered into one of the plague reservoirs could infect a person. That person would likely die within three to five days, but unless the plague infected the lungs from which the bacteria could be spread by coughing (the so-called pneumatic form of bubonic plague), other humans were not at much danger of contracting plague. But the ecology of the disease in Yunnan meant that the danger to humans was never too far away. The plague bacillus was endemic among the vole and field mouse populations, which were somewhat resistant to contracting the disease. The fleas that these rodents hosted then bit the yellow-chested rat, which not only lived in the wild but also during the harvest season ate stored grains and lived in the upper stories or roofs of houses. Even then, as long as the rats were alive and well fed, the fleas tended to stay mostly on the rats. For whatever reason, sometimes the rats began a rapid die-off. When this happened, the fleas jumped to large numbers of new, and human, hosts, some of whom traveled with their hungry fleas for shorter or longer distances—and all of a sudden the deadly bubonic plague would break out, killing a third to half of the infected humans.

Bubonic plague may have existed in Yunnan in the twelfth to fourteenth centuries, and it may have been the origin of the plague that spread to north China and then across the Central Asian steppe to arrive in 1347 with Mongol troops besieging Caffa on the Black Sea, and that hence spread into Europe as the "Black Plague." Historian Carol Benedict thinks that epidemic outbreaks in Yunnan in the eighteenth and nineteenth centuries most likely were bubonic plague. Moreover, she links the spread of the epidemic throughout many regions of Yunnan to the building up of trade routes following the demographic and economic development of Yunnan that we examined in earlier sections of this chapter. "As more and more traders passed through Lijiang prefecture (one of the plague reservoir areas of western Yunnan), they either inadvertently brought plague from Tibet into Yunnan along the Tibetan-Lijiang road, or they passed through an area where plague was already enzootic. Either way, they came into contact with plague-infected fleas and eventually carried them back to the towns and cities in the regional cores." The list of epidemic outbreaks in Yunnan is impressive.[168]

Similar conditions for the existence and spread of plague existed in northeast China on the Manchurian plain, but that part of the story will be taken up in the next chapter. The point here is that Chinese state action toward the southwestern frontier brought in large numbers of Han Chinese settlers who farmed and marketed their surpluses, and miners and loggers, too, who transported their products long distances to supply markets far away from the originally local enzootic reservoirs of plague in Yunnan. Just as people and goods moved along trade routes, so too did epidemic disease. Markets and state action were bringing all of the Chinese empire into closer and more frequent contact, just as China itself was in greater and more frequent contact with the rest of the world, a topic we will take up in the following chapter.

China's Southwest and "Zomia"

Recently James C. Scott has linked the Han Chinese military, political, and ecological conquests in south and southwest China to the peopling of the vast highlands stretching from China's southwest into Southeast Asia that he has dubbed "Zomia." In Scott's view, over the centuries many peoples fled the expanding Chinese state into the hills and mountains further south, seeking to avoid the clutches of the state as well as its taxes and other exactions. "Otherness" might not have been much of issue to these hill peoples, but it certainly was to the state: "Ethnicity and 'tribe' begin exactly where taxes and sovereignty end."[169]

Han Chinese migrants supported by state military power captured river valleys from other peoples, pushing them out to other valleys elsewhere, in the process dislodging peoples who were already there, or pushing them higher up into the hills or mountains, in a very long process that this book has only partially captured.[170] Once refugees were outside the grasp of the state, Scott argues, these peoples adopted subsistence strategies, in part as defensive moves against the state (not just the Chinese but the Burmese and others in Southeast Asia as well)—in particular the tactic of not being settled in one place for long. Shifting, slash-and-burn agriculture thus was a political strategy, as was the planting of tubers and other root crops that could not easily be seized by the "manpower- and grain-amassing strategies of states."[171] Swidden cultivation, in this view, is not a holdover from an earlier social formation but an adaptation to a political environment shaped by the willingness and ability of the Chinese state to wield its power. To that extent, environmental change in China's west, south and southwest highlands wrought at the hands of the non-Chinese peoples there can be seen, in terms of the power of the Chinese state, as "action at a distance."

Debates over Natural Resource Use (and Abuse)

This chapter has provided numerous examples of situations in which Chinese officials had to confront, and many times debate, both the social and economic consequences of particular modes of exploiting the resources of the empire, as well as the wisdom of protecting natural areas and their ecological processes. Officials wondered about the wisdom of destroying dikes in Dongting Lake and the Pearl River delta to maintain hydrological cycles that did not exacerbate flooding.[172] They worried about the implications of continually raising the dikes on the Yellow River, and debated ways of scouring the silt out to keep the Grand Canal working. They understood the effects that planting tobacco in the Lingnan Mountains or maize in the Jiangxi highlands had on soil and erosion, and issued injunctions against those practices. On Taiwan and Hainan islands, officials tried to protect some of the native peoples from the clutches of fortune-seeking lowland-dwelling Han Chinese. And they worried about the causes and consequences of rising grain prices.[173]

Some began to think that the natural bounty they were extracting from the earth was beginning to be exhausted. As early as the mid-eighteenth century, one Wang Taiyue lamented that in copper-bearing hills, "As the underground ways to the ores pierce new depths, [miners] fear, as they cut and drill, to hit marble. . . . If humans take all that there is, if they show no restraint, their force is enough to wear out both the Heaven and Earth." On newly opened land, farmers understood that the soil's fertility was quickly exhausted, and that they had to move on. Although the Qing state extended tax breaks to pioneers in southern Manchuria, a banished Chinese official noted, "It costs dear to develop this waste ground. When you hoe it the first year, it still remains waste. The second year, it becomes mature, and in the third, fourth, and fifth years it is rich. In the sixth or seventh year you abandon it, and hoe some other area."[174]

By the late eighteenth century, concerns about the rise in China's population and the resulting pressures on its land resources prompted an official by the name of Hong Liangqi to warn Qing imperial officials of an impending crisis. A century of peace, he argued, certainly had its benefits, but an overlooked consequence was the doubling of the population every generation, and the subsequent dividing of land and other property into smaller and smaller parcels.

In those circumstances, Hong argued, "[T]he amount [of available farmland and housing] has only doubled or, at the most, increased three to five times, while the population has grown ten to twenty times. . . . Do Heaven-and-earth [nature] have a way of dealing with this situation? Answer: Heaven-and-earth's way of making adjustments lies in flood, drought, and plagues [which reduce the population]. . . . Do the ruler and his ministers have a way of dealing with this situation? Answer: The ruler and his ministers may make [numerous policy] adjustments. . . . In a word, as a long period of peaceful rule, Heaven-and-earth cannot stop the people from reproducing. Yet the resources with which Heaven-and-earth nourish the people are finite."[175] Hong is sometimes called "China's Malthus," after Thomas Malthus, the English author who also proposed that uncontrolled population increases, as he thought marked Qing China, could only be checked by disasters such as famines or wars. Malthus was wrong about China,[176] and Hong's warnings and proposed solutions were ignored.

To be sure, China's human population surged, almost tripling from 225 to 580 million between 1750 and 1950. Those growing numbers indicate that people in the Chinese empire had been able to capture increasing amounts of energy from their environment; agro-ecosystems to support humans replaced ecosystems that had supported other species. Not surprisingly, the resulting human population growth was not spread evenly. The core regions of central and eastern China saw very slow population growth, while frontier regions grew much faster. In part that faster growth came from relaxed controls on fertility and declines in female infanticade within Han Chinese families, and in part from extensive migration from core regions. Ten million or more migrated from central China to Sichuan, and 12 million migrated from north China into Manchuria, with millions more moving shorter distances.[177]

Despite the concerns of Hong and other officials, pressures on China's environment continued and intensified, reaching crisis levels in the nineteenth century. Spreading farms and loyal tax-paying subjects to the furthest corners of the empire enhanced the power and reach of the Qing state, enabling it to attempt to find the final solution to the pesky peoples of the northwest. Economic development more often than not trumped knowledge about ecological problems. Officials even knew that species were going extinct.

By 1800, tigers and elephants—the "star species" we have been watching periodically to gauge the transformation of the Chinese environment from one sustaining healthy ecosystems into farms or denuded hills and mountains—were pushed into the peripheries of the peripheries, and had been extirpated from most of China. The south China tiger held on in a few mountainous redoubts, largely on the border between Guangdong and Jiangxi provinces and in the Fujian mountains. As humans encroached upon and destroyed their habitat, the number of tiger attacks on people surged in the eighteenth and nineteenth centuries, only to drop precipitously as the population of tigers dropped precipitously.[178] The Asian elephant was pushed further into remote areas bordering Yunnan province and Burma (see map 3.1).

One historian has called these disappearances the result of a "three-thousand year war on animals."[179] "War" is probably the wrong metaphor to describe what happened to the wildlife of China. To be sure, tigers and elephants (and other wild animals as well) were indeed hunted and killed, both for protection against their predations and for their marketable body parts. But hunting is not what has driven these species to the brink of extinction and others into oblivion. The culprit rather has been the destruction of their habitat, mostly to make way for farms and for increases in the size and distribution of the Han Chinese population throughout the space that their state could control. To that extent, the loss of China's wildlife has been more like a holocaust than a war.

Despite all these late-imperial indicators of a natural world in distress, literate Chinese apparently did not explore the idea that nature or wilderness, *as nature or wilderness* apart from humans, should be valued or preserved. Insofar as "nature" existed, it did so as an instrument of human society, or, more specifically, of Han Chinese civilization. Nature provided resources that might have been wisely or irresponsibly used, but the idea that wild things should have a right and a place in that world apparently did not arise.[180]

CONCLUSION: POPULATION, MARKETS, THE STATE, AND THE ENVIRONMENT

Over the 500 years considered in this chapter, from 1300 to 1800, China's population quadrupled from some 75–85 million during the years of Mongol rule to about 400 million in 1800 at the height of the Qing dynasty and Manchu rule. The empire expanded to its largest extent, south to the tropical island of Hainan, to Yunnan and Guizhou in the southwest, to Tibet and Xinjiang in the far west, north to Mongolia, and northeast to Manchuria. Under state sponsorship and with military protection, especially during the Ming and Qing dynasties, Han Chinese settlers fanned out from the core agricultural areas in north and south China into these newly colonized regions, and the Han population there increased dramatically at the expense of the non-Chinese indigenous peoples. Continued population growth in the long-settled core areas of north and central China also fueled migration into the hill and mountain regions of south China.

The Chinese empire had reached its ecological limits—frontiers filled up with Han Chinese—and remote regions in the interior also saw significant population increases. Areas that in 1800 were more or less off-limits to Han Chinese—in particular Manchuria and Tibet—would see significant Han Chinese migration in the late nineteenth and twentieth centuries. Markets enabled Chinese in some parts of the empire to specialize in various crops, and to rely on food imports from other regions. Markets also enabled the Qing state to tap resources for its conquest of Zungharia. Chinese-style farming replaced indigenous forms, and markets moved forest products from wood for timber and fuel to aromatics and fungus downhill and downstream to consumers. As we will see at the beginning of the next chapter, China was becoming deforested and experiencing the effects of ecological degradation being driven by the combination of a surging population, efficient markets, and a powerful and expansive colonizing state.

Chapter 6

Environmental Degradation in Modern China, 1800–1949

From 1400 to 1800, China was the most populous political entity on earth with between one-quarter and one-third of the world's total population, and it had the largest economy, both in terms of agriculture and of industrial production. In 1750, China accounted for about one-third of the world's industrial output. During those centuries, which historians often term "the early modern world," China's vast consumption and production constituted a major engine of global economic activity.[1]

That early modern wealth and power was based in large part on the exploitation of China's environmental resources. Previous chapters have shown how the Chinese empire expanded to the north, south, and southwest, pushed at various times by military pressure from nomadic peoples, and at others pulled by the attraction of strategic materials. As the empire expanded its grasp, its various states had sent in Chinese families to transform the local environments into tax-paying farms. That strategy of expansion—which we can only call colonialism because of the various peoples who were incorporated into the empire—worked as long as the empire could expand. During the Ming and the Qing, those limits were reached. In part, limits were set by encounters with other powerful states—the Vietnamese who resisted Ming China's expansion in the early fifteenth century, or Russia in the late seventeenth century. But the limits of empire also had an environmental component, as with the tropical diseases encountered in the south and the southwest, or the arid steppe in the north and northwest.

As those exterior limits were to be tested and reached, populations that might have migrated to borderlands started to exploit inner frontiers—highlands that could not be easily settled or populated before the New World crops made that economically feasible. The demand for resources was beginning to have empirewide ecological effects as a broad environmental crisis mounted in the nineteenth century. Moreover, China began to cast an ecological shadow beyond its own borders.

CHINESE CONSUMPTION AND ITS ECOLOGICAL SHADOWS

To supply its growing population and economy with currency, we saw in the last chapter how from 1500 to 1800 China consumed between one-half and two-thirds of the world's production of silver, initiating massive economic and environmental changes in the mining districts of Mexico and Bolivia and sending prospectors into its own southwestern frontier in search of silver, copper, and other valuable minerals. China produced the world's finest porcelain (so fine it was simply called "China"), the best silks, and even some of the most wearable cottons (along with India). Traders and other adventurers around the world knew that the surest path to getting rich was to "orient" oneself properly and head to Asia where tea, silks, spices, porcelain, and other desirable goods were found stacked in shops and warehouses in Indian and Chinese ports. European traders found their way into the Indian Ocean in 1498, and then through the Straits of Malacca into Chinese waters shortly thereafter. In the sixteenth and seventeenth centuries, Portuguese and Dutch traders got rich buying and selling among Japanese, Chinese, and South Sea ports, followed in the eighteenth and nineteenth centuries by increasing numbers of British, French, and American merchants.[2]

There is a vast literature on the China trade and how it was structured before and after Europeans sailed into China's seas,[3] and some of this will be touched on later in this chapter. But just now, I want to focus briefly on China's trade with regions of the Pacific, which sheds light on China's growing ecological impact beyond its borders.

The Pacific Islands and Sandalwood

Mostly, European and American merchants bought much more from China—increasingly tea—than the Chinese would buy from them, so these merchants constantly had an eye open for anything that might help solve their balance of trade problem. Part of the answer came from exotic products extracted from the Pacific islands. Among the prizes was sandalwood (*Santalum*), an aromatic tree common throughout the Pacific islands that grew to 20 feet tall. The islanders had little use for it but did burn it to clear land for farming. The Chinese, though, had a strong demand for sandalwood, using it for ornamental and pest-repelling chests, furniture, and boxes, and as incense (especially for funerals), perfume, and medicine. Until the turn of the nineteenth century, most of this Chinese demand had been met by supplies from India.

But then the European traders found Pacific island sources to meet Chinese demand: "Traders aware of its worth in [Guangzhou] went first to Fiji (1804–16), then to the Marquesas (1815–20). Next they turned to Hawaii (1811–31) where an efficient royal monopoly expedited depletion, and lastly to Melanesia, especially the New Hebrides (1841–65). In Hawaii kings and chiefs put several thousand commoners to work cutting sandalwood. They burned dry forests to make the precious timber easy to find by its scent (only its heartwood was valuable, so charred trunks were fine). In the heyday of the Hawaiian trade, between 1 and 2 million kilograms of heartwood went to China every year. . . . Everywhere sandalwood disappeared widely and quickly, and in most places it scarcely returned. The commercial opportunities of 150 years ago have made an enduring impact on the species composition of Pacific vegetation."[4]

The European presence wrought extensive environmental damage throughout the Pacific islands. But in effect they were agents servicing China. "Except for whaling, all the nineteenth-century pillaging of the Pacific—for sandalwood, sealskins, *beche-de-mer* [sea slugs, or more delicately "sea cucumbers"], in some cases even timber—was done for the Chinese market. European, American, and Australian merchantmen organized the exchange, in which Pacific island products were acquired for Western manufactured goods, and then exchanged for Chinese silk and tea. From the 1790s to 1850 a world-girdling 'triangular trade' linked the Pacific island economies and ecosystems to Europe, North America, and China, with the most powerful consequences for the smallest and least integrated."[5]

Siberia and Furs

Chinese demand was also high for high-quality animal skins and pelts, especially ermine wolverine found in Siberia, and sea otters from the American West coast. In Beijing, at the north end of the cold North China plain, furs were valued for their ability to give comfort and warmth as well as to demonstrate status. Manchu noblemen demanded furs, a substantial number of which were supplied by the Manchus' "imperial foraging" operations in Manchuria, discussed in chapter 5—and so too did high-ranking Chinese officials. Some furs came from the northern reaches of the Manchu homeland, but either demand exceeded that supply, or the animal sources there were already being depleted by about 1700, when a fabulous new source of furs became available to China.[6]

Russia had been pushing east across Siberia since the late sixteenth century, annexing territory and making the native peoples the Russians encountered and subdued pay *iasak*, or tribute, amounting to about one sable per adult male. John Richards notes that this fur tribute in effect financed the early modern Russian state, since it had little else it could export to Europe to obtain coins and bullion. That need drove Russian explorers further and further east across Siberia until the late seventeenth century when they came into contact with the Qing state which was also pushing northward into the Amur River valley of Siberia. After negotiating a border in the 1689 Treaty of Nerchinsk, trade between Russia and China began. "The Chinese market paid high prices for all varieties of Siberian furs. Ermine and wolverine commanded better prices than sable or fox—although the latter sold well. In return, [Russian] traders could bring back porcelain, silk, gold, silver, tea, precious and semiprecious stones, and ivory."[7]

What percentage of the Russian fur trapping the Chinese accounted for is not known, but Chinese demand for Siberian furs—which Richards called "insatiable"—did contribute to ecological change in Siberia, too. Because the number of people was actually small, the main effect was the slaughter of the fur-bearing animals. By the 1690s, sables had vanished from much of Siberia, and the small bands of Siberian peoples were impoverished by the *iasak* tribute demand, if they weren't decimated by smallpox.[8]

The American West Coast: Sea Otter and Beaver Pelts

China's ecological shadow reached across the Pacific to the American northwest. American and British traders newly arrived at the Columbia River and the access that it gave to the vast natural wealth of what is now the states of Washington and Oregon in the United States were so taken with the idea of the "China market" in the 1820s that they launched several ships loaded with furs from the northwest directly to China's port of Guangzhou. The problem was that the sellers found no market for furs in subtropical south China, and by 1828 the beaver pelt trade failed. What emerged instead was a much more complex system by which American ships traded northwestern furs, timber, and fish among the Pacific islands, including Hawaii, ultimately winding up in Guangzhou with items acquired along the way, including the sandalwood discussed above.[9]

But a fur that did meet a significant Chinese demand was the pelt of the sea otter, obtained from animals whose habitat stretched 4,000 miles along the American west coast from Alaska to Baja California. Whereas the sea otter's sleek black coat brought a high price of forty Spanish dollars in Guangzhou near the end of the eighteenth century, thirty years later they were selling for two. The reason for the drop in price wasn't a drop in Chinese demand, but an explosion in the supply. "Killing sea otters . . . was a very specialized skill and demanded the labor of native hunters," in particular the Aleut and Kodiaks from Alaska. In a very nasty business, Russian procurers held these natives' women and children hostage to force the men to work up and down the west coast for British and American traders. "The entire coastline soon became an extended killing field [and] . . . the region's sea otter population soon faced extinction."[10]

In addition to Chinese consumer demand having ecological consequences as far away as the American west coast, the growing Pacific trade conducted largely on American and British ships began to knit the Pacific region, including the Eurasian and American landmasses that defined its eastern and western edges, into a large market with major hubs in Honolulu and Guangzhou. David Igler shows how these exchanges of goods also transmitted Eurasian diseases such as small pox and influenza to Pacific Islands, often with devastating results to populations that had no experience with these pathogens.[11] In effect, the ships that plied the Pacific began to integrate the entire region into a peculiar kind of ecosystem in which human diseases, technology, ideas, and goods were more easily exchanged across long distances. As we will see, commercial networks involving opium production also enabled plague generated in China's southwest to spread around the world at the end of the nineteenth century.

India and Opium

What sent European and American merchants scurrying around their emerging colonial holdings looking for things the Chinese might buy is that Westerners bought such huge amounts of Chinese tea and porcelain, among other products, that they could not pay for them with goods or manufactures from their homelands. Chinese demand and its farflung supply created incentives for Europeans and Americans to take from nature not to sustain their lives, as hunter-gathers did, but to transform nature into commodities that could be sold in the China market. But those products, and still others, were never enough, despite the ecological damage done to Siberia, the Pacific Islands, and the American northwest in the quest. In the end, what China wanted more than anything else was silver, and European and American clipper ships brought that in increasing piles to the south China port of Guangzhou [Canton] where at annual fairs it was stacked up, assayed, and taken in return for tea and china.

In a European world of competitive nation states, fearful of neighbors and of war, the prevailing political economy summed up as "mercantilism" seemed to make sense: a country ought to conduct its foreign trade so that it would accumulate a surplus of gold and silver to be tapped when needed in time of war. Sending silver to China to pay for tea thus raised strategic concerns. But first Britain, and then the United States, latched onto a commodity that could be produced cheaply in large quantities and exchanged, indirectly and illegally at first, for the Chinese goods warehoused in that great entrepôt of Guangzhou—opium.

John McNeill notes the environmental irony: "By 1850 Chinese tea [now] could be had without hunting down the last seals or sandalwood. Opium provided the key that unlocked Chinese trade. As the British East India Company converted tracts of Bengal to opium production, China's commercial horizons shifted, and the Pacific trade lapsed into insignificance. . . . After decades for hunting or gathering, seals, sandalwood, and sea slugs grew scarce; the China trade had skimmed off the cream of the readily exploitable resources."[12] American clipper ships sailed to Turkey for its opium supplies, sparing the American beaver any further decimation as well; the eastern United States supplied more than enough furs from fur-bearing animals to meet domestic demand as well as export demand from Europe where members of high society wore felt hats, not squirrel-skin caps. As McNeill intimates, the switch in Bengal to poppies (from which opium was extracted) from other crops, cotton in particular, no doubt had ecological implications there, but that story is too far from our concerns here. However, the connection of the opium trade to the outbreak of the world's great late nineteenth-century bubonic plague epidemic is not.

Opium and Global Epidemics

The trade routes spawned by the opium trade globalized two epidemic diseases. One, cholera, was brought to China from India, setting off an empirewide epidemic in 1820–21. Having established a toehold in China, the bacteria that causes cholera lead to six more epidemics in China by 1930.[13] The other epidemic disease—the bubonic plague—spread from southwestern China throughout the world in a great outbreak in 1894. Diseases traveled steamships in all directions around the globe.

In chapter 5, I discussed how environmental conditions in parts of Yunnan province provided the right conditions for the establishment of a reservoir sustaining bubonic plague—a combination that brought together the yellow-chested rat (*Rattus flavipectus*), a particular flea (*Xenopsylla cheopis*) that found a host on the yellow-chested rat, the plague bacillus *Yersinia pestis*, and humans. As Yunnan was brought into the Chinese empire and trade routes increasingly integrated the markets in that province, plague outbreaks too spread within the province. Bubonic plague may well have stayed within Yunnan—had it not been for the opium trade.

Opium was addictive, and hundreds of thousands of Chinese in and around the port city of Guangzhou were consuming significant amounts smuggled in on British and American ships. Given the distances and risks involved, it is not surprising that opium was expensive. Indeed, historians of China credit the consumption of opium with reversing, by 1833, the centuries-long accumulation of silver in Chinese hands. In just a few years, China's treasury was facing shortages of the precious metal.

Used as a medicinal herb, opium had long been grown in parts of China, including Yunnan province. At some point in the late-eighteenth or early-nineteenth century, entrepreneurs began the large-scale planting of opium poppies in Yunnan,[14] processing the resin into opium, and then exporting it over land, by river transport, and by ship east through Guangxi province to Guangdong, the heart of China's opium trade. And along with establishment of those new trade routes linking Yunnan with coastal Guangdong came outbreaks of bubonic plague in the 1860s, 1870s, and 1880s, leading to the great pandemic of 1894 that killed tens of thousands in Hong Kong and Guangzhou, and then spread along steamship routes to India, Vietnam, San Francisco and Glasgow. This was the world's third great outbreak of bubonic plague—the first had been the sixth century "Justinian" plague, and the second the much more famous fourteenth-century "Black Death."[15] Environmental and ecological relationships that had been local to China went viral and global.

Opium and War

The unlocking of the China trade with opium was neither a pleasant nor moral enterprise. The story of the events and processes leading up to China's defeat by the British in the Opium War (1839–42) has been told elsewhere.[16] For the purposes of understanding China's environmental history, the significance of the Opium War is severalfold. First, China's defeat at the hands of the British initiated a century of foreign wars against China. While never conquered and ruled as a colony by one or more "powers," by 1900 China had become what has been termed a "semicolony." The series of treaties that ended the various wars—which the Chinese understandably called "the unequal treaties" because they were forced on its government at the point of a gun—created an institutional framework for the incorporation of China into a global system dominated by Western imperialist powers. As a result, the Chinese state was forced to shift its attention, resources, and energies from traditional statecraft concerns to the much more modern one of protecting the nation state from foreign attack.

It should not be too surprising either that given the high price for imported opium, and energetic, enterprising, and connected Chinese merchants, that Chinese would start to grow and produce their own opium—an early form of "import substitution," if you will. The growing of poppies and the native production of opium first centered on China's southwest, especially Yunnan (where the opium trade was part of the story of the third global plague outbreak), Guizhou, and Sichuan. From these inland provinces, various grades of opium were shipped at first overland and then down either the West River to Guangzhou, or especially for Sichuan opium, down the Yangzi

River to Shanghai. Poppies and opium also spread in the second half of the nineteenth century north into Shaanxi and Gansu, and also found a foothold in Fujian province.[17] By 1900, anywhere between 70 to 90 percent of the world's opium was produced and consumed in China.[18]

This vast expansion of poppy growing does not in itself appear to have had much impact on China's natural environment. Mostly, farmers switched crops, planting poppies on land that had been already been under the plow. "To achieve higher yields and therefore maximum commercial benefits, . . . poppies do best in rich, heavily fertilized soil and with extensive oversight by humans."[19] In regions that planted a second crop of wheat after the rice harvest, rice would continue to be grown, but wheat was replaced with poppies, which had a much higher market return than wheat. As to why the far southwest was a particular center of poppy growing and opium production, David Bello identified both a natural environment conducive to large-scale cultivation of poppies, and weak central government control.[20]

After a brief moment around the turn of the century when Chinese and international efforts curtailed opium production, poppies and opium spread again in the late 1910s, and "by 1922 China was producing more than 80 percent of the world's opium."[21] The new Chinese Republic proved incapable of halting opium production, and in fact generated such tax revenue either directly or indirectly, so that historian Edward Slack calls it "China's narco-economy," bequeathing a very large social and economic problem to the Chinese Communists when they took state power in 1949.

The third way that China's defeat in the Opium War is significant points to the use by the British of a new tool forged at the beginning of their Industrial Revolution—an all-iron, steam-powered gunship called the *Nemesis*.[22] The story of the *Nemesis* is interesting in itself, but what it signifies is that Britain had begun the very rapid escape from the energy constraints imposed by the biological old regime—the one in which China remained until the middle of the twentieth century. Those new sources of energy—first coal, then oil—conferred such power advantages to those that had them that during the nineteenth century, first other European powers and the United States, followed by Japan and more haltingly Russia, adopted the new technologies on pain of their own extinction.[23] These new technologies tap and use such enormous energy that the impact of them and their economies on natural environments is greater than at any previous time in world history. China would not seriously join that new industrial regime until shortly after the victory of the Chinese Communists in 1949, whose rule is the subject of the next chapter. Suffice it to say here that until then, China remained enmeshed in a biological old regime whose natural vitality and ability to support people and their institutions was getting dangerously frail.

Simultaneously, China was racked by internal revolts, rebellions, and revolutions, starting with one of the largest in world history, the Taiping Rebellion (or more properly "revolution") of 1850–65. By the time the Taipings were defeated, some 20–30 million people had died, mostly in the lower Yangzi River region. Foreign invasion, wars, and more revolts saw the end of the last imperial dynasty, the Qing, in 1911. A brief period known as "the Nanjing decade" (1927-37) was about the only time China when had much of a functioning central government, known as the "Guomindang," or Nationalist government, and even that came to an end when the Japanese invaded in 1937 and occupied much of eastern China until 1945. The two major political parties that had emerged in the 1920s, the Chinese Communists and the Chinese Nationalists, or Guomindang, had cooperated in resisting the Japanese, but fought a civil war from 1945 to 1949 to decide which group would rule China: the Communists won, and the Nationalists fled to the island of Taiwan.

Foreign Imperialism and China's Environment

Certainly, the Opium War and subsequent domestic production of opium had significant effects on China's environment. But the impact of foreign imperialism on China was not limited to that aspect alone. Indeed, from the Opium War on through the nineteenth century, first other European countries and then Japan all began extracting various terms from China, leading to the "scramble for concessions" after China's 1895 defeat by Japan. France carved out a "sphere of influence" in Yunnan bordering its existing colony in Indochina; Japan did the same in Fujian province across the strait from its new colony in Taiwan; Germany got Shandong province; Britain had spheres of influence in south China (Hong Kong had already been annexed as a crown colony) and in the Yangzi River valley, where it had a dominant voice in how the city of Shanghai was run; and in the northeast, both Russia and Japan sparred for special influence in Manchuria, ultimately leading to war between them in 1904–5.

In all of those regions, the dominant foreign powers had first dibs on access to Chinese resources, and on shipping them out or building railroads to export them.[24] We should know more about this foreign assault on Chinese resources and its relationship to China's environmental history, but we don't. What glimpses we do have, though, are intriguing enough to raise many questions for further investigation. In the northeast, for instance, Vermeer says that the "Russian and Japanese exploitation of the Manchurian forests early in [the twentieth] century was the most extensive and best organized ever undertaken." During the 1930s and '40s until its defeat in 1945, Japan "plundered 70 million cubic meters of timber [from Manchuria], or one-tenth of China's entire timber reserves at that time."[25]

The 150 years from the height of imperial Qing power in 1800 to the victory of the Chinese communists thus is an exceptionally complex and complicated one, with internal decay, rebellion, and revolution mixed up with foreign invasion. That century and a half was certainly a period of social, political, and economic crisis; it was also a period of environmental crisis that intensified and interlocked the other crises into a more general crisis for China.

ECOLOGICAL DEGRADATION AND ENVIRONMENTAL CRISIS

The centuries of deforestation and destruction of wildlife habitat detailed in the previous chapters did not go unnoticed by Chinese observers. As discussed in chapter 4, China's officials were quite aware of the mounting hydrological problems they were facing, as well as the consequences of deforestation in the mountains above their major river valleys.[26] Perhaps even more interesting, by the early nineteenth century there is evidence that both the idea and reality of species extinction had come to at least one official.[27] In the 1811 edition of a gazetteer from south China, the prefect of Leizhou in southernmost Guangdong province wrote:

> Because local products come from the land [and because there are changes in the land], the local products too change over time. Of the common ones mentioned in the ancient texts, just 80–90 percent exist today; of the rare ones, just 20–30 percent survive. [Today], there is no land that has not changed, so the times are no longer the same either. Northerners record that Leizhou produced teeth and ivory from black elephants, and noted that in Xuwen there were *bao niu* (a kind of buffalo?). The *Records of Jiaozhou* [probably a fourth century CE text] say that Xuwen had the giant centipede . . . The provincial gazetteer records that in the wilds of Leizhou deer were plentiful, and that the "fragrant navel of the civet" could substitute for musk-deer . . . Today these [species] are all extinct. The reason these extinctions were not recorded before is that people then said that extinction was not possible . . . Today it is my task to record for posterity these extinctions in the appendix [to the local products section], [in the hope that my records will be of use] for later research.[28]

One can detect a sense of loss, and that is precisely what species extinction and ecological destruction signify. As Han Chinese captured more and more energy from agricultural sources that relied on the sun, the energy available to other life forms—indigenous peoples, forests, tigers, and elephants alike—declined, sometimes to the point of being insufficient for those species to survive. Tigers disappeared from south China forests by the early nineteenth century, although a few score hung on in remote corners of forests until the twentieth century.[29] At the same time far to the north, after 1822 Manchu Bannermen no longer carted bears and leopards from Manchuria to Beijing, although China's Manchu rulers continued to use live Amur tigers after that for military training exercises.[30]

The removal of forest for farms and the consequent simplification of China's ecosystems into agro-ecosystems led to more than the loss of biodiversity. By the nineteenth century, these processes were also leading to the widespread degradation of the environment. Degradation differs from the loss of biodiversity in that a degraded environment is so changed and depleted of the nutrients needed to support life that ecosystems seldom have the ability to regenerate themselves. Instead, the environment is altered at lower levels of energy, increasingly unable to support complex and life-generating ecosystems. Such a degraded environment creates a crisis for those species whose existence depended on a particular ecosystem, leading to local extirpation or extinction. Because humans are embedded in ecosystems, human institutions have environmental underpinnings that when weakened can precipitate social, economic, and political crises.

As Blaikie and Brookfield point out, land degradation is neither an objective phenomenon nor a natural one. Rather, what constitutes degradation depends to a certain extent on what values a society places on the land; deleterious human interference with natural processes constitute land degradation. From a Chinese point of view, then, deforestation that made way for more valuable farmland did not necessarily

Fig. 6.1. Logging in Late Imperial China *Source:* Needham, *Science and Civilization in China,* vol. 4, part 3, 244. Reprinted with permission.

degrade the land. But erosion of mountainsides and a decline in the productivity of farmland, both of which will be taken up in the next section, do constitute land degradation.[31]

Blaikie and Brookfield argue that not all land is equally susceptible to degradation, and that some land is more easily restored and repaired while other land can be irretrievably degraded. They use the concepts of "sensitivity" and "resilience" to capture this variability of the susceptibility of land to degradation. For instance, land that has low sensitivity to human interruption and that can thus easily bounce back from the effects that entails is more amenable to repair under good human management practices; an example might be wetlands. On the other hand, a land system that is highly sensitive to human alteration and that does not easily repair is likely to degrade quickly and to be very difficult to restore—for example, the arid steppe.

In this chapter, I want to focus on the evidence of deforestation, the consequent river valley flooding in various parts of China, and the ways that land systems in China deteriorated and degraded.

Northwest China

As early as 1850, but certainly during the first half of the twentieth century, the removal of north China's forest cover led to clear signs of environmental degradation in the Wei

River valley and the loess lands to its north and east. Although forests remained in the more inaccessible parts of the Qinling Mountains until the 1930s,[32] in the Wei River valley itself, "trees [were] scarce."[33]

To the east in Shanxi province, an early twentieth-century study observed: "Nowhere is the havoc wrought by deforestation more evident than in [Shanxi province]. Around Taiyuanfu all the once-wooded mountains are bare and bone dry. Down through the province one sees no trees on mountain or foothill save those about temples. . . . Once the tree cover is removed, the rains wash the soil from the hillsides and with it fill the watercourses and choke the valleys. Wherever a brook or a creek debouches into the valley of the Fen it has built with this wash a great alluvial cone. . . . This cone has covered under silt and sand and gravel from a few score acres to several square miles of the former rich bottom lands, and they can never be recovered."[34]

The astounding photographs in figure 6.2 show the effects of the siltation: "Since the bridge was built, 20 feet of wash from deforested hills has been dropped in that watercourse, and the stream, no longer fed from spongy wooded slopes, is a trickle. . . ."[35] The silt probably came from the loess plateau, which had been steadily eroding since the Han dynasty, but which became increasingly eroded in the nineteenth and twentieth centuries (figure 6.3). "From Hankou to Beijing," the German geographer von Richthofen reported in the 1870s, "all mountains and hills are destitute of tree and shrubs and offer a most desolate aspect. . . . If it were not for the [water-storing capacity of the soil formation called] loess, Northern China would already be a desert."[36]

The Huai River Valley

According to David Pietz, before the southern shift of the Yellow River in 1194 CE (see chapter 4), the Huai River valley had been prosperous and economically advanced. A vast irrigation and canal system made it possible to grow rice in a region described as early as the Han dynasty as "teeming with fish, clams, and grains" and as having a dense marketing system.[37] With the shift of the Yellow River to a course south of the Shandong massif after 1194 CE, the Yellow, Huai, and Yangzi River systems became intertwined, to the disadvantage of the Huai River valley. With the mouth of the Huai River blocked by the Grand Canal and the Yellow River, "flood water rolled out onto the agricultural plain. Farmers could only wait for evaporation and seepage to dry their lands."[38]

Despite late sixteenth-century attempts to devise new methods for improving the flow of water through the combined Yellow River/Huai River valley system, between 1400 and 1900 there were 350 large floods in the Huai valley. The increasing deforestation of the region meant that instead of depositing nutrient-rich alluvium, increasingly the floods deposited sterile sand, sometimes 7 to 8 meters deep. Counties that in the Han had been known for their surplus of rice and fish were now "completely abandoned because of salinization—there is not an area which is not a wilderness of weeds and thistles."[39] Plagues of locusts followed.[40]

Locusts, of course, had long been feared as one of the scourges of farmers, with swarming masses periodically devouring the standing crop in county after county. Intensive study of locust behavior in the Ming dynasty finally led to the publication

Fig. 6.2. Siltation in Shanxi Province, ca. 1910 *Source:* Norman Shaw. *Chinese Forest Trees and Timber Supply* (London: T. Fisher Unwin, 1914), facing 126.

of Xu Guangqi's *Treatise on Expelling Locusts*. Xu studied locust life cycles, and concluded that the threat could be minimized when the locusts were in the larval stage and wriggling or jumping on the ground. Human action should shift from damage control to prevention, and the specifics of how to do that were published in his book. Later it was discovered that ducks especially could be useful in eating nearly all the locust larvae. But this approach to controlling locust outbreaks presupposed a society in which officials, local gentry, and commoners would work together to stem a locust threat.[41] By the early twentieth century, local officials were scarce and "good" gentry had become just landlords. Farmers were left pretty much to themselves without the knowledge or organization to handle locusts, let alone floods or droughts.

Not surprisingly, the Huai River valley became progressively poorer and less populated, leading to the endemic peasant unrest described by Elizabeth Perry.[42] Land holding became increasingly concentrated in the hands of a few wealthy families, and

Fig. 6.3. Erosion on the Loess Plateau *Source:* John Lossing Buck, *Land Utilization in China* (Shanghai: The Commercial Press, 1937), facing 186.

even educational and cultural levels declined.[43] Without irrigation, cropping settled on a few hardy crops—winter wheat, sorghum, and soybeans—and without markets, there were few opportunities to make money. By the nineteenth century, most inhabitants existed barely above "minimal subsistence."[44]

The Yellow River and Grand Canal Region

The North China plain was basically flat—it dropped only a foot or so every mile and was described as "flat as a billiard table"[45]—so that water flowed very slowly eastward toward the ocean under any circumstances. Left unrestrained from where the Yellow River leaves the mountains just to the west of present-day Zhengzhou, the River would have meandered all over the North China plain. As it was, Chinese efforts from at least the Zhou period in the eighth century BCE had progressively diked the river to prevent flooding and to open up land for farming. The diking in itself would not have been too problematic had the Yellow River not also carried immense amounts of silt. [46] From its point of origin, the upper reaches of the Yellow River flows through the loess soil region, and as agriculture from Zhou times on removed the rather thin cover of natural vegetation, the amount of yellow silt eroding into the river increased, as did the river's flooding. As the Yellow River entered the essentially flat North China plain, it slowed and the silt settled out, raising the riverbed ever higher and the building of the dikes along with it, to prevent flooding.

Having been heavily deforested by the Han dynasty (see chapter 3), by the turn of the twentieth century, "the plain was entirely free from any tree or shrub, every available inch being taken up by the cultivation of cereals."[47] As we saw in chapter 4, in the twelfth century, political instability and warfare between Song troops and northern invaders led each side to breach the dikes for their own tactical advantage, with most of the river shifting south after 1194. Some water continued to flow north through a channel then called the Daqing River, but the Mongol decision to extend the Grand Canal more or less straight north to their new capital of Dadu (present-day Beijing) meant that after 1288 even that river water was harnessed to canal duty. In the mid-Ming, all remaining Yellow River water was directed south into the course of the Huai River.[48]

The second problem thus was that the Yellow River, flowing slowly across the flat and deforested North China plain to begin with, was bisected by the Grand Canal, forming an immensely complicated intersection near the city of Huaiyin, taking over the lower course of the Huai River, "crowding out and diverting the Huai waters into Hongze Lake and the lakes and marshes that extend from Hongze southward to the Yangzi River."[49] The Grand Canal slowed the flow of an already slow Yellow River, backing up the waters of the Huai River further upriver into the Huai River valley; the silt-laden waters of the Yellow River had a hard time pushing through to the sea, a problem that only worsened with time and the deposition of more silt at the mouth of the river.

During the Ming and much of the early Qing, Hongze Lake was above the Yellow River, so grain boats coming from the south could get a shot of energy with the release of stored Hongze Lake water. That periodic release was part of the hydraulic engineering approach established in the late sixteenth century by a new chief engineer, Pan Jishun, who determined that the fundamental problem with Yellow River flooding, at least in its lower reaches and where it interacted with the Grand Canal and Huai River system, was the buildup of silt. His approach was to narrow the dikes to increase the water speed and hence the continuous scouring of the river bed. Much of north China's hydrology had become one vast interlinked system.[50]

The Grand Canal was more important to the Chinese state than the ecological problems caused by blocking the flow of the Huai River to the sea. The Grand Canal had always been of strategic importance to the Chinese state, tapping the agricultural wealth of the lower Yangzi River region and shipping it north to sustain both the

Fig. 6.4. Dike Repair on the Yellow River *Source:* Charles K. Edmunds, "Shan-tung—China's Holy Land," *The National Geographic Magazine* 35, no. 3 (1919): 237–38.

burgeoning Chinese state and the Chinese military as it sought to defend and control the empire's northern and northwestern borderlands. Without the massive flows of tribute rice from south to north, the Ming would not have been able to build and garrison the Great Wall, and the Manchus in the succeeding Qing dynasty would have been less likely to incorporate Inner Asia—including Zungaria in the far northwest—into their empire. But both were done, and the Grand Canal was an essential piece of the strategic framework that held the empire together. Thus, no emperor since the Mongols could ignore the maintenance of the Grand Canal.[51]

But this extraordinary combination of a flat North China plain, the meandering and diked, silt-laden Yellow River, and the construction and maintenance of the strategically essential Grand Canal, also had significant ecological consequences for the entire region. The canal slowed the drainage of all north China rivers, large and small alike, with increased sedimentation leading to periodic flooding, and then waterlogging, because the waters could not drain. And because fresh water contains dissolved salts (that mostly get flushed out to sea), waterlogged land could easily become saline and less productive, or even useless. "The worst areas become marshes, which in turn become breeding grounds for locusts,"[52] which in their turn devour crops.

The centuries-long ecological degradation of the Huai River valley thus was not caused solely by the shift of the course of the Yellow River. That, no doubt, would have presented some challenges, but the real cause was a combination of the long-standing deforestation of the North China plain, and of the building and maintenance of the Grand Canal. And because of the strategic importance of the Grand Canal to the imperial state, the state was not about to abandon the canal but was going to try to ameliorate the worst effects of an increasingly bad environmental situation. Because the imperial Chinese state had such a huge vested interest in the Grand Canal, and because "the successful operation of the canal-transport system hinged on the state's ability to control the Yellow River,"[53] the imperial state invested vast human, material, and monetary resources to maintain the hydraulic system that was the Yellow River-Grand Canal ecosystem, centering on the region where the Yellow River, Grand Canal, and Huai River/Hongze Lake all converged in Jiangsu province north of the Yangzi River.[54]

That system inexorably degraded in the nineteenth century, as Jane Kate Leonard's study of the Grand Canal crisis of 1824–26 documents.[55] She shows how the technologies that had developed for both the Yellow River and Grand Canal—dikes; the water gates and locks opened and closed by capstans, windlasses, and winches to raise and lower water levels; the flash locks; weirs and glacis over which canal boats could be pulled; lateral and feeder canals; dredging boats; and gabions and rock-mortared revetments to prevent erosion, among countless other ingenious innovations—came under increasing pressure by the late eighteenth century, making not just the prevention of floods but the maintenance of the southern course of the Yellow River, increasingly difficult if not impossible.

The problem was silt building up in the complex of waterworks in the junction region of the Yellow and Huai Rivers, Hongze Lake, and the Grand Canal. By the eighteenth century, several centuries of diking the Yellow River had raised it several meters above the southern section of Grand Canal (known as the Huaiyang Canal), flowing from Hongze Lake south to the Yangzi River, and with its silt content, it was constantly threatening to get even higher. Until the late sixteenth century, the waterworks were managed under a theory of "dividing the channel" of the Yellow River into several smaller ones to disperse floodwaters. All that did, though, was to slow the river and increase the silting.

The approach pioneered in late sixteenth century was to scour the bed of the Yellow River by building narrow dikes to speed the flow and to direct clear water into the Yellow River.[56] The source of the clear water was Hongze Lake, created in 1579 by the construction of the Gaojiayan dike across the Huai,which received more or less silt-free water from the Huai and two other smaller rivers. Hongze Lake was diked on its eastern shore, and the dike was continually raised so that the lake level would be above the Yellow River. That was a recipe for disaster. To make sure that floodwaters did not destroy the system, the Gaojiayan dike was reinforced by a strong rock wall, with several floodgates built into the dike. Further south, five additional gates were installed to spill floodwaters into the Yangzi River.[57]

At its northeastern corner, Hongze Lake was controlled by five locks.[58] Additional locks at the northern neck of the Huaiyang Canal, and a body of water called the "Clear Passage," connected the canal, Hongze Lake, and the Yellow River. As grain boats came north up the canal toward that complex after the fall harvest, water in Hongze Lake would be held back by the locks until the boats had maneuvered into the Clear Passage. The Yuhuang lock to the north kept the Yellow River out as locks let Hongze Lake water into the Clear Passage, raising the water level and the grain boats *above* the level of the Yellow River. When the Yuhuang lock was opened, fresh water gushed into the Yellow River, scouring it of silt, and the grain boats made the short passage on the Yellow River to the Grand Canal.

Over time, Hongze Lake began to silt up, not just from the small amount of silt carried by its tributaries but also by periodic flooding of the Yellow River, which found its way into those tributaries and thus into Hongze Lake; backfilling of Hongze Lake with Yellow River water also contributed. Dredging took care of some of the silt, but as both Hongze Lake and the Yellow River silted and their beds rose, the only way to keep Hongze Lake above the Yellow River was to continually raise its eastern dikes. In Kate Leonard's words, "In spite of the scale and complexity of the canal's water-control network, and advances in the bureaucratic management of the system, the Qing state was losing its battle against the silt [by the late eighteenth century]. The canal, lakes, rivers, and drainage canals were all silted and their beds upraised, and overflow gates were mired in mud."[59] Hongze Lake was "perilously high," and when torrential rains in late 1824 "tore two huge breaches in the dike wall," floodwaters cascaded eastwards into the Grand Canal and beyond that into the flat, low-lying, flood prone eastern part of Jiangsu province. Leonard details the immense effort, led by the Daoguang emperor, to stem the flood and restore the Grand Canal, which was heroically accomplished.

No amount of human effort, though, could stop the Yellow River from its meanders and ultimate shift back north, flowing through channels where it had been prior to 1194. "The final shift occurred between 1851 and 1855, with the main branch of the river moving north in 1852. Devastating floods continued for the rest [of the nineteenth century] as this mighty river established its new bed" to the north of the Shandong massif.[60] The shift north had devastating effects on the North China plain, inaugurating a century of floods, misery, rebellions, and uprisings. Because the imperial state was also dealing with a new kind of threat posed by militarily superior European and American powers, its treasury was strained and its attention taken away from the Grand Canal, which was rendered inoperable and never restored.

And although the Yellow River left the Huai River valley after 1855, according to David Pietz, "the damage it wrought was complete."[61] The Huai was completely cut off from its former bed (the one abandoned by the Yellow River), and because that bed was higher than the Huai itself, the Huai continued to pour into Hongze Lake and to seek access to the sea via an outlet in the southeast corner of Hongze Lake that led to the Yangzi River. Because that was inadequate for the volume of water carried by the Huai, the region was constantly inundated. The only solutions were dredging the Huai's former riverbed or widening the channel to the Yangzi River, neither of which happened: the imperial state was no longer interested in the region, and local leaders lacked the resources.[62] Only after the Chinese Communist victory in 1949 did the state have sufficient manpower, capital, and expertise to attempt to rectify the ecological disaster caused by the Huai River's lack of an adequate outlet to the sea, as we will see in chapter 7.

The North China Plain

With the abandonment of the Grand Canal, the entire region of the North China plain that had been considered strategically central to the imperial state for two millennia entered a period of economic, demographic, and environmental decline. Kenneth Pomeranz calls this process "the making of a hinterland"[63] from the second half of the nineteenth century into the twentieth century, as the concerns of the imperial state shifted from traditional statecraft to the threats posed by Western powers along the China coast.

Prior to the shift of the Yellow River and the end of Grand Canal transport, and because of the strategic importance of the area to the maintenance of the Grand Canal, the region of north China Pomeranz calls "Huang-Yun" (named for the Yellow River and Grand Canal) received building materials and fuel from elsewhere that it could not produce itself. Family farming with few opportunities for marketing led to a large and fairly dense population that consumed more fuel than it could gather from the surrounding countryside. Stone for reinforcing the dikes also came from outside; the imperial state imported all of these resources into Huang-Yun to maintain the Grand Canal.

After 1855 and the abandonment of the Grand Canal, stone and fuel in the form of sorghum stalks both became scarce, leading to more and more devastating floods, and to less, or even no, fuel for heating and cooking. Naturally, "people took from ecologically crucial areas outside the villages—riverbanks, hillsides, wastelands, and former forest lands,"[64] stripping an already bare environment of sources of soil nutrients and sending crop yields plunging. "As peasants ran through not only wood but chaff from their crops, and twigs, roots, and grass from the surrounding land, they were forced to burn dung—an inefficient fuel and a desperately needed fertilizer."[65] By the early twentieth century, "both foreign and Chinese observers were noting that Shandong had no forests left, even on hillsides."[66] As Lowdermilk observed in the 1920s of Shandong's hills, "Each winter, the poor of the villages go into the hills after the grass cover is cut, to dig...out the roots of the summer's growth of grass" for their fuel.[67]

Perversely, in Pomeranz's view, the mounting ecological crisis on the North China plain was not simply caused by population pressures, nor by the environmental problems brought on by the Grand Canal; rather, "it was the abandonment of the old hydraulic system"—i.e., the state-maintained Yellow River/Grand Canal/Huai River/Hongze Lake complex—"that hurt" the region.[68] That is, the imperial state abandoned traditional statecraft concerns with maintaining the Grand Canal to meet greater threats from Western powers. Moreover, without markets and the possibility to specialize and trade cash crops such as cotton (or even opium) for the necessities of life, the ecological impoverishment of north China led to human suffering as well.

Another analysis of north China by Lillian Li, though, suggests that even had the imperial central state devoted all the resources it could to the problems of the Huang-Yun region, the same ecological problems would have cropped up. Around the capital city of Beijing, intense central government concern for maintaining the waterways and preventing flooding nonetheless proved ineffective, and by the turn of the twentieth century the Hai River basin, including the Yongding River, which flowed just past Beijing, was no better off than Huang-Yun or the Yellow River/Grand Canal junction region, all of which shared basic geographical and ecological characteristics. As Li observed of a river in the Beijing capital region, "While the Yongding River was not a central problem of the empire, as the Yellow River was, its critical location posed a problem impossible to ignore."[69]

For nearly 200 years of the Qing dynasty, from around 1700 to 1900, successive emperors and provincial governors expended huge amounts of money and manpower to stabilize the rivers in the capital region by diking, channeling, and dredging out the silt. Professor Li details their efforts in a recent book, and reproduces an impressive mid-eighteenth-century Chinese map that glosses the myriad engineering projects launched to ensure that the rivers did not flood.[70] The end result, in her italicized conclusion, was that "*Altogether in the Qing—during the Kangxi, Yongzheng, and Qianlong eras [1661–1795]—more than 10 million taels of public and private funds had been spent on river construction, and yet catastrophes could not be prevented.*"[71] Then, from the late nineteenth century through the first half of the twentieth century, "the continued deterioration of [the region's] rivers, compounded by unusually heavy precipitation, produced seemingly endless catastrophes." As was true elsewhere on the North China plain, the silt built up, coming in larger quantities as ever more natural land cover and forest was removed for farms; floods were frequent and large. In one of the floods around the turn of the twentieth century, a Western missionary reported: "The area is a vast sea—of which the limit cannot be seen. . . . There is no prospect of water flowing out for more than a year."[72] Water logging and subsequent salinization plagued not just the capital region but also most of the North China plain.

One of the Beijing-area projects that sought to solve the silting problem channeled rivers into two huge swamps called "Eastern Swamp" and "Western Swamp" stretching some 80 miles between the cities of Tianjin and Bao'an, and another 20 miles or more north and south, where the silt would drop out, and the (hopefully) clearer river waters would flow out of the swamp. Hydrologically, of course, the swamps were a catchment basin for annual floodwaters, expanding like a great lung when needed. But to the water engineers of the late imperial Chinese state, these swamps were "solutions" to the problem of siltation in the rivers, and the silt-laden rivers were directed to the swamps. But the swamps were of course extensive, biologically rich ecosystems. Indeed, those swamps may have held the greatest biodiversity of any place on the North China plain since it had first been settled three thousand years earlier. Certainly there were herds of various kinds of Chinese river deer, including sika and musk deer. There may even have been herds of what became known as Peré David's deer, the last surviving members of which were kept in the enclosed imperial hunting grounds just north of the swamps. And with deer come predators—wolves, large cats, perhaps even tigers. One can only imagine the different kinds of waterfowl, including the now-endangered swans, along with pheasants and other swamp-loving birds such as red-winged black birds and oriels. With such a huge water surface, the East and West Swamps no doubt also served as waystations on the flyways of migratory birds. In the waters of the swamps, mollusks, fishes, and turtles of all kinds must been at home there, too.

As the swamps silted up, peasants reclaimed them as farmland. Indeed, by the late nineteenth century, wealthy families in the region claimed and farmed the nutrient-rich former bottomland, and the swamp had shrunk to one-third of its previous size. An important provincial official predicted that it would eventually disappear, and it did. Today, in fact, little water at all flows through any of the rivers around the capital, most of it being captured and retained upstream in reservoirs for the city of Beijing.

"Such is the conclusion," Lillian Li says, "of a long process of environmental change over the centuries." Her explanation deserves extended quotation:

> The eighteenth-century triumphs of hydraulic management—the stabilization of the Yongding River, the control of drainage around the Thousand-Li Dike, the diversion of silted waters to swamps, for example—only encouraged the intense use of the land on or near the swamps and dikes. Cultivators were willing to assume the risk of occasional floods because the silt-laden soil was very fertile. The state cushioned these risks offering famine relief, which included generous tax remissions. As the population settlement became much denser, the human costs and risks became higher each time there was a natural disaster. To a great extent, then, the ecological crisis of the nineteenth century was a product of the very successes of imperial engineering of the eighteenth century, not its failures. The changing riverbeds and topographical monstrosities described in the 1890s flood reports by [missionaries] were the legacy of centuries of channeling and diking. After any major rainfall, the terrain was "like a lake"—a description invoked constantly from the 1890s through the next half century at least. . . . For all the millions of taels that had been spent, the tons of dirt, stone, and straw that had been moved, and the hours of backbreaking work human labor that had been expended since the early Qing, the river situation had only deteriorated. The ambition of "eternal ease after one effort" was nothing but a hollow memory.[73]

The North China plain, including the Huai River valley, of course, had been heavily farmed since the Han dynasty and deforested by the Song, so it is not too surprising that it would have been among the first parts of China to exhibit clear signs of environmental degradation. Certainly, the human attempts at "water control" all backfired in one way or another, creating larger environmental problems and ecological damage than if the rivers and the riparian ecosystems had been left alone. But Han Chinese have been diking rivers on the North China plain since at least the eighth century BCE. Doing so is the Han Chinese way, even if the idea—expressed very early in Chinese history—that nature could, and should, be controlled turns out to have been dangerous not just to natural ecosystems but to humans as well. Where the North China plain once had hundreds of lakes and swamps, by the 1980s only 20 remained. The Qing imperial hunting ground south of Beijing once contained 117 springs and 5 large lakes in the Qianlong era (ca. 1771); today there are none.[74]

The environmental deterioration of the North China plain had social, economic, and political repercussions. Let us start first just with the loss of those swamps. Certainly, the wildlife and the region's biodiversity suffered. But people too relied directly on those swamps, or, more directly, on the animals and plants as sources of food and medicine—deer and fish would have been important sources of nutrients for people. But with the loss of these swamps, as was the case everywhere else in China where natural ecosystems were simplified into farms, the human population, too, lost a natural source of dietary protein that in the best of times would have provided variety and additional nutrients to peoples' diets. As it was, the human population of north China became increasingly tied to food from their farms, and when those harvests failed—as they did with the increased frequency of floods and droughts across the North China plain—people experienced food shortages and entire regions became famine-stricken. The largest of those famines—with millions of causalities—struck in 1876–79, 1917, 1920–21, and 1928–30, earning China the nickname "Land of Famine."[75]

Not surprisingly, banditry was endemic. At various points, that banditry merged with other local and national events to produce rebellions; the largest that originated on the North China plain were the Nian (1851–63), the Boxer Uprising (1899–1900), and the Red Spears (sporadically from 1911 to 1949). Moreover, the Chinese Communist party established a base area there in the 1940s to resist Japanese invaders and then to do battle in a civil war (1945–49) after Japan's defeat.[76] Indeed, ecological degradation contributed significantly to rural poverty, and it should not be too surprising that the poorest parts of rural China provided substantial support to the Communists.[77]

Environmental conditions on the North China plain alone did not cause social disorder, rebellion, and revolution. But as Elizabeth Perry and Joseph Esherick have shown, those social movements cannot be understood or explained without examining the underlying environmental conditions and the processes of ecological degradation.

Yangzi River Valley

In chapter 5, I examined the ecological changes and challenges in central China and in the lower Yangzi region, material we won't repeat in full here. To summarize: deforestation of the highlands led to erosion and the filling in of swamps in the Dongting

Lake region, followed by increasing lowland "reclamation" of land along the shores of Dongting Lake, decreasing its surface area and volume of held water so that it could no longer contain the periodic (and predictable) floodwaters.

To the north of Dongting Lake on the Jianghan plain between the Yangzi River and its tributary the Han River, long-term hydrological changes were also causing severe ecological problems (part of the story of this area was told in chapter 5). Originally a vast marsh that was slowly filled with sediment from the Han and Yangzi Rivers, by the Song it had become "studded with thousands of lakes and small marshes." Diking and poldering transformed the region into highly productive rice producing and exporting farms. But because the land that was reclaimed for the rice paddies originally had been marshland and was lower than the rivers, dikes and polders had to be built higher and higher as sediment raised the riverbeds, and farming communities faced mounting difficulties in draining off annual floodwaters. Increasingly frequent breaks in poorly maintained dikes exacerbated flooding. By the eighteenth century, some fields were becoming permanently waterlogged, and during the nineteenth century water began to reclaim large portions of the region. In response, peasant farmers began growing crops that could be harvested before the floods, or aquatic plants; many abandoned farming altogether and took up fishing instead.[78]

Further downriver, deforestation of the highlands above the southern bank of the Yangzi sent increasingly sterile sand and gravel downhill into the rich rice paddies; to protect those resources, officials prohibited any further upland reclamation, but with dubious results. Similar dynamics unfolded all the way down to Hangzhou and its lakes and highlands.[79] The story of Xiang Lake on Xiaoshan plain just south of the Yangzi River is more emblematic than exceptional. As noted in chapter 4, rice production there had begun in the highlands, and moved into the marshy plains only as growing populations and accumulations of capital made poldering possible. In the Song, the area sported 217 lakes, "the greatest density of lakes in all China," according to Keith Schoppa. In the late Song, a reservoir called Xiang Lake was built to catch, retain, and regulate water supplies flowing from the hills for use in the rice paddies.

Over the succeeding centuries, a dynamic unfolded involving the silting in of Xiang Lake, its periodic dredging by various governmental entities, and encroachments on the lake by wealthy and powerful landlords who wanted to create more farmland. Already stressed by the eighteenth century, in the mid-nineteenth century this "remarkably fragile" system broke down in the wake of social disorders and population loss occasioned by the Taiping Rebellion (1850–65), followed by floods that damaged sluice gates and dikes. In Schoppa's estimation, Xiang Lake might have been saved had there been public-minded officials who wanted to expend the energy to do so, or money for reconstruction. There was neither, and so rice paddies sprouted on the former marsh *cum* lakebed; by 1937 "houses and sheds stood where once the water had been fifty feet deep."[80]

South China

Paradoxically, some of the most degraded of China's lands are in its tropical and semitropical regions. As in the hills south of the Yangzi, from the mid-sixteenth century on, upland specialists migrated into and throughout the hill and mountain regions of south China. Some, especially the Hakka, were more mindful of the fragility of highland environments and took more care to replant forests that had been cut for timber sales down river, while more recent Han migrants, pushed by population pressure out of the lowland valleys, cut down trees and planted nutrient-demanding crops such as maize and tobacco. In the Nanling mountains in northern Guangdong, for instance, according to the 1819 Nanxiong county gazetteer, tobacco had begun to be planted "40 or 50 years ago. . . . The profit obtained is much greater than rice. But the tobacco is all planted on the hilltops. As soon as the land is opened, the soil deteriorates and erodes. Any heavy rain silts the rivers and there is fear of imminent flooding. But because of the large profit it is tolerated. The locals [now] are forbidden to open any new land so as to correct the situation."[81]

That official proscription did little to halt the deforestation and land degradation, as peasant farmers throughout south China "habitually fire[d] most of the burnable slopes in the vicinity of the homes during the dry season each year. The continuation of this practice tends to destroy the majority of species of woody plants and change the aspect of a once richly forested country to that of a hilly or mountainous grassland."[82] Western observers thought that the mountains were fired to bring ash and nutrients down into their fields, but the peasant farmers told the researchers that they burned the fields to deprive snakes, tigers, and thieves of their dens, while Chris Coggins found in Fujian that the practice encouraged the growth of an edible fern that was prized in times of famine.[83] Once the forest cover was removed, especially in the hills and mountains of southern Zhejiang, throughout Guangdong, and in southern Yunnan, heavy monsoon rains quickly leached whatever nutrients remained in the soil, rendering any regrowth of forest impossible.[84] Additionally, the burning off of tropical and subtropical forests unleashed the very tough cogongrass that stifled any other vegetation, turning mountainsides green, but devoid of forest.[85] Even the cogongrass cover did not stop massive slumping after periods of heavy rainfall, where huge parts of hillsides cleaved off and slid downhill.

Southwest China: Yunnan

Parts of the story of the transformation of the environment in China's southwest provinces of Yunnan and Guizhou has been taken up in the previous chapter, and it will be continued in more detail in the next chapter with a consideration of the building of hydroelectric dams on many rivers in the southwest. Here I want to make a few observations about war and the disease environment, in particular malaria.[86] As noted earlier, in the eighteenth century, malaria had foiled Qing military campaigns against Burma. The Japanese invasion of Manchuria in 1931, the civil war between Communists and the Guomindang, coupled with flooding in the lower Yangzi in 1932 led to a 60 percent malaria infection rate there, and 300,000 deaths. In 1933, 30,000 malaria deaths were recorded in a single Yunnan county.[87] After Japan's 1937 attack on China and the entrance of the U.S. into the Pacific War in 1942, the U.S. became committed to keeping the Guomindang in the fight against Japan by supplying war material to Jiang Kaishek's government (which had retreated inland to Chengdu in the Sichuan basin) by building the "Burma Road" from northeastern Burma through Yunnan.

Fig. 6.5. The Zhefang Valley in Yunnan *Source:* Library of Congress Prints and Photographs Division in a collection entitled "Malaria Control in India and China, 1929–40," call number LOT 1786 (M) [P&P].

The American engineers and military personnel encountered malaria, and infection rates reached 50 percent, disabling the men and threatening the project. U.S. Public Health personnel were sent to examine the region, mostly in what was then called the Zhefang Valley. That valley looked like a typical south China rice paddy environment (figure 6.5, left), with the addition of *Anopheles* mosquitoes and malaria. U.S. personnel distributed soap to villages because the suds kept streams "free of mosquitoes for about 100 yards," they dug drainage ditches, sprayed oil on stagnant water, and introduced gambusia minnows into the paddies to eat the mosquito larvae. Additionally, the Americans noted that "the hills are high and out of the mosquito areas," apparently driving some of the locals to begin terracing hillsides to get above the deadly mosquitoes (figure 6.5, right).[88] Whether that worked, or whether transforming the wooded hillsides into rice paddies merely spread the *Anopheles*, is not known. Nor is it known whether those doing the terracing might have been recently arrived Han Chinese fleeing the Japanese invasion who had no experience with malaria.[89]

West China: Sichuan

Several additional examples of environmental degradation following in the wake of the successive waves of deforestation prior to 1949 could be cited.[90] Even the lush rice paddies of the lower Yangzi and the Pearl River delta experienced problems when tons of increasingly sterile sand instead of nutrient-rich alluvium flowed down the hills and mountains, obstructing river channels and flooding the lowland paddies. About the only reference I have found to a human-altered agro-ecosystem that was *not* experiencing environmental degradation was in the Red Basin around Chengdu in Sichuan province (see figure 6.6). According to an early-twentieth-century report on the effects of deforestation in China,

> This portion is densely populated and carefully cultivated, this cultivation not being confined to agriculture alone, but extending to the planting of useful and ornamental trees such as the bamboo, tung, mulberry, cypress, varnish, was, and a variety of fruit-trees. The most important part of the Red Basin is the Cheng[du] plain, which has been described as the most densely area of the earth's surface. The vegetation is in most parts

> of the basin of almost tropical luxuriance owing to the extreme dampness of the climate, which permits, in the Cheng[du] plain, an admirable system of irrigation [the origins of which go back 2,000 years to the Early Empire]. Seen from a height, the plain looks like a forest, for every farm has its grove of bamboo, cypress, palms, and fruit orchards while tung and varnish trees abound. The country along the Min [River] between Kiating and Chungking is also rich in trees, which are described as "of living green, free from insects, and without blight or deformity," thus rendering this part of [Sichuan] an object lesson to regions farther east.[91]

It is somewhat curious that the Red Basin of Sichuan was not experiencing significant problems from silt carried down from rivers flowing out of the mountains to the north and west that formed the eastern portion of Tibet, for as we will see in the next section, large parts of Tibet and the mountainous regions of northern and western Sichuan inhabited by Tibetans in fact had been deforested. But heavy siltation did not cause farmers in the Red Basin problems, and the Qin-era Dujiangyan waterworks continued to function as well.[92]

Tibetan/Qinghai High Mountain Plateau

The history of Tibet and its relationship with China is complex and contentious. Suffice it to say here that the Qing state consolidated its rule over Tibet in the eighteenth century, and incorporated parts of Tibet into its administrative structure, with some being annexed by neighboring provinces and some being organized as the province of Qinghai.

Fig. 6.6. Well-tended Farmland in Sichuan *Source:* Dr. Joseph Beech, "The Eden of the Flowery Republic," *The National Geographic Magazine* 38, no. 5 (1920): 366.

In parts of the Tibetan highlands, in particular the Himalayan Mountains, the climate is too harsh and dry to sustain the growth of trees, but much of the Tibetan plateau not only could sustain birch or juniper forests, but as ecologists now conclude, probably did. That comes as somewhat of a surprise, for as long as most scholars or observers have been able to determine, vast stretches of the Tibetan plateau, as well as south-facing mountain slopes descending further down into Yunnan and Sichuan provinces, were covered not in forest, but in various kinds of meadows and grasslands that Tibetans used as pastures for their herds of yaks, sheep, and goats. Tibetans and other observers assumed that those treeless meadows had always been there. But those assumptions have been proven wrong: "huge areas in the Inner Himalaya [of Tibet] originally bore forests but have been deforested by humans and their livestock."[93]

Over the centuries, Tibetans have removed the original forests, probably by fire, replacing the dense forests with combinations of lower-growing plants that compose useful pasture for their herds. "Regular grazing promotes species with high regenerative capacity like grasses or rosette plants and creeping plants or plants with creeping shoots."[94] Elsewhere, "under moderate grazing, a species-rich, about knee-high, meadowlike vegetation may develop, which we call *flower meadows*, because it is dominated not by grasses but by herbs. It is one of the most beautiful plant communities of the Himalayas."[95] Holzner and Kriechbaum think that Tibetans for centuries followed grazing practices that sustained their meadows and pastures. "This way of herding livestock requires much understanding of, or perhaps a feeling for, animals, vegetation, and the optimal rhythm of grazing and wandering, a knowledge that has been handed down from one generation to the next. . . ."[96] In other words, although Tibetans probably removed the original forest on the plateau and mountainsides, their way of life promoted the establishment and maintenance of meadows, grasslands, and pastures that held the soil in place. Even woodcutting and the cutting of peat from bogs for fuel could have been sustainably managed. Nonetheless, the available evidence suggests that for centuries—maybe going back two thousand years when pollen analysis shows a sharp decline of forests[97]—Tibetans or other peoples on the high plateau have been transforming forests into the grassland environment preferred by their goats, sheep, and yaks.

In Tibetan areas closer to the Red Basin of Sichuan, in particular about a hundred miles north up the Min and Mao'er gai Rivers, Jack Hayes has found significant evidence of the Tibetan use of fire to alter and then maintain their pastures—even on the mountainsides above the Sichuan basin—in the late nineteenth century. Whereas foreign observers from Europe thought that forests were beautiful, and that it was a shame that Tibetans and Chinese removed them for pasture or farms, Hayes concludes that "Tibetans created an 'agro-pastoral regime' based on widespread fire use that lasted throughout the late imperial period even into the late 1930s and early '40s."[98] Thus even though forests had been removed, the mountain sides were not left open and barren but instead were covered with pastureland for Tibetan herds, preventing excessive soil erosion and ecological problems further down river in the Sichuan basin. Serious problems would develop in the late twentieth century, as we will see in chapter 7, when extensive logging with powerful equipment by state forestry bureaus so stripped mountains of forest in western and northern Sichuan that devastating flooding of the Yangzi River valley in 1998 prompted the premier of the People's Republic of China to order an immediate halt to any further logging of old-growth forests.

AGRICULTURAL SUSTAINABILITY

Modern ecologists sometimes point to rice paddies and similar combinations like the "mulberry tree and fish pond" system discussed below as examples of "ecologically sustainable" types of agriculture. To be sure, rice has been harvested in some parts of China from paddies that are a thousand years old, and the paddies themselves have become a form of ecosystem themselves, as noted in chapter 4. But what these observations fail to observe is that the maintenance of these apparently sustainable systems requires inputs of vast amounts of energy from outside of the system. If those extrasystemic energy supplies, in particular in the form of food for humans, were not continuously added, the system would degrade. Indeed, as we will see in the next chapter, scientific analyses show that by 1950 nearly all of China's farmland was deficient in critical nutrients, especially nitrogen.[99] A closer look at the "mulberry tree and fish pond system" will show some of the reasons why.

The Mulberry Tree and Fish Pond Combination

In the wet-rice region of the Pearl River delta, the silk industry there developed on a base that had been created first by the "sand flat" fields (*shatian*) and then a particular combination of fish ponds with fruit trees that has struck twentieth-century scientists as exemplifying a form of ecologically sustainable agriculture.[100] From Song times on, fish ponds had been scooped from the swamplands of the upper Pearl River delta.[101] The mud and the muck raked up into embankments above the flood plain protected the ponds from flooding, while the high water table filled the hole with water, and the pond was stocked with various kinds of carp fry netted from local waters.[102] On the embankments, peasant farmers by 1400 CE had planted mostly fruit trees, giving rise to the "fruit tree and fish pond" combination. The carp fed on organic matter that either dropped or was thrown into the pond, while the muck scooped up from the pond fertilized the fruit trees and the rice fields, and added height to the embankments and more protection for the fish ponds.

The "fruit tree and fish pond" culture provided a ready-made base for expansion of the silk industry when increased demand warranted. And demand for Guangdong silk increased during the last half of the sixteenth century, largely as a result of rising foreign demand. As the demand for silk increased, peasant farmers replaced the fruit trees with mulberry trees, giving rise to the "mulberry embankment and fish pond" system, and then began digging up even more rice paddies to expand the "mulberry embankment and fish pond" system. By 1581, 18 percent of the productive "land" in some counties was fish ponds, and when combined with the mulberry trees on the embankments accounted for about 30 percent of the cultivated land area.[103] The system continued into the 1990s until air pollution from nearby factories killed the silkworms.

The "mulberry (or fruit) embankment and fish pond" system often is cited an example of a sustainable, premodern agricultural ecosystem. In any sustainable ecosystem, natural or otherwise, the mineral and energy resources necessary for life are recycled, and the losses from the system are so small that they can be easily replaced (from the sun or by the weathering of rock or the fixation of nitrogen by bacteria). That, in essence, is what the fish pond system accomplished. Silk worm excrement, leaves from the trees, and other organic material were gathered and thrown into the fish pond, providing food for the carp; the fish were harvested annually, with the muck formed from the fish waste and other decomposed organic matter then scooped out and used to fertilize the mulberry trees and rice fields. In the words of a modern ecologist, "there is a closed nutrient recycling loop via decomposition and mineralization in orchards, fields, and ponds. Nutrient export across the system boundaries takes place only with stream runoff, and with sales of plant or animal products."[104]

The ecologists' view of the mulberry-and-fish-pond system is sound up to a point but omits from the energy flows a critical part of the ecosystem: humans and their energy and nutrient needs, much of which were satisfied by food imports. The peasant farmers raising fish and silk worms had to eat, and the food staple was rice. For much of the last 400 years, the rice consumed by those in silk-producing areas in the Pearl River delta was available locally or was easily obtained from nearby markets. By the end of the sixteenth century, an efficient market system began moving the rice from hundreds of miles away. The mulberry-and-fish-pond system thus was not a closed system but was sustained only by imports of food to sustain the human population of the Pearl River delta.

Certainly, most of the food initially came from nearby sources—perhaps the farmer's own rice paddies that had not been converted into fish ponds. But as time passed and more rice paddies were turned over to sericulture, those farmers had to buy food in markets supplied from ever increasing distances, especially from the eighteenth century on. Exporting organic material outside the system, then, is a major source of instability in an ecosystem, requiring additional inputs to ensure sustainability. From an economic perspective, this exporting of products from one place to another is the essence of marketing and economic development; in the case of agrarian economies, the products by definition are all organic. Commercial development, then, must be seen as one of the primary forces of ecological change: exports of nutrients "across the system boundary" must be replaced by imports from outside the system, or the system is not sustainable. The same is true of rice paddies.

By the nineteenth century, the Chinese agro-ecosystem had probably reached the limits of its ability to capture and funnel energy and nutrients to the human population, and hence had placed a limit on the size of the population. That the Chinese population continued to grow, from about 400 million around 1800 to 583 million in 1953, was largely a result of the extension of agriculture into increasingly marginal and peripheral regions, as we saw in chapter 4; that process would continue through the twentieth century and into the early decades of the People's Republic. The population in the core regions of the North China plain, in the lower Yangzi, and in Lingnan, grew more slowly than China's overall rate of increase,[105] while farming in the hills and mountains led to environmental degradation in those peripheral areas, and to problems of siltation in the low-lying cores.

Resource Constraints, Environmental Management, and Social Conflict

Conflicts over water control and the ecological causes of flooding among various local interests, and between local and national leaders, were but one kind of conflict that strains on environment were causing. Massive migrations of people from areas already densely populated and intensely farmed to more peripheral areas in the southwest, the northeast, and the inland highlands may have alleviated tensions in the areas they left, but those migrations set off conflicts with the indigenous peoples the Chinese farmers encountered. Moreover, as even the inner upland regions filled up, conflicts between upland and lowland interests sharpened. And throughout the core areas of the empire, contests for control of ever-shrinking resources, whether land, water, or forests, sparked lineage feuds in the south and southeast, legal and other contests between local-place organizations, and suspicion of outsiders among villages finding cohesion through religious cult practices. By the second half of the eighteenth century, population growth, efficient markets, and state interests were propelling China toward more intensive use of existing natural resources, to conflict over the use of those resources, and toward the limits of empire. Even ocean fishery stocks were being depleted and fought over, as we will see in more detail later in this chapter.[106]

Deforestation not only degraded the environment but also brought on shortages of timber and wood, critical issues in an agrarian economy still largely fueled by tapping energy stored in trees and other organic material. As early as 1850, there was clear evidence that China was experiencing resource shortages and environmental challenges brought on by the vast environmental changes that China had experienced over the preceding millennia, and that those environmental problems intensified over the next century.

One area that received a significant amount of official attention was the availability—or, more precisely, the growing scarcity—of timber for imperial construction projects. During the Ming dynasty, the emperor had assigned a timber quota for most of China's provinces, implying that the huge timbers needed for the imperial palaces in Beijing and Nanjing could be found throughout the empire. But by the early Qing, timbers from the prized *nanmu* tree were no longer available, and so the emperor had to settle for pine, although in the early eighteenth century, the emperor could requisition some *nanmu* from Sichuan in the west.[107]

Adshead has argued that whereas China may have had the timber resources to fuel a Ming-era boom in felling trees for construction of palaces and huge fleets, by the eighteenth century, when sources of timber for those kinds of projects had been reduced to but three regions of China (Fujian, Hunan, and Sichuan provinces), imperial building projects in the Qing dynasty had to be scaled back because the timber simply was not available: "The conclusion must be that China resolved the timber supply crisis . . . by a permanent reduction in demand, a flight backward into primitivity rather than a flight forward into new sources of supply, new sources of energy."[108]

Paradoxically, additional evidence of the growing shortage of trees for timber comes from a study by Nicholas Menzies designed to show that, even in the midst of "the relentless destruction of what little forest remained . . . [under] certain sets of social, economic, and ecological conditions, forested land was protected, maintained, or managed, in the face of widespread forest clearance and conversion."[109] Menzies examines six cases of forest management: (1) in the Manchu imperial hunting preserve in Manchuria, (2) temple and monastery forests, (3) clan and village commons forests, (4) trees as agricultural products, (5) forests as hosts for other forest products such as mushrooms, and (6) old-growth logging.

There is much that is significant about forest management in Menzies's book, but for our purposes what it also shows is that nearly all of the cases he cites as evidence of forest management (and the preservation of forests) collapsed by the late nineteenth century. The imperial Mulan hunting preserve in Manchuria was abandoned in 1820 and then encroached on afterward; at monasteries monks and abbots conspired with timber merchants to sell their wood; even the most sacred spots found it hard to keep outside forces at bay, leading to extensive land clearance and forest loss. Additionally, "Village forests and clan forests have largely disappeared since the 1911 Revolution and the successive challenges since then to religious [and other] authority,"[110] and old growth stands would have been cut down except for their remote, inaccessible locations and hence high cost to log. The two examples of forest management that appear to have been successful were forests and wood products that were closely integrated into the economy and met some clearly defined market demand. In Jiangxi and northern Fujian, forests were maintained by wealthy local merchants largely because they supplied fuel to the imperial kilns at Jingdezhen, and thereby had a higher economic value as trees than as farmland, and were managed as such. Similarly, some tree species, in particular *cunninghamia*, or the Chinese fir, proved to be economical because they were fast-growing and provided fuel to nearby cities.

By the turn of the twentieth century, then, only the most extraordinary circumstances or protection allowed forests that otherwise would have been logged to remain standing, unless they already had an economic value. That some survived, in particular a few monasteries and their forests, into the twentieth century is important, for as we will see, those relic forests provided researchers with clues to what the forests of China had been before they were all removed or replaced with secondary marketable stands of bamboo or *cunninghamia.*

Even so, there was a decreasing amount of fuel available for people to cook and heat with. Instead of wood, peasant farmers scoured the land for straw, grass, or animal dung to burn.[111] Trees that remained had limbs cut off up the point where people could not reach, and whatever leaf litter fell on the ground too was picked up to burn, thereby depriving the soil of organic nutrients, further impoverishing the environment.

Foreign visitors to China in the late-nineteenth and early-twentieth centuries both noticed and commented on China's deforestation. Some said that "the Chinese detest trees," to which another replied: "On the contrary, no people loves them more: every house has one or several in its courtyard, so that you may expect a village in the district when you see a wood, and the pagodas, which are the only places of public assembly, all possess groves which are usually ancient? In short, you see trees everywhere in the neighborhood of houses—a sufficient proof that they are not unpleasing. Why, then, does the Chinese, who loves to have trees about his house, so pitilessly destroy those at a distance, thus grievously denuding the mountains?"[112]

In that world, resources for the four necessities of life—food, fuel, clothing, and shelter—came from "harvested biomass—from trees, shrubs, and grasses felled, chopped off, or gathered for fuel; from crops cultivated for food, feed, and fuel; from wild plants collected for eating, feeding, and medical use,"[113] all dependent on the ability of plants to capture and transform solar energy via photosynthesis into forms that could be used and consumed directly or indirectly by humans. In that biological old regime, work was performed mostly by human or animal muscle, making it what J. R. McNeill has called a "somatic society."[114] And with forests gone or disappearing, those energy levels were declining.

Erosion and silting of rivers, in Lowermilk's estimation, "has without doubt reduced the aggregate productive capacity of land," especially in north and central China.[115] Despite practices that recycled nutrients back to the farm (see chapter 4), by 1949 nearly all of China's cultivated land was deficient in nitrogen. By the time the Communists came to power in 1949 there was not much farmers could do to increase the input of nitrogen to their fields to increase the food supply, and hence either to produce a surplus to finance industrialization, to raise the standard of living of the existing population, or even to provide sustenance for a growing population from the existing stock of farmland.[116] Indeed, evidence from the first half of the twentieth century indicates that food supplies were inadequate to sustain the population: as much as 15 percent of the male population was so poor that they could not marry, and they died without reproducing.[117] Competition for increasingly scarce resources on both land and water occasioned more and increasingly sharp social conflict. Rural impoverishment stoked the enthusiasm of millions of China's rural people for change and for support for the Chinese Communists to do so, but the impoverished natural environment would not make that an easy task. Among other things, the Chinese Communists were to inherit a seriously degraded natural environment.

Forests as Food Reservoirs

Healthy forests not only provide habitats that preserve biological diversity. Properly managed and sustained, forests not only can provide timber for construction, mining, and housing and pulp for paper, but fuel for heating and cooking. But more than that, forests provide numerous ecological "services," the most important of which are the retention and purification of water to control floodwaters and provide safe drinking supplies, the prevention of soil loss and erosion, and the sequestration of carbon to moderate local and global climate.[118]

But for agricultural societies and peoples, forests are reserves that can be drawn on in times of crisis or food shortage brought on by unforeseen climatic variability, or the destruction of war.[119] As Joachim Radkau notes, "One absolute measure for assessing a culture in economic-ecological terms is whether it guaranteed the subsistence of its population on a sustainable basis. To do that, a culture must possess reserves, which is one of the reasons why forests deserve special consideration." Those cultures which did not preserve forests thus were tempting nature: "It is not without reason that the high forest [i.e., one with trees and bushes of varying ages and heights, providing numerous niches to sustain other species], which demands action guided by the long term, is considered an indicator of the extent to which a society is capable of making provisions for the future." On the other hand, according to Radkau, "In many regions of the world, the destruction of forests triggers disastrous chain reactions: from this perspective it is by and large possible to justify seeing forest preservation as the heart of environmental protection."[120]

Using those standards, China did not protect its forests but valued farms instead—though failing to provide its farming people with a guarantee of subsistence that could be gleaned from forests. Tellingly, where in 1750 about 25 percent of China's land surface had been forested, by 1950 that had shrunk to 5-10 percent. [121] Part of the explanation for what appears now to have been a cavalier and reckless attitude to its forests has to do with the capability of the late imperial state to provide relief to its people in times of harvest failure. For much of its history, the Qing state had indeed constructed and operated an impressive state relief system built around "ever-normal granaries," an empirewide system whereby the state bought and stored grain after the harvest when it was cheap, and sold it on the market when grain prices rose in the spring before the harvest.[122] In exceptional cases, as we will see in the next section, the state mobilized money and grain to areas hit by drought-induced harvest failure. Given these impressive relief credentials, it probably never occurred to the Qing state that the preservation of forests could function as a life preserver for rural people in times of crisis.

But in the second half of the nineteenth century, at the same time that the ability of the Qing state to respond to harvest failure was compromised by both internal rebellion and the pressures of foreign aggressors, one of the strongest global climatic events in 500 years was building—what scientists now call ENSO, the El Niño–Southern Oscillation. Around the turn of the twentieth century, a grand conjuncture of the deforestation of north China and hence the absence of forest reserves, the decline in state capability, and ENSO-induced droughts spelled disaster for millions of Chinese.

INTO THE TWENTIETH CENTURY

ENSO Droughts and Chinese Famines

Chinese have long known that the annual swing in air masses over their land—what we call the monsoon—brings moisture-laden air in the spring and summer in a northeasterly flow from the Pacific Ocean, and the life-giving rains from the tropical south to the more arid north, and then colder, drier air in the winter months. Rain-fed agriculture on the North China plain and the loess plateau thus depends on the regular arrival of the summer monsoon and its rains. Mostly, the summer monsoon arrives, it rains, crops grow, and the autumn harvest sustains the human population in north China. When the monsoon did not arrive, the crops withered, and there was little to harvest—a crisis was building. If the next year's monsoon arrived, the worst of a famine might be avoided. But if the drought continued for a second year, or even a third, then massive famine was nearly ensured.[123]

Climatologists have noted that monsoon climates affect vast stretches of the Afro-Eurasian continent and the eastern and western coasts of South America, and for decades sought an explanation that links them all. That explanation was finally formulated in the 1980s as ENSO (El Niño–Southern Oscillation), better known to Americans as El Niño, that phenomenon named for the warm water that periodically swells along the Peruvian coast around mid to late December (hence the name, El Niño, or "The Child," a reference to the newborn Christ child), and brings heavy rains to parts of North America.

A succinct explanation of ENSO has been provided by Mike Davis, who says that "after the cycle of the seasons itself, ENSO is the most important source of global climate variability . . . capable of bringing hardship to a quarter of the human race on five continents."[124] For sets of reasons that have to do with how solar energy drives global climate and is redistributed around the globe via winds and ocean currents, when otherwise separate pools of warm and cool water on opposite sides of the Pacific merge into a huge warm pool, an El Niño is set off. But an El Niño does not just bring heavy rainfall to North America. The changes in Pacific Ocean water temperatures can also cut off the normal summer monsoons in East and South Asia, as well as northeastern Africa and coastal Brazil as well, in a process called the "global teleconnection" of ENSO.

As soon as climatologists worked out the mechanisms of ENSO, they also began searching historical records in Peru and elsewhere for signs of ENSO events, and developing proxy methods to measure how strong or weak they were. In effect, the more closely teleconnected the ENSO events were, the stronger they were.[125] What this historical reconstruction shows is that exceptionally strong ENSO events caused several droughts in China in the late nineteenth and early twentieth centuries: in 1876–78, 1891, 1899–1900, 1920–21, and 1928–30. These droughts, sometimes preceded or followed by periods of flooding, earned China the nickname "Land of Famine" among foreign relief workers.

We cannot go in depth into each of these disasters, but I would like to begin by at least pointing out the severity of the droughts and the deaths that followed. The 1876–78 drought began in the north China provinces of Shandong and Zhili, and then spread to Shanxi, Henan, and Shaanxi provinces. Those provinces combined had a population of perhaps 80 million; of those, an estimated 9.5–13 million people died. In the 1920–21 drought, there were about 30 million disaster victims, five hundred thousand of whom died. In 1928–30, the drought covered eight to nine north China provinces and counted 57 million victims and 10 million deaths.[126]

These figures are staggering, and when combined with ENSO-spawned droughts in India and elsewhere at the same time, brought global totals of famine deaths for the nineteenth-century droughts alone to an estimated 31.7 to 61.3 million.[127] But it was not the ENSO-induced droughts in themselves that brought such misery and mortality to so many people. In China's case, the century of imperialist wars beginning with the Opium War of 1839–42, coupled with debilitating civil wars and rebellions, had sapped the ability of the Qing state of the ability to mobilize resources to provide relief to the afflicted areas. After the Qing state collapsed in 1911 and China lacked much of a central government of any sort, local areas were thrown back on their own resources and leadership, both of which were overwhelmed. International relief agencies, which began to provide assistance in the early twentieth century, ameliorated the worst of the drought's effects. Even when a relatively robust new government was formed in 1927 under the leadership of Jiang Kaishek and his Nationalist state, he had made deals with warlords in several provinces that kept them in power, and that contributed to the disasters of the drought of 1928–30.

That severe ENSO-induced droughts did not necessarily have to lead to massive mortality is proven by the response of the Qing state to a similarly intense drought in 1742–43. Then, however, the Qing state was relatively young and vigorous, there were no internal revolts to speak of, Western imperialist aggression was 80 years in the future, and both state resources and state capabilities were high. Indeed, Lillian Li dubs this period "The High Qing Model."[128] Not only did the Qing state send waves of officials to investigate the drought in Shanxi province, but it also organized the movement of money and grain to provide relief, set up soup kitchens and released grain from the state granaries to moderate spikes in grain prices, and afterward provided seed, tools, and tax remissions to get agricultural production up and running again.[129]

The recent accounts of China's disaster relief response (or lack thereof) by Will, Davis, and Li rightfully focus on the inability of the Chinese state in the changed political and social circumstances of the late nineteenth and early twentieth centuries to mobilize resources the way the Qing state could in its "golden age" in the eighteenth century. But by the nineteenth century, another factor accounted for the high mortality, too—by then, the forests and swamps that had provided habitat for various wild species had been cut down or filled in. There might have been more farmland, but there were no longer any natural reserves from which drought-stricken farming families might find sustenance—no deer, no fish, no turtles, nothing edible at all. And so as the 1876–78 drought intensified and prices for remaining grain soared, "famine victims resorted to famine 'foods' that had no nutritional value but provided a sense of fullness. People were seen eating clay of a soft stone that they pounded to pieces, mixed with millet husks, and then baked. Trees [around houses] were stripped bare and bark sold for 5 to 7 cash per patty. Ingesting such foods caused people to die of constipation. Grain was three to four times the usual price,"[130] indicating that the wealthy with money could get food and be spared the ravages of the drought and the famine.

North China Famines and Migration to Manchuria and Inner Mongolia

Manchuria was the homeland of the Manchus, the peoples north of the easternmost section of the Great Wall who succeeded in uniting in the seventeenth century, and then invading and conquering the Chinese empire beginning in 1644. Now known as the "three northeastern provinces" of Liaoning, Jilin, and Heilongjiang, the area from which the Manchus drew their strength and support also included Inner Mongolia. After conquering China, the Manchus desired to keep their homeland and that of their Mongol allies free from Chinese influence—a place where they could retain their ancestral customs, to which they could periodically retreat for annual ritual hunts, and where they and their ancestors could be buried. At the time of the Manchu conquest in 1644, there were maybe a million or so Manchus, several hundred thousand of whom occupied and ruled and China; as late at the mid-eighteenth century, there were perhaps a million or so people inhabiting Manchuria, a region as large as the six states of the upper U.S. Midwest (Michigan, Ohio, Indiana, Illinois, Wisconsin, and Ohio)—truly a vast expanse of land.

Moreover, according to James Reardon-Anderson, "Manchuria enjoys extraordinary natural endowments, far beyond those of any other region adjacent to China proper. The topography of Manchuria is defined by a broad central plain surrounded by a horseshoe of mountains that contain abundant and valuable timber, furs, medicinal plants, minerals, and other natural resources. . . . The soils of the plain, aeolian in the west and alluvial in the south and east, are fertile and relatively free of stone. The Manchurian summer is sufficiently warm and long to support a single crop as far north as the Amur River on the Russian border, while ample precipitation during the growing season ensures maximum plant response."[131]

Chinese had long settled in the southernmost regions of Manchuria around the area of Fengtian, but the Manchu rulers of China forbade any further Chinese migration into Manchuria and so in the 1680s built the "Willow Palisade" to delimit the Chinese pale to the south, and the Manchurian homeland to the north. To ensure that Manchuria and Inner Mongolia remain in Manchurian and Mongolian hands, the Manchus devised a landownership regime that divided all the land into "bannerlands" (the homelands of their constituent tribes) and inalienable "estates" owned by Manchu nobles. The idea was that Manchus would own and control the land, and if necessary seek Chinese tenants or serfs to work the land. That turned out to be a failed policy; Chinese proved to be much harder workers than Manchus and, being accustomed to free markets in land and labor, began to organize themselves according to those principles. By 1850, there was little left of Manchu bannerlands or estates, with the institution of private property and markets having taken their place with Chinese beginning to gain access to, and ownership of, Manchu lands.

Then the floodgates opened. With mounting debt from battling the various internal rebellions (the largest and most costly being the Taiping Rebellion, 1850–65), and having to deal with the threats posed by the Western powers, including Russia, which began putting pressure on Manchuria from the north, the Manchu government of China reversed course and adopted a policy of "Moving People to Strengthen the Border" and to increase the tax base. "From 1860 on, Qing policies in the northern territories were dominated by financial and strategic concerns."[132]

Chinese began migrating north into Manchuria, at first as sojourners who would return home after the harvest, but increasingly as entire families from places on the North China plain hard-hit by natural disasters, especially Shandong and Hebei provinces. From a population in 1781 of about 1 million, the population of Manchuria increased to about 2.5 million in 1820, and ballooned to 17 million over the next 90 years. From 1910 to 1940, the population increased again to nearly 40 million. According to Reardon-Anderson, nearly all of this population increase came about because of Chinese migration.[133]

Just to the west of Manchuria in the grasslands of Inner Mongolia, the migration story was much the same. In 1912, the population of Inner Mongolia was slightly more than 2 million, with Han Chinese slightly outnumbering Mongols. By 1990, the population had climbed to 21 million, with six Han for every Mongol. The floodgate of Han migration to Mongolia opened in 1911 when the new Chinese Republic "declared that all Mongol lands belonged to China."[134] As was true almost everywhere Han migrated, "the large-scale changes in land use and the increases in demographic pressures associated with Han colonization did escalate ecological changes within the steppe zone." According to Owen Lattimore, by the 1930s for Han migrants "to produce financial results, land had to be farmed even if it was naturally more suitable for grazing than for ploughing. The good soil is then blown away, and sand begins to work up from below."[135] This part of the story of environmental changes in Manchuria and Inner Mongolia will be continued in the next chapter.

The surge in Chinese migration to Manchuria came largely on the heals of the ENSO-induced droughts and famines of 1876–78, when a million Chinese fled to Manchuria,[136] and in the twentieth century, after the droughts of 1920–21 and 1928–30 (especially the latter). Drought spread across nine provinces, affecting 57 million people, 10 million of whom eventually died. The descriptions and photographs of the situation are harrowing. Starving people susceptible to contracting any number of diseases, including dysentery, flooded the roads; male heads of families sold children and wives; grass and trees were dug up for their roots; cannibalism was reported. Exacerbating the situation was military conflict between the head of the nationalist government, Generalissimo Jiang Kaishek, and his supposed warlord allies that interrupted international and Chinese relief efforts.[137]

Refugees fled north China, many heading to cities, others walking north toward Manchuria, others hopping trains or boats to escape the nightmare, and disembarking in southern Manchuria. In what is somewhat unexpected behavior, though, the Chinese refugees tended to stay in the agricultural regions of southern Manchuria, rather than striking out for the wealth of the mountains encircling the plain. "The highlands of Manchuria offered a wide range of valuable products," Reardon-Anderson says, "to anyone willing to risk the adventure. . . . By the eighteenth century, when most forests in China proper had been stripped bare, the northern territories remained cloaked in what appeared to be endless woodlands. At the upper elevations, the mountains of Manchuria were covered by a taiga (moist, subarctic) forest, dominated by larch in the west and the more valuable cedar and spruce in the east, and at lower levels by oak, walnut, birch, and maple, often of gigantic size." Sable, deer, and tigers abounded in the forests, as did sturgeon and pearl-bearing oysters in its rivers.[138]

Chinese migrants nonetheless preferred to recreate their familiar farmsteads and village landscapes in valleys that promised the greatest returns to agriculture. They clustered by family and native place into compact villages, "protected by walls made first of mud and later brick and stone, and surrounded by fields that expanded from the central core across an unbroken stretch of farmland to the edge of wilderness."[139] A European explorer observed that "every two or three years the Chinese open a new tract for settlement and, as soon as this is occupied by farmers, the border line of cultivation is advanced still farther. In the last seven years [1918–25], it has gone northward forty miles. The Mongols who occupy the frontier regions are simply forced to retreat as the Chinese progress."[140]

Chinese migrants did not set out into the Manchurian wilderness, clearing plots out of the forest like their Shang ancestors had done, or like the many non-Chinese peoples who practiced slash-and-burn agriculture. Neither did these Chinese migrants fleeing drought and famine from the North China plain seem to be aware that the forest offered some subsistence guarantees should the harvest fail. Reardon-Anderson thinks that habits among the north Chinese villagers were so ingrained that none set out into the wilderness as pioneers; nor did Reardon-Anderson find any evidence that the Chinese migrants adapted in any significant ways to their new environment. Rather, "the society and culture of [Manchuria] has been defined more by the transplantation or replication of patterns and practices from China proper than by the innovation or invention of new frontier ways."[141]

And so by the 1930s, "more than half of all potential farmland in Manchuria still awaited the plow, while the percentage of arable land that remained uncultivated increased in a gradient from south to north—27% in Fengtian, 52% in Jilin, and 68% in Heilongjiang."[142] In other words, on the eve of Japan's 1937 invasion of China, there remained vast forests in Manchuria, despite the influx of Chinese migrants who established farming village after farming village, replicating habits, institutions, and customs from north China into Manchuria, pushing the "wilderness" northward, slowly but surely cutting down the forest, not preserving it.

Fujian Forests and Forestry

Manchuria was not the only part of China with some forest left on the eve of the Japanese invasion in 1937. In the last chapter, we discussed Yunnan, where forest remained into the twentieth century, and in chapter 7 I will examine forests in eastern Tibet, western Sichuan, and northwestern Yunnan. Here I want to look at Fujian, the one province in "China proper" that still had some forest left in the 1930s. Chinese migrants had settled in Fujian later than in other places south of the Yangzi River, in part because the inland mountains isolated the coastal strip from the north-south routes that brought Chinese into Guangdong, and in part because the topography did not provide much good land for farming. In chapter 4, we saw the effort needed to drain the coastal swamps that harbored the fierce saltwater crocodile. Moreover, the several rivers that drained the province started in the mountains and flowed quickly the short distance to the sea, without cutting much of a flood plain in valleys. The rivers, though—especially the Min and its tributaries draining the northwester third of the province—did make convenient means of transportation for timber cut from mountain slopes and floated down to the coastal city of Fuzhou.

By the early twentieth century, there was a well-established timber marketing system in the Min River system. Specialized tree fellers working for wages and timber brokers or sawmill owners cut the timber and slid it down specially constructed spillways and chutes to the river. Historian Elena Songster sees the creation of these chutes as evidence of "disproportionately high forest depletion near the rivers,"[143] although she also thinks that timber operations in Fujian did replant or coppice the most highly prized timber tree, the Chinese fir (*cunninghamia*); camphor made up a small percentage of the harvest.[144]

Consciousness of the depleted stocks of China's forests emerged very quickly among the new political elite that tried to fashion a new republic after the fall of the Qing dynasty in 1911. A new "National Forest Law" was promulgated in 1914 calling on all provinces to establish afforestation programs; Fujian province adopted one in 1916. The new government apparently saw adequate timber supplies both as essential both to economic modernization and as a source of tax revenue for the impoverished new state. The problem was that the new republic was so weak that it really could not accomplish much of anything; real power throughout the former Chinese empire had devolved into the hands of warlords. Thus in Fujian "implementation of [their] elaborate afforestation and management plant required a modern infrastructure. In 1916, Fujian not only lacked such an infrastructure, but also was in a state of political chaos."[145] The old timber marketing system continued to function as before.

Political circumstances began to change with the formation in 1927 of Jiang Kai-shek's new Nationalist government. Having broken with his communist allies, Jiang set about creating new governmental institutions, and trying to modernize both the political order and the economy. Like his predecessors, he recognized the value of timber for building a modern economy, and he proclaimed a national arbor day and the establishment of nurseries in Fujian to provide saplings for reforestation. Although this program "actually produced trees," Songster says, the new government regulations of the entire timber industry and high taxes on the timber that reached the port of Fuzhou, coupled with the effects of the Great Depression, strangled the timber industry. Still, reforestation continued into the 1930s, with some success in afforesting the Min riverbank. After Japan invaded China in 1937, the Nationalist government and its forest initiatives evaporated. The old timber marketing networks reappeared, but much of the timber was cut into short sticks for loading onto small boats that could avoid Japanese ships. Moreover, "large-scale reforestation projects could not be maintained under fire."[146]

Fisheries

The history of intensified use, growing scarcity, and hopes for relief by the use of modern scientific concepts of resource management that informed the story of forests in Fujian contains many similarities to the history of offshore fisheries, at least in the Zhoushan archipelago just off the Zhejiang coast, south of where the Yangzi River empties into the East China Sea.[147] The ocean ecology that brought nutrients washed down the rivers into contact with additional nutrients welling up from deep in the ocean provided breeding grounds for four kinds of fish—large and small yellow croaker, hairtail, and cuttlefish—that the growing populations of the lower Yangzi delta added to their diet.

These islands were first fished in the Southern Song dynasty after the capital was moved to Hangzhou (see chapter 4), but more fishermen ventured into these waters about the same time—and for the same reasons—that farmers in overpopulated areas of Zhejiang province abandoned farming in the river valleys and set out to take up lives as the "shed people" (*pengmin*) who exploited highland resources. According to Micah Muscolino, "Opening up highland areas and expanding into offshore fishing grounds were analogous responses to intensified pressure on China's natural resources. In each instance, ecological change brought migration into previously unexploited frontiers. . . . As inland bodies of water disappeared, fishermen turned to lucrative marine fishing grounds."[148]

As the fishermen became better organized, financed, and supported, larger and larger numbers of fish were taken to market. By the late nineteenth century, fish stocks were being depleted, as evidenced by fewer large fish being caught but more and more small fry hauled up in finer and finer nets; competition and conflict broke out among fishermen organized in different local-place organizations. After the turn of the twentieth century, new technologies, in particular outboard motors, and a modernizing elite mobilized by Sun Yat-sen's Nationalist Party and government under Sun's successor Jiang Kaishek, combined to intensify exploitation of the fisheries. Even as evidence continued to mount that the fisheries were being depleted, the modernist faith in "rational management" that science would both protect the natural resource and lead to higher output and hence more tax revenue for the state ran into the reality that the Republican state lacked the ability to implement its plans.

Simultaneously, though, a neighboring state that did have the resources to implement its modernizing vision—Japan—in the 1920s and 1930s pushed into the fishing grounds with newly built steel-hulled fishing trawlers. The catches were large, and provoked conflict with the Zhoushan fishermen and the Republican government. Outgunned (so to speak) by Japan's trawlers, Chinese fishermen sought catches further afield and in deeper waters. "By the mid-1930s," according to Muscolino, "the combined demands of Chinese and Japanese fishing activities had led to a clear decline in the productivity of Zhoushan's yellow croaker fisheries."[149] Overfishing by Chinese boatmen, exacerbated by conflicts among competing groups and even provinces, contributed to the depletion of the fisheries. But war between Japan and China and then the entrance of the United States into the Pacific War brought nearly all coastal fishing to a halt, and provided a space for stocks to recover in the 1940s.[150]

War's Environmental Catastrophes

Within months of the outbreak of war between China and Japan in 1937, Japanese troops took Beijing and the Japanese army began moving south with the goal of taking Wuhan, the wartime capital of Jiang Kaishek's Nationalist government, but first aiming at Zhengzhou. Zhengzhou was not only the site of ancient capitals but also had the newfound strategic importance of sitting astride the Beijing-Hankou railway. Reports of Japanese atrocities, especially the Rape of Nanjing (December 1937–January 1938) preceded the Japanese troops, sowing fear and panic among the Chinese population; the Chinese army was being decimated, and was not able to check the Japanese advance.[151]

To slow the Japanese advance, on June 9, 1938, Jiang Kaishek had his army breach the Yellow River dikes just northeast of Zhengzhou, producing a 70,000–square kilometer flood that spread down the Huai River valley to Hongze Lake and the Grand Canal. The Yellow River dikes there were so large, so well built, and so stout that two attempts to breach them using explosives failed, and only by furiously excavating down was the dike finally breached. Nearly 1 million people drowned, and at least 2 million more fled. Japanese tanks and troops were slowed for a while, but their advance continued. For years, the course of the Yellow River continually shifted, according to American Jack Belden: "In its unpredictable journeyings, the new river has gone on a rampage through eleven counties and three provinces."[152] Hundreds of thousands of villages were washed away, and millions of acres of farmland were covered with silt or waterlogged. When the floodwaters subsided under the parching sun, "the ground turned as hard as brick, and there was no way to plant crops."[153] This war-induced, manmade environmental disaster was immense: more than 4 million victims, millions more in need of relief, and still millions more refugees.[154]

About 1.7 million of those refugees from Hebei province headed west to Shaanxi province and the Wei River valley, an area not under Japanese occupation. Initially clogging the cities of Luoyang and Xi'an (the former Chang'an), Nationalist officials quickly started relocating them to Huanglong Mountain to "reclaim" land and farm. The area had been devastated six decades earlier during the Muslim Rebellion, and there was much of what officials considered "wasteland" waiting to be reopened. By the end of 1938, twenty-five thousand refugees had been resettled there. Following a further drought and famine in 1942–43,[155] additional refugees streamed into Shaanxi from Hebei, and an additional two hundred thousand were relocated to Huanglong Mountain.

In the view of Walter Lowdermilk, an American official of the Soil Conservation Bureau who visited the area in 1942–43, the mountain pastureland of Huanglong Mountain was best suited for animal husbandry, but the refugees had cleared vast tracts of trees, brush, and grass for growing grains, maize, potatoes, and buckwheat. Within a few years, soil eroded down barren hillsides, the nutrients of the soil were exhausted, and people experienced a disease associated with selenium deficiencies. A Chinese source reported that "[w]hen the mountains erode and the rivers [fill up with silt and] grow murky, the harvests from agricultural production are not abundant and erosion problems occur." He predicted that at the current rate of exploitation, Huanglong Mountain would be deforested.[156] Fortunately for the refugees and the forests, the war ended in 1945.

Whereas Jiang Kaishek's Nationalist government had entered the war against Japan as the acknowledged government of China, by the end of the war China's Communist party, under the leadership of their chairman, Mao Zedong, had seen its power and prestige rise to the point that it could challenge Jiang for rule of China. To be sure, Jiang and his forces had born the brunt of the Japanese invasion, retreating inland behind the wall of mountains surrounding Sichuan province after trying to save Nanjing from Japanese occupation. The Chinese Communists, from their base at Yan'an on the loess plateau, began organizing villagers behind Japanese lines and gained their trust, while simultaneously winning the support of urban intellectuals who saw them as fighting the Japanese while Jiang Kaishek had retreated. By 1945, the Chinese Communists had come to govern areas of north China with a population nearing 100 million. When the Nationalists and the Communists could not reach an agreement on a coalition government after the Japanese defeat in September, 1945, civil war broke out. The Chinese Communists won, and on October 1, 1949, the Communist leader Mao Zedong proclaimed the establishment of the People's Republic of China.

CONCLUSION

In the century and a half prior to the Chinese Communist victory in 1949, the evidence clearly points to a widespread environmental crisis in China.[157] The dynamics of population growth, commercialization, and the strategic and fiscal needs of the state sent waves of Chinese migrants into borderlands and inner peripheries where forests were removed and wetlands filled in for farms. Deforestation led to increased siltation and flooding of river plains, loss of nutrients from soil and of its ability to hold water, energy shortages, and constrictions of timber supplies for building. With declining energy levels, the metabolism of China's agro-ecosystems had been slowing, with humans becoming impoverished along with their environment. Competition for increasingly scarce resources on both land and water occasioned more and increasingly sharp social conflict. That impoverishment may have stoked the enthusiasm of countless millions of China's rural people for change and for support for the Chinese Communists to do so, but the impoverished natural environment would not make that an easy task. Among other things, the Chinese Communists inherited a seriously degraded natural environment.

Chapter 7

"Controlling" Nature in the People's Republic of China, 1949–Present

This chapter examines environmental changes to the land, water, and atmosphere during the history of the People's Republic of China, 1949 to the present day. Because the People's Republic created new political, economic, and social institutions through which Chinese interacted with and changed their environment, the first part of this chapter will explore that new context before returning to an examination of environmental changes to the land, forests, and grasslands; to rivers; and to the atmosphere, concluding with a consideration of environmental activism and movements in contemporary China.

SOCIALIST INDUSTRIALIZATION AND SUBDUING NATURE

The victory of the Chinese Communists in 1949 and the formation of their new state, the People's Republic of China, signaled the beginning of a new era marked by a determined state effort to industrialize as rapidly as possible. Despite inheriting a war-ravaged country that was overwhelmingly rural and suffering the consequences of deforestation and environmental degradation, there can be little doubt that the sixty-year history of the People's Republic has seen China transformed from an agrarian society into one of the largest, but arguably most polluted, industrial economies on earth.[1]

To be sure, the policies and practices of the first three decades of the PRC under Communist leader Mao Zedong differed dramatically from those worked out under his successor, Deng Xiaoping. While both claimed to be building a socialist China, Mao distrusted markets and bureaucratic hierarchies, searching instead for a distinctively rapid Chinese (i.e., "Maoist") route to the socialist future, whereas Deng Xiaoping thought that a state controlled by the Communists would be able to use markets and

Map 7.1. China's Provinces, ca. 2010

other "capitalist tools" to build the material prerequisites for a socialist future. Despite significant differences between the two that resulted in intense political infighting and a near civil war, both were committed to the most rapid economic development of China possible. Whatever else may have been heralded or promised in 1949, as parts of a broader modernist agenda, Marxism and socialism in China have provided the ideological support for rapid industrialization in the service of a sovereign state controlled by the Chinese Communist party.

Socialist Industrialization and Its Material Constraints

China's industrialization hinged on surpluses generated from agriculture, and Chinese agriculture was in a bind. Maximum yields from dry-land farming of wheat and millet on the North China plain probably had been reached as early as the Han dynasty, and the waterlogging, salinization, siltation, and sandization caused by hydrological problems cut into those yields. Wet-rice agriculture was much more productive, but those yields probably peaked no later than the eighteenth century.[2] The basic problem was the depletion of critical nutrients—especially nitrogen—from the soil.

Depleted Soils

Despite agricultural practices that recycled nutrients back to the farm (see chapters 4 and 6), by 1949 nearly all of China's cultivated land was deficient in nitrogen.[3] Using the methods then available to Chinese farmers, by the time the Communists came to power in 1949 there probably was not much farmers could do to increase the input of nitrogen to their fields to increase the food supply, and hence either to produce a surplus to finance industrialization, to raise the standard of living of the existing population, or even to provide sustenance for a growing population.[4] Indeed, evidence from the first half of the twentieth century indicates that food supplies were inadequate to sustain the population: as much as 15 percent of the male population was so poor that they could not marry, and they died without reproducing.[5] In short, China's industrialization effort was seriously hampered until the mid-1970s by the lack of synthetic fertilizers to rapidly increase China's agricultural productivity.

Foreign Opposition to Chinese Socialism

Adding to the bind were global factors. Even if the new Communist government had the foreign exchange or credit worthiness to borrow money to buy chemical fertilizer plants on the world market, the United States was in the process of determining that the world communist threat needed to be "contained," and China's decision to intervene in the Korean War (1950–53) on the side of communist North Korea and to fight the United States put China clearly in the camp of the enemy. "Containing" China meant a U.S.-enforced embargo on Chinese access to credit and technology in the capitalist world. The Soviet Union thus was China's only source of foreign aid—as minimal and short-lived as it turned out to be—for its industrialization effort.

A Big and Growing Population (Is Good)

To complicate matters further, the Chinese Communist leader, Mao Zedong (1896–1976), thought that a large and growing population was positive: "It is a very good thing that China has a big population," he wrote in 1949, before his government knew how many Chinese there were. "Even if China's population multiplies many times, she is fully capable of finding a solution; the solution is production."[6] As a Marxist, to Mao more people meant more workers whose labor and creativity could be tapped to grow the economy. When China's first modern census in 1953 returned a total of 583 million, Mao was jubilant. Besides more workers, he thought a large population was a military asset, and that even a nuclear attack from the United States would not be able to wipe out the Chinese. His government encouraged family formation and pregnancies, giving families that had more children bigger rations. Under his rule, China's population rose nearly 250 million to more than 800 million by the time he died in 1976, even while the productivity of agriculture did not—could not, without chemical fertilizer inputs—increase. Total agricultural output did increase, though—as we

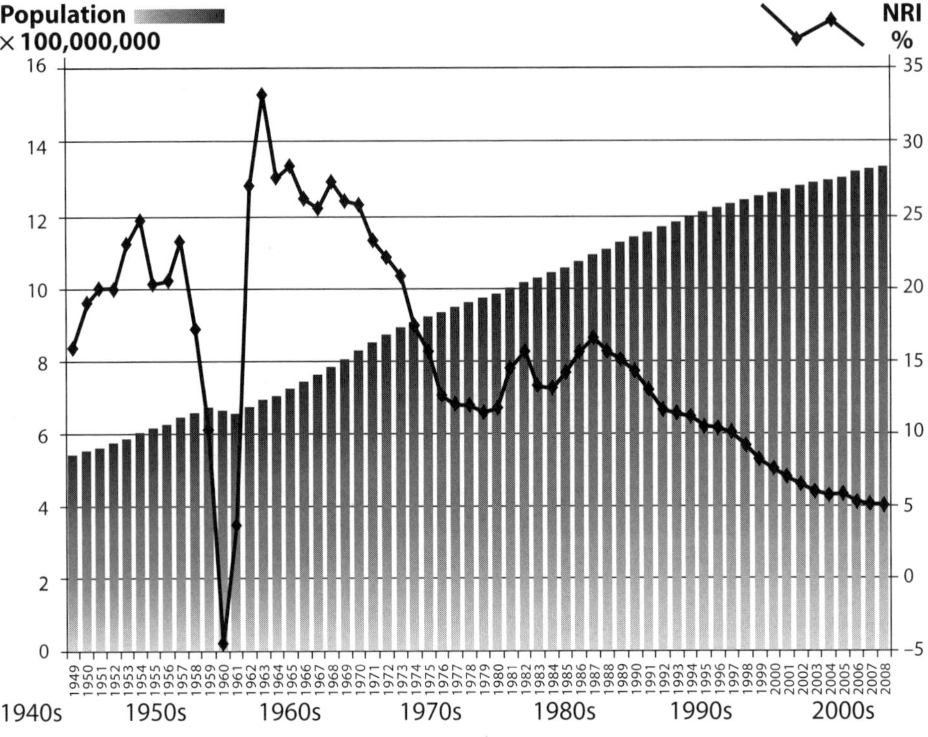

Fig. 7.1. China's Population Size and Growth Rate *Source:* Department of Comprehensive Statistics of National Bureau of Statistics, comp. *Xin zhongguo liushinian tongji ziliao huibian* [China Compendium of Statistics, 1949–2008]. Beijing: China Statistics Press, 2009), 6.

will see—as a result of pushing farming into ever more marginal territories with ever increasing environmental damage to forests, grasslands, and watersheds.

In the early years of the Peoples Republic, dynamics set centuries earlier—a Chinese state emphasizing the combination of agriculture and large farming families creating pressure to push Chinese style farming into ever more marginal areas—thus continued to shape Chinese history, despite Mao's powerful will to change the material circumstances he had inherited.

Nonetheless, the very real material constraints to a successful industrialization effort were immense. But Mao and his most fervent followers came to see those material constraints as, well, immaterial—and to try anyway. That explains much about the history of the People's Republic of China during the nearly thirty-year span of the Mao years, including the massive pressures put on China's environment. Despite achieving industrial growth rates averaging 18 percent per year during the Soviet-inspired First Five-Year Plan (1953–57), Mao was dissatisfied with following the Soviet model because he concluded that its actual results would lead China further away from, rather than closer toward, the promised socialist future. Rapidly collectivized agriculture, he thought, would not only release pent-up peasant enthusiasm for socialism but also result in massive increases in agricultural productivity, even without the needed chemical fertilizer inputs. Mao's wishful thinking was then confirmed by exaggerated harvest reports by local Communist leaders in Hebei province, leading to The Great Leap Forward in 1958 and its disastrous end, and Mao's "retirement" a few years later. His struggle to regain power and push forward with his ideas about the proper way to achieve socialist development culminated in a decade of disruption brought about by "Third Front" industrialization and the Cultural Revolution (1966–76).

Whatever industrial development China was going to have would for several decades depend on the productivity of its agriculture, and the inconvenient limitations that that imposed. As economist Barry Naughton put it, "Here was a system that set all the strategic and systemic settings to maximize the flow of resources into industrialization. It concentrated discretionary power at the top so that leaders could throw resources at whatever their priorities were. The system, in other words, was set up to maximize the potential to 'leap.' But every time the system really began to accelerate, it ran into fundamental problems. The economy would overshoot and hit its head on the ceiling. What was this 'ceiling?' The ceiling was the inability of agriculture to rapidly generate adequate food surpluses."[7] But why couldn't Chinese agriculture be more productive? Mao and the Chinese Communists certainly asked themselves that question many times.

Shortages of Chemical Fertilizer

Chemical fertilizer would have to be an essential part of the solution. It was not that China's Maoist leadership was unconcerned with increasing synthetic chemical fertilizer supplies to solve their agricultural problem, but that that was part of the problem of industrializing—building the modern factories that could manufacture chemical fertilizer. The problem of how to chemically synthesize nitrogen-rich fertilizers had been solved in the early twentieth century by German scientists, and the problem of large-scale commercial manufacturing had been solved by a German industrialist. With world wars and economic depression marring the first half of the twentieth century, the spread of "the Haber-Bosch" process to synthesize ammonia-based chemical fertilizer, as it was known after the inventors, was slow until 1950.[8]

When the Chinese Communists came to power in 1949, China had but two chemical fertilizer factories—one built by the Japanese in the 1930s during their occupation of Manchuria and one near Nanjing built and operated by an American-trained Chinese chemist. Despite plans to increase output of those two plants, a recognition that nearly all of China's farms needed nitrogen inputs, the construction of a handful of additional chemical fertilizer plants in the 1960s that had been started during the Great Leap, and some imports of the expensive material,[9] China simply did not have the domestic capacity to produce adequate supplies of chemical fertilizer. This material constraint meant that only intensifying labor inputs or adding to the amount of farmland could increase agricultural output. The Mao years saw massive combinations of both.

Mass campaigns to encourage peasants to labor longer and harder may have increased agricultural productivity somewhat, but that enthusiasm could be maintained at a fever pitch only for a brief time before exhaustion set in, as the Great Leap Forward demonstrated. Thus actual increases in agricultural output to sustain both a growing population and to produce surpluses necessary for investment in industry thus could come only by increasing the amount of land farmed.

The Chinese Communists had inherited a rural economy that included perhaps 80 million hectares (nearly 200 million acres) of farmland, perhaps 40 percent of which was rice paddies. By 1980 that total probably increased by 50 percent to 120–130 million hectares,[10] with increases coming from forests in China's northeastern and southwestern regions (Manchuria and Yunnan in particular), and grasslands in the north (Mongolia) and the northwest (Gansu and Xinjiang). In other words, in the first thirty years of the People's Republic under the leadership of Mao Zedong, as much new farmland was added as had been under the plow during the first millennium CE (e.g., the Han dynasty to the Song).

As we have seen in chapters 5 and 6, even by the end of the eighteenth century, Chinese farmers were beginning to push into marginal lands, with increasingly deleterious environmental effects. Mountain hillsides, arid grasslands, and tropical forests had already fallen by the time the Communists established their regime. Nonetheless, during the first thirty years of the People's Republic, Mao championed the spread of agriculture to even more marginal land (at least for agriculture), and this continued to be a major force transforming China's environment, as the sections in this chapter on China's forests, grasslands, and water resources will show.

In short, the lack of adequate amounts of chemical fertilizer coupled with ideas and policies that favored a large and growing population and a commitment to the most rapid industrial development possible meant that the leaders of the People's Republic of China pursued policies that rapidly increased the amount of land devoted to agriculture, even if those new lands being brought under the plow, such as was the case for hilly and sloping land or grasslands, degraded the environment.

In terms of the material relation of Chinese to their environment, the year 1949 thus was not much of a watershed. To be sure, the Communist victory brought a powerful new state with the intent and ability to industrialize, as well as the promise of internal peace and security. An apparently stable government with the ability to control its own borders and fate was a significant departure from the experiences of the previous century. But the ongoing need to feed the population—"the conquest of hunger" in Lillian Li's words[11]—continued centuries-long processes that depleted the soil of nutrients, removed forests and grasslands for crops, and pushed farms into ever more marginal areas, including easily eroded mountainsides with slopes exceeding 40 degrees. Added to these pressures were isolation from the world market imposed by the United States because of the Korean War, a belief that a large and growing population was a good thing, and the need to fund industrialization from surpluses generated internally from agriculture.

Because of poverty, technological backwardness, and international isolation (except for support from the Soviet Union, which lasted only until 1960), the Chinese Communists had few options but to focus on developing agriculture as rapidly as possible. The entire country had but two chemical fertilizer plants, few if any farms had machinery, and there was no electricity or small engines for pumps. And yet agriculture and rural peasants were expected to shoulder the weight of transforming China's economy into a modern industrial one. And of course, that meant that the natural environment would have to pay, too. Tragically, these conditions would continue through the 1970s—the entire Mao period—in large part because of the lack of chemical fertilizer. As we will see later in this chapter, that constraint was lifted for Mao's successors as a result of a rather surprising international development involving the United States and its president at that time, Richard Nixon.

In this context, and for understandable reasons, the Chinese Communists thus came to see the forces of nature as neither benign nor helpful. The legacy of droughts, floods, soil depleted of its nutrients, denuded hills, erosion, siltation, and shortages of wood for fuel and building materials, among other environmental nightmares, weighed on the minds of China's new Communist leaders. To them, nature was an enemy—an enemy to be attacked with the same kinds of mass mobilization and military campaigns that had brought them to power. These ideas about nature contributed to a sustained attack on China's forests both for the land that could be converted to agriculture, and for the fuel and timber that could be harnessed for the industrialization drive, and on rivers that were dammed for their stores of water and capacity to generate electricity.

Chinese Communist Ideas about Nature

Embedded within Chinese Communist commitments to rapid industrial development were ideas (some explicit and some implicit) about nature derived from Marxism, the Chinese Communists' own history, China's imperial legacy, and Western science. Despite significant differences among these, and the fact that any tradition contains contradictory elements (making it unwise to essentialize a "Chinese" view of nature),[12] they shared the general modernist disposition that humans were separate from nature, that resources derived from nature were to be used to support humans and their society, and that people should dominate and control nature.

The Idea to Control Nature

China's centralized imperial state, including its predecessors, had long operated on the presumption that to demonstrate and wield power, nature needed to be tamed, if not subdued.[13] The point of political, military, and economic action was the human-centered one of proper governance and social order. In examining Chinese ideas about nature, Robert Weller and Peter Bol point out that "the idea that political authority has fundamental responsibility for maintaining harmonious relations between society and environment has a long history in China. On the other hand, this view did not result in the conscious establishment of environmentally sound practices, largely because human utility always received first consideration."[14] The end result, as we saw in chapter 6, was a largely deforested China and an environmentally degraded landscape.

Marxist ideas about nature and science also contributed to Chinese Communist views. In perhaps their most readily recognizable comment about the place of nature in the human world, or more precisely the capitalist world, Marx and Engels observed in *The Manifesto of the Communist Party* of 1848 that "[t]he bourgeoisie, during its rule of scarce one hundred years, has created more massive and more colossal productive forces than have all preceding generations together. Subjection of Nature's forces to man, machinery, application of chemistry to industry and agriculture, steam-navigation, railways, electric telegraphs, clearing of whole continents for cultivation, canalisation of rivers, whole populations conjured out of the ground—what earlier century had even a presentiment that such productive forces slumbered in the lap of social labour?"[15]

The Chinese Communists also shared with their Guomindang rivals the nineteenth- and early twentieth-century modernist view of science as a tool to control nature, brought to China in the 1920s and 1930s with European and American science advisors, and their newly minted Chinese Ph.D.s (for examples, see the sections on Fujian forestry and the Zhoushan fisheries in chapter 6, as well as on climatologist Zhu Kezhen in chapter 2). Thus Sheldon H. Lu recently identified "the project of Chinese modernity as domination of nature."[16] That view was accentuated even further by the Maoist voluntarist conviction that nature, like human society, was "infinitely malleable," in Laurence Schneider's words, and that the mobilized masses themselves could master science, and hence nature. In this Maoist "discourse, nature and society were equated as objects of change and control; neither was considered to be informed by any permanent structures, qualities, or tendencies; both could be altered and directed from the outside, as it were, by reshaping environments. Doing science and making social revolution became equated metaphorically. . . ."[17] Marxism, Western science, and Maoism all shared the modernist triumphalism of establishing human-directed scientific control over nature.

These views coalesced within a decade after the Chinese Communists came to power in 1949 in what first Rhoads Murphey called the Communists' "war against nature,"[18] and Judith Shapiro later more precisely identified as "*Mao's* war against nature."[19] In Murphey's prescient view (his article was written in 1967), the Chinese Communists thought that "nature is no longer to be accepted but must be 'defied and conquered.'" They designed and implemented policies for agriculture and industry that put a human stamp on their environment, including as examples campaigns to eliminate sparrows because they were thought to be pests, to scatter soot by airplane over the ice and snow in the mountains surrounding the Tarim basin to speed their melting for irrigation, to dam the silt-laden Yellow River in the huge Sanmenxia dam project, and to spread industry from the coastal regions to peripheral areas. Given the huge gap between China and the advanced West, Murphey thought that the mass campaigns to conquer nature gave the peasantry a sense of "national pride" in a "holy war" in which commitment and action were preferable "to inaction or to resignation."

Soviet Lysenkoism

These general ideas were institutionalized in changes brought to the academic field of biology in the 1950s when ideas developed by Stalin's agronomists I. V. Michurin and Trofim Lysenko were imposed on Chinese higher education. Most Chinese biologists had been trained in European and American universities in genetics, evolutionary theory, and experimental biology. This Western approach to science was dismissed by Lysenko and his followers, in Schneider's words, as "totally useless for achieving the only appropriate goal of science—the control of nature and its manipulation for the benefit of the nation and the masses."[20] Lysenkoism dismissed "the old biology" as bourgeois, devoted merely to understanding nature, whereas the aim—adapting a famous Marxist proposition about philosophers[21]—was to change nature.

Lysenko's "transformist belief that all of organic nature is infinitely malleable and subject to human manipulation" harmonized with Mao's ideas about social revolution, and Lysenkoism was adopted as formal party doctrine in 1952. In the critical field of botany and plant science, genetics and experimental plots were abandoned to the idea that food plants could be quickly improved to grow in previously hostile environments, or more abundantly in native ones, in part on the belief that individual plants of the same species would not compete for nutrients. This now thoroughly discredited view no doubt had appeal to Chinese leaders struggling to increase agricultural yields without access to chemical fertilizer. In forestry, Lysenkoist botany "led to some unusual silvicultural and ecological concepts and practices . . . [such as] nest-sowing of seed, group planting, and very close spacing of seedlings. . . ."[22]

Although genetics was reinstated during the Hundred Flowers opening of 1956 and scored important successes in the early 1960s with the development of new strains of seeds that responded to chemical fertilizers, new farm machinery, and irrigation, Maoist attacks on the entire scientific community during the Cultural Revolution decade (1966–76) decimated genetics-informed biology (along with all other science). In Lawrence Schneider's view, it would then take years of post-Mao leadership to "dissolve the Cultural Revolution miasma of contempt and distrust, and to rehabilitate the stature of the scientific community."[23] Although Chinese Communist leaders of the post-Mao reform era repudiated Mao's attempts to control China's scientists, they shared with Mao (and others, for that matter) the modernist belief that the role of science is to understand, control, and manipulate nature for the greater good of human progress.

Post-Mao Reform Era, 1978–Present

China has industrialized most rapidly in the post-Mao era, with annual rates of economic growth averaging between 8 and 12 percent since 1980. Mostly, China's rapid development is attributed to the era that began in late 1978 after China's new leader Deng Xiaoping inaugurated reforms that ultimately saw China opening to the world market, the dismantling of state ownership of land and factories, the elimination of state planning and control, the establishment and protection of private ownership of property, and the use of market mechanisms to set most prices for labor, land, and commodities. Launched from the base created by China's socialist state-directed industrialization, China industrialized rapidly in the 1980s and 1990s, leaping to become a global industrial power by the beginning of the twenty-first century. In the views of many, China has transitioned from a socialist economy in the Mao era to a thoroughly capitalist economy today. If Mao's voluntarism contributed to views of nature as infinitely malleable, Deng Xiaoping's developmentalism conceived of nature as a vast reserve to be plundered for human needs. Both shared the modernist instrumentality that via science humans could—and should—control nature.

Breaks with Maoism

If very real material conditions constrained the ability of Mao's China to industrialize rapidly and contributed to Mao's voluntarist views that material conditions could be overcome by the exercise of pure will, the easing of those Maoist-era material constraints on economic growth has to be considered as a significant factor in China's post-Mao growth. One that is very seldom considered is the chemical fertilizer industry. As we saw earlier in this chapter, the limited availability of chemical fertilizers during the Mao years hindered the improvements to agricultural productivity that were needed to fund investments in industry. That constraint was lifted in a surprising way.

The story involves the historic visit of U.S. President Richard Nixon to China in 1972. Most interpretations of the Nixon opening to China place the event in a geopolitical context: The United States was bogged down in the Vietnam War and wanted a way out, as well as a way to bring pressure on the Soviet Union to enter into more nuclear arms control agreements; China, too, had its military problems with the Soviet Union, and so "the-enemy-of-my-enemy-is-my-friend" logic is usually cited for the historic meeting between Richard Nixon and Chinese Communist leaders Premier Zhou Enlai and Party Chairman Mao Zedong.

Chemical Fertilizer Plants

But the immediate result for China of renewed relations between China and the United States places China's motivations for the détente into the context of its environmental history. The first commercial deal signed immediately after Nixon's visit was China's order for thirteen of the world's largest synthetic ammonia complexes for producing nitrogen-based chemical fertilizer. China purchased additional plants in the 1970s, developed its own capacity to build chemical fertilizer plants in the 1980s, became more or less self-sufficient in the 1990s, and began exporting chemical fertilizer by the turn of the new millennium. In Vaclav Smil's view, with the purchase of those first ammonia-urea complexes, China began to break through what he calls "the nitrogen barrier" to achieve huge increases in agricultural output through the application of vast quantities of chemical fertilizer.[24] That breakthrough coincided with the end of the Mao era and the beginning of the reform era, and provided the huge increases in agricultural productivity necessary to fuel China's subsequent rapid industrialization (see figure 7.2). It is not an accident, as Marxists would say, that the technology most sought by China in the 1970s was the one that would resolve the most fundamental environmental constraint on its ability to industrialize rapidly. The irony is that the breakthrough came during Mao's tenure.

Population Control

Another legacy of the Mao era was China's large and growing population, despite a massive famine accompanying the Great Leap Forward that claimed as many as 33–45 million lives.[25] Many of China's economists and demographers thought that a rapidly growing population would literally eat up any surpluses generated by agriculture and hence stunt China's economic growth. Mao disagreed, and purged a leading

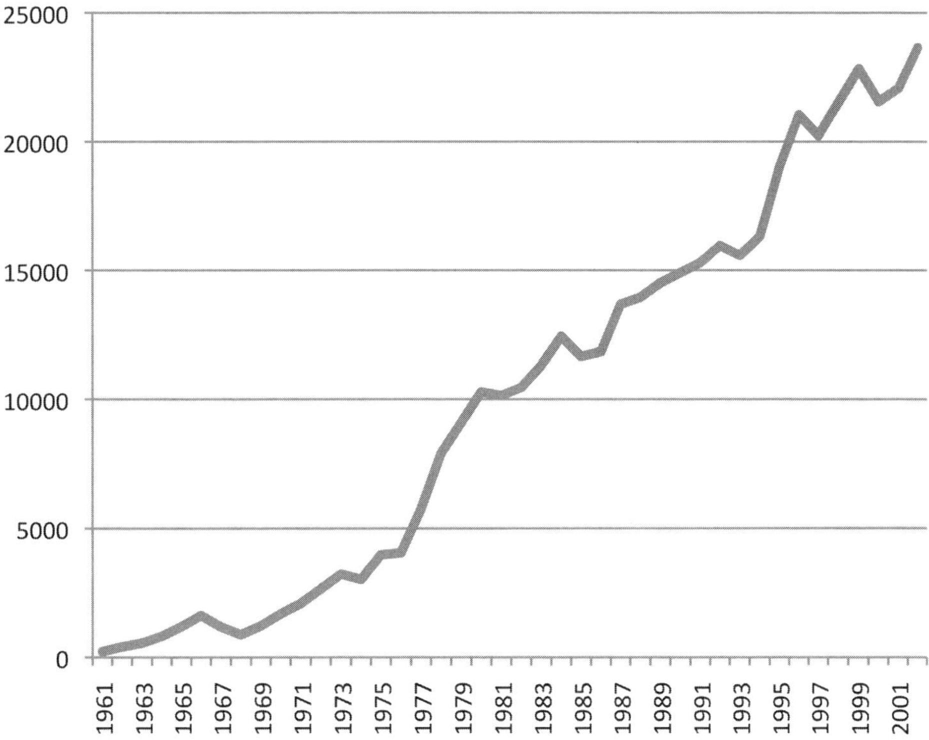

Fig. 7.2. China's Production of Nitrogenous Chemical Fertilizer, 1961–2002 (in thousands of metric tons) *Source:* United Nations Food and Agricultural Organization.

demographer who in the 1950s had proposed limiting China's population growth.[26] Hence the slogan "With Many People, Strength Is Great" governed China's official population policy until the beginning of the reform period in late 1970s after Mao's death.[27]

With Deng Xiaoping in power after Mao's death, the Communist Party heard the calls of those worried about China's population growth rate, and began in 1982 to implement a series of policies to slow the population growth. What is known as China's "One-Child Policy" for the limits it placed on family size, did slow China's population growth rate, mostly because the policy was implemented in cities. Although the rate slowed, China's overall population continued to grow, both because of the huge base that had been established, and because the strictures of the "one-child" policy began to loosen in 1990s as the desire and ability of the Chinese state to control women's reproduction, especially in the countryside, began to wane. Hence, since 1980, China's population has grown by nearly 500 million to about 1.3 billion today.[28] (See figure 7.1.) Moreover, China's population has become increasingly urban, with about 50 percent of the population now living in cities. Over the past thirty years, in other words, a vast rural-to-urban migration of hundreds of millions of people has swelled existing cities, and spawned the construction of hundreds more—new cities of a million or more sprouting annually on former farmland. And this process is likely to continue for quite some time.

Despite the important differences between the Mao years and the reform era—and they are significant and need to be kept in mind—the rest of the chapter will consider changes to land and forests, grasslands and deserts, water, and the atmosphere over the entire period of the People's Republic, and conclude with a consideration of the development of an environmentalist movement and state responses to China's mounting environmental crises.

CHANGES TO FORESTS AND LAND USE

In the century prior to the Chinese Communist victory in 1949, the evidence presented in chapter 6 clearly points to a widespread ecological crisis precipitated largely by deforestation and its consequences such as increased siltation and flooding of river plains, loss of soil nutrients and its ability to hold water, energy shortages, and constrictions of timber supplies for building. With declining energy levels, the metabolism of China's agro-ecosystems was slowing, with humans becoming impoverished along with their environment.

Despite the record of vast deforestation and environmental degradation, not all of the hills and mountains in the eastern half of China had been deforested by 1949. Extensive forests still stood in the northern reaches of Manchuria, in Yunnan to the southwest, in the border region of western Sichuan and eastern Tibet, in southern and central Fujian, in the border of western Hubei and northeastern Sichuan, and in parts of the Qinling mountains in southern Shanxi and northern Sichuan. Additionally, trees were being planted and harvested in at least two hill regions. In the hills bordering Zhejiang and Jiangxi, entrepreneurs had been growing trees for sale downriver to fire the kilns of Jingdezhen. And in southern Hunan province—and probably in the Nanling Mountains of northern Guangxi and Guangdong provinces—the Miao peoples and other Han Chinese who had become upland specialists (e.g., the Yao and the Hakka; see chapter 5) too replanted or coppiced trees that could be harvested every twenty years or so.

Even with its remaining stands of forest, though, China was a heavily deforested country by 1949 (see map 7.2), with somewhere between 5 and 9 percent of its land surface forested. Deforestation presented the rulers of the new People's Republic with two problems: dealing with the consequences of degraded environments and tapping forest resources to support their ambitious plans for economic development. On the eve of the establishment of the People's Republic, China's forest resources were extremely low, not only when compared with the Soviet Union but also in per capita terms compared with the rest of the world, ranking 120th out of 160 nations. As Vaclav Smil put it, "Clearly, China's poor forest resources put the country at a disadvantage in both environmental and economic terms, and the difficulty is compounded by the extremely uneven distribution of forested land"[29]

China's Official Forest-Cover Statistics

China's new rulers understood that their forests had been depleted, and so determined both to estimate how much forest they actually had, and to begin to reforest barren

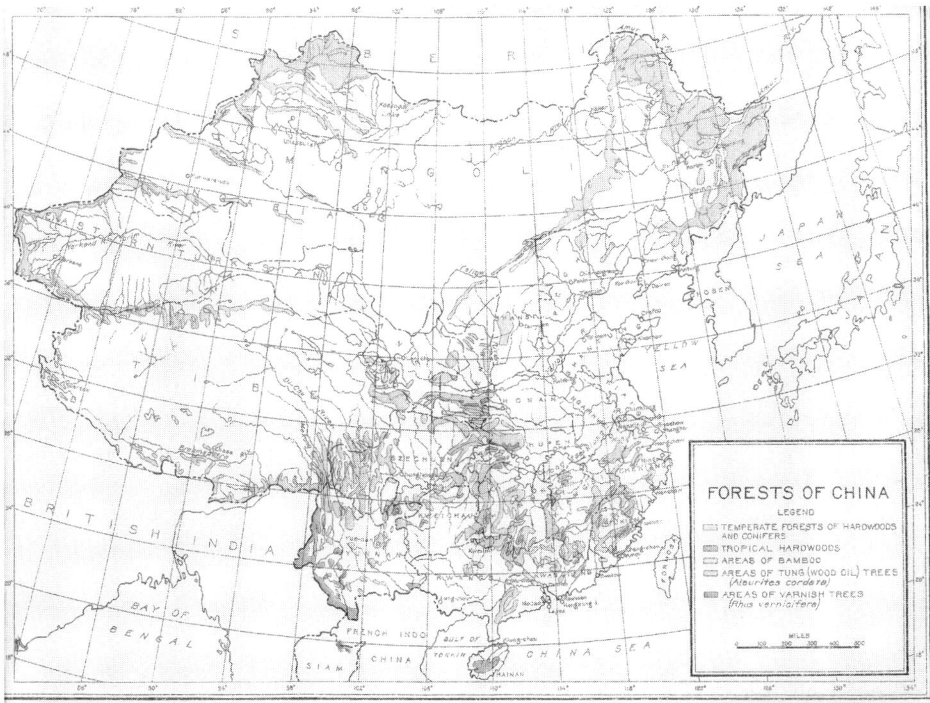

Map 7.2. Forests of China, ca. 1928 *Source:* Library of Congress, Map Division G7821.K1; also http://lccn.loc.gov/2007629493.

ground and slopes. Both of those efforts presented the new state with numerous difficulties and dubious accomplishments.

Problems with the Chinese state's official statistics and definitions complicate the task of examining the use and abuse of forests in the PRC. Western analysts who have examined official Chinese statistics of the extent of forest cover have all identified important issues of interpretation. The main ones have to do with the definition of "forest." Where I have used an implicit definition of "natural forest" (and even that has ambiguities), Chinese official statistics include both stands of natural forest and the extent of land area that are claimed to have been reforested (to be discussed more below). And those reforestation figures have in the past counted the entire area planted with seedlings, not the survival rate. As Richardson notes, "the wild claims during the spring and autumn campaigns in the 1950s and 1960s—with few references to failure—destroyed China's credibility among visiting foresters."[30] Vaclav Smil demonstrates that the actual survival rate was less than 30 percent.[31]

Even among the surviving saplings, the question arises as to when (or whether) that stand constitutes a "forest." Until 1986, the Chinese Ministry of Forestry used a standard of a 40 percent canopy cover as a definition of a "forest," but lowered that to 30 percent, the current standard, thereby vastly increasing China's "forest" by the stroke of a pen.[32] Even when that new, lower standard is met, often the "forest" is comprised of a single species, or of species planted in contiguous belts, not mixed as in a natural forest. That issue becomes important in assessing forests as healthy ecosystems that sustain a wide variety and number of plant and animal species. A "forest" of a single species, whether it is composed of pines or poplars to be pulped for paper, eucalyptus for their aromatic oils, or rubber trees,[33] is more like a monoculture plantation than a forest supporting a variety of wildlife. Indeed, the removal of tropic rain forest in Yunnan for rubber tree plantations may have put the strategically important rubber tires on China's military vehicles, but the habitat of the gibbon was destroyed, and so too were nearly all the gibbons, among other environmental horror stories.[34] To be sure, such a plantation will provide important ecosystem services such as retention of water and soil, and the sequestration of carbon, but few animal species will thrive, let alone survive.

With those problems in mind, let us take an overview of the official figures of China's land surface covered by forest during the People's Republic (figure 7.3).

The story that this graph *appears* to tell is fairly straightforward: From the relatively deforested landscape that the CCP inherited, reforestation and conservation projects during the Mao years increased China's forest cover to 12.7 percent. A rash of tree-cutting by peasant families accounts for the decline from 1977 to 1981, when the ownership of forests and trees was uncertain in the first years of the Deng-era reforms. But then forest cover again climbed from 1980 to 2000 to 18 percent as the new regime of private ownership led to successful afforestation, accompanied by a massive project called the "Three Norths," or the "Green Great Wall," to afforest 37 million hectares of arid steppe across nearly 5,000 km from Heilongjiang province to Xinjiang.

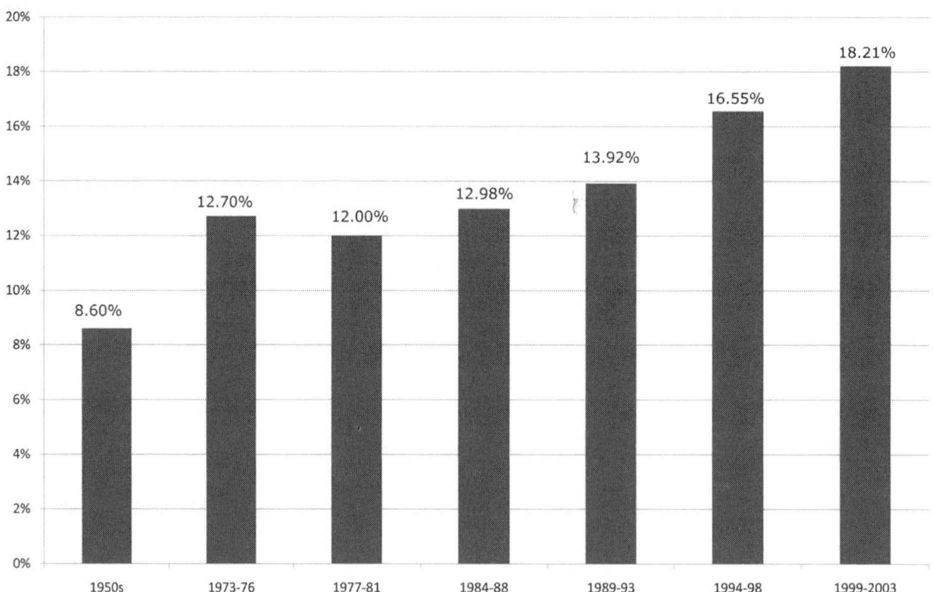

Fig. 7.3. China's Official Forest Cover Statistics, 1950s–1999 *Source:* Dr. Wang Qiming, Counselor for Science and Technology, Embassy of the PRC to India, "Environmental Bio-remediation Programmes in China," March 7, 2008, www.chinaembassy.org.in/eng/kj/P020080313486177342453.ppt.

According to these official statistics, with the exception of the early 1980s, China's forests were consistently expanding, deforestation and its baleful effects were being arrested, and progress toward a sustainably green future was always being made. The problem, of course, is that at each point where China'sofficial forest statistics were published and plans announced for even greater afforestation, almost certainly China's forests actually were deteriorating, and forested areas actually were substantially less than the officials claimed. The 1950s figure of 8.60 percent forest cover, for instance, was most likely more like 5 percent, and the 1979 figure a third less than claimed.[35]

The following assessments made in the 1990s—when forest cover supposedly had increased to 16 percent of China's land surface—give a sense of the disconnect between official statistics and what was happening on the ground (literally).

According to Vaclav Smil, "[T]he Third Forest Census undertaken by the Ministry of Forestry between 1984 and 1988 found a combination of sharply declining forested area, diminishing growing stocks, and poorer quality of timber." "[T]he environmental foundations of China's national existence," he concluded in 1993, "are alarmingly weak, and they continue to deteriorate at high rates."[36]

A year later, Richard Louis Edmonds wrote: "Degradation of vegetation in China has reached a serious stage. . . . [A]s of 1993, it is likely that China's annual harvest of timber still exceeds annual growth and rapid success of remote hillside afforestation is not likely. . . . China *hopes* [emphasis added] current reforestation efforts will make the country self-sufficient in timber by AD 2040. . . . The key question is whether degradation of China's forests will send the whole country into an ecological tailspin before bureaucratic reforms, new technologies or a population decrease can halt current trends."[37]

By the late 1990s, and despite apparent acceptance of international norms regarding the protection and conservation of biodiversity, according to James Harkness, "China's forests and biodiversity are doubly threatened in the 1990s, suffering from both the legacies of the planned economy and the perverse incentives of the current order. Deforestation (and ineffective afforestation) during the Mao years left the country with a seriously depleted resource base, and [now] the wasteful, dying state logging industry threatens to take the last of China's old growth forests with it long before newly planted forests can take their place. Economic growth has brought ever more rapid depletion of wild plant and animal populations, far exceeding the state's regulatory capacity."[38]

Forests not only provide timber for construction, mining, and housing and pulp for paper, but fuel for heating and cooking. Forests are renewable resources, as long as the harvesting is not done in an unsustainable way—and that is a very dubious proposition concerning the history of the People's Republic. But more than that, forests provide numerous ecological "services," the most important of which are the retention and purification of water to control floodwaters and provide safe drinking supplies, the prevention of soil loss and erosion, and the sequestration of carbon to moderate local and global climate.[39] "Because forests have such important monetary and environmental benefits," Qu Geping, the first head of China's Environmental Protection Agency, observed, "careful forest management *should* [emphasis added] receive high priority."[40] The problem is that forest services are seldom if ever given a price in market economies, let alone considered in socialist ones. Mostly, "nature" has been seen a source of "free" resources, where the only costs are those of extraction, and so the history of forests in China after 1949 continued to be one of rapid exploitation and depletion, and hence of continued degradation of China's natural environment.

Forest Ownership Regimes

During the Mao era, the ownership of forests and forestland became increasingly simplified into two categories: state-owned forests and collectively owned ones. The Communist state took over whatever forests had been already state-owned, mainly left over from the imperial and republican eras, but those were quite large enough, and mostly in the areas with the greatest stands of healthy first- and second-growth forest in Manchuria, Yunnan, and western Sichuan/eastern Tibet. As we will see below, an additional category of state-owned forestland was created when biological and nature preserves were established, the first in 1956 but expanding significantly in the post-1978 reform era. But we start with collective ownership of forestland and forests.

Collective Ownership

By 1956, with the rapid movement to collectivize agricultural production, many forests came under collective ownership. To begin with, though, during Land Reform (1950–52), privately owned forests were treated like other property and redistributed to peasant proprietors. Since most of north China had been deforested, the issue there was mostly moot. In the provinces south of the Yangzi, and in Sichuan and Yunnan, there were forest reserves. If not village or lineage owned, these forests tended to be owned by landlords or rich peasants and, if not nationalized by the new state, were confiscated and redistributed along with other land.

Not surprisingly, in anticipation of land reform, landlords and rich peasants felled "their" trees to keep the income in their families' hands. But so, too, did the beneficiaries of land reform—poor peasants and tenants. According to Lester Ross, the new owners "quickly cut down even immature trees. They were induced to do so not only by the high prices for lumber and doubts about the legitimacy of their land tenure, but also by the regime's clear emphasis on grain production which forced many peasants to devote even marginal farmland to the production of staple crops."[41]

The establishment of private peasant ownership of productive agricultural land and forests was not a step toward socialism, and Mao was eager not to allow the institution of private ownership to get firmly established. As soon as Land Reform was completed, CCP cadre began organizing the poorest of the peasants into mutual aid teams, out of which emerged elementary cooperatives by 1955. With Mao's encouragement, those combined in 1956 to form advanced cooperatives, wherein all agricultural productive property, including tools, draft animals, and forests, ceased to be privately owned and came under collective ownership. This change of ownership sparked another round of tree felling because the owners were paid just 15–20 percent of the value of the timber on the grounds that trees were the fruits of nature, not the result of labor.[42]

Larger collectives called "people's communes" emerged in 1958, providing the institutional framework for the Great Leap Forward, a mostly rural mass movement with a goal of industrializing China and catching up with Britain within 15 years. "The system of forest ownership was altered for the fourth time in less than a decade. This time, ownership was transferred from the smaller Agricultural Producers' Cooperatives that, in a number of areas, first liquidated their timber holdings to avoid sharing their property with others. Individual households behaved similarly when faced with the loss of small clusters of trees around their homes and on private plots, which were now regarded as illegitimate vestiges of the small producer society."[43] More will be said about the disastrous impact of the Leap on China's forests in a section below.

Following a quick end to the Great Leap Forward, and despite a devolution of ownership and management of forests from the commune to lower levels of collective ownership, in particular to local governments or to production brigades, in the early 1960s the basic structure (with one exception) of state and collective ownership remained in place through the tumultuous years of the Cultural Revolution and Mao's death in 1976. The exception? Peasant families were allowed to plant fruit and other nontimber trees on their small family plots of cropland, and around their houses, and to have control over those resources. That changed during the Cultural Revolution (1966–76), when even those trees were once again collectivized.

According to Liu Dacheng, these radical and rapid changes in property rights to forestlands and forests "left rural people with a complete lack of confidence in the security of [whatever] ownership rights" they had,[44] and hence to securing income from the felling of trees whenever it appeared that their ownership rights would be abrogated. That happened with individuals who owned wooded plots of land large enough to be called "forests," as well as with the trees planted around houses that lost their security during the Cultural Revolution. Even the first collectives chopped down their trees for the income they could yield when ownership moved up to larger collectives. Thus as far as deforestation was concerned, during the Mao era changes in ownership rather than the form of ownership *per se* had a greater impact. But even these tree cuttings paled in significance to four great spasms of deforestation (to be discussed later) in the service of China's quest to rapidly industrialize.

Distrust of experts informed the Maoist approach to environmental issues in general, and to reforestation in particular. Although Mao endorsed and called for the "greenification" (*lühau*) of China by the rapid planting of trees throughout the country, he did not look to the Ministry of Forestry for that effort. Instead, "the masses" were mobilized. During Land Reform, it was urbanites on Arbor Day. During collectivization (even in the midst of the Soviet-inspired First Five-Year Plan), it was the peasant masses; sometimes the Communist Youth League stood in for the masses. In part this reliance on the masses was necessary because of the small number of China's forestry experts; Ross estimates that there were maybe a couple hundred of them in 1950, and they were all brought to the Ministry of Forestry in Beijing.[45] But mostly the use of peasants reflected the Maoist preference for mass mobilization campaigns, in this case applied to the attempt to gain control over the deteriorating environment by planting trees.[46]

The combination of Lysenkoist biology and the mobilization of peasant masses led not to a socialist upsurge in greenifying China, but to a vast waste of human effort and saplings. Richardson estimates that less than 10 percent of the saplings planted in these mass campaigns actually survived, and that those that did were rapidly "pruned" of their lower branches for fuel. A photograph of a "forest" in rural Guangdong that he took in the early 1960s,[47] showing both the results of a mass reforestation campaign and the continuing erosion, looks much like one I took in 1980 (figure 7.4); both counted as "forest."[48]

The Responsibility System of "Private" Ownership

Where the forest ownership system of the Mao era tended to be fairly simple (but unstable)—state- or collectively owned—forest tenure systems of Deng Xioaping's reform era were more varied and complex. While collective forests were contracted out to peasant households in the early 1980s (called the "responsibility for hills" (*zerenshan* system), as was farmland, the collective retained ownership rights to the land, but the rights of the contracting households to harvest the timber were not clear. Other lands that were classified as "wasteland" or "degraded" were auctioned off to peasant households (the "family plots in the hills" *ziliushan* system) with the encouragement to plant trees, but those arrangements were problematic.[49] Because of the uncertainties in these systems, both underwent numerous changes during the 1980s, with bans on new responsibility contracts to households in 1987.

As had been the case in the Mao era, the major reason for the difficulties with the new responsibility system, according to Liu Dacheng, was that peasant family household uncertainty of the terms of their tenure to forestland and ownership of the trees led to massive and illegal cutting of forests from 1981 to 1988. "They decided to harvest trees as quickly as they could before the government took back control over forests. Thus, there was a dramatic [deforestation] immediately after the introduction of household management."[50] Liu points out, though, that in his view it was the lack of tenure security, not the household management system itself, that led to the illegal cutting and lack of planting of any new trees on their contracted land.[51]

To address these problems, beginning in 1992, county and prefectural governments—ultimately with the blessing and support of the Deng Xiaoping regime—began selling inheritable leases for fifty to one hundred years. That seemed to have addressed the problem of tenure security, but peasant families who leased the forestland confronted two other problems. First, most leased plots were not a single large swath of forestland, but numerous small plots sometimes scattered over several mountains, and certainly not in close proximity, making management and protection of whatever forest products were on those plots difficult. By the end of the 1990s, cooperative agreements among farmers, and with collectives or other companies, had begun to make it possible to plant and manage larger stands of timber.

Nonetheless, a combination of regulations and policies governing the rights to timber limited the incentives to individuals to plant and harvest trees. In 1985, a cutting quota and permitting scheme was instituted, no doubt in response to the rash of illegal logging. Every five years, counties determined what they thought their quota of logs should be and reported that up to the province, which compiled a provincial plan that was then forwarded to the Ministry of Forestry. The Ministry then adjusted

Fig. 7.4. A "Forest" in Eastern Guangdong, 1980 *Source:* Author.

the national quota in light of what it calculated to be sustainably needed, and got the national plan approved by the central government. The readjusted plan was then sent back down, ultimately back down to the county. Quotas were then set not just for volume, but also for five types of wood consumption (commercial timber, farm timber, sideline production, fuel wood, and other uses).

To try to ensure that the quotas are not exceeded, a whole system of cutting permits is in place. Even once a contracting household gets a cutting permit, they need a transport permit to get the logs to market. And even the market for timber and other wood products is controlled. Freely operating markets were closed in 1987 to staunch the tide of deforestation, and since then only state timber companies and forest departments have been allowed to buy timber and to act as wholesaler. All other individuals and companies have been banned from buying directly from the one who obtained the cutting permit to harvest the trees in the first place. "What evidence is available," Liu Dacheng concludes, "indicates that regulations on the cutting, transport, and marketing of wood may help protect existing forests but are a disincentive for farmers to establish new timber plantations."[52] Instead, because rights of tenure and use are more certain and clear for family cropland and areas around houses, more time and effort has gone into planting trees on and around their cropland and farmhouses. "Unfortunately, family plots of croplands are tiny and primarily for growing vegetables. . . . Tree growing in these areas has a limited impact on forest cover."[53]

Nonstate (formerly collective) forestland accounts for 58 percent of China's claimed forested area, and most of this is in the ten provinces of south China (Anhui, Fujian, Guangdong, Guangxi, Guizhou, Hainan, Hubei, Hunan, Jiangxi, and Zhejiang) where the percentage of nonstate forests can reach 90 percent. In Sichuan and Yunnan, nonstate forests account for 65 percent of the total. And on these forestlands at the turn of the twenty-first century, the dynamics detailed by Professor Liu Dacheng prevail. It thus appears that even with secure tenures, peasant farming households will not be a major factor in afforesting China and rehabilitating degraded landscapes.[54]

State-Owned Forests

As noted earlier, state-owned forests are largely natural, are concentrated in the northeast and the southwest, and account for 42 percent of China's claimed forests. Until the Deng-era reforms, economic development under the Maoist regime (including the Soviet-inspired FFYP) saw the forest sector as a supplier of cheap raw materials to support industrialization and to achieve "social objectives, such as regional development and the provision of low-cost construction materials."[55] State forest bureaus rapidly moved to cut timber from the Greater Xing'an Mountains of the northeast, from Yunnan, and from the Jinsha River forest region of Sichuan. "As a consequence," say Wang et al., "while over one billion cubic meters of timber was supplied during the period 1949–79, the country's forest resource base was devastated"[56] by the state forest bureaus.

After the reforms of the Deng era began to shift control of productive resources, including forests, to individuals and capitalist enterprises, state forest bureaus were at somewhat of a disadvantage, and did not cut or sell much of their forest resource. In part that was because the prices offered by the state for timber and other forest products were too low, and in part, as we have seen above, because timber markets were being flooded in any case with rafts of illegally cut timber from newly privatized forest plots.

Deforestation during the PRC: "The Three Great Cuttings" Plus One

The official story implied in China's forest cover statistics obscures four waves of deforestation, two each during the Mao and Deng eras: (1) the Great Leap Forward (1958–60), (2) the campaigns to "Take Grain as the Key Link" and "Learn from Dazhai" during the Cultural Revolution Decade (1966–76), (3) during the early to mid-1980s (possibly to 1988) after the dismantling of collective agricultural production and the introduction of household-based production, and (4) in the 1990s as state-owned forest enterprises and state-established nature preserves cashed in on their forest reserves. Chinese farmers call the former ones the "Three Great Cuttings" (*san da fa*),[57] over and above the "normal" rate of "harvesting." During the First Five-

Year Plan, for instance, the State Forest Bureau reported that 1.332 million hectare of state forests were clear-cut, but only 242,000 hectare replanted (18 percent).[58] So, the "Great Cuttings" added to the on-going state-sponsored deforestation, including the spasms of tree felling after the various changes in forest ownership regimes already discussed.

Great Cutting No. 1—The Great Leap Forward, 1958–60

During the Great Leap, agricultural production was consolidated into twenty-four thousand or so large "peoples communes," which Mao believed were the social formation needed to unleash the productive forces latent in the peasantry, resulting in the industrialization of the countryside and the production of enough steel to surpass Britain within fifteen years. The key technology was the "backyard steel furnaces," primitive affairs that more often than not transformed "good steel into bad" as peasants collected and melted down existing metal objects such as plows and pots into ingots that had so many impurities that they were useless. Nonetheless, the 600,000 furnaces operating by October 1958 needed huge quantities of charcoal, nearly all of which was made by cutting down local forests. In one example from Guangxi province, villagers established 190 charcoal burners, cleared swaths of a subtropical broadleaf evergreen forest, and left a poor-quality, low-stocked secondary forest in its wake.[59] How much forest was cut for the iron furnaces is unclear, but the anecdotal evidence certainly suggests "a lot." An additional amount of forest was lost with the construction of reservoirs.[60] Further west in Yunnan, villagers also recounted the destruction of forests during the Great Leap; there, the timbers were used for posts in a nearby coal mine or to fire a steel furnace.[61]

From Mao's point of view, of course, the people's communes and the industrialization of the countryside were rational approaches to dealing with the problems arising from the separation of town and countryside, peasant and worker, and mental and manual labor. Marx as well had bemoaned the separation of town and countryside, and the degradation of soil that came with the export of food and fiber (and the nutrients that came from the soil) from the countryside to the cities as the nutrients in human waste polluted waterways rather than being recycled back to the farms. But Mao was less concerned with those nutrient cycles than with increasing industrial output—at whatever cost to the environment.

Great Cutting No. 2—The Third Front and the Cultural Revolution, 1966–76

The devastating famine following in the wake of the Great Leap Forward,[62] coupled with security concerns sparked by both the split with the Soviet Union and the U.S. build-up in Vietnam, led CCP leaders to conclude that China needed to achieve industrial and food security to protect against the event of a Soviet or American nuclear attack. These fears led to the development and implementation of a highly secret "Third Front" plan to create a self-sufficient industrial base in remote areas of China's west and southwest, as well as to extensive logging to build the complexes and the railroads.[63] The Third Front included the more open application of the ideal of being "self-reliant" (*zili gengshen*) to having all regions of China becoming self sufficient in grain. That led to the slogan to "Take Grain as the Key Link" and Mao's identification of the Dazhai production brigade in the impoverished and environmentally degraded mountains of southeastern Shanxi province mountains as a national model.

Dazhai was a small village of 160 families that was devastated in a 1963 flood that wiped away the residents' houses, fields, tools, and even fruit trees. The denuded hills undoubtedly were a major factor in the floods, and the village probably looked something like the photos in chapter 6 (figure 6.2) of a bridge and gate tower buried in silt. The local Communist party leader, Chen Yonggui, claimed that Dazhai would accept no outside aid, and mobilized the residents not just to dig out from the flood but also to transform Dazhai and prevent future disasters. With their own labor, they terraced the crumbly loess soil, tunneled through hills for water for irrigation, and spread chemical fertilizer from a local plant on their fields; agricultural yields climbed.

By late 1964, Mao Zedong had singled out Dazhai as a model for the entire country to follow, and within a few years learning from Dazhai had been coupled with the slogan to "Take Grain as the Key Link." Dazhai leader Chen Yonggui shared the view of other Party members that to subdue nature was good and heroic, and perhaps harbored Lysenkoist ideas that grain could be made to grow almost anywhere—taking over river flood plains, grasslands, steep slopes, and sandy beaches.

With encouragement from the top, and in the midst of Mao's Great Proletarian Cultural Revolution, a vast labor-intensive assault on nature to make it yield agricultural bounty quickly led to widespread deforestation. "Early in the Cultural Revolution . . . the state announced that forests were an inefficient land use. Trees were either to be exploited or moved out of the way for the production of both grain and economic crops, such as fruit trees."[64] In the view of the first head of China's State Environmental Protection Agency, "China was overzealous with the campaign. . . . Regardless of the topography, grain production became the all-important priority. . . . Large forested areas were either destroyed to produce grain or neglected, aggravating hydrological cycles and soil erosion."[65]

As a result, in the north and northwest, grasslands were opened to the plow, and with or without irrigation, winds eroded the soil and turned what had been hoped would be farmland into desert: "Under the leadership of the Party," officials in arid Qinghai province declared, "we have finally subdued nature and turned the grasslands that have been desolate for a thousand years into fertile farmland."[66] In mountainous areas with slopes greater than 25 percent, forests were cut down and crops planted, even in rows up and down the slope, increasing the rate of erosion and degradation; terracing in the mountains near Chongqing did not halt the erosion; lakes throughout Hubei were encircled and filled in ("reclaimed"); and the wetlands of the famed Dian Lake near Kunming in Yunnan were filled in for fields, but then ironically became the site of the National Minorities Park.[67] As summarized by Liu Dacheng, these policies "caused large areas of forest and grassland to be cleared and cultivated for food production. . . . [Even] shifting cultivation/swidden agriculture became unsustainable because increasing population pressure on land resulted in much shorter fallow periods. This factor contributed especially to forest loss in the southwest provinces of Yunnan and Sichuan."[68]

The loss of forest in parts of Yunnan came about because in areas where hill people had practiced shifting agriculture, collectivization led to farming on permanent fields. Thus parts of mountains that traditionally had been set aside for shifting cultivation and farmed for a couple of years but then left for 12–15 years for a relatively health forest to regrow were converted to collectively owned and farmed rice paddies.[69]

One wonders whether these Mao-era clearances of forests and grasslands for farms would have been necessary if Chinese had had an alternative way of increasing agricultural output via chemical fertilizers, even though massive applications of those (and pesticides) in the 1980s and 1990s polluted farmland and ran off into nearby water supplies.

Great Cutting No. 3—Deng's Reform Era, 1978–88

As noted above in terms of the discussion of landownership systems, the dismantling of collectivized agriculture and the creation of the "household responsibility system" whereby control over agricultural decision making, farmland, and forestland passed into the hands of peasant families who contracted to do the work coincided with a rash of illegal cutting of forests, especially in the provinces of south and southwest China. This episode in the early to mid-1980s was no small affair. According to Liu Dacheng, this was the "most disastrous period nationwide period of deforestation."[70] Despite the intention of the central government to encourage private farmers to reforest degraded lands and to mindfully harvest their newfound timber wealth, "the results of the forest reform were not what the policy makers had planned or anticipated. Instead of planting trees and improving forest management, significant deforestation occurred in most villages" in south China.[71] "For the first time, rural people were allowed to build their own homes, and over half the rural households did. From 1981 through 1985, housing construction alone consumed a total of 195 million cubic meters of timber, about a year's growth from all of China's forests."[72] In Yunnan, villagers cut timbers to build new more permanent log houses when it became clear that both the village and their houses would not be relocated.[73]

Market-driven Deforestation, 1992–98: The Last Great Cutting?

The Deng-era reforms included extending market reforms to state forest products, but price increases paid for wood products from the state forests during the 1980s had not elicited greater supplies, in part because the market was being flooded with massive supplies from the great illegal cut-off from the contracted-out collective forestland. During the nationwide drive to implement a market economy from 1992–98, however, the state-owned forest companies gained considerable freedom from the Ministry of Forestry (downgraded in 1998 to the State Forestry Administration). "With reduced government interference," Wang et al. conclude, "forest companies were able to respond to market needs and thus improve economic efficiency."[74] With heavy machines and platoons with chainsaws, state forest companies clear-cut great swathes of forested mountains in western Sichuan, the headwaters of the Yangzi River, and in the Qinling Mountains—and in the Amur River watershed in Heilongjiang, seeking to capitalize on the markets for old-growth timber. As far upriver as northwestern Yunnan, loggers clear-cut in the headwaters of the Yangzi River.[75]

A breaking point was reached 1998. From June through early August, an unusual climatic event led to huge downpours of rain across south and central China—up to 68 inches in coastal Guangdong and 50 inches in Jingdezhen—resulting in massive flooding along the Yangzi River. Officials reported 3,656 people killed, 14 million homeless, and 25 million hectares of farmland flooded.[76] Neither Dongting Lake nor Poyang Lake, which normally acted as "lungs" for the Yangzi drainage basin, expanding as necessary to contain annual runoff, could hold the 1998 floodwaters.

The unusual rainfall was the proximate cause of the flooding. The more long-term cause, though, was extensive logging of the old growth forests in the western hills of Sichuan province that denuded the hillsides and sent the unusually heavy rainfall cascading down the mountainsides into the Yangzi River. To address the disastrous flooding, the anger it caused, and its longer-term cause, Premier Zhu Rongji announced an immediate ban on logging in western Sichuan, and shortly afterward extended the ban to additional provinces and municipalities.[77]

It turns out that the forests of primary and secondary stands, mostly in the northeast, in Yunnan, and in western Sichuan/eastern Tibet, contain 93 percent of China's wood volume, are among the healthiest and most diverse ecosystems in China, and are state-owned—and had been designated for logging by 135 state forest bureaus. As with most state-owned enterprises confronted with market forces in the reform era, the state logging companies were short of capital and deeply in debt. So, instead of following sustainable harvesting practices, such as by cutting only swathes and leaving strips both for future harvesting and for reseeding the cut-over portions, state forest bureaus clear-cut up to ridgetops, leaving but a few trees for reseeding. Needless to say, such clear-cutting leads to degradation of the watersheds and increased flooding. Before 1979, it was estimated that a third of all forests cut down were replaced by degraded mountain slopes. James Harkness estimated in 1998 that of the 135 state forest bureaus, 30 had nothing left to cut, and that at the rate of clear cutting state forests, the number would reach 90 forestless state forest bureaus by the year 2000. Adding further pressure to clear cut, local officials—who should have been acting to conserve forest resources—instead encouraged the cutting to reap the greatest tax revenue possible.[78]

There are indications that the 1998 ban on logging has been effective, and, perversely, that that success is affecting forests elsewhere. China is now the world's second largest importer of logs (the first being the world's major consumer of virtually all natural resources, the United States). "[I]n moving to avoid ecological disaster at home, Beijing is causing a catastrophe abroad: to make up for the shortfall in timber, China is devouring forests from Burma to Siberia to Indonesia, much of it in the form of illegal logging."[79] Chinese lumber barons, some possibly former managers of state-owned enterprises, either send their own crews, as into Burma, or contract with illegal loggers, especially in Sumatra and Siberia, and pay local authorities to look the other way as the logs roll out on their way to China.[80]

In a remote border region of Yunnan and Burma, the story of deforestation appears to have been reversed. Despite problems with the way collective land was returned to private ownership in the 1980s, the rash of tree felling for timbers to build new houses, and pressure from the state and outside agencies for villagers to farm fixed plots because it was more "efficient," the dismantling of collective land ownership has allowed some of the Akha people—mostly women—in a part of Xishuangbanna prefecture to begin resurrecting the old methods of shifting agriculture. This return to older traditions has meant that parts of the mountain have been designated for shifting cultivation, and that villagers clear a space for planting for a couple of years, and then leave for 12–15 years to allow the forest to return. Additionally, care has been taken to encourage and protect existing stands of trees that have economic or religious significance. The results so far have been encouraging. A researcher in the late 1990s was shown "different pastures that had not been burned for two, five, and twenty years—all now regenerating forests in various stages." Compared with similarly situated Akha villages in Thailand, the greater diversity of land uses in China has led to greater species-richness as well.[81] These Akha villages in a remote border region of China no doubt are unusual, if not unique, but at least there the trend seen elsewhere in China toward the simplification of landscapes, species, and peoples has been halted, if not reversed.

Grasslands and Desertification

Desertification refers to the process by which land in arid or semi-arid regions that had some form of land cover such as grasses or shrubs loses that cover and becomes bare unproductive land, either with or without shifting sand dunes. Mostly, desertification occurs where there is adequate vegetation and/or rainfall to lead humans to conclude that intensified use of the land is warranted, either by increasing the number or type of animals grazing on the vegetation, or by opening the land to farming. Both the Han-era and the eighteenth-century expansion of the Chinese empire to the north and northwest into steppe areas previously controlled by nomadic peoples brought many of those kinds of lands under Chinese jurisdiction, a relationship that continues today in the provinces and autonomous regions from Inner Mongolia westward through Gansu to Xinjiang (see maps 2.1 and 2.3). The problem of desertification is most acute in those regions, and is the primary reason for the Great Green Wall, discussed above, which is designed to halt the southeasterly march of desertlike conditions toward the capital of Beijing.

To be sure, there are natural deserts in China's north and northwest, the entire region being dubbed by Chinese geographers "the Xinjiang-Inner Mongolia Arid Region"[82] that contain two different kinds of desert: gravelly *gobi* and sandy *shadi* or *shamo*. Mostly, the gravely *gobi* are in the west, with sandy desert zones increasing toward the east.[83] In the Tarim Basin in Xinjiang in the far west is the Taklimakan Desert, "a mostly uninhabitable and impassible arid waste of shifting sand dunes—now of interest for its oil deposits. Around the desert rim lies a chain of fertile oases, watered by . . . rivers flowing from the mountains."[84] Further east are the Gobi, Badian Jaran, Tengger, and Kubuqi deserts spreading across Gansu, northern Shaanxi, and Inner Mongolia. People live and farm along rivers, and have for millennia raised horses and other livestock on the extensive grasslands. But over the past 60 years, pressures have been put on marginal lands that have turned those into desert, quite useless for human activity.

The figures are startling. The annual rate of loss of grasslands has steadily increased from about 1,560 square kilometers in the 1970s to 2,460 square kilometers in the 1990s. More than a quarter of China's landmass was classified as desert in 2000, compared with 15.9 percent just seven years earlier. According to Williams, there is "nearly universal consensus attributing desert expansion in China to human behavior,"[85]but different political regimes have pointed the finger of blame at different forces, including population growth, the conversion of grassland to farmland during the Great Leap Forward and the Cultural Revolution, urbanization, land degradation, historic Qing-era policies, the Maoist regime, and, more recently, global market forces and the privatization of land. Underlying all these, according to Williams, is a tendency to see Mongol customs, practices, and conceptions of the landscape as backward and irrational when compared with reigning Han Chinese or international scientific views.[86]

Since the eighteenth century, Inner Mongolia has been directly governed by the Chinese state, despite a few years of attempted independence in the first half of the twentieth century and its status as an "autonomous region" of the People's Republic. A vast grassland steppe on a rolling tableland about 1,000 meters above sea level, Inner Mongolia is bordered on the northwest by the Altai Mountains, on the east by the Xing'an Mountains (the border with Manchuria), and on the south by the Great Wall. For three thousand years, the Mongolian steppe has been the homeland to nomadic pastoralists, including several notable groups mentioned in early chapters, in particular the Xiongnu in chapter 3, and the Mongols organized by Chinggis Khan in chapter 4, who moved with their herds of horses, sheep, goats, and camels from pasture to pasture.

Toward the end of the Qing dynasty, Mongolia was opened to Chinese migration. In 1912 there were about 1 million Han Chinese and perhaps an equal number of Mongols; by 1990 there were 17 million Chinese and 3 million Mongols, evidence of a long-term process of colonization by Chinese settlers. In the twentieth century, Outer Mongolia first declared itself independent, and then became part of the Soviet Union until its demise in 1991. Inner Mongolia remained attached to China, and was an object in the struggle among the Nationalists, Communists, and Japanese. Mongol forces attempted to gain Inner Mongolian independence, but Chinese Communist forces quickly consolidated their control after 1949 and Innter Mongolia has been ruled as an "autonomous region" since then.

Wealth and social status in the pastoral economy were based not on the ownership of land, since the Mongols moved with their herds from pasture to pasture, but on the size of one's herds. During the first 30 years of the People's Republic, the collectivization of agriculture in Inner Mongolia thus concerned the herds, and the various campaigns to increase agricultural production focused on increasing the size of the herds and the output of grass and hay. The total number of livestock did, in fact, increase rather rapidly—from 16 million in 1957 to more than 30 million by 1965. But the increase came about not simply from increased output but, according to David Sneath, because "the consumption of livestock was strictly limited so that totals would increase rapidly." Where before collectivization herders consumed about 40 percent of their livestock, afterward that consumption fell to about 25 percent.[87]

The collectivization of agriculture in the 1950s, but especially during the Great Leap Forward, began to accelerate the degradation of the grasslands. In addition to failed attempts at farming, "growing numbers of livestock increased the pressure on the grasslands that supported them, and forced pastoralists to make use of more marginal land."[88] The total amount of grassland decreased by 6 million hectares (from 93 to 87 million), but the acreage of "deteriorated grassland" increased dramatically from just more than 1 million hectares in 1965 to nearly 30 million hectares by 1989. According to Sneath, "it is estimated that 85 percent of damage of this sort was due to destructive efforts to reclaim land, overgrazing, and the felling of trees."[89]

The reform era that began after 1978 by Deng Xiaoping's policies unfolded much more slowly in Inner Mongolia. Whereas most of China's agricultural and forested land had come under private management and then ownership during the 1980s, it was not until the 1990s that individual families were allocated rights to specific fixed areas of pasture. This privatization of pastureland not only reversed the collective ownership of the Maoist era of the People's Republic, but also the traditional clan-based structures of access to pastureland that had been in place for prior millennia. As a result, the number of sheep and goats has increased substantially in response to global market demand and price signals, to the extent that the government of Inner Mongolia "considers the pastureland of the region to be saturated, and maintains that this overstocking is the cause of widespread grassland degradation" on more than a third of Inner Mongolia's grassland.[90]

Sneath thinks that the cause of grassland degradation is not simply overgrazing, but the way pastoralism has been managed. "The expansion of cultivation in the last fifty years has removed some of the most fertile land from pastoral use, thus increasing the grazing pressure on more marginal steppe pastures. Large amounts of grassland were also damaged in the failed attempts to cultivate it during the [Great Leap Forward] and Cultural Revolution periods. . . . Lastly, the decrease in the traditional mobility of pastoralists could well be responsible for pasture degradation."[91] Although Williams points out the ambiguities inherent in the concept of "land degradation," he does agree that the grasslands are being degraded, mostly as a result of the extension of the modernist project linking Chinese political economy to the "scientific management" of the grasslands and the transition from a pastoral to a sedentary way of life for Mongols.[92]

A prime example is the history of the region within the great bend of the Yellow River known variously as the Ordos Desert or the Mu-us Sandy Land. This region has been discussed earlier, especially in chapter 5. During the Warring States period, the king of the state of Zhao adopted nomadic ways as well as cavalry to do battle with the Xiongnu, the First Emperor of Qin built the early version of the Great Wall to enclose part of the nomads lands, the Han sent armies to the west to outflank the Xiong-nu warriors, and the Ming confronted the strategic problem of whether or not to use the Yellow River as its northern border, deciding instead to build the Great Wall further south across the Ordos where were farming and Chinese ways of life to defend. From that point forward, "historically, to the north of the Great Wall Mongolian pastoralists rode horses and raised sheep on the grassland. To the south of the Wall, the agricultural Han farmers cultivated crops on winding loess hill slopes."[93]

Toward the end of the Qing dynasty, the Manchu rulers allowed Han Chinese to farm north of the Great Wall. "At first, farmers removed vegetation on fixed sand dunes and ploughed the thin loess layer. They sowed millet seeds in spring and left the fields to grow. They returned in autumn and harvested the sparse yield nourished by the sterile soil. Next spring, strong winds blew on the denuded ground and easily eroded the plowed topsoil layer. The hidden sand in the under-layer was consequently exposed and drifted again. The farmers abandoned the eroded fields and moved on. Desertification was then rapidly developed by the shifting patterns of such nomadic crop-farmers."[94]

After the fall of the Qing dynasty in 1911, Mongols tried to resist further Han Chinese encroachment into their grasslands, and in 1943 did battle with the Nationalist army. "In 1950, Mongolian soldiers again rose against the Communist Party's People's Republic. The last battle was carried out in the Mu-us Sandy Land and the Mongolian troops were annihilated."[95] Han farmers moved in again, especially during the Great Leap Forward, colonizing and claiming the land. Nomadic living was prohibited in the late 1950s, grasslands were fenced in and animals no longer grazed on the open range. The great Han Chinese push into steppe grasslands that had begun two thousand years earlier during the Han dynasty thus continued through the late twentieth century.

After the reforms of the 1980s, farmers acquired ownership of the enclosed grasslands, and with worldwide demand for cashmere skyrocketing, began to intensify the number of goats grazing on the land, replacing sheep. County governments deregulated the price of cashmere, which increased eightfold in the 1980s, while controlling the price of wool, which only doubled, with the predictable result that goats replaced sheep.[96] Where sheep had grazed on the grasses, "goats browsed on even the shoots and roots of shrubs," and so have been identified as the main factor in desertification in the area.[97]

Where investigators in 2001 did find some farmers who "do not raise goats, because goats deteriorate the land," and the government of the PRC in 2002 adopted the China Grassland Act to encourage sustainable land uses and halt further desertification, neither seem to be enough to halt the advance of desert. Investigators who in 2000 found "ruined houses" and "flat plains overtaken by active sand dunes" returned in 2006 to find desertification continuing. They interviewed residents who insisted that the area called Baiyingol, which means "beautiful stream" in Mongolian, as recently as the 1980s had meadows, willow thickets, and wildlife such as foxes and wolves. By 2006, they were gone.[98]

Global market forces contributed to desertification in another way as well. *Ephedra sinica* grows naturally in the arid, sandy habitat. The herb has various medicinal qualities, and ephedirine was used to treat asthma and colds, and was also marketed as a diet aid in Europe and North America. Demand grew rapidly after 2000, and ephedra was cultivated. Cultivated ephedra drove down prices, and those who were gathering the natural herb increased their efforts. Some farmers gave up goat herding for ephedra. But both the cultivation of ephedra and the increased harvest from natural sources "depleted vegetation cover" and contributed to desertification.[99] Overall, Longworth and Williamson conclude, "virtually all natural pastures in China are now [degraded] to some extent," and "large areas of the once lush native pastures have become deserts and the remaining grassland is badly degraded."[100]

Where the harsh climate and geography of China's west for millennia imposed limits on the amount of environmental change humans could bring to the steppe, the developmental commitments of the Chinese state coupled with new productive and communication technologies threaten not just the way of life of pastoral peoples, but the wildlife, too. Halting attempts to establish some wildlife preserves there have yet to yield many results, and many of western China's "amazingly diverse assemblage of terrestrial vertebrates," including birds of prey, hoofed mammals such as gazelles and antelope, and large predators, including leopards and wolves are endangered by the drive for development.[101]

The pastoral life of Mongols in this region thus is in the process of being destroyed.[102] "Some have bought land to manage a pastoral business. Others have chosen crop and dairy farming. Still others have begun to breed the Han Chinese animal, the pig, as a sustainable business. Most people have now abandoned the use of horses."[103] And so ends another non-Han way of life based on learning to live on and with ecosystems that were not fit for Han-style farming, including an appreciation—if not love—for a landscape of intermixed sand with grassland.[104] That precedent is alarming to other pastoral peoples, in particular the Tibetans.

Summary

Over the past century, the pressures on China's forests and grasslands have proven relentless, and more continuous than not. Despite vast differences in their capabilities, the imperial, Republican, and Communist states all have seen forest and steppe ecosystems as resources to be controlled and exploited to enhance state power. Growth of the Han Chinese population pushed cereal farming into non-Chinese peripheries, transforming grasslands and tropical rainforests alike into farms and plantations that provide tax revenue to the state. Forces fueled by the demands of industry and growing domestic consumption led more than one farming family to cut down the last tree on nearby hills for the income it could bring, or the energy it could provide to cook food or keep bodies warm. Rapid industrialization, repeated changes in land tenure regimes, and more-or-less unfettered market forces pushed deforestation.

As a result, few natural forests remain in China, and grasslands have been enclosed with barbed wire. Centuries of exhortations to stem deforestation, to halt the degradation of the environment, and to maintain harmony between man and nature, have been followed by even more deforestation, environmental degradation, and loss of habitat and species. Today, the Asian elephant—once thriving throughout the region—has been displaced to the furthest reaches of China's southwest, the South China tiger is on the verge of extinction, the Yangzi River dolphin is probably extinct, and a couple of Yangzi giant soft-shell turtles in two zoos are all that remain of that species. And those are just the "star species" we know about; hundreds of other species have gone extinct. Biologists estimate that nearly 40 percent of all remaining mammal species in China are endangered, and 70–80 percent of plant species are threatened. As we will see in later in this chapter, battles over preserving the last remain "island" of that diversity in northwestern Yunnan province have become especially sharp because of plans to build dozens of dams on the region's rivers.

STATE NATURE PRESERVES AND THE PROTECTION OF BIODIVERSITY

Even as the Chinese state and the environment were caught in the cross-currents of deforestation in the service of industrialization, some state officials and party cadre understood the need to establish forest reserves and wildlife preserves, and had the influence or power to get them established. That full story has yet to be written, but in brief China's nature reserve system, which began in 1956 with the establishment of the Dinghu Mountain preserve (the site of a former Buddhist temple)[105] near Zhaoqing up the West River from Guangzhou, expanded rapidly during the 1980s.[106] By the end of 2004, there were more than two thousand reserves, accounting for nearly 14 percent of China's total land area.[107] But like the statistics on forest cover, those on nature reserves cover a wide variety of conditions, some of which approach what we might think of as a "nature reserve," while others, such as the Meihuashan tiger reserve in southwest Fujian,[108] epitomize the struggle to maintain and improve a forest habitat capable of sustaining a healthy tiger population, with competing demands of poor villagers struggling to eke out a living in a degraded environment, village and county governments with their own agendas and pressures, and a national state trying to live up to commitments to preserve biodiversity made in the Convention on Biological Diversity of 1992.

Nature Reserves

The international poster child for nature preserves in China is the giant panda.[109] In a forthcoming book, Elena Songster tells the fascinating story by which the giant panda was discovered in the nineteenth century by Western naturalists and then transformed into China's national icon in the 1950s. "In 1962, the Chinese government officially recognized the importance of the giant panda to the nation. That year, the State Council, China's highest governmental body, declared the giant panda a precious and rare species and placed it under 'first-level' national protection. The State Council also advocated the creation of nature reserves designed specifically to protect the giant panda along with eighteen other precious and rare endemic species."[110] Three years later, the Wanglang Nature Reserve in Pingwu county in Sichuan was established, a place well known for pandas and panda habitat—extensive groves of bamboo, almost exclusively the diet of giant pandas—growing in mountainous regions between 2,800 and 4,000 meters above sea level.[111] Ironically, the panda reserve was being established at precisely the same time that the "Learn from Dazhai" campaign of the Cultural Revolution led to cutting down of bamboo forests. According to a scientist at the panda breeding station who grew up in a rural Sichuan county that had both panda habitat, and pandas: "I remember vividly how we cut bamboo and trees to build Dazhai-style terraces and grow grain wherever possible. There was not awareness of the importance of what was lost."[112]

Although China has established two thousand nature reserves and an increasing number of "national parks," most do not function as such.[113] James Harkness has explored what he calls "the political economy of the protected areas." The vast expansion of the nature reserves in the 1980s and 1990s was not accompanied by state funding to support them. One-third are "paper parks" only; large numbers of others have no physical structures, signs, or boundaries; and still others may have an official in charge who resides in the county town, not the reserve. Because of the penury, the Ministry of Forestry has urged the managers and their staff to "fully exploit the resource advantages of nature reserves and on the basis of strengthening conservation, rationally open up utilization, develop your own industries, and increase reserves' abilities for self-accumulation and self-development."[114]

This directive has led to perverse outcomes. Ecotourism leads to the illegal collection of wild plants and animals, road building into remote areas fragments ecosystems, and guesthouses built with scarce conservation funds. Reserve managers not only openly contract with loggers, quarriers, or fishermen to exploit a reserve's resources, but allow profit-making enterprises to be established inside the reserves, including the transformation of lakes and marshes into prawn- and fish-raising operations. The reserve director who pioneered the latter gambit "has earned official praise for the reserve's positive cash flow and has been held up as an example to others."[115] These stories of official policies to protect public resources running into private interests that subvert them recapitulate similar ones from the late imperial period recounted in chapters 4 and 5.

The establishment of nature reserves thus has had contradictory effects. In Yunnan, villagers rushed in to cut down trees that had been maintained sustainably out of fear that that resource would be lost to them. Elsewhere in south China, the replacement of effective community management institutions with weak national ones led to the creation of de facto open areas and overuse of the reserve's resources. Locals had for centuries relied on the forests as sources of food, and have hunted. A strong market over the past decade for body parts of protected species such as tigers has led to active poaching. As Harkness observes: "While China has a Wild Animal Conservation Law, there is no systematic law covering protected areas. As a result, unless they actually apprehend someone who has killed a protected species, nature reserve staff have few options when units with a strong prior claim . . . make inroads into reserves. When offenders are caught, the courts are extremely lenient in all but a few highly publicized cases."[116]

Additionally, many reserves were established without an understanding of the ecosystems necessary to preserve protected species, and hence were too small to begin with. Logging, road building, and fish farming have fragmented ecosystems within other reserves; only in those reserves contiguous to existing forests can species thrive. Mostly, though, "the forests around China's protected areas are being converted so rapidly to other uses that they are becoming embattled islands of diversity."[117]

The largest nature reserve in the world—the Chang Tang Reserve in northwest Tibet—is subject to these pressures. Established by the Chinese state in 1993, the region's 284,000 sq. km was basically unpopulated, but was the home of six wild ungulates, including the wild yak, the Tibetan wild ass, gazelle, antelope, and argali, and blue sheep (all but the last endemic to Tibet). When George Schaller studied Chang Tang in the 1980s, he reported that "in every direction antelope and yak in incredible numbers were seen, some grazing, some lying down. No trees, no sign of man, and this peaceful-looking lake . . . seeming given over as a happy grazing ground to the wild animals." Even so, Schaller could sense change. "Most of what is now the Chang Tang Reserve was uninhabited until 20 years ago. The desolate north remains uninhabited. The south retains one of the last unspoiled grassland ecosystems in the world. However, >3000 families with ~1 million head of livestock now occupy the area. Some herders are giving up tents for permanent huts and are building fences. The future of the grasslands and the wildlife in the reserve as well as the traditional life of the pastoralists will depend on the development of proper management policies and programs."[118] Given the experiences of other of China's nature preserves, that is a tall order.

Recent Reforestation Projects[119]

To address deforestation and environmental degradation, China has engaged in numerous massive reforestation projects. Basically, the story until now has been one of "more trees, fewer forests, less timber." That is, as the millennia-long process of the removal of China's healthy forests continued during the People's Republic, reforestation projects under state, collective, and private auspices have planted huge numbers of seedlings with varying degrees of success. Even when successful, these become more like plantations than forests, and the volume of standing timber has continued to decline as young sticklike stands replace healthy forests and mature trees. Hundreds of thousands of acres of saplings—dead or alive—have been counted as forest cover.

Despite the problematic nature of the mass reforestation campaigns of the Mao years, some analysts hold out hope that the variety of state and private reforestation projects (such as those funded by the World Bank) since then will bear fruit. Prior to the October 2000 launch of the Natural Forest Protection Program, there had been six major state-sponsored campaigns that had as their goal increasing China's forest cover to 20 percent of its area by the year 2000 (given the caveats with that kind of statistic discussed earlier in this chapter). Among the earliest projects was the Coastal Protective Forest Project, begun in the 1950s, designed to stabilize the barren coastal hills in Guangdong and other coastal provinces. A project to reforest the upper and middle reaches of the Yangzi River began in the mid-1990s, and as we have seen, massive flooding in 1998 brought significant changes to forest protection policies there. A 1980s project to reforest the Taihang Mountains—which, as we saw in chapter 3, had been deforested as early as the eleventh century to provide materials for Yellow River dikes—met with little success: "Vegetation cover is low, soil erosion is serious, the environment is worsening and the peasants are very poor," leading to the depressing conclusion that the serious degradation that was documented before 1949 still plagues the region. Another project aims to plant trees of economic value among the villages on the North China plain, while another obligates urban residents to plant trees that are then often uprooted for urban development schemes.[120]

The largest project, and the one that accounts for the bulk of area claimed—and planned to become—afforested in China, is the Three Norths Shelter Project (*sanbei fenghulin*). Stretching nearly 5,000 kilometers from Kashgar in the west to the Great Xing'an Mountains bordering Heilongjiang and Inner Mongolia in the east, and covering 4 million square kilometers, the project calls for afforesting mountains, stabilizing loess land and desert with shrubs, providing fuel wood for populations in oases and other towns, and generally halting the southeasterly advance of desert into north China, Beijing included. Writing in 1994, Edmonds expressed caution about the claims being made for the area planted with trees, shrubs, or grasses, and notes that while "initial reports . . . are optimistic," it will take decades—until 2050—to judge how successful the project has been.[121]

A more recent assessment is more optimistic, in large part because the 1998 Yangzi flooding caught the attention of the central government. Analyst Liu Dacheng of The Nature Conservancy has concluded that the logging bans in the upper Yangzi watershed and the mid- to upper–Yellow River watershed have been enforced: "Forest depletion was effectively controlled, and forest area and growing stock increased. Commercial timber harvesting virtually stopped in the upper Yangtze River and mid-to-upper Yellow River. Annual timber output in the northeast China State-owned Forest Region was reduced by nearly forty percent. . . . Some 3.5 million ha of plantations were established and 4.1 million ha of secondary forests naturally regenerated through mountain land closure."[122]

Liu provides data on other reforestation projects as well, with similar measures of success.[123] Mostly, though, these "forests" are plantations. And while these have important environmental benefits, such as controlling erosion, sequestering carbon, moderating local climates, and stemming desertification, protecting biodiversity is a spin off benefit in just a few areas, Yunnan in particular, which Conservation International has designated one of the world's biodiversity "hot spots" (that is, places defined as being species-rich, with a minimum of 1,500, but having lost 70 percent of its primary vegetation). Incentives to farming households to plant trees to contribute to reforestation efforts have led mostly to the planting of trees of economic value (e.g., fruit trees), not the reestablishment of healthy forests. The state thus formulated a policy limiting such plantings to 20 percent of the total; whether that policy will be followed is questionable. And so, despite the impressive figures for the millions upon millions of hectares of new plantings, such plantations cannot be considered "forests" in the sense of preserving biodiversity. Moreover, the evidence of continuing desertification in the Three Norths Shelter Belt casts doubt on that project's ultimate success.

Wildlife, Consumption, and Epidemic Disease

The establishment of wildlife preserves and the legal framework within which they function, as well as bans on hunting and killing endangered species,[124] clearly indicates that the Chinese state understands that many animal species endemic to China need protection. That some of those reserves could function better goes without saying. The 1998 floods also brought home the message that deforestation was a major cause of that disaster, and that logging those forests in the southwest and northeast had to stop. And the battle over damming the Nujiang River, to be discussed later in this chapter, demonstrates how little forest is left in China to provide ecosystem services to the human population, and habitat to wildlife.

Another threat to wildlife comes from consumption and feasting practices. As some in China have gotten rich (to paraphrase Deng Xiaoping's admonition), many nouveau riche like to flaunt their wealth by hosting lavish feasts for friends, family, and business partners. And many of those feasts feature rare and exotic wildlife to demonstrate the wealth and power of the host. Among the delicacies are cobra snake soup, pangolin (an armadillo-like creature), ostrich, Asian giant soft shell turtle, the Chinese giant salamander, Siamese crocodile, bear paw, and civet cat. Some of these are found outside of China's borders and, like logs, are smuggled in. Along the Russian-Chinese border, according to one report, "not only bear paws but also bear gallbladders—highly valued for their medicinal and aphrodisiac qualities—frogs, tiger bones, deer musk and the genitals of spotted dear are smuggled daily into China."[125]

The market for consumable wildlife in China is considerable. A 1999 survey of people in sixteen Chinese cities found that nearly half had eaten wild animals in the previous year. A similar number of restaurants reported serving dishes made from wild animals. In some cases, the animal parts are already disassembled before arriving in China, as in the case of bear paws. In others, though, the wild animals are captured and brought to urban markets where restaurateurs select fresh meat. Markets with snakes writhing in straw baskets abound, as do markets with pangolin, and, until recently, markets with civet cat.[126]

Civet cats are native to the tropical rainforest of south and southwest China, and have been served up as a delicacy for a very long time. Villagers or other specialists near their habitat capture them, and bring them to market. Some enterprising suppliers in south China even established farms to raise civets—not just as food but also for their musk, an aromatic substance used in perfumes, including Chanel No. 5. But then in late 2002, a restaurant patron fell ill and died of a mysterious new infectious disease soon labeled SARS, for "severe acute respiratory syndrome," setting off fear of a global pandemic because it spread so rapidly from that one case in south China to 24 provinces, autonomous regions, and municipalities. Airliners bound for other countries with people suspected of having been infected or even having traveled in infected regions were quarantined on arrival at their destinations. Scientists suspected, and later proved, that SARS was caused by a virus that had jumped from civet cats to humans. Civet cats were seized from markets and restaurants, tested, and destroyed. By 2006, when the connection between SARS and civet cats was proven and publicized, the number of people reporting that they had eaten civet cat dropped by about 30 percent, but did not disappear altogether, indicating that the animals are still being captured, bred, and sold to restaurants.[127]

Another recent disease infecting humans is avian influenza (H5N1), which jumped from wild migrating waterfowl to domesticated poultry and then to humans. From 2004 to 2009, there have been several cases of humans' contracting Avian flu in China and Thailand, with millions of birds then killed to prevent the spread of the disease. Although the H5N1 virus does not spread from human to human, infectious disease experts fear that the virus could mutate to enable it to spread among humans, setting off a global influenza pandemic.

Both SARS and Avian flu demonstrate that not all habitat for wild animals has been destroyed, for both the civet cat and wild waterfowl still find room in China. But they also show that food chains with people at the top have closely interconnected whatever wildlife is left in China with human consumption, markets, and epidemic disease.

"CONTROLLING" WATER

"Harness the Huai!"

As we saw in chapter 6, the Huai River and its flood plain had been left in ruin after the Yellow River shifted its course back north in the middle of the nineteenth century. A change in course centuries earlier had sent the Yellow River south, taking over the bed of the Huai itself, leading to siltation and the problems that culminated in the nineteenth-century crisis involving the Grand Canal, the Yellow River, and the Huai River. The former outlet of the Huai to the sea had silted up, so it flowed slowly southward to join the Yangzi. Serious rainfall led to extensive flooding throughout the region and, because the Huai "valley" was basically flat with a few indentations, to water logging and salinization. As we saw in chapter 4, those problems on the North China plain go back at least a thousand years.

By the mid-twentieth century, the Huai River valley was densely settled, with 55 million people farming about one-seventh of China's arable farmland. The valley was an important one. Moreover, in the last phases of the civil war, the Chinese Communists had gained the support of the local population in the Huaihai Battle (November 7, 1948–January 10, 1949). And so floods in the summer of 1950 prompted Chinese Communist Party Chairman Mao Zedong to exclaim, "The Huai River must be harnessed!" and to commit the resources of the new state to do just that.

But, short on earth-moving machinery and technical experts (only 270 were available for a plan that called for 1,400 technicians), the Communist state mobilized millions of peasants over the next seven years to move by shovel more than twice as much earth as was moved for the building of the Panama Canal (which was done with steam shovels), and to excavate a 170-kilometer channel to the sea equal in length to the Suez Canal—but dug by hand in one-tenth the time. Although the first task was just to get the floodwaters to drain to the sea, the Minister of Water Conservancy saw that as a waste of precious water that should be retained for irrigation during droughts. In addition to digging a new channel for the Huai, the project included construction of numerous earthen dams on Huai River tributaries to create reservoirs, and diking of critical sections of the Huai River itself to prevent flooding. But, according to Robert Carin, the Communists were "unable to keep the siltation of the Huai River well in hand."[128] The river began in denuded treeless hills further west in southern Henan province, and picked up tons of silt previously laid down by the Yellow River as it meandered across the North China plain. And so, despite the investment of massive amounts of labor and the moving of mountains of earth, the Huai flooded again in 1954, and yet again, quite seriously, in 1956 and 1957. Earthen dams did not hold, the dikes were not high enough, and floodwaters inundated the region.

After seven years of effort, officials of the Huai River Harnessing Commission claimed some progress, but acknowledged the difficulty of their task: "The plains in the Huai River valley . . . were formerly silted by the overflowing of the Yellow River on many occasions. The natural drainage system thus was damaged. Once there is a heavy rainfall here, water logging is in the making as there is no way to drain the rainwater. Owing to such a complicated nature of the Huai River, it can easily be seen that a few reservoirs completed or under construction are not enough to cope with the situation. Furthermore, the harnessing projects of the tributaries were inadequate in the past." Moreover, the same official acknowledged that "the Huai River Harnessing Commission in the beginning was not completely aware of the complicated nature and the long-term requirements in the harnessing of the Huai River."[129]

The Commission called for the state to invest vast amounts of money into the project, beyond the 1 billion yuan already spent. But the official *People's Daily* made it clear, in Carin's words, "that money needed for the current water conservancy projects in the country must be raised principally by the masses themselves" in a new campaign labeled "Less Money, Quicker Results" that soon melded into the Great Leap Forward,[130] the most radical of Mao's attempted solutions to China's poverty.

Despite its problems, the drive toward "harnessing the Huai" became a model for officials in the rest of China to follow. Among the issues resolved in that vast undertaking was whether water conservancy projects were to have flood control as their main objective, and hence the containing and draining of water away from land, or the retention of water for irrigation. Facing that choice was a consequence of centuries of their ancestors' filling in swamps and draining lakes to create the farmland that now needed irrigating. And so, not surprisingly, accumulating water for irrigating farmland became the policy, with flood prevention a secondary consideration. As a result, dams and reservoirs were built in the upper reaches of all of the tributaries to the Huai River. Between 1957 and 1959, more than 100 reservoirs were built in one prefecture in Henan province alone, and extended into the plains as well, totaling some four thousand in the Huai River basin.[131] Indeed, dams and reservoirs were built throughout China. By 1990, China had 83,387 dams, and all but two of China's major rivers had been dammed.[132]

In a much longer historical perspective, of course, the policy of "retaining water" for irrigation would be ironic if its consequences were not so great. As we have seen in previous chapters, much of the environmental history of lowland areas includes the filling in of ponds and lakes to create farmland, encroaching on the larger lakes' ability to absorb and retain floodwaters. By 1949, many of the lakes and ponds in China had disappeared, creating a need for the state to build artificial reservoirs for retaining rainwater and irrigating farmland.

Dam the Yellow River

The Yellow River has long been synonymous with China, from the time Shang and Zhou settlers cleared forest from the North China plain for their farms, and since in the eighth century BCE they tried to protect themselves against Yellow River floods by building earthen dikes. The story of the river and of Chinese attempts to deal with it has continued through each of the chapters in this book, including into this one.

Harnessing the Huai may have been the first priority for China's nascent dam-building corps of engineers, but the Yellow River had greater historical significance. It was even said that its legendary muddiness would only be cleared with the emergence of a great man, and Mao Zedong might well have thought that that man was him. Construction of a dam on the Yellow River did not begin until 1957, under the strong guidance of Soviet advisers, and only after voices that questioned the wisdom of building a dam on the main course of the Yellow River (instead of a series of smaller ones on its tributaries) were silenced in an "Anti-Rightist" campaign that followed the brief opening of the Hundred Flowers.[133]

Ignoring predictions that the huge sediment load of the Yellow River would not only render hydroelectric generators useless but also quickly fill the reservoir with sand, construction began on a 360 meter-high dam at Sanmenxia, just down from where the Wei River joined the Yellow. Sluice gates that had been included in the design were cemented shut, and the dam was completed in early 1962. Hundreds of thousands of acres of farmland were flooded, and nearly three hundred thousand farmers relocated to undesirable land further west. As predicted, the reservoir quickly silted up, and silt even backed up into the Wei River, causing flooding in and around the city of Xian. Silt rendered the generators useless; even reopening the cemented-over sluice gates did not discharge enough silt. Portions of the dam were rebuilt to include tubes at the base to discharge the silt—but nothing worked. According to Judith Shapiro, "Eventually, the dam was so pierced with holes that it became virtually worthless for either flood control or electricity generation."[134]

Environmental Consequences of Dam Building

The policy of damming rivers to create reservoirs to accumulate water for irrigation purposes has had two major consequences. First, a number of those dams were built either without adequate hydrological studies to guide their size, or were of questionable construction, or both. According to an official paraphrased by one critic of dam-building, "all a particular leader had to do was point his finger at a certain place and the decision would be made to build a dam between one mountain and another."[135] To say the dams were dangerous is perhaps an understatement. By 1981, the central government acknowledged that 3,200 dams had collapsed; the largest of those incidents will be discussed shortly.

The other consequence of the policy of "accumulating water" was environmental, and particularly troublesome on the flat North China plain: the water table was raised, increasing both salinization and water logging. Both of those effects were predicted, not just by a hydrologist whose warnings went unheeded and who was punished for saying so, but also by China's premier, Zhou Enlai, who told the communist party cadre at a 1962 conference: "I've been told by doctors that if a person goes without eating for a few days, no major harm will result. But if one goes without urinating for even one day, they will be poisoned. It's the same with land. How can we accumulate water and not discharge it?"[136] Nonetheless, the policy continued.

In the Huai River basin, hundreds of additional dams and reservoirs were built in lower-lying areas so that land that had been reserved for flood diversion could be settled and farmed, which it was. These deadly consequences of the policy of accumulating water came together in August 1975 in the largest and most destructive dam collapse in world history. To be sure, the precipitating cause (literally) was an intense typhoon that unusual weather patterns brought to Henan province on August 4, dumping three feet of rain on the region in just three days. By midnight of August

7, reservoirs on two tributaries to the Huai—the Banqiao reservoir on the Ru River and the Shimantan on the Hong River—were reaching maximum capacity. Within an hour, those two dams each collapsed, sending walls of water moving at 30 miles per hour cascading down the valleys, taking everything in their way, entire villages included. The flood diversion areas down stream could not handle the huge amount of additional water, and those dikes, too, collapsed, resulting in a lake nearly 100 miles long. Eleven million people were affected, and 85,600 killed.

The floodwaters were trapped by the dams lower down on the Huai River, and with millions of people still in the waters, and hundreds of thousands of others suffering from hunger and waterborne diseases such as dysentery and hepatitis, on August 13 the Henan provincial Communist Party secretary pleaded with the central government to dynamite several of the major dams so that the floodwaters could be released. Those dams were destroyed two days later, sending floodwaters down the Huai River and into Anhui province, which was then inundated. A year later, the region had a bumper crop. "Surveying the land carefully, one could see crops everywhere, but what made people's hearts quiver were the small areas where the crops were especially rich and dense"—land where the eighty-five thousand victims' buried bodies fertilized the nitrogen-depleted land.[137]

The Huai River Runs Black

Incredibly, few lessons were learned from that disaster, providing the background not just for the building of the massive Three Gorges dam, which will be discussed in another section, but for continuing environmental disasters along the Huai River occasioned by China's breakneck and largely unregulated industrialization in the 1980s and 1990s. During those two decades, tens of thousands of heavily polluting small factories—paper and pulp mills, monosodium glutamate plants, dyeing operations, tanning mills, chemical factories—have been built in the Huai basin. According to Elizabeth Economy, "they have also freely dumped their waste into the river, making the Huai China's third most polluted river system."[138] Pollution levels similar to those discussed below for the Huai River are also found in the Pearl River delta in south China, and for similar reasons.

Maximizing profit with the blessing of entrepreneurial officials, most factories did not operate waste disposal systems, instead dumping effluent directly into the Huai and its tributaries, which then collected in the reservoirs, where it became increasingly concentrated. Periodically reservoir directors dumped their polluted water, killing fish downstream, and befouling the water so that it was undrinkable. And just two months after the central government announced plans in 1994 to clean up the Huai and to shut polluting factories, a number of factories along the Huai "emptied their waste tanks directly into the river, producing a toxic mix of ammonia and nitrogen compounds, potassium permanante, and phenols . . . The water turned black. . . . Fisheries were destroyed . . . and thousands of people were treated for dysentery."[139]

Again in 1998, the government announced plans to clean up the Huai, and again little was done. The water in the river system was rated "heavily polluted." But the worst was yet to come. The pollutants continued to build in the reservoirs when in

July 2001 heavy rains flooded the Huai's tributaries, and billions of gallons of heavily polluted water flowed into the Huai. Downstream in Anhui province "the river was thick with garbage, yellow foam, and dead fish."[140] The Huai River basin has become such an iconic image of China's polluted rivers that it has been featured in articles on "the death of China's rivers" in *The New York Times*, *The Asia Times*, an online photo essay, and a PBS documentary.[141] Despite the shuttering of hundreds of factories, two years later, in 2003, the water in the Huai was still unsuitable for drinking or fisheries, or in some cases for industrial use—or, even more perversely, given the policy of "accumulating water" in reservoirs, for irrigation.[142]

Deep Drilling on the North China Plain

Flooding to the north of the Huai River in the Hai River basin, in which the capital city of Beijing was cited, also caused waterlogging because of the policy of "accumulating water." But after flooding in the mid-1960s led to the predictable outcomes of waterlogging and salinization, the central government mobilized three hundred thousand laborers to dig drainage ditches, or "new rivers," to drain the floodwaters away, a project completed in 1979.

With the "accumulated water" in reservoirs inadequate to irrigate farmland, in the mid-1960s the state began sinking tube wells into the ground water and aquifers across the North China plain. By 1985, nearly seven hundred thousand wells run by electrical motors had been sunk, expanding irrigated land from 11 to 54 million mu, a 400 percent increase since the founding of the PRC; across the whole North China plain by the new millennium, there were 3.6 million tube wells irrigating flat and ill-drained farmland. The irrigation water increased the salt content of the soils to the extent that by the early 1980s there was a "salt crisis" on some farmland.[143]

Some experts thought that drilling wells up to 300 meters deep to go below the salinated and polluted water table would solve the problem, but others worried about depletion of the deep aquifer. Instead, according to historian Lillian Li, a complex system involving both deep and shallower wells, along with canals and ditches for irrigation, appears to have addressed the problems. However, the whole system now relies on a vast network of agronomists, soil chemists, climatologists, and engineers employing large amounts of electricity and other modern inputs: "This modern management of the [north China] soil may be compared in its intensity and complexity with the traditional water control . . . that had transformed land and agriculture in South China in earlier centuries."[144] The difference is that north China agriculture is now dependent on inputs of vast amounts of money and modern scientific knowledge, a solution that may or may not prove sustainable.

Despite all this massaging of water and soil, water shortages remain a serious problem in north China. Rivers now run dry, and lakes have so shrunk that their ecology has changed to be unable to support fish. Some water was diverted to one of the larger lakes, so that by 1989 reeds would grow and could be cut and fashioned into mats and baskets. In addition to water for irrigation, among the major users that have felt the shortages have been cities and industries, especially in and around Beijing and Tianjin, both of which have grown dramatically in the last two decades.[145] The

Yellow River more often than not now runs dry 500 miles before it reaches its mouth, and the aquifer is now 90 meters below the surface, and still subsiding. Other rivers are dry, and the water table near the Yellow River city of Shijiazhuang is sinking four feet per year, leading some to worry that aquifers beneath the North China plain may be drained within 30 years.[146]

The South-to-North Water Transfer Project

Faced with these water shortages, in the 1990s some water was diverted from the Luan River 100 miles away to Tianjin, but by 2002 an even more aggressive, massive, and controversial plan—the South-to-North Water Transfer Project (SNWTP)—was begun to divert Yangzi River water to the north. Like the Three Gorges Dam on the Yangzi River, which is part of this massive scheme and which will be discussed below, the idea for diverting water from the south to the north long predates its realization, going back at least to the 1950s when Communist Party Chairman Mao Zedong exclaimed, "The south has plenty of water and the north lacks it, so why not borrow some?"

The plan is to move water from the Yangzi River basin to north China via three routes. The eastern route mostly follows the Grand Canal, bringing water north from Jiangsu province. Construction of this section began in 2002 and is scheduled for completion by 2013, but is being delayed because of heavily polluted water from tributaries such as from the Huai River, water not suitable even for irrigation. The central route will divert water from the Three Gorges Dam by holding it back at the Danjiangkou Dam on the Han River; the government had hoped this project would bring water to Beijing and Tianjin in time for the 2008 Olympics, but that date has been pushed back to 2014 as concerns about its environmental impact on the Three Gorges Dam and reservoir have mounted, and as drought in 2008 and 2009 lowered water supplies in the Yangzi River basin. The westernmost route would bring water from the Qinghai-Tibetan highland to the upper reaches of the Yellow River in the hope of irrigating more farmland there. The projected cost for this water project, the largest in world history, is expected to be $US50 billion, even more than the infamous Three Gorges dam to be discussed below.[147]

Like the Three Gorges Dam, the SNWTP has generated considerable environmental concern and opposition. Despite the promise of more water for north China, according to analyst Liu Changming, "where the conveyance canals pass by the discharge gates of water facilities, and in poorly drained areas where there is a high water table, they may cause a rise in the aquifer leading to secondary salinization of the soil." Liu also cites the problems of polluted water and the impact of the intrusion of saltwater into the lower Yangzi estuary, both affecting local fisheries and urban water supply and quality, but thinks that careful planning and engineering can address the problems, leading "to a net improvement by smoothing out the natural distribution of water [in China] both spatially and temporally."[148] As a precaution against such scientific overconfidence, the Three Gorges Dam and the warnings about its environmental impacts are instructive.

The Three Gorges Dam

With construction completed in 2006 and its reservoir nearly filled by 2009, the Chinese government considers the Three Gorges Dam to be its crowning achievement in controlling and using water for human use. Built just west of Yichang in central China where the Yangzi River previously tumbled out of the famous Three Gorges before meandering through flatter land a thousand miles to the ocean, the dam, at more than 300 feet tall and 1.5 miles wide, holding behind it a 350-mile-long reservoir, is the world's largest. The main purposes of the dam are to produce enough electricity from its thirty-two main generators to service the 400 million residents and industries in central China, and to provide flood control in the Yangzi River basin.

First envisioned by Sun Yat-sen at the beginning of the twentieth century and again by Mao Zedong in the 1950s, the Three Gorges Dam was finally proposed in 1992 by Premier Li Peng, a former hydroelectrical engineer who had been educated in the Soviet Union. Because of the scale, cost, and impact on both humans and the environment, the dam sparked controversy from the beginning. One leading voice within China opposing the dam was Dai Qing, a fearless former PLA reporter with high-level Communist party connections.[149] Worldwide publicity and support for her from global environmental NGOs prompted even the World Bank to decline to support the project, but China went ahead anyway with its own resources, although Premier Li did acknowledge that China did not have the technology to build the dam and would have to rely on American, Japanese, and European construction firms.

Choosing to build this signature project on the Yangzi River itself instead of placing numerous smaller dams on tributaries to the great river, promising to relocate 1.3 million residents to villages in choice locations elsewhere but not the cultural relics that would be submerged, and overlooking the concerns of environmentalists for the loss of habitat and species that filling the reservoir was sure to cause, the dam is now operating, generating electricity, and repaying the huge cost of construction. Some of the known environmental costs are already being measured: habitat fragmentation and loss of species. "One exceptional feature of the biodiversity in this region," one scientific team wrote, "is the abundance of ancient, rare, endemic, and endangered species." Mountaintops have become islands in the reservoir, with large predators dying out. Ancient endemic fish species, including the Chinese sturgeon (*Acipenser sinensis*) and the Chinese paddlefish (*Psephurus gladius*) are probably now extinct. The full impact of the dam on the ecosystem will take decades to understand.[150] In an arresting image in which the Three Gorges dam might be seen as a metaphor for the world, the team members write: "Biological species live in increasingly fragmented habitat islands embedded in a matrix of human civilization."[151] And, I would add, are therefore increasingly at risk.

Since construction ended and the reservoir began filling, a series of landslides and riverbank collapses starting in 2003 has sparked concern even in the Chinese government about the potential environmental effects of the dam, including earthquakes. As the reservoir filled, water seeped into the loose soil, destabilizing the land. As more water is added during the summer monsoon but then released afterwards to produce electricity and send water needed for irrigation down river, the water level of the reservoir drops, inducing the landslides that have killed several score of people. Because the reservoir sits astride two earthquake faults, fears have arisen that the fluctuating water level in the reservoir might trigger a quake. One of the dam's engineers has reported that 822 tremors have been registered, none large enough to cause any serious damage.[152] Drought in China's southwest in 2009 delayed filling the reservoir to its 600-foot height capacity, but officials may well be taking that as a reason for a welcome pause. The drought already postponed construction on the central section of the South-to-North Water Transfer Scheme.[153]

Other environmental worries heightened by the dam include climate change. The reservoir is so large that some expect it to alter local temperatures and rainfall patterns, increasing both flooding and drought. Whether or not dam-induced drought led to the lowest water level in the Yangzi in 142 years, ships were stranded in 2008, and schistosomiasis, thought to have increased because of snails' breeding faster on flood plain islands that have not been inundated, has also been reported.[154]

Historic Dujiangyan

If intense international and domestic opposition could not stop the Three Gorges dam, a rather unique combination of circumstances did in fact lead to the decision to cancel construction of one of a series of hydroelectric dams on the Min River in Sichuan province. This dam, which came to be known as the Yangliuhu dam, was slated to be constructed less than a mile upstream from the historic Dujiangyan irrigation system. As noted earlier in chapter 3, the Dujiangyan system had been built in 251 BCE for the purpose of controlling floods and irrigating the fertile Sichuan basin. Astoundingly, the system continues to work to this day with very little upkeep needed.

The Dujiangyan irrigation system had been designated a World Heritage Site by UNESCO in 2000, but when plans to build the hydroelectric dam within sight of Dujiangyan began to move forward in 2003, officials at the Sichuan Province Cultural Relics Bureau, which oversaw Dujiangyan, "were kept in the dark," according to Andrew Mertha.[155] When they did find out, they caused a significant uproar and publicity. Opponents of the dam argued that it would negatively affect the Dujiangyan ecosystem, and even the longstanding irrigation system for the Sichuan basis. Those arguments apparently were not terribly persuasive, but the one that ultimately carried the day was that a hydroelectric dam within eyesight of the historic Dujiangyan irrigation system would be "visual pollution" and sacrifice the historical heritage of the Chinese people. The dam was not built.[156]

The Three Parallel Rivers Region of Yunnan

This section on water concludes with a consideration of environmental issues in the most remote, ecologically diverse, and environmentally threatened region of China—what is now called "The Three Parallel Rivers" region in northwestern Yunnan province (see map 7.3). Indeed, the region is unique in its geology, flora, and fauna.

When the Indian tectonic plate slammed into the Eurasian plate 50 million years ago, rapidly lifting the Tibetan plateau and creating the Himalayan Mountains, the impact wrinkled the earth's crust in what is now the southeastern corner of Tibet and the northern reaches of China's Yunnan province, sandwiched between Myanmar (Burma) and China's Sichuan province. Three of the world's great rivers that have their sources in Tibetan glaciers—the Yangzi, the Mekong (in China the Lancang), and the Salween (the Nu in China)—run south through 6,000-foot-deep gorges made by that folding of the earth's crust, running parallel for about 170 miles—at their closest, merely tens of miles apart.[157]

In 2003, parts of this region were named a World Heritage Site, one of thirty-eight in China.[158] Additionally, the region is environmentally important. According to the World Conservation Monitoring Center of the United Nations, "This vast complex comprises eight clusters of largely mountain-protected areas. . . . It is a landscape of very great topographic, geologic and climatic variety, scenic beauty and unparalleled biologic diversity. There are 118 peaks over 5,000 meters (15,000 feet) high, glaciers, waterfalls and hundreds of small lakes. Owing to its range of elevations, its location on the boundaries of three major bio-geographic realms—east Asia, southeastern Asia, and the Tibetan plateau—and as an ecological corridor between north and south, it contains most of the Palaeartic temperate biomes from alpine to southern sub-tropical. It is an epicentre of Chinese biodiversity with over 6000 species of plants . . . and . . . over 25 [percent] of the world's animal species, many of them relict and endangered."[159]

The biodiversity of the region is made possible by a combination of the range of elevations and unique climatic conditions that bring both the Indian Ocean southwest monsoon and the Pacific ocean southeastern monsoon. Climatic conditions in this relatively small area (about 200 miles north to south, and 100 miles east to west) range from alpine to near-tropical conditions. As a result, the region contains "the most biodiverse and least disturbed temperate ecosystems in the world." There are tropical evergreen broadleaved forests, temperate deciduous and coniferous forests,

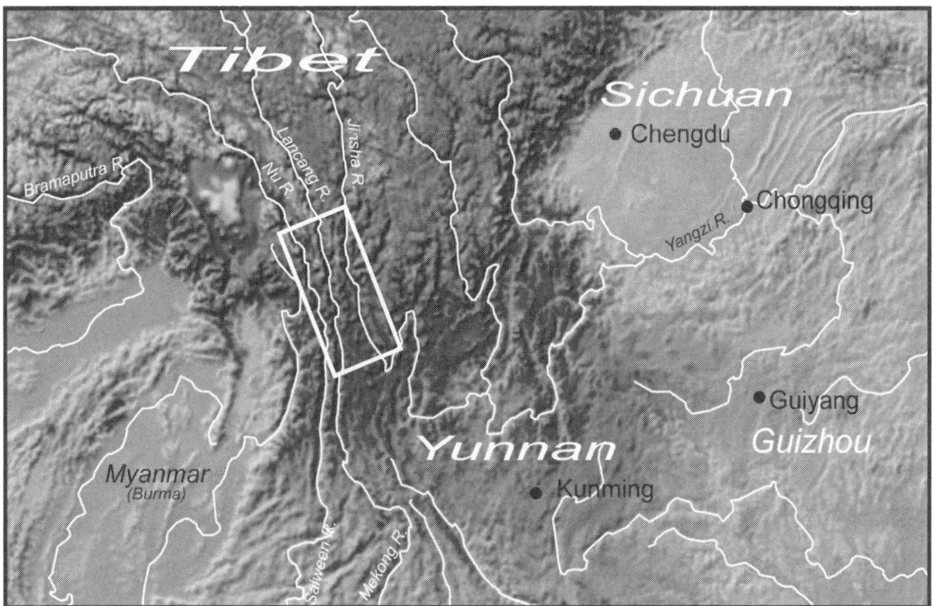

Map 7.3. The Three Parallel Rivers Region of Yunnan Province

alpine meadows, and many ecosystems in between. Not only does the area support a significant proportion of China's animal species but "[m]ost of China's rare and endangered animals occur within it" as well, including three species of monkey, the red panda, both the snow and clouded leopards, and "the richest assemblage of birds in China."[160]

But the Protected Area is not pristine wilderness. With so many ecological niches to support that biological diversity, it is not surprising that the area also is home to a variety non-Chinese peoples numbering about three hundred thousand in all, including Tibetans, Yi, Miao, Bai, Lisu, Pumi, Nu, Dulong, and Naxi.[161] As we have seen elsewhere in this book, different peoples migrated in at various times and learned to exploit different ecological niches, transforming the environment to sustain their populations.[162] In one part of Yunnan, "Bai and Han farmers occupy the best mountain valleys, while Yi villages lie in smaller valleys at higher elevations, and an impoverished Miao hamlet sits alone close to the crest of a mountain." Similar three-tiered divisions of mountain ecosystems were observed elsewhere in Yunnan, too. According to one resident, "The Dai occupy the valleys, the Lisu occupy the foot of the mountains, and the Jingpo are higher up. It's said that all three groups used to battle fiercely till it was settled where each lived, at what height."[163]

The weakest were continually pushed higher into less and less productive land. In the late 1980s, anthropologist Jonathan Unger visited a village situated at 10,000 feet above sea level. Here, wherever "a scrap of mountain slope contains a pocket of soil, hungry peasants have arduously planted small patches of potatoes. Many of these patches are angled at inclines greater than forty-five degrees, and farmers sometimes strap themselves to supporting ropes to avoid falling into the gorges below." In addition to potatoes, these mountain peoples raised sheep for the cash they could earn from sale of the wool. "[E]ach household is desperately trying to increase its own flocks irrespective of the fact that overgrazing is stripping the mountain slopes of grass. Already . . . gullies have begun creasing the stripped high-mountain pastures. . . . This stretch of high country is moving rapidly toward irreversible ecological disaster."[164]

One Chinese observer with a strong interest in "economic development" who supports building dams in the Three Parallel Rivers region over protecting the region from development, said, "I did not see much primitive forest. . . . I have seen patches of farmland on quite steep slopes. . . . Slash-and-burn is the method used to farm such land. . . . [T]he slopes are too steep to plow. And the soil along the Nu [River] is poor. Local people cannot afford to buy fertilizer, so they can only use fire to burn wild grass. And such land can't be used after a few years, so they have to burn another patch. Moreover, the production of that land is very low: 40 to 50 kilograms per mu is quite good. To support one person, five mu must be farmed."[165] These comments were made in the context of an argument that economic development of the region would be good to alleviate what the proponent saw as the poverty of these peoples. Certainly, they were not plugged into the market economy that was booming elsewhere throughout China.

Until recently, there were few roads, and the region was not accessible. The remoteness and ruggedness of the region, together with the steep disease gradient Han Chinese encountered on entering Yunnan province, provided some protection for both the human and natural diversity of the region. But that diversity has been threatened by economic development, in particular by hydropower dams, and, perversely, by turning the World Heritage site and its environs into a tourist attraction.

"Develop the West": The Struggle to Dominate Nature Continues

Launched in 2000 by Premier Zhu Rongji mostly as a tribute to Deng Xiaoping, the campaign to "develop the west" promises to bring investment, jobs, development, and modernity to China's far western regions, including the provinces of Ningxia, Gansu, Shaanxi, Sichuan, Tibet, Qinghai, Xinjiang, Guizhou, and Yunnan. The rationale appears to be that Deng Xiaoping's approach to "let some get rich first" favored eastern and coastal China, and Premier Zhu figured it was time to pay attention to China's impoverished west. Plans called for state investment in infrastructure projects, including highways, railways, airports, pipelines, and telecommunications, but especially hydroelectric projects on rivers cascading out of the Tibetan plateau that would send power back to the most industrially advanced (and electricity-short) regions of central and eastern China.[166] In those plans, Yunnan province looms especially large.

According to Darrin Magee, "Yunnan is construed as a place where hydropower development needs to be waged like a war: China's west will become a base from which strategies and forces for developing electric power will be deployed." Echoing Maoist "conquer nature" rhetoric, official media outlets and China's hydropower companies talked about a "beach assault" when the first dam was built in the 1980s, after which engineering "troops advanced" into Yunnan to tame its "galloping rivers" and build an "electricity mother ship" to provision China's rapidly developing coastal industrial economy, particularly the Pearl River delta region in Guangdong province. As Magee observes, "[o]ne can almost imagine a corps of hydroelectric engineers, dusting their hands clean from chores recently completed at Three Gorges, marching triumphantly westward" into Yunnan.[167]

Others have called the "blind rush" to build dams in the late 1990s–early 2000s throughout China "a scramble for hydropower."[168] A senior fellow at the Chinese Academy of Sciences said "There is a messy free-for-all going on. Nobody seriously considers the consequences. . . . Nobody listens to diverging views. No river is being left undammed."[169] The scramble began in 2002 when the State Power Company of China was privatized and broken into five profit-making enterprises, most headed by people well connected to the ruling Communist Party, unleashing a "hydropower rush" as these companies sought to divvy up China's rivers.[170] In the Three Parallel Rivers Protected Area, Huadian Power got the Nu River, Huaneng Power the Lancang, and Sanxia Power the Upper Yangzi.[171]

The Conquest of Malaria and the Building of Dams

Earlier assaults on Yunnan and Burma in the eighteenth century had been stymied or limited by the steep disease gradient Han Chinese and Manchus from the north encountered, in particular malaria. While there is a long and well-documented history of the Western scientific understanding and treatment of malaria, the Chinese story remains less well known.

As discussed earlier, for centuries the Chinese have known of the medicinal properties of the substance *qinghao*, derived from two variants of artemisia (*Artemisia annua*; known more commonly in the West as sweet wormwood, or mugwort, and *Artemisia apiacea*[172]), using it at least from the fourth century to reduce fevers of all kinds. In 1967, during the Vietnam War, Ho Chi Minh asked Chinese Premier Zhou Enlai for help in developing a malaria treatment for his soldiers trooping down the Ho Chi Minh Trail, where 90 percent came down with a drug-resistant form of malaria. After consulting ancient medical treatises, Chinese scientists succeeded in 1971 in isolating the substance from *Artemisia* that killed even the drug-resistant varieties of malaria; the results were published in 1979 in the *Chinese Medical Journal*, and Chinese since then have had access to a very powerful anti-malarial drug that cut Chinese malaria cases from 2 million in 1980 to ninety thousand in 1990.[173] The dam-building shock troops for the Chinese advance into Yunnan then were armed with a powerful, indigenously developed drug to protect them against malaria.

Just south of the Three Parallel Rivers Protected Area in the middle and lower reaches of the Lancang River, construction of "a cascade of eight hydroelectric power stations . . . has been ongoing since 1986." Magee figures that the total generating capacity of the entire cascade is only slightly less than the Three Gorges dam.[174] The first of those dams, the Manwan, encountered little opposition when it was built, although the tens of thousands of people displaced for its construction harbored grievances concerning their poor treatment that erupted in 2003 after the government announced plans to construct the third of the eight power stations at Xiaowan and a newly formed NGO called Green Watershed led three thousand people to seek a meeting with the power company to air their grievances.[175]

But the most public opposition to Chinese government plans to dam the Three Parallel Rivers arose over the Nu River; analyst Andrew Mertha calls it "The Battle over the Nu River, 2003–present." Of the twenty-eight dams planned for the these three gorges, thirteen were slated for the Nu (see map 7.4), one of only two undammed rivers in China, apparently to be constructed in the World Heritage Area "protected area." But a map of the region shows that the river valleys below 2,000 meters (about 6,000 feet) were purposely omitted from the protected area. According to one report, "United Nations officials were puzzled when Chinese authorities asked that Tiger Leaping Gorge [on the upper reaches of the Yangzi River], one of the main features of the park, be excluded from the [designated protected area]. Why, the officials asked, was the magnificent gorge not to be included? 'To allow for the construction of hydro dams,'" they were told.[176] The United Nations also observed that "a 2006 map of proposed boundary changes showed major alterations in the boundaries and areas originally submitted for World heritage status."[177]

Despite these governmental maneuvers, opponents of the Nu River project apparently have been successful, at least so far, in derailing or postponing, if not killing, the plans to build dams in the gorges. The proposed dam on the upper Yangzi River in Tiger Leaping Gorge, the crowning jewel of the Heritage Area, visited by a reported half-million visitors in 2006, has been moved further upriver to a site in Tibet.[178] According to Magee, work on four of the Nu River dams was likely to begin by the end of 2006. Mertha reports that that in a visit in March 2006 he saw evidence of surveying work at the various proposed dam sites, as well as evidence that the work had been "disguised" ahead of a UNESCO team visit.[179] Thus as of this writing (2011), the status of the Nu River hydropower cascade is unclear.

Even if the dams on the Nu River are never built, the biological and human diversity of the Three Parallel Rivers Protected Area may well be threatened by plans already well advanced to turn the area into privately owned tourist-attracting parks. Paved roads have been built, the area is on the global tourist map, and even the official website of UNESCO World Heritage Centre promotes travel to the region.[180] As noted above, the river valleys below 2,000 meters elevation already are excluded from the World Heritage Site boundaries, and the Chinese government apparently has plans to relocate tens if not hundreds of thousands of the non-Chinese peoples living in the region, and "to preserve" thirty-one of these "traditional villages in order to realise their potential for tourism"[181] and provide employment opportunities for the peoples who will still dress in their customary "native" attire.

Apparently these parks will resemble less the national parks of the United States, which, while preserving habitat and species, nonetheless have been critiqued as "industrial tourism,"[182] than Historic Williamsburg or commercial ski areas, with paved roads, cable cars to the top of glacier-covered peaks, and in at least one place, a horse

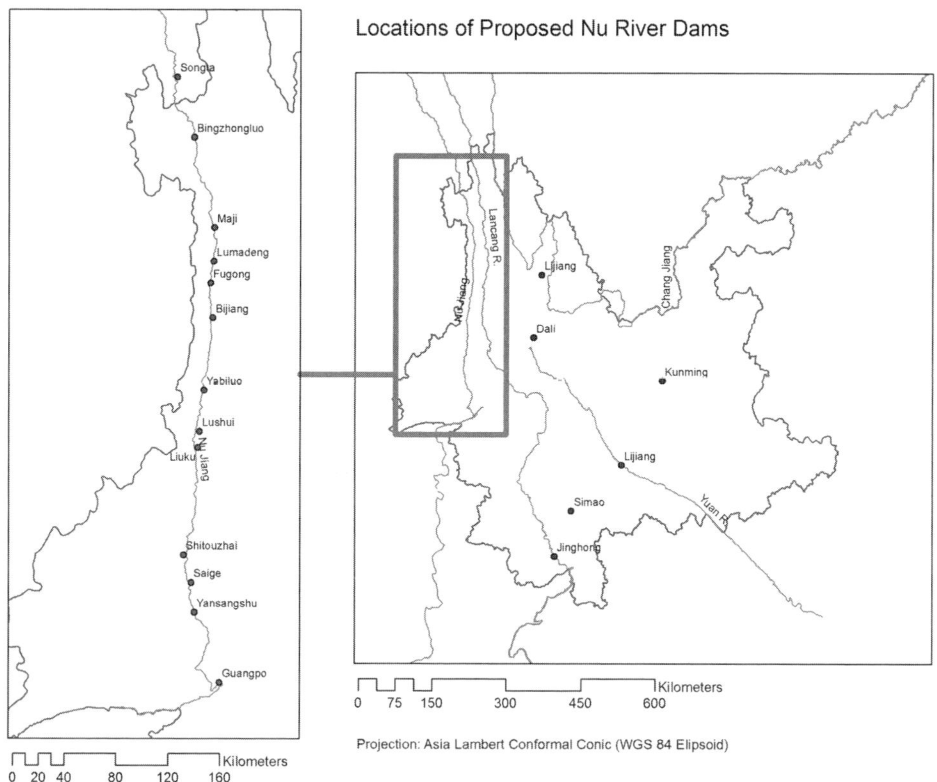

Map 7.4. Proposed Cascade of 13 Dams on the Nu River *Source:* Darrin L. Magee, *New Energy Geographies: Powershed Politics and Hydropower Decision Making in Yunnan, China* (University of Washington Ph.D. thesis, 2006), 169. Dr. Magee graciously redrew that map for publication here.

racetrack where Tibetan locals historically had pastured their horses. To get those plans approved, developers apparently bribed locals or promised them employment.[183]

With a history of deforestation in Yunnan going back to the eighteenth century (see chapters 4–5), coupled with the building of hydropower stations and the rush to develop tourist attractions, what is at stake in the Three Parallel Rivers region is "*one of the world's most important remaining areas for the conservation of the earth's biodiversity*" (italics added).[184] The battles over the Three Parallel Rivers Protected Areas may well be the last stand to protect not just a small habitat island of China's last remaining biological diversity, but the world's. The reason this region has become precious is not just because of the exceptional geological and environmental features that gave rise to its extraordinary biodiversity. In the long-term view of China's environmental history, the region has become a last remaining island of biodiversity precisely because the four thousand-year history of deforesting China and pushing farmland into as many places as could possibly be protected by the Chinese state and its military (or earlier, its *tusi* intermediaries) has greatly simplified ecosystems into agro-ecosystems, and the diversity of human ways of interacting with the environment into a predominately Han Chinese way of doing so.

POLLUTING THE ATMOSPHERE

Powering the Economic Surge—Mostly with Coal

To continue its rapid industrial development, China has needed to generate vast quantities of electricity; indeed, meeting that need was one of the most important rationales for building the Three Gorges and other hydropower dams. Hydropower is one of two main sources of renewable energy China is tapping to produce electricity, the other being wind. But even with the use of solar energy to heat water, and with campaigns to use energy more efficiently, renewable sources combined will meet only 20 percent of China's projected energy needs by 2020.[185] Thus not only is China not backing off from adding to its current total of twenty-two thousand large hydropower dams, it is building an average of one coal-fired power plant per week.

While some of those new plants employ cleaner-burning technology than the inefficient plants they are replacing, they still require coal to be mined and shipped to the power plants. And no matter how advanced they are, these coal-fired plants still emit global warming gases. Even new "green" power-producing technologies such as giant wind turbines, for which China has a large potential,[186] spur the construction of additional coal power plants as backups in case the wind doesn't blow.[187] Not surprisingly, by 2009 China had surpassed the United States as the world's biggest emitter of carbon dioxide, and hence as the world's major contributor to global warming.[188] That astounding transformation mirrors China's rapid industrialization over the past 60 years, but especially in the last three decades.

Coal, iron, and steel are synonymous with both the Industrial Revolution that began in Western Europe in the nineteenth century and the industrialization of the Soviet Union that began in the 1930s under Joseph Stalin. China has vast reserves of coal in fields mostly in the north and northwest. Those supplies had begun to be tapped a thousand years ago during China's aborted industrial revolution during the Song dynasty (see chapter 3), and again in the late nineteenth century when China tried "self strengthening" to build a strong military defense against Western and Japanese imperialism. But the extended development and use of China's coal deposits came only after 1949 when the Chinese Communists launched the First Five-Year Plan to industrialize China (1953–57). Small coal mines and small coal-fired power plants proliferated in the reforms after 1978 when Deng Xiaoping proclaimed, "To get rich is glorious," and China began manufacturing huge quantities of goods not just for its domestic market, but, in particular, for export to other world markets.

By 1989, when China surpassed the Soviet Union to become the world's largest coal producer, 75 percent of the electricity powering China's industry and cities came from burning a billion tons of coal, "largely uncleaned and burned with minimal or no air pollution controls."[189] Until the Deng Xiaoping reform era, most of that coal came from large state-owned enterprises. Since then, thousands of small and mostly illegal mines have opened to supply the surging demand.

Large or small, Chinese coal mines and coal-fired power plants have huge local and global environmental effects. Inferior and unwashed coal accounts for a significant amount of fine particulate pollution, and inefficient burning spews significant amounts of carbon dioxide and sulfur dioxide into the global atmosphere. The impact on the miners themselves is substantial. People's lungs and faces are black, as are local water supplies and the landscape. According to Vaclav Smil, "Large Chinese mines have a long way to go to achieve acceptable levels of coal dust and work safety. The current situation is truly shocking, as chronic bronchitis and pneumoconiosis incapacitate miners in their thirties, and fatal accidents are at least thirty times as frequent per million tonnes of extracted coal as in the USA."[190] Small and illegal mines may be even worse. Local officials are bribed, mine safety is virtually non-existent, and the detritus is simply left on the landscape after the easily worked deposits are abandoned after a few years, leaching into water supplies.

A recent incident illustrates what happens. "When an underground fire killed 35 men at the bottom of a coal shaft last year," *The New York Times* reported on April 11, 2009, "the telltale signs of another Chinese mining disaster were everywhere: Black smoke billowed into the sky, dozens of rescuers searched nine hours for survivors, and sobbing relatives besieged the mine's iron gate. . . . For nearly three months, not a word leaked from the heart of China's coal belt about the July 14 explosion that racked the illegal mine, a 1,000 foot wormhole in Hebei Province, about 100 miles west of Beijing." The mine owner not only paid off the victims' families and local officials, but reporters as well. Nearly four thousand coal miners died in mine accidents in 2008; small mines account for one-third of China's coal production, but 75 percent of miners' deaths.[191]

"Given such a disregard for human safety," Vaclav Smil writes, "it is hardly surprising that the operators of small mines pay scant attention to the environmental consequences of coal extraction. Predictable results include extensive destruction of arable and grazing land, accelerated erosion of topsoils, and increasing air and water pollution . . . Local air pollution has increased. . . . [A]ll of the country's industrial and urban regions have been experiencing unacceptably high air pollution levels, a state attributable to coal's dominance in China's energy supply, to inadequate coal cleaning capacities, and to inefficient combustion."[192]

While carbon dioxide from large and small power plants contributes to global warming, the fine particulates not only befoul the air in China's cities—seven of the world's ten most polluted cities are in China—but the soot enters global air currents and gets deposited around the world, including California. Air filters near Lake Tahoe in the California mountains are darkened with the soot, and most of the "fine particulate" air pollution in the Los Angeles area originates in China.[193]

International pressure to curb emissions of global warming gasses is increasing not just on China, but also on all countries that contribute to the problem (as we will see in a later section on the outcomes of the 2009 and 2010 global climate change conferences). China has indicated both that it is willing to lower emissions, and has begun to invest in wind farms and other so-called green technologies. Even so, China continues to build an average of one new coal-fired power plant per week, and to dam even more of its rivers. And that's even before considering cars and trucks.

Auto-Nation China

China's energy needs and consumption are surging not only because of its rapid transformation into an industrial powerhouse producing and exporting primary producer goods such as steel, cement, and aluminum, as well as boatloads of consumer electronics, clothing, and toys headed mostly toward the United States, but also because its car and truck fleet is growing rapidly. And not from imports. In 2009, China surpassed the United States as the world's largest auto manufacturer by building nearly 14 million cars; China's production is expected to reach 16 million units by 2012. To be sure, U.S. car production was down because of the global recession of 2008–2010, but China's output continues to surge, and it is not likely that the United States will produce 16 million passenger vehicles anytime soon. To move those cars around the country, China has been on a highway-building binge; the total miles of highway have doubled since just 2001 to twenty-three thousand, second only to the United States.[194]

Although some of China's cars are high-mileage, and although all-electric models are coming to market in 2010, accommodating all those cars has required the construction of a national interstate system and support of a global oil and gas industry, replete with exploration, drilling, refining, and distribution to keep the wheels turning; John R. McNeill has analyzed the environmental consequences of that system, and has found that China now contributes significantly to it.[195] About half of China's current demand is supplied by domestic oil fields, with intense exploration for more in the northwestern province of Xinjiang, but China has gone exploring throughout the world, concluding contracts with firms in Canada, Russia, Iraq, Venezuela, and the Sudan, among others.[196]

Here I will not dissect the environmental consequences of China's developing an auto industry and a car-dependent transportation model more like that of the United States than Japan or Western Europe. Suffice it to say that the car-choked streets and "freeways" circling China's cities contribute to local noxious hazes and to global warming, and that China is developing a "car culture" that looks a lot like that in the United States—symbolized most powerfully by the attempted purchase of General Motors' "Hummer" brand of SUV by a Chinese firm[197]—contributing significantly to China's urban air pollution.[198] Here, what I will describe a bit more is China's truck fleet and its contributions to China's pollution problems.

As in the United States, diesel-powered trucks range from smallish bobtail trucks delivering intercity supplies to large freighters carrying goods all over China on the new highway system. The roads of most cities are so clogged with traffic during the day that trucks are banned from entering city limits until night and early morning hours. "Every night, columns of hulking blue and red freight trucks invade China's major cities with a reverberating roar of engines and dark clouds of diesel exhaust so thick it dims headlights."[199]

For several reasons, China's trucks burn a very low-quality and pollutant-laden fuel that deposits soot on the doorsteps of China's urban residents, settlling on their furniture and getting sucked into their lungs. The most important reason is that the Chinese state still controls the price of oil, gas, and diesel fuel, and because it wants to keep the economy growing, it keeps fuel prices for trucks low, both to keep goods moving around the country and as a subsidy to China's export manufacturers. The state may set the price, but China's now-privatized oil firms, such as Sinopec, have to buy the raw material for refining, and so search for low-quality crudes with high sulfur content—130 times as high as diesel sold in the United States—to lower their costs. China's diesels also emit much more nitrogen dioxide, which contributes to photochemical smog, and soot, than U.S. or European models.[200] The pollution is worsened by diesels idling for hours waiting to get the green light to enter cities, or waiting in line to refuel.

The environmental and health consequences are predictable: "International experts say that hundreds of millions of Chinese are exposed every day to [a] potentially lethal mix of soot particles and smog." Refiners have no incentive to upgrade their facilities, because they already lose money on diesel fuel. Building trucks that meet higher pollution standards—which are known in China—doesn't happen because those trucks cost more than cheaper, dirtier ones, even though new. And the Chinese government has not been interested in imposing higher standards, apparently out of fear or concern that higher prices will prompt mob actions from unhappy farmers and truckers. [201]

China and Global Climate Change

Two propositions underlay international efforts to address the issue of global warming: (1) the world's atmosphere has become warmer over the past 150 years, largely because human activity has added to the load of the gases in our atmosphere that contribute to global warming, and (2) global temperatures will continue to rise without human action to slow and then reverse the output of those gases with unknown global environmental consequences. Mostly, the concern is about carbon dioxide released by the burning of fossil fuels for industry and transportation, but methane, too, is a powerful greenhouse gas released in massive amounts by the more than 1 billion cattle in the United States, and by decaying organic matter in Chinese rice paddies. And, as noted above, China has surpassed the United States as the world's largest emitter of the greenhouse gas carbon dioxide.

The first international attempt to set some limits—the 1999 Kyoto Protocol—had limited effect, in part because the United States did not sign the treaty and China was exempted from its strictures because it was a "developing," not already industrially developed, nation. But carbon emissions continue to rise, some think beyond levels at which the climate will remain similar to current conditions. Those concerns led to another attempt, the Copenhagen Summit, held in December 2009. Copenhagen did not result in a draft treaty or any other enforceable international agreement among the 193 countries attending, and many observers thought the international effort to control green house gases had collapsed.[202] After the 2010 summit in Cancun, Mexico, most countries and observers believe that international cooperation has been reestablished, and that progress in limiting green house gases can be made.

Going into the 2009 meeting, China's main contention was that because it is a late industrializer, it is not responsible for creating the global warming problem in the first place (that is attributed to Western Europe, the United States, and Japan), and hence should not be faced with the prospect of slowing or reducing its economic activity to decrease its output of greenhouse gases. Nonetheless, China does recognize the potential problems it, too, will face by global warming, and has offered to set a "binding goal" of cutting output of carbon dioxide per unit of economic growth to 40–45 percent below 2005 levels by 2020. It wants the already industrialized countries to cut emissions 40 percent below 1990 levels by 2020, and to provide China with low-carbon technologies.[203]

Additional measures that China's President Hu Jintao promised in a UN speech include intensifying "our effort to conserve energy and improve energy efficiency." Hu also pointed to China's efforts to develop renewable and nuclear energy, and its efforts to develop a "green economy" and to "energetically increase forest carbon [by] increas[ing] forest coverage by 40 million hectares and forest stock by 1.3 billion cubic meters by 2020 from the 2005 levels."[204]

Going into the 2010 Cancun summit, China was determined to make sure the world knew of its commitments and actions to control emission of global warming gases. The resulting agreements are complex and many issues remain to be resolved, in particular those having to do with the measurement and verification of each country's gas emissions, but China and the United States have both endorsed a draft agreement to cut carbon emissions.[205] China, in addition, is committed to vast reforestation efforts to sequester carbon.

There are reasons to be skeptical of those goals and promises, not the least of which is the actual history of forests in the PRC discussed earlier in this chapter. It is not that President Hu Jintao is not sincere, for he most certainly is that. In 2007 he launched an ambitious campaign known as "Green GDP" which included the environmental costs of China's rapid development in its national accounting of GDP. But the results were so astounding, with the recalculated rates of growth in some provinces then approaching zero, "that the project was banished to China's ivory tower . . . and stripped of official influence."[206]

Tibet, Glaciers, and Desertification

One of the reasons the Chinese government is concerned about global warming is the impact it might have on the Tibetan glaciers that feed not just the Yangzi River, but three more major rivers on which Southeast Asia and India also depend—the Mekong, the Salween, and the Brahmaputra, which feeds the Ganges. As historian Lee Feigon noted, "The confluence of all these rivers in one place means that the runoff from the mountains of Tibet affects the vegetation and agriculture of one of the most fertile and populated areas of the world, home to half the human race. Even minor ecological change in Tibet can therefore have a major impact on vast portions of humanity."[207]

Tibet is a high plateau whose capital, Llasa, sits at higher than 11,000 feet, and is a place characterized by high-altitude ecosystems. The entire region is ringed by mountains, with the Himalayan range, with its peaks well higher than 20,000 feet, the highest on earth. At such a height, there are just fifty frost-free growing days, so agriculture is limited, thus limiting population size—in today's borders, to a bit more than 2 million. Tibet was incorporated into the Chinese empire in the eighteenth century, and after a brief moment of independence in the early twentieth century, was reoccupied by Chinese forces in 1950. Tibet today is about the size of Western Europe, but as an independent empire was much larger, including regions that have subsequently become parts of Chinese provinces. The central and southern regions of Tibet supported agriculture, while Tibetans in other areas tended to be pastoral.

The Tibetan plateau is high and so large that outside of the earth's two polar regions, its glaciers hold the world's largest ice deposits. Global warming, though, has already reduced those glaciers by 7 percent over the past forty years. Chinese glaciologist Yan Tandong, whose research supplied that figure, thinks they will melt even faster over the next twenty-five years: "The retreat over the past 30 years equals the previous 200 years combined." By 2100, he predicts, half of China's glaciers will have melted. Because those glaciers feed the rivers on which over 2 billion Asians rely, Yan thinks that changes on the Tibetan plateau could "ultimately bring about an immeasurable crisis."[208] The rapidly melting glaciers have brought more water to some oases in Xinjiang, allowing pastures and lakes there to rejuvenate—at least for the time being, for although the amount of water has increased, the number of rivers has decreased.[209]

Like Inner Mongolia and other grassland areas discussed earlier in this chapter, Tibet is experiencing various levels of land degradation. The Chinese government thinks the main cause is overgrazing by pastoralists' herds (see also chapter 6). In response, the state has provided incentives to nomadic pastoralists to abandon their lifestyle and to move into the cities, or at least settle in fixed abodes. The government has fenced in some pastureland to keep herds from grazing on more fragile pastures. Whether grazing on hillsides above farmland, or near urban markets, larger numbers of goats, yaks, and sheep make the "thin glacial deposits of loess . . . prone to erosion. . . . [T]he quality of the grasses decreases as close grazing of the nutritious grasses leads to an invasion of the non-nutritious grasses."[210]

Since the economic reforms of 1982, market forces and the growth of an urban population, mostly in Llasa, has created a demand for increased energy, and that, too, is driving environmental change on the Tibetan plateau. Unfortunately, that demand is met mostly with local biomass, including wood from forests and peat dug up from the grasslands. Without coal or other fossil fuels, the only other option for energy production is to build dams for hydroelectricity, but there is considerable opposition to doing so. In pastoral areas, "the overuse of available brush and greater numbers of people lead to the increased collection of animal dung for use as fuel, so removing it from the traditional 'virtuous cycle' of use as fertilizer on the grassland."[211] Changes in land use and evidence of land degradation coupled with decreasing water supplies lead some to worry that large parts of the Tibetan plateau could be subject to processes of desertification.

As is not the case with Mongolia and the lower-elevation steppe regions, though, scientists think the cause of Tibet's desertification is higher temperatures and changing rainfall patterns brought on by global warming. Rain that used to fall in light sustained showers that nurtured the grasslands now falls in downpours, and the grasses dry up. Warming temperatures have begun to melt the permafrost, so that snowmelt and rainfall that stayed once near the surface and provided moisture for the grasses now sinks, lowering the water table for grasses. Creeping deserts and previously unknown dust storms now sweep the plateau.[212]

The Tibetan plateau is not just grassland, but the eastern and southern slopes of the plateau also contain some of China's largest forest reserves. The forests in the eastern part of Tibet called Kham that was incorporated into Sichuan province in the 1950s soon came under pressure from Chinese foresters. According to Lee Feigon, "At the beginning of the 1990s the southeastern parts of what was once Tibet still held some of the largest wooded tracts in China. The clear-cutting of these forests has already [by 1996] decimated half of them. The only saving grace is that the Tibetan loggers are still using handsaws and winches rather than chainsaws and heavy cranes, and are not plowing up the land with earthmovers."[213]

Another significant cause of ecological change in Tibet is the migration of Han Chinese settlers onto the plateau, following the implementation of economic development policies pursued by the central state. Chinese have known for a long time that the Tibet ecosystem is fragile, and that it can be easily disrupted. So, too, have Tibetans, who arguably developed agricultural and pastoral practices that were sustainable for many centuries.[214] In the early eighteenth century, the two thousand Manchu soldiers sent to subdue Tibet strained local resources and greatly inflated commodity prices. In the 1950s, the presence of Chinese Communist troops had a similar impact. Tibet thus has been an object of Chinese scientific research since the 1950s, with expeditions sent to study geographic, climatic, and biological conditions. In the early 1980s, China's Academia Sinica hosted an international scientific conference on Tibet and published two volumes of papers presented at the conference, providing the scientific basis for expanding the Han Chinese presence in Tibet, by, for example, studying the effects of altitude on Chinese subjects, and analyzing the highest points various plants and animals could flourish. As the vice president of the Academia Sinica said in his welcoming remarks, Chinese scientific studies of Tibet aimed "to find out about the scientific basis for the exploration and utilization of the natural resources" of Tibet.[215]

ENVIRONMENTAL PROTESTS, CONSCIOUSNESS, ACTIVISM AND MOVEMENTS

Pollution of China's air, water, and land[216]—along with the seizures of farmland and river valleys to build China's factories and the hydroelectric dams to power them—has spawned tens of thousands of protests, large and small, some effective, many futile, and has prompted environmental activism. Before turning to a broader analysis of Chinese reaction to environmental problems, I will recount several documented incidents that illustrate ordinary people's response to China's mounting environmental problems.

Lake Tai and Crusading Villager Wu Lihong

On the night of April 13, 2007, police and state security forces surrounded the house of Wu Lihong, climbed ladders to his second floor to pry open his windows, and arrested him. The charges may have been trumped up, for his real crime was a decade of environmental activism on behalf of villagers whose livelihoods and water supplies depended on Lake Tai, China's third-largest lake and centrally located in the industrially booming lower Yangzi delta region near Shanghai.

As in the Huai River valley, since the 1980s chemical factories have proliferated along the northern shore of Lake Tai, numbering 2,800 by the early 2000s. And again like the chemical plants in the Huai valley, those along Lake Tai dumped their industrial waste into Lake Tai. The acrid smell attracted the attention of Mr. Wu, who became nauseated in his evening walks and decided to document the evidence of factories dumping the waste into canals that went into Lake Tai. Over the years he amassed evidence of the environmental degradation of the lake, and between 1998 and 2006 he sent 200 letters and complaints to the provincial environmental protection agency alone.

Investigations of the pollution by national authorities in 2001 were managed so as to hide the pollution, so nothing was done. In 2005, Mr. Wu learned that the national press would be investigating, so he contacted China Central TV to promise them the real story; according to the *New York Times*, "Mr. Wu was the star of that report, an environmental celebrity," and in 2006 China's National People's Congress declared him an "Environmental Warrior" (note the use of a war metaphor). With the condition of Lake Tai continuing to deteriorate, in 2007 China's President Hu Jintao and Premier Wen Jiabao ordered a cleanup of Lake Tai by closing half of the most polluting chemical factories. Whether local officials carried out those orders is dubious, but in early 2007 Mr. Wu's village got a distinction as a "Model City for Environmental Protection," despite the city's history of contributing to the problem. That award so enraged Mr. Wu that he assembled evidence of continuing pollution, and prepared to bring the evidence to Beijing and possibly even sue the State Environmental Protection Administration.

That's when local police arrested him. In May of 2007, with Mr. Wu in custody, Lake Tai experienced a massive algae bloom caused by a toxic combination of nitrogen and phosphorous from fertilizer run-off, residues from chemical plants, and sewage. The 2 million residents of the city of Wuxi lost their drinking water, and neighboring cities shut their sluice and canal gates, creating a huge maritime logjam. The central government again intervened, insisting that local officials be fired or demoted. Meanwhile, with no objection from the central government, the prosecution, conviction, and sentencing of Mr. Wu continued; he was likely to be imprisoned until 2010. Local courts and officials are more often interested in protecting local factories for the revenues they generate than in prosecuting them for polluting people's drinking water supplies.[217]

For Clean Water, Peasants Protest a Fertilizer Factory in Gansu

The village of Dachuan in China's northwestern province of Gansu is a long way from Lake Tai, but villagers in that arid region shared with Mr. Wu and the villagers around Lake Tai the problem of their drinking water being polluted, and their animals being killed; the villagers of Dachuan also suspect that their imbibing of the water before understanding the full impact of its pollution was also the cause of a spike in miscarriages and stillborn babies. The story in Dachuan also enfolds over a much longer time period, going back at least four decades.

Somewhat ironically, the cause of the Dachuan villagers' problems was a fertilizer factory that produced much needed chemical fertilizer to raise the yields on their farms. Nonetheless, since the factory was built in 1971, it discharged its wastes into a small stream that runs through Dachuan and its fields before joining the Yellow River. By 1981, that section of the Yellow River, which provided Dachuan its drinking water, had become quite polluted. Blocked from taking legal action to defend their rights to clean water, the villagers began taking collective action such as blockading the factory gates to prevent deliveries. In the 1980s, birth defects and stillborn babies prompted members of the Kong lineage, which happened to claim descent from Confucius (whose family name was Kong), to seek medical attention. "Repeatedly, the doctors told inquirers that it was dangerous to drink from the polluted Yellow River. It could cause, the doctors said, miscarriages and stillbirths as well as mental retardation and stunted growth for children." The village head, who was a member of the Kong lineage and whose wife had had several miscarriages, became convinced that the polluted water was the cause of his personal agony, and led village protests against the factory. From the mid-1980s into the mid-1990s, villagers protested every year.

One incident in 1996 was documented by a visiting social scientist. When a flash flood destroyed a bridge over the stream widened by the polluting waste from the fertilizer plant, villagers marched to the factory gates and asked guards to tell factory officials to come out to talk with them and drink some of the polluted water they brought; the officials refused both. Villagers then began a ten-day barrage of the factory, pumping the polluted water over the wall and ultimately getting the factory officials to agree to repair the bridge and provide capital to sink a new well for safe drinking water.

According to Jun Jing, who observed the 1996 incident and wrote the article this synopsis is based on, the long-term struggle of the Dachuan villagers with the effects of the pollution from the fertilizer factory brought about a "cognitive revolution." According to Jun, "The cumulative effect of this process was a comprehensive understanding of the damaging consequences of water pollution, rather than just one aspect of the problems as in the past. Human health . . . remained the most contentious issue in each phase of the village's struggle against the factory."[218]

A Large-Scale "Environmental Mass Incident"

In April 2005 in a rural area called Dongyang in Zhejiang province, a large-scale mass incident involving thirty thousand to forty thousand villagers "shocked the Chinese authorities, news media, and the general public."[219] After several years of trying to get redress for damages to crops and poisoned air from thirteen chemical companies that had moved into the area in 1999, frustration started to boil in March of 2005 when villagers who tried to speak about the issue with their mayor on "Dongyang Mayor Reception Day" were turned away. Thousands of villagers then built bamboo tents to blockade the industrial zone, only to have hundreds of police and government officials raid the encampment. Their ramshackle blockade nonetheless continued. On April 10, an attempt by 3,500 police and government officials to forcibly remove the bamboo tents and remove the protestors resulted in thirty thousand to forty thousand additional villagers joining in the fray. Dozens were injured, two claimed dead, and several villagers jailed.[220]

Faced with what was a very large mass incident that might threaten state security, the Ministry of Environmental Protection ordered the offending plants shut down or relocated, and numerous officials punished. Additionally, a group of activists in Hangzhou formed a new NGO called "Green Watch" to monitor industrial pollution in Zhejiang province.

Analyst Ma Tianjie places the 2005 Dongyang mass incident in a larger perspective, which also helps us to better understand the three other incidents profiled here. Digging through official data and comments from the Minister for Public Security and the deputy minister of the Ministry of Environmental Protection, Ma reports that rural "mass incidents" in general had jumped from about ten thousand a year in 1994 to seventy-four thousand in 2004.[221] Of those, Ma estimates, five thousand were environmental mass incidents. Ma also helpfully cites a Chinese government source that defined "mass incidents" and classified them by size into four categories from the smallest (five to thirty people) to the largest (more than one thousand people). In other words, at the same time as these three environmentally related incidents were being documented, an additional five thousand "mass incidents" that were not documented erupted across China.[222]

But those figures represent only the tip of the iceberg of Chinese citizen concern and activity arising because of environmental issues. The Ministry of Environmental Protection reported that "environmental disputes" increased from fifty-one thousand in 2004 to 128,000 in 2005. And "environmental complaints" (by letter or by person) increased from 370,000 in 2001 to 616,000 in 2006.[223] These numbers indicate the scale of environmental problems being experienced by the Chinese people in the new millennium.

As Ma notes, environmental degradation thus has become one of the major causes of conflict between the rural Chinese populace and the Chinese state, causing the state some worry, and contributing (as we will see) to changes in state environmental policy. But the underlying cause of rural pollution problems and environmental degradation is not simply China's rapid industrialization, a population growing past 1.3 billion increasingly consumer-driven people, or global demand for Chinese products. Rather, over the past thirty years a significant cause has been the particular constellation of political and economic forces that structure how China industrializes and deals with its associated environmental problems.

Mostly, the explanation revolves around a paradox. Although the People's Republic of China remains a one-party state ruled by the Communist Party, the national center has sent out conflicting signals about industry and environment to the localities where those two interests collide most often. One the one hand, the national state remains a developmental state that has seen its national economy grow at close to double-digit growth since the 1980s, and which recently projected 8 percent annual growth for the foreseeable future. It has also empowered factory owners and local authorities to make that growth happen, and hence to form close alliances between local government and business interests who collude to hide or overlook national environmental standards when building and operating plants, and to cover up offenses when the central government or the media catches wind of them. In a few instances, as in Gansu, there were particular reasons why local leaders sided with rural residents against the factories, and have won some concessions.

Mostly though, in Ma Tianjie's words, "By welcoming heavily polluting industry in a densely populated agricultural region, the local government was behaving like a classic 'entrepreneurial government,' prioritizing revenue generation (the role of an enterprise) over environmental protection (the role of a regulator/public good provider)" in order to increase local tax revenue and to receive kudos and promotions from those higher up.[224] Another study also showed that the mayor's office, generally the place where conflicts would get ironed out, "often favors industrial growth over pollution abatement when economic and environmental goals conflict."[225] Outcomes favoring industrial growth and the resulting pollution and environmental degradation over environmental protection were predicted in the 1990s. According to Abigail Jahiel, "the ethos of the reforms and the political economy constructed to support reform goals are antithetical to solving China environmental problems."[226]

State Responses to Environmental Problems

Thus it is not the case that China's national government has not intended to address its growing environmental problems. Indeed, as the references in this chapter to various environmental protection bureau make clear, China has in fact established environmental protection agencies and begun to create the legal framework within which they can function—whether they do or not depends in large part on the political structures within which they operate.[227]

The first environmental law was promulgated on a trial basis in 1979 as Deng Xiaoping's reform era began to dig out from under the Mao regime. A decade later the law was amended and the trial status removed, and the first National Environmental Protection Agency was created. In 1998 it became the State Environmental Protection Agency (SEPA), and was elevated to a ministerial level in the Chinese state bureaucracy. It was staffed with but a few hundred people, and was charged only with overseeing national-level agencies and programs; as Ma and Ortolano observe, "its role in day-to-day implementation of environmental regulations is limited."[228] In March 2008, SEPA was upgraded to the Ministry of Environmental Protection.[229]

The list of environmental protection laws adopted by China's National Peoples Congress is long, as is the list of "action plans" and "five-year plans" for pollution abatement and environmental protection.[230] Several have been cited in the earlier section on deforestation. Others include the 2006 "National Rural Environmental Protection Action Plan" released by SEPA which including going after poor sanitation, the movement of polluting factories to rural areas, soil contaminated by excess fertilizers and pesticides, and water shortages and contamination.[231]

However, responsibility for enforcement of these national laws and regulations has been decentralized down to the provincial, municipal, and county level, most of which have established Environmental Protection Bureaus, or EPBs. These local-level EPBs receive no funding from SEPA (now MEP), and must generate their own. According to Jonathan Schwartz, "EPBs must therefore rely more heavily on levies and fees collected from polluting factories under their jurisdiction. However, such reliance presents EPBs with a quandary: their task is to lower pollution output, yet success will drive their main revenue source out of existence. Herein lies a perverse disincentive to enthusiastic environmental protection."[232]

The basic problem for China thus has been the disconnect between this national-level structure, and policy implementation on the ground (or in the air, and in the water). As Ma and Ortolando pondered, "Why has China's environment continued to degrade even though the country has a sophisticated set of regulatory programs?"[233] Their basic answer echoes that proposed above: little or no local enforcement.[234] This is where citizen action groups known as environmental "non-governmental organizations," or environmental NGOs, have come into play.

Green NGOs

China's first environmental NGO, Friends of Nature, was founded in 1994. A decade later, SEPA had registered two thousand, but others think that there are only forty or so active. Earlier in this chapter we have encountered two additional ones, Green Watershed and the Nujiang River NGOs.[235]

All Chinese NGOs, including the environmental ones, operate in a structure quite different from those in the United States, Europe, or Japan. Although called "non-governmental," a Chinese NGO is in fact required to be registered, and for it to be registered, it has to be sponsored by a Chinese governmental organization. For the environmental NGOs, that sponsor mostly has been SEPA (now MEP). According to Schwartz, China's NGOs are not only constrained "by the nature of their dependence on government benevolence," but also by the lack of trained staff, access to independent sources of funding, and access to actual data and reports that the government classifies as secret.[236]

In addition to NGOs, China also has what may appear to be an oxymoron, the "government NGO," or GONGO, which gets funding and support from a governmental agency, but operates somewhat independently. Additionally, there are now semi-NGOs that have been established within universities. Two important environmental ones are the Beijing Environment and Development Institute (BEDI) at People's University in Beijing, and the Center for Legal Assistance to Pollution Victims (CLAPV) at Beijing University Center for Law and Politics.[237]

China's environmental activists apparently could use the legal help. As we saw with the case of Wu Lihong above, he did threaten to sue the SEPA and perhaps others, and with the hundreds of thousands of environmental complaints filed, there are a large number of potential lawsuits that could be filed. Legal recourse to sue polluters only opened up in 2007. From then until 2009, though, only individual citizens could sue polluters. As is the case in other countries, the amount of money and technical expertise required often is well beyond the reach of ordinary citizens. But in late July 2009, two of China's provincial courts agreed to hear two cases brought by an environmental NGO called the All-China Environmental Federation; notably, both of these courts are in the Lake Tai region where Wu Lihong got arrested and jailed trying to stop the pollution of the lake.[238]

Environmentalism and Democracy

The Chinese state approved the creation of NGOs not to establish a citizen-based opposition, but rather as a means to better link citizens to the state. Because of the contradiction between national environmental goals and their problematic local implementation, the government had an interest in opening up some political space for environmental NGOs to operate to apply pressure at the local level. The Chinese government does not see these organizations as expressions of democracy, or as precursors to democratization, despite appearances to the contrary. As one SEPA official told Schwartz, "Westerners view Chinese environmental NGOs as a path to greater public participation in a wide range of issues, a crack in the door of eventual democratization."[239] Schwartz notes that the Chinese state is very well aware of that conception, if not possibility, and "makes every effort to ensure that no such democratization develops."[240]

The arrest and jailing of activists calling for more open democratic reform, most recently of Liu Xiaobo,[241] serves as a constant reminder to environmental activists of the limits on their activities. Nonetheless, some commentators have seen in both environmental campaigns and the growing number of green NGOs the beginning of an "environmental movement." But even if China's nascent environmentalism represents a new social movement, it is one that operates within very prescribed limits. According to Guobin Yang, "the environmental movement no longer clearly or mainly targets the state . . . [nor does it] directly challenge political power. It aims to raise environmental consciousness, promote cultural change, and solve environmental problems."[242] If environmentalists cannot directly challenge the state or advocate for the democratic reforms necessary to more effectively protect China's environment, according to Guobin Yang, "activists in the environmental movement consciously try to effect gradual change through practicing—not preaching—democratic values, such as citizen participation, self-responsibility, and reasoned debates."[243]

Return to the "Angry" River

Given the constraints that Chinese citizens and NGOs operate under in trying to effect environmental protection, the results so far in holding off the dams in the Three Parallel Rivers Protected Area, especially on the Nu ("Angry") River, are impressive. No doubt the combination of savvy NGO activism that included extensive media coverage both nationally and internationally, along with the involvement of the United Nations and other international NGOs, caught the attention of Chinese President Hu Jintao and Premier Wen Jiabao, giving them adequate ammunition to hold off the hydropower companies and their advocates in the Chinese government. Whether the halt is permanent or merely a temporary respite while the dam-building forces regroup remains to be seen. But the battle over the Nu River did generate some very interesting debates that reveal the current state of Chinese consciousness about the environment and the relationship of humans to it, as well as the relationship between environmental protection and democracy, that is worthwhile examining as a conclusion to this chapter.

The way the issue of damming the Nu River ultimately was framed may not augur well for the ultimate outcome. The prime figure was a scholar named Fang Shimin, a biochemist and physicist with a Ph.D. from Michigan State University. According to Andrew Mertha, Fang is "something of an apostate" who "has become a vitriolic critic of those who, in his view, do not reason rationally and scientifically."[244] In Fang's view, environmentalists "worship nature" at the expense of the needs of people. A wide-ranging debate in China over "rationalism vs. emotionalism" first opened after the Indian Ocean tsunami of 2004 when one of the leading environmentalist-journalists, Wang Yongchen, took on a member of the Chinese Academy of Science who argued, to quote the title of his article, that "Humans Need Not Worship Nature."

Commenting on the thirty-plus articles that this initial exchange generated, Fang Shimin said the bulk was biased in favor of the "nature worshippers" such as Wang Yongchen, who he charged anthropomorphizes nature and espouses fake science, as opposed to those who practice "real science," as he does. He lit into Wang: "The gist of Wang's 'nature worship' lies in fearing nature, and preventing humans from learning from it, thus being able to utilize, and change nature. This is in conflict with scientific thinking, research and utility."[245] Emotional environmentalists "used bullshit" to "speak outside their area of expertise."[246] If the project of Chinese modernity is the human domination of nature, then these modernist experts exercise their power to silence opposition to that definition of modernity.

Fang not only tried to marginalize Wang Yongchen and "environmentalists" in the debate over dams on the Nu River, he also tried to demolish the ideas and reputation of the scientist who has the greatest knowledge of the Nu River, Professor He Daming, the head of Asian International Rivers Center at Yunnan University in Kunming. According to Mertha, "He has been active in researching rivers in Yunnan for decades and has perhaps more information on the Nu River than any other single person in China."[247] Although He Daming at first voiced opposition to the Nu River dams—and his views were very influential—he became very quiet as the battle ensued, taking the advice of Yunnan government officials, and perhaps university officials too, to keep quiet. "He was being watched by the local authorities who were waiting for him to make a mistake," one that could ruin his career or land him in jail.

But He Daming did publish enough scientific reports to become the object of a fierce attack by Fang Shimin in a speech at Yunnan University. Fang ridiculed He's use of the term "original ecological status river": "Is he making up a new concept so that he can be dressed up as a founder of a new science, and then apply for research funds from the government?" Fang pointed out that the indigenous peoples had burned lots of forest in the gorges for their shifting agriculture. Also, Fang lit into another of He Daming's concepts: "vertical forest and valley area biodiversity," asserting that he had never heard of the terms before and taunting him for making up a new one just to get funding: "Is Professor He going to create 'forest and valley-ology' and become the founder of that research program?"[248]

With the scientific expert on the Nu River marginalized and silenced, the pro-development forces now claim to have science on their side. For those environmental groups that might want access to those scientific studies, the studies have been classified as secret, for "internal use only" (the Chinese term is *neibu*), the release of which type of materials has been used to prosecute offenders for exposing state secrets. That makes it much easier for the pro-development forces to declare that their position, based on "objective, scientific" criteria, is strong. According to Mertha, "This resonates with the Marxist undertow of Chinese political discourse, since Marxism has always been regarded as a 'scientific' theory."[249] The apparent victory of pro-development forces thus disempowers green NGOs and others who question the environmental wisdom of China's unchecked economic developmental trajectory, and places the protection of the biodiversity of the Three Parallel Rivers Protected Region into question.

Can China Go Green?

That question has been asked a lot recently by journalists, analysts, and political pundits. Leading the pack has been American journalist Thomas Friedman of *The New York Times*. In numerous articles and a recent book, he both posed the question and provided evidence.[250] Writing in late 2009, he wrote that "the most important thing to happen in the last eighteen months was that Red China decided to become Green China,"[251] apparently referring to statements in China's Eleventh Five-Year Plan. In other columns, he cited evidence both that Chinese engineers and entrepreneurs were developing so-called green technologies such as solar panels and wind turbines for generating electricity,[252] and that some local Communist Party leaders want to follow a less-polluting way to industrialize.[253]

In the *Wall Street Journal*, Shai Oster wrote an article about Chinese coal-fired electrical plant engineers trying to find ways to keep carbon from being released into the atmosphere while still burning it to generate electricity. These engineers are "part of a broader effort by China to introduce green technology to the world's fastest growing industrial economy—a mission so ambitious it could eventually reshape the business"[254] of coal-fired electricity generation. The BBC also produced a two part series entitled "Can China Go Green?" in which the reporter, "amidst the toxic power stations and burgeoning numbers of cars . . . finds some extraordinary and pioneering green solutions."[255] Friedman also cited the example of a manufacturer of solar panels whose factory happens to sit on (and probably contributes to polluting) Lake Tai. And as noted above, China's wind farms require the construction of coal-fired plants as backup.[256]

Perhaps more than noting a significant change in the pattern of China's pattern of industrialization which has relied on cheap, polluting coal and factories producing vast quantities of stuff for export and dumping the industrial waste into China's land, air, and water—from which a real change would be a welcome sign—these reported anecdotes are being used to cajole and frighten U.S. policymakers into supporting American "green technology" so the United States does not fall behind China or lose the "green technology" edge. To that extent, these views of China continue a centuries-long tradition of seeing China as "the other": to eighteenth-century Enlightenment philosophes as an example of "enlightened despotism" in contrast to their own unenlightened despots; to Malthus as an example of uncontrolled population growth in contrast to the more rational English; to Marx as Asiatic stagnation in contrast to the ruthless innovation of European capitalism, to the post–World War II West as the "communist threat from Red China," and now as a "green threat" to American global supremacy.[257]

But the crowning glory of the ironies rolled up in the stories of China going green faster than the United States or Europe is that so-called green technologies, such as batteries for electric cars and efficient lightbulbs, and especially large wind turbines, all rely on a group of seventeen very rare earth elements, two of which (dysprosium and terbium) are in very short supply and for the moment are found exclusively in China. That might appear to give China the decisive advantage in developing the so-called green technologies and to put a significant fear in the minds of U.S., European, and Japanese policymakers. But here is where the story returns to the main lines of China's environmental degradation developed in this chapter. There is "Just one problem: The elements come from . . . some of the most environmentally damaging mines in [China], in an industry dominated by criminal gangs." In one village, "miners scrape off the topsoil and shovel golden-flecked clay into dirt pits, using acid to extract the rare earths. The acids ultimately wash into streams and rivers, destroying rice paddies and fish farms and tainting water supplies."[258]

Toward a "Harmonious Relationship with Nature"?

As China's environmental degradation and the social and political struggles arising from environmental issues like the pollution of Lake Tai or the preservation of the biodiversity of the Three Parallel Rivers have sharpened, the Chinese Communist state has increasingly called for "harmony." Given the disastrous flooding of 1998, the almost annual drying-up of the Yellow River 500 miles or so from the sea, and planning for the 2008 Olympics, it is not surprising that China's Tenth Five-Year Plan (2001–5) gave "priority to environmental protection," in the words of China's *People's Daily* newspaper. The article quoted an "academician" saying that the "plan describes a beautiful picture for us: a prospering economy, controlled population, well-preserved resources and beautiful environment."[259] In 2003, conservation became "an integral part" of China's elementary school curriculum, and in 2006, the Chinese Communist party proclaimed "promoting harmony between man and nature" an important step in building a "harmonious society." One might hope so, but changing the direction of China's four thousand–year environmental history will require more than repeating nostrums about the "harmony between man and nature."

CONCLUSION

The environmental history of the People's Republic of China documents massive changes and challenges. Deforestation continued through the end of the last millennium before logging in the upper reaches of the Yangzi prompted the state to ban the practice. Although that ban appears to be enforced, illegal imports of timber from Burma, Indonesia, and Russia have picked up. Privatization of land under the Deng Xiaoping regime, coupled with beliefs about "scientific management," have enclosed previously open grasslands, and degradation of vast stretches of the steppe are degrading and becoming desert.

China's wildlife populations continue to decline, with the majority of species native to China now pushed into a remote yet contested corner of Yunnan in China's southwest. All but one of China's majors rivers have been dammed to provide reservoirs for farming and drinking water and, more recently, to produce electricity to fuel China's rapid economic development. Hydroelectric power has never been adequate for China's energy needs, and with those needs now growing exponentially, so too is the burning of coal from China's vast reserves. The rapid development of a personal car culture on top of a diesel-fueled truck fleet to move goods around China as well as to port cities for export has added petroleum to the mix of fossil fuels burned, and in such great quantities over the last decade that China has surpassed the United States as the world's largest contributor of greenhouse gases to the global atmosphere.

Not surprisingly, and somewhat encouraging, in light of the absence of state guarantees of freedom of thought and action, environmental groups have sprung up to do battle with local and regional governments whose economic development plans contribute to the pollution of China's land, water, and air. The central government, too, is concerned about environmental issues, having created the State Environmental Protection Agency and its successor the Ministry of Environmental Protection and encouraging press exposés of abuses. In the last two Five-Year Plans, environmental protection has been featured and quantitative goals for investments have been set. "Conservation" has been added to the elementary school curriculum, and the Party-State has begun unfurling banners promoting both a harmonious society and "harmony between man and nature."

This formulation appears to hark back to the ancient Chinese notions of the "unity of Heaven and humanity" and the "cosmic correspondence" among Heaven, earth, and mankind that lay behind the "Mandate of Heaven." And just as those ideas about the relationship between humans and the environment may have been articulated at times when such a relationship had been disturbed, so, too, is it apparent that the massive environmental crisis and the thousands of mass actions protesting the effects of that crisis is the context for understanding calls for "harmony."

The larger question of changes and continuities over the course of China's long history will be taken up more in the conclusion to the book, but here I want to consider the changes and continuities during the history of the People's Republic, and a bit more broadly over the past century or so. On the one hand, political, social, and economic changes have been dramatic. The last imperial dynasty gave way to the short-lived Republic before social and geopolitical forces gave rise to a successful Chinese Communist movement that seized the levers of state and has operated from 1949 to this day. China under both the Mao regime (1949–76) and the Deng era (1979–present) has pursued the most rapid economic development possible.

And yet the scope and pace of environmental changes do not necessarily or easily fall within those usual patterns of historical periodization. There are at least three ways that an environmental perspective can help us see the history of the People's Republic in a new light. First, the Chinese Communists came to power in the midst of a massive environmental crisis where the nutrients available to be recycled into agriculture to support the human population were declining along with a degraded landscape. The avoidable and disastrous famine accompanying the Great Leap Forward (1959–62) revealed a countryside so depleted of nutrients and so void of space for wildlife that there was little evidence that the millions of starving people could find even rodents or bugs to subsist on. Until the availability of industrially produced chemical fertilizers, China's Communist rulers lived within the same biological constraints as their imperial forerunners, and resorted to the same tactics as they had to increase the human food supply—bringing more land under the plow by removing more forest and plowing up grasslands. Of course, the massive application of chemical fertilizer, in particular of nitrogen-based compounds, may have increased agricultural yields, but those compounds now run off from farms to pollute water supplies.

Second, the resilience of China's environment had been sapped by the preceding millennia of Chinese agricultural-based economic development. That can been seen most clearly in the long process by which swamps, lakes, and river deltas had been transformed from natural reservoirs for China's vast and complex hydrological systems into flood-prone farms and villages. With the natural sponges filled in, China has had to produce huge numbers (at last count more than eighty thousand) of dams to store and release water for agriculture and drinking water. The fragilities of that engineered hydrological system are periodically manifested in dam failures and the massive damage that follows in their wake, and in periodic floods occasioned by heavy (but not unexpected) dumps of monsoonal rain.

Third, the economic, scientific, and ecological presumptions and actions of the People's Republic maintain significant continuities with the broader modernist project equally embraced by the Guomindang leaders of Republican China. They, too, thought both that the environment existed to serve human needs and that on behalf of the state modern rational science and management could control nature, making it yield greater treasures that could be taxed without depleting the resources. The major difference between Republican and Communist China is that the Communist state has created the levers of power to implement its modernist agenda.

And so China today is shaking off the shackles and limitations of the biological old regime, pressing headlong into a fossil-fueled and chemically fertilized future, with all the environmental challenges and promises that come with an industrialized and urbanized world.

Chapter 8

Conclusion

China and Its Environment in World Historical Perspective

Even as China's central government has begun calling for "harmony between man and nature" and implementing environmental protection laws, reports continue that "pollution worsens despite new efforts to control it."[1] This disconnect between an apparent environmental consciousness and the reality of actions that continue to worsen the situation harkens back to a period in Chinese history 2,500 years earlier. Then, as we saw in chapter 2, the North China plain was showing clear evidence of deforestation, marshes and other wetlands were being filled in to create more farmland, some species were becoming scarce, and various thinkers proposed that governments protect natural resources by limiting access to them in order to shepherd those resources for strategic use against other states. Similar worries about resource exhaustion arose amid the mounting environmental crisis in the nineteenth century (chapter 6).

The similarities are sobering. China's current environmental problems have raised popular consciousness and ire, as well as government regulations and actions. Moreover, as in past times of environmental crisis, worries now also are being voiced about whether China is reaching the limits of resource use, especially of water and land.[2] These times of environmental crisis in Chinese history all resulted in calls to establish (or maintain) harmonious relations with nature. That never happened.

Over the millennia covered in this book, the human population of China has accounted for between 25 and 40 percent of the world's total, and today totals more than 1.3 billion people.[3] On its own terms and as a portion of the world's total, China's population was and is large. In comparison with the United States, which has about the same landmass as China, it would be as if there were an additional billion people living in the U.S. It does not take too much to imagine the scope of environmental challenges the United States would face. And so with China.

China's rulers are faced with the problem of balancing economic policies that can improve the life chances and standard of living of its people, with policies that acknowledge and begin to ameliorate its deteriorating environmental underpinnings. As we saw in chapter 7, there is now evidence of both trends. Two recent developments have pointed to the problem of interpreting changes and continuities in China's environmental history, and the variable role of humans and nature in causing environmental change. The first, released by the International Energy Agency, reported that by 2010 China had surpassed the United States as the world's largest consumer of energy. According to the agency's chief economist, this change represents "a new age in the history of energy."[4]

It is indeed big news that China's energy consumption has exceeded that of the United States. For most of the previous century, the United States has consumed the most energy of any country in the world. Other historians have noted the global significance of that fact, both for the industrial and military power that accrued to the United States, but also for the global warming gases that its factories and power plants spewed into the atmosphere. All of those now sit in China's lap as well.

The second recent event was that "record-breaking storms" in the summer of 2010 sent huge amounts of water coursing into the Yangzi River drainage system, raising both water levels in the gigantic reservoir created by the Three Gorges Dam, and fears that the dam will not be able to prevent flooding in central China. The government also ordered that emergency flood preparations begin in the Huai River basin where 50 percent more rain has fallen than in previous yeasr.[5] Again, change or continuity? Human or natural causes? As I argued in chapter 6, flooding is more the result of China's long history of deforestation and the declining ability of its hydrological systems to absorb periodic spikes in rainfall, no matter how "record breaking," although ENSO events and cycles do affect the amount rainfall brought to China in the annual monsoon.

MAIN THEMES IN CHINA'S ENVIRONMENTAL HISTORY

Changes in Land Use and Land Cover

Beyond contemporary interest, then, we can now place developments in contemporary China into a context of its much longer environmental history. There can be no doubt that there has been extensive environmental change in China over the past ten thousand years, and that most of that change has been caused by human action. And until recently, most of that action has been aimed at expanding the amount of China's landmass devoted to agriculture. To be sure, agriculture itself was made possible in the first instance by the mutation of the perennial, wild forms of millet and rice into annuals that depended on humans for their propagation. The changes in land use that then began with the Neolithic agricultural revolution effected significant change in land cover, changing much of China's landscape from natural into agro-ecosystems.[6]

Climate Change

In addition, China's climate has in fact gotten progressively cooler and drier so that even without humans around, the rhinoceroses, crocodiles, tigers, and elephants that inhabited what were then the forests on the North China plain four thousand years ago most likely would not be there today. But they are no longer to be found further south from the Yangzi River valley down to Guangdong and Guangxi provinces where climatic conditions would have enabled them to survive. And the reason for that is that the Chinese first cleared the North China plain for their style of cereal-based farming, then expanded south and west, scraping off whatever forests were in their way. Such massive deforestation counts as one of the largest sustained human efforts in world history.[7]

Water Control

Attempts at water control also absorbed vast amounts of human energy and effort. From the first dikes built along the Yellow River some 2,500 years ago to the Grand Canal and its alteration of the hydrology throughout central and north China to the more than eighty thousand dams built on all but one of China's major rivers over the past 60 years, Chinese hands have been guided by ideas about how to "control water." Paradoxically, as we have seen, nearly all such attempts to "control" water have proven more or less transient as new and even larger challenges arose in the wake of control efforts. Some historians have seen grand "hydrological cycles" in these efforts, often corresponding to the waxing and waning of dynasties. In these interpretations, new dynasties could mobilize the resources necessary to address water issues, and to gain some control over the problems caused by flooding or drought, only to find that the funds, time, and effort put toward maintaining those systems inevitably deteriorated over the centuries until renewed floods and droughts contributed to the fall of the dynasty.[8] ENSO events and cycles may have periodically coincided with these cycles of periodic flood and drought, but the effects of those "natural" disasters surely were mediated through human institutions.

Deforestation

Where China might have experienced hydrological cycles, China's deforestation was a much more progressive, relentless line of march over the past four thousand years. There may have been some pauses in the intensity of the removal of forests for farms, but the push had much force behind it. An interlocking feedback loop between the needs of an aggressive state for more resources to command in its wars against others and a steadily growing population of Han Chinese farmers seeking new lands continually pushed Chinese into frontier areas until the limits of expansion of its empire were reached during the eighteenth century.

Colonization

Much of what counts as China's environmental history thus involves the encounter of Han Chinese with new and unfamiliar environments, landscapes, and peoples. Those encounters were never easy, nor one-way. The myriad ways in which Han Chinese adapted to new environments, and adopted some or all of the techniques the peoples already there had created to obtain their sustenance, probably will never be known, largely because the records we have of those encounters mostly were written and left by Chinese. The overall outcome of those encounters, though, is clear enough: cereal farming on small family plots, supported by the administrative and military power of the Chinese state, spread throughout Chinese-controlled territory.

By the time the Chinese empire reached its maximum size in the eighteenth century, it spanned a vast and biologically diverse territory, ranging from the grasslands to the north and west and the densely forested northeast, to the tropical island of Hainan and the ecologically diverse hills and mountains of Yunnan in the southwest. The Chinese state therefore had under its command, if not its control, a massive array of resources that few states before or since have been able to tap. That diversity lent strength and resiliency to the empire, and China's rulers extracted and used those resources to the fullest extent possible. Nonetheless, one of the consequences of China's colonizing project was not the protection and preservation of that biological richness, but its simplification into fewer and fewer ecosystems.

The Simplification of Ecosystems

The overriding trend in China's environmental history over the past four thousand years has been one of the simplification of natural ecosystems into a particular kind of Chinese agro-ecosystem. China's human population may have accounted for a significant proportion of the world's, but the interaction between those people and the environment began to assume a self-replicating and identifiably Chinese form at least 2,500 years ago, and maybe much earlier. Solar energy that had been captured by plants and animals in hundreds of varying ecosystems supporting a vast diversity of life increasingly came to be claimed by crops planted and harvested by humans. That loss of natural biodiversity was accompanied by a similar loss of human cultural and political diversity as well. With the possible exception of the example provided by the Akha people in China's far southwest (chapter 7), these interactions leading to simplification continue to be played out today, especially among the formerly pastoral peoples of Inner Mongolia, the various peoples in the southwestern province of Yunnan, and in Tibet and Xinjiang in China's far west.

To be sure, changes in land use—from forest to farm, or from pastureland to farm, for instance—do result in significant environmental changes, as we have seen throughout this book, including the elimination of habitat for numerous species and then their extinction or local extirpation, as well as general erosion and desertification. But the simplification of natural environments into a much smaller number of agro-ecosystems, still leaves natural processes intact, if attenuated and captured for human purposes. Except perhaps for land that has become desert with few if any nutrients remaining, most land given over to agriculture is sufficiently resilient that anthropogenic processes of degradation have the prospect of being halted or reversed.

The Sustainability of Agriculture

Indeed, one of the paradoxes of Chinese history has been that while the degradation of its environment has been long-term and palpable, the Chinese farming system itself was remarkably sustainable. Land that was cleared for farms two thousand years ago is still farmed, and swamps and marshes that were drained and enclosed in polders a thousand years ago still produce rice. Historically, Chinese farmers attained that productivity and maintained the viability of their farmland by regular and extensive recycling of nutrients lost to the soil that were deposited nightly in urban bedchambers and public privies and brought back to fertilize farmland. Nonetheless, by the nineteenth century and certainly by the twentieth, there is clear evidence that that system was leading to the progressive, if exceedingly slow, loss of nutrients. By 1950 nearly all of China's farmland was deficient in most nutrients essential for plant growth. Entropy could not be held off forever, although new chemical fertilizers have given Chinese farms a new lease on life. I fear, though, that the combination of China's very long history of environmental degradation, coupled with the vast amounts of industrial and chemical fertilizer pollutants released into the land, water, and air over the past thirty years, may have created a situation in which China's natural environment has progressively lost its resilience and ability to recover from the damages inflicted by humans.

The Problem of 1949: 3,000 Years vs. 30

Among the changes in Chinese history, few appear to be as large as the establishment of the People's Republic of China in 1949. The creation of the PRC marked a significant change in modern Chinese history, ushering in an era dominated by a state strong enough to implement policies pursing the most rapid industrialization possible. Most historians thus see 1949 as significant not just in terms of Chinese history but world history as well.[9]

To be sure, the new Chinese Communist state carried out a thoroughgoing social revolution, centralized political power in its hands, and began to rapidly industrialize, all in the name of achieving socialism. But in terms of China's environmental history, 1949 itself may not have marked that large or immediate a change. Some environmental historians have begun to argue that one important way to periodize human interaction with nature is in terms of the concept of an "energy regime," or the primary ways in which a society taps and utilizes energy.[10] For nearly the entire period covered by this book, Chinese obtained their energy largely from biomass: wood for fuel to keep warm, to refine and forge metal implements, and to boil water to make textiles or concentrate salt; and from crops grown to provide food, mostly for humans. The natural processes of plants stored solar energy until it could be released for human use. The Chinese became very efficient users of stored biomass, but over time those stocks of energy dwindled and became in short supply, both in north China by the eleventh century when coal saw increasing use, and by the nineteenth century when deforestation led to growing fuel shortages. Wind and water, too, were used as sources to power vessels and mechanisms, but like biomass were limited to capturing diurnal and annual flows of solar energy. For the most part, work was performed by human muscle, although by 1200 BCE horses added additional muscle-power, as did water buffalo pulling plows through rice paddies from about 1000 CE on. In this biological old regime, the "prime movers" were human and animal muscle.[11]

The Chinese Communist revolution of 1949 initially did little to change those dynamics. The Chinese Communists may have launched urban industrialization efforts that did succeed to a certain degree, but the limitations of the biological old regime dictated that they intensify their exploitation of energy sources from forest reserves, just as Chinese in past millennia had done. Improvements to agricultural productivity were hampered by the lack of modern fertilizer inputs, and those were not available to the Chinese Communist state until a breakthrough in relations with the United States opened opportunities to import that technology in the mid-1970s. Like other modern industries begun by the Communists, chemical fertilizers relied on electricity produced largely by coal-fired power plants. But unlike other industries, chemical fertilizers removed the ecological ceiling of the biological old regime against which plans for even more rapid industrialization had stalled. These changes coincided with the transition from China's Mao years to the Deng Xiaoping era, to which most analysts attribute (for better or worse) China's dramatic industrial development since 1980. But without chemical fertilizers to increase agricultural output, Deng Xiaoping's exhortations to "Get Rich" would have floundered just as assuredly as did Mao Zedong's calls for "A Great Leap Forward" into the socialist future.

China's Ecological Resilience

The use of chemical fertilizers to increase agricultural output is but one example of a solution to an environmentally imposed constraint on human activity that created a whole new set of ecological problems that succeeding generations inherited and had to deal with. Others include the diking of the Yellow River, which raised the river bed and contributed to hydrological problems on the North China plain; the Grand Canal, which channeled natural river systems but intensified ecological issues and added others, such as salinization of the soil; removing forests for farmland, which contributed to erosion in the highlands and ultimately to a growing energy crisis in the biological old regime; plowing up grasslands to plant more food and to colonize new regions for the Chinese empire; and poldering south China's river valleys and deltas. Each of those human actions had an ecological consequence and sent China's history into new directions and with different dynamics.

Depending on the sensitivity and resilience of the land, the ecological damage of those human actions was mitigated to varying degrees by land management practices. The dikes needed repair, the canals dredging, the fields fertilizing, and the rice paddies tending. The extent to which those practices mitigated disastrous environmental consequences, at least for a while, depended on the amount of energy expended to maintain the new anthropogenically altered ecosystems. One of the laws of physics, which applies equally to ecosystems, is entropy, whereby a system tends toward disorder without the addition of an equal or greater amount of energy to maintain "order." In natural systems, solar energy fuels the earth's ecosystems. To maintain human-engineered systems—social, economic, and agro-ecological—those additional energy inputs have to come from humans, or else the systems deteriorate. Thus as China continued to develop and expand over the millennia, increasingly greater inputs were necessary to keep its systems intact.

One historian has described this situation as a "technological lock-in," whereby the costs of exiting from a particular technological basket were greater than continuously reinvesting in it. This is one way of explaining long-term continuities in Chinese history. Because a technology is the primary means by which humans interact with and change nature, Mark Elvin helpfully goes on to note that such a lock-in ultimately bumps into various environmental or physical constraints.[12]

The chemical fertilizers, the new energy regime dependent on fossil fuels, and the record-setting pace of China's recent industrialization lifted those constraints, and thus constitute a new chapter in China's environmental history. Whereas earlier patterns of China's environmental history had mostly local or regional effects—with the notable exceptions of infectious disease and consumer demand for food stuffs—China's actions now have global environmental repercussions, even though the ill effects of its industrial pollution and changes in land use are felt most directly by its own citizens. China's mounting environmental crisis is a global affair.

THE DRIVING FORCES OF CHINA'S ENVIRONMENTAL CHANGE

As ecologists have demonstrated, the driving forces of environmental change can be classified as direct and indirect. The direct driving forces include natural processes such as evolution, climate change, and volcanic activity, as well as other processes that can have natural or human causes, such as changes in land use and cover, species introduction or removal, technological change, fertilizer use (and abuse), and other agricultural practices. Indirect driving forces include human actions and institutions such as socioeconomic structures and processes, state actions, technology, cultural practices and beliefs, and demographic processes.[13] Moreover, those driving forces are not immutable or given, but have histories themselves.

Increasingly, direct and indirect driving forces have interacted to cause extensive environmental change. The earth's climate, for instance, results from complex natural forces that include both the way the earth itself has formed and evolved, and the interaction of earth systems with solar energy. More recently, human actions arising from industrialization and the change to a new fossil-fuel energy regime that emits vast quantities of greenhouse gases now constitute an additional driver of climate change.

Similarly, human actions have driven local, regional, and global environmental change. Specifically, this book has identified the following kinds of driving forces of environmental change in China's history: the Neolithic transition to agriculture and the interesting interconnections between China's agricultural systems and the development of state power; markets and commerce; technological change; cultural beliefs and practices; and population dynamics. Each of these will be discussed before we conclude with a consideration of China's environmental history in a world historical perspective.

Agriculture and the Chinese State

The ways in which individuals, families, and other social groups claim and exercise rights to use the land are closely connected to the ways in which humans interact with and change natural ecosystems. In terms of China's environmental history, the largest distinction can be made between those who laid claim to specific parcels of land (of whatever size), and those who did not see occupation of a fixed plot of land as necessary or desirable. In the broadest possible terms, the former way of relating to the land characterized the Han Chinese approach, and so concepts and institutions of private property developed.[14] The latter way of relating to the land characterizes many of the non-Han peoples encountered in this book who tended to move from place to place on an annual cycle (as with most steppe pastoralists), or over longer periods of times, as with the various upland and forest peoples who practiced swidden, or shifting agriculture, sometimes returning to the same area every twenty to thirty years or so.

One of the major changes to occur over the part of the world that became China was that as the Chinese empire expanded and imposed its legal and cultural practices over all those within its dominion, Chinese assumptions about land and the highest uses to which it could be put came to replace indigenous understandings. That clearly was a very long-term process, beginning with the Shang state 3,500 years ago and continuing to this day with the formerly pastoral peoples of China's Inner Mongolia Autonomous Region. The affected peoples experienced not just changes to their society, economy, and environment but also to their cultural understandings of who and what they were. Environment and identity were intertwined.

Moreover, Chinese understandings and practices changed over time as well. Neolithic villagers farming on the ecotone between the loess land and forest had fields that could be tilled annually for many years because of the peculiarities of loess soil, and these villagers had to defend their claims to the land against others. To be sure, climate changes in the fifth and fourth millennia BCE prompted villagers to decamp to more favorable locations, but eventually the production and protection of agricultural surpluses gave rise to ruling elites and the Shang state. The royalty of that first state claimed the land and the right to order slaves to work it for their masters. The succeeding Zhou deputed aristocrats to colonize more of the North China plain on behalf of the Zhou king, but the people who did the work of clearing and planting the land did not hold legal title to it—the Zhou aristocracy did. As state competition began to weaken central Zhou authority, new states innovated in military, social, and legal arrangements, and the Qin established both the principle of private property, and the right of farming families to own the land—and, of course, to pay taxes to the state.

That arrangement of a central state collecting taxes from farming families became fundamental to the scope and nature of China's environmental history. To be sure, every so often wealthy and powerful families would accumulate vast amounts of land and force the farming families into serf or serflike status, as happened in the latter half of the Han dynasty and later in the Ming as well. And for a while, the resurgent Sui state effectively eliminated large landlords by redistributing land to peasant families on the basis of family size and land fertility, a practice that continued into the Tang era before a mid-eighth century rebellion curtailed the capabilities of the state. During the Song, once again the wealthy and powerful asserted and accumulated control over land. But the early Ming reestablished peasant rights to land ownership, and although that did not prevent the build up of large landed estates and the loss of freedom for significant numbers of peasant farming families, by the mid-eighteenth century the Qing state settled the question by ensuring that all farming households were both personally free and had the rights to own property and to migrate. The People's Republic eliminated private ownership of land during its first thirty years, but since the 1980s those rights have been extended and given legal status.

Throughout the course of China's imperial and modern history, pressures on the peasant family farm may have led to concentrations of land ownership into a very few hands, and to the loss of freedom for those farming families, but for the most part the fundamental economic unit farming the land tended to be the family unit. As pointed out in chapter 1, there was an underlying ecological reason for that. The particularities of both dry land farming on the North China plain and wet-rice agriculture in the Yangzi River valley and further south meant that Chinese agriculture was to focus on intensive use of the land for cereal production. The most efficient way to manage that land was by making the immediate farming families—and not more removed aristocrats, landlords, or state functionaries—responsible for making the most crucial cropping decisions. Another consequence was that pasture for grazing cattle or horses was minimized, and so the energy captured by food crops allowed the human population to grow ever more dense.

This focus on family farming was in addition the result of state decisions made in the Early Empire. As noted in chapter 3, the Warring States period, despite its well-chosen name, actually saw the rapid growth of cities, commerce, and merchant wealth and culture, so that a very different kind of China might have emerged from that milieu. But the rulers of both the Qin and Han dynasties preferred to be able to base state revenues on the taxation of farmed land rather than to cope with the difficulties involved in taxing commerce.

From very early times, the Chinese state thus had intimate knowledge of the family farm and its significance to the fiscal health of the state. Han-era rulers also discovered that the Chinese family farm was an excellent tool for colonizing newly conquered regions and transforming those environments. The policy of *tun-tian*, or military agricultural colonies, first used by the Han to transform the environment of the northwest from steppe to sown, was then used by nearly every succeeding dynasty to consolidate Chinese rule over frontier regions, whether those were in Lingnan during the Tang, Sichuan during the Song, the southwest during the Ming, or the islands of Hainan and Taiwan during the Qing. The understanding that the Chinese family farm could and should transform alien environments and peoples into more familiar ones, and hence enhance the ability of the Chinese state to control the land and the people, was explicit. Moreover, the farming family not only had control over cropping decisions, but also over family size and composition decisions, a fact that was central to the size and density of China's population, a driving force to be discussed below.

Colonizing and farming new land required vast amounts of resources that farm families could not mobilize by themselves. The Chinese state thus advanced these colonists seed, tools, and draft animals, and often extended tax breaks for several years. But it was not just the state via farmers that brought new lands into agricultural production. During the Middle Empire, wealthy families with access to plenty of capital and labor built the vast polder enclosures that provided the infrastructure to control water that was needed for wet-rice agriculture to succeed in the valleys of the Yangzi River valley, and to transform those vast wetlands into rice paddies. Additionally, Buddhist monasteries, too, accepted gifts of land and money that gave them the wherewithal to clear forests and plant orchards.

This combination of the strategic concerns of the Chinese state with the particularities of its farming system had powerful environmental consequences, revealed most powerfully in map 1.1 (chapter 1) by the International Union for the Conservation of Nature (IUCN) depicting the current range of the tiger. This maps clearly shows that the tiger has been extirpated from within China's boundaries, including the hills and mountains of China's southwest bordering Southeast Asia and comprising China's part of the vast area James C. Scott has called "Zomia." The environment is mostly the same on both sides of the border, so there really is only one explanation why tigers no longer inhabit territory claimed by China: the human transformation of tiger habitat (mostly into farms) under the aegis of the power and reach of the Chinese state. Humans on the other side of the border have found ways of living with tigers (albeit with caution and reverence) in their habitat, whereas the Han Chinese have not.

Markets and Commerce

Despite the early Chinese preference for a stable agrarian society, markets and private property have long been in China's economic and environmental picture. Barbierri-Lowe argues that two thousand years ago Han-era China was already a market economy, while other historians see the major transition to markets coming with the weakening of the Tang state after the mid-eighth century An Lushan Rebellion. While Barbierri-Lowe may be correct about Han China, the end of that empire and the invasion of China by nomadic peoples in the early fourth century marked a significant break in China's history with the reassertion of state control of property and markets under the Sui and early Tang dynasties. After Tang rulers lost the ability to control either, China's history went down a path of increasing private property rights as opposed to state controls, and of an increasing role for market forces in allocating goods and services, and for exploiting natural resources.

By the sixteenth century, China had become a thoroughly market and commodity society.[15] Fortified with New World crops, in particular maize and potatoes but also tobacco and tomatoes, and drawn by markets for timber and paper, migrants headed into the hills and mountain valleys of central and southern China, leading to a vast assault on forests and forest products there, as detailed in chapter 5. Market networks in the southwest also patterned the spread of plague in the eighteenth and nineteenth centuries, and drove the exhaustion of China's east coast fisheries too. After China re-engaged with the world market since 1980, global demand for Chinese products has driven China's rapid industrialization and pollution of land, air, and water. China's market economy made the exploitation of its natural environment much more efficient. For much of the past two thousand years, then, markets have been a driving force of environmental change in China.

Technological Change

If technology is understood as the tools humans use for various purposes, then the kind of technology environmental historians are interested in is that which humans use in their interactions with nature and natural processes. Controlled use of fire to clear farmland thus is a significant technology that numerous peoples in China used, especially in swidden, or shifting, agriculture, a form used throughout Chinese history. Fire was essential as well for cooking and heating, and for refining ores that were combined to make bronze, a technology independently developed at several sites in China as long as four thousand years ago.[16] Hoes, plows, and axes too, first made of wood and sharpened stone but then of bronze and iron, were also part of the agricultural tool basket.

Water control constituted a significant technology that Chinese used in conjunction with settled agriculture to change much of their environment. Initially the Qin and Han road system had linked the vast regions under the control of the Chinese state into a (more or less) unified whole. Maintaining that road system probably required more effort and resources than any Chinese state afterward was willing or able to commit. But when the Sui built the "Grand Canal" in the seventh century, that exceptional infrastructure project linked the North China plain to the vast Yangzi River drainage system, bringing ever more of the empire into regular economic contact and exchange, enabling the exploitation of resources from regions ever further from China's core regions in the north and the east. Much of China's imperial statecraft revolved around maintaining the Grand Canal, and successive states did so until the mid-nineteenth century when long-term ecological processes of degradation coincided with massive social and political disruptions and foreign steamships to render the Canal unsupportable and unnecessary.

The technologies associated with farming and waterways drove much environmental change in China over the millennia from the Neolithic to the twentieth century. Since the mid-twentieth century, rapid industrialization and the use of fossil fuels required a whole new set of extremely powerful technologies that have driven environmental change over the past six decades. Both modes of environmental transformation were set within cultural ideas and practices, and conditioned by the size and distribution of China's population.

Cultural Ideas and Practices

Among the more difficult problems to assess is the extent to which the cultural mores and ideas that people held constituted a driving force of environmental change. On the one hand, people make history by making choices, and those choices are informed by the ideas they hold. On the other hand, "culture" can be such an amorphous concept that it includes either everything or nothing. In terms of China's environmental history, we have discussed the ideas that emerged in ancient China about what the proper relation of humans to nature should be (chapter 3), the ideas about nature that were articulated during the Tang era (chapter 4), and attitudes and ideas about nature that the Chinese Communists held (chapter 7).

In most cases, ideas that made the case for the ways in which humans *should* relate to nature arose at times of significant environmental distress. In ancient China, the use and abuse of forests and wetlands stimulated much thought about limiting the human impact on plants and animals, but did little to change the direction of Chinese society away from more intensive use of natural resources. In the Middle Empire, concerns for the fate and welfare of animals informed by both Buddhism and Confucianism did little to halt deforestation. And recent homilies about China charting a course toward a more harmonious relationship with nature are little more than ideological devices to cover the immense and harmful effects of industrial pollution being visited on people throughout China and, even more broadly, the world.

On the other hand, there are two areas where ideas and cultural practices did matter. One was the Chinese Communist drive to dominate nature and to bend it to human will. The other includes the numerous times when Chinese ideas and institutions were imposed on other peoples who had different cultural ways of relating to their environment. The best well-documented case of that happening is in Chinese relations with the pastoral nomads of the steppe grasslands, a theme that has run throughout China's environmental history.

Population Size and Dynamics

Finally, the size, distribution, and rate of growth of China's human population—its human demography—is an important driver of environmental change. From a population of perhaps 4–5 million during the height of the Shang around 1200 BCE, the population grew to about 50 million two thousand years ago, to as many as 120 million around 1200 CE, to nearly 600 million by 1950, and to 1,300 million (1.3 billion) today. The rates of growth implied by those numbers may have been less because some of that growth may have resulted from the incorporation of various other peoples into the Chinese empire. Also, the size of the population did periodically decline, so China's population history may look more like several waves of peaks and troughs than a single straight line going up. Important declines and population troughs came in the fourth century after the collapse of the early empire, in the fourteenth century in the aftermath of the Mongol conquest, and during the seventeenth-century crisis. Significant increases accompanied social and technological innovations from the fifth century BCE through the establishment of the early empire, the shift of China's population center south with the refinement and spread of wet-rice agriculture from the tenth through the thirteenth centuries, and from the late seventeenth century on with the widespread adoption of New World crops, and the restoration of peaceful conditions following the Chinese Communist victory in 1949.

To sustain a large and growing human population required the transformation of vast amounts of resources captured for human purposes. The combination of China's particular kind of settled farming with an efficient state apparatus allowed the Chinese to be quite successful over long periods of time in growing their population, and hence in transforming their environment. The emphasis of the Chinese state on creating a "fiscally legible" population base, along with a culturally reinforced preference for large families, resulted in high population densities in the north, northwest, and east, and pressures for those lowland farmers to migrate to new regions, providing an additional rationale for China's colonizing drive.

China's population size alone thus should not be seen in isolation as the only driving force of environmental change. Moreover, demographers who have looked at China's population size and growth from the eighteenth century on and concluded that its population was out of control have been proven wrong—Chinese families for at least the past two thousand years have employed various means to manage family size.[17] Like most families anywhere, Chinese families made family-planning decisions in the context of expectations about social and economic conditions in general, and food supplies and prices in particular. That China's population grew thus was a consequence of the Chinese ability to provide not just adequate food supplies for reproduction and replacement of the existing population base, but for its growth. And the combination and interaction of these driving forces over time, not just population dynamics alone, drove China's environmental change.

CHINA'S ENVIRONMENTAL HISTORY IN A WORLD HISTORICAL CONTEXT

Over the millennia considered in this book, China has been both in the world and its history and a part of the world. By the latter, I mean that China can be considered to be one of many similarly constructed discrete entities in the world, and hence can be compared with them; and, by the former, I mean that there is but one world with a common history to which China has contributed. To place China's environmental experience into a world historical context, both perspectives are needed.

In comparative terms, China's environmental history is in many ways distinctive, if not unique, in world history. No other place on earth has such a long and more or less continuous history that is documentable in the same language. Indeed, without those continuities, it would not have been possible to conceive of and write this book. Starting over four thousand years ago with the emergence of an identifiably "Chinese" interaction sphere, as noted in chapter 2, to the People's Republic today, a Chinese state of one form or another has dealt the cards in that part of East Asia. How that hand was played out differed at various points in time, but there can be no doubt of that distinctive aspect of Chinese history. Moreover, in the words of J. R. McNeill, "in comparative perspective the Chinese state . . . appears remarkable for its ecological role. The Chinese imperial state [and, I would add, the modern one too] was a meddlesome one . . . actively seeking to develop resources and rearrange nature so as to maximize tangible and taxable wealth."[18]

No other state in world history has had such a vast range of ecosystems under its purview for such a long period of time. Nor has any state been able to remake its hydrological systems into a vast inland waterway to foster the exploitation of resources from those ecosystems for such a long time. No place on earth has soils that have been worked as continuously over the millennia as China's. Nor have any people had such a long history of experience with epidemic diseases,[19] both adjusting to the pathogens (which also mutated) and exporting them around the world.

China and its history long have been not just part of world historical trends, but often a motive force of world history.[20] The rather unique combination of intensive cereal farming with a powerful and outward-looking state led not just to a large population in relation to the rest of the world but to biological old regime industries such as silk and pottery as well as addictive stimulants such as tea that linked China's economy and hence its environment more broadly to other parts of the world. Other historians have mapped the density of those linkages at the height of the Roman and Han empires, and in the thirteenth century.[21] More recently, A. G. Frank and others have documented the centrality of China to the broad economic, social, and cultural revitalization of the world from about 1400 to 1800,[22] resulting in what historians have called "the early modern world." China's demand for silver as well as sandalwood, furs, and sea slugs and other foodstuffs cast an ecological shadow from Southeast Asia and the Pacific Islands to Europe and the Americas. To change metaphors, China's environmental footprint grew large and left a deep imprint on the earth.[23]

Those distinctions matter, to China and to the world. But China's environmental history was not completely exceptional, exhibiting similarities to other parts of the world in at least two very significant and interlocked ways: in its record of deforestation and in its relations with indigenous peoples (or at least those who were there before the Han Chinese), both of which have been powerful themes in this book. Prior to the emergence and spread of agriculture, an independent development in several parts of the world after the last Ice Age, human populations were small and gleaned their subsistence from forests and savannas. But with agriculture, the production of food surpluses swelled human populations and began the long historical process of removing forests for farms.[24] And in many places around the world, that expansion set up confrontations with indigenous peoples, most of whom fared poorly as a result. China's history sadly is not unique in those regards.

In *Deforesting the Earth*, Michael Williams examines the long historical process by which people around the world have removed the forest from the face of the earth, at first slowly because human populations were neither large nor dense, and because the technologies available (fire and hand axes) limited forest clearance to the temperate regions of the earth where agriculture became the main form of human sustenance. In Europe, by the eighteenth century, the growing shortage of trees for fuel and for timbers for ships sparked concerns about the consequences of further deforestation, and gave birth to significant reforestation projects.[25] Given those pressures on Europe's forests, Joachim Radkau claims that the growing ability of some European states to preserve their old-growth forests is "an indicator of the extent to which a society is capable of making provisions for the future," or to plan for sustainability, in other words.[26] Acutely aware of the limitations on natural resources on its islands, Japan in the seventeenth and eighteenth centuries also halted its deforestation and began to reforest.[27] But in China, awareness of the consequences of deforestation, along with a growing sense that natural resources of all kinds were not limited, did not lead to attempts to slow the onward march of deforestation.

For reasons that historians are now beginning to understand, by the eighteenth century much of world, not just China, was bumping into limits set by environmental conditions. Historian John Richards in *The Unending Frontier* argues that four global trends pushed humanity toward the using up of those natural resources and empty spaces in the early modern world. First, "rising human numbers put increasing pressure on the use of the land," pushing both the more intensive use of existing farmland, but especially the widespread clearance of land for agriculture in frontier regions. Second, greater human mobility along the expanding trade networks spurred by commercialization led to the spread of selected plant and animal species into those frontier regions as farmers planted crops and raised animals in the more exotic frontier regions that were familiar to them. I would add that the most significant species invasion was that of humans themselves. These first two processes led to the third global trend, "the widespread depletion of larger animals, birds, and marine mammals," in part because of habitat destruction, and in part because of what Richards terms "the world hunt" (as in Manchuria in the seventeenth and eighteenth centuries). The fourth global trend in the early modern period was growing scarcities and energy shortages in the more densely populated core areas in states throughout the world.[28] China's environmental history parallels those global trends; but there are significant departures as well.

"The Unending Frontier" is of course an ironic title, for neither the frontier nor natural resources were "unending"—limits were reached. Joachim Radkau also comments on the early modern world confronting environmental limits: "In China, as in Europe, one can detect in the eighteenth century a desire to use natural resources to their limits and to leave no more open spaces, no quiet reserves. As in Europe, this was made easier by crops from the New World, especially the potato and maize."[29] But as we now know from chapter 6, China continued to press its environmental limits into the nineteenth century, and entered a period of ecological crisis brought on by widespread degradation of its environment. Not just in China and Europe, but also throughout much of the world, as John Richards shows, the limits of nature were being reached, and the entire world was laboring under a growing ecological strain.

But the world did not remain stuck in that ecological cul-de-sac, as Kenneth Pomeranz calls it.[30] The Industrial Revolution and the transition to the new energy regime of fossil fuels opened a way out, first for Europe, and then for other parts of the world, China included. But the causes of that transition to the industrial world have been subject to intense scholarly debate. Some see its emergence as the most likely outcome of a long period of preparation in Europe that was bound to happen. Others see the industrial breakthrough as much more contingent, and not at all a necessary development; in other words, the Industrial Revolution might never have happened. And if that were the case, perhaps the entire world would have had to have followed in the path of China's intensive exhaustion of its natural resources, descending as it did in the nineteenth century into ever lower levels of energy use and standards of living for the human population—that might have been the face of the future to the rest of the world, even those which were trying to conserve their resources.

But the industrial world did emerge, first in a corner of Britain, then in other parts of Western Europe, and later in America and other parts of Eurasia. For the past thirty years, China has been on a breakneck pace to catch up industrially with the most advanced parts of the world, and to surpass them in terms of energy use, the size of its national economy, and its per capita income. If China in the eighteenth and nineteenth century showed the world what its future might have looked like without the industrial breakthrough, then China at the beginning of the twenty-first century might once again be showing the world its future should the fossil fuel-driven industrial world continue to shape human relations with our environment. Continued growth of the economy at the expense of preserving significant space for natural ecosystems, as China has made painfully clear with the crowding of most of its remaining biodiversity into the small corner of the Three Parallel Rivers Region of Yunnan province, simply is not sustainable. The reason, J. Donald Hughes argues, is "that the ability of an organism to increase in number and total biomass, and spread geographically, will eventually encounter one of several environmental factors that prevent further increase. Growth is limited by the least available factor, and no resource is infinite."[31]

That consciousness of limitations has emerged at least three times in Chinese history. But just as ideas expressing awareness of those environmental limitations had little effect on the subsequent course of Chinese history 2,500 years ago, so too do I doubt that more recent Chinese calls for a harmonious relationship of its people to the environment will halt, let alone reverse, continued ecological damage. China's ecosystems are increasingly losing their resiliency, so the effects of the pollution of land, air, and water have increasingly severe effects on people, and there is less and less room for error in China. But the behavior of people in China, as elsewhere, continues to evince a willingness to take huge risks with the environment, including the global climate, in order to press forward with rapid economic development. The reason, J. Donald Hughes once observed, is that "many humans, particularly those who wield power, decide that other values, such as short-term survival or profit, are more important to them than long-term survival and sustainability. . . . In most societies, a minority that exploits resources has usurped power from a majority whose genuine, if not always conscious, interest is to maintain the sustainability of resources."[32]

China's long environmental history does not raise high hopes for China's—or the world's—being able to grapple with our common environmental challenges. However, in light of the limitations of our knowledge of the past, and of our powers of prediction, we should have humility in the face of great unknowns. We can be surprised both by new insights we can find by opening new vistas on our common past, and by actions that humans collectively can take to ensure the continued biodiversity of the planet earth, the long-term sustainability of our species as well as others, and the beauty of a natural world that can be enjoyed for generations into the future.

Notes

CHAPTER 1

1. The IUCN Red List of Threatened Species, "*Panthera tigris*," www.iucnredlist.org/apps/redlist/details/15955/0.

2. This is a slightly different view than that provided by Mark Elvin: "[T]he picture is one of . . . Chinese expansion up to natural limits—coasts, steppes, deserts, mountains, and jungles. It was a multimillennial transformation of a variety of habitats by some version of the Chinese style of settlement: cutting down most of the trees for clearance, buildings, and fuel, an ever-intensifying garden type of farming and arboriculture, water-control systems both large and small, commercialization, and cities and villages located as near the water's edge as possible." *The Retreat of the Elephants: An Environmental History of China* (New Haven, CT and London, UK: Yale University Press, 2004), 5.

3. Dee Mack Williams, *Beyond Great Walls: Environment, Identity, and Development on the Chinese Grasslands of Inner Mongolia* (Stanford, CA: Stanford University Press, 2002), ch. 4. A recently published fictional account, *Wolf Totem* (New York, NY: The Penguin Press, 2008), based on author Jian Rong's experiences in Inner Mongolia in the 1960s and 1970s, provides additional insight into Mongol values as well as steppe ecological relationships.

4. That view, of course, is not unique to the Chinese. Many others, too, have set themselves apart from nature, not wanting to see themselves as just one of many different animal species grounded in particular environments. Indeed, just this argument continues to this very day and is one of the reasons environmental historians insist on seeing human institutions and history in their natural environments—we forget about our dependence on natural processes at our peril.

5. For a readable account, see Daniel B. Botkin, *Discordant Harmonies: A New Ecology for the Twenty-first Century* (New York, NY: Oxford University Press, 1990). A more recent textbook approach is found in Colin R. Townsend, Michael Begon, and John L. Harper, *Essentials of Ecology*, 3rd ed. (Malden, MA: Blackwell Scientific, 2008).

6. This list is from Williams, *Beyond Great Walls*, 61.

7. For a brief discussion of "driving forces," see Millennium Ecosystem Assessment, *Ecosystems and Human Well-Being: Synthesis* (Washington, DC: Island Press, 2005), vii.

8. One of the most famous early comments was that of the philosopher Mencius (fl. 300 BCE) on the deforestation of Ox Mountain. For the original text, see Wm. Theodore de Bary and Irene Bloom, comps., *Sources of Chinese Tradition*, 2nd ed., vol. 1 (New York, NY: Columbia University Press, 1999), 151. For an interpretation of that text in a global environmental context, see J. Donald Hughes, *An Environmental History of the World: Humankind's Changing Role in the Community of Life* (London, UK and New York, NY: Routledge, 2001), 66–73. For other examples of ancient Chinese descriptions of environmental change, see Richard Louis Edmonds, *Patterns of China's Lost Harmony: A Survey of the Country's Environmental Degradation and Protection* (London, UK and New York, NY: Routledge, 1994), 22–41.

9. Jack A. Goldstone, "Efflorescences and Economic Growth in World History: Rethinking the 'Rise of the West' and the Industrial Revolution," *Journal of World History* 13, no. 2 (2002): 323–90.

10. On species extinction, see Robert B. Marks, "People Said Extinction Was Not Possible: 2,000 Years of Environmental Change in South China," in *Environmental History: World System History and Global Environmental Change*, ed. Alf Hornberg (Lanham, MD: AltaMira Press, 2007), 41–60.

11. Judith Shapiro calls this *Mao's War against Nature* (New York, NY and Cambridge, UK: Cambridge University Press, 2001).

12. According to a recent count, China has 599 separate categories of ecosystems. See *China's Diversity: A Country Study* (Beijing, CN: China Environmental Science Press, 1998), 2. For slightly different figures, see J. Mackinnon et al., *A Biodiversity Review of China* (Hong Kong, HK: World Wide Fund for Nature International China Programme, 1996), 21.

13. See also Biodiversity Committee of the Chinese Academy of Sciences, "Biodiversity in China: Status and Conservation Needs," www.brim.ac.cn/brime/bdinchn/1.html.

14. *China's Diversity*, 17.

15. Elvin, *Retreat*, 11.

16. John R. McNeill, *Something New under the Sun: An Environmental History of the Twentieth-Century World* (New York, NY: Norton, 2000).

17. For example, I have taught courses using drafts of this book coupled with Patricia Ebrey's *Cambridge Illustrated History of China*, 2nd ed. (New York, NY: Cambridge University Press, 2010).

CHAPTER 2

1. As in the narrative of the "Rise of the West." For a critique, see Robert B. Marks, *The Origins of the Modern World: A Global and Ecological Narrative from the Fifteenth to the Twenty-first Century* (Lanham, MD: Rowman & Littlefield, 2007), 1–20.

2. Kwang-Chih Chang, "China on the Eve of the Historical Period," in *The Cambridge History of Ancient China: From the Origins to 221 B.C*, eds. Michael Lowe and Edward L. Shaughnessy (New York, NY and Cambridge, UK: Cambridge University Press, 1999), 37. Hereafter referred to as CHAC.

3. Xu Guohua and L. J. Peel, eds., *The Agriculture of China* (Oxford, UK and New York, NY: Oxford University Press, 1991), 6–7.

4. Robert Orr Whyte, "The Evolution of the Chinese Environment," in *The Origins of Chinese Civilization*, ed. David N. Keightley (Berkeley and Los Angeles, CA: University of California Press, 1983), 6.

5. For detailed scientific studies of Asia's paleoenvironment, see Robert Orr Whyte, ed., *The Evolution of the East Asian Environment,* 2 vols. (Hong Kong, HK: The University of Hong Kong Centre of Asian Studies, 1984).

6. Zhao Songqiao, *Geography of China: Environment, Resources, Population and Development* (New York, NY: John Wiley and Sons, 1994).

7. Conrad Totman, *Pre-industrial Korea and Japan in Environmental Perspective* (Leiden, NL and Boston, MA: Brill, 2004), 15.

8. Joseph Needham, *Science and Civilization in China*, vol. 6, *Biology and Biological Technology*, part 1: *Botany* (New York, NY: Cambridge University Press, 1988), 33.

9. S. D. Richardson, *Forests and Forestry in China: Changing Patterns of Resource Development* (Washington, DC: Island Press, 1990), 3.

10. A very useful one is Ren Mai'e, *An Outline of China's Physical Geography* (Beijing, CN: Science Press, 1984).

11. Richardson, 39.

12. Nicholas K. Menzies, *Forestry*, vol. 6, part III, *Biology and Biological Technology, Agro-Industries and Forestry*, of Joseph Needham, *Science and Civilization in China* (Cambridge, UK: Cambridge University Press, 1996), 548–49.

13. On the use of forest remnants, especially around Buddhist temples, see Robert B. Marks, *Tigers, Rice, Silk, and Silt: Environment and Economy in Late Imperial South China* (Cambridge, UK and New York, NY: Cambridge University Press, 1998), 37–39.

14. The past tense is used here because we are not certain that tigers have not learned and changed over the millennia of contact with humans. For an intriguing discussion of the Siberian (Amur) tiger, see John Vaillant, *The Tiger: A True Story of Vengeance and Survivial* (New York, NY: Alfred A. Knopf, 2010). The same might well be said of elephants, too.

15. John Seidensticker, "Large Carnivores and the Consequences of Habitat Insularization: Ecology and Conservation of Tigers in Indonesia and Bangladesh," in *Cats of the World: Biology, Conservation, and Management*, eds. S. D. Miller and D. D. Everett (Washington, DC: National Wildlife Federation, 1986), 20–21.

16. See E. O. Wilson, *The Diversity of Life* (Cambridge, MA: Harvard University Press, 1992), 275–78.

17. See Marks, *Tigers*, and Mark Elvin, *The Retreat of the Elephants* (New Haven, CT: Yale University Press, 2004).

18. See H. H. Lamb, *Climate History and the Modern World* (New York, NY: Methuen, 1982), ch. 5. For ancient China, see David Keightley, "The Environment of Ancient China," in CHAC, 30–36, and Robert Orr Whyte, The Evolution of the Chinese Environment," in *The Origins of Chinese Civilization*, ed. Kcightley, 3–19.

19. Keightley, "The Environment," 33–36.

20. For recent examples, see Q.-S. Ge, J.-Y. Zheng, Z.-X. Hao, P.-Y. Zhang, and W.-C. Wang, "Reconstruction of Historical Climate in China: High-Resolution Precipitation Data from Qing Dynasty Archives," *Bulletin of the American Meteorological Society* (May 2005): 671–79, and GE QuanSheng, GUO Xifeng, ZHENG Jingyun, and HAO ZhiXin, "Meiyu in the Middle and Lower Reaches of the Yangtze River since 1736," *Chinese Science Bulletin* 53, no. 1 (January 2008): 107–14.

21. Zhu Kezhen, "Zhongguo jin wuqian nian lai qihou bianqian de chubu yanjiu" (A Preliminary Study of Climatic Change in China over the Past 5000 Years), *Kaogu xue xuebao* no. 1 (1972).

22. The graph is from my book *Tigers, Rice, Silk, and Silt: Environment and Economy in Late Imperial South China* (New York, NY: Cambridge University Press, 1998), 49, and is based on Zhu's article as well as on Manfred Domros and Peng Gongping, *The Climate of China* (Berlin: Springer, 1988), 13.

23. For more on Zhu Kezhen, see (using the old Wade-Giles romanization system), Chiaomin Hsieh, "Chu K'o-chen and China's Climatic Changes," *The Geographic Journal* 142, no. 2 (July 1976): 248–56.

24. E.g., Jean Grove, *The Little Ice Age* (London, UK: Methuen, 1988).

25. Because of China's long historical record, there is now a vast literature reconstructing China's past climates. See Manfred Domros and Peng Gongping, *The Climate of China* (Berlin, DE: Springer, 1988); Raymond S. Bradley and Philip D. Jones, eds., *Climate since a.d. 1500* (New York, NY: Routledge, 1992); Zhang Jiacheng and Lin Zhiguang, *Climate of China* (New York, NY: Wiley, 1992); and Wang Shao-wu and Zhao Zong-ci, "Droughts and Floods in China, 1470–1979," in *Climate and History: Studies in Past Climates and Their Impact on Man*, eds. T. M. L. Wrigley et al. (New York, NY: Cambridge University Press, 1981), 271–87.

26. K. C. Chang, "China on the Eve of the Historical Period," in CHAC, 37–73; Richard Leakey, *The Origin of Humankind* (London, UK: Phoenix, 1995).

27. The HUGO Pan-Asian SNP Consortium, "Mapping Human Genetic Diversity in Asia," *Science* 326 (2009): 1541–45. This DNA mapping analysis concludes that modern humans migrated into East Asia in a single wave from Southeast Asia.

28. Observed about North America by William Cronon, *Changes in the Land: Indians, Colonists, and the Ecology of New England* (New York, NY: Hill and Wang, 1983).

29. For discussions of the "origins of agriculture," see David Christian, *Maps of Time: An Introduction to Big History* (Berkeley and Los Angeles, CA: University of California Press, 2004), ch. 8; and Joachim Radkau, *Nature and Power: A Global History of the Environment* (Cambridge, UK and New York, NY: Cambridge University Press, 2008), ch. 2.

30. Ping-ti-Ho, *The Cradle of the East: An Inquiry into the Indigenous Origins of Techniques and Ideas of Neolithic and Early Historic China, 5000–1000 B.C.* (Chicago, IL: The University of Chicago Press, 1975).

31. Hui-lin Li, "The Domestication of Plants in China: Ecogeographical Considerations," in *The Origins of Chinese Civilization*, ed. Keightley, 21–64; Te-tzu Chang, "The Origins and Early Cultures of Cereal Grains and Food Legumes," *The Origins of Chinese Civilization*, ed. Keightley, 65–94.

32. For a concise account, see Yan Wenming, "The Beginning of Farming," in *The Formation of Chinese Civilization: An Archeological Perspective*, ed. Sarah Allen (New Haven, CT and London, UK: Yale University Press, 2005), ch. 2.

33. Perennials then have to put a lot of their plant resources below ground—getting the root system to water is the only way to make it through the dry season. In the annual mutation, less plant energy goes below ground and more to aboveground structures and seeds; the annual variety needs less of a root system because it does not need to survive the dry season, but an annual does produce lots more seeds to enhance chances of survival. Personal communication from Professor Cheryl Swift, Professor of Botany, Whittier College.

34. Whyte, "The Evolution of the Chinese Environment," 13.

35. Chi-wu Wang, *The Forests of China* (Cambridge, MA: Harvard University Press, 1961), 159.

36. Quoted in Shiba Yoshinobu, *Commerce and Society in Song China* (Ann Arbor, MI: The University of Michigan Center for Chinese Studies, 1970), 8.

37. Quoted in Marks, *Tigers*, 41–42.

38. Francesca Bray, *Agriculture*, in Joseph Needham, *Science and Civilization in China*, vol. 6, part II, (Cambridge, UK and New York, NY: Cambridge University Press, 1984), 481–85.

39. Gary W. Crawford and Chen Shen, "The Origins of Rice Agriculture: Recent Progress in East Asia," *Antiquity* 72 (1998): 858–66.

40. Yan, "The Beginning of Farming," 34–41; Gary W. Crawford and Chen Shen, "The Origins of Rice Agriculture: Recent Progress in East Asia," *Antiquity* 72 (1998): 858–66.

41. Bray, *Agriculture*, 489–95.

42. Steven Mithen, *After the Ice: A Global Human History, 20,000–5000 BC* (Cambridge, MA: Harvard University Press, 2003), 359–69. See also Crawford and Shen, "The Origins of Rice Agriculture," 858–66.

43. Hui-lin Li, "The Domestication of Plants in China: Ecogeographical Considerations," in *The Origins of Chinese Civilization*, ed. Keightley, 43.

44. Three recent studies of malaria include Sonia Shah, *The Fever: How Malaria Has Ruled Humankind for 500,000 Years* (New York, NY: Farrar, Straus, and Giroux, 2010); James L. A. Webb, Jr., *Humanity's Burden: A Global History of Malaria* (New York, NY: Cambridge University Press, 2009); and Randall M. Packard, *The Making of a Tropical Disease: A Short History of Malaria* (Baltimore, MD: The Johns Hopkins University Press, 2007).

45. Elizabeth Hsu, "The History of *qing hao* in the Chinese *materia medica*," *Transaction of the Royal Society of Tropical Medicine and Hygiene* (2006), 505–8.

46. Yoshinobu Shiba, "Environment versus Water Control: The Case of the Southern Hangzhou Bay Are from the Mid-Tang through the Qing," in *Sediments of Time: Environment and Society in Chinese History*, eds. Mark Elvin and Liu Ts'ui-jung (Cambridge, UK and New York, NY: Cambridge University Press, 1998), 137–38.

47. For photographs, see Cressey, 80, 133.

48. There has been considerable controversy over whether or not the loess highlands were ever forested, with K. C. Chang arguing that they were and Ping-ti Ho arguing that they were not. See K. C. Chang, CHAC, 43; Ping-ti Ho, *The Cradle of the East: An Inquiry into the Indigenous Origins of Techniques and Ideas of Neolithic and Early Historic China, 5000–1000 B. C.* (Chicago: University of Chicago Press, 1975). My view reflects Ho's slightly revised view as stated in "The Paleoenvironment of North China—A Review Article," *Journal of Asian Studies* 43, no. 4 (August 1984): 725–26—that the loess highlands were "a semiarid steppe," but that the Yellow River valley and North China plain to the east "were substantially forested."

49. Li, "The Domestication of Plants," 23.

50. Menzies, *Forestry*, 558. Menzies's view has been confirmed by a recent palynological study: "From the data accumulated we suggest that there were no forests on the [loess] Plateau during the last hundred thousand years, except during some comparatively short intervals when the climate was more suitable for forest growth [e.g., during the last glaciation]." Xiangjun Sun, Changqing Song, Fengyu Wang, and Mengrong Sun, "Vegetation History of the Loess Plateau of China during the Last 100,000 Years Based on Pollen Data," *Quaternary International* 37 (1997): 25–36.

51. Chun Chang Huang, Jiangli Peng, Qunying Zhou, and Shu'e Chen, "Holocene Pedogenic Change and the Emergence and Decline of Rain-Fed Cereal Agriculture on the Chinese Loess Plateau," *Quaternary Science Reviews* 23 (2004): 2525–35. I thank Nicholas Menzies for bringing this article to my attention.

52. See Zhang Zhongpei, "The Yangshao Period: Prosperity and the Transformation of Prehistoric Society," *The Formation of Chinese Civilization: An Archeological Perspective*, ed. Sarah Allen (New Haven, CT and London, UK: Yale University Press, 2005), 68–71.

53. Ho, *The Cradle of the East*, 49–50.

54. Bray, *Agriculture*, 442.

55. See Richard Pearson, with the assistance of Shyr-Charng Lo, "The Ch'ing-lien-kang [Qing-lian-kang] Culture and the Chinese Neolithic," and William Meacham, "Origins and Development of the Yueh Coastal Neolithic: A Microcosm of Culture Change on the Mainland of East Asia," both in *The Origins of Chinese Civilization*, ed. Keightley.

56. Bray, *Agriculture*, 47.

57. Chang, "The Origins and Early Cultures of the Cereal Grains and Food Legumes," in *The Origins of Chinese Civilization*, ed. Keightley, 80–81. See also Ho, *Cradle of the East*, 76–78.

58. Meacham, "Origins and Development of the Yueh," 153.

59. Ho, *Cradle of the East*, 116–20.

60. Li Liu, *The Chinese Neolithic: Trajectories to Early States* (Cambridge, UK: Cambridge University Press, 2004), 27–31.

61. Ibid., 186; see also 31, 193, 197.

62. Ibid., 30.

63. Mark Edward Lewis, *The Flood Myths of Early China* (Albany, NY: State University of New York Press, 2006).

64. *Ji Min Yao Shu*, quoted in Bray, *Agriculture*, 97.

65. Deduced from data in Song Zhenhao, "Xia Shang renkou chutan" [A preliminary investigation of population size during the Xia and Shang dynasties], *Lishi yanjiu* 1991.4: 92–106.

66. Chang, "China on the Eve of the Historical Period," in CHAC, 58.

67. Ibid., 59.

68. Ho, *Cradle of the East*, 89.

69. See K. C. Chang, "Sandai Archeology and the Formation of States in Ancient China: Processual Aspects of the Origins of Chinese Civilization," in *The Origins of Chinese Civilization*, ed. Keightley, 495–522; K. C. Chang, *Shang Civilization* (New Haven and London: Yale University Press, 1980), esp. part II; and K. C. Chang, "The Rise of Kings and the Formation of City-States," *The Formation of Chinese Civilization: An Archeological Perspective*, ed. Sarah Allen (New Haven, CT and London, UK: Yale University Press, 2005), ch. 5.

70. The *Zuo Zhuan*, as quoted in Chang, "China on the Eve of the Historical Period," in CHAC, 64.

71. This is not to imply that the use of bronze caused the social changes that led to "civilization," for clearly identifiable civilizations developed in the pre-Columbian Americas without metals of any kind.

72. Noel Barnard, "Further Evidence for Support of the Hypothesis of the Indigenous Origins of Metallurgy in Ancient China," in *The Origins of Chinese Civilization*, ed. Keightley, 237–77. See also Paul Wheatley, *The Pivot of the Four Quarters: A Preliminary Inquiry into the Origins and Character of the Ancient Chinese City* (Chicago, IL: Aldine Publishing Co., 1971), 36.

73. For a readable discussion of how those geological processes led to coal and oil deposits, see Anthony N. Penna, *The Human Footprint: A Global Environmental History* (Malden, MA: Wiley-Blackwell, 2010).

74. Robert Bagley, "Shang Archeology," in CHAC, 141,

75. Ursula Marius Franklin, "On Bronze and Other Metals in Early China," in *The Origins of Chinese Civilization*, ed. Keightley, 279–96.

76. For a useful discussion and map, see Barnes, *The Rise of Civilization in East Asia*, 122.

77. Chang, *Shang Civilization*, 152

78. Bagley, "Shang Archeology," 136–37.

79. Ibid., 156–57.

80. For a description of Erlitou and photos of the early bronzes produced there, see Lu Liancheng and Yan Wenming, "Society during the Three Dynasties," *The Formation of Chinese Civilization: An Archeological Perspective*, ed. Sarah Allen (New Haven, CT and London, UK: Yale University Press, 2005), 144–50.

81. Bagley, "Shang Archeology," 160.

82. Wheatley, *Pivot*, 76.

83. Chang, *Shang Civilization*, 248.

84. Significant numbers have been translated in David N. Keightley, *The Ancestral Landscape: Time, Space, and Community in Late Shang China (ca. 1200–1045 B.C.)* (Berkeley, CA:

University of California–Berkeley Center for Chinese Studies, 2000). The first cache of oracle bones was discovered in 1899. A recent discovery near Jinan, Shandong province, unearthed four more. "China Unearthed Shang Oracle Bones Again, 104 Years after the First Discovery," http://englishpeopledaily.com.cn/200304/09.

85. Keightley, *The Ancestral Landscape*, 149.

86. Quoted in K. C. Chang, ed., *Food in Chinese Culture: Anthropological and Historical Perspectives* (New Haven, CT: Yale University Press, 1977), 32.

87. E. N. Anderson, *The Food of China* (New Haven, CT: Yale University Press, 1988), 20.

88. Patricia Ebrey, *The Cambridge Illustrated History of China* (Cambridge, UK and New York, NY: Cambridge University Press, 1999), 25–27.

89. Chang, *Shang Civilization*, 148–49.

90. David Keightley, "The Late Shang State: When, Where, and What," in *The Origins of Chinese Civilization*, ed. Keightley, 538–39.

91. Magnus Fiskesjö, "On the 'Raw' and the 'Cooked' Barbarians of Imperial China," *Inner Asia* 1 (1999): 139–68.

92. Song Zhenhao, "Xia Shang renkou chutan" [A preliminary investigation of population size during the Xia and Shang dynasties], *Lishi yanjiu* 1991.4: 92–106. See also Ge Jianxiong, ed., *Zhongguo renkou shi* [China's population history], vol. 1, 216–81.

93. Quoted in Bray, *Agriculture*, 127.

94. Bray, *Agriculture*, 159–61. Bray notes that a bronze plow was found in Tonkin (currently northern Vietnam), contemporaneous with Shang-era China, and that those states had contact.

95. Quoted in Chang, *Shang Civilization*, 225.

96. Quoted in Chang, *Shang Civilization*, 226–27.

97. Elvin, *Retreat of the Elephants*, 44.

98. Quoted in Chang, *Shang Civilization*, 254–55.

99. See the illustrations in the *Cambridge History of Ancient China*, 199.

100. Ibid., 142.

101. Ibid., 143.

102. For examples, see Edmund Burke III, "The Big Story: Human History, Energy Regimes, and the Environment," in *The Environment and World History*, eds. Edmund Burke III and Kenneth Pomeranz (Berkeley and Los Angeles, CA: University of California Press, 2009), 33–53; and I. G. Simmons, *Global Environmental History* (Chicago, IL: University of Chicago Press, 2008).

103. John R. McNeill, *Something New under the Sun: An Environmental History of the Twentieth-Century World* (New York, NY: W. W. Norton, 2000), 11–12.

104. Keightley, *Ancestral Landscape*, 15–16.

105. Keightley, *Cambridge History of Ancient China*, 36.

CHAPTER 3

1. According to political scientists Cioffi-Revilla and Lai, "warfare and politics are cross-cultural universals that originated as pristine social phenomena—invented ex novo, not adopted by diffusion—in at least three 'protobellic' areas [places where war emerged] of the ancient world: Mesopotamia, China, and Mesoamerica." Claudio Cioffi-Revilla and David Lai, "War and Politics in Ancient China, 2700 B.C. to 722 B.C." *The Journal of Conflict Resolution* 39, no. 3 (1995): 467.

2. For a discussion of this kind of energy regime, see J. R. McNeill, *Something New under the Sun: An Environmental History of the Twentieth-Century World* (New York, NY: Norton, 2000), 10–12.

3. Gina L. Barnes, *The Rise of Civilization in East Asia: The Archeology of China, Korea and Japan* (London: Thames and Hudson, 1999), 107.

4. Richard Louis Edmonds, *Patterns of China's Lost Harmony: A Survey of the Country's Environmental Degradation and Protection* (London, UK and New York, NY: Routledge, 1994), 29; see also Mark Elvin, *Retreat of the Elephants*, 10.

5. According to Anthony Barierri-Low, "Early imperial China provides an example of an economy that, while still strongly agrarian and redistributive, was also home to burgeoning commercial activity. More than any other civilization in the ancient world, early imperial China operated under a money economy, where nearly everything could be purchased with standardized coins produced in vast quantities by state mints. . . . Though, in theory, the Chinese state wished to suppress commercialization in favor of agriculture, they nevertheless established market laws and regulations that greatly facilitated commerce. Recently unearthed legal texts now show that the early imperial Chinese state possessed a developed body of enforceable contract law that ensured market reliability, protected property rights, and lowered the kind of transaction costs that Douglas North has written were a hindrance to greater market activity in other premodern economies." Anthony J. Barbierri-Low, *Artisans in Early Imperial China* (Seattle, WA and London, UK: University of Washington Press, 2007), 18.

6. David W. Anthony, *The Horse, the Wheel, and Language: How Bronze-Age Riders from the Eurasian Steppes Shaped the Modern World* (Princeton: Princeton University Press, 2007), 199–201, 221–24, 237, 267, 311. There is much debate on the origins and nature of pastoral nomadism, horse riding, and war making across the Central Asian steppe. In addition to Anthony, see Michael Frachetti, *Pastoral Landscapes and Social Interaction in Bronze Age Eurasia* (Berkeley and Los Angeles, CA: University of California Press, 2009), and Christopher Beckwith, *Empires of the Silk Road: A History of Central Eurasia from the Bronze Age to the Present* (Princeton, NJ: Princeton University Press, 2009). I am particularly grateful to David Christian for bringing the latter two books to my attention, and for sharing with me his review essay of all three, "'Pots are not people': Recent books on the Archeology and History of Central Asia," forthcoming.

7. Thomas J. Barfield, *The Nomadic Alternative* (Upper Saddle River, NJ: Prentice Hall, 1993), 131.

8. Owen Lattimore, *The Inner Asian Frontiers of China* (Boston, MA: Beacon Press, 1967), 21–23.

9. Barfield, *The Nomadic Alternative*, 136.

10. Francois Bourliere, *The Land and Wildlife of Eurasia* (New York, NY: Time Incorporated, 1964), 85, 87, 102–3, 104–5. A sensitive and insightful 20th-century account of the ecological relationships in the eastern Mongolian steppe among the Mongols, horses, wolves, gazelles, marmots, mice, and raptors is given in a fictional account by Jian Rong, *Wolf Totem*, Howard Goldblatt, trans. (New York, NY: The Penguin Press, 2008).

11. George B. Schaller and Gu Binyuan, "Ungulates in Northwest Tibet," *National Geographic Research and Exploration* 10, no. 3 (1994): 266–93.

12. Andrew C. Isenberg, *The Destruction of the Bison: An Environmental History, 1750–1920* (New York, NY: Cambridge University Press, 2000), 25.

13. Nicola Di Cosmo, *Ancient China and Its Enemies: The Rise of Nomadic Power in East Asian History* (Cambridge, UK: Cambridge University Press, 2002), 23.

14. Anthony, *The Horse, the Wheel, and Language*, 300.

15. Barfield, *The Nomadic Alternative*, 133.

16. See also Di Cosmo, *Ancient China and Its Enemies*, 28

17. Barfield, *The Nomadic Alternative*, 137.

18. According to Di Cosmo, "the transition to actual pastoral nomadism as practiced by horseback riders was probably not completed until the beginning of the first millennium B.C., and the first Scythian mounted archers appear on the scene only in the tenth or ninth century B.C." Di Cosmo, *Ancient China and Its Enemies*, 27.

19. Barfield, *The Nomadic Alternative*, 134–35.

20. Ibid., 140–44.

21. Ibid., 145–50.

22. Ibid., 144–45, 149.

23. Ibid., 149.

24. Martin Fiskesjö, "On the 'Raw' and the 'Cooked' Barbarians of Imperial China," *Inner Asia* 1 (1999): 139–68.

25. Heather Peters, "Tattooed Faces and Stilt Houses: Who Were the Ancient Yue?" in Victor Mair ed., *Sino-Platonic Papers* no. 17 (1990): 1–27.

26. See, for example, Stevan Harrell, *Ways of Being Ethnic in Southwest China* (Seattle: Washington University Press, 2001), esp. part 1; and Magnus Fiskesjö, "Rescuing the Empire: Chinese Nation-Building in the Twentieth Century," *European Journal of East Asian Studies* 5, no. 1 (2006), 15–44.

27. E. G. Pulleyblank, "The Chinese and Their Neighbors in Prehistoric and Early Historic Times," in *The Origins of Chinese Civilization*, ed. Keightley, 411–66.

28. Lothar von Falkenhausen, *Chinese Society in the Age of Confucius (1000–250 BC): The Archeological Evidence* (Los Angeles, CA: Cotsen Institute of Archeology, University of California–Los Angeles, 2006), ch. 5.

29. Stephen F. Sage, *Ancient Sichuan and the Unification of China* (Albany, NY: State University of New York Press, 1992), 35.

30. Von Falkenhausen, *Chinese Society in the Age of Confucius*, 240, 244–52.

31. Quoted in Elvin, *Retreat of the Elephants*, 43.

32. Hsu, "The Spring and Autumn Period," *CHAC*, 550.

33. Quoted in Hsu, "The Spring and Autumn Period," *CHAC*, 576.

34. Bray, *Agriculture*, 161

35. Shaughnessey, "Western Zhou History," 326–28.

36. Early Zhou rulers differed on whether Heaven had given the mandate to the king's family, or to the king only. The debate was settled for the latter, and Chinese rulers henceforth were then known as the "Son of Heaven." *Ibid.*, 315.

37. James Legge, *The Works of Mencius* (London, UK: Trübner, 1861), vol. 2, 156. A longer and slightly modified translation is quoted in Elvin, *Retreat of the Elephants*, 11.

38. Elvin, *Retreat of the Elephants*, 101.

39. Cho-yun Hsu, *Ancient China in Transition* (Stanford, CA: Stanford University Press, 1965), 111.

40. Di Cosmo, *Ancient China and Its Enemies*, 31–32, 39, 45–47.

41. Donald B. Wagner, *Iron and Steel in Ancient China* (Leiden, NL: E. J. Brill, 1993), 60–106, 406–7.

42. Wagner, *Iron and Steel in Ancient China*, 258.

43. Barbierri-Low, *Artisans in Early Imperial China*, 98–99.

44. Donald B. Wagner, personal e-mail communication.

45. Allan Rickett, *Guanzi: Political, Economic, and Philosophical Essays from Early China: A Study and Translation* (Princeton, NJ: Princeton University Press, 1985), vol. 1, 228.

46. Ibid., 230.

47. Ibid., 112, 254.
48. Ibid., 265–67.
49. Quoted in Chang, *Food in Chinese Culture*, 42.
50. Von Falkenhausen, *Chinese Society in the Age of Confucius*, 258.
51. Quoted in Nicola di Cosmo, "The Northern Frontier in Pre-Imperial China," in *CHAC*, 949.
52. Di Cosmo, *Ancient China and Its Enemies*, 87.
53. Ibid., 90.
54. Quoted in Di Cosmo, *Ancient China and Its Enemies*, 110.
55. Joseph Needham, *Science and Civilization in China*, vol. 4, part III, *Civil Engineering and Nautics* (Cambridge, UK: Cambridge University Press, 1971), 53.
56. Di Cosmo, "The Northern Frontier in Pre-Imperial China," 953.
57. Quoted in Needham, *Civil Engineering and Nautics*, 53.
58. Sechin Jagchid and Van Jay Symons, *Peace, War and Trade along the Great Wall* (Bloomington, IN: Indiana University Press, 1989).
59. Di Cosmo, *Ancient China and Its Enemies*, 156–57.
60. For the central role of the Qin conquest of Sichuan in the unification, see Sage, *Ancient Sichuan and the Unification of China*.
61. Ma Zhongliang, Song Chaogang, and Zhang Qinghua, *Zhongguo senlin de bianqian* [Changes to China's Forests] (Beijing, CN: Zhongguo Linye Chubanshe, 1997), 15.
62. Di Cosmo, *Ancient China and Its Enemies*, 174–86. For details, see Chun-shu Chang, *The Rise of the Chinese Empire*, vol. 1, *Nation, State, and Imperialism in Early China, ca. 1600 B.C.–A.D. 8* (Ann Arbor, MI: The University of Michigan Press, 2007), 193–201.
63. Chang, *Rise of the Chinese Empire*, vol. 1, *Nation, State, and Imperialism in Early China*, 158
64. Di Cosmo, *Ancient China and Its Enemies*, 190–96.
65. Chang, *Rise of the Chinese Empire*, vol. 1, 155.
66. Ho, *The Cradle of the East*, 91–120.
67. Chang, *Rise of the Chinese Empire*, vol. 1, 151, 159, table 6, 164–73. Where the trainers of horsemen and cavalrymen came from is unclear, but probably from those with such skills—the peoples of the steppe.
68. For details, see Chang, *Rise of the Chinese Empire*, vol. 1, chapters 4–5 and Chun-shu Chang, *Rise of the Chinese Empire*, vol. 2, *Frontier, Immigration, and Empire in Han China, 130 B.C.–A.D. 157* (Ann Arbor, MI: The University of Michigan Press, 2007).
69. A predecessor of the Han colonization scheme may well have been Qin policies and efforts after conquering the state of Shu in the Sichuan basin. Although the details are lacking, after the conquest Qin officials carried out a major land reform, giving land not just to the indigenous peasantry but to several tens of thousands, perhaps a hundred thousand, migrants sent from Qin. "Shu was thoroughly remade as an image of Qin, only more so, repopulated with a tide of immigrants from Qin itself and the central plains." See Sage, *Ancient Sichuan and the Unification of China*, 132–34, 196.
70. Chang, *Rise of the Chinese Empire* vol. 1, 211–12.
71. Ibid., ch. 5.
72. Ibid., 212.
73. Ibid., 237.
74. See the photographs in Chun-shu Chang, *Rise of the Chinese Empire*, vol. 2, plate 3.
75. For an interesting analysis of two differing Dust Bowl narratives, see William Cronon, "A Place for Stories: Nature, History, and Narrative," *The Journal of American History* 78, no. 2 (Mar 1992): 1347–76.
76. Quoted in Needham, *Civil Engineering and Nautics*, 7.
77. Needham, *Civil Engineering and Nautics*, 16, 19–21.

78. Quoted in Needham, *Civil Engineering and Nautics*, 25.

79. Needham, *Civil Engineering and Nautics*, 17.

80. Lattimore, *Inner Asian Frontiers*, 172–73.

81. This paragraph and the next are based on S. A. M. Adshead, *China in World History*, 2nd ed. (New York, NY: St. Martin's Press,1995), ch. 1.

82. Quoted in *Fan Sheng-chih Shi: An Agricultural Book of China written by Fan Sheng-chih in the First Century B.C.*, trans. and commented on by Shih Sheng-han (Beijing, CN: Science Press, 1959), 49 n. 7.

83. Alfred Crosby, *The Columbian Exchange: Biological and Cultural Consequences of 1492* (Westport, CT: Greenwood Press, 1972).

84. Bin Yang, "Horses, Silver, and Cowries: Yunnan in Global Perspective," *Journal of World History* 15, no. 3 (2004): 281–322.

85. Cho-yun Hsu, *Ancient China in Transition*, "Conclusion," 175–80.

86. On agriculture, see Cho-yun Hsu, *Han Agriculture: The Formation of Early Chinese Agrarian Economy* (Seattle, WA: University of Washington Press, 1980).

87. Bray, *Agriculture*, 179.

88. For a first-hand account of farming techniques, see *Fan Sheng-chih Shu.*

89. *Fan Sheng-chih Shu*, 49.

90. Francesca Bray, "Agricultural Technology and Agrarian Change in Han China," *Early China* vol. 5 (1980), 4.

91. Ma, Song, and Zhang, *Zhongguo senlin de bianqian*, 37.

92. Quoted in Elvin, *Retreat of the Elephants*, 122.

93. See Elvin, *Retreat of the Elephants*, 122–23, and Pierre-Etienne Will, "Clear Waters versus Muddy Waves: The Zheng-Bai Irrigation System of Shaanxi Province in the Late Imperial Period," in *Sediments of Time*, eds. Mark Elvin and Liu Ts'ui-jung (Cambridge and New York, NY: Cambridge University Press, 1998), 283–343, for the story of the Zheng Guo canal. See also Mark Elvin, "Three Thousand Years of Unsustainable Growth: China's Environment from Archaic Times to the Present," *East Asian History*, vol. 6 (1993), 7–46

94. Sage, *Ancient Sichuan and the Unification of China*, 148.

95. Needham, *Civil Engineering and Nautics*, 299–306; Marks, *Tigers*, 34.

96. This section is drawn from Needham, *Civil Engineering and Nautics*, 227–54. For a very brief discussion, see also Elvin, "Three Thousand Years of Unsustainable Growth."

97. Heiner Roetz, "On Nature and Culture in Zhou China," in *Concepts of Nature: A Chinese-European Cross-Cultural Perspective*, eds. Hans Ulrich Vogel and Gunter Dux (Leiden, NL: Brill, 2010), 203, n. 20.

98. Needham, *Civil Engineering and Nautics*, 235.

99. K. C. Chang, *Food in Chinese History*, 67–68, 73.

100. Mark Edward Lewis, *Sanctioned Violence in Early China* (Albany, NY: State University of New York Press, 1990), 150.

101. Ibid., 151

102. Ibid., 151–52.

103. Ibid., 154.

104. For a biography of that advisor and his influence on the creation of the centralized Chinese state, see Derk Bodde, *China's First Unifier: A Study of the Ch'in Dynasty as Seen in the Life of Li Ssu* (Leiden, NL: E. J. Brill, 1938).

105. The discussion of "nature" in this paragraph comes from Robert P. Weller, *Discovering Nature: Globalization and Environmental Culture in China and Taiwan* (Cambridge, UK: Cambridge University Press, 2006), 20–23.

106. For a discussion of these difficulties, and an exploration of the concept of "nature" in the late imperial period that does shed light on these earlier considerations, see Paolo Santangelo,

"Ecologism versus Moralism: Conceptions of Nature in Some Literary Texts of Ming-Qing Times," in *Sediments of Time*, eds. Mark Elvin and Liu Ts'ui-jung, 617–56.

107. For an exhaustive list of the latter, see Christoph Harbsmeier, "Towards a Conceptual History of Some Concepts of Nature in Classical Chinese: *ZI RAN* and *ZI RAN ZHI LI*," in *Concepts of Nature: A Chinese-European Cross-Cultural Perspective*, eds. Hans Ulrich Vogel and Gunter Dux (Leiden, NL: Brill, 2010), 220–54.

108. Helwig Schmidt-Glintzer, "On the Relationship between Man and Nature in China," in *Concepts of Nature*, eds. Hans Ulrich Vogel and Gunter Dux, 526–27.

109. Two places to start are the essays in Mary Evelyn Tucker and John Berthrong, eds., *Confucianism and Ecology: The Interrelation of Heaven, Earth, and Humans* (Cambridge, MA: Harvard University Press, 1998), and Hans Ulrich Vogel and Gunter Dux, eds., *Concepts of Nature: A Chinese-European Cross-Cultural Perspective* (Leiden, NL: Brill, 2010).

110. For a brief discussion, see Heiner Roetz, "On Nature and Culture in Zhou China," in *Concepts of Nature*, eds. Hans Ulrich Vogel and Gunter Dux (Leiden, NL: Brill, 2010), 198–200.

111. Examples of Chinese landscape painting can be found in nearly any art history textbook, but especially good representations can be found in Wen C. Fong and James Y. C. Watt, eds., *Possessing the Past: Treasures from the National Palace Museum, Taipei* (New York, NY: The Metropolitan Museum of Art, 1996); two catalogues from special exhibitions from the collection of the National Palace Museum in Taipei, *Xia jing shanshui hua tezhan tulu* [A Special Exhibition of Summer Landscape Paintings] (Taipei, CN: National Palace Museum, 1993), and *Dong jing shanshui hua tezhan tulu* [A Special Exhibition of Winter Landscape Paintings] (Taipei, CN: National Palace Museum, 1996); and several works by James Cahill, including the overview in *The Painter's Practice: How Artists Lived and Worked in Traditional China* (New York, NY: Columbia University Press, 1994).

112. John B. Henderson, "Cosmology and Concepts of Nature in Traditional China," in *Concepts of Nature*, eds. Hans Ulrich Vogel and Gunter Dux, 181–97; Mark Elvin uses the concept of "moral meteorology" in *Retreat of the Elephants*, 414–20.

113. Heiner Roetz, "On Nature and Culture in Zhou China," 201.

114. Ibid., 209.

115. Zhuangzi, quoted in Heiner Roetz, "On Nature and Culture in Zhou China," 205.

116. See the long quotation from the Daoist text the *Huainanzi* in Elvin, *Retreat of the Elephants*, 109–10.

117. *Sources of Chinese Civilization*, 2nd edition, 151.

118. J. Donald Hughes, *An Environmental History of the World: Humankinds Changing Role in the Community of Life* (New York, NY: Routledge, 2001), 72.

119. Roetz, "On Nature and Culture in Zhou China," 213.

120. Quoted in Elvin, *Retreat of the Elephants*, 102–3.

121. Quotes from *The Guanzi*, quoted in Elvin, *Retreat of the Elephants*, 105–6.

122. Quoted in Anderson, *The Food of China*, 33.

123. Charles Sanft, "Environment and Law in Early Imperial China (Third Century BCE–First Century CE): Qin and Han Statutes Concerning Natural Resources," *Environmental History* 15 (2010): 708–09. Sanft argues that while these and similar statutes had the intent of conservation, "these did not result in effective, long-term protection" (715). Given the evidence that this book will amass, that might be somewhat of an understatement.

124. Quoted in Anderson, *The Food of China*, 33.

125. Cho-yun Hsu, *Ancient China in Transition*, 134.

126. Cho-yun Hsu, *Han Agriculture*, 108.

127. The following paragraphs are based on William H. McNeill, *Plagues and Peoples* (Garden City NY: Anchor Books, 1976), 26–61, 117–19.

128. Donald R. Hopkins, *The Greatest Killer: Smallpox in History* (Chicago, IL: The University of Chicago Press, 2002), 18, 103–5.

129. Quoted in McNeill, *Plagues and Peoples*, 118.

130. Quoted in Arthur F. Wright, *Buddhism in Chinese History* (New York, NY: Atheneum, 1969), 19–20.

131. For an insightful discussion of macro- and micro-parasites, see McNeill, *Plagues and Peoples*, 5–7.

132. Howard S. Levy, "Yellow Turban Religion and Rebellion at the End of the Han," *Journal of the American Oriental Society* 74, no. 4 (1956), 214–27.

CHAPTER 4

1. For an overview, see Herold J. Wiens, *Han Chinese Expansion in South China* (Hamden, CT: The Shoe String Press, 1967).

2. Paul J. Smith, *Taxing Heaven's Storehouse: Horses, Bureaucrats, and the Destruction of the Sichuan Tea Industry, 1074–1224* (Cambridge, MA: Harvard University Press, 1991), 3.

3. L. S. Yang, *Studies in Chinese Institutional History* (Cambridge, MA: Harvard-Yenching Institute, 1961), 126.

4. Quoted in David A. Graff, *Medieval Chinese Warfare, 300–900* (London, UK and New York, NY: Routledge, 2002), 47.

5. Arthur F. Wright, *The Sui Dynasty* (New York, NY: Knopf, 1978), 24.

6. Quoted in Arthur F. Wright, *Buddhism in Chinese History* (Stanford, CA: Stanford University Press, 1959), 42.

7. Graff, *Medieval Chinese Warfare*, 56.

8. For those seeking a brief sampling, see Graff, *Medieval Chinese Warfare,* ch. 3.

9. Graff, *Medieval Chinese Warfare*, 60.

10. Etienne Balazs, *Chinese Civilization and Bureaucracy*, ed. and intro. Arthur F. Wright (New Haven, CT: Yale University Press, 1977), 107.

11. Sing Chew, *The Recurring Dark Ages: Ecological Stress, Climate Changes, and System Transformation* (Lanham, MD: AltaMira Press, 2007).

12. Francesca Bray, *Agriculture*, 96–98.

13. Graff, *Medieval Chinese Warfare*, 64.

14. Ping-ti Ho, "Lo-yang A.D. 495–534: A Study of Physical and Socio-economic Planning of a Metropolitan Area," *Harvard Journal of Asiatic Studies* 26 (1966): 52–101.

15. For a chilling description, see Jonathan Schell, *The Fate of the Earth* (New York, NY: Knopf, 1982).

16. T. H. Barrett, *The Woman Who Discovered Printing* (New Haven: Yale University Press, 2008), 57–59.

17. For a translation of one of those texts, see James R. Ware, *Alchemy, Medicine, Religion in the China of A. D. 320: The Nei P'ien of Ko Hung (Pao-p'u tzu)* (Cambridge, MA: The M.I.T. Press, 1966). Ware also translates Ge's autobiography.

18. Elisabeth Hsu, "Reflections on the 'discovery' of the antimalarial qinghao," *British Journal of Clinical Pharmacology* 61, no. 6 (2006): 666–70.

19. Wiens, *Han Chinese Expansion in South China*, 140–41.

20. For an exhaustive look at the state of Chinese medical treatments of malaria around 1300 CE that does not include Ge Hong and his remedy based on qinghao, see Saburo Miyasita, "Malaria (yao) in Chinese Medicine during the Chin and Yuan Periods," *Acta Asiatica: Bulletin of the Institute of Eastern Culture* 36 (March 1979): 90–112.

21. Wright, *The Sui Dynasty*, 26.

22. Graff, *Medieval Chinese Warfare*, 77.

23. Shiba Yoshinobu, "Environment versus Water Control: The Case of the Southern Hangzhou Bay Area from the Mid-Tang through the Qing," in *The Sediments of Time: Environment and Society in China*, eds. Mark Elvin and Ts'ui-jung Liu (New York, NY: Cambridge University Press, 1997), 141.

24. Franscesa Bray, *The Rice Economies: Technology and Development in Asian Societies* (Berkeley and Los Angeles, CA: University of California Press, 1994), 28–29. Emphasis added.

25. For the full argument, see Bray, *The Rice Economies*, ch. 6.

26. Shiba, "Environment versus Water Control," 135.

27. Herbert Franke and Denis Twitchett, eds., *The Cambridge History of China*, vol. 6, *Alien Regimes and Border States* (New York, NY: Cambridge University Press, 1995).

28. Arthur F. Wright, *The Sui Dynasty*, chs. 1–2.

29. E.g., Denis Twitchett, ed., *The Cambridge History of China*, vol. 3, *Sui and T'ang China, 589–906*, Part I (Cambridge and New York, NY: Cambridge University Press, 1979); Wright, *The Sui Dynasty*; Graff, *Medieval Chinese Warfare*.

30. Wright, *The Sui Dynasty*, 163.

31. See Joseph Needham, *Science and Civilization in China*, vol. 4, part 3, *Engineering and Nautics* (Cambridge, UK and New York, NY: Cambridge University Press, 1971), 306–320; and Wright, *The Sui Dynasty*, 177–81.

32. Needham, *Engineering and Nautics*, 319.

33. Wright, *The Sui Dynasty*, 179–80.

34. On all of these peoples, see Edward H. Schafer, *The Vermilion Bird: T'ang Images of the South* (Los Angeles and Berkeley, CA: University of California Press, 1967), chs. 1–3. See also Wiens, *Han Chinese Expansion in South China*, esp. chs. 2–3.

35. Quoted in Schafer, *The Vermilion Bird*, 51, 52.

36. Liu Yuxin, translated and quoted in Schafer, *The Vermilion Bird*, 54–55.

37. Schafer, *The Vermilion Bird*, 61.

38. Ibid., 69.

39. Weins, *Han Chinese Expansion in South China*, 193–94.

40. Ma Zhongliang, Song Chaogang, and Zhang Qinghua, *Zhongguo senlin de bianqian* [Changes to China's Forests] (Beijing, CN: Zhongguo Linye Chubanshe, 1997), 22.

41. Schafer, *The Vermilion Bird*, 195.

42. Ibid., 173–76.

43. Ibid., 160–62.

44. These three paragraphs on Fujian are drawn from Hugh R. Clark, "Wu Xing Fights a Jiao: An Allegory of Cultural Tensions" (paper presented at the 2009 AAS annual meeting, Chicago, IL). In this paper, Professor Clark unravels the fascinating story of how a Chinese folk tale both recapitulates the "heroic" role of a Chinese official in taming a wild frontier and points to real tensions between the indigenous Yue people and the new Han Chinese in-migrants.

45. As suggested by James C. Scott, *The Art of Not Being Governed: An Anarchist History of Upland Southeast Asia* (New Haven, CT: Yale University Press, 2009), 138–41.

46. Weins, *Han Chinese Expansion in South China*, 335.

47. Schafer, *The Vermilion Bird*, 65, 77, 102.

48. This section is excerpted from Robert B. Marks, *Tigers, Rice, Silk, and Silt: Environment and Economy in Late Imperial South China* (Cambridge and New York, NY: Cambridge University Press, 1998), 71–76.

49. On the history of malaria, see three recent books: James L. A. Webb Jr., *Humanity's Burden: A Global History of Malaria* (New York, NY: Cambridge University Press, 2009); Sonia Shah, *The Fever: How Malaria Has Ruled Humankind for 500,000 Years* (New York,

NY: Sarah Crichton Books, 2010); and Randall M. Packard, *The Making of a Tropical Disease: A Short History of Malaria* (Baltimore, MD: Johns Hopkins Press, 2007).

50. Brian Maegraith, *Adams and Maegraith: Clinical Tropical Diseases* (Oxford, UK: Blackwell Scientific, 1989), 201.

51. Zhou Quofei, quoted in Marks, *Tigers*, 72.

52. Maegraith, *Clinical Tropical Diseases*, 201.

53. Quoted in Marks, *Tigers*, 75.

54. For a brief account of ancient Chinese cholera, see Kerrie L. MacPherson, "Cholera in China, 1820–1930," in *Sediments of Time*, eds. Elvin and Liu, 492–99.

55. Zhang Yixia and Mark Elvin, "Environment and Tuberculosis in Modern China," in *Sediments of Time*, eds. Elvin and Liu, 521–23.

56. Denis Twitchett, "Population and Pestilence in T'ang China," in *Studia Sino Mongolia: Festshrift für Herbet Franke*, ed. Wolfgang Bauer (Weisbaden, DE: Steiner, 1979), 42.

57. Ibid., 43–45.

58. Ibid., 47.

59. Ibid., 50–51.

60. Yoshinobu, "Environment versus Water Control," 141, 151–58.

61. Mira Ann Mihelich, *Polders and the Politics of Land Reclamation in Southeast Chinese during the Northern Sung Dynasty (960–1126)* (Cornell University Ph.D. dissertation, 1979), 192–93. Mihelich claims that a total of 34 million acres were reclaimed, an area the size of Kansas. Those figures may instead be for Chinese "acres," or *mu*, which were about one-sixth of an English acre, which would still be about 5.6 million acres.

62. Ling Zhang, "Ponds, Paddies and Frontier Defence: Environmental and Economic Changes in Northern Hebei in Northern Song China (960–1127)," *Journal of Medieval History*, 14.1 (2011): 21–43.

63. According to one expert, "There are many factors that result in the modification of any given variety. Plants as a rule are notorious hybridizers. Because of the transference of pollen by wind, insects or other agencies cannot be adequately controlled, hybridization has gone on uninterruptedly, and the rice plant is no exception. The resultant combinations, stable or unstable, complicate the varietal picture. Mutations certainly must have added numbers to the list. Selection, conscious or natural, has released latent differences which under conditions of a new environment, accidental or controlled, have been given an opportunity to express themselves. These germinal differences, stemming from hereditary reservoirs, may express other differences imposed on them by a peculiar kind of environment. These new differenced are not themselves inherent in the germ plasm, but are responses to a particular environment and may persist as long as the environment remains consistent. Lowland cultivation, upland cultivation, and length of growing season are only three of the modifying influences which call forth definite morphological and physiological expressions." Quoted in Ping-ti Ho, "Early-Ripening Rice in Chinese History," *The Economic History Review*, New Series 9, no. 2 (1956): 210 n. 1.

64. Li Bozhong, "Was There a 'Fourteenth-Century Turning Point'? Population, Land, Technology, and Farm Management," in *The Song-Yuan-Ming Transition in Chinese History*, eds. Paul Jakov Smith and Richard von Glahn (Cambridge, MA: Harvard University Asia Center, 2003), 150–53, 159–61.

65. Ho, "Early-Ripening Rice in Chinese History," 201.

66. Ibid., 211–14, 215.

67. Alfred W. Crosby, *Ecological Imperialism: The Biological Expansion of Europe, 900-1900* (New York, NY: Cambridge University Press, 1986), 28. For an engaging exploration based on English history, see Richard Mabey, *Weeds: In Defense of Nature's Most Unloved Plants* (New York, NY: HarperCollins, 2011).

68. Bray, *Agriculture*, 300. For examples of the implements, see pages 302–317.

69. Sima Qian, quoted in Bray, *Agriculture*, 99.

70. Ibid., 318.

71. Ibid., 299.

72. Liu Xun, quoted in Cai Renkui, Ni Dashu, and Wang Jianguo, "Rice-Fish Culture in China: The Past, Present, and Future," in Kenneth T. MacKay ed., *Rice-fish Culture in China* (Ottawa: International Development Research Centre, 1995), 4.

73. Wu Neng, Liao Guohou, Lou Yulin, and Zhong Gemei, "The Role of Fish in Controlling Mosquitoes in Ricefields," in MacKay, *Rice-Fish Culture*, 213; Wang Jianguo and Ni Dashu, "A Comparative Study of the Ability of Fish to Catch Mosquito Larva," in MacKay, *Rice-Fish Culture*, 218–219.

74. William H. McNeill, *Plagues and Peoples* (Garden City, NJ: Anchor Press, 1976), 5–13.

75. Mark Elvin, *The Pattern of the Chinese Past* (Stanford, CA: Stanford University Press, 1971), 116.

76. Sheng-han Shih, *A Preliminary Survey of the Book Ch'i Min Yao Shu, an Agricultural Treatise of the Sixth Century* (Beijing, CN: Science Press, 1962).

77. For a discussion of the complexities of the problem of landownership in the Song era, see Denis Twitchett, *Land Tenure and the Social Order in T'ang and Sung China* (London: University of London School of Oriental and African Studies, 1962); Mark Elvin, "The Last Thousand Years of Chinese History: Changing Patterns in Land Tenure," *Modern Asian Studies* 4, no. 2 (1970): 97–114; Peter J. Golas, "Rural China in the Song," *The Journal of Asian Studies* 39, no. 2 (1980): 291–325; and Joseph P. McDermott, "Charting Blank Spaces and Disputed Regions: The Problem of Sung Land Tenure," *The Journal of Asian Studies* 44, no. 1 (1984): 13–41.

78. Golas, "Rural China in the Song," 309.

79. Ibid., 302.

80. Jacques Gernet, *Buddhism in Chinese Society: An Economic History from the Fifth to the Tenth Centuries*, trans. Franciscus Verellen (New York, NY: Columbia University Press, 1995), 7. Gernet points out that these great establishments do not include the 30,000–40,000 small sanctuaries with a monk or two.

81. Ibid., 115.

82. Ibid., 116–17.

83. Quoted in ibid., 20.

84. Ibid., 17.

85. Denis Twirchett, "The Monasteris and China's Economy in Medieval Times," *Bulletin of the School of Oriental and African Studies* 19, no. 3 (1957): 535–41.

86. Twitchett, "The Monasteries and China's Economy in Medieval Times," 536–37.

87. Gernet, *Buddhism in Chinese Society*, 100.

88. Ibid., 102.

89. James Cahill, *The Painter's Practice: How Artists Lived and Worked in Traditional China* (New York, NY: Columbia University Press, 1994), 98–100. See also James Cahill, *Hills Beyond a River: Chinese Painting of the Yüan Dynasty* (New York, NY: Weatherhill, 1976).

90. Quoted in Wen C. Fong and James Y. C. Watt, *Possessing the Past: Treasures from the National Palace Museum, Taipei* (New York, NY: The Metropolitan Museum of Art, 1996), 127–28.

91. Edward H. Schafer, "The Conservation of Nature under the T'ang Dynasty," *Journal of the Economic and Social History of the Orient* 5, no. 3 (1962): 298. Schafer is probably wrong in deducing from his sources that "the most civilized of all arts [writing] . . . was responsible

for the deforestation of much of north China." As we have seen so far, clearing forests for farms was a much more powerful force, and as historian Ling Zhang points out later in this chapter, maintaining dikes to maintain the Yellow River in its course is more likely the cause of denuding the Taihang Mountains.

92. Ibid., 301–2.

93. Ibid., 308.

94. Joanna Handlin Smith, "Societies for Liberating Animals," in *The Art of Doing Good: Charity in Late Ming China* (Berkeley and Los Angeles, CA: University of California Press, 2009), 15–42.

95. The term is from Mark Elvin, *The Pattern of the Chinese Past*, Part 2, 111–99.

96. Denis Twtichett, "Chinese Social History from the Seventh to the Tenth Centuries: The Tunhuang Documents and Their Implications," *Past and Present*, no. 35 (1966): 40–42.

97. F. W. Mote, *Imperial China, 900–1800* (Cambridge, MA: Harvard University Press, 1999), 133–34.

98. Quoted in Michael Freeman, "Sung," in *Food in Chinese Culture: Anthropological and Historical Perspectives*, ed. K. C. Chang (New Haven, CT: Yale University Press, 1977), 151.

99. Ibid., 127.

100. E. A. Anderson, *The Food of China* (New Haven, CT: Yale University Press, 1988), 67–68.

101. Robert Hartwell, "A Revolution in the Chinese Iron and Coal Industries during the Northern Sung, 960–1126 A.D.," *The Journal of Asian Studies* 21, no. 2 (1962), 159–60.

102. Hartwell, "A Revolution in the Chinese Iron and Coal Industries," 155–58.

103. Ibid., 161.

104. Ibid.

105. Mark Elvin, *The Pattern of the Chinese Past*, Part 2, 111–99.

106. In *The Pattern of the Chinese Past*, Elvin posited a "high-level equilibrium trap" as the reason an industrial revolution did not occur in China. For a broader discussion, see Jack Goldstone, "Efflorescences and Economic Growth in World History: Rethinking the 'Rise of theWest' and the Industrial Revolution," *Journal of World History* 13, no. 2 (2002): 323–389.

107. Robert Hartwell, "A Cycle of Economic Change in Imperial China: Coal and Iron in Northeast China, 750–1350," *Journal of the Economic and Social History of the Orient*, no. 10 (1967): 151.

108. By the late imperial period, at least. See Magnus Fiskesjö, "On the 'Raw' and the 'Cooked' Barbarians of Imperial China," *Inner Asia* 1 (1999): 147.

109. The following paragraphs on Sichuan are based on Richard von Glahn, *The Country of Streams and Grottoes: Expansion, Settlement, and the Civilizing of the Sichuan Frontier in Song Times* (Cambridge MA: Harvard University Press, 1987).

110. Ibid., 33.

111. Ibid., 191.

112. Scott, *The Art of Not Being Governed.*

113. Fiskesjö, "On the 'Raw' and the 'Cooked,'" 139–168. See also Scott, *The Art of Not Being Governed*, chs. 4–6.

114. Direct evidence is provided by Lin Niangsong, "Sui Tang Wu Dai senlin shu lue" [The extent of forests in the Sui, Tang, and Five Dynasties periods], *Nongye kaogu* [Agricultural archeology], no. 1 (1995): 218–25.

115. Edward H. Schafer, "War Elephants in Ancient and Medieval China," *Oriens* 10, no. 2 (1957): 289.

116. Mark Elvin, *Retreat of the Elephants*, 10, 12–14.

117. Marks, *Tigers*, 44–45.

118. Frank Leeming, "Official Landscapes in Traditional China," *Journal of the Economic and Social History of the Orient* 23, no. 1/2 (1980): 153–204.

119. Ling Zhang, "Manipulating the Yellow River and the State Formation of the Northern Song Dynasty (960–1127)," *Environment and Climate in China and Beyond*, ed. Carmen Meinhert (Leiden, NL: Brill, forthcoming).

120. Roetz, "On Nature and Culture in Zhou China," in *Concepts of Nature*, eds. Vogel and Dux, 203 n. 20.

121. Jiongxin Xu, "A Study of the Long-Term Environmental Effects of River Regulation on the Yellow River of China in Historical Perspective," *Geografiska Annaler, Series A, Physical Geography* 75, no. 3 (1993): 61–72.

122. The following is based on Christian Lamouroux, "From the Yellow River to the Huai: New Representations of a River Network and the Hydraulic Crisis of 1128," in *Sediments of Time*, eds. Elvin and Liu, 545–84.

123. Ibid., 546–48.

124. This story is teased out from Mark Elvin and Su Ninghu, "Action at a Distance: The Influence of the Yellow River on Hangzhou Bay since A.D. 1000," in *Sediments of Time*, eds. Elvin and Liu, 344–407.

125. This section is based on a wonderfully researched articled by Ling Zhang, "Changing with the Yellow River: An Environmental History of Hebei, 1048–1128," *Harvard Journal of Asiatic Studies* 69, no. 1 (2009): 1–36.

126. Ibid., 12.

127. Ibid., 24.

128. Ibid., 26.

129. Ibid., 12.

130. Ibid., 16.

131. Quoted in ibid., 28.

132. Quoted in ibid., 32.

133. Ibid., 34.

134. This section is excerpted from Marks, *Tigers*, 66–70; see also Robert B. Marks, "Geography Is Not Destiny: Historical Contingency and the Making of the Pearl River Delta," in *The Good Earth: Regional and Historical Insights into China's Environment*, eds. Abe Ken-ichi and James Nickum (Kyoto, HK: Kyoto University Press, 2009), 1–28.

135. Excerpted from Marks, *Tigers*, 76–79.

136. Excerpted from Marks, *Tigers*, 80–82.

137. Ho, "Lo-yang," 52. That is the number of cities recorded in Chinese sources as having been built, destroyed, abandoned, or still in use.

138. For Kaifeng, see Robert Hartwell, "A Cycle of Economic Change in Imperial China," 102–59; and Lawrence J. C. Ma, *Commercial Development and Urban Change in Sung China (960–1279)* (Ann Arbor, MI: University of Michigan Department of Geography, 1971); Pei-yi Wu, "Memories of Kaifeng," *New Literary History* 25, no. 1 (1994): 47–60. For Hangzhou, see Jacques Gernet, *Daily Life in China on the Eve of the Mongol Invasion 1250–1276*, H. M. Wright trans. (Stanford, CA: Stanford University Press, 1962).

139. This section on Chang'an is based on Arthur F. Wright, *The Sui Dynasty* (New York, NY: Alfred Knopf, 1978), 85–90; and Edward H. Schafer, "The Last Years of Ch'ang-an," *Oriens Extremus* 10 (1963): 133–79.

140. Schafer, "Ch'ang-an," 170.

141. Ibid., 152–53.

142. Edward H. Schafer, "Hunting Parks and Animal Enclosures in Ancient China," *Journal of Economic and Social History of the Orient* 11, no. 3 (1968): 318–43.

143. Ibid., 343.

144. Ibid., 342.

145. Elvin, *Retreat of the Elephants*, xvii.

146. Implied from J. R. McNeill, *Something New under the Sun*, comparing 336–340 with 310–311.

147. J. Donald Hughes, *An Environmental History of the World: Humankind's Changing Role in the Community of Life* (London, UK and New York, NY: Routledge, 2001), 8–9.

148. Radkau, *Nature and Power*, 2.

149. Frank H. King, *Farmers of Forty Centuries, or Permanent Agriculture in China, Korea, and Japan* (Madison, WI: Mrs. F. H. King, 1911), 194.

150. In her work on a nineteenth-century cholera outbreak, Kerrie L. MacPherson quoted an eighteenth-century English source who observed that because Chinese usually boiled water before drinking and carefully handled nightsoil, "the danger of contamination" was likely to have been reduced to "a minimum." MacPherson, "Cholera in China," 503.

151. Yong Xue, "'Treasure Nightsoil as if It Were Gold'": Economic and Ecological Links Between Urban and Rural Areas in Late Imperial Jiangnan," *Late Imperial China* 6, no. 1 (2005): 41–71.

152. E. N. Anderson, *The Food of China* (New Haven, CT: Yale University Press, 1988), 102.

153. King, *Farmers of Forty Centuries*, 167–70.

154. Pierre Poivre, *Travels of a Philosopher* (trans. from the French, London, UK 1769), 153.

155. Radkau, *Nature and Power*, 103–4.

CHAPTER 5

1. The devastation of Sichuan province was especially great, with recorded population there tumbling more than 90 percent from nearly 3 million households to only one hundred twenty thousand between 1200 and 1300. Paul J. Smith, "Commerce, Agriculture, and Core Formation in the Upper Yangzi, 2 A. D. to 1948," *Late Imperial China* 9, no. 1 (1988): 1–3.

2. Herbert Frank and Denis Twitchett, eds., *The Cambridge History of China*, vol. 6, *Alien Regimes and Border States, 907–1368* (New York, NY: Cambridge University Press, 1994), 362. Hereafter CHOC.

3. CHOC, vol. 6, 36.

4. Quoted in Dee Mack Williams, *Beyond Great Walls: Environment, Identity, and Development on the Chinese Grasslands of Inner Mongolia* (Stanford, CA: Stanford University Press, 2002), 67–68.

5. Quoted in ibid., 68.

6. The Mongols turned "large tracts" of north China into pasture before Kubilai Khan prohibited the practice because it reduced grain production and increased Mongol reliance on rice imports from the south. Herbert Franz Schurman, trans., *Economic Structure of the Yuan Dynasty*, (Cambridge, MA: Harvard University Press, 1956), 29–30.

7. William McNeill, *Plagues and Peoples*, 143–46; Robert Gottfried, *The Black Death* (New York, NY: The Free Press, 1983), 35.

8. Radkau, *Nature and Power*, 155; Carol Benedict, *Bubonic Plague in Nineteenth-Century China* (Stanford, CA: Stanford University Press, 1996), 7–10.

9. The problem of assessing the impact of Mongol rule on China is broached in F. W. Mote, *Imperial China, 900–1800* (Cambridge, MA: Harvard University Press, 1999), chs. 17–20.

10. Anthony Barbierri-Lowe argues that China had a market economy at least since the Han dynasty: "More than any other civilization in the ancient world, early imperial China operated under a money economy, where nearly everything could be purchased with standardized coins produced in vast quantities by state mints. . . . Though, in theory, the Chinese state wished to suppress commercialization in favor of agriculture, they nevertheless established market laws and regulations that greatly facilitated commerce. Recently unearthed legal texts now show that the early imperial Chinese state possessed a developed body of enforceable contract law that ensured market reliability, protected property rights, and lowered the kind of transaction costs that Douglas North has written were a hindrance to greater market activity in other premodern economies." Barbierri-Lowe, *Artisans in Early Imperial China*, 18.

11. See especially G. William Skinner, "Marketing and Social Structure in Rural China," Parts I, II, and III, *Journal of Asian Studies* Vol. 24, No. 1 (Nov, 1964), 3–43; Vol. 24, No. 2 (Feb, 1965), 195–228; and Vol. 24, No. 3 (May, 1965), 363–399.

12. Shiba, *Commerce and Society in Song China*, 140, 141.

13. For an early assessment of the interesting evidence, see Denis Twitchett, "Chinese Social History from the Seventh to the Tenth Centuries: The Tunhuang Documents and Their Implications," *Past and Present*, no. 35. (1966): 28–53.

14. For brief discussions, see Valerie Hansen, *The Open Empire: A History of China to 1600* (New York, NY: W. W. Norton, 2000); and Patricia Ebrey, *The Cambridge Illustrated History of China* (New York, NY: Cambridge University Press, 1998).

15. Jean Grove, *The Little Ice Age* (London, Methuen, 1988).

16. See the essays in Trevor Aston, ed., *Crisis in Europe, 1560–1660* (New York, NY: Doubleday, 1967); and in Geoffrey Parker and Leslie Smith, eds., *The General Crisis of the Seventeenth Century* (London, UK: Henley and Boston, 1978). The extent to which a "general crisis" extended to Asia is taken up in a set of essays in a special issue of *Modern Asian Studies* 24, no. 4 (1990): 625–97.

17. See especially Andre Gunder Frank, *ReOrient: Global Economy in the Asian Age* (Los Angeles and Berkeley, CA: University of California Press, 1998).

18. William S. Atwell, "Time, Money, and Weather: Ming China and the 'Great Depression' of the Mid-Fifteenth Century," *The Journal of Asian Studies* 61, no. 1 (2002): 83–113.

19. The concepts of "frontier" and "borderlands" are more ambiguous than not. For a discussion that is broader than the title implies, see Hugh R. Clark, "Frontier Discourse and China's Maritime Frontier: China's Frontiers and the Encounter with the Sea through Early Imperial History," *Journal of World History* 20, no. 1 (March, 2009): 1–33. For a discussion of "border," see Janet C. Sturgeon, *Border Landscapes: The Politics of Akha Land Use in China and Thailand* (Seattle, WA: University of Washington Press, 2005), 4–7.

20. That Chinese peasants were free to migrate in response to demographic pressures or economic pulls or pushes distinguishes China from much of the rest of the early modern world, where restrictions on freedom prevented migration. As Kenneth Pomeranz points out, this difference was significant for the ways in which China's economy developed (or didn't) in the eighteenth and nineteenth centuries. Kenneth Pomeranz, *The Great Divergence: China, Europe and the Making of the Modern World Economy* (Princeton, NJ: Princeton University Press, 2000.

21. Bin Yang, "Horses, Silver and Cowries: Yunnan in Global Perspective," *Journal of World History* 15, no. 3 (2004): 281–98.

22. Ibid., 298–322.

23. John E. Herman, "The Cant of Conquest: *Tusi* Offices and China's Political Incorporation of the Southwest Frontier," in *Empire at the Margins: Culture, Ethnicity, and Frontier in Early Modern China*, eds. Pamela Kyle Crossley, Helen F. Siu, and Donald S. Sutton (Berkeley and Los Angeles, CA: University of California Press, 2006), 135.

24. For a sampling of the contemporary understandings of all these peoples, see Stevan Harrell, *Ways of Being Ethnic in Southwest China* (Seattle, WA: University of Washington Press, 2001).

25. Magnus Fiskesjö, "On the 'Raw' and the 'Cooked' Barbarians of Imperial China," *Inner Asia* 1 (1999): 145–46.

26. Li Daoyong, "The Kammu People in China and Their Social Customs," *Asian Folklore Studies* 43, no. 1 (1984): 15–28.

27. Sturgeon, *Border Landscapes*, 8. See 120–22 for a fuller description of the cultivation practices and 123–26 for a description of the region's geography, forests, and wildlife.

28. John E. Herman, *Amid the Clouds and Mist: China's Colonization of Guizhou, 1200–1700* (Cambridge, MA: Harvard University Press, 2007), 21.

29. Ibid., 66–70.

30. C. Patterson Giersch, *Asian Borderlands: The Transformation of Qing China's Yunnan Frontier* (Cambridge, MA: Harvard University Press, 2006), 20.

31. James C. Scott, *The Art of Not Being Governed: An Anarchist History of Upland Southeast Asia* (New Haven, CT: Yale University Press, 2009), ch.1.

32. Elvin, *Retreat of the Elephants*, 216.

33. Geneticists now think that modern humans migrated into East Asia in a single wave from Southeast Asia. The greatest human diversity thus is found there and in China's south and southwest, and decreases as human populations migrated north. See The HUGO Pan-Asian SNP Consortium, "Mapping Human Genetic Diversity in Asia," *Science* 326 (December 11, 2009): 1541–45.

34. Nicholas Menzies, "The Villagers' View of Environmental History in Yunnan Province," in *Sediments of Time*, eds. Elvin and Liu, 112–113.

35. Giersch, *Asian Borderlands*, 22–24.

36. Laura Hostetler, *Qing Colonial Enterprise: Ethnography and Cartography in Early Modern China* (Chicago, IL: University of Chicago Press, 2001), 105–114, 135–148.

37. Herman, "The Cant of Conquest, 135–68.

38. Herman, *Amid the Clouds and Mist*, 10.

39. Ibid., 87.

40. Ibid., 136.

41. Ibid., 131.

42. In addition to the books by Giersch and Herman listed above, see also Leo Shin, *The Making of the Chinese State: Ethnicity and Expansion on the Ming Borderlands* (New York, NY: Cambridge University Press, 2006). Not all the violence and land grabs were Han Chinese taking from the locals. There was plenty of conflict among them as well, in part because a chieftain could covet his neighbor's land and expect Chinese support (or benign neglect) when going after it, and in part because the Chinese state often was too unfamiliar with what was actually going on to distinguish between internative warfare and "rebellion" against the Ming state.

43. David Faure, "The Yao Wars in the Mid-Ming and Their Impact on Yao Ethnicity," in *Empire at the Margins*, eds. Crossley, Siu, and Sutton, 176.

44. Elvin, *Retreat of the Elephants*, 227.

45. Quoted in Elvin, *Retreat of the Elephants*, 229–30.

46. Herman, "The Cant of Conquest," 151.

47. Quoted in Hostetler, *Qing Colonial Enterprise*, 113.

48. Ibid., 121–22.

49. James Lee, "Food Supply and Population Growth in Southwest China, 1250–1850," *Journal of Asian Studies* 41, no. 4 (1982): 712.

50. For this complicated story, see Richard von Glahn, *Fountain of Fortune: Money and Monetary Policy in China, 1000–1700* (Berkeley and Los Angeles, CA: University of California Press, 1996).

51. Dennis O. Flynn and Arturo Giraldez, "Cycles of Silver: Global Economic Unity through the mid-18th Century," *Journal of World History* 13 (2002): 391–428.

52. Herman, *Amid the Clouds and Mist*, 142.

53. Nearly 10,000 tons per year. E-tu Zen Sun, "Ch'ing Government and the Mineral Industries before 1800," *The Journal of Asian Studies* 27, no. 4 (1968): 841.

54. Xu Dixin and Wu Chengming, eds., *Chinese Capitalism, 1522–1840* English edition ed. and annot. C. A. Curwen (New York, NY: St. Martin's Press, 2000), 287.

55. Ibid.

56. Owen Lattimore, *Studies in Frontier History: Collected Papers, 1928–1958* (London, UK: Oxford University Press, 1962), 108–9.

57. Arthur Waldron, *The Great Wall of China: From History to Myth* (Cambridge, UK and New York, NY: Cambridge University Press, 1990), 62–63.

58. Ibid., 64.

59. Ibid., 87.

60. Ibid., 91.

61. Eduard B. Vermeer, "Population and Ecology along the Frontier in Qing China," in *The Sediments of Time*, eds. Elvin and Liu, 238.

62. There has been much debate on the extent and causes of the "general crisis." See the essays in Trevor Aston, ed., *Crisis in Europe, 1560–1660* (New York, NY: Doubleday, 1967); and in Geoffrey Parker and Leslie Smith, eds., *The General Crisis of the Seventeenth Century* (London: Henley and Boston, 1978). The extent to which a "general crisis" extended to Asia is taken up in a set of essays in a special issue of *Modern Asian Studies* 24, no. 4 (1990). As William Atwell has aptly observed, the concept of "general crisis" is somewhat ambiguous as used in the literature on Europe. Let us start with the idea of "crisis." As used initially among European historians looking at the seventeenth century, the term tended toward imprecision, leading to the helpful criticism that "it must be realized that nowadays the crisis is often merely an affirmation of the undisputable fact that something happened in the seventeenth century; the crisis has become a synonym for what historians concerned with other centuries call 'history.'" Building on this critique, Theodore Rabb offered a definition of "crisis" that Atwell subsequently adopted in his analyses of seventeenth-century East Asia: for the term "crisis" to retain any meaning at all, the crisis must be shortlived—maybe in historical perspectives as long as two decades—and it must be distinct both from what precedes and follows. Atwell then proceeds to argue that the crisis period "falls between the early 1630s and the late 1640s." For south China, the timing of the crisis was a bit later, beginning in the mid-1640s and extending into the late 1650s. The other part of the concept—"general"—is also laden with ambiguity. It can mean either an event that occurred broadly over a large expanse of territory, such as all of China or East Asia, or a conjuncture of crises affecting a region deeply throughout its society, economy, and polity, to mention just a few of its possible facets. In two excellent essays exploring the extent of the general crisis in East Asia, Atwell adopts the former definition, stressing the breadth of the crisis across a wide geographic area. As will be used here, though, "general" will signify depth: four and perhaps five different kinds of crises cutting across most aspects of life and livelihood afflicted the people of south China in the middle of the seventeenth century. A demographic crisis, brought about in part by food shortages, epidemic disease, and warfare, resulted in a significant loss of population; an economic crisis was caused in part by declining agricultural production but also by a break in overseas trade and monetary fluctuations, all of which fueled unemployment; banditry and piracy coupled with uprisings of tenants and tenant-serfs ripped the social fabric; and the political crisis of the fall of the Ming and the consolidation of the Qing, which brought state-sponsored warfare with its attendant death and destruction to south China. An intellectual and cultural crisis could be added to the list, but such an exploration extends beyond the bounds of this study. Our

purpose here will be first to describe these crises, and then to examine their consequences. See William S. Atwell, "A Seventeenth-Century 'General Crisis' in East Asia?" *Modern Asian Studies* 24, no. 4 (1990): 664–65; see also his "Some Observations on the 'Seventeenth-Century Crisis' in China and Japan," 223–44.

63. Jean Grove, *The Little Ice Age* (London, UK: Methuen, 1988), 1.

64. Marks, *Tigers*, 139–40.

65. In discussing the effects of the seventeenth-century crisis on Manchuria, Frederic Wakeman speculates that "the pressure upon the Manchus to find new sources of food must have been increased by the growing cold of the 'little ice age,'" which in turn "may have played no small part in spurring the Manchus to military conquest." *The Great Enterprise* (Berkeley and Los Angeles, CA: University of California Press, 1985), 58, 48.

66. For detailed evidence, see Marks, *Tigers*, ch. 6.

67. Marks, *Tigers*, 138–40.

68. Helen Dunstan, "The Late Ming Epidemics: A Preliminary Survey," *Ch'ing-shih wen-t'i* 3, no. 3 (1975): 14.

69. Ibid., 14–32.

70. James B. Parsons, *Peasant Rebellions in the Late Ming Dynasty* (Tucson, AZ: University of Arizona Press, 1970).

71. For that story, Wakeman, *The Great Enterprise*.

72. Richard L. Edmonds, "The Willow Palisade," *Annals of the Association of American Geographers* 69, no. 4 (1979): 599–621.

73. David Bello, "The Cultured Nature of Imperial Foraging in Manchuria," *Late Imperial China* 31, no. 2 (2010): 4.

74. Vermeer, "Population and Ecology on the Frontier," 239.

75. Bello, "Imperial Foraging," 3.

76. Ibid., 12, 20–23, 24.

77. To place the Manchurian experience in the broader context of "the world hunt," and to make comparisons with the Russians in Siberia, see John F. Richards, *The Unending Frontier: An Environmental History of the Early Modern World* (Berkeley and Los Angeles, CA: University of California Press, 2003).

78. This section is based on parts of a book of the same title, Peter C. Perdue, *China Marches West: The Qing Conquest of Central Eurasia* (Cambridge, MA: The Belknap Press of Harvard University Press, 2005). See also a brief statement in Vermeer, "Population and Ecology along the Frontier," 245.

79. Perdue, *China Marches West*, 283.

80. Ibid., 285.

81. On the steppe ecology, see also Joseph Fletcher, "The Mongols: Ecological and Social Perspectives," *Harvard Journal of Asiatic Studies* 46, no. 1 (1986): 11–50.

82. Perdue, *China Marches West*, 45–48, 91–92.

83. Peter C. Perdue, "Military Mobilization in Seventeenth- and Eighteenth-Century China, Russia, and Mongolia," *Modern Asian Studies* 30, no. 4 (1996): 759.

84. For a discussion of the ways in which differing "ecologies of production" influenced the policies of the Qing state, see Peter C. Perdue, "Nature and Nurture on Imperial China's Frontiers," *Modern Asian Studies* 43, no. 1 (2009), 245–267.

85. Edward H. Shafer, *Shore of Pearls* (Berkeley and Los Angeles, CA: University of California Press, 1970), 28.

86. Quoted in Schafer, *Shore of Pearls*, 11.

87. Anne Alice Csete, *A Frontier Minority in the Chinese World: The Li People of Hainan Island from the Han through the High Qing* (SUNY-Buffalo Ph.D. dissertation, 1995), 39. For a more accessible source, see Anne Csete, "Ethnicity, Conflict, and the State in Early to

Mid-Qing: The Hainan Highland, 1644–1800," in *Empire at the Margins*, eds. Crossley, Siu, and Sutton, 229–52.

88. See also Fiskesjö, ""On the 'Raw' and the 'Cooked" Barbarians," 143–44.

89. Csete, *A Frontier Minority in the Chinese World*, 19.

90. Ibid., 58.

91. Ibid., 62.

92. Ibid., 91–92.

93. Ibid., 99.

94. Catherine Schurr Enderton, *Hainan Dao: Contemporary Environmental Management and Development on China's Treasure Island* (UCLA Ph.D. dissertation, 1984), map 3.1, 69.

95. Csete, *A Frontier Minority* 118.

96. Ibid., 119.

97. Quoted in ibid., 184.

98. Ibid., 191.

99. Quoted in ibid., 205.

100. Quoted in ibid., 207.

101. Quoted in ibid., 210.

102. Enderton, *Hainan Dao*, 73.

103. For another look at Taiwan's environmental history, see John F. Richards, *The Unending Frontier: An Environmental History of the Early Modern World* (Berkeley and Los Angeles, CA: University of California Press, 2003), 89–111.

104. John Robert Shepherd, *Statecraft and Political Economy on the Taiwan Frontier, 1600–1800* (Stanford, CA: Stanford University Press, 1993), 37–38. See also Magnus Fiskesjö, ""On the 'Raw' and the 'Cooked" Barbarians," 144–45.

105. Liu Ts'ui-jung, "Han Migration and the Settlement of Taiwan: The Onset of Environmental Change," in *Sediments of Times*, eds. Elvin and Liu, 167–70.

106. Shepherd, *Statecraft and Political Economy on the Taiwan Frontier*, 33.

107. Ibid., 38.

108. See also Liu, "Han Migration and the Settlement of Taiwan," 166, 175, 179.

109. For a discussion of various Chinese views of Taiwan, see Emma Jinhua Teng, *Taiwan's Imagined Geography: Chinese Colonial Travel Writing and Pictures, 1683–1895* (Cambridge, MA: Harvard University Press, 2004).

110. Shepherd, *Statecraft and Political Economy on the Taiwan Frontier*, ch. 7.

111. Ibid., 161.

112. Ibid., 304–5, 306.

113. Ibid., ch. 10.

114. Richards, *The Unending Frontier*, 110.

115. Shepherd, *Statecraft and Political Economy on the Taiwan Frontier*, 359.

116. Ibid., 360.

117. For aspects of Taiwan's environmental history since 1950, see Kuo-tung Ch'en, "Nonreclamation Deforestation in Taiwan, c. 1600–1976," in *Sediments of Time*, eds. Elvin and Liu, 693–727; and An-Chi Tung, "Hydroelectricity and Industrialization: The Economic, Social, and Environmental Impacts of the Sun Moon Lake Power Plants," in *Sediments of Time*, eds. Elvin and Liu, 728–55.

118. James C. Scott borrowed and expanded upon a term used by James Z. Lee, whose work on the southwest I have cited in this chapter as well; see *The Art of Not Being Governed*, 91–94.

119. Ibid., 9.

120. Vermeer, "Population and Ecology on the Frontier," 257.

121. See Marks, *Tigers*, ch. 9; and William Rowe, *Saving the World: Chen Hongmou and Elite Consciousness in Eighteenth-Century China* (Stanford, CA: Stanford University Press, 2001), 59–65.

122. See Vermeer, "Population and Ecology on the Frontier," 259–66; and Marks, *Tigers*, ch. 8.

123. Alfred W. Crosby, *The Columbia Exchange: Biological and Cultural consequences of 1492* (Westport, CT: Greenwood Press, 1972).

124. Ping-ti Ho, "The Introduction of American Food Plants into China," *American Anthropologist*, New Series 57, no. 2, part 1 (1955): 191–201. More recently, a Chinese demographer, Cao Shuji, has taken issue with Ho's interpretation. For a brief summary, see Vermeer, "Population and Ecology on the Frontier," 266.

125. G. William Skinner, "Introduction" to Sow-Theng Leong, *Migration and Ethnicity in Chinese History: Hakkas, Pengmin, and their Neighbors*, ed. Tim Wright (Stanford, CA: Stanford University Press, 1997), 7.

126. Ibid.

127. Ibid., 47.

128. Ibid., 97.

129. Stephen Averill, *Revolution in the Highlands: China's Jinggangshan Base Area* (Lanham, MD: Rowman & Littlefield, 2006), 25.

130. Ibid., 26–27.

131. Ibid., 27.

132. Ibid., 27.

133. This section on Hubei is based on Pierre-Etienne Will, "State Intervention in the Administration of a Hydraulic Structure: The Example of Hubei Province in Late Imperial Times," in *The Scope of State Power in China*, ed. Stuart Schram (New York, NY: St. Martin's Press, 1985), 295–347.

134. Will, "State Intervention," 308–9.

135. This section on Hunan is based on Peter C. Perdue, *Exhausting the Earth: State and Peasant in Hunan, 1500–1850* (Cambridge, MA: Harvard University Press, 1987). See also Richards, *The Unending Frontier*, 120-125.

136. Donald S. Sutton, "Ethnicity and the Miao Frontier in the Eighteenth Century," in *Empire at the Margins*, eds. Crossley, Siu, and Sutton, 190. For a brief assessment, see Vermeer, "Population and Ecology on the Frontier," 245–46.

137. Richards, *The Unending Frontier*, p. 133.

138. Ibid., 137.

139. Sutton, "Ethnicity and the Miao Frontier in the Eighteenth Century," 190-92.

140. Perdue, *Exhausting the Earth*, 211.

141. Keith Schoppa, *Xiang Lake—Nine Centuries of Chinese Life* (New Haven, CT: Yale University Press, 1989).

142. Perdue, *Exhausting the Earth*, 97.

143. Ibid., 86–87.

144. Ibid., 223.

145. Ibid., 200–202

146. This section is based on work by Anne Osborne, *Barren Mountains, Raging Rivers: The Ecological and Social Effects of Changing Landuse on the Lower Yangzi Periphery in Late Imperial China* (Columbia University Ph.D. dissertation, 1989) and "Highlands and Lowlands: Economic and Ecological Interactions in the Lower Yangzi Region under the Qing," in *Sediments of Time*, eds. Elvin and Liu, 203–34. See also Richards, *The Unending Frontier*, 126-131.

147. Osborne, *Barren Mountains, Raging Rivers*, 41.

148. Ibid., 162.

149. Skinner, "Introduction," 13.

150. Osborne, *Barren Mountains, Raging Rivers*, 158–67.

151. Ibid., 167.

152. Ibid., 175.

153. Ibid., 169–70. See also Mark Elvin, "Three Thousand Years of Unsustainable Growth: China's Environment from Archaic Times to the Present," *East Asian History* 6 (1993): 7–46.

154. Osborne, "Economic and Ecological Interaction," 218–19. See also Mark Elvin, "Three Thousand Years of Unsustainable Growth," 34–35 for a lament from another official.

155. Ibid., 229.

156. See Frederick W. Mote, *Imperial China*, 902–3 for an overview, and for more detail Kent C. Smith, *Ch'ing Policy and the Development of Southwest China: Aspects of Ortai's Governor-Generalship, 1726–31* (Yale University Ph.D. dissertation, 1970).

157. Giersch, *Asian Borderlands*, 128–45, 165–78.

158. Paul J. Smith, *Taxing Heaven's Storehouse: Horses, Bureaucrats, and the Destruction of the Sichuan Tea Industry, 1074–1224* (Boston, MA: Harvard University Press, 1991), 24–25.

159. This and the previous paragraph are based on Robert Gardella, *Harvesting Mountains: Fujian and the China Tea Trade, 1757–1937* (Berkeley and Los Angeles, CA: University of California Press, 1994), 9–10, 21–31, 33–40.

160. Quoted in Evelyn Rawski, *Agricultural Change and the Peasant Economy of South China* (Cambridge, MA: Harvard University Press, 1972), 51.

161. Quoted in Gardella, *Harvesting Mountains*, 43.

162. David A. Bello, "To Go Where No Man Could Go for Long: Malaria and the Qing Construction of Ethnic Administrative Space in Frontier Yunnan," *Modern China* 31, no. 3 (2005): 283–317.

163. Quoted in Bello, "Malaria and the Qing," 296.

164. Quoted in ibid., 283.

165. Quoted in ibid., 283–84.

166. Ibid., 300.

167. Ibid., 306, 310.

168. Carol Benedict, *Bubonic Plague in Nineteenth-century China* (Stanford, CA: Stanford University Press, 1996), 19–20, 29.

169. Scott, *The Art of Not Being Governed*, x–xi, 138–141.

170. For more detail and examples, see Wiens, *Han Chinese Expansion in South China*, 186. I have changed Romanization of Chinese words into standard pinyin.

171. Scott, *The Art of Not Being Governed*, 178.

172. For additional examples, see William T. Rowe, "Water Control and the Qing Political Process," *Modern China* 14, no. 4 (1988): 353–87; and Peter Perdue, "Lakes of Empire: Man and Water in Chinese History," *Modern China* 16, no. 1 (1990): 119–29.

173. See two works by Helen Dunstan, "Official Thinking on Environmental Issues and the State's Environmental Roles in Eighteenth-Century China," in *Sediments of Time*, eds. Elvin and Liu, and *Conflicting Counsels to Soothe the Age: A Documentary Study of Political Economy in Qing China* (Ann Arbor, MI: University of Michigan Press, 1996).

174. Both quotes are from sources translated in Mark Elvin, "Introduction," in *Sediments of Time*, eds. Elvin and Liu, 11.

175. Hong Liangqi, "China's Population Problem," in *Sources of Chinese Tradition* 2nd ed., vol. 1, eds. de Bary and Bloom (New York, NY: Columbia University Press, 2005), 175.

176. James Z. Lee and Wang Feng, *One Quarter of Humanity: Malthusian Mythology and Chinese Realities* (Cambridge: Harvard University Press, 1999).

177. Ibid., 115–118.

178. See Marks, *Tigers*; Chris Coggins, *The Tiger and the Pangolin: Nature, Culture, and Conservation in China* (Honolulu, HI: University of Hawai'i Press, 2003).

179. Elvin, *Retreat of the Elephants*, ch. 2, p. 11.

180. The history of ideas is highly complex and the work (mostly) of cultural, intellectual, and social historians. Among the various sources already listed in this and previous chapters, those interested in late imperial ideas about nature can consult two chapters in Ulrich and Dux, eds., *Concepts of Nature*: Georges Métailié, "Concepts of nature in Traditional Chinese Meteria Medica and Botany (Sixteenth to Seventeenth Century," 345–367, and Benjamin Elman, "The Investigation of Things (*gewu*), Natural Studies (*gezhixue*), and Evidential Studies (*kaozhengxue*) in Late Imperial China, 1600–1800)," 368–399, as well as Elvin, "Introduction," in *Sediments of Time*, eds. Elvin and Liu, 13.

CHAPTER 6

1. See Andre Gunder Frank, *ReOrient: Global Economy in the Asian Age* (Berkeley and Los Angeles, CA: University of California Press, 1998); Kenneth Pomeranz, *The Great Divergence: China, Europe, and the Making of the Modern World Economy* (Princeton: Princeton University Press, 2000); R. Bin Wong, *China Transformed: Historical Change and the Limits of European Experience* (Ithaca, NY: Cornell University Press, 1997); Robert B. Marks, *The Origins of the Modern World: A Global and Ecological Narrative from the Fifteenth to the Twenty-first Century* (Lanham, MD: Rowman & Littlefield, 2007).

2. See Frank, *ReOrient*.

3. See, for example, Takeshi Hamashita, *China, East Asia and the Global Economy: Regional and Historical Perspectives* (New York, NY: Routledge, 2008).

4. J. R. McNeill, "Of Rats and Men: A Synoptic Environmental History of the Island Pacific," *Journal of World History* 5, no. 2 (1994): 322.

5. Ibid., 319.

6. Bello, "Imperial Foraging."

7. Richards, *The Unending Frontier*, 537.

8. Richards, 536, 538, 540–41.

9. Richard Mackie, *Trading beyond the Mountains: The British Fur Trade on the Pacific 1793–1843* (Vancouver: UBC Press, 1997), 51–55. See also James R. Gibson, *Otter Skins, Boston Ships, and China Goods: The Maritime Fur Trade of the Northwest Coast, 1785–1841* (Seattle, WA: University of Washington Press, 1992).

10. David Igler, "Diseased Goods: Global Exchanges in the Eastern Pacific Basin, 1770–1850," *American Historical Review* 109, no. 3 (2004): 714–15.

11. Ibid, 693–719.

12. McNeill, "Of Rats and Men," 325–26.

13. Kerrie L. MacPherson, "Cholera in China, 1820–1930," in *Sediments of Time*, eds. Elvin and Liu, 487–519.

14. This continued into the 1950s. See the vignettes in Nicholas Menzies, "The Villagers' View of Environmental History in Yunnan," in *Sediments of Time*, eds. Elvin and Liu, 115–19.

15. This section connecting opium to plague is based on Carol Benedict, *Bubonic Plague in Nineteenth-Century China* (Stanford, CA: Stanford University Press, 1996).

16. See especially Frederic Wakeman, Jr., *The Fall of Imperial China*; almost any textbook on modern China contains one or more serviceable chapters on the Opium War.

17. Joyce A. Madancy, *The Troublesome Legacy of Commission Lin: The Opium Trade and Opium Suppression in Fujian Province, 1820s–1920s* (Cambridge, MA: Harvard University Press, 2003).

18. Edward R. Slack, *Opium, State, and Society: China's Narco-economy and the Guomindang, 1924–1937* (Honolulu. HI: University of Hawai'i Press, 2001); Li, Xiaoxiong, *Poppies and Politics in China: Sichuan Province, 1840s to 1940s* (Newark, DE: University of Delaware Press, 2009); Allan Baumler, *The Chinese and Opium under the Republic: Worse Than Floods and Wild Beasts* (Albany, NY: State University of New York Press, 2007); Carl Trocki, *Opium, Empire, and the Global Political Economy: A Study of the Asian Opium Trade* (London, UK: Routledge, 1999). Nearly all scholarly work has focused on the production and consumption of opium, with very little attention given to the growing of poppies, which may or may not have had significant environmental consequences.

19. Li, *Poppies and Politics in China*, 30.

20. David Bello, *Opium and the Limits of Empire: Drug Prohibition in the Chinese Interior, 1729–1850* (Cambridge, MA: Harvard University Press, 2005), 222–23.

21. Slack, *Opium, State, and Society*, 4.

22. Daniel Headrick, *The Tools of Imperialism: Technology and Imperialism in the Nineteenth Century* (New York, NY: Oxford University Press, 1981); for a synopsis, see Marks, *Origins of the Modern World*, 2nd ed., 115–17.

23. Kenneth Pomeranz calls this change *The Great Divergence*; and John R. McNeill sees it as *Something New under the Sun*.

24. For the somewhat different case of Xinjiang, see Jeffrey Kinzley, "Oil and the Making of an Economic Borderland: Xinjiang, Republican China, and the Russian/Soviet Empire, 1912–1921," paper presented at 2011 AAS annual convention, Honolulu, HI.

25. Eduard B.Vermeer, "Population and Ecology along the Frontier in Qing China," in *Sediments of Time*, eds. Elvin and Liu, 252–54.

26. For additional examples, see Vermeer, "Population and Ecology along the Frontier," 272–77.

27. Robert B. Marks, "People Said Extinction Was Not Possible: 2,000 Years of Environmental Change in South China," in *Environmental History: World System History and Global Environmental Change*, ed. Alf Hornberg (Lanham, MD: AltaMira Press, 2007), 41–59.

28. Quoted in Marks, *Tigers*, 331–32.

29. Marks, *Tigers*, ch. 10.

30. Bello, "Imperial Foraging," 10.

31. This paragraph and the next are based on Piers Blaikie and Harold Brookfield, "Defining and Debating the Problem," in *Land Degradation and Society*, eds. Piers Blaikie and Harold Brookfield (New York, NY: Methuen, 1987), 1–26.

32. For descriptions of the deforestation of the Wei River valley, see Eduard B. Vermeer, *Economic Development in Provincial China: The Central Shaanxi since 1930* (Cambridge and New York, NY: Cambridge University Press, 1988), ch. 4.

33. Norman Shaw, *Chinese Forest Trees and Timber Supply* (London, UK: T. Fisher Unwin, 1914), 134.

34. Ibid., 125.

35. Ibid., 128–29.

36. Quoted in W. C. Lowdermilk, "Forestry in Denuded China," *The Annals of the American Academy of Political and Social Science* 152 (November 1930), 138.

37. David A. Pietz, *Engineering the State: The Huai River and Reconstruction in Nationalist China, 1927–1937* (New York, NY and London, UK: Routledge, 2002), 7.

38. Ibid., 10.

39. Ibid., 15.

40. Elizabeth Perry, *Rebels and Revolutionaries in North China, 1845–1945* (Stanford, CA: Stanford University Press, 1980), note p. 16.

41. Tim Sedo, "Environmental Governance and the Public Good in Xu Guangqi's *Treatise on Expelling Locusts*," paper presented at 2011 AAS annual conference, Honolulu, HI.

42. Perry, *Rebels and Revolutionaries in North China*.

43. Pietz, *Engineering the State*, 15–16.

44. Perry, *Rebels and Revolutionaries in North China*, 42.

45. Quoted in Perry, *Rebels and Revolutionaries in North China*, 19.

46. When "the River" became known as the "Yellow" River—in the Han or only later in the Tang—is a matter of some scholarly dispute. See Rotz, "On Nature and Culture in Zhou China," in Vogel and Dux eds., *Concepts of Nature*, p. 203 n. 20.

47. Quoted in Joseph W. Esherick, *The Origins of the Boxer Uprising* (Berkeley and Los Angeles, CA: University of California Press, 1987), 1.

48. Tim Wright and Ma Junya, "Sacrificing Local Interests: Water Control Policies of the Ming and Qing Governments and the Local Economy of Huaibei, 1495–1949," *Modern Asian Studies*, forthcoming.

49. Jane Kate Leonard, *Controlling from Afar: The Daoguang Emperor's Management of the Grand Canal Crisis, 1824–1826* (Ann Arbor, MI: Center for Chinese Studies, University of Michigan Press, 1996), 9.

50. Randall A. Dodgen, *Controlling the Dragon: Confucian Engineers and the Yellow River in Late Imperial China* (Honolulu, HI: University of Hawai'i Press, 2001), 11–23.

51. On his first "southern tour" in 1684, the Kangxi emperor was being transported down the Grand Canal and observed the massive flooding and human misery caused by the breakdown of the Yellow River/Grand Canal system, and asked the director-general of the river conservancy who was with him what it would take to fix the problems. "More than 1 million taels [ounces of silver]," the emperor was told. Or using corvee labor summoned by local magistrates, it "would certainly be over ten years before it was finished." Because of the significance of the Grand Canal, the Kangxi emperor decided to proceed expeditiously. See Antonia Finnane, *Speaking of Yangzhou: A Chinese City, 1550–1850* (Cambridge, MA: Harvard University Press, 2004), 149–50.

52. Phillip C. C. Huang, *The Peasant Economy and Social Change in North China* (Stanford, CA: Stanford University Press, 1985), 60.

53. Leonard, *Controlling from Afar*, 41.

54. For descriptions of several of the incidents of Yellow River flooding, the role of "Confucian engineers," and execution of strategies to stem the flood and improve the situation, see Dodgen, *Controlling the Dragon*, esp. chs. 4–5.

55. The following is based on Leonard, *Controlling from Afar*, ch. 1.

56. The story of the Ming official Pan Jixun who developed these ideas is told in Pietz, *Engineering the State*, 11–15; and in Randall Dodgen, "Hydraulic Evolution and Dynastic Decline: The Yellow River Conservancy, 1796–1855," *Late Imperial China* 12, no. 2 (1991): 36–63. See also Dodgen, *Controlling the Dragon*, chs. 1–2.

57. In addition to Leonard, *Controlling from Afar*, see Finnane, *Speaking of Yangzhou*, 152–71 for a description not just of the hydraulic infrastructure but also of the complex bureaucratic machinery necessary to manage the Yellow River conservancy and the Grand Canal, as well as of the place of salt drying in the economy of the region.

58. For a map of this exceptionally complex intersection, see Leonard, *Controlling from Afar*, xix.

59. Leonard, *Controlling from Afar*, 48.

60. Ibid., 49.

61. Pietz, *Engineering the State*, 17.

62. Ibid., 17–18. The story of attempts to "control" the Huai River continued after the establishment of the People's Republic of China, and will be taken up in chapter 7. Briefly, in the spring of 1950, Mao Zedong called for a mass movement to "harness" the Huai River, with ambiguous results. Mao ordered the "mountains to bend their tops, and the rivers to give way." Millions of peasants dug a new outlet to the Yangzi, dug reservoirs to hold floodwaters, and built dikes to constrain the river, but severe flooding in 1954 called into question the efficacy of those efforts. See James Nickum, *Hydraulic Engineering and Water Resources in the People's Republic of China* (Stanford, CA 1977); Robert Carin, *River Control in Communist China* (Hong Kong, HK 1962); and Jasper Becker, "The Death of China's Rivers," *AsiaTimesOnline*, August 26, 2003. In the post-Mao reform era, chemical plants sited on former rice paddies dumped tons of toxic waste into ill-prepared holding ponds which burst in a 2001 flood, poisoning the waters downstream, prompting mass protests, and lending the title to Elizabeth Economy's book, *The River Runs Black: The Environmental Challenge to China's Future* (Ithaca, NY: Cornell University Press, 2004); see chapter 1 for the story of the Huai River.

63. Kenneth Pomeranz, *The Making of a Hinterland: State, Society, and Economy in Inland North China, 1853–1937* (Berkeley and Los Angeles, CA: University of California Press, 1993).

64. Ibid., 122.

65. Ibid., 127.

66. Ibid., 137.

67. Lowdermilk, "Forestry in Denuded China," p. 137.

68. Pomeranz, *The Making of a Hinterland*, 151.

69. Lillian Li, *Fighting Famine in North China: State, Market, and Environmental Decline, 1690s–1990s* (Stanford, CA: Stanford University Press, 2000), 41.

70. Ibid., 46–47.

71. Ibid., 67.

72. Quoted in Li, *Fighting Famine in North China*, 68.

73. Li, *Fighting Famine in North China*, 19.

74. Zuo Dakang and Zhang Peiyuan, "The Huang-Huai-Hai Plain," in B. L. Turner et al. eds, *The Earth as Transformed by Human Action: Global and Regional changes in the Biosphere over the Past 300 Years* (New York, NY: Cambridge University Press, 1990), 476.

75. Li, *Fighting Famine in North China*, ch. 10. Li also demonstrates the extraordinary extent to which first the Chinese state provided effective famine relief, how those efforts failed in the late nineteenth and early twentieth centuries, and how international organizations provided famine relief.

76. On the Nian, the Red Spears, and the Chinese Communists, see Perry, *Rebels and Revolutionaries*. On the Boxers, see Esherick, *The Origins of the Boxer Uprising*.

77. On the connections among environmental degradation, rural poverty, and Communist base areas, see Yan Ruizhen and Wang Yuan, *Poverty and Development: A Study of China's Poor Areas* (Beijing, CN: New World Press, 1992).

78. Jiayang Zhang, "Environment, Market, and Peasant Choice: The Ecological Relationships in the Jianghan Plain in the Qing and the Republic," *Modern China* 32, no. 1 (2006): 31–63. Zhang makes the addition important point that peasant cropping choices increasingly were influenced in the first instance by the changing environment and hence their subsistence needs, and only secondarily by market opportunities.

79. See also Lyman P. Van Slyke, *Yangtze: Nature, History, and the River* (Reading, MA: Addison-Wesley Publishing Co., Inc.,1988), esp. 20–27.

80. Keith Schoppa, *Xiang Lake: Nine Centuries of Chinese Life* (New Haven, CT: Yale University Press, 1989), 6, 65, 190.

81. Quoted in Marks, *Tigers*, 311.

82. Albert N. Steward, "The Burning of Vegetation on Mountain Land, and Slope Cultivation in Ling Yuin Hsien, Kwangsi Province, China," *Lingnan Science Journal* 13, no. 1 (1934): 1.

83. Chris Coggins, *The Tiger and the Pangolin: Nature, Culture, and Conservation in China* (Honolulu, HI: University of Hawai'i Press, 2003), 147–48.

84. According to geologist Walter Parham, "The process of degradation follows a predictable path. When vegetation is removed in these regions, the exposed soil bakes in the sun; it reaches temperatures so high that seeds and sprouts are killed or stunted. Since new vegetation cannot be established easily, soil organic matter is reduced, and the soil becomes desiccated. Soil organic matter decreases quickly as soil temperature and biotic decomposition rates increase. Further, removal of vegetation and litter by farmers for fuel inhibits buildup of new organic matter. Soil organic matter plays a large role in retaining nutrients in a form available to plants. Even small decreases in soil organic matter have a pronounced negative effect on the soil's fertility. Granite underlies most of South China and when the original topsoil is removed by erosion, the surface becomes a mixture of aluminum-rich clays and quartz sand that contain very few minerals useful to plant life. The loss of vegetative cover and soil organic matter leaves the soil subject to damage from intense tropical rainfall. With little organic matter in the soil, clay particles are moved by raindrops and plug soil pores, thus inhibiting water infiltration and increasing runoff and erosion. Residual boulders of fresh granite (core stones) as large as automobiles sometime slide and tumble down hillsides when the surrounding soft weathered material is eroded during heavy rains. The finer-grained eroded sediments damage aquatic productivity and bury what were once freshwater and near-shore marine aquatic breeding grounds. The remaining coarser, sandy material of the weathered granite yields soils of low fertility. Stripped of vegetation that would otherwise have absorbed or slowed the flow of water, the water pours rapidly into streams and rivers, cutting deep ravines in the soft, deeply weathered granite." Walter Parham, "Degraded Lands: South China's Untapped Resource," *FAS Public Interest Report: The Journal of the Federation of American Scientists* 54, no. 2 (2001). www.fas.org/faspir/2001/v54n2/resource.htm.

85. Marks, *Tigers*, pp. 319–21.

86. There is a long and interesting history of the relationship among warring in China, malaria, and malaria cures, going back to the fourth century CE and continuing through the Vietnam War and China's development of a new anti-malarial drug derived from two variants of artemisia (*Artemisia annua*; known more commonly in the West as sweet wormwood, or mugwort, and *Artemisia apiacea*). Elisabeth Hsu, "The History of *qing hao* in the Chinese *materia medica*," *Transactions of the Royal Society of Tropical Medicine and Hygiene* 100 (2006), pp. 505–508.

87. James L. A. Webb, *Humanity's Burden: A Global History of Malaria* (New York, NY: Cambridge University Press, 2009), p. 156.

88. The quotes in this paragraph are from handwritten notes on the back side of the photographs in figure 6.5. The photographs are at the Library of Congress Prints and Photographs Division in a collection entitled "Malaria Control in India and China, 1929–40," call number LOT 1786 (M) [P&P].

89. On the history of malaria, see Webb, *Humanity's Burden*. See also Russell, *War and Nature*, pp. 112–17.

90. Shaw, *China's Forest Trees*; Vaclav Smil, *The Bad Earth* (Armonk, NY: M.E. Sharpe, 1984); and Richard Louis Edmonds, *Patterns of China's Lost Harmony: A Survey of the Country's Environmental Degradation and Protection* (London: Routledge, 1994).

91. Shaw, *China's Forest Trees*, 141.

92. Ruth Mostern, "The Dujiangyan Waterworks," Association for Asian Studies annual meeting, March 26–29, 2009, Chicago, IL. For a brief description, see Mark Edward Lewis, *The Early Chinese Empires: Qin and Han* (Cambridge, MA: Harvard University Press, 2007), 35–36.

93. Wolfgang Holzner and Monika Kriechbaum, "Man's Impact on the Vegetation and Landscape in the Inner Himalaya and Tibet," in *Sediments of Time*, eds. Elvin and Liu, 100.

94. Ibid., 71.

95. Ibid., 73.

96. Ibid., 89–91.

97. Jack Hayes, "Rocks, Trees and Grassland on the Borderlands: Tibetan and Chinese Perceptions and Manipulations of the Environment along Ecotone Froniers, 1911–1982," paper presented at March, 2011 AAS Annual Meeting, Honolulu, HI.

98. Jack Hayes, "Fire Disasters on the Borderland: Qing Dynasty Chinese, Tibetan and Hui Fire Landscapes in Western China, 1821–1911," paper presented at the AAS Annual Meeting, March 2010, Philadelphia, PA.

99. Jung-Chao Liu, *China's Fertilizer Economy* (Chicago, IL: Aldine Publishing Co., 1970), 104–5.

100. "A complete, scientific, man-made ecosystem," in the words of Zhong Gongfu, "Zhujiang sanjiaozhou de 'sang ji yu tang'—yige shui lu xianghu zuoyong de rengong shengtai zitong" [The 'mulberry tree and pond' system of the Pearl River delta—an artificial water and land ecological system] *Dili xuebao* 35, no. 3 (1980): 200–209.

101. Zhong, "The Mulberry Tree and Pond System," 200–201.

102. In the twentieth century, five kinds of fish were reared in the ponds, all from fry secured from local rivers. See William E. Hoffman, "Preliminary Notes on the Fresh-Water Fish Industry of South China, Especially Kwangtung Province," *Lingnan Science Journal* 8 (Dec. 1929): 167–68.

103. Marks, *Tigers*, 119.

104. E. F. Bruenig et al., *Ecological-Socioeconomic System Analysis and Simulation: A Guide for Application of System Analysis to the Conservation, Utliization, and Development of Subtropical Land Resources in China* (Bonn: Deutsches Nationalkomitee für das UNESCO Programm de Mensch und die Biosphäre, 1986), 176.

105. Bozhong Li, *Agricultural Development in Jiangnan, 1620–1850* (New York, NY: St. Martin's Press, 1998), 19–22; Marks, *Tigers*, 279–281; Pomeranz, *The Great Divergence*, 287–88. On the Chinese demographic system and the ways in which rural families controlled family size, see James Z. Lee and Wang Feng, *One Quarter of Humanity: Malthusian Mythology and Chinese Realities* (Cambridge, MA: Harvard University Press, 1999).

106. Micah Muscolino, "The Yellow Croaker War: Fishery Disputes between China and Japan, 1925–1935, *Environmental History* 13 (April 2008): 305–24; Micah Muscolino, *Fishing Wars and Environmental Change in Late Imperial and Modern China* (Cambridge, MA: Harvard University Press, 2009).

107. Vermeer, "Population and Ecology along the Frontier," 247–51.

108. S. A. M. Adshead, "An Energy Crisis in Early Modern China*." Ch'ing-shi wen-t'i* [*Late Imperial China*] 3, no. 2 (1974): 20–28.

109. Nicholas K. Menzies, *Forest and Land Management in Imperial China* (New York, NY: St. Martin's Press, 1994), 1–2.

110. Ibid., 87.

111. See Marks, *Tigers*, 320, for an example.

112. As reported in Shaw, *China's Forest Trees*, 21.

113. Vaclav Smil, *China's Environmental Crisis*, 36.

114. McNeill, *Something New under the Sun.*

115. Lowdermilk, "Forestry in Denuded China," 129.

116. For more on the place of nitrogen in Chinese agriculture, see Vaclav Smil, *China's Past, China's Future: Energy, Food, Environment* (New York, NY: RoutledgeCurzon, 2004), 109–20.

117. Edwin Moise, "Downward Social Mobility in Pre-Revolutionary China," *Modern China* 3, no. 1 (1977): 8.

118. For a succinct discussion, see Qu Geping and Li Jinchang, *Population and the Environment in China*, 55–57.

119. For a specific example, see Elvin, *Retreat of the Elephants*, ch. 9, esp. 307–318.

120. Radkau, *Nature and Power*, 21, 24.

121. The 1750 figure is derived from Ling Daxie, "Wo guo senlin ziyuan de bianqian," *Zhongguo nongshi* 1983 No. 2: 26-36. For 1950, official statistics figure China about 13 percent forested, but others think the forest cover was about half that. See Vaclav Smil, *The Bad Earth*, pp. 10-12. Richardson, *Forests and Forestry in China*, p. 89; and Smil, *China's Environmental Crisis*, p. 60.

122. See Pierre-EtienneWill and R. Bin Wong, *Nourish the People: The Civilian State Granary System in China, 1650–1850* (Ann Arbor, MI: University of Michigan Press, 1991); and Marks, *Tigers*, ch. 8.

123. For a discussion of the connections between ENSO events and harvests in China, see Robert B. Marks and Georgina Endfield, "Environmental Change in the Tropics in the Past 1000 Years," in *Quaternary Environmental Change in the Tropics*, eds. Sarah Metcalf and David Nash (Oxford, UK: Blackwell Publishing, forthcoming).

124. Mike Davis, *Late Victorian Holocausts: El Niño Famines and the Making of the Third World* (London, UK and New York, NY: Verso Press, 2001), 239.

125. Ibid., 240–45, 270–72.

126. Figures are based on Li, *Fighting Famine in North China*, 284.

127. Davis, *Late Victorian Holocausts*, 7.

128. Li, *Fighting Famine in North China*, ch. 8.

129. The detailed story of this episode is provided by Pierre-Etiennne Will, *Bureaucracy and Famine in Eighteenth-Century China* (Stanford, CA: Stanford University Press, 1990). For more concise accounts, see Li, *Fighting Famine in North China*, ch. 8; and Davis, *Late Victorian Holocausts*, 280–85.

130. Li, *Fighting Famine in North China*, 273.

131. James Reardon-Anderson, *Reluctant Pioneers: China's Expansion Northward, 1644–1937* (Stanford, CA: Stanford University Press, 2005), 9.

132. Ibid., 73.

133. Ibid., 97–101.

134. Dee Mack Williams, *Beyond Great Walls: Environment, Identity, and Development on the Chinese Grasslands of Inner Mongolia* (Stanford, CA: Stanford University Press, 2002), 28.

135. Quoted in ibid., 28–29.

136. Reardon-Anderson, *Reluctant Pioneers*, 110.

137. Li, *Fighting Famine in North China*, 303–7.

138. Reardon-Anderson, *Reluctant Pioneers*, 103–4.

139. Ibid., 140.

140. Quoted in ibid., 142.

141. Ibid., 100.

142. Ibid., 107.

143. E. Elena Songster, "Cultivating the Nation in Fujian's Forests: Forest Policies and Afforestion Effort in China, 1911–1937," *Environmental History* 8 (July 2003): 456.

144. Ibid., 457–58.

145. Ibid., 462.

146. Ibid., 468.

147. This section on fisheries is based on Micah S. Muscolino, *Fishing Wars and Environmental China in Late Imperial and Modern China* (Cambridge, MA: Harvard University Press, 2009).

148. Ibid., 22.

149. Ibid., 122.

150. Ibid., 151, 174–78.

151. Diana Lary, "The Waters Covered the Earth: China's War-Induced Natural Disasters," in *War and State Terrorism: The United States, Japan, and the Asia-Pacific in the Long Twentieth Century*, eds. Mark Selden and Alvin Y. So (Lanham, MD: Rowman & Littlefield, 2004), 143–47.

152. Quoted in Micah Muscolino, "Violence against the People and the Land: Refugees and the Environment in China's Henan Province, 1938–45," *Environment and History*, forthcoming.

153. Ibid., 8–9.

154. After the war and with the help of the UNRRA (United Nations Relief and Rehabilitation Administration), the breach was closed and by late 1946 the Yellow River resumed its northerly course. Lary, "The Waters Covered the Earth," 156.

155. For a brief description, see Lary, 158–62.

156. Quoted in ibid., 18–19.

157. There is some controversy surrounding the use of the concept of "environmental crisis" by historians. For an insightful and stimulating discussion, see Richard C. Hoffman, Nancy Langston, James C. McCann, Peter C. Perdue, and Lise Sedrez, "*AHR* Conversation: Environmental Historians and Environmental Crisis," *The American Historical Review* 113, no. 5 (Dec. 2008), pp. 1431–65.

CHAPTER 7

1. See, for example, Eduard Vermeer, "Industrial Pollution in China and Remedial Policies," *China Quarterly* no. 156 (December 1998): 952–85. By the turn of the twenty-first century, sixteen of the world's twenty most polluted cities were in China. "Smoggy Skies: Environmental Health and Air Pollution," Woodrow Wilson International Center for Scholars, China Environment Forum, 2008. Other examples of industrial pollution will be taken up in the sections in this chapter on "Controlling Water" and "Polluting the Atmosphere." For an early exposé of pollution in Mao's China, see Vaclav Smil, *The Bad Earth: Environmental Degradation in China* (Armonk, NY: M. E. Sharpe, 1984).

2. Li Bozhong, "Changes in Climate, Land, and Human Efforts: The Production of Wet-Field Rice in Jiangnan during the Ming and Qing Dynasties," in *Sediments of Time*, eds. Elvin and Liu, 447–84.

3. Jung-Chao Liu, *China's Fertilizer Economy* (Chicago, IL: Aldine Publishing Co., 1970), 104–5.

4. For more on the place of nitrogen in Chinese agriculture, see Vaclav Smil, *China's Past, China's Future: Energy, Food, Environment* (New York, NY: RoutledgeCurzon, 2004), 109–20.

5. Edwin Moise, "Downward Social Mobility in Pre-Revolutionary China," *Modern China* 3, no. 1 (1977): 8.

6. Mao Zedong, quoted in Shapiro, *Mao's War against Nature*, 31.

7. Barry Naughton, *The Chinese Economy: Transitions and Growth* (Cambridge, MA: The MIT Press, 2007), 79.

8. Vaclav Smil, *Enriching the Earth: Fritz Haber, Carl Bosch, and the Transformation of World Food Production* (Cambridge, MA: The MIT Press, 2004). Smil estimates that without the invention of the process for synthesizing ammonia, and without fertilizing fields with the nitrogen so fixed into a form usable by farmers and taken up by plants, the human population of the world would not be much more than 2.5 billion people. In other words, food grown by artificial fertilizers made possible the addition of more than 3.5 billion people to the world's population (so far), a significant portion of which is Chinese.

9. Liu, *China's Fertilizer Economy*, 5–10, 50.

10. These land figures have been calculated from data provided in Kang Chao, *Man and Land in Chinese History: An Economic Analysis* (Stanford, CA: Stanford University Press, 1986), 87; and Vaclav Smil, *China's Environment Crisis: An Inquiry into the Limits of National Development* (Armonk, NY: M. E. Sharpe, 1993), 52–56. As Smil notes, these land statistics are open to question and interpretation. Official Chinese statistics distinguish between "cultivated land" (*geng di*) and "sown area" (*bozhong mianji*), although the distinction between those two categories is not made. Those statistics show that while the cultivated land area (*geng di*) did not increase much from 1949 to 1976 (staying around 100 million hectare), the sown area did—from about 120 million to 150 million hectare. Department of Comprehensive Statistics of National Bureau of Statistics, comp., *Xin zhongguo liushinian tongji ziliao huibian* [China Compendium of Statistics 1949-2008] (Beijing, CN: China Statistics Press, 2009), p. 6.

11. Lillian Li, *Fighting Famine in North China*, 342.

12. At any given particular historical moment, people in China held a wide variety of views about nature and the relationship of people to the environment. As Mark Elvin observed, "A systematic study of Chinese views of nature . . . at least in late-imperial times for which materials are abundant—reveals almost the entire possible spectrum of attitudes. There were Qing-dynasty enthusiasts for gigantic engineering projects, even more demented than Li Peng's Sanxia (Three Gorges) Dam. There were those who believed that nature should be attacked in military fashion. Others argued that humans should accommodate themselves to the pattern of natural processes without forcing matters. Others again saw nature as savage towards humankind, or indifferent. . . . Others again saw nature as benevolent. . . . [T]here was no single set of attitudes towards nature that could legitimately be called 'Chinese.'" Mark Elvin, "The Environmental Legacy of Imperial China," *China Quarterly* no. 156 (December 1998): 755. The classic statement on ideas about the environment in "the West" is Lynn White, "The Historical Roots of Our Ecological Crisis," *Science*, New Series 155, no. 3767 (1967): 1203–7.

13. Robert B. Marks, "Asian Tigers: The Real, the Symbolic, the Commodity," *Nature and Culture* 1, no. 1 (2006): 63–87.

14. Robert P. Weller and Peter K. Bol, "From Heaven-and-Earth to Nature: Chinese Concepts of the Environment and Their Influence on Policy Implementation," in *Energizing China: Reconciling Environmental Protection and Economic Growth*, eds. Michael B. Elroy, Chris P. Nielsen, and Peter Lyon (Cambridge, MA: Harvard University Press, 1998), 473. As they further point out: "China is not the only place where a unitary view of nature and society nevertheless supports anthropocentric activity. Seeing humanity and nature as part of a single system can easily support the human right to alter that system" (497 n. 2).

15. Karl Marx and Frederick Engels, *Manifesto of the Communist Party*, in *The Marx-Engels Reader*, ed. Robert C. Tucker (New York, NY: W. W. Norton, 1978), 477. Until quite recently,

most readings of Marx and Engels have cited their embrace of a "Promethean industrial outlook in which human progress corresponds to ever-greater human domination and control over nature," in the words of Paul Burkett, *Marx and Nature: A Red and Green Perspective* (New York, NY: St. Martin's Press, 1999), 5. Burkett attempts to reconstruct a Marxism that is relevant to ecology and an analysis and critique of environmental problems, and so critiques the common view of Marx as either irrelevant to ecology and/or hostile to environmental protection. So too does John Bellamy Foster, *Marx's Ecology: Materialism and Nature* (New York, NY: Monthly Review Press, 2000). That convincing new interpretations can be developed (largely on the basis of a reading of *Capital* and Marx's consideration of capitalist agriculture and the impoverishment of the soil by the movement of food and fiber from the countryside to cities; see especially Foster, ch. 5) should not obscure the point that Chinese Communists (and others) who wanted the fastest possible development of the forces of production did take a Promethean message from Marx. Marx seems to have made a distinction between the irrational exploitation of nature under capitalist relations of production and the rational control of nature under socialism (see Foster, 159–65), but either way, it seems to me, human control of nature was central to Marx's concerns: labor + nature = value. See also Howard L. Parsons, *Marx and Engels on Ecology* (Westport, CT: Greenwood Press, 1977).

16. Sheldon H. Lu, "Introduction: Cinema, Ecology, Modernity," in *Chinese Ecocinema in the Age of Environmental Challenge*, eds. Sheldon H. Lu and Jiayan Mi (Hong Kong, HK: Hong Kong University Press, 2009), 11.

17. Laurence Schneider, *Biology and Revolution in Twentieth-Century China* (Lanham, MD: Rowman & Littlefield, 2003), 3, 272.

18. Rhoads Murphey, "Man and Nature in China," *Modern Asian Studies* 1, no. 4 (1967): 313–33.

19. Shapiro, *Mao's War against Nature*.

20. Schneider, *Biology and Revolution*, 4–5

21. From the XI Thesis on Feurerbach: "The philosophers have only *interpreted* the world, in various ways; the point, however, it to *change* it." Tucker, *The Marx–Engels Reader*, 145.

22. S. D. Richardson, *Forestry in Communist China* (Baltimore, MD: The Johns Hopkins Press, 1966), 144.

23. Ibid., pp. 205–6.

24. Vaclav Smil, *China's Past, China's Future: Energy, Food, Environment* (New York, NY: RoutledgeCurzon, 2004), 115–16.

25. That is the range of "excess" deaths estimated in two recent studies. See Cao Shuiji, *Da Jihuang 1959–1961 nian de Zhongguo renkou* [The Great Famine: China's population in 1959–61] (Hong Kong, HK: Shidai guoji chuban youxian gongsi, 2005), and Frank Dikötter, *Mao's Great Famine: The History of China's Most Devastating Catastrophe, 1958–1962* (New York, NY: Walker and Co., 2010). There is an environmental perspective from which to view the famine of 1959–61. The reports from of the famine from the Huai River basin, including the provinces of Henan, Hebei, and Anhui are truly harrowing. In Jasper Becker's words, "peasants [in Xinyang prefecture] had nothing to eat but tree bark, wild grasses, and wild vegetables." In a part of Anhui also on the Huai River plain, the communal kitchens served nothing but wild grasses, peanut shells, and sweet potato skins; cannibalism was reported (Becker, 117, 118–19, 135, 137–40). According to Lillian Li, in Hebei province "people ate wild 'vegetables,' that is, grasses, weeds, and bark, as well as corncobs and chaff. Other food substitutes . . . included soybean flour, sweet potato stalks, cottonseed cakes, and starches made of leaves and grasses. Peasants would grind the dried food substitutes, such as tree bark of corncobs, into a powder, and then cook them by boiling or steaming so they could be swallowed. Green herbs, leaves, and grass roots could be boiled without preparation. Feeling their stomachs to be empty, famine victims often resorted to

easting nonedible matter that could not be digested and could have adverse consequences. One was call *guanyin tu* (the bodhisattva earth, or Buddha's soil); others were cotton or sawdust. Such famine 'foods' provided a temporary feeling of fullness, but they had a disastrous impact on the digestive systems" (Li, 360–61). The countryside was so barren, at least in north China, that there weren't even any mice or rats, and peasants poked sticks into holes to find their warrens and possibly any food that they had stored. These reports of what people resorted to all point to an exceedingly degraded and impoverished natural environment on the North China plain. Outside of their fields, there wasn't enough land or habitat to sustain any other wild creatures—there are no reports that I have come across that people resorted to eating frogs, birds, lizards, insects, or even worms—nothing. If those had been there, they would have been captured and eaten. That they weren't testifies not just to the cruelty of a human-induced famine, but also to the complete collapse of natural ecosystems. Mao may have been culpable, but with more robust natural ecosystems, unknown numbers of Hubei people might well have survived.

26. For the story, see Shapiro, *Mao's War against Nature*, 36–48.

27. For discussions of the connection between population growth and environmental issues, see also Vaclav Smil, *China's Environmental Crisis: An Inquiry into the Limits of National Development* (Armonk, NY: M. E. Sharpe, 1993); and Qu Geping and Li Jinchang, *Population and the Environment in China*, trans. Kiang Batching and Go Ran (Boulder, CO: Lynne Reinner, 1994).

28. Judith Banister, *China's Changing Population* (Stanford, CA: Stanford University Press, 1987); Matthew Connelly, *Fatal Misconception: The Struggle to Control World Population* (Cambridge, MA: Belknap, 2008).

29. The statistics and quote are from Vaclav Smil, *The Bad Earth*, 11.

30. Richardson, *Forests and Forestry in China*, 89.

31. Smil, *China's Environmental Crisis*, 60.

32. Richardson, *Forests and Forestry in China*, 89.

33. Ken-Ichi Abe, "Collaged Landscape: History and Political Ecology of Forests in Yunnan," in *The Good Earth*, eds. Abe and Nickum, 124–35; Shaoting Yin, "Rubber Planting and Eco-Environmental/Socio-cultural Transition in Xishuangbanna," in *The Good Earth*, eds. Abe and Nickum, 136–43.

34. On the rubber plantations and their environmental consequences, see Shapiro, *Mao's War against Nature*, 169–85.

35. Vaclav Smil, *The Bad Earth*, 10–12.

36. Vaclav Smil, *China's Environmental Crisis: An Inquiry into the Limits of National Development* (Armonk, NY: M. E. Sharpe, 1993), 62–63, 66.

37. Richard Louis Edmonds, *Patterns of China's Lost Harmony: A Survey of the Country's Environmental Degradation and Protection* (London, UK and New York, NY: Routledge, 1994), 58–59.

38. James Harkness. "Recent Trends in Forestry and Conservation of Biodiversity in China," *The China Quarterly*, no. 156 (December 1998), 929.

39. For a succinct discussion, see Qu Geping and Li Jinchang, *Population and the Environment in China*, 55–57.

40. Ibid., 56.

41. Lester Ross, *Forestry Policy in China* (University of Michigan Ph.D., 1980), 79–80.

42. Ibid., 94.

43. Ibid., 133.

44. Liu Dachang, "Tenure and Management of Non-State Forests in China since 1950: A Historical Review," *Environmental History* 6 (April 2001): 239–63.

45. Ross, *Forestry Policy in China*, ch. 3.

46. Mao's approach also differed from that of Stalin and the Soviet Union. See Stephen Brain, "The Great Stalin Place for the Transformation of Nature," *Environmental History* 15 (October 2010): 670–700.

47. Richardson, *Forestry in Communist China*, unnumbered and unpaginated photograph caption of a forest plantation in Guangdong province.

48. See also the photo in Marks, *Tigers*, 36.

49. In at least one instance in Yunnan province, such an "auction," which was supposed to open up the sale of state resources to anyone who could pay for them, was "secret" and resulted in the passing of a state resource into the hands of a politically connected leader. Janet Sturgeon, *Border Landscapes: The Politics of Akha Land Use in China and Thailand* (Seattle, WA: University of Washington Press, 2005), 91–94.

50. Liu, "Tenure and Management," 250.

51. For an alternative view, see Maurice Meisner, *The Deng Xiaoping Era: An Inquiry into the Fate of Chinese Socialism 1978–1994* (New York, NY: Hill and Wang, 1996), 248.

52. Liu, "Tenure and Management," 256.

53. Ibid.

54. Sen WANG et al., "Mosaic of Reform: Forest Policy in Post-1978 China," *Forest Policy and Economics* 6 (2004), and the extensive listing of World Bank environmental projects on its website.

55. Ibid.: 77.

56. Ibid.: 74.

57. James Harkness, "Recent Trends in Forestry and Biodiversity in China," *The China Quarterly* (1998): 914.

58. Vaclav Smil, *The Bad Earth*, 16.

59. Liu Dacheng, "Reforestation after Deforestation in China," in *The Good Earth: Regional and Historic Insights into China's Environment*, eds. Ken-ichi and Nickum, 90–105. See also Judith Shapiro, *Mao's War against Nature*, ch. 2.

60. Qu Geping and Li Jinchang, *Population and the Environment in China*, 57.

61. Nicholas Menzies, "The Villagers' View of Environmental History in Yunnan Province," in *Sediments of Time*, eds. Elvin and Liu, 115, 118.

62. The causes of the famine—natural, or political—are disputed. For an indictment of Mao's Great Leap Forward policies, see Jasper Becker, *Hungry Ghosts: Mao's Secret Famine* (New York, NY: First Owl Books, Henry Holt and Co., 1998). For the latest assessment, see Dikötter, *Mao's Great Famine*.

63. On "The Third Front" in general, see Barry Naughton, "The Third Front: Defence Industrialization in the Chinese Interior," *China Quarterly*, no. 115 (1988), 351–86. Judith Shapiro explores the environmental consequences of that strategy in *Mao's War against Nature: Politics and the Environment in Revolutionary China* (New York, NY: Cambridge University Press, 2001), ch. 4.

64. Sturgeon, *Border Landscapes*, 152.

65. Qu Geping, in *Population and the Environment in China*, 61. Sharply differing views of Dazhai can be found in William Hinton's, *Shenfan: The Continuing Revolution in a Chinese Village* (New York, NY: Random House, 1983), 682–93; in a later article, "Dazhai Revisited," *Monthly Review* 39, no. 10 (1988); and in Judith Shapiro, *Mao's War against Nature*, ch. 3.

66. Quoted in Peter Ho, "Mao's War against Nature? The Environmental Impact of the Grain-First Campaign in China," *The China Journal*, no. 50 (July 2003): 51.

67. These examples and more can be found in Judith Shapiro, *Mao's War against Nature*, ch. 3; Qu Geping and Li Jinchang, *Population and the Environment in China*; and Vaclav

Smil, *The Bad Earth*, ch. 1. A contrary view is developed by Peter Ho, "Mao's War against Nature?" 37–59.

68. Liu, "Reforestation after Deforestation," 91.

69. Sturgeon, *Border Landscapes*, 18–21.

70. Ibid.

71. Ibid., 92.

72. Sandra Postel and Lori Heise, *Reforesting the Earth*, Worldwatch Paper 83 (Washington, DC: Worldwatch Institute, 1988), 51–52.

73. Sturgeon, *Border Landscapes*, 163, 153–56.

74. Wang et al., "Mosaic of Reform: Forest Policy in Post-1978 China," 74, 77.

75. Li Bo, "Jinsha in Yunnan: Environmental and Cultural Protection in the Development of Tourism," in *The China Environment Yearbook (2005): Crisis and Breakthrough of China's Environment*, eds. Liang Conjie and Yang Dongping (Leiden, NL: Brill, 2007), 396.

76. National Climatic Data Center, http://lwf.ncdc.noaa.gov/oa/reports/chinaflooding/chinaflooding.html#SITES.

77. Elizabeth Economy, *The River Runs Black: The Environmental Challenge to China's Future* (Ithaca, NY: Cornell University Press, 2004), 121.

78. James Harkness, "Recent Trends in Forestry and Conservation of Biodiversity in China," *China Quarterly*, no. 156 (December 1998): 924–26.

79. Brook Lamer and Alexandra A. Seno, "A Reckless Harvest: China Is Protecting Its Own Trees, But Has Begun Instead To Devour Asia's Forests," *Newsweek*, January 27, 2003. URL http://newweek.com/id/62877. China's demand for timber is but one of the causes of the increasing deforestation of Sumatra's lowland tropical rain forests. Cutting pulp for paper and clearing forest for palm oil production are major factors. See also Chang Li, "Memorandum Concerning the Asia Pulp and Paper Co. Ltd (APP) Incident," in *The China Environment Yearbook*, eds. Liang Congjie and Yang Dinging (Leiden, NL: Brill, 2007), pp. 103–116.

80. Lamer and Seno, "A Reckless Harvest."

81. Sturgeon, *Border Landscapes*, 166, 193–95, 209–15.

82. Xu Guohua and L. J. Peel, eds., *The Agriculture of China* (Oxford, UK: Oxford University Press, 1991), 4.

83. Williams, *Beyond Great Walls*, 25.

84. James A. Millward and Peter C. Perdue, "Political and Cultural History of the Xinjiang Region through the Late Nineteenth Century," in *Xinjiang: China's Muslim Borderland*, ed. S. Frederick Starr (Armonk, NY: M. E. Sharpe, 2004), 30.

85. Williams, *Beyond Great Walls*, 15.

86. Ibid., ch. 2

87. David Sneath, *Changing Inner Mongolia: Pastoral Mongolian Society and the Chinese State* (Oxford: Oxford University Press, 2000), 83, 85.

88. Ibid., 85.

89. Ibid., 86.

90. Ibid., 135–36

91. Ibid., 136.

92. Williams, *Beyond Great Walls*, ch. 3.

93. Kobayashi Tatsuaki and Yang Jie, "Eco-historical Background and the Modern Process of Desertification in the Mu-us Sand Land with Reference to Pastoral Life," in *The Good Earth*, eds. Abe and Nickum, 243–44.

94. Ibid., 249. For a fictionalized account that captures much truth about the transformation of the grasslands of Inner Mongolia, see Jian Rong, *Wolf Totem*, Howard Goldblatt trans. (New York, NY: The Penguin Press, 2008).

95. Ibid., 250.

96. John Longworth and Gregory J. Williamson, *China's Pastoral Region: Sheep and Wool, Minority Nationalities, Rangeland Degradation and Sustainable Development* (Canberra, AU: The Australian Centre for International Agricultural Research, 1993), 311

97. Ibid., 254.

98. Ibid., 258–61.

99. Ibid., 260–63.

100. Ibid., 82, 332–33.

101. Richard B. Harris, *Wildlife Conservation in China: Preserving the Habitat of China's Wild West* (Armonk, NY: M. E. Sharpe, 2008).

102. Sneath argues that some five hundred thousand Mongols continue to practice pastoralism elsewhere in Inner Mongolia (Sneath, x).

103. Ibid., pp. 264–65.

104. Williams, *Beyond Great Walls*, ch. 4.

105. Among the most important forest preserves in China were Buddhist temples, mostly belonging to those in south China. North China had been largely deforested by the Song, and during the Tang, Buddhist temples had actually been among the entities most responsible for deforesting their regions. In the south, though, where Buddhist temples had been founded as early as the seventh century in what were then remote mountains, several maintained and protected their thousands of hectares of forest well into the twentieth century. And it was not as if these temples and their forests did not come under attack. During the mid-nineteenth century, Taiping armies attacked and burned Buddhist temples near Guangzhou because they were "idolaters," and during the Cultural Revolution, most temples were shuttered, their temples trashed, and their forests cut or burned. An interesting exception was the Nanfang temple in northern Guangdong, founded in the early Tang by the revered Ninth Patriarch, Hui Neng. For reasons that are somewhat unclear, Premier Zhou Enlai personally intervened and used his position and prestige to protect the Nanfang temple and its grounds. The forests of the Nanfang temple, and those of others that also managed to avoid destruction, provided Chinese botanists with a storehouse of knowledge—and seeds—with which to reconstruct the composition of the original forest communities. See Marks, *Tigers* (1998).

106. Harkness, "Recent Trends in Forestry and Biodiversity in China," 918.

107. "Nature Reserves," http://english.gov.cn/2006-02/08/content_182512.htm.

108. Chris Coggins, *The Tiger and the Pangolin: Nature, Culture, and Conservation in China* (Honolulu, HI: University of Hawai'i Press, 2003).

109. See especially two books by George Schaller, *The Great Pandas of Wolong* (Chicago, IL: University of Chicago Press, 1985) and *The Last Panda* (Chicago, IL: University of Chicago Press, 1993).

110. E. Eleana Songster, *Panda Nation: Nature, Science, and Nationalism in the People's Republic of China,* ch. 1, 56–57.

111. Curiously though, it turns out that bamboo periodically dies off after flowering. One such die-off in 1975 came to Chinese scientific notice when pandas started dying of starvation. Another bamboo die-off occurred in 1983. Because of the constructed link between pandas and China's modern national identity, pandas and their preserves get special attention from the central government. Other wild animal preserves are not so lucky. On the bamboo die-off, see Songster, ch. 5.

112. Quoted in Shapiro, *Mao's War against Nature*, 109.

113. For an account of a recent trek to the Laojunshan National Park in western Yunnan—where there were few professional park rangers and the eight thousand people living there did

not know they were in a "national park," see Mike Ives, "Scoping Out New Playgrounds," *Los Angeles Times*, January 9, 2011, L1, L5.

114. Harkness, "Recent Trends in Forestry and Biodiversity in China," 919.

115. Ibid., 920.

116. Ibid., 922.

117. Ibid., 923.

118. George B. Schaller and Gu Binyuan, "Ungulates in Northwest Tibet," *National Geographic Research & Exploration* 10, no. 3 (1994): 267, 268, 285, 274.

119. The idea of state support for afforestation projects was not new to the PRC. Even Yuan Shikai, the first president of the Republic of China and a failed monarchist, in 1914 established China's first National Forest Law. Nor was the disconnect between official state plans for afforestation and actual results peculiar to the PRC. E. Elena Songster, "Cultivating the Nation in Fujian's Forests: Forest Policies and Afforestation Efforts in China, 1911–1937," *Environmental History* 8 (July 2003): 454, 468.

120. Edmonds, *Patterns of China's Lost Harmony*, 51–57.

121. Ibid., 55–56.

122. Liu, "Reforestation after Deforestation," 95–96.

123. For a list of the ten major forestry programs and their goals, see also Wang et al., "Mosaic of Reform," 76.

124. In the border region with Burma, China's ban on killing protected species led at least one hunter to regularly roam into Burma to hunt and kill leopards; others hunted deer and smaller animals. Sturgeon, *Border Landscapes*, 161.

125. Andrew E. Kramer, "At the Russia-China Border, Bear Paws Sell Best," *The New York Times*, June 29, 2010, http://nytimes.com/2010/06/30/world/asia/30animals.

126. "Civets, Other Wildlife Off the Chinese Menu," *Associated Press*, April 18, 2006, http://www.msnbc.com/id/12371160/.

127. Qiu Quanlin, "Scientists Prove SARS-Civet Cat Link," *China Daily*, November 23, 2006, http://www.chinadaily,com.cn.china/2006–11/23/content.

128. Robert Carin, *River Control in Communist China* (Hong Kong, HK: Union Research Institute, 1962), 13.

129. Ibid., 23.

130. Ibid., 30–31.

131. Yi Si, "The World's Most Catastrophic Dam Failures: The August 1975 Collapse of the Banqiao and Shimantan Dams," in *The River Dragon Has Come! The Three Gorges Dam and the Fate of China's Yangtze River and Its People*, ed. Dai Qing (Armonk, NY: M. E. Sharpe, 1998), 30.

132. Shui Fu, "A Profile of Dams in China," in *The River Dragon Has Come!*, ed. Dai Qing, 18–24.

133. See Shapiro, *Mao's War against Nature*, 48–62, for the extraordinary story of hydroengineer Huang Wanli, his opposition to the Sanmenxia dam, and the consequences he and his family suffered.

134. Shapiro, *Mao's War against Nature*, 63.

135. Shui Fu, "A Profile of Dams," 20–21.

136. Ibid., 21.

137. Yi Si, "The World's Most Catastrophic Dam Failures," 25–38.

138. Economy, *The River Runs Black*, 2.

139. Ibid., 4.

140. Ibid., 1.

141. Jim Yardley, "Industrial Pollution Destroys Fish Farms in Rural Area," *The New York Times*, September 12, 2004; Jasper Becker, "The Death of China's Rivers," *Asia Times*, August 26, 2003; Stephen Voss, "Industrial Pollution Kills Hundreds along the Huai River Basin in China," http://www.stephenvoss.com/stories/ChinaWaterPollution/story.html. The PBS documentary is "Shifting Nature," program 3 of the four-part series "China from the Inside."

142. Economy, *The River Runs Black*, 8.

143. Li, *Fighting Famine in North China*, 367–69.

144. Ibid., 369.

145. Ibid., 370.

146. Jim Yardley, "Beneath Booming Cities, China's Future Is Drying Up," *The New York Times*, September 28, 2007.

147. Zhang Quanfa, "The South-to-North Water Diversion Project," *Frontiers in Ecology and the Environment* 3, no. 2 (2005): 76; Shai Oster, "Water Project in China Is Delayed," *The Wall Street Journal*, December 31, 2008, A4.; Jasper Becker, "The Death of China's Rivers"; "Factbox: Facts on China's South-to-North Water Transfer Project," Thomson Reuters http://reuters.com/assets, February 26, 2009.

148. Liu Changming, "Environmental Issues and the South-North Water Transfer Scheme," *The China Quarterly*, no. 156 (December 1998): 904–6.

149. Two of her important books have been translated into English: Dai Qing, *Yangtze! Yangtze! Debate over the Three Gorges Project* (London, UK: Earthscan, 1994); Dai Qing, *The River Dragon Has Come!*

150. Jianguo Wu, Jianhui Huang, Xingguo Han, Xianming Gao, Fengliang He, Mingxi Jiang, Zhigang Jiang, Richard B. Primack, Zehao Shen, "The Three Gorges Dam: An Ecological Perspective," *Frontiers on Ecology and the Environment* 2, no. 5 (2004): 241–48.

151. Jianguo Wu, Jianhui Huang, Xingguo Han, Zongqiang Xie, Xianming Gao, "Three Gorges Dam—Experiment in Habitat Fragmentation?," *Science* 300 (May 23, 2003): 1239–40.

152. Mara Hvistendahl, "China's Three Gorges Dam: An Environmental Catastrophe?" *Scientific American*, March 25, 2008.

153. James T. Areddy, "Drought Poses Obstacle for Giant Chinese Dam," *The Wall Street Journal*, November 18, 2009, A12.

154. Hvistendahl, "China's Three Gorges Dam."

155. Andrew C. Mertha, *China's Water Warriors: Citizen Action and Policy Change* (Ithaca, NY: Cornell University Press, 2008), 99.

156. See Mertha, *China's Water Warriors*, 94–109, for a narrative and analysis of the Dujiangyan story.

157. The Yangzi River (known in Yunnan province as the Jinsha River) turns east, but the Lancang River (which becomes the Mekong), continues south for 3,000 miles through Yunnan province and into Laos, forming the border with Thailand, before coursing through Cambodia and the Mekong delta in southern Vietnam on its way to the South China Sea. The Nu River flows for 1,250 miles through Yunnan province before entering Myanmar and becoming known as the Salween, coursing an additional 500 miles before emptying into the Gulf of Martaban.

158. UNESCO World Heritage Centre, "Three Parallel Rivers of Yunnan Protected Areas," http://whc.unesco.org/en/list/1083.

159. United Nations Environment Programme, World Conservation Monitoring Center, "Three Parallel Rivers of Yunnan Protected Areas," www.unep-wcmc.org.

160. Ibid.

161. These ethnic designations contain very complex histories and politics. For an informed discussion, see Jonathan Unger, "Not Quite Han: The Ethnic Minorities of China's Southwest," *Bulletin of Concerned Asian Scholars* 29, no. 3 (1997): 67–98.

162. For agricultural calendars of one village located 1,600 meters above the Nu River, see Nicholas K. Menzies, "Villagers' View of Environmental History," in *Sediments of Time*, eds. Elvin and Liu, 120–22.

163. Unger, "Not Quite Han," 70.

164. Jonathan Unger, "Life in the Chinese Hinterlands under the Rural Economic Reforms," *Bulletin of Concerned Asian Scholars* 22, no. 2 (1990): 9.

165. Fang Zhouzi, quoted in Mertha, *China's Water Warriors*, 137.

166. For a brief description of the scheme to "develop the west," see Williams, *Beyond Great Walls*, 52.

167. Darrin L. Magee, *New Energy Geographies: Powershed Politics and Hydropower Decision Making in Yunnan, China* (University of Washington Ph.D. thesis, 2006), 112–14.

168. One more consequence of the suppression of the voice of opposition to the first megadam project, the Sanmenxia on the Yellow River; see Shapiro, *Mao's War against Nature*, 62–65.

169. Xue Ye and Wang Yongchen, "Highly Controversial Hydropower Development in Western China," in *The China Environment Yearbook (2005): Crisis and Breakthrough of China's Environment*, eds. Liang Congjie and Yang Dongping (Leiden, NL: Brill, 2007), 66.

170. Mertha, *China's Water Warriors*, 45–48.

171. Ibid., 45–48.

172. Elisabeth Hsu, "The History of *qing hao* in the Chinese *materia medica*," *Transactions of the Royal Society of Tropical Medicine and Hygiene* no. 100 (2006): 505–8 discusses both the history of *qing hao* and the confusion over the shrubs *Artemisia. apiacea* and *A. annua*.

173. For a very brief account of the development of antimalarial drugs in China, see Sonia Shah, *The Fever: How Malaria Has Ruled Humankind for 500,000 Years* (New York, NY: Sarah Crichton Books, Farrar, Strauss and Giroux, 2010), 110–14. Less helpful is Randall M. Packard, *The Making of a Tropical Disease: A Short History of Malaria* (Baltimore, MD: Johns Hopkins University Press, 2007).

174. Magee, *New Energy Geographies*, 125–55.

175. Mertha, *China's Water Warriors*, 110–15.

176. Quoted in Mertha, Ibid., 116.

177. United Nations Environment Programme, World Conservation Monitoring Center, "Three Parallel Rivers of Yunnan Protected Areas," www.unep-wcmc.org.

178. Nujiang River NGO, "Treasured Gorge Survives—for Now," February 29, 2008, http://www.nujiang.ngo.cn/Dynamics-en/treasured-gorge-survives-for-now.

179. Mertha, *China's Water Warriors*, 142. Darren Magee confirmed to me in a telephone conversation in July 2011 that preliminary work continues on those four dam sites, including geologic testing to see if the dams will hold.

180. UNESCO World Heritage Centre, "Three Parallel Rivers of Yunnan Protected Areas," http://whc.unesco,org/en/list/1083.

181. United Nations Environment Programme, World Conservation Monitoring Center, "Three Parallel Rivers of Yunnan Protected Areas," www.unep-wcmc.org.

182. See the chapter of the same title in Edward Abbey, *Desert Solitaire* (various printings).

183. Li Bo, "Jinsha in Yunnan: Environmental and Cultural Protection in the Development of Tourism," in *The China Environment Yearbook (2005): Crisis and Breakthrough of China's Environment*, eds. Liang Congjie and Yang Dongping (Leiden, NL: Brill, 2007), 393–405.

184. UNESCO World Heritage Centre, "Three Parallel Rivers of Yunnan Protected Areas," http://whc.unesco,org/en/list/1083.

185. See two Worldwatch Institute reports: "Renewable Energy and Energy Efficiency in China: Current Status and Prospects for 2020," Worldwatch Report 182 (Washington, DC:

Worldwatch Institute, 2010), table 16, p. 37; and "Powering China's Development: The Role of Renewable Energy," Worldwatch Special Report (Washington, DC: Worldwatch Institute, 2007).

186. Michael B. McElroy, Xi Lu, Chris P. Nielsen, Yuxuan Wang, "Potential for Wind-Generated Electricity in China," *Science* 325 (September 11, 2009): 1378–80.

187. "China's Wind Farms Come with a Catch: Coal Plants," *The Wall Street Journal*, September 28, 2009.

188. Elisabeth Rosenthal, "China Increases Lead as Biggest Carbon Dioxide Emitter," *The New York Times*, June 14, 2008. Cement plants contribute 20 percent of China's carbon dioxide emissions.

189. Smil, *China's Environmental Crisis*, 117.

190. Smil, *China's Past, China's Future*, 16.

191. Sharon LaFraniere, "Graft in China Covers Up Toll of Coal Mines," *The New York Times* April 11, 2009.

192. Smil, *China's Past, China's Future*, 17.

193. Keith Bradsher and David Barboza, "Pollution from Chinese Coal Casts Shadow around Globe," *The New York Times*, June 6, 2006, 1.

194. For a fascinating (if sometimes terrifying) account of driving throughout China on its new interstate highways, see Peter Hessler, *Country Driving: A Journey through China from Farm to Factory* (New York, NY: HarperCollins Publishers, 2010). See also Ted Conover, "Capitalist Roaders," *The New York Times Magazine*, July 2, 2006, 32.

195. McNeill, *Something New Under the Sun*, 296–324.

196. Smil, *China's Past, China's Future*, 21.

197. John Stoll, Sharon Terlep, and Neil King Jr., "China Firm to Buy Hummer," *The Wall Street Journal*, June 3, 2009, http://online.wsj.com/article/SB124393928530076283.html. Other indicators are massive traffic jams: a record of 140 on the evening of September 17, 2010, in Beijing, and the late August 2010 ten-thousand-car, 60-mile jam north of Beijing that lasted ten days. *The New York Times*, September 25, 2010, A6.

198. Described in Conover, "Capitalist Roaders," 32. As Conover concludes (55): "It is reminiscent of a fading romance in American life, this crush of the automobile, and it is fun to see. But in this area, American culture seems more mature than Chinese culture, and with the benefit of hindsight and statistics, it is not hard to spot a multicar pileup in the making. While I was in Beijing, the journal *Nature* reported that the city's air pollution was much worse than previously thought. Concentrations of nitrogen dioxide have increase 50 percent over the past 10 years, and the buildup is accelerating. . . . Beijing's sulfur dioxide levels in 2004 were more than double New York's, and airborne-particulate levels more than six times as high. Last year [2005] China enacted its first comprehensive emissions law, but it is expected to have little effect on the transport sector's copious carbon-dioxide emissions. . . ."

199. Keith Bradsher, "Trucks Power China's Economy, at a Suffocating Cost," *The New York Times*, December 8, 2007.

200. Ibid.

201. Ibid.

202. Jeffrey Ball, "Summit Leaves Key Questions Unresolved," *The Wall Street Journal*, December 21, 2009, A17.

203. "Where Countries Stand on Copenhagen," BBC World Service, December 3, 2009.

204. "Hu Jintao's Speech on Climate Change," *The New York Times*, September 23, 2009.

205. For the background and documents generated by the 2010 Cancun conference, see United Nations Framework Convention on Climate Change http://unfccc.int/2860.php; for a brief background account of China's positions, see "Cancun Climate Change Summit: China's

Journey from Copenhagen," http://www.guardian.co.uk/environment/2010/dec/01/cancun-climate-change-summit-china.

206. Joseph Kahn and Jim Yardley, "As China Roars, Pollution Reaches Deadly Extremes," *The New York Times*, August 26, 2007.

207. Lee Feigon *Demystifying Tibet: Unlocking the Secrets of the Land of the Snows* (Chicago, IL: Ivan R. Dee, Inc., 1996), 8.

208. Quoted in Michael Zhao and Orville Schell, "Tibet: Plateau in Peril," *World Policy Journal* (fall 2008): 172–173.

209. Ibid., 179.

210. Graham E. Clark, "Tradition, Modernity, and Environmental Change in Tibet," in *Imaging Tibet: Perceptions, Projections, and Fantasies*, eds. Thierry Dodin and Heinz Räther (Boston, MA: Wisdom Press, 2001), 350.

211. Ibid.

212. Ibid., 178–79.

213. Feigon, *Demystifying Tibet*, 152.

214. For a unique case, see Toni Huber, *The Cult of Pure Crystal Mountain: Popular Pilgrimage and Visionary Landscape in Southeast Tibet* (New York, NY: Oxford University Press, 1999), esp. 196–201, 208–10, 218.

215. Qian San-qiang, "Opening Speech for Symposium on Qinghai-Xizang (Tibet) Plateau," in *Geological and Ecological Studies of Qinghai-Xizang Plateau* (Beijing, CN: Science Press, 1981), vol. 1, xv.

216. For an earlier assessment, see *Clear Water, Blue Skies: China's Environment in the New Century* (Washington, DC: The World Bank, 1997).

217. Joseph Kahn, "In China, a Lake's Champion Imperils Himself," *The New York Times*, October 14, 2007.

218. Jun Jing, "Environmental Protests in Rural China," in *Chinese Society: Change, Conflict, and Resistance*, eds. Elizabeth J. Perry and Mark Selden (New York, NY: Routledge, 2000), 148.

219. Ma Tianjie, "Environmental Mass Incidents in China: Examining Large-Scale Unrest in Dongyang, Zhejiang," in Woodrow Wilson International Center for Scholars, *China Environment Series 10 (2008–2009)* (Washington, DC: Woodrow Wilson Center, 2009), 33–49.

220. For addition description, see also Mark Magnier, "As China Spews Pollution, Villagers Rise Up," *Los Angeles Times*, Scptember 3, 2006, A9.

221. Howard French, "Land of 74,000 Protests (but Little Is Ever Fixed)," *The New York Times*, August 24, 2005.

222. Ma Tianjie, "Environmental Mass Incidents in China," 33–34.

223. Ibid., 35.

224. Ibid., 44.

225. Xiaoying Ma and Leonard Ortolando, *Environmental Regulation in China: Institutions, Enforcement, and Compliance* (Lanham, MD: Rowman & Littlefield, 2000), 63.

226. Abigail R. Jahiel, "The Contradictory Impact of Reform on Environmental Protection in China," *The China Quarterly*, no. 149 (March 1997): 81.

227. See, for example, Christina Larson, "In China, a New Transparency on Government Pollution Data," *Yale Environment 360*, http://e360.yale.edu/content/print.msp?id=2352.

228. Ma and Ortolando, *Environmental Regulation in China*, 9.

229. Ma, "Environmental Mass Incidents in Rural China," 35.

230. Michael S. Liu, *Environmental Protection in China: International Influence and Policy Change*, M.A. thesis, San Diego State University, 2003.

231. Xiaoqing Lu and Bates Gill, "Assessing China's Response to the Challenge of Environmental Health," in Woodrow Wilson International Center for Scholars, *China Environment Series 9 (2007)* (Washington, DC: Woodrow Wilson Center, 2007), 3–18.

232. Jonathan Schwartz, "Environmental NGOs in China: Roles and Limits," *Pacific Affairs* 77, no. 1 (2004): 33.

233. Ma and Ortolando, *Environmental Regulation in China*, 8.

234. Ibid., 126–29.

235. For additional environmental NGOs, see Green Earth Volunteers, http://eng.greensos.cn; and Christina Larson, "China's Emerging Environmental Movement," *Yale Environment 360* http://e360.yale.edu/content/print.msp?id=2018.

236. Schwartz, "Environmental NGOs in China," 38–42.

237. Ibid., 42–45.

238. Jonathan Shieber, "Courting Change: Environmental Groups in China Now Have the Ability to Sue Polluters: But Will They?" *The Wall Street Journal*, December 7, 2009, R11.

239. Schwartz, "Environmental NGOs in China," 46.

240. Ibid., 46.

241. Andrew Jacobs, "In Sentence of Activist, China Gives West a Chill," *The New York Times*, December 26, 2009.

242. Guobin Yang, "Is There an Environmental Movement in China? Beware of the 'River of Anger,'" in *Active Society in Formation: Environmentalism, Labor, and the Underworld in China* (Washington, DC: Woodrow Wilson Center International Center for Scholars, Asia Program Special Report no. 124, September 2004), 6.

243. Ibid.

244. Mertha, *China's Water Warriors*, 135.

245. Quoted in ibid., 136.

246. Quoted in ibid., 138.

247. Ibid., 119.

248. Quoted in ibid., 137–38.

249. Mertha, 146. For a more extended discussion of the relationship between democracy and environmental protection, see Shapiro, *Mao's War against Nature*, especially 64–65, 195–208.

250. In addition to the articles cited below, see Thomas L. Friedman, *Hot, Flat, and Crowded: Why We Need a Green Revolution, and How It Can Renew America* (New York, NY: Farrar, Straus and Giroux, 2008), esp. ch. 15, "Can Red China become Green China?" 343–67.

251. Thomas L. Friedman, "The New Sputnik," *The New York Times*, September 27, 2009.

252. Thomas L. Friedman, "Postcard from South China," *The New York Times*, August 31, 2008.

253. Thomas L. Friedman, "China's Sunshine Boys," *The New York Times*, December 6, 2006.

254. Shai Oster, "World's Top Polluter Emerges as Green-Technology Leader," *Wall Street Journal*, December 15, 2009, A1, A12.

255. Jonathan Porritt, "Can China Go Green?" BBC World Service Documentaries, http://www.bbc.co.uk.worlservice/documentaries/2009/12/191201_wednesdaydoc_chinagreen.shtml.

256. *The Wall Street Journal*, September 28, 2009.

257. For a critique of the general idea of China's challenge to U.S. global power, see Bruce Cumings, "'The Rise of China'?" in *Radicalism, Revolution, and Reform in Modern China: Essays in Honor of Maurice Meisner*, eds. Catherine Lynch, Robert B. Marks, and Paul G. Pickowicz (Lanham, MD: Lexington Books, 2010), 185–208.

258. Keith Bradsher, "Earth-Friendly Elements, Mined Destructively," *The New York Times*, December 26, 2009, A1, B5. *The Wall Street Journal* of September 25, 2010 reported that a

U.S. corporation called Molycorp is planning to reopen a rare-earth mine in Mountain Pass, California.

259. *People's Daily*, http://englishpeoplesdaily.com.cn, March 13, 2001.

CHAPTER 8

1. Andrew Jacobs, "As China's Economy Grows, Pollution Worsens Despite New Efforts to Control It," *The New York Times*, July 29, 2010, A4.

2. The worries about water are most evident in the annual drying up of the Yellow River and the building of the massive "south-to-north water transfer project," both discussed in chapter 7. The issue of whether or not China is running out of land has arisen in the peculiar form of foreign press reports on Chinese activities in Africa. Two online articles by Loro Horta started the speculation: "Food Security in Africa: China's New Rice Bowl," *Ocnus Net* http://ocnus.net/artman2/publish/Africa_8/Food_Security; and "The Zambezi Valley: China's First Agricultural Colony?" The Center for Strategic and International Studies http://csis.org/print/18426, originally posted June 8, 2008. Horta's pieces were followed up by articles in the *Financial Times* (Jamil Anderlini, "China Eyes Overseas Land in Food Push," May 8, 2008), the *Guardian* (David Smith, "The Food Rush: Rising Demand in China and West Sparks African Land Grab," July 3, 2009), and a UPI post ("Food and Water Drive African Land Grab," April 29, 2010). On the one hand, these reports seem plausible given reports about the decline in the amount of arable in China. On the other hand, scholarly investigations do not support the claims of China's "African land grab." Deborah A. Bräutigam and Tang Xiaoyang, "China's Engagement in African Agriculture: 'Down to the Countryside,'" *The China Quarterly* 199 (Sep. 2009): 686–706; and Deborah A. Bräutigam, *The Dragon's Gift: The Real Story of China in Africa* (New York, NY: Oxford University Press, 2009), esp. ch. 10 "Foreign Farmers: Chinese Settlers in Rural Africa."

3. Today, with 1.3+ billion people, that percentage is slowly declining to around 20 percent, largely because the rate of growth of China's population has slowed, while that of other parts of the world has surged.

4. *The Wall Street Journal*, July 20, 2010, A1, C10. The data included all forms of energy, but both the mix of the sources of energy, and per capita usage, differed significantly. The United States relies on coal to meet 22 percent of its energy needs, while China's reliance on coal has climbed from 57 percent in 2000 to two-thirds in 2010. In the U.S., each person on average consumed the equivalent of 7 to 8 tons of oil annually, while in China the figure was 1.7 tons per person, implying that there is significant room for even more energy consumption and production in China as its standard of living continues to rise.

5. *The Wall Street Journal*, July 20, 2010, A12. See also Edward Wong, "Water Levels Near Record at Three Gorges Dam in China," *The New York Times*, July 19, 2010.

6. For a discussion and case studies around the world, see B. L. Turner II and William B. Meyer, *Changes in Land Use and Land Cover: A Global Perspective* (New York, NY: Cambridge University Press, 1994).

7. The rapid deforestation of tropical lands in just the past fifty years probably exceeds both the rate and extent of China's deforestation. See Michael Williams, *Deforesting the Earth: From Prehistory to Global Crisis* (Chicago, IL: University of Chicago Press, 2003), esp. ch. 13. I say "probably" because making the comparison is difficult, since Williams does not include statistical data on twentieth-century China.

8. Pierre-Etienne Will, "State Intervention in the Administration of a Hydraulic Structure: The Example of Hubei Province in Late Imperial Times," in *The Scope of State Power in China*, ed. Stuart Schram (New York, NY: St. Martin's Press, 1985), 295–347.

9. Clive Ponting, *The Twentieth Century* (New York, NY: Henry Holt, 1999).

10. Edmund Burke III, "The Big Story: Human History, Energy Regimes, and the Environment," in *The Environment and World History*, eds. Edmund Burke III and Kenneth Pomeranz (Berkeley and Los Angeles, CA: University of California Press, 2009); I. G. Simmons, *Global Environmental History*, Chicago, IL: University of Chicago Press, 2008.

11. Vaclav Smil, *Energy in World History* (Boulder, CO: Westview Press, 1994), esp. ch. 6.

12. Mark Elvin, "Three Thousand Years of Unsustainable Growth: China's Environment from Archaic Times to the Present," *East Asian History* 6 (1993), 7–46.

13. For a summary, see Millennium Ecosystem Assessment, *Ecosystems and Human Well-being, Synthesis* (Washington, DC: Island Press, 2005), vii.

14. For an earlier, and somewhat quirky but at times insightful book on this linkage, see Leon E. Stover, *The Cultural Ecology of Chinese Civilization: Peasants and Elites in the Last of Agrarian States* (New York, NY: Mentor Books, 1974).

15. Timothy Brook, *The Confusions of Pleasure: Commerce and Culture in Ming China* (Berkeley and Los Angeles, CA: University of California Press, 1998).

16. For the history of fire, see the various works by Stephen J. Pyne, especially *World Fire: The Culture of Fire on Earth* (Seattle, WA: University of Washington Press, 1997).

17. James Z. Lee and Wang Feng, *One Quarter of Humanity: Malthusian Mythologies and Chinese Realities, 1700–2000* (Cambridge, MA: Harvard University Press, 1999).

18. J. R. McNeill, "China's Environmental History in World Perspective," in *Sediments of Time* eds. Elvin and Liu, 36.

19. Ibid., 31–37.

20. In addition to the instances cited in this book, William McNeill argues that global rise of market economies started in Song-era China. "'The Rise of the West' after Twenty-five Years," *Journal of World History* 1, no. 1 (1991).

21. See Janet Abu-Lughod, *Before European Hegemony* (New York, NY: Oxford University Press, 1989); Sing C. Chew, *World Ecological Degradation: Accumulation, Urbanization, and Deforestation, 3000 B.C.—A. D. 2000* (Lanham, MD: AltaMira Press, 2001), 75.

22. Andre Gunder Frank, *ReOrient* (Berkeley and Los Angeles, University of California Press, 1999); Kenneth Pomeranz, *The Great Divergence: China, Europe, and the Making of the Modern World Economy* (Princeton, NJ: Princeton University Press, 2000).

23. Anthony N. Penna, *The Human Footprint: A Global Environmental History* (Malden, MA: Wiley-Blackwell, 2010).

24. For an overview, see Clive Ponting, *A New Green History of the World* (New York, NY: Penguin Books, 1997), chs. 1–4.

25. Michael Williams, *Deforesting the Earth*, esp. ch. 7.

26. Joachim Radkau, *Nature and Power: A Global History of the Environment* (New York, NY: Cambridge University Press, 2008), 21.

27. Conrad Totman, *The Green Archipelago: Forestry in Pre-Industrial Japan* (Columbus, OH: Ohio University Press, 1998).

28. John F. Richards, *The Unending Frontier: An Environmental History of the Early Modern World* (Berkeley and Los Angeles: University of California Press, 2003), 4–11.

29. Ibid., 111.

30. Pomeranz, *The Great Divergence.*

31. J. Donald Hughes, *An Environmental History of the World: Humankind's Changing Role in the Community of Life* (London, UK and New York, NY: Routledge, 2001), 5, 209–11.

32. Ibid., 8–9.

Select Bibliography

Abe, Ken-ichi and James Nickum eds. *The Good Earth: Regional and Historical Insights into China's Environment*. Kyoto, HK: Kyoto University Press, 2009.

Adshead, S. A. M. "An Energy Crisis in Early Modern China." *Ch'ing-shi wen-t'i [Late Imperial China]* 3, no. 2 (1974): 20–28.

Allen, Sarah. *The Formation of Chinese Civilization: An Archeological Perspective*. New Haven, CT and London, UK: Yale University Press, 2005.

Anderson,E. N. *The Food of China*. New Haven, CT: Yale University Press, 1988.

Anthony, David W. *The Horse, the Wheel, and Language: How Bronze-Age Riders from the Eurasian Steppes Shaped the Modern World*. Princeton, NJ: Princeton University Press, 2007.

Atwell, William S. "Time, Money, and Weather: Ming China and the 'Great Depression' of the Mid-Fifteenth Century." *The Journal of Asian Studies* 61, no. 1 (2002): 83–113.

Averill, Stephen. *Revolution in the Highlands: China's Jinggangshan Base Area*. Lanham, MD: Rowman & Littlefield, 2006.

Balazs, Etienne. *Chinese Civilization and Bureaucracy*, ed. and intro. Arthur F. Wright. New Haven, CT: Yale University Press, 1977.

Banister, Judith. *China's Changing Population*. Stanford, CA: Stanford University Press, 1987.

Barbierri-Low, Anthony J. *Artisans in Early Imperial China*. Seattle, WA and London, UK: University of Washington Press, 2007.

Barfield, Thomas J. *The Nomadic Alternative*. Upper Saddle River, NJ: Prentice Hall, 1993.

Barnes, Gina L. *The Rise of Civilization in East Asia: The Archeology of China, Korea and Japan*. London, UK: Thames and Hudson, 1999

Barrett, T. H. *The Woman Who Discovered Printing*. New Haven, CT: Yale University Press, 2008.

Baumler, Allan. *The Chinese and Opium under the Republic: Worse Than Floods and Wild Beasts*. Albany, NY: State University of New York Press, 2007.

Becker, Jasper. *Hungry Ghosts: Mao's Secret Famine*. New York, NY: First Owl Books, Henry Holt and Co., 1998.

Beckwith, Christopher. *Empires of the Silk Road: A History of Central Eurasia from the Bronze Age to the Present*. Princeton, NJ: Princeton University Press, 2009.

Bello, David A. "To Go Where No Man Could Go for Long: Malaria and the Qing Construction of Ethnic Administrative Space in Frontier Yunnan." *Modern China* 31, no. 3 (2005): 283–317.

———. "The Cultured Nature of Imperial Foraging in Manchuria," *Late Imperial China* 31, no. 2 (2010): 1–33.

———. *Opium and the Limits of Empire: Drug Prohibition in the Chinese Interior, 1729–1850*. Cambridge, MA: Harvard University Press, 2005.

Benedict, Carol. *Bubonic Plague in Nineteenth-Century China*. Stanford, CA: Stanford University Press, 1996.

Biodiversity Committee of the Chinese Academy of Sciences. "Biodiversity in China: Status and Conservation Needs." www.brim.ac.cn/brime/bdinchn/1.html

Blaikie, Piers and Harold Brookfield eds. *Land Degradation and Society*. New York, NY: Methuen, 1987.

Botkin, Daniel B. *Discordant Harmonies: A New Ecology for the Twenty-first Century*. New York, NY: Oxford University Press, 1990.

Bräutigam, Deborah A. *The Dragon's Gift: The Real Story of China in Africa*. New York, NY: Oxford University Press, 2009.

Bräutigam, Deborah A. and Tang Xiaoyang. "China's Engagement in African Agriculture: Down to the Countryside." *The China Quarterly* 199 (Sep. 2009): 686–706.

Bray, Francesca *Agriculture*, vol. 6, part II of Joseph Needham, *Science and Civilization in China*. Cambridge, UK and New York, NY: Cambridge University Press, 1984.

———. *The Rice Economies: Technology and Development in Asian Societies*. Berkeley and Los Angeles, CA: University of California Press, 1994.

Brook, Timothy. *The Confusions of Pleasure: Commerce and Culture in Ming China*. Berkeley and Los Angeles, CA: University of California Press, 1998.

Bruenig E. F. et al. *Ecological-Socioeconomic System Analysis and Simulation: A Guide for Application of System Analysis to the Conservation, Utliization, and Development of Subtropical Land Resources in China*. Bonn: Deutsches Nationalkomitee für das UNESCO Programm de Mensch und die Biosphäre, 1986.

Burke, Edmund III and Kenneth Pomeranz eds. *The Environment and World History*. Berkeley and Los Angeles, CA: University of California Press, 2009.

Cahill, James. *Hills Beyond a River: Chinese Painting of the Yüan Dynasty*. New York, NY: Weatherhill, 1976.

———. *Painter's Practice: How Artists Lived and Worked in Traditional China*. New York, NY: Columbia University Press, 1994.

Carin, Robert. *River Control in Communist China*. Hong Kong, HK, 1962.

Chang, Chun-shu. *The Rise of the Chinese Empire*. 2 vols. Ann Arbor, MI: The University of Michigan Press, 2000.

Chang, K. C. ed. *Food in Chinese Culture: Anthropological and Historical Perspectives*. New Haven, CT: Yale University Press, 1977.

Chang, K. C. *Shang Civilization*. New Haven, CT and London, UK: Yale University Press, 1980.

Changming, Liu. "Environmental Issues and the South-North Water Transfer Scheme." *The China Quarterly*, no. 156 (December 1998): 899–910.

Chao, Kang. *Man and Land in Chinese History: An Economic Analysis*. Stanford, CA: Stanford University Press, 1986.

Chen, Jung. *Zhongguo senlin shiliao* [Historical source materials on China's forests]. Beijing, CN: Zhongguo linye chuban she, 1983.

China's Diversity: A Country Study. Beijing, CN: China Environmental Science Press, 1998.

Clark, Hugh R. "Frontier Discourse and China's Maritime Frontier: China's Frontiers and the Encounter with the Sea through Early Imperial History." *Journal of World History* 20, no. 1 (March, 2009): 1–33.

Coggins, Chris. *The Tiger and the Pangolin: Nature, Culture, and Conservation in China.* Honolulu, HI: University of Hawai'i Press, 2003.

Crawford, Gary W. and Chen Shen. "The Origins of Rice Agriculture: Recent Progress in East Asia." *Antiquity* 72 (1998).

Crosby, Alfred W. *Ecological Imperialism: The Biological Expansion of Europe, 900–1900.* New York, NY: Cambridge University Press, 1986.

———. *The Columbian Exchange: Biological and Cultural Consequences of 1492.* Westport, CT: Greenwood Press, 1972.

Crossley, Pamela Kyle, Helen F. Siu, and Donald S. Sutton, eds. *Empire at the Margins: Culture, Ethnicity, and Frontier in Early Modern China.* Berkeley and Los Angeles, CA: University of California Press, 2006.

Csete, Anne Alice. *A Frontier Minority in the Chinese World: The Li People of Hainan Island from the Han through the High Qing.* SUNY-Buffalo Ph.D. dissertation, 1995.

Dai Qing ed. *The River Dragon Has Come! The Three Gorges Dam and the Fate of China's Yangtze River and Its People.* Armonk, NY: M. E. Sharpe, 1998.

Dai Qing. *Yangtze! Yangtze! Debate over the Three Gorges Project.* London, UK: Earthscan, 1994.

Davis, Mike. *Late Victorian Holocausts: El Niño Famines and the Making of the Third World.* London, UK and New York, NY: Verso Press, 2001.

Di Cosmo, Nicola. *Ancient China and Its Enemies: The Rise of Nomadic Power in East Asian History.* New York, NY: Cambridge University Press, 2002.

Dikötter, Frank. *Mao's Great Famine: The History of China's Most Devastating Catastrophe, 1958–1962.* New York, NY: Walker and Co., 2010.

Dodgen, Randall A. *Controlling the Dragon: Confucian Engineers and the Yellow River in Late Imperial China.* Honolulu, HI: University of Hawai'i Press, 2001.

Dodin, Thierry and Heinz Räther eds. *Imaging Tibet: Perceptions, Projections, and Fantasies.* Boston, MA: Wisdom Press, 2001.

Domros, Manfred and Peng Gongping. *The Climate of China.* Berlin, DE: Springer, 1988.

Dunstan, Helen. "The Late Ming Epidemics: A Preliminary Survey," *Ch'ing-shih wen-t'i* [*Late Imperial China*] 3, no. 3 (1975): 1–59.

Ebrey, Patricia. *The Cambridge Illustrated History of China.* Cambridge, UK and New York, NY: Cambridge University Press, 1999.

Economy, Elizabeth. *The River Runs Black: The Environmental Challenge to China's Future.* Ithaca, NY: Cornell University Press, 2004.

Edmonds, Richard Louis. *Patterns of China's Lost Harmony: A Survey of the Country's Environmental Degradation and Protection.* London and New York, NY: Routledge, 1994.

Elroy, Michael B. Chris P. Nielsen, and Peter Lyon eds. *Energizing China: Reconciling Environmental Protection and Economic Growth.* Cambridge, MA: Harvard University Press, 1998.

Elvin, Mark. "The Environmental Legacy of Imperial China." *China Quarterly* no. 156 (December 1998): 733–756.

———. "Three Thousand Years of Unsustainable Growth: China's Environment from Archaic Times to the Present." *East Asian History*, vol. 6 (1993): 7–46.

———. *The Pattern of the Chinese Past.* Stanford, CA: Stanford University Press, 1971.

———. *The Retreat of the Elephants: An Environmental History of China.* New Haven, CT and London, UK: Yale University Press, 2004.

Elvin, Mark and Liu Ts'ui-jung eds. *Sediments of Time: Environment and Society in Chinese History*. New York, NY: Cambridge University Press, 1998.

Enderton, Catherine Schurr. *Hainan Dao: Contemporary Environmental Management and Development on China's Treasure Island*. UCLA Ph.D. dissertation, 1984.

Fan Sheng-chih Shu: An Agricultural Book of China written by Fan Sheng-chih in the First Century B.C. Shih Sheng-han trans. Beijing, CN: Science Press, 1959.

Feigon, Lee. *Demystifying Tibet: Unlocking the Secrets of the Land of the Snows*. Chicago, IL: Ivan R. Dee, Inc., 1996.

Fiskesjö, Magnus. "On the 'Raw' and the 'Cooked' Barbarians of Imperial China." *Inner Asia* 1 (1999): 139–68.

Fletcher, Joseph. "The Mongols: Ecological and Social Perspectives." *Harvard Journal of Asiatic Studies* 46, no. 1 (1986): 11–50.

Flynn, Dennis O. and Arturo Giraldez. "Cycles of Silver: Global Economic Unity through the mid-18th Century." *Journal of World History* 13 (2002): 391–428.

Fong, Wen C. and James Y. C. Watt, eds. *Possessing the Past: Treasures from the National Palace Museum, Taipei*. New York, NY: The Metropolitan Museum of Art, 1996.

Frachetti, Michael. *Pastoral Landscapes and Social Interaction in Bronze Age Eurasia*. Berkeley and Los Angeles, CA: University of California Press, 2009.

Frank, Andre Gunder. *ReOrient: Global Economy in the Asian Age*. Los Angeles and Berkeley: University of California Press, 1998.

Franke, Herbert and Denis Twitchett, eds. *The Cambridge History of China*, vol. 6, *Alien Regimes and Border States*. New York, NY: Cambridge University Press, 1995.

Gardella, Robert. *Harvesting Mountains: Fujian and the China Tea Trade, 1757–1937*. Berkeley and Los Angeles, CA: University of California Press, 1994.

Gernet, Jacques. *Buddhism in Chinese Society: An Economic History from the Fifth to the Tenth Centuries*, trans. Franciscus Verellen. New York, NY: Columbia University Press, 1995.

Giersch, C. Patterson. *Asian Borderlands: The Transformation of Qing China's Yunnan Frontier*. Cambridge, MA: Harvard University Press, 2006.

Goldstone, Jack A. "Efflorescences and Economic Growth in World History: Rethinking the 'Rise of the West' and the Industrial Revolution." *Journal of World History* 13, no. 2 (2002): 323–389.

Graff, David A. *Medieval Chinese Warfare, 300–900*. London, UK and New York, NY: Routledge, 2002.

Grove, Jean. *The Little Ice Age*. London, UK: Methuen, 1988.

Hamashita, Takeshi. *China, East Asia and the Global Economy: Regional and Historical Perspectives*. New York, NY: Routledge, 2008.

Harkness, James. "Recent Trends in Forestry and Conservation of Biodiversity in China." *The China Quarterly*, no. 156 (December 1998): 911–934.

Harrell, Stevan. *Ways of Being Ethnic in Southwest China*. Seattle, WA: Washington University Press, 2001.

Harris, Richard B. *Wildlife Conservation in China: Preserving the Habitat of China's Wild West*. Armonk, NY: M. E. Sharpe, 2008.

Hartwell, Robert. "A Cycle of Economic Change in Imperial China: Coal and Iron in Northeast China, 750–1350." *Journal of the Economic and Social History of the Orient*, no. 10 (1967): 102–159.

———. "Demographic, Political, and Social Transformations of China, 750-1550." *Harvard Journal of Asiatic Studies,* Vol. 42, No. 2 (Dec., 1982): 365–442.

———. "Markets, Technology ad the Structure of Enterprise in the Development of the Eleventh-Twelfth Century Chinese Iron and Steel Industry." *The Journal of Economic History* 26, no. 1 (March 1966): 29–58.

———. "A Revolution in the Chinese Iron and Coal Industries during the Northern Sung, 960–1126 A.D." *The Journal of Asian Studies* 21, no. 2 (1962): 153–162.

Hayes, Jack. "Fire Disasters on the Borderland: Qing Dynasty Chinese, Tibetan and Hui Fire Landscapes in Western China, 1821–1911." Paper presented at the 2010 AAS Annual Meeting, Philadelphia, PA.

———. "Rocks, Trees and Grassland on the Borderlands: Tibetan and Chinese Perceptions and Manipulations of the Environment along Ecotone Froniers, 1911–1982." Paper presented at the 2011 AAS Annual Meeting, Honolulu, HI.

Herman, John E. *Amid the Clouds and Mist: China's Colonization of Guizhou, 1200–1700*. Cambridge, MA: Harvard University Press, 2007.

Ho, Peter. "Mao's War against Nature? The Environmental Impact of the Grain-First Campaign in China." *The China Journal*, no. 50 (July 2003): 37–59.

Ho, Ping-ti. *The Cradle of the East: An Inquiry into the Indigenous Origins of Techniques and Ideas of Neolithic and Early Historic China, 5000–1000 B.C.* Chicago, IL: The University of Chicago Press, 1975.

———. "Early-Ripening Rice in Chinese History." *The Economic History Review*, New Series 9, no. 2 (1956): 37–59.

———. "The Introduction of American Food Plants into China." *American Anthropologist*, New Series 57, no. 2, part 1 (1955): 191–201.

———. "Lo-yang A.D. 495–534: A Study of Physical and Socio-economic Planning of a Metropolitan Area." *Harvard Journal of Asiatic Studies* 26 (1966): 52–101.

———. "The Loess and the Origin of Chinese Agriculture." *The American Historial Review* 75, no. 1 (October 1969): 1–36.

Hoffman, Richard C., Nancy Langston, James C. McCann, Peter C. Perdue, and Lise Sedrez. "*AHR* Conversation: Environmental Historians and Environmental Crisis." *The American Historical Review* 113, no. 5 (December 2008): 1431–65.

Hostetler, Laura. *Qing Colonial Enterprise: Ethnography and Cartography in Early Modern China*. Chicago, IL: University of Chicago Press, 2001.

Hsu, Cho-yun. *Ancient China in Transition*. Stanford, CA: Stanford University Press, 1965.

———. *Han Agriculture: The Formation of Early Chinese Agrarian Economy*. Seattle, WA: University of Washington Press, 1980.

Hsu, Elisabeth. "The History of *qing hao* in the Chinese *materia medica*," *Transaction of the Royal Society of Tropical Medicine and Hygiene* 100 (2006): 505–8.

———. "Reflections on the 'discovery' of the antimalarial qinghao." *British Journal of Clinical Pharmacology* 61, no. 6 (2006): 666–70.

Huang, Phillip C. C. *The Peasant Economy and Social Change in North China*. Stanford, CA: Stanford University Press, 1985.

Huber, Toni. *The Cult of Pure Crystal Mountain: Popular Pilgrimage and Visionary Landscape in Southeast Tibet*. New York, NY: Oxford University Press, 1999.

Hughes, J. Donald. *An Environmental History of the World: Humankind's Changing Role in the Community of Life*. New York, NY: Routledge, 2001.

Jagchid, Sechin and Van Jay Symons. *Peace, War and Trade along the Great Wall*. Bloomington, IN: Indiana University Press, 1989.

Jahiel, Abigail R. "The Contradictory Impact of Reform on Environmental Protection in China." *The China Quarterly*, no. 149 (March 1997): 81–103.

———. "The Organization of Environmental Protection in China." *The China Quarterly*, no. 156 (1998): 757–787.

Jun Jing. "Environmental Protests in Rural China." In Elizabeth J. Perry and Mark Selden eds., *Chinese Society: Change, Conflict, and Resistance*. New York, NY: Routledge, 2000: 143–160.

Keightley, David N. ed. *The Origins of Chinese Civilization*. Berkeley and Los Angeles, CA: University of California Press, 1983.

Keightley, David N. *The Ancestral Landscape: Time, Space, and Community in Late Shang China (ca. 1200–1045 B.C.)*. Berkeley, CA: University of California–Berkeley Center for Chinese Studies, 2000.

King, Frank H. *Farmers of Forty Centuries, or Permanent Agriculture in China, Korea, and Japan*. Madison, WI: Mrs. F. H. King, 1911.

Lary, Diana. "The Waters Covered the Earth: China's War-Induced Natural Disasters." In Mark Selden and Alvin Y. So eds., *War and State Terrorism: The United States, Japan, and the Asia-Pacific in the Long Twentieth Century*. Lanham, MD: Rowman & Littlefield, 2004: 143–170.

Lattimore, Owen. *The Inner Asian Frontiers of China*. Boston, MA: Beacon Press, 1967.

———. *Studies in Frontier History: Collected Papers, 1928–1958*. London, UK: Oxford University Press, 1962.

Lee James Z. and Wang Feng. *One Quarter of Humanity: Malthusian Mythology and Chinese Realities*. Cambridge: Harvard University Press, 1999.

Lee, James. "Food Supply and Population Growth in Southwest China, 1250–1850." *Journal of Asian Studies* 41, no. 4 (1982): 711–746.

Leeming, Frank. "Official Landscapes in Traditional China." *Journal of the Economic and Social History of the Orient* 23, no. 1 (1980): 153–204.

Leonard, Jane Kate. *Controlling from Afar: The Daoguang Emperor's Management of the Grand Canal Crisis, 1824–1826*. Ann Arbor, MI: Center for Chinese Studies, University of Michigan Press, 1996.

Leong, Sow-Theng. *Migration and Ethnicity in Chinese History: Hakkas, Pengmin, and their Neighbors*, ed. Tim Wright. Stanford, CA: Stanford University Press, 1997.

Lewis, Mark Edward. *The Early Chinese Empires: Qin and Han*. Cambridge MA: Harvard University Press, 2007.

———. *The Flood Myths of Early China*. Albany: State University of New York Press, 2006.

———. *Sanctioned Violence in Early China*. Albany: State University of New York Press, 1990.

Li, Bozhong. *Agricultural Development in Jiangnan, 1620–1850*. New York, NY: St. Martin's Press, 1998.

———. "Was There a 'Fourteenth-Century Turning Point'? Population, Land, Technology, and Farm Management." In Paul Jakov Smith and Richard von Glahn eds., *The Song-Yuan-Ming Transition in Chinese History*, eds. Cambridge, MA: Harvard University Asia Center, 2003: 135–175.

Li, Lillian. *Fighting Famine in North China: State, Market, and Environmental Decline, 1690s–1990s*. Stanford, CA: Stanford University Press, 2007.

Li, Xiaoxiong. *Poppies and Politics in China: Sichuan Province, 1840s to 1940s*. Newark, DE: University of Delaware Press, 2009.

Liang Conjie and Yang Dongping eds., *The China Environment Yearbook (2005): Crisis and Breakthrough of China's Environment*. Leiden, NL: Brill, 2007.

Liang, Fangzhong. *Zhongguo lidai hukou, tiandi, tianfu tongji* [China's historical statistics on population, land, and taxes]. Shanghai, CN: Renmin Chuban She, 1980.

Lin, D. Y. "China." In Stephen Haden-Guest, John K. Wright, and Eileen M. Teclaff eds., *A World Geography of Forest Reserves*. New York, NY: The Ronald Press Co., 1956: 529–550.

Ling, Daxie. "Wo guo senlin ziyuan de bianqian" [Changes in our country's forest resources]. *Zhongguo nongshi* [Chinese agricultural history] 1983 No. 2: 26–36.

Liu Dachang. "Tenure and Management of Non-State Forests in China since 1950: A Historical Review." *Environmental History* 6 (April 2001): 239–63.

Liu, Jung-Chao. *China's Fertilizer Economy*. Chicago, IL: Aldine Publishing Co., 1970.

Liu, Li. *The Chinese Neolithic: Trajectories to Early States*. Cambridge, MA: Cambridge University Press, 2004.

Longworth, John and Gregory J. Williamson. *China's Pastoral Region: Sheep and Wool, Minority Nationalities, Rangeland Degradation and Sustainable Development*. Canberra: The Australian Centre for International Agricultural Research, 1993.

Lowdermilk, W. C. "Forestry in Denuded China." *The Annals of the American Academy of Political and Social Science*, vol. 152 (Nov. 1930): 127–141.

Lowe, Michael and Edward L. Shaughnessy, eds. *The Cambridge History of Ancient China: From the Origins to 221 B.C.* New York, NY and Cambridge, UK: Cambridge University Press, 1999.

Lu, Sheldon H. and Jiayan Mi, eds. *Chinese Ecocinema in the Age of Environmental Challenge*. Hong Kong, HK: Hong Kong University Press, 2009.

Lu, Xiaoqing and Bates Gill. "Assessing China's Response to the Challenge of Environmental Health." Woodrow Wilson International Center for Scholars, *China Environment Series 9 (2007)*. Washington, DC: Woodrow Wilson Center, 2007: 3–18.

Ma, Tianjie. "Environmental Mass Incidents in China: Examining Large-Scale Unrest in Dongyang, Zhejiang." Woodrow Wilson International Center for Scholars, *China Environment Series 10 (2008–2009)*. Washington, DC: Woodrow Wilson Center, 2009: 33–49.

Ma Zhongliang, Song Chaogang, and Zhang Qinghua, *Zhongguo senlin de bianqian* [Changes to China's Forests]. Beijing, CN: Zhongguo Linye Chubanshe, 1997.

Ma, Lawrence J. C. *Commercial Development and Urban Change in Sung China (960–1279)*. Ann Arbor, MI: University of Michigan Department of Geography, 1971.

Ma, Xiaoying and Leonard Ortolando. *Environmental Regulation in China: Institutions, Enforcement, and Compliance*. Lanham, MD: Rowman & Littlefield, 2000.

MacKay, Kenneth T. ed. *Rice-fish Culture in China*. Ottawa, ON: International Development Research Centre, 1995.

Mackinnon, John et al. *A Biodiversity Review of China*. Hong Kong, HK: World Wide Fund for Nature International China Programme, 1996.

Madancy, Joyce A. *The Troublesome Legacy of Commission Lin: The Opium Trade and Opium Suppression in Fujian Province, 1820s–1920s*. Cambridge, MA: Harvard University Press, 2003.

Magee, Darrin L. *New Energy Geographies: Powershed Politics and Hydropower Decision Making in Yunnan, China*. University of Washington Ph.D. dissertation, 2006.

Marks, Robert B. "Asian Tigers: The Real, the Symbolic, the Commodity." *Nature and Culture* 1, no. 1 (2006): 63–87.

———. "Geography Is Not Destiny: Historical Contingency and the Making of the Pearl River Delta." In Abe Ken-ichi and James Nickum eds., *The Good Earth: Regional and Historical Insights into China's Environment*. Kyoto, HK: Kyoto University Press, 2009: 1–28.

———. "People Said Extinction Was Not Possible: 2,000 Years of Environmental Change in South China." In Alf Hornberg ed., *Environmental History: World System History and Global Environmental Change*. Lanham, MD: AltaMira Press, 2007: 41–59.

———. *The Origins of the Modern World: A Global and Ecological Narrative from the Fifteenth to the Twenty-first Century*. Lanham, MD: Rowman & Littlefield, 2007.

———. *Tigers, Rice, Silk, and Silt: Environment and Economy in Late Imperial South China*. Cambridge, UK and New York, NY: Cambridge University Press, 1998.

Marks, Robert B. and Georgina Endfield. "Environmental Change in the Tropics in the Past 1000 Years." In Sarah Metcalf and David Nash eds., *Quaternary Environmental Change in the Tropics*. Oxford, UK: Blackwell Publishing, forthcoming.

McNeill, J. R. "Of Rats and Men: A Synoptic Environmental History of the Island Pacific." *Journal of World History* 5, no. 2 (1994): 299–349.

———. *Something New under the Sun: An Environmental History of the Twentieth-Century World*. New York, NY: Norton, 2000.

McNeill, William H. *Plagues and Peoples*. Garden City, NY: Anchor Books, 1976.

Menzies, Nicholas K. *Forest and Land Management in Imperial China*. New York, NY: St. Martin's Press, 1994.

———. *Forestry*, vol. 6, part III, *Biology and Biological Technology, Agro-Industries and Forestry*, of Joseph Needham, *Science and Civilization in China*. Cambridge, UK: Cambridge University Press, 1996.

Mertha, Andrew C. *China's Water Warriors: Citizen Action and Policy Change*. Ithaca, NY: Cornell University Press, 2008.

Mihelich, Mira Ann. *Polders and the Politics of Land Reclamation in Southeast Chinese during the Northern Sung Dynasty (960–1126)*. Cornell University Ph.D. dissertation, 1979.

Millennium Ecosystem Assessment. *Ecosystems and Human Well-Being: Synthesis*. Washington, DC: Island Press, 2005.

Mote, F. W. *Imperial China, 900–1800*. Cambridge, MA: Harvard University Press, 1999

Murphey, Rhoads. "Man and Nature in China." *Modern Asian Studies* 1, no. 4 (1967): 313–33.

———. "Deforestation in Modern China." In Richard P. Tucker and John F. Richards eds., *Global Deforestation and the Nineteenth Century World Economy*. Durham, NC: Duke University Press, 1983: 111–28.

Muscolino, Micah. *Fishing Wars and Environmental Change in Late Imperial and Modern China*. Cambridge, MA: Harvard University Press, 2009.

———. "The Yellow Croaker War: Fishery Disputes between China and Japan, 1925–1935." *Environmental History* 13 (April 2008): 305–24.

———. "Violence against the People and the Land: Refugees and the Environment in China's Henan Province, 1938–45." *Environment and History*, forthcoming.

Naughton, Barry. *The Chinese Economy: Transitions and Growth*. Cambridge, MA: The MIT Press, 2007.

Needham, Joseph. *Science and Civilization in China*, vol. 6, *Biology and Biological Technology*, part 1: *Botany*. New York, NY: Cambridge University Press, 1988.

———. *Science and Civilization in China*, vol. 4, part III, *Civil Engineering and Nautics*. New York, NY: Cambridge University Press, 1971.

Nickum, James. *Hydraulic Engineering and Water Resources in the People's Republic of China*. Stanford, CA: Stanford University Press, 1977.

———. "Is China Living on the Water Margin?" *The China Quarterly*, no. 156 (1998): 880–898.

Osborne, Anne. *Barren Mountains, Raging Rivers: The Ecological and Social Effects of Changing Landuse on the Lower Yangzi Periphery in Late Imperial China*. Columbia University Ph.D. dissertation, 1989.

Penna, Anthony N. *The Human Footprint: A Global Environmental History*. Malden, MA: Wiley-Blackwell, 2010.

Perdue, Peter C. *China Marches West: The Qing Conquest of Central Eurasia*. Cambridge, MA: The Belknap Press of Harvard University Press, 2005.

———. *Exhausting the Earth: State and Peasant in Hunan, 1500–1850*. Cambridge, MA: Harvard University Press, 1987.

———. "Lakes of Empire: Man and Water in Chinese History." *Modern China* 16, no. 1 (1990): 119–29.

———. "Military Mobilization in Seventeenth- and Eighteenth-Century China, Russia, and Mongolia." *Modern Asian Studies* 30, no. 4 (1996): 557–793.

———. "Nature and Nurture on Imperial China's Frontiers." *Modern Asian Studies* 43, no. 1 (2009): 245–267.

Peters, Heather. "Tattooed Faces and Stilt Houses: Who Were the Ancient Yue?" In Victor Mair ed., *Sino-Platonic Papers* no. 17 (1990): 1–27.

Pietz, David A. *Engineering the State: The Huai River and Reconstruction in Nationalist China, 1927–1937*. New York, NY and London, UK: Routledge, 2002.

Pomeranz, Kenneth. *The Great Divergence: China, Europe, and the Making of the Modern World Economy*. Princeton, NJ: Princeton University Press, 2000.

———. *The Making of a Hinterland: State, Society, and Economy in Inland North China, 1853–1937*. Berkeley and Los Angeles, CA: University of California Press, 1993.

Ponting, Clive. *A New Green History of the World*. New York, NY: Penguin Books, 1997.

Qu Geping and Li Jinchang. *Population and the Environment in China*, trans. Kiang Batching and Go Ran. Boulder, CO: Lynne Rienner, 1994.

Radkau, Joachim. *Nature and Power: A Global History of the Environment*. Cambridge, UK and New York, NY: Cambridge University Press, 2008.

Rawski, Evelyn. *Agricultural Change and the Peasant Economy of South China*. Cambridge, MA: Harvard University Press, 1972.

Reardon-Anderson, James. *Reluctant Pioneers: China's Expansion Northward, 1644–1937*. Stanford, CA: Stanford University Press, 2005.

Richards, John F. *The Unending Frontier: An Environmental History of the Early Modern World*. Berkeley and Los Angeles, CA: University of California Press, 2000.

Richardson, S. D. *Forestry in Communist China*. Baltimore, MD: The Johns Hopkins Press, 1966.

———. *Forests and Forestry in China: Changing Patterns of Resource Development*. Washington, DC: Island Press, 1990.

Rickett, Allan. *Guanzi: Political, Economic, and Philosophical Essays from Early China: A Study and Translation*. Princeton, NJ: Princeton University Press, 1985.

Rong, Jian. *Wolf Totem*. Howard Goldblatt trans. New York, NY: The Penguin Press, 2008.

Ross, Lester. *Forestry Policy in China*. University of Michigan Ph.D. dissertation, 1980.

Rowe,William T. "Water Control and the Qing Political Process." *Modern China* 14, no. 4 (1988): 353–87.

Saburo Miyasita, "Malaria (yao) in Chinese Medicine during the Chin and Yuan Periods." *Acta Asiatica: Bulletin of the Institute of Eastern Culture* 36 (March 1979): 90–112.

Sage, Stephen F. *Ancient Sichuan and the Unification of China*. Albany, NY: State University of New York Press, 1992.

Sanft, Charles. "Environment and Law in Early Imperial China (Third Century BCE–First Century CE): Qin and Han Statutes Concerning Natural Resources." *Environmental History* 15 (2010): 701–721.

Schafer, Edward H. "Hunting Parks and Animal Enclosures in Ancient China." *Journal of Economic and Social History of the Orient* 11, no. 3 (1968): 318–43.

———. "The Conservation of Nature under the T'ang Dynasty." *Journal of the Economic and Social History of the Orient* 5, no. 3 (1962): 279–308.

———. *Shore of Pearls*. Berkeley and Los Angeles, CA: University of California Press, 1970.

———. *The Vermilion Bird: T'ang Images of the South*. Berkeley and Los Angeles, CA: University of California Press, 1967.

Schaller, George B. and Gu Binyuan. "Ungulates in Northwest Tibet." *National Geographic Research and Exploration* 10, no. 3 (1994): 266–93.

Schaller, George. *The Great Pandas of Wolong* (Chicago, IL: University of Chicago Press, 1985

———. *The Last Panda*. Chicago, IL: University of Chicago Press, 1993.

Schneider, Laurence. *Biology and Revolution in Twentieth-Century China*. Lanham, MD: Rowman & Littlefield, 2003.

Schoppa, Keith. *Xiang Lake—Nine Centuries of Chinese Life*. New Haven, CT: Yale University Press, 1989.

Schurman, Herbert Franz, trans. *Economic Structure of the Yuan Dynasty*. Cambridge, MA: Harvard University Press, 1956.

Schwartz, Jonathan. "Environmental NGOs in China: Roles and Limits." *Pacific Affairs* 77, no. 1 (2004): 28–49.

Scott, James C. *The Art of Not Being Governed: An Anarchist History of Upland Southeast Asia*. New Haven, CT: Yale University Press, 2009.

Sedo, Tim. "Environmental Governance and the Public Good in Xu Guangqi's *Treatise on Expelling Locusts*." Paper presented at 2011 AAS annual conference, Honolulu, HI.

Shapiro, Judith. *Mao's War against Nature: Politics and the Environment in Revolutionary China*. New York, NY and Cambridge: Cambridge University Press, 2001.

Shaw, Norman. *Chinese Forest Trees and Timber Supply*. London, UK: T. Fisher Unwin, 1914.

Shepherd, John Robert. *Statecraft and Political Economy on the Taiwan Frontier, 1600–1800*. Stanford, CA: Stanford University Press, 1993.

Shiba, Yoshinobu. *Commerce and Society in Song China*. Ann Arbor, MI: The University of Michigan Center for Chinese Studies, 1970.

Shih, Sheng-han. *A Preliminary Survey of the Book Ch'i Min Yao Shu, an Agricultural Treatise of the Sixth Century*. Beijing, CN: Science Press, 1962.

Shin, Leo. *The Making of the Chinese State: Ethnicity and Expansion on the Ming Borderlands*. New York, NY: Cambridge University Press, 2006.

Skinner, G. William. "Marketing and Social Structure in Rural China," Parts I, II, and III, *Journal of Asian Studies* Vol. 24, No. 1 (Nov, 1964), 3–43; Vol. 24, No. 2 (Feb, 1965), 195–228; and Vol. 24, No. 3 (May, 1965), 363–399.

Slack, Edward R. *Opium, State, and Society: China's Narco-economy and the Guomindang, 1924–1937*. Honolulu, HI: University of Hawai'i Press, 2001.

Smil, Vaclav. *The Bad Earth: Environmental Degradation in China*. Armonk, NY: M. E. Sharpe, 1984.

———. *China's Environment Crisis: An Inquiry into the Limits of National Development*. Armonk, NY: M. E. Sharpe, 1993.

———. *China's Past, China's Future: Energy, Food, Environment*. New York, NY: RoutledgeCurzon, 2004.

———. *Enriching the Earth: Fritz Haber, Carl Bosch, and the Transformation of World Food Production*. Cambridge, MA: The MIT Press, 2004.

Smith, Joanna Handlin. *The Art of Doing Good: Charity in Late Ming China*. Berkeley and Los Angeles, CA: University of California Press, 2009.

Smith, Paul J. "Commerce, Agriculture, and Core Formation in the Upper Yangzi, 2 A.D. to 1948." *Late Imperial China* 9, no. 1 (1988): 1–178.

———. *Taxing Heaven's Storehouse: Horses, Bureaucrats, and the Destruction of the Sichuan Tea Industry, 1074–1224* (Cambridge, MA: Harvard University Press, 1991

Sneath, David. *Changing Inner Mongolia: Pastoral Mongolian Society and the Chinese State* (Oxford, UK: Oxford University Press, 2000

Songster, E. Elena. "Cultivating the Nation in Fujian's Forests: Forest Policies and Afforestion Effort in China, 1911–1937." *Environmental History* 8 (July 2003): 452–473.

———. *Panda Nation: Nature, Science, and Nationalism in the People's Republic of China* (book manuscript in preparation).

Sturgeon, Janet C. *Border Landscapes: The Politics of Akha Land Use in China and Thailand.* Seattle, WA: University of Washington Press, 2005.

Tan, Qixiang, chief ed. *Zhongguo lidai dituji* [Historical Atlas of China], 8 vols. Beijing, CN: Ditu Chuban She, 1987.

Teng, Emma Jinhua. *Taiwan's Imagined Geography: Chinese Colonial Travel Writing and Pictures, 1683–1895*. Cambridge, MA: Harvard University Press, 2004.

Totman, Conrad. *The Green Archipelago: Forestry in Pre-Industrial Japan*. Columbus, OH: Ohio University Press, 1998.

———. *Pre-industrial Korea and Japan in Environmental Perspective*. Leiden, NL and Boston, MA: Brill, 2004.

Townsend, Colin R., Michael Begon, and John L. Harper. *Essentials of Ecology*, 3rd ed. Malden, MA: Blackwell Scientific, 2008.

Trocki, Carl. *Opium, Empire, and the Global Political Economy: A Study of the Asian Opium Trade*. London, UK: Routledge, 1999.

Tuan, Yi-fu. *China*. Chicago, IL: Aldine, 1969.

Tucker, Mary Evelyn and John Berthrong, eds. *Confucianism and Ecology: The Interrelation of Heaven, Earth, and Humans*. Cambridge, MA: Harvard University Press, 1998.

Turner, B. L. et al. eds. *The Earth as Transformed by Human Action: Global and Regional changes in the Biosphere over the Past 300 Years*. New York, NY: Cambridge University Press, 1990.

Twitchett, Denis, ed. *The Cambridge History of China*, vol. 3, *Sui and T'ang China, 589–906*, Part I. Cambridge, UK and New York, NY: Cambridge University Press, 1979.

Twitchett, Denis. "Chinese Social History from the Seventh to the Tenth Centuries: The Tunhuang Documents and Their Implications." *Past and Present*, no. 35 (1966): 28–53.

———. *Land Tenure and the Social Order in T'ang and Sung China*. London, UK: University of London School of Oriental and African Studies, 1962.

———. "The Monasteries and China's Economy in Medieval Times." *Bulletin of the School of Oriental and African Studies* 19, no. 3 (1957): 535–41.

———. "Population and Pestilence in T'ang China." In Wolfgang Bauer ed., *Studia Sino Mongolia: Festshrift für Herbet Franke*. Weisbaden, DE: Steiner, 1979: 35–68.

Unger, Jonathan. "Life in the Chinese Hinterlands under the Rural Economic Reforms." *Bulletin of Concerned Asian Scholars* 22, no. 2 (1990): 4–17.

———. "Not Quite Han: The Ethnic Minorities of China's Southwest." *Bulletin of Concerned Asian Scholars* 29, no. 3 (1997): 67–98.

Van Slyke, Lyman P. *Yangtze: Nature, History, and the River*. Reading, MA: Addison-Wesley Publishing Co., Inc.,1988.

Vermeer, Eduard B. *Economic Development in Provincial China: The Central Shaanxi since 1930*. Cambridge and New York, NY: Cambridge University Press, 1988.

———. "The Mountain Frontier in Late Imperial China: Economic and Social Developments in the Bashan." *T'oung Pao*, Vol. LXXVII, 4–5 (1991): 300–329.

Vogel, Hans Ulrich and Gunter Dux eds. *Concepts of Nature: A Chinese-European Cross-Cultural Perspective*. Leiden, NL: Brill, 2010.

von Falkenhausen, Lothar. *Chinese Society in the Age of Confucius (1000–250 BC): The Archeological Evidence*. Los Angeles, CA: Cotsen Institute of Archeology, University of California–Los Angeles, 2006.

von Glahn, Richard. *The Country of Streams and Grottoes: Expansion, Settlement, and the Civilizing of the Sichuan Frontier in Song Times*. Cambridge MA: Harvard University Press, 1987.

Wagner, Donald B. *Iron and Steel in Ancient China*. Leiden, NL: E. J. Brill, 1993.

Wakeman, Frederick. *The Great Enterprise: The Manchu Reconstruction of Imperial Order in Seventeenth-Century China*, 2 vols. Berkeley and Los Angeles, CA: University of California Press, 1985.

Waldron, Arthur. *The Great Wall of China: From History to Myth*. Cambridge, UK and New York, NY: Cambridge University Press, 1990.

Wang, Chi-wu. *The Forests of China*. Cambridge, MA: Harvard University Press, 1961.

Ware, James R. *Alchemy, Medicine, Religion in the China of A. D. 320: The Nei P'ien of Ko Hung (Pao-p'u tzu)*. Cambridge, MA: The M.I.T. Press, 1966.

Webb, James L. A. Jr. *Humanity's Burden: A Global History of Malaria*. New York, NY: Cambridge University Press, 2009.

Weller, Robert P. *Discovering Nature: Globalization and Environmental Culture in China and Taiwan*. Cambridge, UK and New York, NY: Cambridge University Press, 2006.

Whyte, Robert Orr ed. *The Evolution of the East Asian Environment,* 2 vols. Hong Kong, HK: The University of Hong Kong Centre of Asian Studies, 1984.

Wiens, Herold J. *Han Chinese Expansion in South China*. Hamden, CT: The Shoe String Press, 1967.

Will, Pierre-Etienne and R. Bin Wong. *Nourish the People: The Civilian State Granary System in China, 1650–1850*. Ann Arbor, MI: University of Michigan Press, 1991.

Will, Pierre-Etienne. *Bureaucracy and Famine in Eighteenth-Century China*. Stanford, CA: Stanford University Press, 1990.

———. "State Intervention in the Administration of a Hydraulic Structure: The Example of Hubei Province in Late Imperial Times." In Stuart Schram ed., *The Scope of State Power in China*. New York, NY: St. Martin's Press, 1985), 295–347.

Williams, Dee Mack. *Beyond Great Walls: Environment, Identity, and Development on the Chinese Grasslands of Inner Mongolia* (Stanford, CA: Stanford University Press, 2002.

Williams, Michael. *Deforesting the Earth: From Prehistory to Global Crisis*. Chicago, IL: University of Chicago Press, 2003.

Wong, R. Bin. *China Transformed: Historical Change and the Limits of European Experience*. Ithaca: Cornell University Press, 1997.

Wright, Arthur F. *Buddhism in Chinese History*. New York, NY: Atheneum, 1969.

———. *The Sui Dynasty*. New York, NY: Knopf, 1978.

Wright, Tim and Ma Junya. "Sacrificing Local Interests: Water Control Policies of the Ming and Qing Governments and the Local Economy of Huaibei, 1495–1949." *Modern Asian Studies*, forthcoming.

Xu Dixin and Wu Chengming, eds. *Chinese Capitalism, 1522–1840*. English edition ed. and annot. C. A. Curwen. New York, NY: St. Martin's Press, 2000.

Xu Guohua and L. J. Peel, eds., *The Agriculture of China*. Oxford, UK and New York, NY: Oxford University Press, 1991.

Xu, Jiongxin. "A Study of the Long-Term Environmental Effects of River Regulation on the Yellow River of China in Historical Perspective." *Geografiska Annaler, Series A, Physical Geography* 75, no. 3 (1993): 61–72.

Xue, Yong. "'Treasure Nightsoil as if It Were Gold': Economic and Ecological Links Between Urban and Rural Areas in Late Imperial Jiangnan." *Late Imperial China* 6, no. 1 (2005): 41–71.

Yan Ruizhen and Wang Yuan. *Poverty and Development: A Study of China's Poor Areas*. Beijing, CN: New World Press, 1992.

Yang, Bin. "Horses, Silver, and Cowries: Yunnan in Global Perspective." *Journal of World History* 15, no. 3 (2004): 281–322.

Yang, Guobin. "Is There an Environmental Movement in China? Beware of the 'River of Anger.'" In *Active Society in Formation: Environmentalism, Labor, and the Underworld in China*. Washington, DC: Woodrow Wilson Center International Center for Scholars, Asia Program Special Report no. 124, September 2004.

Yang, L. S. *Studies in Chinese Institutional History*. Cambridge, MA: Harvard-Yenching Institute, 1961.

Zhang, Jiacheng. *The Reconstruction of Climate in China for Historical Times*. Beijing, CN: Science Press, 1988.

Zhang Jiacheng and Lin Zhiguang. *Climate of China*. New York, NY: Wiley, 1992.

Zhang, Jiayang. "Environment, Market, and Peasant Choice: The Ecological Relationships in the Jianghan Plain in the Qing and the Republic." *Modern China* 32, no. 1 (2006): 31–63.

Zhang, Ling. "Changing with the Yellow River: An Environmental History of Hebei, 1048–1128." *Harvard Journal of Asiatic Studies* 69, no. 1 (2009): 1–36.

———. "Manipulating the Yellow River and the State Formation of the Northern Song Dynasty (960–1127)." In Carmen Meinhert ed., *Environment and Climate in China and Beyond* (Leiden, NL: Brill, forthcoming in 2012).

———. "Ponds, Paddies and Frontier Defence: Environmental and Economic Changes in Northern Hebei in Northern Song China (960–1127)." *Journal of Medieval History*, vol. 14, no. 1 (2011): 21–43.

Zhao Songqiao. *Geography of China: Environment, Resources, Population and Development*. New York, NY: John Wiley and Sons, 1994.

Index